D1273023

THOMAS JEFFERSON

GARLAND REFERENCE LIBRARY
OF SOCIAL SCIENCE
(VOL. 184)

THOMAS JEFFERSON
A Comprehensive, Annotated Bibliography of Writings About Him (1826–1980)

Frank Shuffelton

GARLAND PUBLISHING, INC. • NEW YORK & LONDON
1983

Library of Congress Cataloging in Publication Data

Shuffelton, Frank, 1940–
    Thomas Jefferson : a comprehensive, annotated
bibliography of writings about him (1826–1980)

    (Garland reference library of social science ;
v. 184)
    Includes index.
    1. Jefferson, Thomas, 1743–1826—Bibliography.
I. Title. II. Series.
Z8452.S55   1983   016.9734'6'0924   83-48200
[E332]
ISBN 0-8240-9078-0

Printed on acid-free, 250-year-life-paper
Manufactured in the United States of America

CONTENTS

For Frank B,
My first Democrat

INTRODUCTION

This is the first attempt in nearly fifty years at a comprehensive bibiliography of the writings about Thomas Jefferson, and it is the first critically annotated comprehensive bibliography ever to appear. In view of the immense number of pages that have been devoted to Jefferson since his death, this should come as no surprise; as early as the 1940's a scholar as good as William Peden confessed to being daunted by the enormous amount of material that had already appeared. Although this bibliography contains nearly two and a half times as many entries as any previous effort, it refrains from calling itself complete, settling for the more realistic term, comprehensive. Bibliographies are seldom ever complete; they merely await the inevitable appearance of the undiscovered material. Given these metaphysical limits to bibliography, however, this work aims to present the fullest map yet of the scholarly and popular reception of Thomas Jefferson, a man of no narrow scope himself.

The first major attempt to cover the material on Jefferson appeared in 1905 when Richard Holland Johnston included his bibliography as a supplement to the final volume of the *Writings of Thomas Jefferson* edited by Andrew A. Lipscomb and Albert E. Bergh. Johnston's was a fine piece of scholarship, especially on the years from Jefferson's death in 1826 through the remainder of the nineteenth century; although his listings are augmented here, nearly everything he described came to light just as he described it. Not all the bibiliographies I consulted were so unfailingly accurate. W. Harvey Wise, Jr., and John W. Cronin brought out their *Bibliography of Thomas Jefferson* in 1935 with 1,248 citations, but this turned out to be only a relatively modest update of Johnston and overlooked a good deal of material. Neither of these bibliographies is annotated. Still, Wise and Cronin must be regarded as the last attempt, if an unsuccessful one, at a genuinely comprehensive listing of the material on Jefferson.

The next attempt at an extensive bibliography was Eugene L. Huddleston's *Thomas Jefferson: A Reference Guide* which appeared in 1982 and cited approximately 1400 items with annotations. Although the author claims in his preface to be "comprehensive," the definition of comprehensiveness as well as the actual practice undermines that claim. This bibliography purports to focus on "all major scholarship" but in fact admits a fair amount of popular material which supposedly is "mostly excluded," and it overlooks a considerable body of scholarly material, particularly that having to do with Jefferson's interests in science, the arts, and architecture. Influenced by Merrill Peterson's *The Jefferson Image in the American Mind*, it swerves from strictly scholarly criteria for inclusion out of a desire to depict Jefferson's reputation, particularly along the lines Peterson had laid out. This leads to the inclusion of peripheral material, or at least material considered too peripheral for inclusion in this bibliography. (This is probably no serious flaw, for defining the limits of inclusion is one of the most difficult problems in creating a bibliography, and a cautious generosity is often more useful than overly scrupulous discrimination. The items this reference guide doesn't include pose a more serious problem.) Since the annotations "aim at objectivity," however, it is often difficult to separate the peripheral and popular from the more scholarly and central. A few errors in bibliographic description, e.g., confusion of author's names, of editions, etc., also occur.

There are also a number of other bibliographies, often accompanying scholarly monographs, which have proved useful. Especially worth noticing is William B. O'Neal's *An Intelligent Interest in Architecture* covering material dealing with Jefferson as an architect, and since it includes items that merely refer to Jefferson in passing and are thus not included here, it is useful as a guide to the growing recognition of his importance in architectural history. Also, Peterson's *Jefferson Image* includes a "Guide to Sources" that is a treasury of references to items charting the course of Jefferson's reputation, and like O'Neal's book it lists items that only allude to Jefferson and are not listed here. Its usefulness is limited, however, by its offering incomplete and sometimes erroneous bibliographic information for its references.

This bibliography, then provides the most comprehensive coverage to date of the writing about Jefferson from his death to the present. Earlier bibliographers paid not a great deal of attention to items in languages other than English. Although I am least confident about comprehensiveness in regard to foreign language material, I did turn up items in sixteen languages besides English. In addition to earlier bibliographies, I have consulted a wide variety of indexes covering publications in biography, the humanities and social sciences, law, education, and fine arts; guides to periodical literature; and specialized scholarly bibliographies such as *Writings in American History* and the *MLA Bibliography*. I have consulted the holdings of the Harvard libraries, Boston Public Library, New York Public Library, the Cornell University Library, Princeton University Library, the library of the American Philosophical Society, the Library of Congress, the University of Virginia Library, and the Virginia State Historical Society Library, turning up valuable and interesting material in all of these. Stack access to a number of these libraries allowed me to find material not listed in card catalogues under Jefferson.

A comprehensive bibliography such as this cites two rather different kinds of item: the first sort ideally is written with a scholarly intention for a scholarly audience and contains an apparatus such as footnotes, references, etc., while the other is aimed at a popular readership which may not have much previous knowledge of Jefferson or his times. Not all material, of course, conforms to one or the other of these polar ends of what is in fact a broad spectrum of writing about Jefferson. Some material prepared for a lay audience, an article in a journal like *American Heritage* for instance, is based upon careful research but is presented without the usual scholarly apparatus, while books and articles ripe with footnotes are upon occasion derivative or insipid. Dumas Malone's six-volume biography of Jefferson is a landmark of scholarship which has also attracted a wide popular audience.

Scholars will always find useful in some way any well-written, informed and informative statement about Jefferson, regardless of its manner of presentation. But even the derivative, the merely popular, or the trivial item deserves a place in a bibliography claiming comprehensiveness. First, because such material is occasionally cited in scholarly indexes or bibliographies, it needs to be described for what it is and cleared out of scholars' way. Second, such material, as Peterson has shown in *The Jefferson Image*, claims an interest in its own right; material with little intrinsic scholarly value can still be quite informative about the development of public opinion in reference to both Jefferson himself and his interests. Popular articles on Jefferson, while holding little of interest for a serious Jefferson scholar, can tell us much about things as diverse as America's changing tastes in architecture, national concern for the separation of church and state, the fate of public education, or evolving issues of the Constitution. These popular articles are a barometer of the nation's attention levels. In other words, a comprehensive bibliography such as this records the material of interest to serious Jefferson scholars and directs them away from items unsuitable for their purposes, but it also lists material which is the basis for a kind of sociology of popular knowledge, notes toward understanding of an American *mentalité*.

Criteria for Inclusion

I have attempted to list every article, dissertation, and book dealing with Thomas Jefferson in a substantial way which has appeared since his death in 1826 and through 1980. I have also attempted to cite books containing at least one chapter specifically on Jefferson (or a section of approximately chapter length). Within these parameters I used the following criteria to determine which items to include in this bibliography:

(1) Previous listing in some index, bibliography, or library card catalogue under "Thomas Jefferson."

(2) Previous listing under "Monticello" or "Declaration of Independence." Items listed under "Monticello" almost always turned out to deal in some way with Jefferson's life there, but, curiously enough, items on the Declaration of Independence would upon occasion completely ignore its Jeffersonian origins and thus not qualify for inclusion in this listing. This cold shoulder to Jefferson came usually where the author was politically conservative and wished to rescue the Declaration from its radi-

cal draftsman. After checking references to other writings of Jefferson such as *Notes on the State of Virginia*, I determined they were typically cross-referenced under his name and that only "Monticello" and "Declaration of Independence" were useful additional references to trace.

(3) All works with the word "Jeffersonian" in the title. Here a large number of items were rejected when the term was used as a general chronological label, i.e., for anyone or any event in the years 1790 to 1825, or in some cases as a general political tag when the work turned out to have little direct reference to Jefferson.

(4) Works dealing with the period of Jefferson's mature years which might by inference be supposed to contain substantial material directly relevant to him, e.g., histories of the presidency or of foreign affairs and diplomacy. Again, items were rejected when there was no substantial coverage of Jefferson himself, so histories of his presidency which include chapters on his leadership of his party or his role in the Louisiana Purchase were included whereas histories which focus on events independently of him as agent or actor were rejected. I did not include studies of figures like Hamilton or Madison which inevitably contain a great deal of attention, at least in passing, to Jefferson unless was at least a chapter concerned directly with him. Under this criterion books about minor figures are more likely to qualify for inclusion than those about major figures; Madison is of considerable interest in his own right and is so treated, but Philip Mazzei or William Short are of interest because they were friends of Jefferson, and writers on them focus on this relationship.

Exclusion of works considered under criteria (3) and (4) above required individual acts of judgment, but items qualifying under the first criterion, previous bibliographic listings, were included even when they seemed to be of only peripheral interest. In such cases, however, the annotation should suggest this peripheral quality, since one of the uses of a bibliography such as this is to separate the wheat from the chaff. Similarly, although the bibliography includes items written for a juvenile audience, much of it previously referenced, it clearly identifies such material as juvenile fiction or non-fiction. This bibliography does not ordinarily include encyclopedia or biographical dictionary entries, newspaper publications, or book reviews, although it does cite review essays. (It has also included items from the *New York Times Magazine* and *Christian Science Monitor Magazine* because they are listed in the *Guide to Periodical Literature*.) Although the coverage here is comprehensive for the years 1826 through 1980, a few important items appearing in 1981 or 1982 are represented, the final volume of Malone's biography and Noble Cunningham's *The Image of Thomas Jefferson*, for instance.

Organization

The materials cited in this bibiliography are divided into five sections, as described below, according to their central concern or focus, and they are arranged alphabetically by author (or title if the author is unknown) within their sections and annotated. The annotations are of necessity brief, but they aim at giving some notion of the content and leading argument of a cited item, and in many cases they offer some critical judgment about the item's scholarly value or importance. Not all items are annotated, nor are all minor, derivative sketches scolded for being so. Items without annotation often seemed so bland and familiar as not to require any special description, and in other cases the place of publication should warn the reader what to expect. *Reader's Digest* or the *DAR Magazine* fulfill a purpose, but they do not pretend to further scholarly inquiry. More important are affirmative signals I have used like "intelligent," "suggestive," or "definitive" which point to those items which should be especially useful for students and scholars pursuing Jeffersonian studies. When a citation follows an asterisk in the right margin, I have not physically seen that item.

BIBLIOGRAPHIES: This first, brief section lists separately published bibliographies which list either Jefferson's printed writings or material on him or provide indexes and calendars of his papers.

BIOGRAPHICAL STUDIES: The second section lists materials having mainly a biographical focus or intention. Among the difficulties inherent in dividing writings about Jefferson into discrete subject categories is their tendency to resist easy categorization. Does an item on Jefferson's theory of education belong with studies of his ideas or with studies of his educational activities? Isn't everything ultimately of biographical interest? Recognizing these problems, I have included in the biographical section items which are either straightforwardly presented as biography or which confine themselves to a narrative rather than an analytic account of Jefferson's activities and interests. Thus, an article describing his life in Philadelphia while drafting the Declaration would typically end up in this section, but an essay on how or why he composed it would be included with items dealing with his political activities, and an article analyzing his prose style in the Declaration will appear in the final section on the arts.

There are a great many articles of the "Thomas Jefferson, A Wonderful Man" variety, and they belong here; the biographical section, because of this, probably has the greatest admixture of the important and trivial. Items dealing with the growth of Jefferson's reputation as testified by the erection of memorials, statues, etc., are included in this section, and it also includes items concerned with the problems of Jefferson biography. In the last decade since the appearance of Fawn Brodie's *Thomas Jefferson* much of this has focused on his relationship with members of the Hemings family, the Callendar scandals, and the validity of Brodie's claims about his sexual activity. I should state here my own skepticism regarding the Brodie thesis because it does affect the judgments in my annotations. The evidence offered seems inconclusive to me, and if it cannot be proved that Jefferson was not the father of Sally Heming's children, strong evidence does exist pointing to another as her lover.

POLITICAL STUDIES: This section includes materials dealing with Jefferson's political activities. Items concerned essentially with his political theories will be found in the next section, but those centering on the significance his ideas had for his practice of political leadership will be found here. This includes material on, among other subjects, the political implications of the Declaration, his diplomatic mission to France, his career as secretary of state, vice-president, and president, his authorship of the Kentucky Resolutions, and his response to the problem of slavery. In the last two decades notable work has been done on the slavery issue and on his conduct of the presidency. This seems appropriate in light of the struggles for civil rights in the 60's and the problematic career of the presidency in the 70's.

PHILOSOPHICAL APPROACHES AND STUDIES IN THE HISTORY OF IDEAS: This section contains items concerned with Jefferson's ideas, the intellectual influences on him, and his intellectual influence on others. It includes material which attempts to portray him as a thinker in various strands of the Enlightenment tradition, accounts of his political theories, of his religious notions, and of his ideas about citizenship, economics, education, race, separation of church and state, and war and peace.

PRACTICAL AND FINE ARTS, SCIENCE AND EDUCATION: This section details Jefferson's interests in art, architecture, music, cooking, agriculture, gardening, literature, science, and his activities to encourage public education. His design of Monticello and its furnishings has been a continuing fascination for Americans, and a large number of popular articles on the subject appear in this section. Also of enduring interest are his plans for the University of Virginia, both architectural and organizational. This section also cites materials dealing with the controversy over the architecture of the Jefferson Memorial. It also includes representations of Jefferson *in* the arts: his appearance in drama and novels, poems about him, music celebrating him, and his portraiture in both two and three dimensional representation.

INDEX: Since a number of items cited in this bibliography might reasonably appear in more than one category, users should consult the subject index for material relevant to their specific interests. The subject index is followed by an alphabetically-arranged list of authors of the items cited. This list includes entries for joint authors of articles but does not list corporate authors, e.g., U.S. Senate. All items are identified by their citation number in this bibliography.

The Papers of Thomas Jefferson

One extremely important source is not cited in these pages and should be noted here. Beginning in 1950 under the general editorship of Julian P. Boyd, *The Papers of Thomas Jefferson* have been appearing from the Princeton University Press. As of 1982, under the editorship of Charles Cullen since Boyd's death, it has arrived at twenty volumes, the most recent covering papers from April through August of 1791; announced for publication is volume 21 which will be a general index for the first twenty volumes. (Separate "throwaway" indexes have been issued for volumes 1–6, 7–12, and 13–18, but the new index should super-cede these both in completeness and usefulness.) When com-plete in sixty volumes, this should be the definitive edition of Jefferson's writings. In addition to his public papers and his letters, it includes letters written to him and extensive scholarly notes and commentary. These notes, many of which swell to the proportions of extended essays, are not listed separately in this bibliography. Anyone writing on Jefferson who deals with any aspect of his life in years covered by the *Papers* should consult these volumes, both for the Jefferson texts and for the scholarly apparatus. (For those interested, the subject index of this bibli-ography references items pertaining to the genesis and progress of the *Papers* edition.)

I should like to thank all those who assisted me in my re-search. I am grateful to the librarians of all the libraries I noted above as contributing to my researches, and in addition I wish to thank the librarians of Lafayette College and Dickinson College who gave me access to materials in their collection. I am grateful to the librarians of my own University of Rochester Libraries, particularly so to Phyllis Andrews. Julius Barclay, rare book li-brarian of the University of Virginia, was exceptionally consid-erate and supportive, and the friendly assistance of Carol Bierly and Amy L. White was much appreciated. James A. Bear, Jr., curator of Monticello, was of more help than I can possibly credit here. He has a truly Jeffersonian desire to encourage scholarship as well as a tough-mindedness, sense of humor, and spirit of hospitality that Mr. Jefferson could not fail to approve. I am also grateful to his staff, William Beiswanger, Elizabeth Braswell, Lucia Goodwin, and Charles Granquist, who answered ques-tions and gave of their time. In my travels from library to library I was materially helped and entertained by David and Patricia Levin, Charlotte Morse, Ray and Claudine Nelson, and Mar-garet Wells; their generous hospitality gave me more time to fill in lots of file cards. Also helpful were Philip Weimerskirch, James Spenko, and Peter Dzwonkoski, who sent material my way, and Bruce Johnson and J. Paul Hunter, who gave me leave when I needed it. Cindy Warner and Catherine Strassner typed heroically and with good humor. They caught most of my typos; any errors that remain are all mine. Jane Shuffelton put up with my enthusiasm and absences, and Amy and George listened to a lot of stories about "TJ."

University of Rochester
May 8, 1983

ABBREVIATIONS

In the interest of saving space some frequently used journal titles and terms have been abbreviated as follows:

AHR   *American Historical Review*
APS   American Philosophical Society
DAI   *Dissertation Abstracts International*
MVHR   *Mississippi Valley Historical Review*
Notes   *Notes on the State of Virginia*
PMHB   *Pennsylvania Magazine of History and*
               Biography
TJ   Thomas Jefferson
Univ.   University
VMHB   *Virginia Magazine of History and Biography*
VQR   *Virginia Quarterly Review*
WMQ   *William and Mary Quarterly*

Thomas Jefferson

I. BIBLIOGRAPHIES

I. BIBLIOGRAPHIES.

1. Adams, Randolph G. "Notes and Queries." <u>Colophon</u>. n.s. 3(1938), 134-39.

   Contains 7 bibliographic notes on TJ, his papers, and <u>Notes</u>.

2. Bishop, Arthur, ed. <u>Thomas Jefferson, 1743-1826: Chronology-Documents-Bibliographic Aids</u>. Dobbs Ferry: Oceana, 1971. pp. 122.

   A "research tool ... for the student;" very basic.

3. "Books, Films, Records on Thomas Jefferson." <u>Scholastic</u>. 42(April 12, 1943), 4+.

4. <u>Classified List of Manuscripts, Books, Correspondence, Etc. of Thomas Jefferson, Offered by Purchase to the United States by Sarah N. Randolph</u>. Washington: Government Printing Office, 1889. pp. 5.

   Includes 3660 letters by TJ, manuscripts of the Farm Book, Garden Book, book of cases, fee book, and much else.

5. Cooke, Jacob E. "The Federalist Age: A Reappraisal" in <u>American History; Retrospect and Prospect</u>, ed. George Athan Billias and Gerald N. Grob. New York: Free Press, 1971. 85-153.

   A useful bibliographical essay on the politics of the period from 1789-1815. Another version printed as "The Federal Era: Hamiltonian or Jeffersonian?" in <u>Interpretations of American History</u>, ed. Grob and Billias. New York: Free Press, 1972. 243-59.

6. Cuthbert, Norma, comp. "Jefferson Collection" in <u>American Manuscript Collections in the Huntington Library for the History of the Seventeenth and Eighteenth Centuries</u>. San Marino, Cal.: Huntington Library, 1941. 28-32.

7. Doumato, Lamia. <u>Architect Thomas Jefferson: A Selected Bibliography</u>. Monticello, Ill.: Vance Bibliographies, 1980. pp. 9.

8. Duncan, Richard R. and Dorothy M. Brown. "Theses and Dissertations on Virginia History: A Bibliography." <u>VMHB</u>. 79(1971), 55-109.

   TJ Items on pp. 77-80.

9. Duncan, Richard R., Dorothy M. Brown and Ralph D. Nurnberger. "Theses and Dissertations on Virginia History: A Supplementary Bibliography." <u>VMHB</u>. 83(1975), 346-67.

10. Edwards, Everett E. <u>Selected References on Thomas Jefferson and His Contribution to Agriculture</u>. Washington: Department of Agriculture, 1944. pp. 7.

11. Foster, W. E. "Jefferson's Administrations." Providence Public Library Monthly Reference Lists. 3(1883), 21-22.

12. Gillespie, David and Michael H. Harris. "A Bibliography of Virginia Library History." Journal of Library History. 6(1971), 72-90.

    Section on TJ lists 39 items.

13. Huddleston, Eugene L. Thomas Jefferson, A Reference Guide. Boston: G. K. Hall, 1982. pp. xxiii, 374.

    Annotates about 1300 items, both scholarly and popular; not critical, occasionally inaccurate, but useful for students.

14. Index to the Thomas Jefferson Papers. Washington: Library of Congress, 1976. pp. xxiii, 155.

    Indexes papers in the L. C. collection as contained in the 65 reel microfilm which appeared in 1974. Paul G. Sifton's "Introduction" gives the provenance of the collection.

15. The Jefferson Bicentennial, 1743-1943. A Catalogue of the Exhibition at the Library of Congress. Washington: Government Printing Office, 1943. pp. iii, 171.

    500 entries. Includes introduction by Archibald MacLeish and an address by Felix Frankfurter.

16. Johnston, Richard Holland. A Contribution to a Bibliography of Thomas Jefferson in The Writings of Thomas Jefferson, ed. Andrew A. Lipscomb and Albert Ellery Bergh. Washington: Thomas Jefferson Memorial Association, 1905. 20: iv, 73 (separately paginated).

    Also separately printed.

17. Krout, John Allen. "Jefferson's Contribution to the Constitution." Outlook. 145(1927), 288a (inside rear cover).

18. Massachusetts Historical Society. Catalogue of Manuscripts of the Massachusetts Historical Society. Boston: G. K. Hall, 1969. 4:164-271.

    Catalogue for Jefferson mss. in the collection.

19. O'Neal, William B. A Checklist of Writings on Thomas Jefferson as an Architect. Publication No. 15. Charlottesville: American Association of Architectural Bibliographers, 1959. pp. 18.

    Also issued as Secretary's News Sheet, No. 43, University of Virginia Bibliographical Society. Approximately 150 entries.

4

20. O'Neal, William B. An Intelligent Interest in Architecture: A
Bibliography of Publications about Thomas Jefferson as an Architect,
together with an Iconography of the Nineteenth-Century Prints of the
University of Virginia. Charlottesville: Univ. Press of Virginia, 1969.
pp. viii, 150.

(American Association of Architectural Bibliographers Papers. No. 6).
Lists articles and books that mention TJ even in passing and are not
within the scope of this bibliography. Well annotated and very useful.

*21. Select List of References on Thomas Jefferson. Washington: Library of
Congress, 1919. pp. 8.

71 citations; see also list of additional references, 1931. pp. 2.

22. Tanner, Douglas W., ed. Guide to the Microfilm Edition of the
Jefferson Papers of the University of Virginia, 1732-1828.
Charlottesville: Univ. of Virginia Library, 1977. pp. 96.

Includes Index.

23. Thomas Jefferson and Architecture. Charlottesville: Alderman Library,
1953. pp. 4.

Mimeographed check list of materials in the Alderman Library.

24. "Thomas Jefferson—Bibliography." Education for Victory. 2(March 20,
1944), 6.

25. Thurlow, Constance and Francis L. Berkeley, Jr. The Jefferson Papers
of the University of Virginia: A Calendar Compiled by
Constance E. Thurlow and Francis L. Berkeley, Jr. With an Appended
Essay by Helen D. Bullock on the Papers of Thomas Jefferson.
Charlottesville: Univ. of Virginia Library, 1950. pp. xi, 343.

26. Thurlow, Constance E., et. al. The Jefferson Papers of the University
of Virgina: Part I. A Calendar Compiled by Constance E. Thurlow
and Francis L. Berkeley, Jr. of Manuscripts Acquired Through 1950.
Part II. A Supplementary Calendar Compiled by John Casteen and
Anne Freudenberg of Manuscripts Acquired 1950-1970.
Charlottesville: University Press of Virginia, 1973. pp. xvi, 497.

Most recent calendar of papers held at the Univ. of Virginia.

27. Tompkins, Hamilton Bullock. Bibliotheca Jeffersoniana: A List of
Books Written by or Relating to Thomas Jefferson. New York:
Putnam's 1887. pp. 187.

28. U.S. Department of State. Bureau of Rolls and Library. Arrangement
of the Papers of Madison, Jefferson, Hamilton, Monroe, and Franklin.

Miscellaneous Index. Bulletin No. 5. Washington: Department of State, 1893.

29. U.S. Department of State. Bureau of Rolls and Library. Calendar of the Correspondence of Thomas Jefferson. Part I. Letters from Jefferson. Bulletin No. 6. Washington: Department of State, 1894. pp. vi, 541.

Letters are listed under the names of TJ's correspondents.

30. U.S. Department of State. Bureau of Rolls and Library. Calendar of the Correspondence of Thomas Jefferson. Part II. Letters to Jefferson. Bulletin No. 8. Washington: Department of State, 1895. pp. iii, 593.

31. U.S. Department of State. Bureau of Rolls and Library. Calendar of the Correspondence of Thomas Jefferson. Part III. Supplement. Bulletin No. 10. Washington: Department of State, 1903. pp. iii, 270.

Includes an index to all three parts.

32. Verner, Coolie. A Further Checklist of the Separate Editions of Jefferson's Notes on the State of Virginia. Charlottesville: Bibliographical Society of the University of Virginia, 1950. pp. 26.

Earlier checklist implied in the title is the unpublished memoranda of Harry Clemons, Librarian of the Univ. of Virginia.

33. Wise, W. Harvey, Jr. and John W. Cronin. A Bibliography of Thomas Jefferson. Washington: Riverford Publishing, 1935. pp. 72.

34. Woodward, Frank E. Reference List of Works Relating to Thomas Jefferson. Malden, Mass., 1906. pp. 4.

35. "Writings about Jack Jouett's Ride and Tarleton's Raid on Charlottesville; Compiled August 1951, from materials in the University of Virginia Library, for Twentieth Century Fox Film Corporation at the request of Frank McCarthy." Charlottesville: Univ. of Virginia Library, 1951. pp. 3.

II. BIOGRAPHICAL STUDIES

II. BIOGRAPHICAL STUDIES

36. Abbott, John S. C. "Thomas Jefferson" in Lives of the Presidents of the United States of America, From Washington to the Present Time. Boston: B.B. Russell, 1867. 97-147.

    Anecdotal sketch, emphasizing TJ's humane and generous qualities.

37. Abbott, Lawrence F. "Thomas Jefferson." The Outlook. 143(1926), 131-33.

    Biographical sketch.

38. Abbott, Lawrence F. "Thomas Jefferson, The Aristocrat" in Twelve Great Modernists. New York: Doubleday, 1927. 95-124.

    John Marshall is "The Democrat"!

39. Abernethy, Thomas Perkins. "Beacon on Monticello." VQR. 19(1943), 288-91.

    Review essay, claiming TJ's accomplishments are a result of his "intellectuality" and his character.

40. Abrams, Rochonne. "Meriwether Lewis: Two Years with Jefferson, the Mentor." Missouri Historical Society Bulletin. 36(October 1979), 3-18.

    Lewis as TJ's private secretary and protege; biographical.

41. Adair, Douglass. "The Jefferson Scandals" in Fame and the Founding Fathers: Essays by Douglass Adair, ed. Trevor Colbourn. New York: Norton, 1974. 160-91.

    One of the best arguments to date exonerating TJ from the charges of sexual misconduct with Sally Hemings. Adair suggests Peter Carr was the father of Sally's children and discusses the implications of this for TJ.

42. Adair, Douglass. "The New Thomas Jefferson." WMQ. 3rd ser. 3(1946), 123-33.

    Review essay examines TJ's changing reputation.

43. Adair, Douglass. "Trivia III." WMQ. 3rd ser. 12(1955), 332-34.

    "Post Office Degrades Jefferson from a 3¢ to a 2¢ Status" in the Eisenhower administration. Only partly tongue in cheek.

44. Adams, Elizabeth L. "The Jefferson Bicentenary." More Books. 18(1943), 151-62.

9

On exhibition at Boston Public Library; prints 10 unpublished letters with background comment.

45. Adams, James Truslow. The Living Jefferson. New York: Scribner's, 1936. pp. vii, 403.

TJ "was, and still is, the greatest and most influential American exponent of both Liberalism and Americanism." Goes on to define TJ's liberalism, follow its progress through American history, and call for a great liberal leader in the 1930's, since FDR took a Hamiltonian turn.

46. [Adams, Randolph G.] Thomas Jefferson, 1743-1943: A Guide to the Rare Books, Maps & Manuscripts Exhibited at the University of Michigan. Ann Arbor: William L. Clements Library, 1943. pp. 32.

47. "Adams—Jefferson." The Outlook. 143(1926), 305-06.

Brief note on the correspondence.

48. Advisory Committee on the Papers of Thomas Jefferson. "Minutes of a meeting ... held in Princeton, February 14, 1945." Princeton, 1945. pp. 9.

Discusses editorial problems; mimeographed copy, in the McGregor Library, Univ. of Virginia.

49. Alba, Pedro de. De Bolivar a Roosevelt, Democracia y Unidad de America. Ciudad de Mexico: Cuadernos Americanos, 1949. 11-30.

Discusses TJ's democratic principles, his correspondence with Dupont de Nemours, and "El Testamento de Jefferson" on slavery and its consequences.

50. Alba, Pedro de. "Jefferson's Correspondence with DuPont de Nemours." Bulletin of the Pan American Union. 77(April 1943), 192-96.

General account.

51. "Mr. Albee, Meet Mr. Jefferson." Nation. 118(1924), 195.

Criticizes the proposal by the chairman of the Thomas Jefferson Memorial Foundation to make Monticello "an active agency of relentless war against the dangerous radicalisms of our time."

52. Alderman, Edwin A. "A Madison Letter and Some Digressions." North American Review. 217(1923), 785-96.

Mostly digressions, one of which discusses TJ's trip to the south of France and his admiration of the Maison Carrée.

53. Alderman, Edwin A. "Thomas Jefferson." Univ. of Virginia Alumni Bulletin. 3rd ser. 17(1924), 270-72.

54. Alexander, Edward P. "Jefferson and Kosciuszko: Friends of Liberty and Man." PMHB. 92(1968), 87-102.

Describes the friendship, gives detail on Kosciuszko's later career.

55. Allen, Margaret V. "The Political and Social Criticism of Margaret Fuller." South Atlantic Quarterly. 72(1973), 560-78.

TJ's was the "only one mind among America's political sons that really interested her during the formative years of her education." Little on TJ.

56. Allison, John Murray. Adams and Jefferson: the Story of a Friendship. Norman: Univ. of Oklahoma Press, 1966. pp. xiv, 350.

Pleasant but not especially probing account of the relationship done from printed sources.

57. Alvord, Clarence Walworth. "Thomas Jefferson, Apostle of Democracy." The Contemporary Review. 130(1926), 39-45.

Sketch, claims TJ "was the father of party government in a democracy."

58. "American Leaders. No. 1. Thomas Jefferson." United States Review. 4(1855), 371-84.

Biographical sketch. Journal continues The Democratic Review.

59. Anderson, Dice Robins. "The Teacher of Jefferson and Marshall." South Atlantic Quarterly. 15(1916), 327-43.

On George Wythe, discusses relationship with TJ.

60. Anniversary Dinner at Monticello, April 12, 1964 In Memory of Thomas Jefferson. Monticello: Thomas Jefferson Memorial Foundation, 1964. pp. (8).

Contains note on "Jefferson's Canons of Conduct" by James A. Bear, Jr.

61. Anniversary Dinner at Monticello, April 11, 1965 In Memory of Thomas Jefferson. Monticello: Thomas Jefferson Memorial Foundation, 1965. pp. (16).

Contains "Some of Thomas Jefferson Randolph's Recollections of His Grandfather" by James A. Bear, Jr.

62. Anniversary Dinner at Monticello April 11, 1968 In Memory of Thomas

Jefferson. Monticello: Thomas Jefferson Memorial Foundation, 1968. pp. (16).

Contains note by James A. Bear, Jr. on "The Jefferson Lottery."

63. Anniversary Dinner at Monticello April 13, 1969 in Memory of Thomas Jefferson. Monticello: Thomas Jefferson Memorial Foundation, 1969. pp. (16).

Note by James A. Bear, Jr. on TJ's calling and invitation cards.

64. Anniversary Dinner at Monticello April 12, 1970 In Memory of Thomas Jefferson. Monticello: Thomas Jefferson Memorial Foundation, 1970. pp. (12).

Note on Monticello in "The Confederate Period" by James A. Bear.

65. Anniversary Dinner at Monticello April 12, 1973 In Memory of Thomas Jefferson. Monticello: Thomas Jefferson Memorial Foundation, 1973. pp. (12).

Contains "Trial Chronology of the Organization of the Thomas Jefferson Memorial Foundation" by James A. Bear, Jr.

66. Anniversary Dinner at Monticello, April 13, 1975 In Memory of Thomas Jefferson. Monticello: Thomas Jefferson Memorial Foundation, 1975. pp. (9).

Note by Walter Muir Whitehill on "Mr. Jefferson's Codfish."

67. Anniversary Dinner at Monticello, April 12, 1976 In Memory of Thomas Jefferson. Monticello: Thomas Jefferson Memorial Foundation, 1976. pp. (5).

Note by James A. Bear, Jr. on TJ's portable writing desk.

68. Anniversary Dinner at Monticello, October 14, 1976 in Memory of Thomas Jefferson. Monticello: Thomas Jefferson Memorial Foundation, 1976. pp. (7).

Contains Lucia Goodwin's "Two Monticello Childhoods" on the reminiscences of Thomas Jefferson Randolph and Virginia Randolph Trist, two of TJ's grandchildren.

69. Anniversary Dinner at Monticello, April 13, 1980 in Memory of Thomas Jefferson. Monticello: Thomas Jefferson Memorial Foundation, 1980. pp. (5).

Note by Lucretia Ramsey Bishko, "A Dinner at Monticello," describing 1820 visit by John S. Skinner, editor of the American Farmer.

70. Antrim, Doron K. "Our Musical Presidents." Etude. 58(1940), 299, 337, 349.

    Insignificant and poorly informed.

71. Ardery, William B. "The 'Other Ride' of the Revolution." American History Illustrated. 6(October 1971), 41-42.

    Brief account of Jack Jouett's ride.

72. Aring, Charles D. "Adams and Jefferson, a Correspondence." History Today. 21(1971), 609-18.

    Descriptive.

73. Armbruster, Maxim Ethan. "Thomas Jefferson" in The Presidents of the United States: A New Appraisal from Washington to Kennedy. New York: Horizon, 1960. 69-82.

    Nothing new; reprinted with new subtitles for new presidents.

74. Arnold, Richard K. Adams to Jefferson and Jefferson to Adams: A Dialogue from Their Correspondence 1812-1826. San Francisco: Jerico Press, 1975. pp. 38.

75. Arnold, Winifred. "The Jefferson Sisters." Woman's Home Companion. 47(September 1920), 54-55.

    Note on TJ's daughters and his relationships with them.

76. At the City of Jefferson, Missouri, January 6, 1913, Ceremonies Were Had on the Occasion of the Presentation of a Bronze Bust of Thomas Jefferson as a Memorial to Louis Nicholas Krauthoff and Sophia Riseck Krauthoff. New York: H.K. Brewer Co., 1913. pp. 23.

77. Bagby, George W. "Waifs from Monticello." Lippincott's Magazine. 4(1869), 205-07.

    Describes a few leaves from one of TJ's account books, claiming they illustrate his "particularity in manners of business" and his considerate attention to his slaves.

78. Bailey, Thomas A. "Jefferson and Madisonian Democracy" in Voices of America: The Nation's Story in Slogans, Sayings, and Songs. New York: Free Press, 1976. 39-50.

    Discusses slogans and songs associated wilth TJ during the election of 1800 and the subsequent eight years.

79. Bailyn, Bernard. "Boyd's Jefferson: Notes for a Sketch." New England Quarterly. 33(1960), 380-401.

Review essay on the first 15 volumes of The Papers which "contain more than enough material for a re-estimation," particularly in the volumes covering his time abroad. Two controlling groups of traits emerge: a "conventionality of mind and behavior" in the face of European culture and society, but "in his direct, tactical involvement with public affairs, he was as unconventional, as imaginative, resourceful, and tough as the best, or worst, of Old World politicians."

80. Baird, W. "The Domestic Life of Thomas Jefferson, Compiled from Family Letters and Reminiscences. By his Great-grandaughter, Sarah N. Randolph." Southern Magazine. 10(1872), 495-502.

Review essay using the occasion to praise TJ for his efforts to resist the Federal usurpation of state's powers which had produced the recent difficulties.

81. Bakeless, John. Lewis & Clark: Partners in Discovery. New York: Morrow, 1947. pp. xii, 498.

Chapters 1, 6, and 7 deal with TJ's appointment of Lewis as his secretary and with the purchase of Louisiana.

82. Bakeless, John and Catherine. "Thomas Jefferson" in Signers of the Declaration. Boston: Houghton Mifflin, 1969. 71-79.

Superficial.

83. Banks, Louis Albert, ed. "Thomas Jefferson" in Capital Stories about Famous Americans. New York: The Christian Herald, 1905. 319-28.

Anecdotes.

84. Banks, Louis Albert. "Thomas Jefferson" in The Story of the Hall of Fame, Including the Lives and Portraits of the Elect and of Those Who Barely Missed Election. New York: The Christian Herald, 1902. 106-18.

85. Banks, Louis Albert. "Thomas Jefferson" in Youth of Famous Americans. New York: Eaton and Mains, 1902. 41-47.

86. Barkley, Alben W. "'This is the Fourth of July; Jefferson Still Lives.'" Vital Speeches. 9(1943), 628-31.

Jefferson Day speech at the Univ. of Virginia, June 4, 1943.

87. Barnes, Harry Elmer. The New History and the Social Studies. New York: Century, 1925. 235-47.

Personalities of Hamilton and TJ discussed as an illustration "of the application of the newer psychology to historical biography." TJ, an introvert in the Jungian mode, was terrified of his father, "a gruff giant with a tremendous temper," and he obtained "considerable of psychic release ... by assaults upon kings." Reworking of material in 88 infra.

88. Barnes, Harry Elmer. "Some Reflections on the Possible Service of Analytical Psychology to History." Psychoanalytic Review. 8(1921), 22-37.

   Contends TJ has "anti-authority" and "inferiority" complexes.

89. Barr, Stringfellow. "L'Influence Française sur Jefferson." Le Moniteur Franco-Américain. 14(January 1930), 13, 17.

90. Barre, W. L. "Thomas Jefferson" in Lives of Illustrious Men of America, Distinguished in the Annals of the Republic as Legislators, Warriors, and Philosophers. Cincinnati: W.A. Clarke, 1859. 118-68.

   Sympathetic sketch.

91. Barrett, Clifton Waller. Thomas Jefferson, The American. Charlottesville: Thomas Jefferson Memorial Foundation, 1979. pp. 15.

   Biographical sketch; Independence Day Address.

92. Barrett, Marvin. Meet Thomas Jefferson. New York: Random House, 1967. pp. 86.

   Juvenile.

93. Barry, Joseph. "Jefferson in Paris." Saturday Review. 3(January 10, 1976), 20-22.

   TJ as visitor in Paris; derivative.

94. Barry, William T. Speech of William T. Barry, Esq., on the Death of Adams, Jefferson, and Shelby. Delivered in Lexington on Tuesday, Fifteenth August, One Thousand Eight Hundred and Twenty Six. Lexington, Ky.: John Bradford, 1826. pp. 24.

   Isaac Shelby died on July 18th; pays particular attention to the death-bed scenes of TJ and Adams.

95. Bartley, Thomas Welles. The Address of T. W. Bartley, Before the Jefferson National Monumental Association. Delivered October 16, 1882. Washington, 1882. pp. 7.

   Call for a monument to TJ in Washington, D.C.

96. Barman, Sol. "Thomas Jefferson" in Madmen and Geniuses: The Vice Presidents of the United States. Chicago: Follett, 1974. 21-25.

   Trivial.

15

97. Basso, Hamilton. "Farewell and Hail to Thomas Jefferson" in
    Mainstream. New York: Reynal and Hitchock, 1943. 23-43.

    Unconvincing discussion of TJ as a "Rousseauist."

98. Battle, George Gordon. New York and Jefferson, An Address. n.p.,
    1926. pp. 11.

    Speech at Monticello, cataloguing TJ's links with New York.

99. Bear, James A. Jr. "Accounts of Monticello: 1780-1878, A Selective
    Bibliography." Magazine of Albermarle County History. 21(1963),
    13-27.

    Checklist of first hand accounts, arranged chronologically.

100. Bear, James A., Jr. "The Hemings Family of Monticello." Virginia
     Cavalcade. 29(Autumn 1979), 78-87.

     Carefully researched account of the Hemings family in TJ's time
     reveals a set of able, intelligent workers.

101. Bear, James A., Jr., ed. Jefferson at Monticello. Charlottesville:
     Univ. of Virginia Press, 1967. pp. xiv, 144.

     Collects Isaac Jefferson's Memoirs of a Monticello Slave and
     Hamilton Wilcox Pierson's Jefferson at Monticello, with an intro-
     duction by the editor.

102. Bear, James A., Jr. "The Last Few Days in the Life of Thomas
     Jefferson." Magazine of Albemarle County History. 32(1974), 63-79.

     Well-researched account of the death and burial of TJ.

103. Bear, James A., Jr. "Mr. Jefferson's Nails." Magazine of Albemarle
     County History. 16(1958), 47-52.

     On TJ's nail-making business. Technically successful, its accounts
     were not well managed, and since all due bills were not collected, it
     probably lost money in its later years.

104. Bear, James A., Jr. "Monticello, Home of Thomas Jefferson." Stamps.
     94(March 31, 1956), 446-48.

     Account related to the issue of the 20¢ Monticello postage stamp on
     April 13, 1956.

105. Bear, James A., Jr. "Monticello—Jefferson's Palladian Retreat."
     Museum News. 39(February 1961), 20-23.

     Short account of the house as it was in TJ's time and a discussion of
     research resources used in restoration and preservation.
16

106. Bear, James A., Jr. "Thomas Jefferson and the Ladies." Augusta Historical Bulletin. 6(Fall 1970), 4-19.

Thoughtful account of TJ's relations with women. Finds him "more thoughtful than sentimental, more conventional and utilitarian than advanced.

107. Beard, Charles A. "Jefferson in America Now." Yale Review. n.s. 25(1935), 241-57.

Argues that conservative appeals to TJ's authority against the New Deal are mistaken in their understanding of him.

108. Beard, Reed. "Thomas Jefferson" in Brief Biographies of American Presidents, Embracing an Authentic Account of the Lives and Times of Our Presidents from the Ancestry of Washington to Cleveland's Administration. Lafayette, Ind.: Spring, Emerson, and Co., 1886. 102-42.

109. Beck, James M. The Memory of Jefferson, An Address Delivered at a Stated Meeting of the Sons of the Revolution in the District of Columbia on the 150th Anniversary of the Birth of Thomas Jefferson. Washington: Government Printing Office, 1928. pp. 8.

Laudatory oration.

110. Beck, James M. The Scholar in Polictics. An Oration Delivered at Celebration of the One Hundred and Seventy-first Anniversary of the Birthday of Thomas Jefferson on Founders Day, April 13, 1914, at the University of Virginia. n.p., 1914. pp. 27.

Rambling praise.

111. Bedini, Silvio A. Declaration of Independence Desk, Relic of Revolution. Washington: Smithsonian Institution Press, 1981. pp. vii, 112.

112. Bell, Landon C. Thomas Jefferson, An Address Before the Columbus Chapter of the National Society of the Daughters of the American Revolution, n.p. n.d. pp. 19.

Loosely organized survey.

113. Bellot, H. Hale. "Thomas Jefferson in American Historiography." Transactions of the Royal Historical Society. 5th ser. 4(1954), 135-55.

Considers the treatment particularly after the Civil War of TJ as prophet of national democracy and the embarassing question of his responsibility for the concept of nullification. Claims there has been no effect reinterpretation of TJ's ideas in light of the distinction drawn between allegiance to the rule of law and primary trust in the rule of the people.

114. Beloff, Max. "A 'Founding Father': The Sally Hemings Affair." Encounter. 43(September 1974), 52-56.

Inconclusive discussion of Fawn Brodie's claims.

115. Beloff, Max. Thomas Jefferson and American Democracy. London: Hodder and Stoughton, 1948. pp. xi, 271.

A volume in the Teach Yourself History Library, points out the difficult questions about TJ but evades answering them.

116. Benjamin, Mary. "More Fun!" Collector. 65(1952), 194-95.

Describes an invitation from TJ, in Meriwether Lewis' hand, to DeWitt Clinton for "dinner and chess."

117. [Bennett, Lerone]. "Thomas Jefferson's Negro Grandchildren." Ebony. 10(November 1954), 78-80.

Descendents of Joseph Fossett, supposedly a son of Sally Hemings and TJ. Photographs.

118. Bennett, Paul L. "A Virginian and a Man from Massachusetts." New York Times Magazine. July 3, 1955. 5.

Brief sketch of TJ and John Adams.

119. Benson, Samuel P. "Origin of Article VIII., Literature in the Constitution of Maine." Collections of the Maine Historical Society. 7(1876), 239-42.

Governor William King stated that TJ wrote "the substance if not the exact words" of the article on education in the Maine Constitution.

120. Bérenger, Henry. "Jefferson and France" in Paroles d'Amérique. Abbeville: Imprimerie F. Paillart, 1926. 41-66.

Tribute to TJ's affection for France.

121. Bernard, John. "Recollections of President Jefferson" in Retrospectives of America 1797-1811. New York: Harper, 1887. 232-42.

"His heart was warmed with a love for the whole human race; a bonhomie which fixed your attention the instant he spoke ... his conversational powers capable of discussing moral questions of deepest seriousness, or the lightest themes of humor and fantasy."

122. Bernhard, Karl, Duke of Saxe-Weimar-Eisenach. Reise Sr. Hoheit der Herzogs Bernhard zu Sachsen-Weimar-Eisenach durch Nord-Amerika in den Jahren 1825 und 1826. Hrsg. von Heinrich Luden. Weimar: Wilhelm Hoffman, 1828. 1: 296-99.
18

These pages describe a visit to the Univ. of Virginia and Monticello in November 1825, noting especially TJ's art collection.

123. Betts, Edwin Morris and James A. Bear, Jr. "Introduction" to The Family Letters of Thomas Jefferson. Columbia: Univ. of Missouri Press, 1966. 3-14.

Discusses TJ's family life and family. Letters printed in this collection are annotated and arranged chronologically.

124. Beutin, Ludwig. "Hamilton und Jefferson." Historische Zeitschrift. 177(1954), 495-516.

Surveys twentieth-century historical writing on TJ and Hamilton, arguing that treatment of them reflects both the prejudices of the writers and an increasing scholarly sophistication.

125. Bevan, Edith Rossiter, ed. "Thomas Jefferson in Annapolis, November 25, 1783—May 11, 1784." Maryland Historical Magazine. 41(1946), 115-24.

Transcribes his expense account while delegate to Congress.

126. Biddle, Nicholas. Eulogium on Thomas Jefferson, Delivered Before the American Philosophical Society, on the Eleventh Day of April 1827. Philadelphia: Robert H. Small, 1827. pp. 55.

TJ was a force for reason, science, and enlightened leadership. One of the most interesting of the eulogies.

*127. Bierstadt, Edward Hale. "Was Jefferson Right?" Reviewer. 2(1922), 301-05.

128. Bigelow, John. "Jefferson's Financial Diary." Harper's Magazine. 70(1885), 534-42.

Detailed description with extracts from TJ's account book from 1791-1803.

129. Bigelow, John. "Thomas Jefferson" in The Louisiana Purchase of 1803: A History from the Earliest Explorations to the Present Time, of the Territory Acquired by the Louisiana Purchase; Together With Some Account of the Famous Men Connected Therewith, ... New York: Encyclopedia Brittanica Co., 1904. 9-21.

130. Binger, Carl. "Conflicts in the Life of Thomas Jefferson." American Journal of Psychiatry. 125(1969), 1098-1106.

Argues that TJ "achieved an extraordinary mastery of his life." Also suggests TJ and Hamilton were competing for the love of a father figure (Washington) and this rivalry was complicated by their mutual admiration. Lyman H. Butterfield in reply generally agrees, but points to TJ's deficient sense of humor, his avoidance of conflict, his silences. Suggestive exchange.

131. Binger, Carl. Thomas Jefferson: A Well-Tempered Mind. New York: Norton, 1970. pp. 209.

Psychological study claiming to demonstrate the inner harmony of TJ's mind as a result of his reconciliation of masculine, aggressive, executive characteristics with feminine, aesthetic, care-taking attributes.

132. "A Biographical Sketch of Thomas Jefferson" in The Thomas Jefferson Bible; Being, as Entitled by Him, "The Life and Morals of Jesus Extracted Textually from the Gospels of Matthew, Mark, Luke, and John." With a Valuable Appendix of Biblical Facts. Chicago: George W. Ogilvie, 1904. pp. xxii, 161.

133. Birch, John J. "The Ride of Jack Jouett, the Hero of Virginia." Americana. 23(1929), 454-57.

Ride to warn TJ of Tarleton's approach to Monticello.

134. Birdwell, A. W. Thomas Jefferson, Author of American Liberty. Houston: Star Engraving Co., 194?. pp. 14.

Sketch.

135. Birthday Celebration in Honor of Thomas Jefferson (1743-1826), Independence Hall, Independence Square, Philadelphia, Pennsylvania, Monday, April 13, 1964, 3:00 P.M. Hancock, N.H.: Thomas Jefferson Society, 1964. Broadside.

One of the activities of this short-lived group; featured speech was "TJ and the Constitution" by Davis Young Paschall.

136. Bishop, H. O. "Twenty Minutes with Jefferson." National Republic. 25(February 1938), 1-2, 16.

TJ gives a lesson in Americanism.

137. Bizardel, Yvon. "Les Americains de l'An II." Informations & Documents. 216(1965), 24-29.

How TJ and other Americans in Paris coped with the Revolution.

138. Bizardel, Yvon and Howard C. Rice, Jr. "'Poor in Love Mr. Short.'" WMQ. 3rd ser. 21(1964), 516-32.

Account of the "sentimental life" of TJ's protege and secretary in France, 1784-1789, deals with the relationship between Short and TJ.

139. Bliven, Bruce, "Our Legacy from Mr. Jefferson." <u>Reader's Digest</u>. 82(March 1963), 160-68.

    Superficial; rpt. in <u>A Mirror for Greatness</u>. New York: McGraw Hill, 1975. 107-35 in revised form.

140. Bloss, George M. D. "Jefferson, the Second Vice-President and the Third President of the United State" in <u>Historic and Literary Miscellany</u>. Cincinnati; R. Clarke and Co., 1875. pp. 62-67.

    Laudatory sketch.

141. Bogart, William H. ("Sentinel"). <u>Who Goes There? or, Men and Events</u>. New York: Carleton, 1866. 37-40.

    Anecdotes about TJ stressing his sociability.

142. Bok-Van Bork, Jacoba Johanna. "Thomas Jefferson" in "Bijdrage tot de Psychologie van den Staatsman." Ph.D. dissertation. Univ. of Amsterdam, 1924. 37-64.

    Printed: Haarlem: H.D. Tjeenk Willink & Zoon, 1924. Psychological portrait, but based on Morse's and Parton's lives of TJ.

143. Bolton, Sarah Knowles. "Thomas Jefferson" in <u>Famous American Statesmen</u>. New York: Crowell, 1888. 67-98.

    Chapter in a companion book to her <u>Poor Boys Who Became Famous</u>; often reprinted.

144. Bonnell, Ulane. "The World of Franklin and Jefferson." <u>Manuscripts</u>. 28(1976), 213-15.

    Describes an exhibit which opened in Paris in January, 1975.

145. Booth, Edward Townsend. "Thomas Jefferson: Piedmont Villa" in <u>Country Life in America as Lived by Ten Presidents of the United States</u>. New York: Knopf, 1947. 76-103.

    Life at Monticello. TJ, like Washington, "took too broad and impersonal a view of farming. He and Washington, in effect, ran two very expensive agricultural experiment stations."

146. Borne, O. S. "Jefferson and the Dark Days of '14." <u>National Magazine</u>. 11(1900), 551-56.

    Fanciful portrait of TJ in despair, unaware of the Treaty of Ghent; blames the war on him.

147. Bottorf, William K. "Mr. Jefferson Tours New England." <u>New England Galaxy</u>. 20(no. 3, 1979), 3-7.

148. Bottorf, William K. Thomas Jefferson. Boston: Twayne, 1979. pp. 162.

A volume in the Twayne United States Authors Series; competent introduction which pays particular attention to his aesthetic interests and literary gifts.

149. Bowen, Dorothy. "Thomas Jefferson—1743-1943: A Bicentennial Exhibition." Huntington Library Quarterly. 6(1943), 495-504.

Account of material from the Huntington on exhibit there.

150. Bowers, Claude G. "Founder's Day Address." Univ. of Virginia Alumni Newsletter. 16(April 1928), 185-93.

TJ is a "living, vital principle" who opposes the enemies of democracy at home and abroad.

151. Bowers, Claude G. The Founders of the Republic. Chicago: American Library Association, 1927. pp. 36.

An introduction to a course of readings which includes Bower's Jefferson and Hamilton.

152. Bowers, Claude G. "Jefferson and the American Way of Life" in The Heritage of Jefferson. New York: International Publishers, 1944. 13-29.

Argues for TJ as a revolutionist, iconoclast, and radical who defined the American way of life.

153. Bowers, Claude G. Patriotic Editorials Written ... Expressly for The Sesqui-Centennial of American Independence and the Thomas Jefferson Centennial Commission. New York: Thomas Jefferson Memorial Foundation, 1926. unpag.

Fund raising effort for Monticello.

*154. Bowers, Claude G. "Thomas Jefferson" in High Moment, ed. Wallace Brockway. New York: Simon and Schuster, 1955. 129-46.

155. Bowers, Claude G. Thomas Jefferson; An Address Before the Democratic Women's Luncheon Club of Philadelphia, February 7th 1927. [Philadelphia, 1927]. pp. 21.

156. Bowers, Claude G. "Thomas Jefferson of Monticello." New York Times Magazine. February 28, 1943. 5, 33.

157. Bowers, Claude G. The Young Jefferson, 1743-1789. Boston: Houghton Mifflin, 1945. pp. xxx, 544.

The first volume in Bowers' biographic trilogy, but the last written; concentrates on the "human Jefferson" as the foundation for the successes of the later political Jefferson.

158. Boyd, Julian P. "Adrienne Koch: Historian." Maryland Historian. 3(1972), 5-8.

Evaluates an eminent Jefferson scholar's work on TJ.

159. Boyd, Julian P. The Enduring World of Thomas Jefferson. Williamsburg: College of William and Mary, 1963. pp. 20.

"What the world of Jefferson has to offer us ... is only an abstraction and an example drawn from an era that may be wholly irrelevant in the world we face."

160. Boyd, Julian P. "Introduction" to The Jeffersonian Cyclopedia, ed. John P. Foley. New York: Russell and Russell, 1967.

Rpt. separately; comments on the range of TJ's opinions and the usefulness of Foley's compilation.

161. Boyd, Julian P. A Geranium for Lyman. Princeton: Princeton Univ. Press, 1951. pp. 6.

Farewell note to Lyman Butterfield, recalls TJ's gift to Margaret Bayard Smith of a potted geranium when he left Washington in 1809.

162. Boyd, Julian P. "Jefferson's Final Testament of Faith." New York Times Magazine. April 10, 1949. 11, 33-39.

On the June 21, 1826 letter to R. S. Weightman.

163. Boyd, Julian P. "Jefferson's French Baggage, Crated and Uncrated." Proceedings of the Massachusetts Historical Society. 83(1971), 16-27.

Account of the shipment in 1790 of TJ's acquisitions in France.

164. Boyd, Julian P. "Mr. Jefferson to Dr. Rush with Affection." Quarterly Journal of the Library of Congress. 1(no. 2, 1944), 3-9.

Discusses context and prints correct copy of the letter of September 23, 1800 to Rush in which he swears eternal hostility against tyranny over the mind of man.

165. Boyd, Julian P. "The Relevance of Thomas Jefferson for the Twentieth Century." American Scholar. 22(1953), 61-76.

Applauds TJ's faith in principle, in the rights of man, and in knowledge, but notes that, paradoxically, increasingly exact, predictive social knowledge may be the next threat to human freedom.

166. Boyd, Julian P. "Report to the Thomas Jefferson Bicentennial Commission on the need, scope, proposed method of preparation, probable cost, and possible mens of publishing a comprehensive edition of the Writings of Thomas Jefferson." Washington?: 1943. pp. 32 (mimeographed).

Boyd was historian of the Commission; this report helped lay the way for the Princeton edition of the Papers.

167. Boyd, Julian P. "The Smooth Handle"; A Challenge to the Organization Man. Williamsburg: College of William and Mary, 1957. pp. 10.

Rpt. from Seminar, An Academic Journal. 2(Spring 1957). TJ illustrates the proper behavior of a citizen in a republic, a challenger of conventional beliefs but a respecter of the people's right to govern themselves.

168. Boyd, Julian P. "Some Animadversions on Being Struck by Lightning." Daedalus. 86(May 1955), 49-56.

On editing the Papers of Thomas Jefferson.

169. Boyd, Julian P. The Spirit of Christmas at Monticello. New York: Oxford Univ. Press, 1964. pp. (60).

Surveys the variety of Christmas celebration in 18th-century Virginia and discusses in particular TJ's visit at Christmas, 1759, to Colonel Nathaniel Dandridge. TJ, however, does not mention in his letters festive activities at Christmas, even though he clearly practiced some of the traditions. Best piece on this subject.

170. Boyd, Julian P. "Thomas Jefferson Survives." American Scholar. 20(1951), 163-73.

Even so, few of the voices now claiming TJ's authority are authentic echoes of his.

171. Boyd, Julian P. and Alfred L. Bush. "While the Art of Printing Is Left to Us, Science Can Never Be Retrograde" in "Let Every Sluice of Knowledge be Open'd and set a Flowing" A Tribute to Philip May Hamer .... New York, 1960. unpag.

Three page discussion of TJ's letter to William Green Munford, June 18, 1799; facsimile and transcription.

172. Boykin, Edward. "Affectionately Yours, Thomas Jefferson." Ladies Home Journal. 81(November 1964), 136-42.

Introductory note and family correspondence selected from the author's To the Girls and Boys, q.v.

173. Boykin, Edward, comp. Thomas Jeffeson Quiz Book. Washington: Thomas Jefferson Bicentennial Commission, 1943. pp. 30.

91 questions and answers for students.

174. Boykin, Edward. To the Girls and Boys, Being The Delightful, Little-Known Letters of Thomas Jefferson to and from His Children and Grandchildren. New York: Funk and Wagnalls, 1964. pp. x, 210.

Historical notes and commentary accompany the letters.

175. Brackenridge, Henry M. A Eulogy on the Lives and Characters of John Adams and Thomas Jefferson. By the Hon. H. M. Brackenridge. Pensacola: W. Hasell Hunt, 1826. pp. 18.

Touches comprehensively on the careers and accomplishments of both Adams and TJ and delivers equal praise.

*176. Brent, Robert A. Mr. Jefferson of Virginia; Renaissance Gentleman in America. Quezon City?, 1966? pp. xii, 150.

Has a "Foreward" by Edward Mattos and "On Jefferson" by I. P. Soliongco.

177. Brent, Robert A. "Nicholas Philip Trist—A Link Between Jefferson and Jackson?" Southern Quarterly. 1(no. 2, 1963), 87–97.

Sketch of Trist as TJ's secretary and grandson-in-law and friend of Jackson.

178. Brent, Robert Arthur. "Nicholas Philip Trist's Search for a Career." M.A. thesis. Univ. of Virginia, 1947. pp. 92.

A short biographical sketch of Trist, who was TJ's last private secretary and who married his granddaughter, Virginia Randolph.

*179. Bridges, David L. "A Historical Study of Thomas Jefferson." M.A. thesis. North Texas State Univ., 1958.

180. Bridgwater, Dorothy. "A New Letter to Thomas Jefferson." Yale Univ. Library Gazette. 30(July 1955), 29–30.

Letter of Harry Innes, November 29, 1781, noted as unlocated in the Papers, 6:159.

181. Bright, Robert Southall. Address ... Before the Society of the Descendants of the Signers of the Declaration of Independence, on the Occasion of the One Hundred and Thirty-fourth Anniversary of the Adoption of the Declaration. n.p., 1910? pp. 21.

TJ as philosopher of free enterprise and individualism.

182. Brodie, Fawn M. "The Great Jefferson Taboo." American Heritage. 22(June 1972), 48-57, 97-100.

Claims that the evidence showing TJ as the father of Sally Hemings' children, while not conclusive, is suggestive.

183. Brodie, Fawn M. "Jefferson Biographers and the Psychology of Canonization." Journal of Interdisciplinary History. 2(1971), 155-71.

Review essay of bigraphical volumes by Dumas Malone and Merrill Peterson, criticizing them for being "extremely protective of (TJ's) inner life," particularly in regard to his sex life and Sally Hemings.

184. Brodie, Fawn M. "The Political Hero in America: His Fate and His Future." VQR. 46(1974), 46-60.

Discusses the difficulties in maintaining American political heroes; even TJ is in question because of his attitudes toward blacks and the Sally Hemings affair.

185. Brodie, Fawn M. Thomas Jefferson: An Intimate History. New York: Norton, 1974. pp. 591.

Controversial biography focusing on TJ's private life and its relation to his public life. Has been criticized both on the grounds of historical accuracy and psychological method, but if the claims for TJ's sexual liaisons are fully unsupported, the handling of his response to the death of his wife and his dealing with grief is interesting.

186. Brodie, Fawn M. "Thomas Jefferson's Unknown Grandchildren: A Study in Historical Silence." American Heritage. 27(October 1976), 28-33, 94-99.

On Sally Hemings' descendants and family traditions linking them to TJ as ancestor; a more assertive continuation of claims made in the author's Thomas Jefferson.

187. Brogan, Denis W. "The Ghost of Jefferson." Fortnightly. 146(July 1936), 88-92.

Explaining to a British audience why American politicians of different persuasions all appeal to the authority of TJ.

188. Brogan, Denis W. "Thomas Jefferson" in American Themes. London: Hamish Hamilton, 1948. 175-80.

Review essay occasioned by Saul Padover's biography; suggests that TJ's self-chosen epitaph is not a rejection of public honors but an underlying "scepticism of the permanence of any political form."

189. Broglie, Axelle de. "Jefferson's Pursuit of Happiness." Réalités.

250(September 1971), 39–45.

TJ's life at Monticello. Illustrated.

190. Brooks, Elbridge Streeter. "Thomas Jefferson" in <u>Historic Americans</u>. New York: Crowell, 1899. 100–14.

*191. Brooks Erastus. <u>Address by Hon. Erastus Brooks. What True Democracy Means: as Illustrated in the Life and Character of Thomas Jefferson. Delivered Before the Jefferson Club of New Brighton, S.I. ... Printed for Circulation on the Birthday Anniversary April 2, 1884.</u> Tompkinsville, N.Y.: Richmond County Democrat Steam Job Print, 1884. pp. 27.

192. Brooks, Geraldine. "Martha Jefferson, Daughter of Thomas Jefferson" in <u>Dames and Daughters of the Young Republic</u>. New York: T. Y. Crowell, 1901. 176–215.

193. Brooks, Van Wyck. "Thomas Jefferson" in <u>The World of Washington Irving</u>. New York: Dutton, 1944. 133–51.

TJ an important referential figure throughout, but here drawn as a democratic idealist shaped by the French Enlightenment and "the earliest crystallization of what might be called the American prophetic tradition, of Whitman's Pioneers, the 'trust thyself' of Emerson and Lincoln's mystical faith in the wisdom of the people."

194. Brougham, Henry Peter, Lord. "Professor Tucker's <u>Life of Jefferson</u>." <u>Edinburgh Review</u>. 66(1837), 156–86.

Review essay proclaiming TJ as the greatest American after Washington and Franklin.

195. Brougham, Henry Peter, Lord. "Thomas Jefferson" in <u>Historical Sketches of Statesmen Who Flourished in the Time of George III. Third Series</u>. London: Richard Griffin and Co., 1843. 280–90.

196. Brown, B. Bolton. "Thomas Jefferson at Monticello." <u>Mentor</u>. 13(October 1925), 37–44.

Photographic illustrations.

197. Brown, Marel. "Monticello Was Jefferson's Dream Home." <u>Home Life</u>. 4(August 1950), 4, 10–13.

198. Brown, Margaret Washington. "The Story of the Declaration of Independence Desk and How It Came to the National Museum." <u>Annual Report of the Board of Regents of the Smithsonian Institution ... 1953</u>. Washington: Government Printing Office, 1954. 455–62.

Provenance of TJ's portable desk and an account of the copies made of it.

199. Browne, C. A. "Elder John Leland and the Mammoth Cheshire Cheese." Agricultural History. 18(1944), 145-53.

Leland thought up and organized the presentation of the mammoth cheese on New Years Day, 1802.

200. Browne, Edythe H. "The Great Simplicity of Jefferson." Commonweal. 4(1926), 261-62.

TJ as friend of the common man.

201. Bruce, David K. E. "Thomas Jefferson" in Seven Pillars of the Republic. [Garden City, N.Y.]: privately printed, 1936.

Brief sketch, rpt. in Revolution to Reconstruction. Garden City: Doubleday, Doran, 1939. 85-133.

202. Bruce, Philip Alexander. "President Thomas Jefferson" in The Virginia Plutarch. Chapel Hill: Univ. of North Carolina Press, 1929. 2:19-37.

203. Bryan, John H. Orations on the Death of Thomas Jefferson and John Adams. Delivered at the Request of the Citizens of Newbern, on the 17th and 24th July, 1826. By the Hon. John H. Bryan and the Hon. John Stanley. Newbern, N.C.: Watson and Machen, 1826. 3-10.

Bryan's oration on TJ was delivered on July 17th.

204. Bryan, Mina R. "Thomas Jefferson Through the Eyes of His Contemporaries." Princeton Univ. Library Chronicle. 9(1948), 219-24.

Discussion of firsthand accounts and anecdotes about TJ.

205. Bryan, William Jennings. Speech of William Jennings Bryan With Address of Welcome by Edward M. Shepard at the Brooklyn Democratic Club. Brooklyn: Brooklyn Democratic Club, 1907. pp. 26.

If TJ were here now, he would oppose monopolies and vote Democratic.

206. Bryant, Arthur. "Thomas Jefferson" in The American Ideal. London: Longmans, Green, 1936. 1-145.

Biographical sketch.

207. Bryce, James. "Third President and Founder of the University of Virginia" in University and Historical Addresses. New York: Macmillan, 1913. 109-24.

Univ. of Virginia founder's Day speech, praising TJ's variety and his interest in education.

*208. Budd, Henry. "Thomas Jefferson" in St. Marys Hall Lectures and Other Papers. Philadelphia: H.T. Coates and Co., 1898. 242-63.

209. Budd, Henry. Thomas Jefferson: An Address delivered on the occasion of the birthday of Jefferson, under the auspices of the Jeffersonian Society of Philadelphia, at the Odd Fellows Temple, April 15th, 1901. [Philadelphia, n.d.]. pp. 36.

TJ still best example of presidential conduct at a time when "centralization and imperialism together threaten ... our very life as a republic."

210. Budka, Metchie J. E. "Minerva Versus Archimedes." Smithsonian Journal of History. 1(Spring 1966), 61-64.

TJ was asked in 1802 to choose a design for the U.S. Military Philosophical Society.

211. "Builders of America; Picture Biography." Scholastic. 41(November 16, 1942), 13.

TJ in comicstrips.

212. [Bulfinch, Thomas]. "Jefferson's Private Character." North American Review. 91(1860), 107-18.

Review of Randall's biography; revelation of TJ's private life justifies high opinion formed by readers of his Writings in 1829 and after.

213. Bullard, F. Lauriston. "Lincoln as a Jeffersonian." More Books. 23(1948), 283-300.

Documents Lincoln's knowledge of TJ; notes that TJ and Lincoln were in essential agreement on the advantages of gradual emancipation and the colonization of freed slaves.

214. Bullock, Helen D. My Head and My Heart: A Little Chronicle of Thomas Jefferson and Maria Cosway. New York: Putnam, 1945. pp. xvii, 235.

Charming account of TJ's friendship with Maria Cosway, but does not satisfactorily come to grips with the complexities of his character or of the historical context.

215. Bullock, Helen Duprey. "The Papers of Thomas Jefferson." American Archivist. 4(1941), 238-49.

Account of archival collections of TJ's papers.

216. [Bumstead, Samuel A.]. "A Description of Jefferson." <u>VMHB</u>.
      24(1916), 309-10.

      Amusing account of meeting TJ on a road near Monticello in 1822.

217. Butler, Nicholas Murray. <u>Is Thomas Jefferson the Forgotten Man? An
      Address delivered at the Parrish Art Museum, Southampton, Long
      Island, September 1, 1935</u>. New York: Carnegie Endowment for
      International Peace, n.d. pp. 16.

      Less about TJ than an attack upon governmental regulation and taxa-
      tion; an anti-New Deal Jefferson.

218. Butler, Nicholas Murray. "Un fondateur des États Unis; Thomas
      Jefferson réprésentant de l'esprit démocratique." <u>Correspondant</u>.
      n.s. 263(April 10, 1925), 23-42.

219. Butterfield, Lyman. "The Dream of Benjamin Rush: The Reconciliation
      of John Adams and Thomas Jefferson." <u>Yale Review</u>. 40(1951),
      297-319.

      Good account of how Rush fostered the reconciliation of TJ and
      Adams.

220. Butterfield, Lyman H. "The Jefferson-Adams Correspondence in the
      Adams Manuscript Trust." <u>Quarterly Journal of the Library of
      Congress</u>. 5(February 1948), 3-6.

      Comments on the friendship and the location of mss. letters.

221. Butterfield, L. H. and Howard C. Rice, Jr. "Jefferson's Earliest Note
      to Maria Cosway with Some New Facts and Conjectures on His
      Broken Wrist." <u>WMQ</u>. 3rd ser. 5(1948), 26-33.

      Suggests possibility TJ injured his wrist while visiting the Desert de
      Retz on September 16, 1786. Interesting description of the Desert.

222. Butterfield, L. H. "July 4 in 1826." <u>American Heritage</u>. 6(1955),
      102-04.

      U.S. came of age in the summer of 1826 because deaths of TJ and
      Adams "awakened in every thoughtful citizen a consciousness of the
      republican ideals the two patriots had exemplified."

*223. Buttre, Lilian C. "Jefferson" in <u>American Portrait Gallery. With
      Biographical Sketches of Presidents, Statesmen,...</u> . New York:
      J. C. Buttre, 1877. 1:141-42.

224. "Buying Monticello." <u>House Beautiful</u>. 33(January 1913), 50.

      "Mixed sentiments" about Mrs. Littleton's scheme to acquire
      Monticello.

225. Byrd, Harry Flood. Thomas Jefferson and American Democracy. Charlottesville: Thomas Jefferson Memorial Foundation, 1972. pp. (12).

Conventional generalities.

226. C. F. "The Home of Thomas Jefferson." Philomathean Monthly (Bridgewater College, Va.). 4(1899), 57-59.

Sketch, probably from secondary sources.

227. Cable, Mary and Annabelle Prager. "The Levys of Monticello." American Heritage. 29(February 1978), 30-39.

Good popular account of the care of Monticello by Commodore Uriah Phillips Levy and his nephew Jefferson Monroe Levy, who owned the house from 1836 until 1923.

228. Cambreleng, C. C. "Eulogy Pronounced in the City of New York, July 17th, 1826" in A Selection of Eulogies ... . Hartford: D. F. Robinson & Co., 1826. 59-70.

Emphasizes the death of Adams and TJ on the 50th anniversary of the Declaration as God's "manifesting to us his special favor and protection, apparently revealing to all mankind that this is his chosen land."

229. Campbell, Mrs. A. A. "Monticello." Confederate Veteran. 28(1920), 129-30.

230. Campbell, Charles. "Thomas Jefferson" in History of the Colony and Ancient Dominion of Virginia. Philadelphia: Lippincott, 1860. 603-06.

Sketch, little on TJ as governor.

231. Campbell, Helen L. Famous Presidents: Washington, Jefferson, Madison, Lincoln, Grant. Boston: Educational Publishing Co., 1903. 53-87.

School text.

232. Campbell, Helen L. Thomas Jefferson, The Sage of Monticello. Boston: Educational Publishing Co., 1899. pp. 32.

Juvenile.

233. Capen, Oliver Bronson. "Thomas Jefferson" in Country Homes of Famous Americans. New York: Doubleday, Page, 1905. 145-54.

TJ's life at Monticello; loose with the facts. Illustrated.

234. Cappon, Lester J. "A Postscript from Monticello, July 4, 1826." Papers of the Albemarle County Historical Society. 1(1940-41), 25-30.

A report from TJ's death bed.

235. Cappon, Lester J. "Preface" and "Introduction" to The Adams-Jefferson Letters; The Complete Correspondence Between Thomas Jefferson and Abigail and John Adams. Chapel Hill: Univ. of North Carolina Press, 1959. 1:xxv-li.

On editorial procedures and a survey of the Adams-TJ relationship.

236. Carlton, Mabel Mason and Henry Fisk Carlton. "Thomas Jefferson, Author of the Declaration" in The Story of the Declaration of Independence. New York: Scribner's, 1926. 55-65.

Juvenile.

237. [Carlton, Mabel Mason]. Thomas Jefferson: An Outline of His Life and Service with the Story of Monticello, the Home He Reared and Loved. New York: Thomas Jefferson Memorial Foundation, 1924. pp.21.

"The Monticello Papers, No. 1."

238. Carlton, Mabel Mason. Thomas Jefferson, Lover of Liberty. Boston: John Hancock Mutual Life Insurance Co., 1922. pp. 16.

239. Carmer, Carl, ed. "Apostle of Freedom" and "Scientist, Writer, Inventor" in Cavalcade of America, The Deeds and Achievements of the Men and Women Who Made Our Country Great. New York: Crown/Lothrop, Lee and Shepard, 1956. 42-49.

Stories adapted from radio plays broadcast on the "Cavalcade of America" program.

240. Carmer, Carl. Thomas Jefferson and the Mockingbird Motif. Macon, Ga.: Southern Press, 1964. pp. v, 12.

Using an anecdote about TJ and his pet mockingbird, contends biographers need to be more sensitive to folklore and folklife.

241. [Carpenter, Stephen Cullen]. Memoirs of the Hon. Thomas Jefferson, Secretary of State, Vice President, and President of the United States of America; Containing a Concise History of Those States from the Acknowledgement of Their Independence: With a View of the Rise of French Influence and French Principles in That Country. [New York]: For the Purchaser, 1809. 2 vols. iv, 404; 434.

Federalist attack, not authentic memoirs.

242. Carriere, J. M. and L. G. Moffatt. "A Frenchman Visits Albemarle, 1816." Papers of the Albemarle County Historical Society. 4(1943-44), 39-55.

Baron de Montlezun visits TJ, Monroe and Madison.

243. Casey, Robert E., comp. The Declaration of Independence; Illustrated Story of Its Adoption, With the Biographies and Portraits of the Signers ... Supplemented with Illustrated Story of the Lives of Washington, Franklin, Jefferson & Other Patriots of the Revolution. Fredericksburg, Va.: Privately Printed, 1927?. pp. 192.

Picture book.

244. Catlin, George E. Gordon. "Thomas Jefferson" in Great Democrats. ed. A. Barratt Brown. London: Ivor Nicholson and Watson, 1934. 385-98.

If TJ is the "especial hierophant of the natural rights of man," natural rights as a theoretical basis of democracy were undermined by Bentham by the time TJ died, even though Jeffersonianism is compatible with utilitarianism.

*245. Cavanagh, Catherine Frances. "The Youth of Jefferson." New Age. 6(1907), 29-32.

Not located; cited in Writings on American History (1907), #1452.

246. Chamberlain, Mellen. "The Authentication of the Declaration of Independence, July 4, 1776." Proceedings of the Massachusetts Historical Society. 2nd ser. 1(1885), 273-98.

The Declaration was not signed on the Fourth as Adams and TJ later remembered, but on August 2, or later in some cases.

247. Chandler, J. A. C. "Jefferson and William and Mary." WMQ. 2nd. ser. 14(1934), 304-07.

Sketchy.

248. Chandler, J. A. C. "Thomas Jefferson" in Makers of Virginia History. New York: Silver Burdett, 1904. 233-46.

School text: see also next entry.

249. Chandler, Julian Alvin Carroll and Olive P. Chitwood. "Thomas Jefferson. 1743-1826" in Makers of American History. New York: Silver Burdett, 1904. 176-86.

250. Chanut, J. "Jefferson" in Nouvelle Biographie Générale depuis les Temps les Plus Reculés jusqu'à Nos Jours. Paris: Firmin Didot Frères, 1861. 611-31.

251. Chapman, Charles C. "Thomas Jefferson" in Portraits and Biographies of the Governors of Illinois, and of the Presidents of the United States. Chicago: Chapman Brothers, 1885. 27-32.

252. "Charlottesville, Virginia Is 'The Jefferson Country'." American Motorist. 22(April 1945), 22.

253. Charpentier, John. "Thomas Jefferson à Paris." Revue Politique et Littéraire. 58(1919), 311-14.

   Notes the range of TJ's attitudes toward French culture and his sympathy for the French people.

254. Cheatham, Edgar and Patricia. "Monticello." The Sohion (Sohio Oil Co.). August 1976. 13-15.

   Version of this sketch also appears in Pace (Piedmont Airlines). January/February 1977. 21-23, 35.

255. Cheatham, Edgar and Patricia. "Reunion at Monticello." Early American Life. 8(December 1977), 40-43.

   On TJ's friendship with Lafayette and their meeting in 1824.

256. Chianese, Mary Lou. "Thomas Jefferson: Enlightened American." Daughters of the American Revolution Magazine. 109(1975), 417-23.

   Sketch emphasizing his role as "a member of the Enlightenment;" insignificant.

257. Chiang, C. Y. Jesse. "Understanding Thomas Jefferson." International Review of History and Political Science. 14(August 1977), 51-61.

   Biographical sketch; nothing new.

258. Chinard, Gilbert. Les amitiés américaines de Madame d'Houdetot, d'apres sa correspondance inédite avec Banjamin Franklin et Thomas Jefferson. Paris: Champion, 1924. pp. viii, 62.

   TJ's correspondence with the Countess d'Houdetot from 1785 to 1808, mostly before 1790, illuminated with extensive commentary.

259. Chinard, Gilbert. "La Correspondance de Madame de Staël avec Jefferson." Revue de Littérature Comparée. 2(1922), 621-40.

   Prints letters of Madame de Staël for the first time in the original French; TJ's replies are in English.

260. Chinard, Gilbert, ed. The Correspondence of Jefferson and DuPont de Nemours with an Introduction on Jefferson and the Physiocrats. Baltimore: Johns Hopkins Press, 1931. pp. cxxiii, 293.

Useful introduction studies relationship between TJ and DuPont
de Nemours and their shared interests.

261. Chinard, Gilbert. "Hommage á Thomas Jefferson." Renaissance.
1(1943), 347-58.

Discusses the European response to TJ.

262. Chinard, Gilbert. "Jefferson's Influence Abroad." MVHR. 30(1943),
171-86.

TJ, unlike Franklin, shunned popularity while in Europe, but through
his letters, writings, and example he exerted a widespread influence.

263. Chinard, Gilbert, ed. The Letters of Lafayette and Jefferson With An
Introduction and Notes. Baltimore: Johns Hopkins Press/Paris: Les
Belles Lettres, 1929. pp. xiv, 443.

Introductory material puts the correspondence in historical and biographical context; letters in French are also translated.

264. Chinard, Gilbert. Thomas Jefferson, the Apostle of Americanism.
Boston: Little, Brown, 1929. pp. xviii, 548.

Revised edition published Boston, 1939. Argues that the major influences on TJ's political thinking were classical and English sources,
and that his ideas were essentially formed by the time he encountered most of the French thinkers he read.

265. Chinard, Gilbert. Trois amities francaises de Jefferson, d'apres sa
correspondance inedite avec Madame de Brehan, Madame de Tesse et
Madame de Corny. Paris: Societe d'edition "Les Belles Lettres,"
1927. pp. vi, 242.

An historical introduction, "Jefferson en France," and a biographical
introduction to each correspondence. Notes.

266. Christian, Sheldon. "Why No One Signed on July 4th." Tradition.
1(1958), 52-70.

Untangling for a popular audience TJ's mistaken reminiscences.

267. Chryssikos, George J. Thomas Jefferson. New York: The Author,
1949. pp. 18.

TJ "belongs in such company—the company of Plato and St. Paul."
He would be surprised to find himself ranked in this company, given
his opinions about them.

268. Claiborne, Craig. "The Epicure of Monticello." Cheers. 23(April
1976), 8-14.

Everything TJ was and aspired to be gave him "the necessary temper-
ament to become an eminent and dedicated gourmet." Good wine,
good company, fresh food, and moderation.

269. Clark, Champ. "Jefferon's Versatility" in The Writings of Thomas
Jefferson, ed. Lipscomb and Bergh. Washington: Thomas Jefferson
Memorial Association, 1903. ll:i-vi.

270. Clark, George Rogers. "Letter of General George Rogers Clark to
Dr. Samuel Brown for His Transmission to Thomas Jefferson, re
Cresap and Logan." Bulletin of the Cresap Society. 14(1949), no. 7,
3-4; no. 8, 1-2.

Exonerates Michael Cresap from the murder of Logan's family but
claims Logan's speech as reported by TJ is authentic.

271. Clark, Graves Glenwood. Thomas Jefferson, Friend of Liberty.
Richmond: Johnson Publishing Co., 1947. pp. 176.

Juvenile.

272. Clark, Kenneth. The Concept of Universal Man. Ditchley Park:
Ditchley Foundation, 1972. pp. 19.

TJ and Franklin considered as men whose interests covered every
branch of human activity and of nature.

*273. Claudel, Paul. "Jefferson et Lafayette." Le Moniteur Franco-Améri-
caine. 14(January 1930), 11.

274. Clemens, Cyril. "At Home With Thomas Jefferson." Hobbies. 64(April
1959), 108.

Describes visit of Sir Augustus John Foster to Monticello.

275. Cleveland, Grover. "The Principles of Thomas Jefferson" in The Writings and Speeches of Grover Cleveland, ed. George F. Parker. New
York: Cassell Publishing, 1892. 480-83.

5 letters attesting in general terms to his esteem for TJ.

276. Cobb, Joseph B. "Thomas Jefferson" in Leisure Labors: or Miscellanies
Historical, Literary, and Political. New York: Appleton, 1858. 5-
130.

Long unfriendly sketch; "We regard him as the masterspirit of former
mischievous inculcations, and his influence as the main promoting
cause of all succeeding political malversations of 'the progressive
Democracy'."

277. Cochran, Isabel Mason. The Ride of Captain Jack Jouett, Junior, of

Charlottesville, to Save Thomas Jefferson and the Virginia Legislature. Charlottesville, 1926? pp. 15.

278. Cochran, Isabel Mason Chamberlain. Thomas Jefferson. Charlottesville: Surber-Arundale, Co., 1926. pp. 20.

Sketch, with an account of Tarleton's raid.

279. Cochran, Joseph Wilson. The Tide and Thomas Jefferson. Bradenton, Fla.: Franklin Press, 1956. pp. 11.

Biographical sketch; "tide" as in tide of events. Minor.

280. Cole, Redmond S. Our Debt to Jefferson: An Address ... Before the City Club of Tulsa, Oklahoma, April 12, 1924. n.p., 1924. pp. 4.

281. Coleman, Elizabeth Dabney. "Peter Carr of Carr's-Brook (1770-1815)." Papers of the Albemarle County Historical Society. 4(1942), 5-23.

Biographical sketch of TJ's nephew and ward.

282. Coleman, McAlister. "Thomas Jefferson, First of the Democrats" in Pioneers of Freedom. New York: Vanguard, 1929. 15-36.

Sketch in a volume written for the Pioneer Youth of America.

283. Coles, Harry L. "Some Recent Interpretations of Jeffersonian America." Indiana Historical Society Lectures 1969-1970. (1970), 63-88.

Reviews major reevaluations of TJ since the progressives and presents them both as correction and vindication of Henry Adams' History.

284. College of William and Mary. Thomas Jefferson Day Schedule of Events, Sunday, October 6, 1957. Williamsburg: College of William and Mary, 1957. Broadside.

Event also sponsored by the Univ. of Virginia and the Thomas Jefferson Memorial Foundation.

285. Colman, Edna M. "First Administration of Thomas Jefferson," "Second Administration of Thomas Jefferson" in Seventy-Five Years of White House Gossip, From Washington to Lincoln. Garden City: Doubleday, Page, 1925. 73-95.

Usual anecdotes and a fair amount of misinformation.

286. "Colonial Virginia and the Father of Thomas Jefferson." Watson's Jeffersonian Magazine. 1(1907), 1087-91.

Sketch of Peter Jefferson as Virginia yeoman.

287. Colver, Anne. Thomas Jefferson, Author of Independence. Champaign, Ill.: Garrard, 1963. pp. 80.

   Juvenile.

288. Commager, Henry Steele. Crusaders for Freedom. Garden City: Doubleday, 1962. 52-58.

   Juvenile; emphasizes TJ as proponent of religious freedom.

289. Commager, Henry Steele. "He Opened All Eyes to the Rights of Man." New York Times Magazine. April 9, 1944. 18, 36-37.

290. Commager, Henry Steele. "Jefferson and the Book Burners." American Heritage. 9(August 1958), 65-68.

   Portrays Federalist opposition to national purchase of TJ's library. Rpt. in author's The Search for a Usable Past. New York: Knopf, 1967. 99-105.

291. Commager, Henry Steele. "Our American Heritage: Jefferson and Hamilton." Senior Scholastic. 39(December 1, 1941), 13.

   Reconciles them in their common love of country.

292. Commager, Henry Steele. "Thomas Jefferson, 1743-1943." Scholastic. 42(April 12, 1943), 3.

293. Commager, Henry Steele. "Thomas Jefferson Still Survives." Publisher's Weekly. 143(1943), 1504-06.

   Note reviewing studies of TJ.

294. Commemorative Program To the Freedom of the Press and the People's Right to Know, June 18, 1960. Charlottesville, 1960. unpag.

   Sigma Delta Chi journalism fraternity honors TJ; minor note.

295. Conde, Jose Alvarez. "Monticello: El Hogar de Thomas Jefferson." Circus Social de Cuba. 12(December 1955), 62-65.

296. Congleton, James Edward. "James Thomson Callender, Johnson and Jefferson." Johnsonian Studies. (1962), 161-72.

   Callender began his career in England by publishing two attacks on Samuel Johnson.

297. Conklin, Edwin G. "Inroduction to the Jefferson Bicentennial Program." Proceedings of the APS. 87(1943), 199-200.

298. Conway, John Joseph. "Thomas Jefferson" in Footprints of Famous Americans in Paris. London: John Lane, 1912. 15-24.

Sketch, not particularly informative.

299. Conway, Moncure D. "Jefferson Papers Recently Found at Washington." Athenaeum. No. 3750(1899), 353-55.

Discusses letters written over nearly a fifty year period.

300. Cooke, John Esten. "Jefferson as a Lover." Appleton's Journal. 12(1874), 230-32.

Romanticized account of TJ in the Williamsburg days.

301. Cooke, John Esten. "Jefferson, The 'Apostle of Democracy'" in Virginia. A History of the People. Boston: Houghton Mifflin, 1883. 405-09.

Slight sketch.

302. Cooke, John Esten. "Thomas Jefferson." Southern Literary Messenger. 39(1860), 321-41.

Biographical sketch.

303. Cooke, John Esten. "The Writer of the Declaration. A Familiar Sketch." Harper's Magazine. 53(1876), 211-16.

Focus on the young TJ, much romanticized.

304. Coolidge, Archibald Cary. "Jefferson and the Problems of Today." Minutes of the Eighth Meeting of the Monticello Association. (1921), 10-14.

TJ believed in the brotherhood of man; "... the 'federation of the world' would be for him no mere empty phrase." Rpt. in Univ. of Virginia Alumni Bulletin. 3rd ser. 14(July 1921), 53-58.

305. Coolidge, Harold Jefferson. "An American Wedding Journey in 1825." Atlantic. 143(1929), 354-66.

Describes the wedding journey from Monticello to Boston of TJ's granddaughter, Ellen Randolph Coolidge.

306. Coolidge, Harold Jefferson. Thoughts on Thomas Jefferson: Or, What Jefferson Was Not. Boston: Club of Odd Volumes, 1936. pp. 45.

Collection of short notes on TJ's character.

307. Coolidge, Thomas Jefferson. "Jefferson in His Family" in The Writings of Thomas Jefferson, ed. Lipscomb and Bergh. Washington: Thomas Jefferson Memorial Association, 1903. 15:i-vii.

308. Coolidge, T. Jefferson. "Remarks by T. Jefferson Coolidge, in

presenting a large collection of Jefferson Papers." <u>Proceedings of the Massachusetts Historical Society</u>. 2nd series. 12(1899), 264-73.

Brief description of and extracts from letters and papers presented to the MHS.

309. Copeland, Thomas Wellsted. "Burke, Paine, and Jefferson" in <u>Our Eminent Friend, Edmund Burke: Six Essays</u>. New Haven: Yale Univ. Press, 1949. 146-89.

Focuses on the relationship between Burke and Paine in 1787-89; Paine passed information on the French Revolution on to Burke, including a letter from TJ to Paine, dated July 11, 1789.

*310. Cottler, Joseph. "The Arch-Rebel, Thomas Jefferson" in <u>Champions of Democracy</u>. Boston: Little, Brown, 1936.

311. Cottler, Joseph. <u>Thomas Jefferson</u>. Evanston, Ill.: Row, Peterson, 1950. pp. 36.

Juvenile.

312. Cousins, Norman. "The Higher Patriotism." <u>Saturday Review</u>. 53(July 4, 1970), 20.

What TJ would think of America now.

313. Craighill, Robert T. <u>The Virginia "Peerage," or Sketches of Virginians Distinguished in Virginia's History</u>. Richmond: William Ellis Jones, 1880. 1:143-227.

Washington was the father of his country, but TJ was the "author of the Republic."

314. Crane, John. <u>Thomas Jefferson, Author of the Declaration of Independence, of the Statute of Virginia for Religious Freedom, and Father of the University of Virginia</u>. Washington: Pan American Union, 1948. pp. 32.

Illustrated sketch; no. 5 in the American Historical Series.

315. Cridlin, W. B. <u>Thomas Jefferson, Patriot, Statesman, Scientist</u>. Richmond: W. C. Hill Printing Co., 1924. pp. 8.

"Written for use in Public Schools of Virginia, Week of April 6-13, 1924."

316. Criss, Mildred. <u>Jefferson's Daughter</u>. New York: Dodd Mead, 1948. pp. ix, 278.

Juvenile biography of Martha Jefferson Randolph.

317. Crowley, Francis J., ed. "Madame de Staël and the United States." *Modern Philology.* 52(1955), 201-02.

   Prints with informative comment a letter from de Staël to TJ, dated February 12, 1817.

318. Cummings, Amos J. *A National Humiliation; A Story of Monticello. ... Reprinted from the "Sun".* n.p., 1903? pp. (8).

   On the need to acquire Monticello for the nation; "... the mansion itself is decaying." Originally in *New York Sun*, August 24, 1902, and rpt. at least once after 1912.

319. Cunningham, Noble E., Jr. "The Diary of Frances Few, 1808-1809." *Journal of Southern History.* 29(1963), 345-61.

   Washington diary of Gallatin's niece, who dined with TJ.

320. Current, Richard N. "The Lincoln Presidents." *Presidential Studies Quarterly.* 9(1979), 25-35.

   Lincoln often quoted TJ as presidential authority for his own decisions.

321. Curtis, William Eleroy. *The True Thomas Jefferson.* Philadelphia: Lippincott, 1901. pp. 395.

   A Biography in a series designed to present great Americans "in entertaining form, free from glamour." A deglamorized TJ is nearly indistinguishable from a Hamiltonian view.

322. Cushing, Caleb. *Eulogy on John Adams and Thomas Jefferson Pronounced in Newburyport, July 15, 1826.* Cambridge: Hilliard & Metcalf, 1826. pp. 60.

   Also in *A Selection of Eulogies ...* . Hartford: D.F. Robinson, 1826. 18-57. Praises their role as the great men of "the congress of seventy-six," who in a time of revolutionary excitement were the authors of a national literature of liberty.

323. Cuthbert, Norma B. "Poplar Forest: Jefferson's Legacy to His Grandson." *Huntington Library Quarterly.* 6(1942), 333-56.

   Prints for the first time letters from TJ to John Wayles Eppes and Francis Eppes regarding the disposition of Poplar Forest; with commentary.

324. Cutter, Abram E. "Edward Gibbons and Thomas Jefferson." *New England Historical and Genealogical Register.* 29(1875), 233-37.

   Traces a remote family connection.

325. Dabney, Virginius. "Facts and the Founding Fathers, Thomas Jefferson." Vital Speeches. 41(April 15, 1975), 389-92.

Criticism of Fawn Brodie and Gore Vidal for defaming the Founders.

326. Dabney, Virginius. "From Cuckoo Tavern to Monticello." The Iron Worker. 30(Summer 1966), 1-13.

Rpt. Charlottesville: Jack Jouett Chapter National Society Daughters of the American Revolution, 1966. pp. 11. Account of Jack Jouett's ride, "a significant minor exploit."

327. Dabney, Virginius. "Jack Jouett's Ride." American Heritage. 13(December 1961), 56-59.

Good popular account.

328. Dabney, Virginius. The Jefferson Scandals: A Rebuttal. New York: Dodd Mead, 1981. pp. x, 154.

Somewhat frantic refutation of Fawn Brodie, Gore Vidal, and Barbara Chase-Riboud.

329. Dabney, Virginius and Jon Kukla. "The Monticello Scandals: History and Fiction." Virginia Cavalcade. 29(Autumn 1979), 52-61.

Rejects the Callender scandals about TJ and Sally Hemings as given new currency by Fawn Brodie.

330. Dabney, William Minor. "Jefferson's Albemarle: History of Albemarle County, Virginia, 1727-1819." Ph.D. dissertation. Univ. of Virginia, 1951. pp. 228.

331. Dallas, George Mifflin. Oration on the Centennial Anniversary of the Birth of Thomas Jefferson, Delivered at the County Court House, Philadelphia, April 3, 1843. ... Published by Request of the Meeting. Philadelphia: Mifflin & Parry, 1843. pp. 8.

TJ the "Patriarch of our party," whose election was the people's "first authentic and emphatic ratification of the entire Democratic creed."

332. Dana, Emma Lilian. "Thomas Jefferson, The Friend of the People" in Makers of America: Franklin, Washington, Jefferson, Lincoln. New York: Immigrant Publication Society, 1915. 95-138.

For new Americans; "More than anyone else among our patriot fathers, Jefferson expressed the ideals that we call American."

333. Dangerfield, George. "Jefferson and Madison." New Republic. 123(September 4, 1950), 18-20.

Review essay warning those who wish to fly to TJ's bosom for comfort, "it isn't a very comfortable place."

334. Daniel, Frederick. "Virginia Reminiscences of Jefferson." Harper's Weekly. 48(1904), 1766-68.

Collects reminiscences from people in the Charlottesville area who supposedly remembered TJ; interesting if not reliable.

*335. Daniel, John W. "Thomas Jefferson" in White House Gallery of Official Portraits of the Presidents. New York: Gravure Company of America, 1906.

336. Daniels, Jonathan. Ordeal of Ambition: Jefferson, Hamilton, Burr. Garden City: Doubleday, 1970. pp. x, 446.

Pro-Burr, treatment of TJ biased accordingly.

337. Darden, Norman. "Sally Hemings, Myth or Mistress." Virginia Cardinal. 5 (March 1975), 20-21.

Contends TJ's descendants tried to hide the truth; assumes Hemings affair without question.

338. Darden, Norman. "Thomas Jefferson and the Mulatto Mistress." Metro: Hampton Roads Magazine. 5(July 1975), 45-48.

Enthusiastic support for the Fawn Brodie thesis.

339. Dauer, Manning J. "The Two John Nicholases, Their Relationship to Washington and Jefferson." AHR. 45(1939), 338-53.

Historians have not always distinguished between John Nicholas, the Republican member of Congress from 1793-1801, and John Nicholas of Albemarle, Federalist and long time clerk of the county court. The latter Nicholas exposed the Langhorne forgery to Washington, but ascribed it to TJ instead of its real author, Peter Carr.

340. Daugherty, Sonia. The Way of an Eagle. An Intimate Biography of Thomas Jefferson and His Fight for Democracy. New York: Oxford Univ. Press, 1941. pp. 352.

Invented dialogue in the costume drama manner and fanciful psychologizing. Rpt. as Thomas Jefferson: Fighter for Freedom and Human Rights. New York: Ungar, 1961. pp. 352.

341. Daveis, Charles Stewart. An Address Delivered at Portland on the Decease of John Adams and Thomas Jefferson, August 9, 1826. pp. 55.

TJ's greatest achievement as president was the Louisiana Purchase,

Adams's was the navy, but their real monument is the country itself.

342.   Davenport, William L. "Faithful Are the Wounds of a Friend."
       American Bar Association Journal. 64(1978), 227-31.

       Account of the TJ-Adams friendship.

343.   Davis, Betty Elyse. Monticello Scrapbook: Little Stories of the Chil-
       ren and Grand-Children of Thomas Jefferson. New York: M. S. Mill,
       1941. pp. 62.

       Sentimental anecdotes for young readers.

344.   Davis, Burke. Getting to Know Thomas Jefferson's Virginia. New York:
       Coward, McCann and Geoghegan, 1971. pp. 69.

       Juvenile; social and political life in TJ's Virginia and a biographical
       sketch.

345.   Davis, Burke. "The Pen" in Three for Revolution. New York: Harcourt
       Brace Jovanovich, 1975. 59-90.

       Young readers; emphasizes TJ's "farm boy" origins and covers his life
       up through the Declaration.

346.   Davis, Burke. A Williamsburg Galaxy. Williamsburg: Colonial
       Williamsburg, 1968. 171-83.

       Biographical sketch.

347.   Davis, John W. "Thomas Jefferson" in Virginia Born Presidents:
       Addresses Delivered on the Occasions of Unveiling the Busts of
       Virginia Born Presidents at Old Hall of the House of Delegates
       Richmond, Virginia. New York: American Book Co., 1932. 47-56.

348.   Davis, Richard Beale, ed. Correspondence of Thomas Jefferson and
       Francis Walker Gilmer 1814-1826. Columbia: Univ. of South Carolina
       Press, 1946. pp. 163.

       Introduction focuses on Gilmer and his role in finding faculty for TJ's
       university.

349.   "Death of Jefferson and Adams." Niles Register. 30(1826), 329, 345,
       368-75.

       TJ's death noted on July 8, Adams's on July 15, and the number for
       July 22 notices various "Testimonies of Respect for the Deceased
       Patriarchs."

350.   "Debtor's Letter." Newsweek. 58(August 14, 1961), 19.

Facsimile of a letter to Craven Peyton, dated Nov. 27, 1803, asking for an extension of a loan, is often mistaken for the original.

351.   Dedication Ceremonies of a Memorial Tablet to Thomas Jefferson marking the site of his office when first Secretary of State of the United States of America, Wednesday, May twenty-fifth nineteen and forty-nine. Philadelphia: Strawbridge and Clothier, 1949. unpag.

        Program.

352.   "Defending the Founders." Time. 105(February 17, 1975), 22-23.

        Report of Virginius Dabney's Charter Day Address at William and Mary College; see # 325 above.

353.   Detweiler, Philip F. "The Changing Reputation of the Declaration of Independence: The First Fifty Years." WMQ. 3rd ser. 19(1962), 557-74.

        Argues that attitudes toward the Declaration correspond directly with those held about its author.

354.   Devries, Julian. "Thomas Jefferson" in Lives of the Presidents. Cleveland: World, 1940. 33-53.

355.   Dewey, John, ed. The Living Thoughts of Thomas Jefferson. New York: Longmans, 1940. pp. 173.

        Selections from TJ with a thirty page introduction by Dewey, who presents him as an intellectual committed to action and as a private man with a public life.

356.   Dewey, Frank L. "Thomas Jefferson's Law Practice." VMHB. 85(1977), 289-301.

        Intelligently discusses TJ's law practice, based upon an examination of his casebook, fee book, and account books.

357.   DeWitt, William R. A Sermon on the Death of the Patriots and States-men, Thomas Jefferson and John Adams, Delivered by the Rev. W. R. DeWitt, Pastor of the Presbyterian Congregation, Harrisburg, in the German Reformed Church, on Friday, the 22nd of July, 1826, in Com-pliance with a Request of the Citizens of Harrisburg. Harrisburg: Cameron & Krause, 1826. pp. 16.

358.   Diamond, Sigmund, ed. "Some Jefferson Letters." MVHR. 28(1941), 225-42.

        Letters (1809-23) to George Ticknor and David Bailie Warden, with introduction and notes.

359. Diaz Vasconcelos, Luis Antonio. "El Padre del Dolar Americano. Tomas Jefferson" in Unos Americanos ... y Faltan Muchos. Guatemala: Tipographia Nacional, 1944. 144-47.

"Lecturas para muchachas."

360. Dickore, Marie, ed. Two Letters from Thomas Jefferson to His Relatives the Turpins Who Settled in the Little Miami Valley in 1797. Oxford, Ohio: The Oxford Press, 1941. pp. 16.

TJ advises a cousin on study for the law and reports on balloon ascensions.

361. Didier, Eugene L. "Thomas Jefferson as a Lawyer." Green Bag. 15(1903), 153-59.

Somewhat fanciful sketch.

362. Dix, Dorothy. "Monticello-Shrine or Bachelor's Hall?" Good Housekeeping. 58(April 1914), 538-41.

Encourages Mrs. Martin W. Littleton's campaign to acquire Monticello for the nation.

363. Dix, John P. "Thomas Jefferson, Father of American Democracy." Social Studies. 38(1947), 357-66.

Superficial sketch written for high school history teachers.

364. Dix, John P. "Washington and Jefferson's Contemporaries." Social Studies. 39(1948), 106-15.

Insignificant.

365. Donaldson, Thomas. The House in Which Thomas Jefferson Wrote the Declaration of Independence. Philadelphia: Avil Printing, 1898, pp. 119.

Uncritical antiquarianism, but useful.

366. "Donation by the State of Louisiana to the Family of Thomas Jefferson." Louisiana Historical Quarterly. 8(1925), 52.

Transcribes act of the legislature in 1827 donating $10,000 in bonds to TJ's family.

367. Donovan, Frank. The Thomas Jefferson Papers. New York: Dodd Mead, 1963. pp. ix, 304.

TJ's career narrated by piecing together bits of his own writing; selections are too brief, commentary jejune.

46

368. Donovan, Frank. "The Tragic Loves of Thomas Jefferson" in The Women in Their Lives; The Distaff Side of the Founding Fathers. New York: Dodd Mead, 1966. 205-53.

Popular; dismisses scandals about Sally Hemings and gives an account of TJ's relations with wife, daughters, and Maria Cosway.

369. [Dorsheimer, William]. "Thomas Jefferson." Atlantic Monthly. 2(1858), 706-17; 789-803.

Review essay finds Randall's biography of TJ verbose and dull but agrees with his highly favorable assessment of TJ.

370. Dos Passos, Cyril Franklin. "Notes on the 10 cents Jefferson, 1870-1879." Original Papers on Philatelic Themes Presented by Invitation: American Philatelic Congress. 22(1956), 47-55.

Philatelic notes on stamps bearing TJ's portrait.

371. Dos Passos, John. The Head and Heart of Thomas Jefferson. New York: Doubleday. 1954. pp. vi, 442.

Biography covering TJ's life through his service as Secretary of State.

372. Dos Passos, John. "A Portico Facing the Wilderness" in The Ground We Stand On: Some Examples from the History of a Political Creed. New York: Harcourt Brace, 1941, 228-55.

Sketch of TJ as he was when the Marquis de Chastellux met him in 1782, at Monticello.

373. Dos Passos, John. "Thomas Jefferson and the World of Today." Congressional Record. 109, no. 44(Thursday, March 21, 1963), 4428-32.

Argues that if the organization of society has changed, human nature has not, and TJ still can teach us about democracy. A passion for freedom is the best weapon against communism.

374. Dos Passos, John. Thomas Jefferson: The Making of a President. Boston: Houghton Mifflin, 1963. pp. 184.

Juvenile.

375. Douglas, Carlyle C. "The Dilemma of Thomas Jefferson." Ebony. 30(August 1975), 60-66.

Claims TJ did not consistently practice the doctrines of equality he preached in the Declaration; accepts TJ's paternity of Sally Heming's children as fact.

47

*376. Douglass, P. "Curricular Making of Thomas Jefferson." Improving College and University Teaching. 19(Autumn 1971), 261-62.

377. Douty, Esther. Mr. Jefferson's Washington. Champaign, Ill.: Garrard, 1970. pp. 96.

Juvenile; traces history of Washington, D.C. unti 1809 with emphasis on life during TJ's administration.

378. Dowdey, Clifford. "He Lives at Monticello." Holiday. 12(December 1952), 72-73, 81, 152-57.

379. Duer, William Alexander. An Eulogy on John Adams and Thomas Jefferson, Pronounced by Request of the Common Council of Albany, at the Public Commemorative of Their Deaths, Held in That City on Monday the 31st of July, 1826. Albany: National Observer, 1826. pp. 20.

Also in A Selection of Eulogies ... . Hartford: D. F. Robinson, 1826. "In this splendid coincidence of events, ... what grateful and ingenuous heart hesitates to acknowledge an omniscient and benignant Providence?"

380. Duke, Richard Thomas Walker, Jr. "The Private Life of Thomas Jefferson." Minutes of the Eighth Meeting of the Monticello Association. 1921. 6-10.

Rpt. in Univ. of Virginia Alumni Bulletin. 3rd ser. 14(July 1921), 47-53. General praise.

381. Dumbauld, Edward. "Jefferson's Residence in Richmond." VMHB. 60(1952), 323-26.

When TJ was governor, he probably rented a house on the northwest corner of what is now the intersection of 12th and Franklin.

382. Dumbauld, Edward. "Les demeures parisiennes de Thomas Jefferson." French-American Review. 1(1948), 68-75.

"Translated in part from Thomas Jefferson, American Tourist."

383. Dumbauld, Edward. Thomas Jefferson, American Tourist. Norman: Univ. of Oklahoma Press, 1946. pp. xv, 266.

Thorough study of TJ's travels; offers valuable insights on his personality and character and information on conditions and items of interest in the places he visited.

384. Dumbauld, Edward. "Thomas Jefferson and the City of Washington" in Records of the Columbia Historical Society of Washington D.C. The Fiftieth Volume, ed. Francis Coleman Rosenberger. Washington: The Society, 1980. 67-80.

Discusses TJ's connections with the city of Washington, including his roles in creating and establishing the national capital, his architectural activities, and his life as a resident.

385. Dumbauld, Edward. "Thomas Jefferson and Pennsylvania." Pennsylvania History. 5(1938), 157-65.

Biographical conjunctions.

386. Dumbauld, Edward. "Thomas Jefferson in Princeton." Princeton Alumni Weekly. 43(April 9, 1943), 5-6.

He passed through several times, was there with the Congress.

387. Dumbauld, Edward. "Where Did Jefferson Live in Paris?" WMQ. 2nd ser. 23(1943), 64-68.

"At present a complete answer cannot be given."

388. Dunning, E. O. "Private Character of Thomas Jefferson." New Englander. 19(1861), 648-73.

Review of Randall's Life. Attacks Bulfinch's North American Review article, claiming that TJ "Whatever may be said of his intellectual eminence or distinguished public services, has certainly, never been esteemed for moral purity or practical piety."

389. [Duycinck, Evert]. "Jefferson and Coleridge." Historical Magazine. 9(1865), 24-25.

Describes Coleridge's notes in vol. IV of the 1829 London edition of the Memoirs ... . Coleridge thought he was "onesided."

390. Duycinck, Evert. "Thomas Jefferson" in National Portrait Gallery of Eminent Americans. New York: Johnson, Fry & Co., 1862. 1:117-34.

391. Dwight, Nathaniel. "Thomas Jefferson" in Sketches of the Lives of the Signers of the Declaration of Independence. Intended Principally for the Use of Schools. New York: Harper, 1830. 287-97.

Rpt. after 1851 as The Lives of the Signers of the Declaration of Independence.

392. Dwight, Theodore. The Character of Thomas Jefferson as Exhibited in His Own Writings. Boston: Weeks, Jordan & Co., 1839. pp. xi, 371.

"... the main purpose of the writer will be to show, that the estimate which the federalists formed of his principles and character, political, moral and religious, was not merely justified but strictly correct."

393. E. E. "Interesting Letters from Jefferson and Jackson." Historical Magazine. 2nd ser. 8(1870), 50.

Identifies a namesake of TJ, Thomas Jefferson Grotjan, to whom he wrote a letter later commented upon and approved of by Andrew Jackson.

394. [Eames, Charles and Ray]. The Worlds of Franklin and Jefferson. Washington: American Revolution Bicentennial Commission, 1976. Broadside.

Accordion fold broadside, issued in conjunction with the exhibit of the same title, has a bar calendar showing events in TJ's lifetime and life spans of contemporaries.

395. Early, R. H. "A Notable Trio of the Nineteenth Century.—Burk. Hening. Jefferson" in By-Ways of Virginia History: A Jamestown Memorial Embracing a Sketch of Pocahontas. Richmond: Everett Waddey Co., 1907. 71-84.

Fragmented antiquarian musings.

396. Early, Ruth H. "Thomas Jefferson, Citizen of 'Poplar Forest'." Univ. of Virginia Alumni Bulletin. 3rd ser. 15(1922), 374-80.

397. Eastman, Fred. "Thomas Jefferson" in Men of Power: Sixty Minute Biographies. Nashville: Cokesbury Press, 1938. 1:9-50.

398. Eaton, Clement. "A Mirror of the Southern Colonial Lawyer: The Fee Books of Patrick Henry, Thomas Jefferson, and Waightstill Avery." WMQ. 3rd ser. 8(1951), 520-34.

Discusses TJ's conduct of his law practice.

399. Eaton, William. "A Poem on John Adams and Thomas Jefferson" in Searsburgh Poetry. Williamstown, Mass.: For the author, 1827. 34-37.

Doggerel verse eulogy by a precursor of Julia Moore; seems to think TJ wrote the Constitution.

400. Edwards, Mike. "Thomas Jefferson: Architect of Freedom." National Geographic Magazine. 149(1976), 231-59.

Heavily illustrated sketch.

401. Egan, Clifford. "How Not to Write a Biography: A Critical Look at Fawn Brodie's Thomas Jefferson." Social Science Journal. 14(April 1977), 129-36.

Criticizes Brodie's use of evidence and contradictory speculation.

402. Eichner, James A. Thomas Jefferson, the Complete Man. New York: Franklin Watts, 1966. pp. xv, 157.

Juvenile.

403. Ellett, Elizabeth F. "Jefferson's Administration" in The Court Circles of the Republic, or the Beauties and Celebrities of the Nation: Illustrating Life and Society under Eighteen Presidents; Describing the Social Features of the Successive Administrations From Washington to Grant; ... Hartford: Hartford Publishing Co., 1869. 57-79.

Comments on TJ's ladies and fashion in Washington, 1801-08.

404. Elliott, Mary Mallet. Colonial Days in Virginia. A Souvenir of the Sesquicentennial. Yorktown, 1931. pp. 56.

Has sketches on TJ and "How Jack Jouett Saved Thomas Jefferson."

405. Elliott, Milton J. "Mr Jefferson's Mountaintop Home." Commonwealth The Magazine of Virginia. 28(November 1961), 20-23, 38.

Emphasizes present day operation of Monticello.

406. Ellis, Edward S. "Thomas Jefferson" in Lives of the Presidents of the United States: Designed for Study and Supplementary Reading. Revised by J. O. Hall. Chicago: A. Flanagan, 1913. 25-33.

407. Ellis, Edward S. "Thomas Jefferson" in Makers of Our Country. Philadelphia: J. E. Potter and Co., 1894. 127-33.

408. Ellis, Edward S. Thomas Jefferson, A Character Sketch ... with Anecdotes, Characteristics, and Sayings. Milwaukee: H. G. Campbell, 1898. pp. 112.

Juvenile, with apocryphal anecdotes. Another edition, Chicago: University Association, 1898. pp. 112.

409. Ellis, Edward S. Thomas Jefferson, A Character Sketch ... With Supplementary Essay by G. Mercer Adam. Milwaukee: Campbell, 1903. pp. 180.

Reprints #408 with additions. A hodge-podge for students.

410. Ellis, Edward S. "Thomas Jefferson, Third President, 1801-1809" in Lives of the Presidents of the United States. Chicago: A. Flanagan, 1897. 25-33.

411. Emmons, William. Sacred to the Memory of the Patriots John Adams and Thomas Jefferson, Who Died July 4, 1826. Eulogy Pronounced at Salem, July 27, 1826. n.p., 1826. pp. 4.

*412. "Les Enfants Malheureux de Jefferson." Connaisance des Arts. 235(1971), 31.

413. Entziklopediya Bol'shaya Sovetskaya. "A Soviet View of Six Great Americans." American Heritage. 11(October 1960), 64-74.

     Includes translation of entry on TJ from the Large Soviet Encyclopedia and an accompanying comment by Richard B. Morris.

414. Erikson, Erik H. Dimensions of a New Identity: The 1973 Jefferson Lectures in the Humanities. New York: Norton, 1974. pp. 125.

     Considers TJ as a founding personality of a new national identity; he was a Protean man who was always himself and provided a model and rationale for national liberation into adulthood.

415. Eskew, Garnett Laidlaw. "Jefferson's Virginia." Travel. 39(June 1922), 15, 40-42.

416. Espenshade, A. H. "Jefferson—One of the Founders." St. Nicholas. 55(1928), 535, 574.

417. Evans, Charles H. "Thomas Jefferson" in Kings Without Crowns or Lives of American Presidents With a Sketch of the American Constitution. Edinburgh: William P. Nimmo. 1884. 65-90.

     Uncritical sketch.

418. Evans, Marny. "'All My Wishes End at Monticello'." American Home. 74(July 1971), 41-49, 78-80.

419. [Everett, Alexander Hill]. "Character of Jefferson." North American Review. 40(1835), 170-232.

     Review essay on Rayner's Life of Thomas Jefferson and William Sullivan's Remarks on Article IX in the ... North American Review. Mostly answers Sullivan, who is attacking an article by Everett.

420. Everett, Alexander H. A Defence of the Character and Principles of Mr. Jefferson; Being an Address Delivered at Weymouth, Mass., at the Request of the Anti-Masonic and Democratic Citizens of That Place, On the Fourth of July, 1836. Boston: Beals and Greene, 1836. pp. 76.

Turns into a history of parties in America; sees TJ as standing for Liberty, Hamilton for Law.

421. Everett, Edward. An Address Delivered at Charlestown, August 1, 1826, In Commemoration of John Adams and Thomas Jefferson. Boston: William L. Lewis, 1826. pp. 36.

"the declining period of their lives presents ... a new spectacle of moral sublimity" as they overcame their differences.

422. Faber, Doris. "Jane Randolph Jefferson" in Mothers of American Presidents. New York: New American Library, 1968. 232-35.

Sketchy, dwelling upon TJ's apparent "coldness" toward his mother.

423. Faris, John T. "Thomas Jefferson, Statesman" in Makers of Our History. Boston: Ginn, 1917. 68-79.

School text; only one paragraph on his presidency.

424. Farnum, George R. "Thomas Jefferson—Apostle of Democracy." Lawyer. 6(September, 1942), 13-14.

An inspiration to loyal Americans.

425. Federal Writers' Project. Jefferson's Albemarle: A Guide to Albemarle County and the City of Charlottesville, Virginia. n.p., 1941. pp. vi, 157.

American Guide Series volume pays particular attention to sites associated with TJ.

426. Fenner, Mildred Sandison and Eleanor Fishburn. "Thomas Jefferson, Educator." National Education Association Journal. 32(April 1943), 99-100.

Colorful but not very informative.

427. Fenner, Mildred Sandison and Eleanor C. Fishburn. "Thomas Jefferson" in Pioneer American Educators. Washington: National Education Association, 1944. 9-16.

Biographical sketch.

*428. Ferguson, John and Tim Benton. Thomas Jefferson. Bletchley: Open University Press, 1972. pp. 79.

British; prepared for the Age of Revolution Course Team.

429. Fetter, Frank Whitson. "The Revision of the Declaration of Independence in 1941." WMQ. 3rd ser. 31(1974), 133-38.

Explains how and why the text of the Declaration was altered when it was inscribed on the Jefferson Memorial in 1941.

430. Fields, Joseph Edward. "Birthplace of the Declaration." Manuscripts. 7(1955), 140-44.

On the house where TJ drafted the Declaration.

431. Finkelnburg, Gustavus A. "Thomas Jefferson as a Lawyer." American Law Review. 39(1905), 321-29.

Surveys TJ's career as a lawyer; his belief in a "higher law" is evidence that he lived in "the romantic period of our history."

432. "51 to Go." Time. 55(May 22, 1950), 110.

Notes publication of volume one of the Jefferson Papers.

433. Fishwick, Marshall. "Dinner with Mr. Jefferson." Ford Times. 66(October 1973), 22-27.

TJ as host.

434. Fishwick, Marshall. "Thomas Jefferson" in Gentlemen of Virginia. New York: Dodd Mead, 1961. 125-43.

Anecdotal.

435. Fiske, John. "Thomas Jefferson, the Conservative Reformer" in Essays Historical and Literary. New York: Macmillan, 1902. 1:143-81.

TJ is "the earnest but cool-headed representative of the rural English free-holders that won magna Charta and overthrew the usurpations of the Stuarts."

436. Firestone, Linda and Whit Morse. The Firestone/Morse Guide to Jefferson's Country: Charlottesville and Albemale County. Richmond: Good Life Publishers, 1977. pp. 151.

First 45 pages cover TJ, Monticello, and the Jeffersonian foundation of the Univ. of Virginia.

437. The First Jubilee of American Independence; and, Tribute of Gratitude to the Illustrious Adams and Jefferson. Newark, N.J.: M. Lyon & Co., 1826. pp. 60.

"Tribute" on pp. 45-60 includes address delivered July 14, 1826, by Philip Courtland Hay.

438. Fitzpatrick, F. B. "Helps for Grade Teachers: The Higher Grades. Things Worth Knowing about Thomas Jefferson." Virginia Journal

of Education. 19(1926), 365–66.

Questions and answers.

439. Fleming, Anne Taylor. "Jefferson Swindle." Newsweek. 85(March 10, 1975), 11.

Accuses TJ of spoiling Americans by leading them to expect happiness as a birthright. Silly.

440. Fleming, Thomas. "At Home With Mr. Jefferson." Reader's Digest. 90(July 1968), 170–76.

Monticello described.

441. Fleming, Thomas. "Jefferson at Monticello." Boys' Life. 65(June 1975), 32–35.

442. Fleming, Thomas. The Man from Monticello: An Intimate Life of Thomas Jefferson. New York: Morrow, 1969. pp. v, 409.

Popular biography; nothing new.

443. Fleming, Thomas. "Monticello's Long Career—From Riches to Rags to Riches." Smithsonian. 4(June 1973), 62–69.

Account of the Thomas Jefferson Memorial Foundation's successful effort to acquire and restore Monticello.

444. Fleming, Thomas J. Thomas Jefferson. New York: Grossett and Dunlap, 1971. pp. 182.

Juvenile.

445. Fleming, Thomas. "Thomas Jefferson's New England Granddaughter." Yankee. 41(May 1977), 65–67, 140–48.

On Ellen Randolph Coolidge.

446. Flower, B. O. "Jefferson's Service to Civilization During the Founding of the Republic." Arena. 29(1903), 500–18.

TJ established "the reign of popular government and robust Americanism."

447. Flower, Milton E. "Letter from Henry S. Randall to James Parton on Jefferson and the 'Dusky Sally Story'" in James Parton, The Father of Modern Biography. Durham, N.C.: Duke Univ. Press, 1951. 236–39.

Prints in full the letter accusing Peter Carr of being Sally Hemings' lover; Randall's authority was Thomas Jefferson Randolph.

448. Foley, John P. "Outdoor Life of the Presidents. No. 2. Thomas Jefferson." Outing. 13(1889), 250-59.

Sketch of TJ as horseman, gardener, natural historian.

449. Ford, Paul Leicester. "The French Revolution and Jefferson." The Nation. 61(1895), 61.

Prints letter of October 28, 1795 to James Madison.

450. Ford, Paul Leicester. "Jefferson in Undress." Scribner's Magazine. 12(1892), 509-16.

Uses extracts from TJ's account books in a discussion of his private life.

451. Ford, Paul Leicester. Thomas Jefferson. Cambridge: A. W. Elson, 1904. pp. 37.

Introduction, followed by texts of 1st inaugural address, Declaration of Independence, and A Bill for Establishing Religious Freedom. "Recognition of the principles for which he fought does not, however, imply endorsement of his methods and instruments."

452. Ford, Worthington C. "Letter to Samuel Adams. Is It Jefferson's?" The Nation. 70(1900), 298-99.

Ford inquires about the authenticity of a letter known only in a late transcription.

453. Ford, Worthington C., ed. Thomas Jefferson Correspondence Printed from the Originals in the Collections of William K. Bixby. Boston: Privately printed, 1916. pp. xiv, 322.

454. Forman, S. E. The Life and Writings of Thomas Jefferson Including All of His Important Utterances on Public Questions Compiled From State Papers and from His Private Correspondence. Indianapolis: Bowen-Merrill, 1900. pp. 474.

Short biography, followed by a selection of TJ's writings arranged alphabetically by topic.

455. Forsyth, John. Eulogium on Adams and Jefferson, Delivered at the Request of the Citizens of Augusta. Augusta, Ga.: Brantly and Clarke, 1826. pp. 8.

456. Foster, Sir Augustus John. Jeffersonian America: Notes on the United States of America, Collected in the Years 1805-6-7 and 11-12. Edited with an Introduction by Richard Beale Davis. San Marino, Cal.:

Huntington Library, 1954. pp. xx, 356.

British diplomat visits Monticello, pp. 143-61; TJ discussed there and passim. Interesting but predictably biased.

457. Frankfurter, Felix. "The Permanence of Jefferson" in The Jefferson Bicentennial, 1743-1943. A Catalogue of the Exhibition at the Library of Congress. Washington: Government Printing Office, 1943. 3-12.

Declares that TJ should be treated as a source of energy for American democracy and not as a book of rules for specific situations.

458. Freidel, Frank. "Thomas Jefferson, Third President 1801-1809" in Our Country's Presidents. Washington: National Geographic Society, 1966. 30-37.

459. Frey, Herman S. Thomas Jefferson. Washington: For the author, 1976. pp. 8.

460. Friederich, Werner P. "Der Philosoph der Revolution: Thomas Jefferson" in Werden und Wachsen der U.S.A. in 300 Jahren. Bern: A Francke, 1939. 48-54.

461. Friedman, Daniel. "Meet Rob Coles." Albemarle Monthly. 2(June/July 1979), 12-16.

Report on a descendant of TJ who acts his ancestor in a play, "Meet Thomas Jefferson."

462. Friis, Herman R. "Baron Alexander von Humboldt's Visit to Washington, D.C., June 1 through June 13, 1804." Records of the Columbian Historical Society. 1960-62. Washington: The Society, 1963. 1-35.

Detailed account of Humboldt's visit and meeting with TJ.

463. Frost, John. "Thomas Jefferson" in The Presidents of the United States; from Washington to Fillmore. Comprising Their Personal and Political History. Boston: Phillips, Sampson, 1852. 77-102.

464. Fuentes, German Alvarez. Thomas Jefferson y Su Tiempo. Miami: Rex Press, 1977. pp. 180.

465. Gaines, William H., Jr. "From Desolation to Restoration: The Story of Monticello Since Jefferson." Virginia Cavalcade. 1(Spring 1952), 4-8.

466. Gaines, William H., Jr. "Thomas Jefferson's Favorite Hideaway." Virginia Cavalcade. 5(Summer 1955), 36-39.

On Poplar Forest.

467. Gaines, William H., Jr. Thomas Mann Randolph: Jefferson's Son-in-Law. Baton Rouge: Louisiana State Univ. Press, 1966. pp. vi, 203.

Biography of Martha Jefferson's husband contains much on life in TJ's family.

468. Ganter, Herbert L. "William Small, Jefferson's Beloved Teacher." WMQ. 3rd ser. 4(1947), 505-11.

Small was professor of natural philosophy at William and Mary; this is the best separate piece on him.

469. [Gardner, Joseph L., ed]. The Founding Fathers: Thomas Jefferson. A Biography in His Own Words. New York: Newsweek/Harper and Row, 1974. pp. 416.

A scissors and paste job with excellent illustrations.

470. Garnett, W. E. "Lets Celebrate Jefferson's Birthday." Virginia Journal of Education. 50(March 1957), 22-23.

471. Garrett, Wendell D. "Bicentennial Outlook: The Monumental Friendship of Jefferson and Adams." Historic Preservation. 28(April-June 1976), 28-35.

Conventional account.

472. Garrett, Wendell D. Thomas Jefferson Redivivus. Barre, Mass.: Barre Publishers, 1971. pp. 192.

Photographs by Joseph Farber, quotations by TJ, connecting text by Garrett. Handsome illustrations.

473. Garwood, Wilmer St. John. Thomas Jefferson: Su Vida y Su Obra. Buenos Aires: Instituto Cultural Argentina-Norteamericano, 1939.

Pamphlet explaining the American way.

474. Genet, George Clinton. Washington, Jefferson, and "Citizen" Genet, 1793. New York, 1899. pp. 52.

Focus on Genet, by a descendent who defends his behavior, and criticizes TJ.

475. Georigiady, Nicholas P. and Louis G. Russo. Events in the Life of Thomas Jefferson. Milwaukee: Independents Publishing Co., 1966. unpag.

Juvenile.

476. Gilpin, Henry D. A Biographical Sketch of Thomas Jefferson. Philadelphia, 1828. pp. 245-372.

From the Biography of the Signers of the Declaration of Independence, but pagination different from below. Positive view of TJ, but aware that he is still a figure who can arouse party differences.

477. [Gilpin, Henry Dilwood]. "Jefferson" in Biography of the Signers to the Declaration of Independence, ed. John Sanderson. Philadelphia: R. W. Pomeroy, 1827. 7:9-148.

478. [Gilpin, Henry Dilwood]. "Thomas Jefferson" in The National Portrait Gallery, eds. James B. Longacre and James Herring. Philadelphia: Henry Perkins, 1835. unpag.

Presents TJ as the republican hero of simple habits, liberal temper, devoted to democratic principles.

479. Girouard, Mark. "Monticello, Virginia, The Home of Thomas Jefferson from 1771 to 1826." Country Life. 133(1963), 106-110.

Intelligent account focusing on TJ's innovations and contrivances, some successful, some not.

480. Glass, Anna Cleghorne. "Poplar Forest, Home of Thomas Jefferson." Daughters of the American Revolution Magazine. 85(1951), 761-62.

481. Gleason, Gene. "The Longest Independence Day." The Iron Worker. 40(Winter 1976), 2-7.

Account of the memorial ceremonies to TJ and Adams after their deaths.

482. Glenn, Thomas Allen. "Monticello" in Some Colonial Mansions and Those Who Live in Them; With Genealogies of the Various Families Mentioned. Second Series. Philadelphia: Henry T. Coates, 1899. 192-241.

Illustrated with circa 1895 photographs; sketch of TJ's life at Monticello.

483. Godwin, Mills E. Some Thoughts on the Fourth of July. Charlottesville: Thomas Jefferson Memorial Foundation, 1971. pp. (12).

Generalities on TJ and the Declaration.

484. Godwin, Parke. "Jefferson" in Homes of American Statesmen: With Anecdotical, Personal and Descriptive Sketches, by Various Writers. New York: G. P. Putnam, 1854. 79-94.

"He conquered, as Emerson says in speaking of the force of character over and above mere force of some special faculty, because his arrival anywhere altered the face of affairs."

485. Goetzmann, William. "Savage Enough to Prefer the Woods: The Cosmopolite and the West" in Thomas Jefferson: The Man ... His World ... His Influence, ed. Lally Weymouth. New York: Putnam's 1973. 107-27.

Surveys the variety of TJ's interest in the American West.

486. Golladay, V. Dennis. "Jefferson's 'Malignant Neighbor,' John Nicholas, Jr." VMHB. 86(1978), 306-19.

John Nicholas, Jr. told Washington that TJ was the author of the Langhorne letter of 1797, and he may have been James Callender's chief informant.

487. Gooch, Richard Barnes. The Anniversary Address of the Jefferson Society, of the University of Virginia, Delivered on the 13th of April, 1840 ... . Charlottesville: J. Alexander, 1840. pp. 15.

Triumph of style over content; only touches on TJ.

488. Goodman, Nathan G. "Thomas Jefferosn, A Really Wonderful, Allround Man. 1743-1826." Historical Outlook. 17(1926), 365-66.

Myths and platitudes for social science teachers.

489. Goodrich, Charles A. "Thomas Jefferson" in Lives of the Signers to the Declaration of Independence. New York: William Reed, 1829. 380-405.

490. Goodrich, Samuel Griswold. "Letter XI" in Recollections of a Lifetime, or Men and Things I have Seen: in a Series of Familiar Letters to a Friend. New York: Miller, Orton, and Mulligan, 1856. 1:106-26.

Anecdotes illustrating New England's reaction to TJ's election in 1800. Federalist nostalgia from Peter Parley.

491. Goodwin, Katherine Calvert. "Where the Declaration of Independence Was Written." Daughters of the American Revolution Magazine. 59(1925), 405-09.

492. Gorman, Ann C. "Poplar Forest, Thomas Jefferson's Other Home." Lynchburg, The Magazine of Central Virginia. 12(December/January 1980/81), 16-20.

Describes Poplar Forest as TJ built it and as it is now.

493. Govan, Thomas P. "Alexander Hamilton and Julius Caesar: A Note on the Use of Historical Evidence." WMQ. 3rd ser. 32(1975), 475-480.

Despite TJ's letter to Benjamin Rush of Jan. 16, 1811, considerable evidence exists that Hamilton did not admire Caesar and would have been unlikely to have praised him over TJ's trinity of Bacon, Newton and Locke.

494. Graff, Henry F. Illustrious Americans: Thomas Jefferson. Morristown, N.J.: Silver Burdett, 1968. pp. 240.

Includes a 32 page "Picture Portfolio."

495. Graham, Pearl M. "Thomas Jefferson and Sally Hemings." Journal of Negro History. 46(1961), 89-103.

Contends that "He preached against miscegenation ... but practiced it." Evidence adduced is not entirely convincing.

496. Grampp, William D. "Everman His Own Jeffersonian." Sewanee Review. 52(1944), 118-26.

Varying interpretations of TJ are possible because of "the plural character of his thought," and "Because his system is infinitely mutable," he is the founding father most often turned to whenever the "present stands in need of a great democrat."

497. "The Grave of Jefferson." The Idea and Literary Gazette Charlottesville). 1(January 1843), 14-15.

Account of a visit to the grave in about 1828.

498. Gray, Francis Calley. Thomas Jefferson in 1814, Being an Account of a Visit to Monticello, Virginia by Francis Calley Gray. With Notes and Introduction by Henry S. Rowe and T. Jefferson Coolidge, Jr. Boston: Club of Odd Volumes, 1924. pp. 84.

Gray visited Monticello in company with George Ticknor; comments particulary on the furnishings of Monticello and the library.

499. Gregory, Richard Claxton (Dick). "The Myth of the Founding Fathers" in No More Lies: The Myth and Reality of American History. New York: Harper and Row, 1971. 64-100.

Criticizes the hypocrisy of the Founders who continued slavery; discusses the correspondence of TJ and Benjamin Banneker.

500. Gregory, Stephen S. Thomas Jefferson: An Address Before the Iroquois Club, April 13th 1901. n.p., 1901?. pp. 15.

Biographical sketch; praises TJ for being above the "greed" which

61

now threatens society.

501. Gressman, Eugene. "How Disloyal Was Thomas Jefferson?" New Republic. 127(July 14, 1952), 13-14.

What a McCarthy-era loyalty board would do to TJ.

*502. Grosvenor, Charles Henry. "Thomas Jefferson" in The Book of the Presidents, with Biographical Sketches. Washington: Continental Press, 1902.

503. Griggs, Edward Howard. "Jefferson: The Democratic American: in American Statesmen, An Interpretation of Our History and Heritage. Croton-on-Hudson, N.Y.: Orchard Hill Press, 1927. 118-74.

Biographical sketch; "... Jefferson stands for just that range of ideas that most need re-emphasis at the present hour ... if we are to keep the soul of democracy in our great, ever more powerful, more highly organized, centralized and authoritative Republic."

504. Grundy, Felix. "Eulogy, Pronounced at Nashville Tennessee, August 3, 1826" in A Selection of Eulogies ... . Hartford: D. F. Robinson & Co., 1826. 287-97.

Concentrates on TJ as the "great apostle of civil liberty."

505. Grzelonski, Bogdan, ed. Jefferson/Kosciuszko Correspondence. Warsaw: Interpress, 1978. pp. 127.

Informative introduction covers Kosciuszko's life and his friendship with TJ. Full annotation. Letters of Kusciuszko which were originally written in French are printed in both original and in English translation.

506. Guernsey, A. H. "Thomas Jefferson and His Family." Harper's Monthly. 43(1871), 366-80.

Review essay occasioned by Sarah Randolph's Domestic Life.

*507. Gunn, John W. The Life of Thomas Jefferson. Girard, Kan.: Haldeman-Julius, n.d.

Little Blue Book no. 769.

508. Gurney, Gene and Clara. Monticello. New York: Franklin Watts, 1966. pp. 74.

TJ and his house, for tourists.

509. H. W. "Great Americans and Why (Thomas Jefferson)." American Catholic Quarterly Review. 49(1924), 16-22.

Sketch of TJ as author of the Declaration.

510. Haber, Francis. _David Baillie Warden. A Bibliographical Sketch of America's Cultural Ambassador in France._ Washington: Institute Francaise de Washington, 1954. pp. 44.

Warden, on diplomatic service in France from 1804 on, corresponded with TJ on scientific matters and sent news on the savants of Paris. Only a little on this, however.

511. Hadley, Arthur T. "The 'Pol' and the Philosopher... Thomas Jefferson" in _Power's Human Face; A Unique American History._ New York: Morrow, 1965. 17-35.

TJ caught "in the act of power" by authorial commentary on snippets of correspondence.

512. Haiman, Miecislaus. _Kosciuszko, Leader and Exile._ New York: Polish Institute of Arts and Sciences in America, 1946. pp. vii, 183.

Focus on Kosciuszko; uses correspondence of TJ with him and discusses their relationship.

513. Hale, Edward Everett. "Memories of a Hundred Years." _The Outlook._ 70(1902), 320-32.

Federalist memories of TJ recounted, among others.

514. Hale, Edward Everett. "Thomas Jefferson, The Pioneer of Democracy in America" in _Noble Living and Grand Achievement: Giants of the Republic._ Philadelphia: J. C. Winston and Co., 1895. 115-28.

Similar material in _Illustrious Americans,_ ed. Hale. Philadelphia: International Publishing, 1896. 115-30.

515. Hale, Edward Everett. "With Jefferson's Manuscripts." _Book News._ 14(1895), 65-67.

Commentary on TJ's correspondence.

516. Hale, Harrison. "The United Front." _Scientific Monthly._ 58(1944), 233-34.

Lavoisier, Jefferson and DuPont considered as symbols of our science, government, and industry.

517. Hale, Salma. "Salma Hale Papers." _Massachusetts Historical Society Proceedigs._ 46(1913), 402-09.

Hale visited TJ at Monticello in May, 1818, and later sent him several pamphlets on the Unitarian-orthodox debate, for which TJ thanked him and gave his own opinion about Christ.

518. Hale, William Bayard. "Presidential Inaugurations at Four Crises."
      World's Work. 25(1913), 508-14.

      Pp. 509-12 recount events of TJ's first inauguration.

519. Hall, Gordon Langley. Mr. Jefferson's Ladies. Boston: Beacon Press,
      1966. pp. xvi, 239.

      Sentimental study of the women in TJ's life: his wife, daughters,
      Maria Cosway. Inaccurate in detail.

520. Halsey, Ashley, Jr. "How Thomas Jefferson's Pistols Were Restored."
      The American Rifleman. 117(November 1969), 21-22.

521. Halsey, Ashley, Jr. and John M. Snyder. "Jefferson's Beloved Guns."
      The American Rifleman. 117(November 1969), 17-20.

      TJ as hunter, shooter, and owner of firearms.

*522. Halstead, Murat. "Jefferson's Journalism in His Letter-Writing Habit"
      and "Jefferson's Personal Part in Purchasing Louisiana" in Pictorial
      History of the Louisiana Purchase and the World's Fair at St. Louis.
      Philadelphia: National Publishing Co., 1904. 43-56, 77-86.

523. Hamilton, J. G. deRoulhac. "Jefferson and Adams at Ease." South
      Atlantic Quarterly. 26(1927), 359-72.

      Genial portrayal of TJ and Adams in retirement.

524. Hamilton, J. G. deRoulhac. "Mr. Jefferson Visits the Sesquicentennial."
      VQR. 3(1927), 38-47.

      What would TJ have thought of the U.S. of 1926? He would have con-
      demned the Volstead Act, the Watch and Ward Society, anti-evolu-
      tionists, and Andrew Mellon.

525. Hamilton, J. G. deRoulhac. "Ripened Years: Thomas Jefferson—Time
      Treated Him Kindly." Century Magazine. 114(1927), 476-85.

      TJ as contented senior citizen.

526. Hammond, Jabez D. Life and Opinions of Julius Melbourn: With
      Sketches of the Lives and Characters of Thomas Jefferson, John
      Quincy Adams, John Randolph, and Several Other Eminent American
      Statesmen. Edited by a Late Member of Congress. Syracuse, N.Y.:
      Hall & Dickson, 1847. pp. 239.

      Pp. 63-78 describe a purported visit to Monticello in 1815, including
      a dinner party at which TJ entertained Melbourn, a freed slave,

John Marshall, Elder John Leland, and Samuel Latham Mitchill, all at the same table. Antislavery fiction which has been uncritically accepted as true.

527. Hannon, Stuart L. "The Mind of Thomas Jefferson." Foreign Service Journal. 32(March 1955), 20-21.

528. Haraszti, Zoltan. "Jefferson's Bill of Religious Freedom." Boston Public Library Quarterly. 7(1955), 221-23.

Note describing its enactment; the Boston Library claims to have the only known copy of the earliest printing of the Bill.

529. Harnit, Fanny. "Monticello." Daughters of the American Revolution Magazine. 50(1917), 158-62.

*530. Harper, Samuel H. An Eulogium on the Late Thos. Jefferson & Jno. Adams, Pronounced in New Orleans, Aug. 16, 1826 .... New Orleans: Lyman and Beardslee, 1826. pp. 24.

531. Harris, Ramon I. "Thomas Jefferson: Female Identification." American Imago. 25(1968), 371-83.

Contends TJ's life is to be explained in terms of a female identification with his mother which represented "an identification with the aggressor." Interesting, but less than convincing.

532. Harrison, Frederic, ed. "Thomas Jefferson" in The New Calendar of Great Men: Biographies of the 558 Worthies of All Ages and Nations in the Positivist Calendar of Auguste Comte. London: Macmillan, 1892. 574-75.

533. Harrison, Lowell H. "Some Thomas Jefferson—John Breckinridge Correspondence." Filson Club History Quarterly. 42(1968), 252-77.

Historical and biographical introductions point out how the correspondence reveals the increasing importance of Breckinridge as a Jeffersonian leader and friend prior to his death in 1806.

534. Harrison, Mary Louise. "The Sage of Monticello." Daughters of the American Revolution Magazine. 52(1918), 32-36.

Brief description of the house.

*535. Hash, Ronald J. "Slavery on Thomas Jefferson's Plantations." M.A. thesis. Millersville State College, 1969.

536. Haskins, Caryl Parker. Mr. Jefferson and Wide America. Charlottesville: Thomas Jefferson Memorial Foundation, 1977. pp. 20.

TJ's life illustrates a theme of diversity of experience played off against a constancy of democratic belief.

537. Hawgood, John A. "The Papers of Thomas Jefferson." History. 40(1955), 273-85.

Intelligent review of the contents of the first seven volumes of the Jefferson Papers.

538. [Hawkes, Francis Lister]. "Character of Mr. Jefferson." New York Review. 1(1837), 1-58.

Printed separately as A Criticism on Tucker's 'Life of Jefferson'. New York, 1837. pp. 58. Review essay on Tucker's biography attacks TJ for supposed irreligion, dissimulation, and for cribbing from documents such as the Mecklenburg Declaration when writing the Declaration of Independence. This article provoked considerable response.

539. Hay, Robert P. "The Glorious Departure of the American Patriarchs: Contemporary Reactions to the Deaths of Jefferson and Adams." Journal of Southern History. 35(1969), 543-55.

Deaths of Adams and TJ were taken as a providential sign of Divine approval of the republic.

540. Hazelton, Jean Hanvey. "The Hemings Family of Monticello." unpub. paper. Claremont Graduate School, 1960. pp.19.

Copy in Univ. of Virginia Library. Detailed account of the Hemings family, relying mostly on the Farm Book and a few other sources, including Madison Heming's supposed autobiography.

541. Heller, Francis H. "Monticello and the University of Virginia, 1825: A German Prince's Travel Notes." Papers of the Albemarle County Historical Society. 7(1946-47), 29-35.

The Duke of Saxe-Weimar-Eisenach visits TJ; see item # 122.

542. Hemings, Madison. "Life among the Lowly." Pike County Republican (Waverly, Ohio). March 13, 1873. 4.

Rpt. in Brodie, Thomas Jefferson (1974), 471-76, as "Reminiscences of Madison Hemings." Supposedly the autobiography of one of Sally Heming's children. Handle with care.

543. Hemphill, John M., III., ed. "Edmund Randolph Assumes Thomas Jefferson's Practice." VMHB. 67(1959), 170-71.

Prints a circular issued by Randolph announcing assumption of TJ's law practices, with critical endorsements by James Parker.

544. Hemphill, William Edwin. "Thomas Jefferson and His Personal Property Taxes." Virginia Cavalcade. 1(Spring 1952), 18-19.

Records in the State Library show taxes on land and personal property taxes which provide information on the way of life at Monticello.

545. Henderson, Josie Duncan. Thomas Jefferson at Home. Charlottesville: The author, 1954. pp. 15.

Fanciful sketch.

546. Hendrickson, Walter B. "Thomas Jefferson—Up From Slander." Social Education. 18(1954), 244-48.

Argues that biographers from George Tucker to Dumas Malone and Nathan Schachner have progressively corrected the slanders of the Federalists and the historians they influenced.

547. Henkels, Stan V. "Jefferson's Recollection of Patrick Henry." PMHB. 34(1910), 385-418.

Correspondence with William Wirt, who was collecting material for his biography of Henry; no introduction or annotation.

548. Henry, William Wirt. Character and Public Career of Patrick Henry. Comments upon Mr. Jefferson's Letter. Richmond?, 1867. pp. 8.

Responding to an article in the Richmond Dispatch, defends Henry and calls for publication of all of TJ's correspondence with William Wirt. In one letter TJ had claimed Henry was "avaritious and rotten-hearted."

549. "Heroes: Jefferson's 200th." Time. 41(April 12, 1943), 22-23.

"Now on the 200th anniversary of his birth, Jefferson once more occupies the place he deserves in American history."

550. Higginson, Thomas Wentworth. "The Early American Presidents." Harper's Magazine. 68(1884), 548-60.

Historical sketch.

551. Hirst, Francis W. Life and Letters of Thomas Jefferson. New York: Macmillan, 1926. pp. xviii, 588.

English author's admiring biography; attacks the Hamiltonian charges that TJ did not understand public finance.

*552. Historical Account of the Washington Monument in the Capitol Square, Richmond, Va. With Biographical Sketches of Thomas Jefferson,

John Marshall, Patrick Henry, George Mason, Thomas Nelson, and Andrew Lewis; also a Brief Notice of the Houdon Statue of Washington. Richmond: W. A. R. Nye, 1869, pp. 16.

553. Hoar, George Frisbie. "Special Introduction" in The Writings of Thomas Jefferson, ed. Lipscomb and Bergh. Washington: Thomas Jefferson Memorial Association, 1903. 1:vii-xiii.

Notes that the proof of TJ's greatness can be seen in the attempts of every variety of political opinion in the U.S. to ground itself in his writings.

*554. [Hoge, James]. Proceedings of the United States Court, Gentlemen of the Bar, and Citizens of Columbus, in Testimony of Respect for the Late Thomas Jefferson & John Adams; also, the Discourse Delivered on the Occasion by the Rev. James Hoge. Published by Order of the Bar. Columbus, Ohio: George Nashee & Co., 1826, pp. 20.

555. Holland, Corabelle A. "The Jefferson Memorial in Wales." American Foreign Service Journal. 10(1933), 396-97.

Unveiling of a memorial tablet for TJ in Glyceiriog.

556. Holliday, Carl. "The Amazing Versatility of Jefferson." Overland Monthly. 88(1930), 359-60.

Sketch.

557. Holliday, Carl. "The Man Who Wrote the Declaration." Methodist Quarterly Review. 73(1924), 453-68.

Biographical sketch; TJ's big flaw was his occasionally impractical idealism.

558. Hollis, Christopher. "Thomas Jefferson" in The American Heresy. London: Sheed and Ward, 1927. 6-81.

America's heresy is the rejection of the Jeffersonian concept of the state in favor of Hamiltonian principles; TJ is broadly praised, partly by minimizing almost all of his contemporaries.

559. Holloway, Laura C. "Martha Jefferson" in The Ladies of the White House; or, In the Home of the Presidents. Being a Complete History of the Social and Domestic Lives of the Presidents from Washington to the Present Time—1789-1881. Philadelphia: Bradley and Co., 1881. 126-70.

Account of Martha Jefferson Randolph.

560. Holmes, Prescott. "Thomas Jefferson" in Lives of the Presidents. Philadelphia: Henry Altemus, 1898. 46-67.

Juvenile.

561. Holmgren, Rod. "Jefferson's Debt." American Mercury. 88(February 1959), 83-85.

Brief account of the 1826 lottery.

562. Holway, John. "Trzy Legaty Jeffersona." Ameryka. 150(July 1971), 48-50.

"Three Gifts of Jefferson," in Polish; followed by a description of Monticello.

563. Hosmer, Charles B., Jr. "The Levys and the Restoration of Monticello." American Jewish Historical Quarterly. 53(1964), 219-52.

Good account of the Thomas Jefferson Memorial Foundation's genesis and campaign to purchase Monticello.

564. Houghton, W. M. "Open Letter to Mr. Jefferson." American Mercury. 37(1936), 273-76.

Conservative's lament; the New Deal has "violated all your principles."

565. Howard, George Elliott. "Thomas Jefferson, the Father of American Democracy" in Biography of American Statesmanship: An Analytical Reference Syllabus. Lincoln: Univ. of Nebraska, 1909. 31-34.

Notes for a course given in 1907-08 and 1908-09 to study "nation-building through the lives of the builders."

566. Howe, Henry. Historical Collections of Virginia. Charleston, S.C.: Babcock & Co., 1845. 164-72.

Section on Albemarle County is largely given over to TJ and his works; derivative.

567. Hubbard, Elbert. "Thomas Jefferson" in Little Journeys to the Homes of American Statesmen. New York: G. P. Putman's, 1898. 223-58.

Frequently reprinted. TJ offers "an almost ideal example of simplicity, moderation and brotherly kindness."

568. Hubbard, Elbert and John J. Lentz. Thomas Jefferson; A Little Journey by Elbert Hubbard, and an Address by John J. Lentz, Being two attempts to help perpetuate the memory and pass along the influence of the Great American. East Aurora: Roycrofters, 1906. pp. 105.

Rpt. of Hubbard (1898); the Lentz 4th of July address seeks to counter the argument that TJ was a conservative aristocrat, claiming that "he was at all times the radical of radicals."

*569. Hubbard, Simeon. A Dirge: On the Death of Our Illustrious 2d and 3d Presidents, hastily Composed on Hearing That of the Latter. Norwich, Conn.: Office of the Norwich Courier, 1826. broadside.

570. Hudson, Rector. "Captain Christopher Hudson Insures Jefferson's Safety." Tyler's Quarterly. 22(1940), 97-101.

Hudson warned TJ of Tarleton's approach, but only after Jack Jouett had already delivered his warning.

*571. Humphrey, Heman. "Review of A Selection of Eulogies..." in Miscellaneous Discourses and Reviews. Amherst: J.S. & C. Adams, 1834. 361-92.

Review of funeral eulogies for TJ and Adams.

572. Hutchins, Frank and Cortelle. Thomas Jefferson. New York: Longmans, 1946. pp. vii, 279.

Biography for teenagers.

573. "Ideals of This Great Champion of the Common Man Live On." Scholastic. 42(April 12, 1943), 2.

574. "Impressive Ceremonies Will Launch Jefferson Papers." Publisher's Weekly. 157(1950), 1500-01.

Note on ceremony at Library of Congress to celebrate Volume 1 of the Papers.

575. "In Honor of Jefferson." Missouri Historical Review. 37(January 1943), 193-96.

Accounts of testimonials to TJ in Missouri or by Missourians.

*576. Ingersoll, Charles Jared. Recollections, Historical, Political, Biographical, and Social, of Charles J. Ingersoll. By Experience, Presenting Annals, With Portraiture of Personages of This Country, From Genet's Arrival in 1792, to the Purchase of Louisiana in 1803. Philadelphia: Lippincott, 1861. pp. x, 458.

Cited in Johnston, not seen.

577. Irwin, Frank, ed. Letters of Thomas Jefferson. Tilton, N.H.: Sanbornton Bridge Press, 1975. pp. 260.

28 page biographical introduction; insignificant.

578.	Izard, Ralph. "Letters of Ralph Izard. Communicated by Worthington C. Ford, of Boston." South Carolina Historican and Genealogical Magazine. 2(1901), 199-204.

Rpt. separately as Some Letters of Ralph Izard to Thomas Jefferson. Charleston: Walker, Evans, & Cogswell, 1901. pp. 13. Letters written while TJ was in France; no editorial comments or notes.

*579.	"Iz pisem Tomasa Dzheffersona. Po stranitsam istorii." Literaturnaya Gazeta. June 13, 1953.

USSR; "From the letters of Thomas Jefferson. Through the pages of history."

580.	J. B. C. "Thomas Jefferson." American Whig Review. 12(1850), 33-46, 182-88, 290-99, 367-76, 471-89.

Review essay occasioned by the edition of TJ's Memoirs, Correspondence, Miscellanies (1849). Praises TJ but criticizes the editor for including the "Anas," of which we should have been spared.

581.	J. S. "Jefferson and His Times." National Magazine. 13(1858), 20-32.

"The model Democrat and President."

582.	J. T. C. "Mr. Rives' Address." Southern Literary Messenger. 13(1847), 574-76.

"Criticizes Wm. Rives' address to the alumni of the Univ. of Virginia for his "unlimited laudation" of TJ, who "in this country at least ... has done more to injure religion than any person who ever lived."

583.	Jackson, Donald. "On the Death of Meriwether Lewis's Servant." WMQ. 3rd ser. 21(1964), 445-48.

Letters to and from TJ concerning John Pernier, Lewis's free mulatto servant, who was accused by some of Lewis's murder.

584.	Jackson, Joseph. Where Jefferson Wrote the Declaration of Independence. Philadelphia: Penn National Bank, 1924. pp. 18.

Corner of Seventh and Market Streets, site of J. Graff's house.

*585.	James, John W. Eulogy on Thomas Jefferson, Delivered at the Columbian College, D.C., on the Fourth of October, 1826, By John W. James, a Member of the Senior Class. Washington, 1826. pp. 8.

*586.	James Marquis. "Thomas Jefferson Goes Shopping" in They Had Their Hour. Indianapolis: Bobbs-Merrill, 1934. 85-100.

587. [Jefferson, Isaac]. "A Slave's Memory of Mr. Jefferson." American Heritage. 10(October 1959), 112.

Brief extract from Memoirs of a Monticello Slave: As Dictated to Charles Campbell. see #708.

588. Jefferson Club of St. Louis. The Pilgrimage to Monticello. The Home and Tomb of Thomas Jefferson, By the Jefferson Club of St. Louis, Mo. October 10 to 14, 1901. St. Louis: Curran Printing Co., 1902. pp. 78.

Interesting bit of social history, describing group trip to Monticello, where they erected a monument commemorating the Louisiana Purchase.

589. Jefferson National Expansion Memorial Association, St. Louis. Executive Committee. A Memorial to Thomas Jefferson and the National Expansion of the United States of America. St. Louis: The Committee, 1934. pp. 16.

Promotional pamphlet linking TJ to national expansion and St. Louis in order to justify the monument there.

590. Jefferson National Expansion Memorial Association, St. Louis. Thomas Jefferson and the Pioneers to Whom We Owe Our National Expansion. (St. Louis, 1935?). pp. (24).

Limited edition promotional brochure which includes a drawing of the proposed memorial, a grandiose project looking as if it had been a project of Albert Speer. They settled for the Gateway Arch.

591. "Jefferson" in Biographie Universelle et Portative des Contemporains, ou Dictionnaire Historique des Hommes Vivants, et des Hommes Morts depuis 1788 jusqu'à Nos Jours ... Publié sous le Direction de MM. Rabbe, Vielh de Boisjolin, et Sainte-Preuve. Paris: F. G. Levrault, 1834. 2:2165-67.

592. "Jefferson." Russell's Magazine. 3(1858), 107-29; 4(1859), 205-11.

Review essay on the first two volumes of Randall's Life; holds TJ responsible for "the universal democracy, unrestrained ..." and attempts to rescue Burr's reputation. rpt. DeBow's Review. 24(1858), 508-36.

593. "Jefferson and Madison." Harper's Weekly. 29(1885), 363.

Describes the tombs of the two men.

594. "Jefferson and Radicalism." National Republic. 18(June 1930), 12.

Conservative editorial, rescuing TJ from modern radicals.

595. "Jefferson Bicentennial." Hobbies. 48(April 1943), 4.

Notes various celebratory activities.

596. "Jefferson Family." Tyler's Quarterly Historical and Genealogical Magazine. 6(1925), 199-201, 264-70; 7(1925), 49-54.

Genealogy of the descendants of Thomas Jefferson (?-1687) of Henrico, TJ's great-grandfather.

597. Jefferson Invites You to Charlottesville. Charlottesville: Chamber of Commerce, 1926? pp. (16).

598. "Jefferson Letter: Indians present old script to Princeton Library." Life. 21(December 2, 1946), 44.

Otoe Indians present letter written by TJ in 1806.

599. "Jefferson Memorial Woes: Strike Is Latest in the Series of Rows Harassing Project." Newsweek. 14(August 28, 1939), 22.

*600. The Jefferson Monument. Correspondence Relating Thereto. n.p., 1883. pp. 3.

Letters from James Rollins and Mary B. Randolph.

601. "Jefferson's Adieu." Manuscripts. 7(1955), 213.

Prints what purports to be perhaps TJ's last written words, an eight-line poetic farewell to Martha Jefferson Randolph. Gives provenance of mss. Uncritical.

602. Jefferson's Birthday in Paris, April 12-13, 1919. The Centennial Celebration of the Overseas Alumni. Paris: Univ. of Virginia European Bureau, 1919. pp. 48.

603. "Jefferson's Memoirs and Correspondence." Edinburgh Review. 51(1830), 496-526.

Review essay which considers TJ's writings as a mirror of American society; "he will be a necessary witness, whenever we survey the successive constitutional questions which have so furiously divided parties in America." rpt. in Selections from the Edinburgh Review. Paris: Baudry, 1835. 2:366-75.

604. "Jefferson's Monticello" in American Tradition: A House & Garden Guide. New York: House & Garden, 1976. 52-56.

605. The Jefferson Monument Magazine. 1(October 1849) to 2(June 1851).

Literary magazine conducted by students of the Univ. of Virginia with the object of erecting a monument to TJ. Little material pertaining to him contained here, however.

606. "Jefferson's Persistence." Watson's Jeffersonian Magazine. 1(1907), 997-98.

TJ's continuing relevance as author of the Declaration.

607. Jeffries, Ona Griffin. "The Pell-Mell System: Thomas Jefferson" in In and Out of the White House: An Intimate glimpse into the social and domestic aspects of the presidential life from Washington to the Eisenhowers. New York: Wilfred Funk, 1960. 39-52.

Entertaining in the White House, including some recipes. Minor.

608. Jellison, Charles A. "James Thomson Callender: 'Human Nature in a Hideous Form'." Virginia Cavalcade. 29(Autumn 1979), 62-69.

Touches on Callender's circulation of the Sally Hemings rumors.

609. Jellison, Charles A. "That Scoundrel Callender." VMHB. 67(1959), 295-306.

Sketch of the career of James Thomson Callender.

610. Jenkins, Charles Francis. Jefferson's Germantown Letters Together with Other Papers Relating to His Stay in Germantown During the Month of November, 1793. Philadelphia: Campbell, 1906. pp. xxiv, 194.

TJ was in Germantown because of the yellow fever epidemic in Philadelphia of the previous summer. Historical introduction and notes supplement sixty-three letters written at this time, TJ's accounts, the Ana entries describing cabinet meetings in Germantown, and Walter R. Johnson's eulogy of July 20, 1826.

611. Jobe, Brock W. "Governor's Palace Wine Cellars: Jefferson Knew Them and Enjoyed Their Wines" in Jefferson and Wine, ed. R. deTreville Lawrence, Sr. The Plains, Va.: Vinifera Wine Growers Association, 1976. 134-43.

Information on the plan and contents of the wine cellar in the Williamsburg governor's palace.

612. Johnson, Alfred, Jr. Eulogy Delivered at Belfast, August 10, 1826, on John Adams and Thomas Jefferson, at the Request of the Citizens of Belfast. Belfast, Me.: E. Fellowes, 1826. pp. 28.

613. Johnson, Ann Donegan. The Value of Foresight: The Story of Thomas Jefferson. La Jolla, Cal.: Value Communications, 1979. pp. 63.

Juvenile biography; TJ moralized.

614. Johnson, Gerald W. "The Changelings." VQR. 19(1943), 236-55.

On the character of TJ and Hamilton and their changing reputations; claims their visions were mutually compensating.

615. Johnson, Walter Rogers. An Oration Delivered at Germantown, Pennsylvania, on the 20th July, 1826, in the Presence of the Citizens of Germantown, Roxborough, Bristol, and Penn Townships, Assembled to Commemorate the Virtues and Services of Thomas Jefferson and John Adams. Philadelphia: Robert H. Small, 1826. pp. 25.

A particularly dramatic oration in which an aged narrator extolls for a youthful audience the similar excellencies of the two patriarchs.

616. Johnson, William. Eulogy on Thomas Jefferson, Delivered August 3, 1826, in the First Presbyterian Church of Charleston. Charleston: C. C. Stebbing, 1826. pp. 38.

Also in A Selection of Eulogies.... Hartford: D. F. Robinson, 1826. Full consideration of TJ's career and a defense of his policies, particulary claiming him to be a friend of commerce as opposed to speculation. Comments on the poverty of his later years.

617. Johnston, John T. M. "Thomas Jefferson, The Father of Democracy" in World Patriots. New York: World Patriots Co., 1917. 259-84.

618. Johnston, Johanna. Thomas Jefferson, His Many Talents. New York: Dodd Mead, 1961. pp. 160.

Juvenile biography.

*619. Jones, Alfred Haworth. "The Jefferson Papers and the Usable Past" in La France et l'Esprit de 76, ed. Daniel Royot. Clermont-Ferrand: Assn. pour les Publications de la Faculte de Lettres et Sciences Humaines, 1977. 125-30.

620. Jones, Charles W. Jeffersonian Democracy. Address ... on the Life and Work of Thomas Jefferson, Delivered on the Occasion of the Celebration of the 138th Anniversary of the Birth of Thomas Jefferson by the Essex County Democratic Club, Newark, N.J. Washington: Thomas McGill & Co., 1881. pp. 11.

621. Jones, Joseph Seawell. A Defense of the Revolutionary History of the State of North Carolina from the Aspersions of Mr. Jefferson. Boston: C. Bowen, 1834. pp. 343.

Defends the Mecklenburg Declaration; written from secondary sources, mostly Federalist. See Edwin Miles' 1957 article, noted below.

75

622.　Jouett, Edward S. "Jack Jouett's Ride." Filson Club History Quarterly. 24(1950), 142-57.

Standard account of Jouett's ride, with additional biographical and genealogical information on him.

623.　Judson, Clara Ingram. Thomas Jefferson, Champion of the People. Chicago: Wilson and Follett, 1952. pp. 224.

Juvenile biography.

624.　Judson, L. Carroll. "Thomas Jefferson" in A Biography of the Signers of the Declaration of Independence, and of Washington and Patrick Henry; With an Appendix Containing the Constitution of the United States and Other Documents. Philadelphia: J. Dobson and Thomas Cowperthwait, 1839. 13-24.

Rpt. in his Sages and Heroes of the American Revolution. Philadelphia: The Author, 1851. 191-205. Sympathetic sketch defending TJ from charges of infidelity.

625.　Kalkbrenner, Jurgen. "Jefferson's German Wine Choices, his Vineyard Tour, 1788" in Jefferson and Wine, ed. R. deTreville Lawrence, Sr. The Plains, Va.: Vinifera Wine Growers Association, 1976. 74-80.

TJ's favorites were Johannisberger and Rudesheimer; he found the hocks "acid."

626.　Kammen, Michael. "The Founding Fathers: In Search of Fame and Identity." Reviews in American History. 3(1975), 196-205.

Provocative review essay on Douglass Adair, Fame and the Founding Fathers, and Erik Erikson, Dimensions of a New Identity, takes issue with Adair's interpretation of the Sally Hemings scandal, among other points.

627.　Kammen, Michael. "Thomas Jefferson's America—and Ours." Occasional Review. 2(Autumn 1974), 107-26.

Review essay; thoughtful response to Fawn Brodie and others.

628.　Kane, Joseph Nathan, comp. "Thomas Jefferson" in Facts about the Presidents: A Compilation of Biographical and Historical Data. New York: H. W. Wilson, 1968. 25-32.

2nd edition; earlier edition, not seen, appeared in 1959.

629.　Kaplan, Lawrence S. "Reflections on Jefferson as a Francophile." South Atlantic Quarterly. 79(1980), 38-50.

Claims that TJ's Francophilia did not compromise his position as a public man, but that it did give later historians a handy theme around which to organize praise and criticism.

630. Karsten, Peter. Patriot-Heroes in England and America: Political Symbolism and Changing Values over Three Centuries. Madison: Univ. of Wisconsin Press, 1978. pp. ix, 257.

   TJ's reputation discussed passim, but especially pp. 95-109. Finds that "Lincoln is the patriot-hero of order-conscious, cosmopolitan statists; Jefferson of freedom-conscious, localistic antistatists."

631. Kean, Jefferson Randolph. "The Origin of the Monticello Graveyard." Minutes of the Ninth Meeting of the Monticello Association. 1922. 9-20.

   First interment was TJ's friend Dabney Carr.

632. Kean, Robert H. "History of the Graveyard at Monticello" in Collected Papers of the Monticello Association, ed. George Green Shackelford. Princeton: Princeton Univ. Press, 1965. 3-26.

   Printed separately, Charlottesville: Thomas Jefferson Memorial Foundation, 1972. pp. 24.

633. Kelley, Joseph J., Jr. and Sol Feinstone. "Patrician and Slave: The Women in Thomas Jefferson's Life" in Courage and Candlelight: The Feminine Spirit of '76. Harrisburg, Pa.: Stackpole, 1974. 205-31.

   Trivial.

634. Kellogg, Charles E. "Appreciation of Thomas Jefferson on the Occasion of the Two Hundredth Anniversary of His Birth." Journal of the American Society of Agronomy. 36(1944), 371-72.

*635. Kelly, Edward James. The Thomas Jefferson Memorial, Washington, D.C. Alexandria, Va.: Action Publications, 1949. pp. 30.

636. Kemp, Verbon E. "Thomas Jefferson Memorial Foundation." Commonwealth, The Magazine of Virginia. 10(March 1943), 14-16.

   Brief history of progress made in restoring Monticello.

637. Kerchendorfer, Paul R. "Jefferson's 'Writing Box,' Officially the Declaration Box." National Historical Magazine (formerly D.A.R. Magazine). 72(July 1938), 12-15.

638. Kibler, J. Luther, Jr. "Jack Jouett, Jr. and Christopher Hudson." Tyler's Quarterly. 23(1941), 49-57.

Response to Rector Hudson's article in Tyler's (1940).

639. Kimball, Fiske. "In Search of Jefferson's Birthplace." VMHB.
      51(1943), 313-25.

      Account of excavations at Shadwell.

640. Kimball, Fiske. "Monticello, Home of Thomas Jefferson." Journal
      of the 4th Annual National Antiques Show (New York). 1948. p. 4.

      TJ the inventor and collector.

641. Kimball, Marie. "Europe Comes to Jefferson." The American-German
      Review. 15(February 1949), 15-17, 30.

      Describes TJ's friendships with Hessian prisoners of war lodged in
      Albemarle County in 1779, particularly General von Riedesel and his
      wife, Baron von Geismar, and Jean Louis de Unger.

642. Kimball, Marie. "Feast Days at Monticello." McCall's. 83(November
      1955), 42-47, 84.

      TJ as host at Monticello, illustrated.

643. Kimball, Marie. Jefferson: The Road to Glory, 1743-1776. New York:
      Coward-McCann, 1943. pp. ix, 358.

      Carefully researched biography, the fruit of a career of Jefferson
      scholarship. Two later volumes carry TJ to 1789.

644. Kimball, Marie. Jefferson: War and Peace, 1776 to 1784. New York:
      Coward-McCann, 1947. pp. ix, 398.

      Second of three volumes on TJ. Long discussions of his authorship of
      Notes on the State of Virginia on 259-305.

645. Kimball, Marie. Jefferson: The Scene of Europe, 1784 to 1789.
      New York: Coward-McCann, 1950. pp. ix, 357.

646. Kimball, Marie. "Jefferson in Paris." North American Review.
      248(1939), 73-86.

      On TJ's social life.

647. Kimball, Marie G. "Jefferson's Farewell to Romance." VQR. 4(1928),
      402-19.

      Account of TJ's relationship with Maria Cosway; Head wins out over
      Heart.

648. Kimball, Marie. "A Playmate of Thomas Jefferson." North American Review. 213(1921), 145-56.

TJ's relationship with his granddaughter, Ellen Wayles Randolph.

649. Kimball, Marie Goebel. "Thomas Jefferson's Rhine Journey." The American-German Review. 13(1946-47): October, 4-7; December, 11-14; February, 4-8.

Account of TJ's journey to the Hague in 1788; he was especially interested in vineyards and winemaking.

650. Kimball, Marie Goebel. "Unpublished Correspondence of Madame de Stael with Thomas Jefferson." North American Review. 208(1918), 63-71.

Brief introduction to 3 letters by Mme. de Stael and 4 by TJ.

651. King, Wiliam V. "Foreword to Story 'Was I Jefferson?'" n.p. 1958. broadside.

In support of the tale of Isom Richard Lamb, see below.

652. [Kingsley, W. V.]. "Thomas Jefferson." National Quarterly Review. 30(1875), 283-303.

Systematically minimizes TJ's character and achievements; holds him responsible for the Civil War because the Declaration planted the seed of liberty.

653. Kinnaird, Anne. "A Treasure House of the Past." Southern Magazine (Wytheville, Va.). 2(no. 8, 1935), 26-27, 45.

Describes collections in the St. Louis Jefferson Memorial.

654. Kirk, Russell. "Jefferson and the Faithless." South Atlantic Quarterly. 40(1941), 220-27.

Contends Horace Gregory is mistaken in calling Mencken, Sandburg, Vachel Lindsay, and Edgar Lee Master Jeffersonians, since they share little with TJ.

655. Kirkland, John Thornton. "A Discourse in Commemoration of John Adams and Thomas Jefferson; Delivered Before the American Academy of Arts and Sciences, October 30, 1826." American Academy of Arts and Sciences, Memoirs. new series. 1(1833), iii-xxxi.

656. Klare, Ralph E. "Monticello, Where Thomas Jefferson Introduced to Colonial Virginia Many Facets of Our 1963 Living Comforts." Hoosier Motorist. 50(January/February 1963), 6-7.

657.   Klingberg, Frank J. and Frank W. Klingberg, eds. The Correspondence
       Between Henry Stephens Randall and Hugh Blair Grigsby, 1856-1861.
       Berkeley: Univ. of California Press, 1952. pp. ix, 196.

       Randall's biography of TJ appeared in 1858; both men were ardent
       Jeffersonians and their correspondence is full of discussion about
       Randall's book and his subject.

658.   Knapp, Samuel Lorenzo. An Address Delivered in Chauncy Place
       Church before the Young Men of Boston, August 2, 1826, in Com-
       memoration of the Deaths of Adams and Jefferson. Boston:
       Ingraham & Hewes, 1826. pp. 31.

       Also in A Selection of Eulogies ... . Hartford: D. F. Robinson, 1826.
       173-92. One of the most rhetorically ornate of the eulogies.

659.   Knoles, George H. "Thomas Jefferson: Crusader for Freedom." Social
       Studies. 33(1942), 297-304.

       Sketch on TJ's "struggles to maintain and extend human enlighten-
       ment."

*660. Knox, George W. "Alexander Hamilton and Thomas Jefferson" in
       Thirty-one Orations Delivered at Hamilton College from 1864 to
       1895, ed. Melvin Gilbert Dodge. New York: Putnam's, 1896. 73-78.

661.   Knudson, Jerry W. "Thomas Jefferson and James Callender: The Myth
       of Black Sally." Negro History Bulletin. 32(November 1969), 15-22.

       Account of Callender and his animus toward TJ.

662.   Koch, Adrienne, ed. Jefferson. Englewood Cliffs, N.J.: Prentice-Hall,
       1971. pp. viii, 180.

       Collection of reprinted material in the Great Lives Observed series.

663.   Koch, Adrienne. "The Versatile George Tucker." Journal of Southern
       History. 29(1963), 502-12.

       Essay review which focuses on the historiographic accomplishments
       of Tucker, a biographer of TJ.

664.   Kohler, Max J. "Unpublished Correspondence Between Thomas
       Jefferson and Some American Jews." Publications of the American
       Jewish Historical Society. 20(1911), 11-30.

       Comments briefly on TJ's correspondence with American Jews,
       reprints a variety of letters with a few notes.

*665. Kohut, George C. "Jefferson and the Jews." New Era. 6(1905?),
       481-91.

Not located.

666.   Komroff, Manuel. Thomas Jefferson. New York: Messner, 1961.
        pp. 191.

        Juvenile biography.

667.   Kozlowski, W. M. "Niemcewicz en Amérique et sa correspondance
        inédite avec Jefferson (1797-1810)." Revue de Littérature
        Comparée. 8(1928), 29-45.

        Describes the relationship and prints correspondence between TJ and
        Julien Ursyn Niemcewicz, Polish poet, patriot, and friend of
        Kosciuszko.

668.   Kuenzli, Esther Wilcox. The Last Years of Thomas Jefferson.
        Hicksville, N.Y.: Exposition Press, 1974. pp. 92.

        TJ after 1809; uncritically sympathetic sketch.

669.   Kukla, Jon. "Flirtation and Feux d'Artifices: Mr. Jefferson,
        Mrs. Cosway, and Fireworks." Virginia Cavalcade. 26(Autumn 1976),
        52-63.

        Maria Cosway and TJ attended a fireworks display by the Ruggieris
        on the day they first met.

670.   Kuper, Theodore Fred. "Address on Thomas Jefferson." Proceedings
        of the Fifth National Convention of the Future Farmers of America.
        Held at Kansas City, Missouri, November 11-17, 1932. 37-40.

        What TJ was, including a farmer.

671.   Kuper, Theodore Fred. "Collecting Monticello." Manuscripts. 7(1955),
        216-23.

        Account of the efforts of the Thomas Jefferson Memorial Foundation
        to acquire Monticello.

672.   Kuper, Theodore Fred. Jefferson the Giant. New York: Thomas
        Jefferson Memorial Foundation, 1926. pp. (16).

        "Monticello Papers Number Seven." Brief life for visitors to the
        shrine.

673.   Kuper, Theodore Fred. "Jefferson and Italy: The Vital Contacts Be-
        tween Two Great Peoples." Atlantica. 15(December 1933), 8-10, 37.

        Discusses TJ's connections with Italy: Mazzei, Carlos Bellini, and
        his trip there in 1787.

674. Kuper, Theodore Fred. "Thomas Jefferson Ordered the Life of Houdon Insured." New England Pilot. 25(May-August 1940), 267-70.

TJ had John Adams insure the life of Houdon when he came to America to model the statue of Washington.

675. Kuper, Theodore Fred. Thomas Jefferson Still Lives. An Outline of the Life of the Architect of Our American Heritage. With an Introduction by Irving Dillard. New York: Arthur Price Foundation, 1968. pp. 32.

676. Kuper, Theodore Fred. "Thomas Jefferson the Lawyer." Lawyers Guild Review. 3(March/April 1943), 30-36.

Survey.

677. Kusielewicz, Eugene F. "The Jefferson-Niemcewicz Correspondence." Polish Review. 2(n. 4, 1957), 7-21.

Prints the letters with notes, including 3 letters recently discovered.

678. Lafayette, Marie Joseph, Marquis de. "Thomas Jefferson." Independent. 55(1903), 26-27.

Prints without comment a letter on TJ's death, dated September 17, 1826, and sent to Arnold Scheffer.

679. "Lafayette et Jefferson." Revue des Sciences Politiques. 53(1930), 607-12.

Review essay occasioned by Chinard's Letters of Lafayette and Jefferson.

680. Lagemann, John Kord. "How Jefferson Spent the First Fourth." Colliers. 132(July 4, 1953), 50-53.

Fanciful sketch of events in 1776.

681. Lamb, Isom Richard. Was I Jefferson? Pomona, Cal.: The Author, 1959. pp. vi, 526.

A Californian who was hypnotized by his dentist and discovered that he had been TJ in a previous existence. Since the first event he remembered is shaking Aaron Burr's hand at his trial in Richmond, this seems unlikely. Probably only a few copies of this distributed; one at Virginia Historical Society.

682. Langhorne, Elizabeth. "The Other Hemings." Albemarle Magazine. 3(October/November 1980), 59-66.

82

Good article for a popular audience; criticizes Brodie's evidence and reasoning.

683. Lansdale, Nelson. "House on the Nickel." House and Garden. 103(February 1953), 80-85.

Monticello, illustrated.

684. Lasch, Christopher. "The Jeffersonian Legacy" in Thomas Jefferson: The Man ... His World ... His Influence, ed. Lally Weymouth. New York: Putnam's, 1973. 229-45.

Argues that in our time "Jeffersonian traditions have survived only as a minor current of opposition among those who retain an old-fashioned commitment to equality, ... or who believe ... that the rights of free speech and free inquiry have not been altogether superseded by the exigencies of world power."

685. "Last Words of Jefferson." Univ. of Virginia Alumni Bulletin. 6(1900), 79-80.

686. Lawson, Lyle. "At Home with Tom Jefferson." Modern Photography. 40(September 1976), 102-03, 147-50.

Monticello for the photographer.

687. Leach, Beverly B. "Thomas Jefferson the Gourmet." Commonwealth, The Magazine of Virginia. 39(February 1972), 34-37.

TJ as a host.

688. [Lee, Henry]. "The Late Mr. Jefferson." Niles Register. 31(1826), 197-200.

Account of TJ's death; 2 letters from TJ to Lee relative to the Revolutionary War in Virginia in 1780-81.

689. Lee, Henry. Observations on the Writings of Thomas Jefferson, With Particular Reference to the Attack They Contain on the Memory of the Late Gen. Henry Lee. New York: Charles DeBehr, 1832. pp. 237.

Rpt. "With an Introduction and Notes by Charles Carter Lee," Philadelphia: J. Dobson, et. al., 1839. pp. 262. In the 1829 edition of TJ's Writings his letter to George Washington of June 19, 1796, refers to a supposed political scandal monger; an editor's note states, "Here in the margin of the copy, is written, apparently at a later date, 'Gen. H. Lee.'" Lee rapidly moves from a defense of his father into a general attack upon TJ.

690. Lee, Susan and John. Thomas Jefferson. Chicago: Children's Press, 1974. pp. 47.

Juvenile.

691. Lemesle, Charles. Éloge de Thomas Jefferson, Ancien Président des Etats-Unis de l'Amérique du Nord, Membre Honoraire de la Societé Linnéenne de Paris. Paris: Au Secretariat de la Societé Linnéenne, 1827. pp. 11.

"Extrait des Annales Linnéennes pour 1826." Praises TJ's interest in science and notes his connections in the international community.

692. Lengyel, Cornel. Four Days in July: The Story Behind the Declaration of Independence. New York: Doubleday, 1958. pp. 360.

Quasi-fictional account of the period leading up to the acceptance of the Declaration and its publication.

693. Levasseur, Antoine. Lafayette in America in 1824 and 1825. Philadelphia: Carey and Lea, 1829. 1:212-21.

Describes Lafayette's visit to TJ at Monticello.

694. Levy, Jefferson M. "Monticello, the Home of Thomas Jefferson." Yearbook ... 1912-13. New York: Sons of the American Revolution, Empire State Society, 1913. 68-74.

The owner of Monticello defends his possession.

695. Lewis, Alfred Henry. "Jefferson's Grand Day: A Pregnant Scene from the Drama of American Independence." Everybody's Magazine. 7(1902), 561-70.

Romanticized, dramatic, and inaccurate version of the Fourth of July, 1776.

696. Lilienthal, Helen and David. "Thomas Jefferson One Hundred Years After." The Outlook. 143(1926), 322-24.

Review essay.

697. Lincoln, Abraham. "To Henry L. Pierce and Others" in Collected Works of Abraham Lincoln, ed. Roy P. Basler. New Brunswick: Rutgers Univ. Press, 1953. 3:374-76.

Famous letter replying to an invitation to attend a celebration in Boston of TJ's birthday; "The principles of Jefferson are the definitions and axioms of a free society." Given wide circulation at the time in the Republican press; cited here in a readily available and authoritative edition.

698. Lincoln, Robert W. "Thomas Jefferson" in Lives of the Presidents of the United States, and of the Signers of the Declaration of

Independence. New York: N. Watson, 1833. 97-130.

Variously reprinted.

699. Lindsay, Barbara. "Henry Adams' History: A Study in Limitations."
Western Humanities Review. 8(1954), 99-110.

Argues that Adams turns his history of TJ's and Madison's administrations into "an ironic demonstration of the futility of human aspirations.

700. Lingelbach, Anna Lane. "Jefferson Today." Current History. n.s.
5(1943), 225-28.

701. Linn, William, The Life of Thomas Jefferson, Author of the Declaration of Independence, and Third President of the United States.
Ithaca, N.Y.: Mack and Andrus, 1834. pp. 267.

"A compilation exclusively." Pro-Jeffersonian.

702. Littell, Mary Clark. "Mrs. Thomas Jefferson, Mistress of Monticello."
Virginia Record. 78(December 1956), 15-16.

Biographical sketch of Martha Wayles Jefferson.

703. Little, Charles J. "Thomas Jefferson. April 13, 1743—July 4, 1826."
The Chautauquan. 14(1891), 141-45.

Biographical sketch playing off general praise against specific criticism.

704. Little, Robert. A Funeral Sermon on the Death of John Adams and
Thomas Jefferson, Ex-Presidents of the United States, Preached on
Sunday Evening, July 16, 1826, in the First Unitarian Church,
Washington City. Washington: Bartow & Brannan, 1826, pp. 22.

Pays particular attention to TJ and defends his religious opinions;
argues that the simultaneous death is a sign of God's orderly gover-
nance of the universe.

705. Littleton, Mrs. Martin W. Monticello. n.p., 1912. unpag.

Attempt to raise money and congressional support for public acquisition of Monticello.

706. Littleton, Mrs. Martin W. One Wish. n.p., 1911. pp. (16).

Her wish is to make Monticello a national shrine; an opening shot in
the campaign to acquire Monticello.

85

707. Lizanich, Christine M. "'The March of This Government': Joel Barlow's Unwritten History of the United States." WMQ. 3rd ser. 33(1976), 315-30.

TJ encouraged Barlow to write a history of the Revolution from a republican point of view. Four essays, printed here for the first time, survive of Barlow's effort.

708. Logan, Rayford W., ed. Memoirs of a Monticello Slave: As Dictated to Charles Campbell in the 1840's by Isaac, One of Thomas Jefferson's Slaves. Charlottesville: Tracy W. McGregor Library, 1951. pp. 45.

Published simultaneously in WMQ. 3rd ser. 8(1951), 561-82. Introduction discusses the history of this mss. from the Univ. of Virginia Library and compares it to an apparently later mss. in the William and Mary Library. Isaac claimed that Sally Hemings and some other of the Hemings "was old Mr. Wayles' children."

709. Long, Edward John. "Shadwell—Jefferson's Birthplace." The Iron Worker. 26(Autumn 1962), 1-7.

On the attempt to determine what Shadwell looked like in TJ's time and to reconstruct it.

710. Long, E. John. "Thomas Jefferson, Master Craftsman." The Carpenter. 82(July 1962), 10-14.

TJ as handyman.

711. Long, H. Jack. "Last Letters from the Valiant." Manuscripts. 28(1976), 195-201.

Describes TJ's and Adams's last letters; insignificant.

712. "Long Tom Lives to See the Day." Collier's. 110(July 4, 1942), 70.

Account of TJ's death, highly colored.

713. Lord, John. "Thomas Jefferson. Popular Sovereignty" in Beacon Lights of History. New York: Fords, Howard, and Hulbert, 1894. 7:221-76.

Sketch with underlying Federalist bias.

714. Loring, George B. Celebration of the Birth-day of Thomas Jefferson, at Salem Mass., April 1st, 1859. Oration By Dr. Geo. B. Loring. Salem: The Advocate Office, 1859. pp. 23.

Oration celebrates TJ as politician, statesman, and philanthropist; the pamphlet also details the rest of the ceremony organized by the the National Democrats of Essex County.

715. [Lossing, Benson J]. "Jefferson Caricatured." American Historical Record. 1(1872), 63–66.

On a caricature of TJ putting the Constitution upon an "Altar to Gallic Despotism" after the disclosure of the Mazzei letter.

716. Lossing, Benson J. "Monticello." Harper's Monthly Magazine. 7(1853), 145–60.

Account of a visit to Monticello in the early 1850's and of TJ's life there.

717. Lossing, Benson J. "Thomas Jefferson" in Biographical Sketches of the Signers of the Declaration of American Independence: The Declaration Historically Considered; ... . New York: George F. Coolidge & Brother, 1848. 174–83.

Often reprinted and similar material in other Lossing collections; also note pp. 244–309 which sketch the historical background of the Declaration, examine the charges against George III, and find them valid.

718. Lossing, Benson J. "Thomas Jefferson, the Third President of the United States" in Lives of the Presidents of the United States. New York: H. Phelps & Co., 1847. 39–48.

*719. Luca, A. Toussaint. "Thomas Jefferson 1743-1826" in Ceux qui ont fait l'Amérique: ... . Paris: G. Roustan, 1918. 145–84.

720. Ludlow, J. M. "A Gallery of American Presidents." Macmillan's Magazine. 12(1865), 292–94.

Superficial sketches of early presidents, including TJ.

721. Ludlow, L. L. "The Vision of Jefferson." Vital Speeches. 6(1940), 479–80.

TJ is "the greatest humanitarian 19 centuries have produced since the great human God trod the hills of Nazareth."

722. Ludlum, David M. "The Washington and Jefferson Snowstorm." Weatherwise. 10(December 1957), 187–88, 212.

The snowstorm which began on the day TJ returned to Monticello with Martha Wayles Jefferson was the worst in 150 years.

*723. Lustrac, Jean de, Baron. Jefferson et la France. Bergerac, 1960. pp. 32.

Not located.

724.   Lydenberg, Harry Miller. "What Did Macaulay Say About America?" _Bulletin of the New York Public Library._ 29(1925), 459-81.

Best account of Macaulay's famous letter to Henry S. Randall and its reception in the popular press; prints all of Macaulay's correspondence with Randall, including a partial retraction.

725.   Lyne, Cassie Moncure. "A Romance of Monticello." _National Republic._ 19(October 1931), 24-25.

TJ's wedding gift to Ellen Randolph Coolidge.

726.   Lyman, T. P. H. _The Life of Thomas Jeffeson, Esq., LL.D., Late Ex-President of the United States. Arranged and Compiled from Original Documents._ Philadelphia: D. & S. Neall, 1826. pp. xi, 111.

Apologetic biography of TJ as one of those who "not only go for men in the vast catalogue of nations; but they are men upon the list of reason, and of Heaven."

727.   McAdie, Alexander. "Thomas Jefferson at Home." _Proceedings of the American Antiquarian Society._ n.s. 40(1931), 27-46.

Contends that by nature TJ was a private person deeply attached to his family.

728.   Macaulay, Thomas B. "A Timely Letter from Lord Macaulay (Written in 1857 to a Correspondent in America)." _American Mercury._ 35(1935), 378-79.

Prints without comment Macauley's letter to Henry S. Randall, stating, "I cannot reckon Jefferson among the benefactors of mankind."

729.   McCabe, James D. "Thomas Jefferson" in _The Centennial Book of American Biography, Embracing the Biographies of the Great Men Whose Deeds Illustrate the First One Hundred Years of American Independence._ Philadelphia: P. W. Ziegler, 1876. 145-77.

730.   MacConkey, Dorothy Ingling. "Bicentennial Presidents and Their Role Models: A Sociological View." _Daughters of the American Revolution Magazine._ 110(1976), 508-512, 642.

TJ's role model was George Wythe.

731.   McConnell, Jane and Burt. "Martha Wayles Skelton Jefferson, Who Did not Live to See the White House" in _Our First Ladies, From Martha Washington to Mamie Eisenhower._ New York: Crowell, 1953. 33-41.

She "would have been proud" of TJ "had she lived;" superficial.

732. McCorvey, T. C. "Long's Portraits of the Virginia Presidents."
      Nation. 57(1893), 307.

      Describes George Long's account of visits with TJ in 1825.

733. McCorvey, Thomas Chalmers. "Thomas Jefferson and His Political
      Philosophy" in Alabama Historical Sketches. Charlottesville:
      Univ. of Virginia Press, 1960. 185-207.

      Biographical sketch, only of interest for containing a 4 paragraph
      reminiscence of TJ by George Long, one of the original University
      professors.

734. McCracken, Henry Mitchell. "Thomas Jefferson" in The Hall of Fame.
      New York: Putnam's, 1901. 107-12.

*735. McFee, Inez. "Thomas Jefferson" in American Heroes From History.
      Chicago: A. Flanagan Co., 1913.

736. McIlwaine, Bill. "Letters Jefferson Didn't Write." Saturday Evening
      Post. 226(January 16, 1954), 108.

      On the facsimile of the Nov. 27, 1803 letter distributed by the
      Richmond Morris Plan Bank.

737. MacIvor, Ivor. "So We Commemorate the Big Cheese." Saturday
      Evening Post. 226(April 3, 1954), 88.

      Note on the mammoth cheese.

738. Mackall, Leonard L. "A Letter from the Virginia Loyalist John
      Randolph to Thomas Jefferson Written in London in 1779." Proceed-
      ings of the American Antiquarian Society. 30(1920), 17-31.

      Discusses Randolph's background and friendship with TJ; prints the
      letter with notes.

739. Mackay, Charles. The Founders of the American Republic, A History
      and Biography With a Supplementary Chapter on Ultra-Democracy.
      Edinburgh: Wm. Blackwood, 1885. 208-92.

      Positive view of TJ which shows him as more friendly to the British
      people and more opposed to slavery than he probably was in fact.

740. McKee, George Holladay. "Was Revolutionary American Dry?"
      Commonweal. 16(1932), 609-12.

      TJ liked wine but disapproved of hard liquor.

741. McKee Thomas Hudson. "Biography of Thomas Jefferson, Historical Notes, and Inaugural Addresses" in Presidential Inaugurations from George Washington to Grover Cleveland. Washington: Statistical Publishing Co., 1893. 16-24.

742. McKittrick, Eric. "The View From Jefferson's Camp." New York Review of Books. 15(December 17, 1970), 35-38.

Review essay on Malone's Jefferson the President: First Term and Peterson's Thomas Jefferson and the New Nation. Reflects intelligently on dealing with the more ambiguous aspects of TJ's character and career, particularly his sexual life and his two political failures, the governorship and the Embargo.

743. MacLeish, Archibald. "The Ghost of Thomas Jefferson" in Riders on the Earth: Essays and Recollections. Boston: Houghton Mifflin, 1978. 57-65.

Argues that TJ gave American freedom as a purpose, a purpose that Americans have betrayed in the years since 1945.

744. Macleod, Ann K. "Monticello, Dreams and Daybooks on a Little Hill." Virginia Country. Summer/Fall 1979. 48-51.

Then and now at Monticello.

745. McPherson, Elizabeth Gregory. "Unpublished Letters from North Carolinians to Jefferson." North Carolina Historical Review. 12(1935), 252-83, 354-80.

Brief introduction and extensive notes; letters deal with foreign affairs and political matters for the most part.

746. Macomber, Hattie E. Thomas Jefferson. Boston: Educational Publishing, 1898. pp. 32.

"Young Folks Library of Choice Literature."

747. Maelor, Arglwydd. Thomas Jefferson Trydydd Arlywydd America. Dinbych: Gwasg Gee, 1980. pp. 80.

In Welsh.

748. Maggio, Samuel. "Parent: Jefferson's Burgundy 'Wine Man'" in Jefferson and Wine, ed. R. deTreville Lawrence, Sr. The Plains, Va.: Vinifera Wine Growers Association, 1976. 48-55.

Brief introduction to a selection of correspondence dealing with his wine agent in Beaune, M. Parent.

90

749. Malden, Henry. "Jefferson" in Distinguished Men of Modern Times. London: Charles Knight, 1838. 4:344-57.

750. Malkin, Arthur Thomas. "Jefferson" in The Gallery of Portraits with Memoirs. London: Charles Knight, 1837. 7:153-61.

    Sketch with portrait.

751. Malone, Dumas. "At Home with Thomas Jefferson." New York Times Magazine. July 1, 1956. 8-9, 18-19.

    Description of life at Monticello; reply by L. Loeb, July 22, 1956. p. 4.

752. Malone, Dumas, ed. Correspondence Between Thomas Jefferson and Pierre Samuel duPont de Nemours, 1798-1817. Boston: Houghton Mifflin, 1930. pp. ix, 210.

    Translations by Linwood Lehman. Annotated, but slightly less complete than Chinard's edition of the correspondence.

753. Malone, Dumas. "He Dedicated Us to Liberty." New York Times Magazine. April 13, 1941. 9.

754. Malone, Dumas and Richard B. Morris. "If Jefferson and Hamilton Were Alive Today." Nations Business. 64(July 1976), 40-46.

    Interviews with Malone and Morris on how TJ and Hamilton would see us now.

755. Malone, Dumas. "Introduction" to Autobiography of Thomas Jefferson. New York: Capricorn Books, 1959. 1-18.

    Adapted from Malone's Jefferson the Virginian.

756. Malone, Dumas. "Jefferson and Lincoln." Abraham Lincoln Quarterly. 5(1949), 327-47.

    Compares the TJ and Lincoln legends and how they relate to what appear to be the facts; also compares them as writers—TJ's words appeal to the mind, not emotions, and if they are graceful, they lack Lincoln's eloquence.

757. Malone, Dumas. "Jefferson and the New Deal." Scribner's Magazine. 93(1933), 356-59.

    "... the times require a Jeffersonian Hamilton or a Hamiltonian Jefferson..." FDR is no strict Jeffersonian, but TJ would probably "bestow his apostolic blessing ... as the new President buckles on his Hamiltonian sword."

91

758.   Malone, Dumas. Jefferson and His Time: Jefferson the Virginian.
        Boston: Little Brown, 1948. pp. xx, 484.

        The first volume of the best biography of TJ; covers until 1784.
        Malone goes into great detail on TJ's life, but has a tendency to en-
        gage in what might seem special pleading in regard to some of TJ's
        more questionable actions. This tendency is more noticeable in the
        later volumes (but not the final one), and since Malone scrupulously
        presents all the facts, a reader is not obliged to accept his judgments
        blindly.

759.   Malone, Dumas. Jefferson and His Time: Jefferson and the Rights of
        Man. Boston: Little Brown, 1951. pp. xxix, 523.

        Covers TJ's years in France and his service as Secretary of State,
        1784-1792.

760.   Malone, Dumas. Jefferson and His Time: Jefferson and the Ordeal of
        Liberty. Boston: Little Brown, 1962. pp. xxx, 545.

        Covers the years 1792-1801, until TJ's inauguration as president.

761.   Malone, Dumas. Jefferson and His Time: Jefferson the President: First
        Term, 1801-1805. Boston: Little Brown, 1970. pp. xxix, 539.

762.   Malone, Dumas. Jefferson and His Time: Jefferson the President:
        Second Term, 1805-1809. Boston: Little Brown, 1974. pp. xxxi, 704.

763.   Malone, Dumas. Jefferson and His Time: The Sage of Monticello.
        Boston: Little Brown, 1981. pp. xxiii, 551.

        Covers the years from 1809 to TJ's death in 1826; reflections on what
        TJ accomplished in his presidency show a good critical sense, and the
        accounts of TJ's troubles in his last years are quite moving. A
        strong conclusion to a masterly biography.

764.   Malone, Dumas. "The Jefferson Faith." Saturday Review of Literature.
        26(April 17, 1943), 4-6.

        Essay review; claims that TJ is "most appealing ... as a symbol of
        personal liberty, and as such he is often misunderstood."

765.   Malone, Dumas. "Jefferson Goes to School at Williamsburg." VQR.
        33(1957), 481-96.

        Discussion of TJ's education at William and Mary College and subse-
        quent years in Williambsburg.

766.   Malone, Dumas. "Mr. Jefferson and the Living Generation." American
        Scholar. 41(1972), 587-98.

92

TJ's relevance for the present day.

767. Malone, Dumas. "Mr. Jefferson and the Traditions of Virginia. VMHB. 75(1967), 131-42.

Annual Address to the Virginia Historical Society in 1967.

768. Malone, Dumas. "Mr. Jefferson's Private Life." Proceedings of the American Antiquarian Society. 84(1974), 65-72.

Prints a letter of Ellen Randolph Coolidge, TJ's granddaughter, refuting the Callender libels and claiming Peter and Samuel Carr were cohabitating with Betty and Sally Hemings.

769. Malone, Dumas. "Mr. Jefferson to Mr. Roosevelt: An Imaginary Letter." VQR. 19(1943), 161-77.

TJ reviews his presidential career as a model for his eventual successor; he approves of FDR.

770. Malone, Dumas and Steven H. Hochman. "A Note on Evidence: The Personal History of Madison Hemings." Journal of Southern History. 41(1975), 523-28.

Contends that Hemings' account of his life and his paternity "was solicited and published for a propagandist purpose."

771. Malone, Dumas. An Outline of the Life of Thomas Jefferson, 1743-1826. Charlottesville: Univ. of Virginia, 1924. pp. 14.

Published as Univ. of Virginia Record. Extension Service. 8(no. 7, 1924).

772. Malone, Dumas. Patriots: Old and New. Charlottesville: Thomas Jefferson Memorial Foundation, 1975. pp. 12.

TJ's faith in popular government was part of a love for his country which did not demand uniformity among his fellow citizens.

773. Malone, Dumas. "Polly Jefferson and Her Father." VQR. 7(1931), 81-95.

Account of the relationship between TJ and daughter Maria Jefferson Eppes.

774. Malone, Dumas. "Prophet of the American Way" in The American Story: The Age of Exploration to the Age of the Atom, ed. Earl Schenk Miers. Great Neck, N.Y.: Channel Press, 1956. 83-88.

Biographical sketch.

775. Malone, Dumas. "The Relevance of Mr. Jefferson." VQR. 37(1961), 331-49.

Thoughtful meditation upon the uncertain aspects of TJ's reputation and his permanent importance as a spokesman for the rights of man.

776. Malone, Dumas. "The Return of a Virginian." VQR. 27(1951), 528-43.

Account of TJ's return from his mission to France.

777. Malone, Dumas. "Thomas Jefferson" in Dictionary of American Biography, ed. Malone. New York: Scribners, 1933. 10:17-35.

Malone on TJ in a nutshell.

778. Malone, Dumas, T. V. Smith, and Lyman Bryson. "Thomas Jefferson, Notes on the State of Virginia (as Broadcast October 11, 1953)." Invitation to Learning Reader. 5(1954), 287-92.

Roundtable discussion.

779. Malone, Dumas. "Thomas Jefferson Still Survives." New York Times Magazine. July 2, 1950. 8+.

780. Malone, Dumas. "Was Washington the Greatest American?" New York Times Magazine. February 16, 1958. 11+.

Compares TJ and Washington and makes claim for the greatness of the former.

781. Malone, Thomas. "The Man Who Wrote the Declaration." Independent. 117(1926), 11-12.

782. "Man from Monticello." Time. 105(May 10, 1975), 6-7.

Sketch.

783. Marienstras, Élise. "Thomas Jefferson et la naissance des États-Unis." L'Histoire. 19(1980), 30-39.

TJ as "une figure emblematique de l'Amerique."

784. Marraro, Howard R. "The Four Versions of Jefferson's Letter to Mazzei." WMQ. 2nd ser. 22(1942), 18-29.

Prints with introduction the original version of the notorious letter, its Italian translation, subsequent French version, and ultimate translation back into English, arguing that some of the provocative qualities of the published version are a result of the translation and not in TJ's original.

785. Marraro, Howard R., ed. "Jefferson Letters Concerning the Settlement of Mazzei's Virginia Estate." MVHR. 30(1944), 235–42.

      TJ's difficulty in remitting proceeds of Mazzei's property to his heirs in Italy.

786. Marraro, Howard R. "Unpublished Correspondence of Jefferson and Adams to Mazzei." VMHB. 51(1943), 111–33.

      Annotated letters.

787. Marraro, Howard R., ed. "An Unpublished Jefferson Letter to Mazzei." Italica. 35(June 1958), 83–87.

      Prints with commentary and notes a letter dated August 2, 1791, mostly concerned with Mazzei's financial affairs and what TJ can do to help him.

788. Marraro, Howard R. "Unpublished Mazzei Letters to Jefferson." WMQ. 3rd ser. 1(1944), 374–96.

      Twenty-eight out of thirty letters printed were sent to TJ from Italy between 1793 and 1815.

789. Marsh, Philip M. "Freneau and Jefferson: The Poet-Editor Speaks for Himself about the National Gazette Episode." American Literature. 8(1936), 180–89.

      Claims Freneau "made no editorial bargain with Jefferson, but had founded his paper independently, his interest in the translator's office and Jefferson being only incidental to his main purpose."

790. Marsh, Philip M. "The Griswold Story of Freneau and Jefferson." AHR. 51(1945), 68–73.

      Finds no evidence for any subsidy, undue influence, or editorial guidance on TJ's part towards Freneau's handling of the National Gazette as later charged by Griswold.

791. Marsh, Philip. "Jefferson and the Invasion of Virginia." VMHB. 57(1949), 322–26.

      Author of a letter to Fenno's Gazette defending TJ's conduct was probably John Beckley, who was in Richmond and Charlottesville during the Arnold and Tarleton raids.

792. Marsh, Philip M. "The Jefferson-Madison Vacation." PMHB. 71(1947), 70–72.

      TJ's and Madison's letters show that their trip in 1791 to Lake Champlain and Vermont was for pleasure, not politicking or trying to avoid John Adams.
95

793.   Marsh, Philip M. "Jefferson's Retirement as Secretary of State."
        PMHB. 69(1945), 220-24.

        Argues that TJ planned as early as April 1, 1791, to retire from his
        cabinet post in March, 1793, but he prolonged his stay—rather than
        shortening it as some have held—because of Hamilton's attacks.

794.   Marsh, Philip M. "John Beckley, Mystery Man of the Early
        Jeffersonians." PMHB. 72(1948), 54-69.

        Little on TJ, focus on Beckley, first clerk of the House of Represen-
        tatives, then appointed by TJ as librarian to Congress.

795.   Marsh, Philip. "The Manuscript Franklin Gave to Jefferson." APS
        Library Bulletin. 1946. 45-48.

        Surmises that TJ may have remembered accurately a passage in
        Franklin's autobiography concerning Lord North although it is not in
        the published version, since Franklin gave him that section of the
        mss.

796.   Marsh, Philip. "'The Vindication of Mr. Jefferson'." South Atlantic
        Quarterly. 45(1946), 61-67.

        Author of "The Vindication" in Dunlap's American Advertiser of 1792
        was James Monroe, and he got the better of his opponent, Hamilton.

797.   Martin, Asa E. "The Sage of Monticello: Thomas Jefferson, March 4,
        1809—July 4, 1826" in After the White House. State College, Pa.:
        Penns Valley Publishers, 1951. 51-75.

        Conventional sketch of TJ in retirement.

798.   Martin, H. Christopher. "Philip Mazzei: Jefferson's Vigneron and
        Revolutionary Patriot" in Jefferson and Wine, ed. R. deTreville
        Lawrence, Sr. The Plains, Va.: Vinifera Wine Growers Association,
        1976. 9-16.

        Discusses Mazzei's viticultural work in behalf of TJ.

799.   Martin, Pete. "Jefferson's True Love." Saturday Evening Post.
        218(April 13, 1946), 22+.

        Monticello.

800.   Marx, Rudolph, M.D. "Thomas Jefferson" in The Health of the Presi-
        dents. New York: Putnam's, 1960. 43-66.

TJ is close to the Senecan ideal of a sound mind in a healthy body. His "ideas of preventive medicine were far advanced for his time." Interesting account of TJ's various fractures, his headaches, his so-called rheumatism.

801. Mason, F. Van Wyck. "Independence Forever!" Collier's. 128(July 7, 1951), 14, 73-75.

Death of TJ and Adams.

802. Mason, J. E. "Thomas Jefferson." American Monthly Magazine. 3(1893), 404-19.

Address delivered before the Mary Washington Chapter, D.A.R.; laudatory biographical oration.

803. Masters, Edgar Lee. "Thomas Jefferson" in The New Star Chamber and Other Essays. Chicago: Hammersmark Publishing Co., 1904. 51-64.

TJ is not much celebrated because "Latterly ... the root and branch of despotism have flourished to some extent in this land..." TJ presented as radical defender of individual rights.

804. Mayo, Barbara. "Twilight at Monticello." VQR. 17(1941), 502-16.

TJ in his last years as seen from the letters of his granddaughter, Virginia Randolph, who married Nicholas Trist in 1824.

805. Mayo, Bernard. Another Peppercorn for Mr. Jefferson: Fall Convocation, University of Virginia, Charlottesville, October 15, 1976. Charlottesville: Thomas Jefferson Memorial Foundation, 1977. pp. 28.

Celebrates TJ's social graces, charm, and friendliness.

806. Mayo, Bernard, ed. Jefferson Himself, The Personal Narrative of a Many-sided American. Boston: Houghton Mifflin, 1942. pp. xv, 384.

Biography created by skillful arrangement of TJ's own writings. Rpt. Charlottesville: Univ. of Virginia Press, 1970.

807. Mayo, Bernard. "Lafayette and Jefferson: Twilight Reminscences at Monticello." Gazette of the American Friends of Lafayette. 17(December 1953), 3-6.

Account of the visit of Lafayette to Monticello.

808. Mayo, Bernard. Myths and Men: Patrick Henry, George Washington, Thomas Jefferson. Athens: Univ. of Georgia Press, 1959. pp. xii, 71.

"The Strange Case of Thomas Jefferson" looks at the ironies of his reputation as a "democratic demon."

809. Mayo, Bernard. "A Peppercorn for Mr. Jefferson." VQR. 19(1943), 222-35.

Sketches of TJ as a man of the people, humorist, and host.

810. Mayo, Bernard. Thomas Jefferson and His Unknown Brother Randolph. Charlottesville: Tracy W. McGregor Library, 1942. pp. 41.

28 letters exchanged between TJ and his brother during the years 1807-1815. Excellent introduction points out that Randolph (1755-1815) was hardly TJ's intellectual equal, "but ... Thomas Jefferson's relations with his brother were ever characterized by an affectionate solicitude."

811. Mazzei, Philip. "Memoirs of the Life and Voyages of Doctor Philip Mazzei." WMQ. 2nd ser. 9(1929), 161-74, 247-64; 10(1930), 1-18.

Translated excerpts from Mazzei's Memoirs relating to his life in Virginia and friendship with TJ.

812. Meacham, William Shands. "Thomas Jefferson and the Greatest Party of Four." Commonwealth, The Magazine of Virginia. 34(April 1967), 23-27.

Sketch of TJ's friendship with Governor Fauquier, William Small, and George Wythe.

813. Mead, Edward C. "Monticello—The Home of Thomas Jefferson" in Historic Homes of the Southwest Mountains, Virginia. Philadelphia: Lippincott, 1898. 21-40.

Chatty account; see also pp. 41-74 for accounts of Pantops, Lego, Shadwell, and Edgehill.

814. Mead, Edwin Doak. "The Editor's Table." New England Magazine. n.s. 23(1900), 228-40.

Notices the Old South Lectures for 1900, first of which was "Thomas Jefferson, the First Nineteenth-Century President." Reviews TJ's career as president favorably.

815. Mead, Edwin D. "Jefferson and the Democratic Party." Unity. 99(July 25, 1927), 293-95.

The Democrats' numerous Jefferson Day dinners of 1927 revealed little of the spirit of TJ despite the genuine need for it.

816. Mead, Robert G., Jr. "Thomas Jefferson y la America Latina." La Nueva Deomcracia. 34(January 1954), 40-46.

Surveys TJ's views of events in Latin America.

817. Mearns, David. "Mr. Jefferson to His Namesakes." Quarterly Journal of the Library of Congress. 14(November 1956), 1-5.

Describes three pages of inscription by TJ in a copy of Cicero's De re publica, all addressed to Thomas Jefferson Smith, identity unknown.

*818. Melbo, Irving R. "Thomas Jefferson" in Our America; A Textbook for Elementary School History and Social Studies. Indianapolis: Bobbs-Merrill, 1937.

819. "Mementoes of Jefferson." Hobbies. 48(April 1943), 9.

The Jeffersoniana collection of Herman H. Diers.

820. Menzies, Sir Robert. Jefferson Oration; Speech by the Prime Minister of Australia. Charlottesville: Thomas Jefferson Memorial Foundation, 1963. pp. 23.

Credits TJ with an influence on Australian democracy.

821. Merriam, Harold G. "Some Founders of the American Republic." Landmark. 1(1919), 440-44.

Sketch of TJ.

822. Merrill, Boynton, Jr. Jefferson's Nephews: A Frontier Tragedy. Princeton: Princeton Univ. Press, 1976. pp. xv, 462.

Account of the vicious murder of a slave by Lilburne and Isham Lewis, sons of TJ's sister Lucy. Gives information on TJ's relationships with other members of his family.

823. Merwin, Henry Childs. Thomas Jefferson. Boston: Houghton Mifflin, 1901. pp. 164.

Riverside Biographical Series. Focuses on public career, takes a moderate position.

824. Michael, William H. The Declaration of Independence: Illustrated Story of Its Adoption with the Biographies and Portraits of the Signers and of the Secretary of Congress. Washington: Government Printing Office, 1904. pp. 99.

825. Middlebrook, Samuel. "They Ganged Up on Jefferson" in The Eagle Screams, by Coley Taylor and Samuel Middlebrook. New York:

Macaulay, 1936. 67-99.

Studies the assassination of TJ's character by his political enemies, particularly during his presidency.

826.   Midgley, Louis. "The Brodie Connection: Thomas Jefferson and
        Joseph Smith." Brigham Young University Studies. 20(1979), 59-67.

        Argues that the faults of Brodie's Thomas Jefferson should make non-
        Mormon historians reconsider her earlier biography of Joseph Smith.

827.   Miers, Earl Schenck. The Story of Thomas Jefferson. New York:
        Grosset and Dunlap, 1955. pp. 179.

        Juvenile biography.

828.   Miers, Earl Schenck. That Jefferson Boy. New York: World Publishing,
        1970. pp. 143.

        Juvenile biography of TJ up to the signing of the Declaration.

829.   Miles, Edwin A. "Joseph Seawell Jones of Shocco—Historian and
        Humbug." North Carolina Historical Review. 34(1957), 483-506.

        Jones wrote A Defense of the Revolutionary History of the State of
        North Carolina, vindicating the priority of the Mecklenburg Declara-
        tion and attacking TJ.

830.   Miller, Hope Ridings. "Miscegenation and Mr. Jefferson" in Scandals
        in the Highest Office: Facts and Fictions in the Private Lives of Our
        Presidents. New York: Random House, 1973. 55-107.

        Well-informed if somewhat inconclusive discussion of the legacy of
        the Callender scandals; charges against TJ cannot be definitely dis-
        proved, although the accusers can be shown to rely on "arbitrary
        inferences and distorted facts."

831.   Miller, Joseph. "Thomas Jefferson" in Jefferson, Washington, Lincoln,
        and Lee, America's Big Four. Alhambra, Cal.: Miller Books, 1972.
        1-3.

832.   Miller, Sue Freeman. "Christmas at Monticello." Albemarle Monthly
        Magazine. 2(December/January 1979), 59-61.

        Derives from Boyd's Spirit of Christmas.

833.   Miller, Vincent. "Perspective on the Founders." National Review.
        14(February 12, 1963), 117-19.

        Review essay of books on Adams, Hamilton, and TJ, claiming "he
        wove into our life a dangerously wafty idealism."

834. Milton, George Fort. "Thomas Jefferson, A Force in the World of Today and Tomorrow." Bulletin of the Missouri Historical Society. 1(July 1945), 3-13.

Survey's TJ's public life.

835. Mintz, Max M. "A Conversation Between Thomas Jefferson and Gouverneur Morris: The Author of the Declaration of Independence and the Penman of the Constitution." Connecticut Review. 9(November 1975), 21-26.

Fictional dialogue, making TJ argue for a graduated income tax; Morris calls it tyrannic expropriation of property.

836. Mitchell, Broadus. "Hamilton and Jefferson Today." VQR. 10(1934), 394-407.

Hamilton defended against Jeffersonian aspersions; neither TJ nor Franklin Roosevelt see the American situation as clearly as Hamilton did in his emphasis on "centralized sovereignty" in politics and economics.

837. Mitchill, Samuel Latham. A Discourse on the Character and Services of Thomas Jefferson. More Especially as a Promoter of Natural Science. Pronounced by Request, before the New York Lyceum of Natural History, on the 11th October, 1826. New York: G. & C. Carvill, 1826. pp. 67.

Concentrates on TJ's public activities. Comments at length on the Notes and notices his connections and communications with the American Philosophical Society. Claims that in his efforts to acquire information about the Louisiana Purchase he "placed himself before the world as one of the most substantial promoters of statistical, natural, and physical science."

838. Moley, Raymond. "The Star in the West." Newsweek. 22(December 27, 1943), 88.

TJ and Lafayette presented an image of American liberty to a troubled Europe.

839. Monsell, Helen Albee. Tom Jefferson: A Boy in Colonial Days. Indianapolis: Bobbs-Merrill, 1939. pp. 168.

Juvenile biography in the Childhood of Famous Americans Series. Often reprinted.

840. Montague, Andrew J. "Jefferson as a Citizen of the Commonwealth of Virginia" in The Writings of Thomas Jefferson, ed. Lipscomb and Bergh. Washington: Thomas Jefferson Memorial Association, 1903. 5:i-xiii.

841. Monticello Association. The Annual Report of the Monticello Association. 1914—.

The Monticello Association is a society of descendants of TJ and proprietors of the graveyard at Monticello. The reports contain information on the upkeep of the graveyard and material of a genealogical or historical nature; items directly pertinent to TJ are listed here separately.

842. "Monticello" in The Collegian. Conducted by a Committee Elected by the Students of the University of Virginia. Charlottesville: James Alexander, 1839. 367-68.

Early visit when the Levys were at home.

843. "Monticello: Home on a Mountaintop." Senior Weekly Reader. 23(February 26, 1969), 4-5.

844. The Monticello Family. Catalogue of an Exhibition Held at the University of Virginia Museum of Fine Arts April 12—May 13, 1960. Charlottesville: Thomas Jefferson Memorial Foundation, 1960. pp. 14.

Note on the family and a catalogue of exhibited portraits.

845. "Monticello, The Cinderella Mansion." Impact (Mopar/Chrysler Auto). February, 1974. pp. 3, 13-15.

TJ's innovations.

846. "Monticello, The Home of Jefferson, Near Charlottesville, Virginia." Harper's Weekly. 10(1866), 345.

Two engraved views, brief description of condition of Monticello and TJ's grave in 1866.

847. "Monticello, Virginia; Statements on Both Sides of the Controversy Concerning the Proposed Public Ownership of the Home of President Jefferson." American Scenic and Historic Preservation Society, Annual Report. 19(1914), 517-41.

In 1912 the Thomas Jefferson Memorial Association petitioned Congress to buy Monticello, but its owner, Jefferson M. Levy, refused to sell. Printed here are statements by the Association, Levy, and a report prepared for Levy by W. K. Semple on "The Care of Monticello by Its Owner," which describes the property as of 1912.

848. "Monticello, Where 'All My Wishes End'." News from Home. 4(no. 2, 1943), 6-7.

TJ's life at Monticello, illustrated.

849. Moore, John Hammond. Albemarle: Jefferson's County, 1727-1976. Charlottesville: Univ. Press of Virginia, 1976. pp. xii, 532.

County history with considerable space given to TJ's role in Albemarle, but nothing new.

850. Moreau, Henry. "Les Fondateurs de l'Union Americaine et la Crise Actuelle." Correspondant. 54(1861), 315-36.

Review essay occasioned by Witt's book on TJ and Guizot's Etude sur Washington, accepts Witt's analysis of TJ.

851. Morgan, Henry. A Description of the Peaks of Otter, With Sketches and Anecdotes of Patrick Henry, John Randolph and Thomas Jefferson, and Other Distinguished Men, Who Have Visited the Peaks of Otter, or Resided in that Part of the State; Also a Description of the Natural Bridge and Other Scenery in Western Virginia. Lynchburg: Virginia Job Office, 1853. pp. 94.

Anecdotes of TJ on 47-52 and a poem, "The Tomb of Jefferson."

852. Morgan, James. "Thomas Jefferson" in Our Presidents. New York: Macmillan, 1924. 20-32.

853. Morison, Samuel Eliot. "John Adams and Thomas Jefferson" in By Land and By Sea: Essays and Addresses by Samuel Eliot Morison. New York: Knopf, 1953. 219-30.

Comparative biographical sketches portraying their friendship; first printed in New England Society of Pennsylvania, Forty-Seventh Annual Report.

854. Morrill, Justin S. "Thomas Jefferson" in Self-Consciousness of Noted Persons. Boston: Ticknor, 1887. 24-26.

By "self-consciousness" the author means self-praise; private edition published in 1882.

*855. Morris, Charles. "Thomas Jefferson, The Author of the Declaration of Independence" in Heroes of Progress in America. Philadelphia: Lippincott, 1909.

856. Morris, Nellie Hess. "The Great Committee, and Its Great Chairman of the 'Masterly Pen'." Potter's American Monthly. 7(1876), 17-22.

Biographical sketch of members of the committee to write the Declaration.

857. Morris, Richard B. "Thomas Jefferson: The Intellectual as Revolutionary" in Seven Who Shaped Our Destiny: The Founding Fathers as Revolutionaries. New York: Harper, 1973. 115-49.

TJ was not always an effective administrator, inconsistent as a principled statesman, but "the most successful politician of his age." A somewhat unfocused essay, touching on many aspects of TJ's career.

858.   Morris, Terry. "Thomas Jefferson's Untold Love Story." Coronet. 12(May 1974), 22-28.

Maria Cosway and the Head vs. Heart letter; insignificant.

859.   Morse, John T., Jr. Thomas Jefferson. Boston: Houghton Mifflin, 1883. pp. vi, 351.

In the American Statesmen Series; often reprinted, influential, and vigorously critical biography from a basically Federalist point of view.

860.   Moscow, Henry. Thomas Jefferson and His World. New York: American Heritage, 1960. pp. 153.

American Heritage Junior Library.

861.   Moulton, F. R. "Dedication of the Jefferson Memorial." Scientific Monthly. 56(1943), 478-91.

862.   Moulton, Robert H. "In Memory of Thomas Jefferson." Technical World Magazine. 19(1913), 712-13.

On the Jefferson Memorial Building in Forest Park, St. Louis.

863.   Muirhead, James F. "Jefferson's Virginian Home." Landmark. 4(1922), 103-07.

864.   Mullen Robert R. "When, in the Course of Human Events ... ." Christian Science Monitor Magazine. April 10, 1943. 7, 14.

TJ and human freedoms.

865.   Munson, Lyman E. "Comparative Study of Jefferson and Lincoln." Connecticut Magazine. 8(1903), 49-56, 324-29.

Traces similarities, mostly trivial or contrived.

*866.   Murdock, Myrtle M. "The Thomas Jefferson Memorial" in Your Memorials in Washington. Washington: Monumental Press, 1952.

867.   Murphy, Mabel Ansley. "The Friend of the People: Thomas Jefferson" in American Leaders. Philadelphia: The Union Press, 1920. 53-62.

Juvenile.

868. Muse, Benjamin. "Dinner Conversation at Monticello." New South. 22(Winter 1967), 46-50.

On Julius Melbourn and his supposed visit to TJ; author takes this as fact. See #526 above.

869. Muzzey, David Saville. "Jefferson Underwrites Democracy." Liberty: A Magazine of Religious Freedom. 38(no. 3, 1943), 5-9.

Biographical sketch, emphasizing TJ's advocacy of individual rights.

870. Muzzey, David Saville. Thomas Jefferson. New York: Scribner's, 1918. pp. vii, 319.

Foucs is on TJ's political career; tone is laudatory.

871. Muzzey, David Saville. "Thomas Jefferson—Humanitarian." American Review. 4(1926), 36-44.

"The master passion of Thomas Jefferson's life was human freedom."

872. Nash, Roderick. "Thomas Jefferson" in From These Beginnings: A Biographical Approach to American History. New York: Harper and Row, 1978. 1:101-48.

TJ's life as background to narrative of American history.

873. "National Monument to Thomas Jefferson." Independent. 77(January 1914), 60-63.

Photograph of Monticello and account of Mrs. Littleton's efforts to make it a national shrine.

874. Nelson, Virginia Armistead. "Thomas Jefferson and the Sureties of Magna Carta." Southern Literary Messenger. 2(1940), 255-58.

TJ was descended from ten of the Magna Carta sureties.

875. Netto, Medeiros. Thomas Jefferson, Conferência Realisado na Associacão Brasileira de Educacão, em 24 de Maio de 1943. Rio de Janeiro: Jornal do Commercio, 1943. pp. 52.

Survey of TJ's democratic principles.

876. Nevins, Allan. "Jefferson—Mentor for Our Times." New York Times Magazine. February 21, 1943. 12, 23.

877. "New Bust of Jefferson." Magazine of History. 14(1911), 364.

Note on decision of Virginia D.A.R. to put a bust of TJ in Memorial Continental Hall.

105

878. "The New York Review of Mr. Jefferson Reviewed. By a Southerner. With an Editorial Introduction." Southern Literary Messenger. 4(1838), 209-14.

    Reply to the strictures of Francis Lister Hawkes; see #538.

879. Nichols, Ashton. "A Country Place: 'Poplar Forest'." Country Magazine. 2(March 1981), 48-51.

880. Nichols. Frederick Doveton. "Jefferson's Retreat: Poplar Forest." The Iron Worker. 37(Spring 1974), 2-13.

    One of the best popular accounts of Poplar Forest; illustrated.

881. Nicolay, Helen. The Boy's Life of Thomas Jefferson. New York: Appleton-Century, 1933. pp. xi, 360.

882. Nicolay, Helen. "Diplomats and a Democrat" in Our Capital on the Potomac. New York: Century, 1924. 71-93.

    TJ in Washington, D.C.

883. Nicolay, John G. "Thomas Jefferson's Home." Century Magazine. 34(1887), 643-53.

    The building of Monticello.

884. Nock, Albert Jay. Jefferson. New York: Harcourt Brace, 1926. pp. 340.

    Although somewhat uncritical in its use of the Beard thesis, this is a shrewd and perceptive assessment of TJ. More a study of character than a formal biography, but organized along biographical lines.

885. Nock, Albert Jay. "Mr. Thomas Jefferson." Saturday Review of Literature. 6(1930), 631.

    Review of Chinard's Thomas Jefferson; cautions against confusing Jeffersonism with Americanism.

886. Ogden, Octavius N. An Anniversary Oration, Delivered on the 13th of April, 1836, at the Request of the Jefferson Society of the University of Virginia. Charlottesville: James Alexander, 1836. pp. 35.

    "On the new continent, the moral and intellectual creation seems to have been fashioned after the same bold sublimity of outline, that characterized the works of external nature."

887. Olgin, Joseph. Thomas Jefferson: Champion of the People. Boston: Houghton Mifflin, 1960. pp. 192.

106

Juvenile.

888. Orico, Osvaldo. "Thomas Jefferson" in Homens da America, Libertadores de Povos do Continente. Rio de Janeiro: Editora Getulio Costa, 1944. 65-82.

889. Oshiba, Ei. Thomas Jefferson. Kobe: Gakushu Bunku Co., 1951. pp. 191.

In Japanese.

890. Otis, William Bradley. "Thomas Jefferson" in Great American Liberals, ed. Gabriel Richard Mason. Boston: Starr King Press, 1956. 17-24.

TJ a great leader produced by a great crisis.

891. Ottenburg, Louis. "A Testamentary Tragedy: Jefferson and the Wills of General Kosciuszko." American Bar Association Journal. 44(January 1958), 22-26.

Kosciuszko left four wills and three estates in three countries when he died in 1817; TJ, named executor in the first will, declined the executorship because of his age. It took 30 years to settle the estate.

892. "Our Jefferson Heritage." Christian Century. 60(1943), 415-16.

TJ's heritage is his devotion to liberty, religious freedom, faith in education, and warnings against the encroachments of centralized government.

893. "Outline Sketch of Thomas Jefferson." Watson's Jeffersonian Magazine. 5(1910), 552-61.

894. Padgett, James A. "The Letters of Doctor Samuel Brown to President Jefferson and James Brown." Register of the Kentucky State Historical Society. 35(1937), 99-130.

Introduction identifies Brown as a Virginian gone West who carried on a long correspondence with TJ; annotated.

895. Padover, Saul K. "The American as Democrat: Thomas Jefferson" in The Genius of America, Men Whose Ideas Shaped Our Civilization. New York: McGraw-Hill, 1960. 55-68.

896. Padover, Saul K. "Introduction" in A Jefferson Profile as Revealed in His Letters. New York: John Day, 1956. ix-xiv.

"The philosopher of freedom and happiness."

897. Padover, Saul K. Jefferson. New York: Harcourt Brace, 1942. pp. 459. 107

898. Padover, Saul K. Jefferson. New York: New American Library, 1952. pp. 192.

Abridged by the author from the version published in 1942.

899. Padover, Saul K. Jefferson, A Great American's Life and Ideas. Hong Kong: Highland Press, 1956. pp. 290.

Text in Chinese.

900. Padover, Saul K. "Jefferson Still Survives." New York Times Magazine. April 8, 1962. 28+.

Reply by B. B. Baines, May 13, 1962. 4.

901. Padover, Saul K. "Jefferson vs. Totalitarianism." American Mercury. 57(1943), 318-19.

The Communists' claim of TJ as progenitor is "brassy charlatanism."

902. Page, Rosewell. "Thomas Jefferson and the Declaration of Independence." Virginia Journal of Education. 19(1926), 343-45.

Sketch of TJ as he was in 1776; minor.

903. [Page, Thomas J]. "Jefferson and Macaulay." Virginia University Magazine. 4(1860), 515-24.

904. Page, Thomas Nelson. Tommaso Jefferson, Apostolo Della Liberta (1743-1826). Con Prefazione del Sen. Maggiorino Ferraris. Firenze: R. Bemporad & Figlio, 1918?. pp. 111.

Brief biography, intended as part of a series to explain to Italian readers their new WWI ally, the U.S.

905. Palmer, Phyllis M. "Jefferson's Pursuit of Independence." Mount Holyoke Alumnae Quarterly. 59(Summer 1975), 78-81.

Biographical sketch.

906. Parris, Leonard. "Designer of Ideals." Senior Scholastic. 71(November 1, 1957), 11.

907. Parisot, Jacques Theodore. "Jefferson" in Biographie Universelle, Ancienne et Moderne .... Paris: Michaud Frères, 1841. 145-59.

908. Parker, Alton B. "Jefferson's Faith in the People" in The Writings of Thomas Jefferson, ed. Lipscomb and Bergh. Washington: Thomas Jefferson Memorial Association, 1903. 10:i-xii.

909. Parker, Theodore. "Thomas Jefferson" in <u>Historic Americans</u>. Boston: H. B. Fuller, 1870. 235-95.

A lecture on TJ, never delivered. TJ "exhibited no spark of genius, nor any remarkable degree of original talent," but "His strength lay in his understanding the practical power." He was notable as a consistent opponent of slavery and as a believer in the common man.

910. Parton, James. "College Days of Thomas Jeffeson." <u>Atlantic Monthly</u>. 29(1872), 16-33.

First of twenty-two installments later published in 1874 as <u>The Life of Thomas Jefferson</u>. Listed here in order of publication rather than alphabetically.

911. Parton, James. "Jefferson a Student of Law." <u>Atlantic Monthly</u>. 29(1872), 179-97.

912. Parton, James. "Thomas Jefferson a Virginia Lawyer." <u>Atlantic Monthly</u>. 29(1872), 312-31.

913. Parton, James. "Jefferson in the House of Burgesses of Virginia." <u>Atlantic Monthly</u>. 29(1872), 395-412.

914. Parton, James. "Jefferson in the Service of Revolutionary Virginia." <u>Atlantic Monthly</u>. 29(1872), 517-34.

915. Parton, James. "Jefferson in the Continental Congress." <u>Atlantic Monthly</u>. 29(1872), 676-94.

916. Parton, James. "Jefferson a Reformer of Old Virginia." <u>Atlantic Monthly</u>. 30(1872), 32-49.

917. Parton, James. "Jefferson Governor of Virginia." <u>Atlantic Monthly</u>. 30(1872), 174-92.

918. Parton, James. "Thomas Jefferson as a Sore-Head." <u>Atlantic Monthly</u>. 30(1872), 273-88.

919. Parton, James. "Jefferson American Minister in France." <u>Atlantic Monthly</u>. 30(1872), 405-24.

920. Parton, James. "Jefferson's Return from France in 1789." <u>Atlantic Monthly</u>. 30(1872), 547-65.

921. Parton, James. "Meeting of Jefferson and Hamilton." <u>Atlantic Monthly</u>. 30(1872), 704-19.

922. Parton, James. "The Cabinet of President Washington." <u>Atlantic Monthly</u>. 31(1873), 29-44.

923. Parton, James. "Thomas Jefferson Secretary of State." Atlantic Monthly. 31(1873), 163-79.

924. Parton, James. "The Quarrel of Jefferson and Hamilton." Atlantic Monthly. 31(1873), 257-75.

925. Parton, James. "The Exploits of Edmond Genet in the United States." Atlantic Monthly. 31(1873), 385-405.

926. Parton, James. "The Presidential Campaign of 1796." Atlantic Monthly. 31(1873), 542-60.

927. Parton, James. "The French Imbroglio of 1798." Atlantic Monthly. 31(1873), 641-60.

928. Parton, James. "The Presidential Election of 1800." Atlantic Monthly. 32(1873), 27-45.

929. Parton, James. "The Art of Being President Gathered from the Experience of Thomas Jefferson." Atlantic Monthly. 32(1873), 129-48.

930. Parton, James. "President Jefferson's Chief Measures." Atlantic Monthly. 32(1873), 298-318.

931. Parton, James. "Thomas Jefferson's Last Years." Atlantic Monthly. 32(1873), 393-412.

932. Parton, James. Life of Thomas Jefferson, Third President of the United States. Boston: James R. Osgood, 1874. pp. vi, 764.

An apologetic biography, the most important to appear between Randall's and Morse's.

933. Parton, James. "Thomas Jefferson" and "The Wife of Thomas Jefferson" in People's Book of Biography: or, Short Lives of the Most Interesting Persons of All Ages and Countries. Hartford: A. S. Hale & Co., 1868. 566-73.

934. Parton, James. "Thomas Jefferson" in The Presidents of the United States, 1789-1902, by John Fiske, Carl Schurz, Robert C. Winthrop, George Ticknor Curtis, George Bancroft, John Hay, and Others, ed. James Grant Wilson. New York: Appleton, 1902. 62-87.

935. Pate, H. Clay. "Monticello" in The American Vade Mecum, or the Companion of Youth, and Guide to College. Cincinnati: Morgan & Co., 1852. 157-60.

Notes dilapidation of the tomb; also see pp. 13-28 on TJ and the University.

110

936. "Patrick Henry. 1. A Memorandum by Thomas Jefferson. 2. Mr. Jefferson and Patrick Henry. 3. Thomas Jefferson and His Contemporaries." Historical Magazine. n.s. 2(1867), 90-96.

Prints controversy from the New York World, 2 August, 1867, and 3 August, 1867, over TJ's notes on Patrick Henry prepared for William Wirt, Henry's biographer.

937. Patterson, Augusta O. "Monticello." Town and Country. 101(November 1947), 98-105, 136.

Illustrated spread.

938. Patton, John S. "Monticello." University of Virginia Alumni Bulletin. 3rd ser. 7(October 1914), 633-46.

Description and history of Monticello; rpt. separately, n.p., n.d. pp. 14.

939. Patton, John S. and Sallie J. Doswell. Monticello and Its Master. Charlottesville: Michie Press, 1925. pp. 78.

Monticello then and now; printed under the auspices of the Thomas Jefferson Memorial Foundation.

940. Paulding, C. G. "Ten Little Indians: Jefferson's Letter to the Indian Chiefs." Commonweal. 45(December 6, 1946), 182-83.

Account of the Otoe Indian gift of a TJ letter to Princeton Univ. Library.

941. Peattie, Donald Culross. "Thomas Jefferson, Architect of Democracy." Reader's Digest. 42(April 1943), 1-5.

Sketch rpt. in the author's Lives of Destiny. Boston: Houghton Mifflin, 1954. 18-23.

942. Peck, Mamie Downard. Thomas Jefferson and His Home, Monticello. Corsicana, Texas: Marr Publishing, 1928.

Part of the campaign to acquire Monticello; a bit late.

943. "Pecuniary Embarrassments of Jefferson." Niles Register. 30(1826), 35, 281, 390-91.

Notices the progress of a lottery arranged in TJ's behalf.

944. Peden, William. "A Book Peddler Invades Monticello." WMQ. 3rd ser. 6(1949), 631-36.

Samuel Whitcomb, Jr.'s amusing account of his interview with TJ in 1824.

945. Peden, William. "The Jefferson Monument at the University of Missouri." Missouri Historical Review. 72(1977), 67-77.

History of TJ's grave marker and how the original ended up at the Univ. of Missouri.

946. "The Pedigree of Peter Jefferson." The Researcher. 1(1926), 33-34.

947. Perkins, John L. "Thomas Jefferson and John Adams in 1822." Potter's American Monthly. 4(1875), 413-14.

Prints a letter from each to the other, with minimal comment.

948. Perry, Frances M. and Henry W. Elson. Four Great American Presidents, No. 1: Washington, Jefferson, Jackson, Lincoln: A Book for American Readers. New York: J. M. Stradling & Co., 1905. 111-207.

Juvenile.

949. Peterson, Arnold. "Thomas Jefferson" in Reviling of the Great. New York: New York Labor News Co., 1949. 9-18.

TJ slandered by the clergy and the "top bourgeoisie."

950. Peterson, Helen Stone. "The President's Daughters." Virginia Cavalcade. 13(Autumn 1963), 18-22.

Biographical sketch of Martha and Maria.

951. Peterson, Maud Howard. "The Home of Thomas Jefferson." Munsey's Magazine. 20(1899), 608-19.

Numerous photographic illustrations, ca. 1899, of Monticello; descriptive text.

952. Peterson, Merrill D. Adams and Jefferson: A Revolutionary Dialogue. Athens: Univ. of Georgia Press, 1976. pp. xiv, 146.

An account of the long and sometimes troubled friendship of an enlightened Puritan and a man of the Enlightenment. Intended for a general audience, of interest to scholars.

953. Peterson, Merrill D. "Adams and Jefferson: A Revolutionary Dialogue." Wilson Quarterly. 1(Autumn 1976), 108-29.

Adapted from the previous item.

954. Peterson, Merrill D. "Bowers, Roosevelt, and the 'New Jefferson'." VQR. 34(1958), 530-43.

Discusses Claude Bower's career as a promoter of TJ, the impact of his Jefferson and Hamilton, and FDR's use of the refurbished image of TJ for political purposes.

955. Peterson, Merrill D. "Henry Adams on Jefferson the President." VQR. 39(1963), 187-201.

"... the validity of Adams' interpretation of Jefferson hinges on the validity of his basic assumption: that he was a theorist and a doctrinaire." Nevertheless, Adams' work is a great example of the historian's art.

956. Peterson, Merrill D. "Introduction" to The Portable Thomas Jefferson. New York: Viking, 1975. xi-xli.

A judicious, comprehensive, and well-balanced introduction to the life and achievements of TJ.

957. Peterson, Merrill D. "The Jefferson Image, 1829." American Quarterly. 3(1951), 204-20.

Analyzes the effect of the publication of the first collected edition of TJ's writings.

958. Peterson, Merrill D. "The Jefferson Image in the American Mind, 1826-1861." Ph.D. dissertation. Harvard Univ., 1950. pp. 404.

Revised, expanded, and published as The Jefferson Image in the American Mind (1960).

959. Peterson, Merrill D. The Jefferson Image in the American Mind. New York: Oxford Univ. Press, 1960. pp. x, 548.

The best study of TJ's reputation and influence, although since its focus is on the reputation, it tends to slight any genuine Jefferson influences in favor of studying the semi-magical invocations of TJ's name. An essential book. Extensive bibliography lists items invoking TJ's name or alluding to him which are too peripheral for listing here.

960. Peterson, Merrill D. "Thomas Jefferson" in The Patriots, The American Revolution Generation of Genius, ed. Virginius Dabney. New York: Atheneum, 1975. 79-81.

961. Peterson, Merrill D. "Thomas Jefferson: A Brief Life" in Thomas Jefferson: The Man ... His World ... His Influence, ed. Lally Weymouth. New York: Putnam's, 1973. 13-38.

962. Peterson, Merrill D. Thomas Jefferson and the American Revolution. Williamsburg: Virginia Independence Bicentennial Commission, 1976. pp. ix, 77.

963.	Peterson, Merrill D. Thomas Jefferson and the Dimensions of Liberty, 1776-1976. A Poynter Pamphlet. Bloomington, Ind.: The Poynter Center, 1975. pp. 12.

Tribute to TJ's defense of the personal, intellectual dimension of liberty and of its socio–economic and political dimensions.

964.	Peterson, Merrill D. Thomas Jefferson and the New Nation, A Biography. New York: Oxford Univ. Press, 1970. pp. xvi, 1072.

The best one volume biography.

965.	Peterson, Merrill D., ed. Thomas Jefferson, A Profile. New York: Hill and Wang, 1967. pp. xxii, 263.

Collection of eleven essays by various hands, all previously published.

966.	Pettengill, Samuel B. Jefferson, The Forgotten Man. New York: America's Futures Inc., 1938. pp. xvii, 249.

An anti-New Deal TJ by a Democratic congressman who felt the New Deal of 1932 was "essentially Jeffersonian" but had moved away "to the principles of centralized government." Focus is on the New Deal, not TJ.

967.	Pew, Marlen. "Monticello Free Press Shrine Dedicated by Distinguished Newspapermen." Editor and Publisher. 74(October 24, 1931), 5-6, 56-57.

Account of ceremonies and the speeches of Claude G. Bowers and James M. Beck.

968.	Philips, Edith. Louis Hue Girardin and Nicholas Gouin Dufief and Their Relations with Thomas Jefferson: An Unknown Episode of the French Emigration in America. The Johns Hopkins Studies in Romance Literatures and Languages. Extra Volume No. III. Baltimore: Johns Hopkins Press, 1926. pp. 8, 75.

Dufief had little to do with TJ, but Girardin carried on a somewhat interesting correspondence with him and played an active, if minor, part in the cultural life of his adapted country.

969.	Phillips, Edward Hake. "Timothy Pickering's 'Portrait' of Thomas Jefferson." Essex Institute Historical Collections. 94(1958), 309-27.

Describes Pickering's vigorously unflattering opinion of TJ and claims it is of value because, given its prejudices, it sees through "the garb of idealistic philosophy with which Jefferson clothed himself."

970.	Pierson, Hamilton W. "Jefferson at Monticello." Historical Magazine. 5(1861), 366-69.

Memoirs of Edmund Bacon, overseer at Monticello from 1806 until 1822, and letters to him from TJ.

972. Pilling, Ron. "'... Permit Me Again to Suggest That You Receive the Olive Branch ...'." American History Illustrated. 15(no. 8, 1980), 30-35.

973. Pitts, Carolyn. "Washington, Jefferson, and Lafayette in Germantown." Germantowne Crier. 1(December 1949), 11-12.

Note on their stay there during the 1793 yellow fever epidemic; minor.

974. Plumer, William. "Thomas Jefferson and Company." Historical New Hampshire. 23(Summer 1968), 29-31.

Critical account by a New Hampshire Federalist of dinners given by TJ and Madison for Anthony Merry, British minister.

975. Poole, Gwinette. "Papers of Jefferson to Be Published in Fifty-two Volumes." Commonwealth, The Magazine of Virginia. 17(August 1950), 14-16.

976. Poppen, Richard S. Thomas Jefferson. The Declaration of Independence and Letters, Addresses, Excerpts and Aphorisms Selected from His Writings With a Short Biography and An Outline of the Two Principal Parties. St. Louis, 1904.

"The purpose of this hand-book is to bring Thomas Jefferson, the wisest exponent of true Democracy closer to the hearts of the people, whom he loved so well."

977. Potter, Henry. "Eulogy, Pronounced in Fayetteville, North-Carolina, July 20th, 1826" in A Selection of Eulogies ... . Hartford: D. F. Robinson & Co., 1826. 129-38.

Praises especially TJ's authorship of the Virginia act of religious toleration.

978. Pound, Ezra. "The Jefferson-Adams Correspondence." North American Review. 244(1938), 314-24.

Admittedly random notes discussing TJ in relation to the Mediterranean paideuma, money, Flaubert, etc. in support of the claim that TJ and Adams were civilized men in a civilized world. rpt. in Pound, Selected Prose, 1909-1965. New York: New Directions, 1973. 147-58, as "The Jefferson-Adams Letters as a Shrine and a Monument."

979. Powell, Edward Alexander. A Virginia Pilgrimage. Roanoke, Va.: Stone Printing, 192?. pp. 68.

Pp. 34-41 on TJ, Univ. of Virginia, and Monticello; he was "never so happy as when living the life of a landed gentleman."

980. Powell, E. P. "The Friendship of John Adams and Thomas Jefferson." New England Magazine: An Illustrated Quarterly. n.s. 16(1897), 179-93.

981. Powell, Edward Payson. "A Study of Thomas Jefferson." Arena. 3(1891), 712-73.

TJ a democratic model for young Americans, as opposed to Hamilton.

982. Pratt, Richard. "Around Charlottesville." Ladies Home Journal. 65(November 1948), 44-49.

On Monticello.

983. "The President's Phaeton." Carriage Journal. 14(Autumn 1976), 63-65.

Correspondence about and plans for a carriage TJ had built.

984. "President Jefferson Plays Host to a Couple of Pennsylvania Dutchmen." Pennsylvania Dutchman. 3(March 15, 1952), 2.

Congressman Andrew Gregg takes two Pennsylvania Germans to call on the President; sounds like folklore.

985. Princeton University Library Trustees Committee Dinner. January 29th 1943. Princeton: Princeton Univ. Press, 1943. pp. 8.

"Dinner a la Jefferson together with a Letter from Monticello. June 7, 1817."

986. Proceedings of the Committee Appointed by the Citizens of New York, At Their Meeting Held for the Relief of Mr. Jefferson. New York, 1826. pp. 8.

Announces a scheme to help TJ by purchasing lottery tickets, then destroying them; published in May, just before his death.

987. "Programs Portraying Jefferson Contributions: Opportunity for School Activity." Education for Victory. 2(March 3, 1944), 20.

988. "Proposal of a Public Museum of Science Erected in St. Louis as a Monument to Thomas Jefferson." Science. n.s. 82(1935), 522-23.

"A towering monument symbolizing the spirit of Jefferson and the ideal of American democrary, arresting the eye of visitors from afar, a sign of the forward look of the people of St. Louis."

989.	Pryor, John Carlisle. "Thomas Jefferson and the Golden Age of the Old Dominion." Virginia Law Register. n.s. 13(1928), 513-25.

Laudatory sketch.

990.	Pula, James S. "The American Will of Thaddeus Kosciuszko." Polish American Studies. 34(1977), 16-25.

TJ named an executor, but he declined to serve.

991.	Pulley, Judith Ross. "An Agent of Nature's Republic Abroad: Thomas Jefferson in Pre-Revolutionary France." Essays in History. 11(1966), 5-26.

TJ's appreciation of French culture and love for her people did not blind him to the attractive aspects of 18th-century France; discusses his French associates.

992.	Pulley, Judith. "The Bittersweet Friendship of Thomas Jefferson and Abigail Adams." Essex Institute Historical Collections. 108(1972), 193-216.

TJ took Mrs. Adams seriously as a knowledgeable and intelligent person, but he never regained the rapport with Abigail that he did with John.

993.	Quadros, Jose Antonio. Discurso Pronunciado ... en Ocasion de Solemnizarse el "Dia de las Americas" Sobre la Personalidad de Thomas Jefferson. Montevideo: Camara de Representantes, 1948. pp. 18.

994.	Quinby, Laurie J. Jefferson-Lincoln Symposium of What Constitutes Americanism. Los Angeles: Davis Printing, 1936. pp. 14.

Conjuration of the figures of TJ and Lincoln to guard against some uncertain danger; New Deal? Plutocrats? Confused.

995.	Radcliff, Robert R. "Thomas Jefferson, Chessplayer." Chess Life. 36(April 1981), 24-28.

Account of TJ's interest in chess.

996.	Randall, Henry S. The Life of Thomas Jefferson. New York: Derby and Jackson, 1858. 3 vols. pp. xxiv, 645; xii, 694; xii, 731.

Major biography written in the nineteenth century; Randall had access to sourses unavailable to earlier writers and sought information from people who had known TJ.

997.	Randall, J. G. "When Jefferson's Home Was Bequeathed to the United States." South Atlantic Quarterly. 23(1924), 35-39.

On Uriah P. Levy's will, disposing of Monticello.

998. Randall, Samuel Jackson. An Address Delivered Before the Literary Societies of Dickinson College, Carlisle, Penna., Ninety-eighth Commencement. n.p.: George H. McCully & Co., 1882. pp. 20.

Laudatory biographical survey of TJ.

999. Randolph, Sarah N. The Domestic Life of Thomas Jefferson. Compiled from Family Letters and Reminiscences. New York: Harper Bros., 1871. pp. xiii, 432.

The private Jefferson, by his great-granddaughter. Still useful, often reprinted.

1000. Randolph, Sarah N. "Mrs. Thomas Mann Randolph" in Worthy Women of Our First Century, ed. Mrs. O. J. Wister and Miss Agnes Irwin. Philadelphia: Lippincott, 1877. 9-70.

Biographical sketch of Martha Jefferrson Randolph.

1001. Randolph, Thomas Jefferson. Jefferson Papers. Memorial of Thomas Jefferson Randolph, of Virginia, in Regard to the Purchase and Publication by Congress of the Manuscripts of Mr. Jefferson. December 30, 1847. Read and Laid on the Table. 30th Congress, 1st Session. House of Representatives Miscellaneous, No. 7.

Offers for sale a collection of about forty thousand letters and three boxed volumes of opinions as Secretary of State.

1002. Randolph, Thomas Jefferson. The Last Days of Jefferson. Charlottesville: Jeffersonian Print, 1873. Broadside.

Comments on James Parton's article in the Atlantic Monthly (#931 above); criticizes numerous inaccuracies in Edmund Bacon's reminiscences and defends Thomas Mann Randolph.

1003. Raumer, Frederick von. "Thomas Jefferson" in America and the American People. New York: J. and H. G. Langley, 1846. 87-109.

Sketch by a German traveler and historian, sympathetic to the American experiment.

1004. Rayner, B. L. Sketches of the Life, Writings, and Opinions of Thomas Jefferson; With Selections of the Most Valuable Portions of His Voluminous and Unrivaled Private Correspondence. New York: A. Francis and W. Boardman, 1832. pp. 556.

First full length biography of TJ.

1005. Raynor, E. C. "Communication: Jefferson and John Leland." Granite Monthly. 8(1885), 240.

Rejects the accusation that TJ paid Leland for the mammoth cheese.

1006. Recéption de la statue de Thomas Jefferson, troisième président des États-Unis, oeuvre de David d'Angers offerte à la ville d'Angers par Hon Jefferson M. Levy, citoyen Américaine, le samedi, 16 septembre 1905. Mesnil: Typ. Firmin-Didot et cie., 1905. pp. 59.

Proceedings in French and English.

1007. Reckley, Gladys. "The Shadwell Reconstruction." Commonwealth, The Magazine of Virginia. 28(March 1961), 20.

Account of efforts to find site of house TJ was born in and to build an approximate reconstruction.

1008. Reed, Stanley F. "Thomas Jefferson." Daughters of the American Revolution Magazine. 99(1965), 584-85.

1009. Reid, Whitelaw. One Welshman, A Glance at a Great Career. London: Macmillan, 1912. pp. 59.

Career of that great Welsh-American, TJ; the inaugural address of the autumn session of the University College of Wales, Aberystwyth, in 1912, controversial because of its Hamiltonian-Federalist point of view. See Peterson, The Jefferson Image, p. 339.

1010. Reid, Whitelaw. "Thomas Jefferson" in American and English Studies. New York: Scribner's, 1913. 2:37-70.

Version of One Welshman of the previous year.

1011. "Reflections Suggested by the Obsequies of John Adams and Thomas Jefferson." Christian Examiner. 3(1826), 315-30.

Interesting essay-review of ten eulogies on TJ and Adams.

1012. "The Remarkable Mr. Jefferson." The Humble Way (Humble Oil Co.). Summer, 1962. 13-17.

TJ's talents on display at Monticello.

1013. Remington, Frank L. "The Amazing Mr. Jefferson." The Link, A Magazine for Armed Forces Personnel. 31(July 1973), 5-10.

1014. Revis, Anne. "Mr. Jefferson's Charlottesville." National Geographic Magazine. 97(1950), 553-92.

Charlottesville past and present and TJ's impress upon it.

1015. Rhinesmith, W. Donald. "Henry Stephens Randall and His Life of Thomas Jefferson." Essays in History. 10(1965), 5-28.

How Randall wrote his three-volume biography of TJ.

1016. Rhinesmith, W. Donald. "Henry Stephens Randall: Nineteenth-Century Democrat and Biographer of Jefferson." M.A. thesis. Univ. of Virginia, 1965. pp. 169.

Chapter V, "Writing a Biography," discusses Randall's authorship of his life of TJ.

1017. Rhodes, Thomas L. The Story of Monticello, As Told by Thomas L. Rhodes, For Nearly Forty Years Superintendent of Monticello, to Frank B. Lord. Washington: American Publishing Co., 1928. pp. 94.

Sketch of TJ's life, account of Monticello through the years by Jefferson M. Levy's superintendent.

1018. Rice, Howard C., Jr. "Chastellux at Monticello, 1782." Antiques. 98(July 1970), 42-43.

1019. Rice, Howard C., Jr. L'Hotel de Langeac, Jefferson's Paris Residence, Residence de Jefferson a Paris, 1785-1789. Paris: Librarie Henri Lefebfre; Monticello: Thomas Jefferson Memorial Foundation, 1947. pp. 25. 14 illustrations.

Bi-lingual description with drawings and engravings of TJ's residence for most of his stay in Paris.

1020. Rice, Howard C., Jr. "Jefferson in Europe a Century and a Half Later: Notes of a Roving Researcher." Princeton Univ. Library Chronicle. 12(Autumn 1950), 19-35.

Describes efforts to find TJ manuscripts and related materials in 1946-48; sheds light on TJ's experiences in Europe.

1021. Rice, Howard C., Jr. "Thomas Jefferson à Strasbourg (1788)." Cahiers Alsaciens d'Archéologie d'Art et d'Histoire. 1(1958), 137-53.

Fascinating account of what TJ managed to do in 3 days.

1022. Rice, Howard C., Jr. Thomas Jefferson's Paris. Princeton: Princeton Univ. Press, 1976. pp. ix, 156.

Handsomely illustrated, authoritative account of where TJ went and what he saw in Paris.

1023. Rice, Howard C., Jr. "Thomas Jefferson's Paris." University A Princeton Quarterly. 72(1977), 19-24.

Adapted from the book of the same title.

1024. Rice, Howard C., Jr. "Les Visites de Jefferson au Mont-Valérien."

Société Historique de Suresnes. Bulletin. 3(no. 13, 1954), 46-49.

TJ visited the monastery at Mount Calvary, another name for Mount Valerien in Suresnes, near Paris.

1025. Richards, Norman. The Story of Monticello. Chicago: Childrens Press, 1970. pp. 30.

Juvenile.

*1026. Richardson, James D. "Thomas Jefferson." New Age. 6(1907), 18-24, 114-22, 224-30.

Cited in Writings on American History (1907), # 1454.

1027. Ridpath, John Clark. "Three Epochs of Democracy and Three Men." Arena. 19(1898), 543-63.

TJ the "father of American Democracy."

1028. Riordan, Gertrude Frances. The Little Desk of Independence. Phoenix, Ariz.: The Author, 1976. pp. (32).

1029. Robbins, Roland Wells. "Report on 1955 Archaeological Exploration at Shadwell, Birthplace of Thomas Jefferson ... April 5-May 27 ... June 15-July 1, 1955." n.p., 1955. pp. 35, 6.

Mimeographed report on excavations which located the probable site of TJ's birthplace.

1030. Robins, Edward. "A Disappointment in Love: Legends from Virginia" in Romances of Early America. Philadelphia: George W. Jacobs, 1902. 101-18.

Sentimentalized account of TJ's flirtation with Rebecca Burwell.

1031. Robins, Elizabeth. "The Old Jefferson House, Philadelphia." Harper's Weekly. 27(1883), 228.

House at S.W. corner of Seventh and Market about to be razed; picture.

*1032. Robins, Sally Nelson. "Thomas Jefferson" in Love Stories of Famous Virginians. Richmond: Dietz Printing, 1923.

1033. Robinson, William A. "A Misused Quotation." AHR. 33(1927), 81-83.

A description by Theodore Dwight of "The great object of Jacobinism" was cited by several historians, including Henry Adams, as illustrative of Federalist views of TJ's administration; actually,

Dwight was talking about the imaginary state projected in William Godwin's Political Justice.

1034. Robinson, William E. Speech of Hon. William E. Robinson of New York, in the House of Representatives, Friday, March 14, 1884. n.p., 1884? pp. 16.

Points out that extremely generous pensions have been awarded to the widows of Tyler, Polk, Lincoln, and Garfield in the same year one was refused to TJ's last living grandchild.

1035. Roby, Norman S. "Thomas Jefferson, A Bicentennial Celebration of America's First Wine Expert." Vintage Magazine. 6(January 1976), 23-28.

TJ's interest in wine.

1036. Rodgers, William. "Autographs: The Man of Monticello." Hobbies. 85(August 1980), 100-01.

TJ's was a "poor man's autograph" for years, now one of the most valuable of the founding fathers.

1037. Rogers, Fred B. "A Guide to Health—'An Epistle to a Friend' (Thomas Jefferson) by Charles Willson Peale." Transactions and Studies of the College of Physicians of Philadelphia. 4th ser. 28(1960), 94-99.

Focus on Peale and his pamphlet on preserving health; asserts TJ was "ailing" in 1802, mostly because he seems to misread Peale's preface.

1038. Rogers, James Frederick. "The Athletic Author of the 'Declaration.'" Saint Nicholas. 42(1915), 791-93.

TJ as a clean living man.

1039. Roosevelt, Franklin D. "Address at the Dedication of the Thomas Jefferson Memorial, Washington, D.C. April 13, 1943." in The Public Papers of and Addresses of Franklin D. Roosevelt, ed. Samuel I. Rosenman. 1943 volume. New York: Harper's, 1950. 162-64.

TJ as the "Apostle of Freedom."

1040. Roosevelt, Franklin D. "Is There a Jefferson on the Horizon?" American Mercury. 61(1945), 277-81.

A review of Bowers' Jefferson and Hamilton originally appearing in the New York Evening World, December 3, 1925. "...for some years I have been, frankly, fed up with the romantic cult which has since the publication of an historical novel, surrounded the name of Alexander Hamilton."

122

1041. Rosenberger, Francis Coleman, ed. Jefferson Reader: A Treasury of Writings about Thomas Jefferson. New York: Dutton, 1953. pp. 349.

Interesting collection of pieces from various points of view and dealing with the many sides of TJ.

1042. Rossiter, Clinton. "Which Jefferson Do You Quote?" Reporter. 13(December 15, 1955), 33-36.

Describes "seven Jeffersons," anti-statist, civil libertarian, etc. The real TJ, he claims, was a progressive, not a limitationist.

1043. Rosten, Leo. "They Made Our World ... 2 ... Jefferson." Look. 27(July 30, 1963), 52-53.

Sketch.

1044. Rothert, Otto A., ed. "A Report of the Dedication of the Inscriptions on the Thomas Jefferson Statue, Louisville, July 4, 1943; Included are: A News Story by Miss Marion Porter, A Letter by Mr. Isaac W. Bernheim, An Address by Mr. Hambleton Tapp." Filson Club History Quarterly. 17(1943), 189-201.

Dedication of Jeffersonian quotations on the base of the statue Bernheim had donated in 1901.

1045. Rowan, Stephen N. An Address, Delivered July 12, 1826, in the Middle Dutch Church, at the Request of the Common Council, on Occasion of the Funeral Obsequies of John Adams and Thomas Jefferson. New York: William Davis, Jr., 1826. pp. 36.

General praise without considering TJ and Adams in any detail.

1046. Rozwenc, Edwin Charles. "Henry Adams and the Federalists" in Teachers of History: Essays in Honor of Laurence Bradford Packard, ed. H. Stuart Hughes. Ithaca: Cornell Univ. Press, 1954. 123-45.

Examines Adams' History and rejects the view that he was a crypto-Jeffersonian.

1047. Rullière, H. "Le Jeffersonisme and les Jeffersoniens." La Revue. 129(1918), 213-24, 478-90.

Biographical sketch. "Je suis convaincu que ce sera surtout après cette guerre—'La guerre des guerres'—que les idées préconisées par le grand révolutionnaire et homme d'Etat américaine, seront réellement comprises."

*1048. Rullière, H. "Thomas Jefferson." Wetenschappelijke Bladen. 1(1919), 129-58.

1049. Rusinowa, Izabella. "Wstep" in Tadeusz Kosciuszko Thomas Jefferson Korespondencja (1798-1817), prz. Agnieszka Glinczanka, Jozef Paszkowski. Warsaw: Panstwowy Instytut Wydawniczy, 1976. 5-19.

1050. Rusk, Dean. Mason and Jefferson Revisited. An Address by the Honorable Dean Rusk ... On the Occasion of the Prelude to Independence at the Eighteenth-Century Capitol, Williamsburg, Virginia. Williamsburg: Colonial Williamsburg Foundation, 1966. pp. 23.

The ideas of TJ and George Mason are still powerful.

1051. Rusling, James F. "Thomas Jefferson." Methodist Quarterly. 41(1859), 59-73.

Praises TJ for everything except his religious views.

1052. Russell, Phillips. Jefferson, Champion of the Free Mind. New York: Dodd Mead, 1956. pp. viii, 374.

Well-written, popular biography, but derivative.

1053. Russell, Phillips. "Thomas Jefferson, Social Architect" in Harvesters. New York: Brentano's, 1932. 215-58.

Biographical sketch.

1054. Russell, William E. "Jefferson and His Party Today." The Forum. 21(1896), 513-24.

The Democratic Party needs to reassert TJ's principles, especially when it opposes as now a party of class, sectional and private interests.

1055. Rutherfoord, John Coles. An Oration Delivered Before the Jefferson Society of the University of Virginia, on the 13th of April, 1843. Charlottesville: James Alexander, 1843. pp. 13.

100th anniversay of TJ's birth; his principles fostered progress and the advance of freedom.

1056. Ryan, G. J. "Monticello, A Patriotic Shrine Preserved for the Children of America." Journal of American History. 26(1932), 65-66.

1057. Sachs, Jules R. "Thomas Jefferson in Paris." The American Society Legion of Honor Magazine. 26(1955), 55-75.

Rambling discussion of TJ in Paris, emphasizing the impact of its cultural life; minor.

1058. Sainte-Beuve, Charles Augustin. "Thomas Jefferson" in Premiers

<u>Lundis</u>. Paris: Michel Lévy Frères, 1874. 1:126-53.

Review essay originally appearing February 4, 1833, on L. P.
Conseil's <u>Melanges</u> ... .

1059. Sainte-Beuve, Charles Augustin. <u>Thomas Jefferson et Tocqueville.</u>
Avec une <u>Introduction par Gilbert Chinard</u>. Princeton: Princeton
Univ. Press for Institut Francais de Washington, 1943. pp. 43.

Reprints two reviews of Conseil's <u>Melanges</u> ..., originally appearing
in 1833 in the <u>National</u>. "En Jefferson, Sainte-Beuve voyait un de
'ces guides de génie' qui devoit aider à l'avenement de 'cette liberté
européene, dont l'enfantement s'opère depuis plus de quarante ans
dans le sang et dans les larmes de tous.'"

1060. Sandburg, Carl. "Jefferson's Surest Memorial" in <u>Home Front Memo</u>.
New York: Harcourt Brace, 1943. 260-62.

The best memorial is not in marble but in the democratic spirit.

1061. Sarles, Frank B. "The Jefferson National Expansion Memorial."
<u>Journal of the West</u>. 7(1968), 193-202.

Account of the activities of the Jefferson National Expansion
Memorial Association, begun in 1933-34, to establish a monument to
TJ, the Louisiana Purchase, and the opening of the trans-Mississippi
West.

1062. "Saving Monticello." <u>Literary Digest</u>. 70(August 27, 1921), 24-25.

Proposes that Monticello be acquired for a "country White House."

1063. Schachner, Nathan. "Jefferson: The Man and the Myth." <u>American</u>
<u>Mercury</u>. 65(1947), 46-52.

"Jefferson's place among the progenitors of the democratic way is
unassailable."

1064. Schachner, Nathan. <u>Thomas Jefferson</u>. New York: Appleton-Century,
1951. 2 vols. pp. xiii, 559; vii, 561-1070.

An intelligent, generally sympathetic biography.

1065. Schmidtchen, P. W. "Apostle of American Democracy; Thomas
Jefferson." <u>Hobbies</u>. 74(August 1969), 104-05, 116-17.

Sketch of TJ as aristocratic democrat, slaveowner, and deist.

1066. Schmucker, Samuel M. <u>The Life and Times of Thomas Jefferson</u>.
Philadelphia: John E. Potter, 1857. pp. xiii, 400.

125

Often reprinted biography which finds as TJ's chief fault "a pusillanimous and morbid terror of popular censure, and an insatiable thirsting after popular praise" which kept him from recognizing the depravity of most humans. Title pages of early editions spell author's name as Smucker.

1067. Schouler, James. Thomas Jefferson. New York: Dodd Mead, 1893. pp. vi, 252.

Balanced account of TJ's life: "Jeffersonism is modern America."

1068. Schulte, Nordholt J. W. "Adams en Jefferson als Getuigen van Hun Tijd." Tijdschrift voor Geschiedenis. 83(1970), 212-25.

"Adams and Jefferson as Witnesses of Their Time." TJ more than Adams can be taken as a reliable witness because of his objectivity, not his natural reserve keeps him from giving many facts in his writing.

1069. Scott, Clinton Lee. "Thomas Jefferson, 1743-1826" in These Live Tomorrow: Twenty Unitarian Universalist Biographies. Boston: Beacon Press, 1964. 47-60.

Sketch emphasizing his Unitarian sympathies.

1070. Scribner, Robert Leslie. "Mr. Jefferson's Rock Bridge." Virginia Cavalcade. 4(Spring 1955), 42-47.

Account of TJ's ownership of the Natural Bridge and its visitors.

1071. Scruggs, C. G. "Thomas Jefferson's Monticello." Progressive Farmer. 88(January 1973), 87-88.

1072. A Selection of Eulogies Pronounced in the Several States, In Honor of Those Illustrious Patriots and Statesmen, John Adams and Thomas Jefferson. Hartford: D. F. Robinson and Norton and Russell, 1826. pp. 426.

Contains nineteen eulogies, the most well known being Webster's and Wirt's. Eulogies are listed separately here.

1073. Selesky, Harold E. "Additional Material Relating to Ezra Stiles." Yale University Library Gazette. 50(1975), 112-22.

New acquisitions include three letters written in 1786 by TJ to Stiles discussing political questions and scientific concerns. Also thanks Stiles for the honorary degree bestowed in that year.

1074. Sergeant, John. An Oration Delivered in Independence Square, in the City of Philadelphia, on the 24th of July, 1826, in Commemoration of Thomas Jefferson and John Adams. Philadelphia: H. Carey and I. Lea, 1826. pp. 44.

Also in A Selection of Eulogies ... . Hartford: D. F. Robinson, 1826. "Henceforward the names of Jefferson and Adams can never be separated from the Declaration of Independence." TJ and Adams offered as exemplars of the principles of the Declaration.

*1075. Serpell, Jean K. "Thomas Jefferson: His Relationship with France." M.A. thesis. Stetson Univ., 1957.

1076. "The Sesqui-Centennial of the Declaration of Independence; Thomas Jefferson as the Central Figure." Virginia Journal of Education. 19(1926), 372-73.

Notes ceremonies to honor TJ.

1077. Severance, Frank H., ed. "A Bundle of Thomas Jefferson's Letters Now First Published." Publications of the Buffalo Historical Society. 7(1904), 1-32.

Letters to Francis Adrian van der Kemp transcribed with extensive comment and annotation. Correspondence centers on TJ's "Syllabus of the Doctrines of Jesus."

1078. Sevostianov, G. N. and A. I. Utkin. Tomas Dzhefferson. Moscow: Izdatel'stvo "Mi'sl'", 1976. pp. 390.

In Russian.

1079. Shackelford, George Green, ed. Collected Papers to Commemorate Fifty Years of the Monticello Association of the Descendants of Thomas Jefferson. Princeton: Princeton Univ. Press, 1965. pp. ix, 292.

Individual essays by various hands on the history of the graveyard, the Association, TJ's ancestry, each of his children and grandchildren.

1080. Shackelford, George Green. "Mr. Jefferson's Grandchildren." Magazine of Albemarle County History. 33/34(1975-76), 163-72.

Sketches of the children of Martha Jefferson Randolph and Maria Jefferson Eppes.

1081. Shackelford, George Green. "New Letters Between Hugh Blair Grigsby and Henry Stephens Randall, 1858-1861." VMHB. 64(1956), 323-57.

Letters discuss Randall's Life of Jefferson; introduction and notes.

1082. Shackelford, George Green. "William Short, Jefferson's Adopted Son, 1758-1849." Ph.D. dissertation. Univ. of Virginia, 1955. pp. 566.

The only full-length biography of Short.

1083. Shaffer, Kenneth R. "Copy to Mr. Jefferson About the Sale of His Library." Indiana Quarterly for Bookmen. 1(1945), 55-59.

Jonathan Williams, president of the APS, regrets TJ did not donate his library to the Society.

1084. Shannon, Joseph B. Speech of the Hon. Joseph B. Shannon of Missouri in the House of Representatives April 13, 1934. Washington: Government Printing Office, 1934. pp. 16.

Laudatory biographical address.

*1085. Shaw, C. P. "The Jefferson Memorial Road." Univ. of Virginia Alumni Bulletin. 3(1903).

1086. Shaw, John Angier. Eulogy on John Adams and Thomas Jefferson, Delivered August 2, 1826, By Request of the Inhabitants of Bridgewater. Taunton, Mass.: Samuel W. Mortimer, 1826. pp. 20.

Also in A Selection of Eulogies .... Hartford: D. F. Robinson, 1826. 155-71.

1087. Shaw, Peter. "Blood Is Thicker Than Irony: Henry Adams' 'History'." New England Quarterly. 40(1967), 163-87.

"Henry Adams' portrait of Jefferson in the History may be read as one of a series of Adams fathers by Adams sons."

1088. Sheean, Vincent. Thomas Jefferson, Father of Democracy. New York: Random House, 1953. pp. 184.

Juvenile biography.

1089. [Sheldon, F.]. "Parton's Life of Jefferson." North American Review. 118(1874), 405-15.

Review essay criticizing Parton for errors in taste and "painting his angel all white and his devil all black." Instead, TJ was a clever party manager who was an impractical visionary too often motivated by vanity and rhetoric.

1090. Shenker, Israel. "Monticello, Like No Other Home in America." Travel and Leisure. 1(June/July 1971), 65-72, 76.

1091. Shenkir, William G., Glenn A. Welsch, and James A. Beard, Jr. "Thomas Jefferson: Management Accountant." The Journal of Accountancy. 133(April 1972), 33-47.

TJ was a meticulous record keeper and his personal record keeping seems to have influenced his desire for reliable and understandable public financial data.

1092. Shepperson, Archibald B. "Thomas Jefferson Visits England and Buys a Harpsichord" in Humanistic Studies in Honor of John Calvin Metcalf. Charlottesville: Univ. of Virginia, 1941. 80-106.

Good account of TJ's diplomatic visit in 1786; detailed information on his political and cultural adventures.

1093. Sherman, E. David. "Geriatric Profile of Thomas Jefferson (1743-1826)." Journal of the American Geriatric Society. 25(1977), 112-17.

Notes TJ's impressive activity in retirement, after 1809.

1094. Sherman, Stuart P. "Thomas Jefferson: An English Interpretation" in The Main Stream. New York: Scribner's, 1927. 17-27.

Review essay on the fortunes of TJ's reputation, now on rise again with the publication of Francis W. Hirst's biography.

1095. Sherman, Stuart P. "Thomas Jefferson: A Revaluation" in The Main Stream. New York: Scribner's, 1927. 28-36.

Review essay on Nock's Jefferson; admires TJ as "a philosopher and man of culture."

1096. [Shields, W. S.]. "General Lafayette's Visit to Monticello and the University." Virginia University Magazine. 4(1859), 113-25.

Eye-witness account.

1097. Shippen, Rebecca Lloyd. "Inauguration of President Thomas Jefferson, 1801." PMHB. 25(1901), 71-76.

Description of events.

1098. Showalter, J. D. "The Fame of Jefferson and the University of Virginia Sought to Be Sold." Watson's Jeffersonian Magazine. 3(1909), 785-88.

TJ betrayed because the president of the University sought donations from Andrew Carnegie and Thomas Fortune Ryan.

1099. Sidey, Hugh. "Oh, For Another Stargazing Gardener." Time. 107(April 26, 1976), 19.

Virtues of TJ as opposed to those of 1976 presidential candidates.

1100. Sidey, Hugh. "What Would Jefferson Say?" Time. 112(December 4, 1978), 40.

Interview with Dumas Malone on what TJ would think of the present.

1101. Sifton, Paul G. "The Provenance of the Jefferson Papers." American Archivist. 40(1977), 17-30.

Informative article on the vicissitudes of TJ's papers.

1102. [Simpson, Lloyd D.]. Notes on Thomas Jefferson, By a Citizen of Maryland. Philadelphia: Sherman & Co., 1885. pp. 182.

Analyzes TJ's character in order to prove that he more than anyone else has fostered "the restlessness, the self-assertion, the restiveness under parental control, the diminished reverence for all that is sacred and venerable," etc. which now exists among us.

1103. Simpson, Stephen. The Lives of George Washington and Thomas Jefferson: With a Parallel. Philadelphia: Henry Young, 1833. pp. 389.

Washington in the field and Jefferson in the cabinet accomplished a revolution without parallel in history for its grandeur.

1104. [Simpson, Stephen]. The Life of Thomas Jefferson. With a Portrait and a Parallel (Washington and Jefferson Compared). Philadelphia: J. G. Russell, 1844. pp. 189-389.

Reissue of the Jefferson section of the previous item with a new title page but retaining the old pagination.

1105. Smelser, Marshall. "Mr. Jefferson in 1801" in The Democratic Republic 1801-1815. New York: Harper and Row, 1968. 1-20.

A sketch of TJ as he appeared in 1801, leading up to the inaugural speech which is presented as a keynote to the era. Considers the speech in terms of its reception by some of TJ's contemporaries.

1106. Smith, Bessie White. "Thomas Jefferson" in The Romances of the Presidents. Boston: Lothrop, Lee, and Shepard, 1932. 38-51.

TJ courts Rebecca Burwell and Martha Wayles Skelton.

1107. Smith, Charles Card. "The Life of Thomas Jefferson. By Henry S. Randall, LL.D. ... ." North American Review. 91(1860), 107-18.

TJ's true character was revealed after his death by publication of his letters and testimony of those who knew him intimately.

1108. Smith, Datus C., Jr. "The Jefferson Monument: The Nation's No. 1 University Press Project." Saturday Review of Literature. 33(May 6, 1950), 12-13, 61.

Story of the Jefferson Papers project at Princeton Univ. Press.

1109. Smith, Dorothy Hunt and Mina Ruese. "He Wrote the Declaration."
       Christian Science Monitor Magazine. June 30, 1945. 3.

       On the projected edition of the Papers.

1110. Smith, Glenn Curtis. "Jefferson on the Press." Tyler's Quarterly.
       27(1945), 13-16.

       TJ advocated a free press but deplored the malignity and vulgarity of
       the press in his time.

1111. Smith, Helen Ainslie. "Jefferson" in One Hundred Famous Americans.
       New York: G. Routledge and Sons, 1889. 68-73.

1112. Smith, Margaret Bayard. The First Forty Years of Washington Society.
       New York: Scribner's 1906. pp. xii, 424.

       TJ dealt with throughout; Margaret Bayard of the Federalist
       Delaware Bayards married Samuel Harrison Smith, editor of The
       National Intelligencer, and came to admire TJ, described in the pre-
       face as "her life's hero."

1113. Smith, Margaret Bayard. "Washington in Jefferson's Time." Scribner's
       Magazine. 40(1906), 292-310.

       Adapted from the previous item.

1114. Smith, Page Jefferson: A Revealing Biography. New York: American
       Heritage, 1976. pp. 310.

       Numerous illustrations; a popular biography attempting to do some of
       the same things Fawn Brodie did, get at TJ's emotional life, etc., but
       with less success and no documentation.

1115. Smith, Paul H. "Time and Temperature: Philadelphia, July 4, 1776."
       Quarterly Journal of the Library of Congress. 33(1976), 294-99.

       Discusses the time of day when the debate on the Declaration con-
       cluded and the weather on the 4th.

1116. Smith, Samuel. "Eulogy, Pronounced in Baltimore, Maryland, July 20th
       1826" in A Selection of Eulogies ... . Hartford: D. F. Robinson, 1826.
       71-90.

       Claims TJ's last words were "I resign my Soul to my God, and My
       daughter to my country!"

1117. Smith, Samuel Harrison. Memoirs of the Life, Character and Writings
       of Thomas Jefferson; Delivered in the Capitol, Before the Columbian
       Institute, on the Sixth of January, 1827, and Published at Their
       Request. Washington: S. A. Elliott, 1827. pp. 38.

Extensive survey of TJ's life.

1118.   Smith, Sheldon. "Eulogy, Pronounced at Buffalo, New York, July 22nd,
        1826" in A Selection of Eulogies ... . Hartford: D. F. Robinson, 1826.
        91-96.

1119.   Smyth, Clifford. Thomas Jefferson, The Father of American
        Democracy. New York: Funk and Wagnalls, 1931. pp. 176.

        In the Builders of America Series; sentimental and uncritical.

1120.   Sokolsky, Eric. "Thomas Jefferson" in Our Seven Greatest
        Presidents. New York: Exposition, 1964. 29-39.

1121.   Sparks, Edwin Erle. "Thomas Jefferson, The Exponent of Democracy"
        in The Men Who Made the Nation; An Outline of United States
        History from 1760 to 1865. New York: Macmillan, 1901. 218-54.

        Account of TJ's presidency, portraying him as a disappointed
        theorist.

1122.   Spencer, John Bassett. "Thomas Jefferson and the Climax of the
        Revolution." Daughters of the American Revolution Magazine.
        58(1924), 289-94.

        TJ's life before the Declaration.

1123.   Spivey, Herman E., ed. "William Cullen Bryant Changes His Mind: An
        Unpublished Letter about Thomas Jefferson." New England
        Quarterly. 22(1949), 528-29.

        Bryant in an 1859 letter calls TJ "one of the wisest political philoso-
        phers of his time."

1124.   Sprague, Joseph E. An Eulogy on John Adams and Thomas Jefferson,
        Pronounced August 10, 1826, at the Request of the Town of Salem.
        Salem, Mass.: Warwick Palfrey, Jr., 1826. pp. 48.

        Also in A Selection of Eulogies ... . Hartford: D. F. Robinson, 1826.
        235-71. TJ's "noblest effort, though unsuccessful, has been for the
        emancipation of slaves." Claims that it rained on July 4, 1826, and
        the rainbow "gave assurance that the offerings of these patriots had
        been accepted."

1125.   Sprague, Peleg. Eulogy on John Adams and Thomas Jefferson,
        Pronounced in Hallowell, July, 1826, at the Request of the
        Committees of the Towns of Hallowell, Augusta, and Gardiner.
        Hallowell, Maine: Glazier & Co., 1826. pp. 22.

        Also in A Selection of Eulogies ... . Hartford: D. F. Robinson, 1826.
        139-53. The Declaration considered "as a great, solemn, political

act, ... demands our highest veneration," and its truth has changed the world. TJ and Adams became "the patriarchs of America, and saw their children in the land of promise."

1126. [Stanard, William G.]. "Lilburne-Randolph-Jefferson." VMHB. 26(1918). 321-24.

Genealogy of TJ's mother.

1127. Stanford, John. A Discourse on the Death of the Honorable Thomas Jefferson and John Adams. Delivered in the Chapel at Bellevue, N. York. New York: E. Conrad, 1826. pp. 20.

Text of the sermon is Zechariah 1:5, "Your Fathers, Where are they?" turns this into a jeremiad. One of the more interesting eulogies.

1128. Stanley, Augustus Owsley. Character and Services of Thomas Jefferson and Alexander Hamilton; Speech ... in the House of Representatives, March 25, 1908. Washington: Government Printing Office, 1908. pp. 31.

1129. Staughton, William. Sermon Delivered in the Capitol of the United States; on Lord's Day, July 16, 1826; at the Request of the Citizens of Washington, on the Death of Mr. Jefferson and Mr. Adams. Washington: Columbian Office, 1826. pp. 32.

1130. Stenberg, Richard R. "The Jefferson Birthday Dinner, 1830." Journal of Southern History. 4(1938), 334-45.

Does not discuss use of TJ by either the Jacksonians or Calhounians.

1131. Stephenson, Nathaniel Wright. "Jefferson and the Real Purpose of Democracy" in Lectures on Typical Americans and Their Problems. Scripps College Papers III. Claremont: Scripps College, 1930. 1-19.

Americans have been untrue to TJ's example because democracy has run wild and taken over the evils of aristocracy without its virtues.

1132. Sterling, Peter Roman. "Society in Jefferson's Day." National Republic. 17(October 1929), 28, 40.

TJ upsets Anthony Merry.

1133. Stevens, Charles. Funeral Eulogy, on the Characters of Thomas Jefferson and John Adams. Pronounced on the 1st August, 1826, Before the Inhabitants of Pineville, S.C. And Published at Their Request. Charleston: Philip Hoff, 1826. pp. 18.

1134. [Stewart, Robert Armistead]. "Jefferson and His Landlord." The Researcher. 1(October 1926), 5-8.

Note on TJ's living arrangements in Richmond while governor; rpt. in Sons of the Revolution in State of Virginia Semi-Annual Magazine. 9(January 1931), 13-18.

1135.   Stockton, Frank R. "The Later Years of Monticello." The Century Magazine. 34(1887), 654-58.

The fate of Monticello after TJ's death and its condition in 1887.

1136.   Stoddard, William O. John Adams and Thomas Jefferson. New York: White, Stones, and Allen, 1887. pp. viii, 358.

TJ on pp. 175-358; focuses on years before TJ's presidency and takes his side.

1137.   Stokes, William E., Jr., ed. "Mr. Jefferson Comes Home." Magazine of Albemarle County History. 12(1952), 46-49.

Ceremonies at presentation of a copy of the Sully portrait to the Albemarle County Court House.

1138.   Stone, Gene. The Story of Thomas Jefferson. New York: Barse and Hopkins, 1921. pp. 182.

"Famous Americans for Younger Readers."

1139.   Strachey, John St. Loe. "Representative Americans" and "Jefferson" in American Soundings. London: Hodder and Stoughton, 1926. 171-86.

TJ and Lincoln are the men most representative of American life; quotes from Notes to argue that TJ is "sound in heart and head" on slavery.

1140.   Stratton, Ella Hines. "Thomas Jefferson" in The Men Who Have Risen to the White House; Containing the Childhood, Early Education, Occupations, Characteristics, and Achievements of All the Presidents of the United States. Philadelphia: National Publishing Co., 1903. 45-53.

Juvenile.

*1141.   Stratton, Ella Hines. "Thomas Jefferson" in True Stories of Our Presidents. Philadelphia: National Publishing Co., 1901. 45-53.

1142.   [Strother, John M.] "Thomas Jefferson." Virginia University Magazine. 3(1859), 271-88.

Review essay of Randall's biography.

1143.   Sullivan, Mark. "Seeing America With Jefferson's Eyes." World's Work.

52(1926), 328-32.

A greater density of population makes many of TJ's theories inade-
quate for modern America.

1144. Swift, Lindsay. "Our Literary Diplomats. Thomas Jefferson." The
Bookbuyer. 20(1900), 289-91.

Conventional sketch.

1145. Swindler, R. E. "Thomas Jefferson and Slavery." Southern Magazine.
1(February 1935), 6-7, 44.

TJ was a good master who favored emancipation.

1146. Talbert, Ernest Lynn. In the Spirit of Jefferson; Essays and Reviews.
New York: Exposition, 1951. pp. 68.

Little on TJ; one essay calls on his authority to denounce loyalty
oaths in universities; another is on "Kate Smith and Jeffersonian
Democracy."

1147. Tansill, Charles Callan. The Secret Loves of the Founding Fathers.
New York: Devin-Adair, 1964. 81-121.

Superficial account of TJ's romantic interests.

1148. Tarr, Harry A. "Builders of American Democracy. 7. Thomas
Jefferson: Believer in the Common Man." Scholastic. 37(November
11, 1940), 15-16.

1149. Tator, Henry H. An Oration Commemorative of the Character of
Thomas Jefferson. Albany: Joel Munsell, 1852. pp. 22.

Overblown rhetoric.

1150. Tauber, Gisela. "Reconstruction in Psychoanalytic Biography:
Understanding Thomas Jefferson." Journal of Psychohistory.
7(1979), 187-207.

Argues that the ambivalence of dependence "fired his need to
destroy the symbols of the maternal womb and to put new ones up
simultaneously, even more beautiful in appearance." Discusses the
relevance of Ovid and Petrarch, implications seen in A Summary
View, the Declaration, and his interest in building. Stimulating
but not everyone will accept the author's assumptions about psycho-
historical method.

1151. Taylor, Cornelia Jefferson. "Gleanings from the Life of Thomas
Jefferson." American Monthly Magazine. 2(January 1893), 29-34.

Miscellaneous notes by a descendant.

1152. Taylor, Olivia. "Dear Ghosts of Lego and Monticello." Papers of the Albemarle County Historical Society. 3(1943), 17-32.

Diffuse reminiscences of the early 20th century, including lore about TJ.

1153. Taylor, Olivia A. "The Jefferson Family." Annual Report of the Monticello Association. 1954. 15-19.

Genealogy of TJ; in the Reports for 1955-59 the author gives genealogic lists for "The Descendents of Thomas Jefferson."

1154. Temple, W. K. Monticello, The Home of Thomas Jefferson. n.p., n.d. Broadside.

Defends Jefferson Levy as a restorer of Monticello and describes the property, circa 1912.

1155. Tener, George. "Tour Notes on Wines and Vines in France and Italy 1787" in Jefferson and Wine, ed. R. deTreville Lawrence, Sr. The Plains, Va.: Vinifera Wine Growers Association, 1976. 107-120.

TJ's notes with comment.

1156. Terrier, Max. "The Carriages of Jefferson in Europe." The Carriage Journal. 14(Autumn 1976), 59-62.

Describes the coach TJ had built by John Kemp, discusses English and French coach-making, illustrations of other coaches of the period.

1157. "Th: Jefferson on Birch Bark." The Yorker. 19(no. 4, 1961), 12-13.

Transcription with notes of TJ's letters written on birch bark to Martha Jefferson Randolph and her husband and sent from his New England tour.

1158. Thomas, Charles M. "Date Inaccuracies in Thomas Jefferson's Writings." MVHR. 19(1972), 87-90.

Inaccuracies in vol. 6 of the Writings, ed. P. L. Ford.

1159. Thomas, Elbert. "World Citizen." New Masses. 47(April 13, 1943), 19-20.

On TJ's message to "a world of free, cooperative men."

1160. Thomas Jefferson Bicentennial Commission. Thomas Jefferson, Author of the Declaration of Independence, Of the Statute of Virginia for Religious Freedom and Father of the University of Virginia.

136

April 13, 1743—April 13, 1943. Washington: Thomas Jefferson Bicentennial Commission, 1943. pp. 35.

Illustrated pamphlet; life of TJ.

1161. Thomas Jefferson Memorial Foundation. Independence Day Exercises Held by the Thomas Jefferson Memorial Foundation at Monticello ... July 4, 1936. New York?: Thomas Jefferson Memorial Foundation, 1936. pp. (8).

Brief remarks from Franklin D. Roosevelt, Carter Glass, George C. Perry.

1162. Thomas Jefferson Memorial Foundation. The Story of the Thomas Jefferson Memorial Foundation, Dedicated to the Preservation of Monticello, The Home of Thomas Jefferson Situated at Charlottesville, Virginia. New York: Thomas Jefferson Memorial Foundation, 1926. pp. 12.

1163. Thomas Jefferson Society. The Thomas Jefferson Society of the United States of America. Hancock, N. H.: The Society, 1963?, broadside.

Announces the purpose of the Society to disseminate the principles of TJ; director is Albert Levitt.

1164. "Thomas Jefferson." The Dutch Boy Painter. 19(July 1926), 109-09.

1165. "Thomas Jefferson." New England Historical and Genealogical Register. 11(1857), 193-97.

Brief, admiring sketch, emphasizing his services in the revolutionary period.

1166. "Thomas Jefferson, A Man Who Believed in Other Men." News from Home. 4(no. 2, 1943), 4-5.

1167. "Thomas Jefferson and the Declaration of Independence." American Scene (Tulsa, Oklahoma). 16(no. 4, 1976), 4-7.

1168. "Thomas Jefferson and the Human Design." Fortune. 28(November 1943), 156-57.

Biographical sketch.

1169. "Thomas Jefferson and The Law." The Lawyer. 6(May 1943), 6.

Note on Library of Congress exhibit.

1170. "Thomas Jefferson and Wine in Early America in San Francisco." Sunset. 156(April 1976), 58-59.

137

Note on exhibit at the Wine Museum.

1171. "Thomas Jefferson as a Lawyer." The Columbia Jurist. 2(1886), 479-80.

Slight sketch.

1172. "Thomas Jefferson—Draughtsman of American Ideals." The Independent. 117(1926), 13-16.

Mostly illustrations.

1173. Thomas Jefferson, Man of Achievement. Fiskeville, R. I.: Interlaken Mills, 1959. pp. (7).

New Year's greeting, illustrated sketch of TJ's life and interests.

1174. The Thomas Jefferson Memorial. Alexandria, Va.: Action Publications, 1949. pp. 29.

Account for tourists, brief biographical sketch.

1175. "Thomas Jefferson Number." The Amateur Reporter. 1(April 1927), 1-32.

Published by the student body of Jefferson Jr. High School, Charleston, W. Va.

1176. "Thomas Jefferson, 1743-1943." Life. 14(April 12, 1943), 62-75.

Illustrated biographical sketch.

1177. "Thomas Jefferson: Suggestions for April Reading." National Education Association Journal. 39(1950), 306-09.

1178. "Thomas Jefferson, Third President, 1801-9" in The Presidents from the Inauguration of George Washington to the Inauguration of Gerald Ford, ed. Robert G. Ferris. Washington: National Park Service, 1976. 71-77.

1179. "Thomas Jefferson, Troisiéme Président de États Unis." Revue Brittanique. 4th ser. 11(1837), 52-72.

Biographical sketch translated from North American Review.

1180. "Thomas Jefferson—Welshman." Literary Digest. 116(December 2, 1933), 40.

Tablet erected in Wales honoring TJ because of his Welsh ancestry.

1181. Thomas Jefferson's Birthday. Program and Selections for Its Cele-
       bration. Montgomery: Alabama State Department of Education,
       1909. pp. 32.

       Suggested order of exercises for schools to use in celebrating TJ's
       birthday.

1182. Thomas Jefferson's Birthday Program and Selections for Its Celebration
       Wednesday, April 13, 1910, in the Schools of Alabama. Montgomery:
       Alabama Department of Education, 1910. pp. 40.

       Similar to previous item, but different items for the suggested exer-
       cises. Only two of these located, but they may have been published
       for some years after this, as late as 1935.

1183. Thomas Jefferson's Monticello. Charlottesville: Thomas Jefferson
       Memorial Foundation, n.d. Broadside.

       Accordion-fold broadside for visitors to Monticello has been reprinted
       in several revised versions since mid-1920's.

1184. "Thomas Jefferson's Monticello." Wide Track World (Pontiac Motor
       Division). 7(July 1976), 4-7.

1185. "Thomas Jefferson's Monticello, America's First Modern Home." House
       and Garden. 148(January 1976), 48-53.

1186. Thompson, Daniel Pierce. Green Mountain Boy at Monticello: A Talk
       with Jefferson in 1822. Introduction by Howard C. Rice, Jr.
       Brattleboro: Book Cellar, 1962. pp. 35.

       The Vermont novelist's youthful visit to TJ; discussion mainly turned
       on the "social revolution" then taking place in Virginia and on educa-
       tion. Met TJ on the campus of the University then under construc-
       tion.

1187. Thompson, Daniel Pierce. "A Talk with Jefferson." Harper's Magazine.
       26(1863), 833-35.

       Account of his visit with TJ in 1822.

1188. Thompson, Richard W. Recollections of Sixteen Presidents From
       Washington to Lincoln. Indianapolis: Bowen-Merrill, 1894. 37-63.

       In spring of 1825 he saw TJ shop in Charlottesville; takes a
       Hamiltonian view of his life.

1189. Thornton, William F. "Eulogy, Pronounced at Alexandria, District of
       Columbia, August 10, 1826" in A Selection of Eulogies ... . Hartford:
       D. F. Robinson, 1826. 329-46.

Praises TJ's "extraordinary power of intense reflection."

1190.   Thornton, William Mynn. Who Was Thomas Jefferson? Address
         Delivered Before the Virginia State Bar Association, August 12th,
         1909. Richmond: Richmond Press, 1909. pp. 32.

         Biographical sketch of "the great apostle of American Democracy."

1191.   Thornton, William M. "Who Was Thomas Jefferson?" Tennessee Bar
         Association Proceedings. 32(1913), 122-47.

         Repeat performance of the previous item.

1192.   Thorpe, Francis N. "Adams and Jefferson: 1826-1926." North
         American Review. 223(1926), 234-47.

         Discusses the differing reputations of TJ, who deserves to have been
         so well remembered as he has been, and Adams, who deserves better
         than he received.

1193.   Ticknor, George. "Visit to Jefferson at Monticello" in Life, Letters,
         and Journals of George Ticknor. Boston: James R. Osgood, 1876.
         1:34-38.

         Ticknor visited TJ on February 4-7, 1815, and sent a rather full
         account to his father, printed here.

1194.   Tillinghast, Joseph Leonard. Eulogy Pronounced in Providence, July 17,
         1826, Upon the Characters of John Adams and Thomas Jefferson,
         Late Presidents of the United States, By Request of the Municipal
         Authorities. Providence: Miller & Grattan, 1826. pp. 28.

         Praises TJ for the omitted anti-slavery passage in the Declaration.

1195.   Tillman, Terry. The Monticello Question and Answer Book.
         Charlottesville: Kaminer and Thompson, 1975. pp. 11.

1196.   Tinkcom, Margaret Bailey. "Caviar along the Potomac: Sir Augustus
         John Foster's 'Notes on the United States,' 1804-12." WMQ. 3rd ser.
         8(1951), 68-107.

         See item # 456.

1197.   Tompkins, E. P. "The Will of Patrick Henry, the Negro Caretaker of
         the Natural Bridge." VMHB. 58(1950), 134-35.

         Henry was one of TJ's slaves.

1198.   Torrence, Clayton, ed. "Letters of Sarah Nicholas Randolph to Hugh
         Blair Grigsby." VMHB. 59(1951), 315-36.

TJ's great-granddaughter discusses writing an account of his life and papers in possession of the family.

1199.   "Touring Europe with Thomas Jefferson." Life. 52(June 15, 1962), 64-75.

Follows the route of TJ's 1787 trip to Southern France and Italy.

1200.   Townsend, George Alfred ("Gath"). Monticello and Its Preservation Since Jefferson's Death, 1826-1902. Washington: Gibson Bros. Printers, 1902. pp. 56.

Defends Jefferson Monroe Levy's care of Monticello.

1201.   Townsend, Virginia F. "Thomas Jefferson" in Our Presidents or the Lives of the Twenty-Three Presidents of the United States. New York: Worthington, 1889. 59-102.

"Of the first three Presidents Thomas Jefferson had, perhaps, the most lovable personality."

1202.   Trent, William P. "Thomas Jefferson." Columbia University Quarterly. 16(1914), 392-98.

Laudatory speech at unveiling of a statue of TJ.

1203.   True, Katherine M. "The Romantic Voyage of Polly Jefferson." Harper's. 129(1914), 489-97.

Account of Maria Jefferson's trip to join her father in Paris.

1204.   "The True Thomas Jefferson." The Outlook. 70(1902), 239-41.

Review essay on W. E. Curtis's book of this title. TJ was the greatest genius of his age, but Washington was the greater man. TJ was essentially a doctrinaire, but he lived in an age that needed a doctrinaire.

1205.   Truett, Randle B. Monticello, Home of Thomas Jefferson. Including Some Photographs by Samuel Chamberlain. New York: Hastings House, 1957. pp. 70.

A picture book.

1206.   Tucker, George. Defence of the Character of Thomas Jefferson Against a Writer in the New York Review and Quarterly Church Journal. By a Virginian. New York: William Osborn, 1838. pp. 46.

Reply to Francis Lister Hawkes' critical review of Tucker's biography.

1207.   Tucker, George. The Life of Thomas Jefferson, Third President of the

United States. With Parts of His Correspondence Never Before Published, and Notices of His Opinions on Questions of Civil Government, National Policy, and Constitutional Law. Philadelphia: Carey, Lea and Blanchard, 1837. 2 vols. pp. xx, 545; viii, 525.

Tucker was Professor of Moral Philosophy at the University of Virginia, and was given access to family papers and received information from Martha Jefferson Randolph. The first important biography.

1208.   Tudury, Moran. "Mr. Jefferson." Bookman. 64(1926), 31-34.

Biographical sketch.

1209.   Trumbull, Archibald Douglas. "Jefferson and the Declaration." Saint Nicholas. 53(1926), 843-45.

Romanticized account of the writing, for young readers.

1210.   Turner, Edward. "Eulogy Pronounced at Portsmouth, New-Hampshire, August 10, 1826" in A Selection of Eulogies ... . Hartford: D. F. Robinson, 1826. 273-85.

1211.   Tuttle, Kate A. "The First Bell and Clock of the University." University of Virginia Alumni Bulletin. 5(1889), 111-13.

TJ planned for the bell and clock.

1212.   "Two Architects of Independence: Thomas Jefferson and Benjamin Franklin." UNESCO Courier. 29(July 1976), 14-19.

Sketch.

1213.   Tyler, John. A Funeral Oration on the Death of Thomas Jefferson, Delivered at the Request of the Citizens of Richmond, on the 11th of July, 1826. Richmond: Shepherd & Pollard, 1826. pp. 12.

Also in A Selection of Eulogies ... . Hartford: D. F. Robinson, 1826. TJ praised as a philosophic democrat who will be remembered for the Declaration; quotes from TJ's letter of June 24 to Roger C. Weightman

1214.   Tyler, Lyon G., ed. "Some Contemporary Accounts of Eminent Characters." WMQ. 17(1908), 1-8.

Excerpts a paragraph from Francis T. Brooke's "A Narrative of My Life For My Family" on TJ.

1215.   Umbreit, Kenneth. "Thomas Jefferson" in Founding Fathers, Men Who Shaped Our Tradition. New York: Harper, 1941. 1-103.

Undistinguished short biography.

1216. U. S. Commission for the Celebration of the Two-Hundredth Anniversary of the Birth of Thomas Jefferson. "Report ... Pursuant to Section 7 of Public Resolution No. 100, Seventy-sixth Congress." 77th Congress, 1st Session. Senate Document No. 12. Washington: Government Printing Office, 1941. pp. 3.

Recommends programs to celebrate TJ's 200th.

1217. U. S. Congress. Joint Committee on the Library. "Report on Bill S. 4087, Relative to the Proposed Purchase of the Manuscript Papers and Correspondence of Thomas Jefferson." 51st Congress, 1st Session. Senate Report No. 1365. Washington: Government Printing Office, 1890. pp. 3.

Favors acquisition of papers now in the possession of Sarah N. Randolph and gives a short list.

1218. U. S. Congress. "Joint Resolution to Provide for the Appointment of a National Agricultural Jefferson Bicentenary Committee to Carry Out Appropriate Exercises and Activities in Recognition of the Services and Contributions of Thomas Jefferson to the Farmers." 78th Congress, 1st Session. Senate Joint Resolution No. 47. Washington: Government Printing Office, 1944. pp. 2.

1219. U. S. Congress. "Letter from the Secretary of State to Hon. D. W. Voorhees, Chairman of the Committee on the Library, Transmitting Letter of the Attorney-General in Relation to the Obstacles in the way of erecting a monument over the grave of Thomas Jefferson." 46th Congress, 2nd Session. Senate Miscellaneous Document No. 88.

1220. U. S. Congress. "Proceedings Had in the Senate and House of Representatives, April 23, 1880, On the Occasion of the Presentation of Thomas Jefferson's Writing-Desk to the United States By the Heirs of the Late Joseph Coolidge, Jr." 47th Congress, 1st Session. House of Representatives Miscellaneous Document No. 44. Washington: Government Printing Office, 1882. pp. 37.

1221. U. S. Congress. Joint Committee on the Library. "Report to Accompany Bill S. No. 278, "A Bill Authorizing the Purchase and Publication of the Papers and Manuscripts of the Late Thomas Jefferson." 30th Congress, 1st Session. Senate Rep. Com. No. 167. Washington: Government Printing Office, 1848. pp. 3.

Recommends purchase and preservation of papers in the hands of T. J. Randolph and briefly describes them.

1222. U. S. House of Representatives. Committee on the Library. "Papers Of Thomas Jefferson. (To Accompany Bill H.R., No. 627)." 29th Congress, 2nd Session. House of Representatives Report No. 39. Washington: Ritchie & Heiss, 1847. pp. 2.

Essentially the same as the preceding item.

1223.   U. S. House of Representatives. Library Committee. Site for the
        Thomas Jefferson Memorial; Hearing ... on H. J. Res. 337.
        Washington: Government Printing Office, 1937. pp. 129.

        Defenders of cherry blossoms speak out.

1224.   U. S. House of Representatives. Committee on Pensions. "Report to
        Accompany Bill H. R. 999, 'A Bill Granting a Pension to the Sole
        Surviving Grandchild of the Author of the Declaration of Indepen-
        dence.'" 48th Congress, 1st Session. House Report No. 38.
        Washington: Government Printing Office, 1884. pp. 3.

        Proposal to grant a pension to Septimia Randolph Meikleham.

1225.   U. S. House of Representatives. Committee on Pensions. "Views of the
        Minority on H. R. No. 999, Granting a Pension to Mrs. Septimia R.
        Meikleham, Only Surviving Granddaughter of Thomas Jefferson. Jan.
        22, 1884." 48th Congress, 1st Session. House of Representatives
        Report No. 38, Part 2. Washington: Government Printing Office,
        1884. pp. 3.

        Opposed to granting civil pensions as a matter of principle.

1226.   U. S. House of Representatives. Rules Committee. Public Ownership
        of Monticello; Hearings ... on S. Con. Res. 24, Wednesday, July 24,
        1912. Washington: Government Printing Office, 1912. pp. 78.

        Mrs. Martin W. Littleton has her say.

1227.   U. S. House of Representatives. "Purchase of Monticello. Report to
        Accompany H. J. Res. 390." 63d Congress, 3rd Session. House of
        Representatives Report No. 1441. Washington: Government Printing
        Office, 1915. pp. 2.

        Proposes a Jefferson Memorial Commission to see after purchasing
        Monticello for the nation. See also 63d Congress, 2d Session. Senate
        Report No. 366.

1228.   U. S. Library of Congress. "Commemoration of the 200th Anniversary
        of the Birth of Thomas Jefferson, April 13, 1943. A collection of the
        press-releases, the Exhibit catalogue, the musical and theatrical
        programs, etc., issued in connection with the occasion." Washington,
        1943. unpag.

        A unique scrapbook with all printed ephemera issued by the Library,
        plus photographs; in Rare Books Division of the Library.

1229.   U. S. Library of Congress. The Jefferson Bicentennial 1743-1943.
        Washington: Library of Congress, 1943. broadside.

List of exhibits at the library and a note by Archibald Macleish.

1230. U. S. President [Rutherford B. Hayes]. "The Desk upon Which Mr.
       Jefferson Wrote the Declaration of Independence. Message from the
       President of the United States. Transmitting the desk upon Which
       the Declaration of Independence Was Written, Accompanied by a
       Letter from the Hon. Robert C. Winthrop, presenting the same to the
       United States." 46th Congress, 2nd Session. House of Represen-
       tatives Ex. Doc. No. 75. Washington: Government Printing Office,
       1881.

1231. U. S. Senate. Library Committee. Public Ownership of Monticello,
       Hearing ... on S. J. Res. 92, A Joint Resolution Providing for the
       Purchase of the Home of Thomas Jefferson at Monticello, Virginia.
       Washington: Government Printing Office, 1912. pp. 57.

       Mrs. Martin W. Littleton appeals to the Senate.

1232. U. S. Senate. Committee on Public Buildings and Grounds. Purchase
       of Monticello; Hearing ... on S. J. Res. 153, A Bill Directing the
       Secretary of the Treasury to Acquire by Purchase the Estate Known
       as Monticello, ... Washington: Government Printing Office, 1917.
       pp. 26.

       The DAR interests itself in TJ and Monticello.

1233. U. S. Senate. Committee on Public Buildings and Grounds. "Report to
       Accompany Joint Resolution S. R. 6. 'That the Committee on Public
       Buildings and Grounds Be Instructed to Consider the Expediency of
       Providing for the Protection of the Statue of Jefferson Now in the
       Open Air in the Grounds of the Executive Mansion, the Same Being a
       Work of Art by an Eminent French Sculptor." 43d Congress, 1st
       Session. Senate Report No. 138. Washington: Government Printing
       Office, 1874. pp. 5.

       Gives interesting account of Uriah P. Levy's gift of 1834 and its sub-
       sequent history.

1234. U. S. Senate. "Report: The Select Committee to whom was referred a
       bill concerning Martha Randolph, daughter and only surviving child of
       Thomas Jefferson." 22nd Congress, 1st Session. Senate document
       No. 107. Washington, 1832. pp. 5.

       Proposes to relieve her financial difficulties with a grant of western
       land; discusses TJ's economic sacrifices for his country.

1235. U. S. Sesquicentennial of the American Independence and the Thomas
       Jefferson Centennial Commission. "Report of the ... Commission."
       70th Congress, 1st Session. Senate Document No. 54. Washington:
       Government Printing Office, 1928. pp. 76.

Programs and texts of speeches given under various phases of this patriotic extravaganza.

1236. U. S. Sesquicentennial of American Independence and the Thomas Jefferson Centennial Commission. Official Plan for the NATION-WIDE CELEBRATION of the One Hundred and Fiftieth Anniversary of the Adoption of the Declaration of American Independence. Washington: Government Printing Office, 1926. pp. 12.

*1237. "The University of Missouri: First State University in the Louisiana Purchase." The University of Missouri Bulletin. 54(no. 37, 1954). unpag. (General Series, 1954, no. 29).

Information on Jeffersonian relics at the University.

1238. University of the State of New York. Slides and Photographs Study 56: Thomas Jefferson. Albany: Univ. of the State of New York Press, 1925. pp. 23.

Slides illustrating TJ's life and prepared text.

1239. [Upshur, Abel P.]. "Mr. Jefferson." Southern Literary Messenger. 6(1840), 642-50.

Essay review of Tucker's Life; comments on the difficulty of TJ getting a fair hearing.

1240. Upton, Harriet Taylor. "The Family of Jefferson" in Our Early Presidents, Their Wives and Children, from Washington to Jackson. Boston: D. Lothrop, 1891. 149-88.

Appeared earlier in Wide Awake. 26(March 1888), 249-59. Conventional sketch.

1241. Vance, Joseph C. "Knives, Whips and Randolphs on the Court House Lawn." Magazine of Albemarle County History. 15(1956), 28-35.

Best account of Charles L. Bankhead's attack on his brother-in-law, Thomas Jefferson Randolph, in February 1819. Bankhead had mistreated his wife, TJ's granddaughter, and TJ and the family had tried to intervene.

1242. Vance, Joseph Carroll. "Thomas Jefferson Randolph." Ph.D. dissertation. Univ. of Virginia, 1957. pp. 269.

Biography of TJ's favorite grandson who managed his farms after the War of 1812 and became the executor of his estate upon his death.

1243. Vance, Marguerite. Patsy Jefferson of Monticello. New York: E. P. Dutton, 1948. pp. 154.

Juvenile biography of Martha Jefferson Randolph, focuses on years in France; heavily fictionalized.

1244. Van Der Linden, Frank. The Turning Point: Jefferson's Battle for the Presidency. Washington: Robert B. Luce, 1962. pp. x, 371.

The "story of the public battles and the secret intrigues which enabled Thomas Jefferson to win the presidency in 'the Revolution of 1800'" and "of the romance between Margaret Bayard and Samuel Harrison Smith."

1245. Van Loon, Hendrik Willem. "I Get a Cable to Return to America, and So THOMAS JEFFERSON Is the Last of Our Guests as Well as the Most Honored of All" in Van Loon's Lives. New York: Simon and Schuster, 1942. 855-83.

An imaginary conversation with "the greatest American who ever lived."

1246. Van Loon, Hendrik Willem. Thomas Jefferson, The Serene Citizen from Monticello Who Gave Us an American Way of Thinking and Who Gained World-wide Renown by His Noble Understanding of That Most Difficult of All the Arts, The Art of Living as He Felt that It Should Be Practiced in the Republic of Which He Was One of the Founders. New York: Dodd Mead, 1943. pp. 106.

Chatty sketch; rpt. in 1962 in Fighters for Freedom: Jefferson and Bolivar.

1247. van Pelt, Charles B. "Thomas Jefferson and Maria Cosway." American Heritage. 22(August 1971), 22-29, 102-03.

1248. van Vollenhoven, C. Gijsbert Karel overzee. Rotterdam: W. L. & J. Brusse, 1926. pp. 20.

Introduction in Dutch; prints letters of Gijsbert Karel van Hogendorp to TJ, written from 1784-1786.

1249. Van Wyck, P. V. R. Address of P.V.R. Van Wyck, and Oration by Peyton Wise, Delivered Before the Irving Lyceum ... July 3, 1856, at the New Library Building of W.W. Corcoran, Esq.. Washington: Henry Polkinhorn, 1856. pp. 23.

Van Wyck's address is a biographical sketch of TJ.

1250. Verner, Coolie. "Thomas Jefferson." Convergence. 3(no. 4, 1970), 88-90.

1251. Vest, George G. Thomas Jefferson, An Address. Delivered at Columbia, Mo., on June 4, 1885. St. Louis: Buxton & Skinner, 1885. pp. 24.

Laudatory and rhetorical view of TJ's career.

1252. Vest, George G. Thomas Jefferson. An Address. Delivered Before the Jefferson Club, of St. Louis, Missouri, October 31, 1895, on the occasion of unveiling a bust in bronze of Thomas Jefferson, the work of Benjamin Harney, Esq., a member of the Club. St. Louis: The Jefferson Club, 1895. pp. 21.

Laudatory rhetoric linking TJ with the present day Democratic Party and not the Republicans or Populists.

1253. Via, Betty Davis. Monticello's Animal Kingdom. Charlottesville: For the author, 1967. pp. (32).

Domestic and wild animals at Monticello in TJ's time; juvenile.

1254. Via, Betty Davis. Thomas Jefferson and the Indians. Charlottesville: The author, 1969. pp. (32).

Juvenile; fanciful.

1255. Via, Betty Davis. Thomas Jefferson's Letters to Young People. n.p., 1956. broadside.

Brief notes and extracts from TJ's letters.

1256. Via, Vera V. "Mr. Jefferson's Uneasy Rest." Virginia Cavalcade. 11(Winter 1961), 27-32.

The Monticello graveyard.

1257. [Victor, O. J.]. "Thomas Jefferson." Knickerbocker Magazine. 52 (1858), 359-62, 479-84.

Review essay of Randall's Life; the first section on TJ's youth is generally admiring, but the second section is a sharp attack on his "inconsistencies."

1258. Vogt, Per. Thomas Jefferson. Oslo: Johan Grundt Tanum, 1946. pp. 344.

Biography in Norwegian.

*1259. Voorhees, Daniel W. "Thomas Jefferson" in Forty Years of Oratory ... Lectures, Addresses, and Speeches. Indianapolis: Bowen-Merrill, 43-77.

1260. Wade, Mary Hazelton. The Boy Who Loved Freedom: The Story of Thomas Jefferson. New York: Appleton, 1930. pp. vii, 235.

Juvenile biography.

148

1261. Wagner, Julia. <u>Thomas Jefferson, The Man and Patriot</u>. Washington: Creative Arts Studio, 1949. pp. 16.

A script for an accompanying filmstrip.

1262. <u>Walking With Thomas Jefferson Through Philadelphia History</u>. Philadelphia: Strawbridge & Clothier, 1949. folding broadside.

Account of TJ's various stays in Philadelphia; minor.

1263. Wallace, M. G. "Monticello." <u>American Monthly Magazine</u>. 22(1903), 106-07.

1264. Walne, Peter. "Mr. Jefferson's Visits to Hertfordshire." <u>Hertfordshire Countryside</u>. 30(no. 2, 1975), 16-17.

TJ visits Moor Park; interesting account.

1265. Walter, L. Rohe. <u>Thomas Jefferson American Credo Stamp Ceremony, May 18, 1960</u>. n.p., 1960. pp. 8.

First day of issue ceremony in Charlottesville for postage stamp bearing TJ's vow of hostility against every form of Tyranny.

1266. Ward, Paul W. "Washington Weekly." <u>Nation</u>. 142(1936), 267-68.

Criticizes proposals to spend 30 million for a TJ memorial in St. Louis.

1267. Warren, Charles. "Fourth of July Myths." <u>WMQ</u>. 3rd ser. 2(1945), 237-72.

TJ misremembered the date of signing the Declaration; also notes early celebrations of the Fourth as an expression of party spirit.

1268. Warren, Charles. "How Jefferson's Death Was Reported in the Campaign of 1800" in <u>Odd Byways in American History</u>. Cambridge: Harvard Univ. Press, 1942. 127-35.

Rumor based on the death of a slave of the same name.

1269. Warner, Charles Willard Hoskins. "Jefferson's Williamsburg Friends" in <u>Road to Revolution: Virginia's Rebels from Bacon to Jefferson</u>. Richmond: Garrett and Massie, 1961. 131-42.

Derivative account of Small, Wythe, and Fauquier.

1270. Wasserman, Felix M. "Six Unpublished Letters of Alexander von Humboldt to Thomas Jefferson." <u>Germanic Review</u>. 29(1954), 191-200.

Describes the letters in the Library of Congress and discusses
Humboldt's interest in TJ and the United States.

*1271. Watson, Henry C. "Thomas Jefferson" in Lives of the Presidents of the
        United States. Boston: Kelly & Bro., 1853. 200-54.

1272.   Watson, Ross. "Thomas Jefferson's Visit to England, 1786." History
        Today. 27(1977), 3-13.

        Informative, detailed account of TJ's visit which, says the author,
        strengthened his anti-British prejudices; his introduction to English
        gardens was the only positive result of the trip.

1273.   Watson, Thomas E. The Life and Times of Thomas Jefferson. New
        York: Appleton, 1903. pp. xxii, 534.

        TJ as courageous fighter of religious bigotry, class despotism, and all
        other kinds of oppression; intended in part as a reply to Theodore
        Roosevelt's characterization of TJ in his Winning of the West.
        Revised edition published in 1927.

1274.   Watson, Thomas E. Thomas Jefferson. Boston: Small, Maynard, 1900.
        pp. xv, 150.

        In the series "Beacon Biographies of Eminent Americans."

1275.   Weaver, Bettie Woodson. "Mary Jefferson and Eppington." Virginia
        Cavalcade. 19(Autumn 1969), 30-35.

        TJ's younger daughter at her aunt's home.

1276.   Weaver, George Summer. "Thomas Jefferson. Third President of the
        United States" in The Lives and Graves of Our Presidents. Chicago:
        Elder, 1884. 119-62.

        Sketch ends with a call for "some patriotic national association" to
        take over Monticello.

1277.   Webster, Daniel. A Discourse in Commemoration of the Lives and
        Services of John Adams and Thomas Jefferson, Delivered at Faneuil
        Hall, Boston, August 2, 1826. Boston: Cummings, Hilliard, & Co.,
        1826. pp. 62.

        Frequently reprinted; credits TJ with authorship of the Declaration
        and Adams with putting it through Congress. Their lives, spent in
        gaining for us the blessings of liberty, remind us of the duties which
        have devolved upon us from our fathers.

1278.   Webster, Daniel. "Memorandum of Mr. J's Conversations" in Private
        Correspondence. Boston: Little Brown, 1857. 1:364-73.

Webster visited Monticello in December, 1824; TJ talked about
Patrick Henry and his experience in France among other topics.

1279. Webster, Nathan Burnham. Thomas Jefferson. Philadelphia:
Lippincott, 1890. pp. 7.

Separate printing of Chambers' Encyclopedia entry.

1280. Wecter, Dixon. "Thomas Jefferson, the Gentle Radical" in The Hero
in America, A Chronicle of Hero Worship. New York: Scribner's,
1941. 148-180.

Examines TJ's reputation with particular attention to his canonizing
by the New Deal.

1281. Weeks, Elie. "Thomas Jefferson's Elk Hill." Goochland County Historical Society Magazine. 3(Spring 1971), 6-11.

Account of TJ's purchases at Elk Hill from 1778 to 1799, when he sold
his property there; conjectural drawing by Calder Loth.

1282. Weisman, Morris. "Thomas Jefferson." Commercial Law Journal.
48(1943), 32-35.

Sketch.

1283. Wertenbaker, Thomas Jefferson. "Glimpses of Thomas Jefferson."
Emory University Quarterly. 9(1953), 48-55.

Sketch.

1284. West, Murray. "Jeffersonianism." New Republic. 127(November 24,
1952), 4.

If TJ were here, he'd be "a good Truman Democrat."

1285. Weymouth, Lally, ed. Thomas Jefferson: The Man ... His World ...
His Influence. New York: Putnam's, 1973. pp. 254.

Introduction to the numerous aspects of TJ with essays by several
hands, noted separately here.

1286. Wharton, Anne Hollingsworth. "Jeffersonian Simplicity" in Social Life
in the Early Republic. Philadelphia: Lippincott, 1902. 102-03.

TJ as host in Washington, D. C.

1287. Wharton, Isaac T. An Oration Delivered on the Fourth of July, 1827,
in the State House, in the City of Philadelphia, ... Philadelphia,
1827. pp. 16.

Refers to the death of TJ and Adams, ends by asking "how far we are living up to Mr. Jefferson's doctrines."

1288. "Where Was the Declaration of Independence Written?" Potter's American Monthly. 4(1875), 62-63.

Editor's note commenting on disputed locations; replied to by Agnes Y. McAllister, pp. 223-25, who argues for the house on the southwest corner of Seventh and Market Streets.

1289. Whitehill, Jane. "The Papers of Thomas Jefferson." PMHB. 85(1961), 78-81, 211-15.

Review essay of the first 15 volumes of the Papers discusses editorial decisions and the insights offered by the material into the character of TJ.

1290. Whitehill, Walter Muir. "The Union of New England and Virginia." VQR. 40(1964), 516-30.

TJ's connections with New England: John Adams, George Ticknor, Ellen Randolph Coolidge.

1291. Whitney, David C. "Thomas Jefferson" in The American Presidents. New York: Doubleday, 1969. 27-40.

1292. Whitton, Mary Ormsbee. "Thomas Jefferson and the Rights of Women" in First First Ladies 1789-1865: A Study of the Wives of the Early Presidents. New York: Hastings House, 1948. 39-53.

TJ, his wife and daughters; he was conservative in regard to women's rights, and "the saga of the three Jefferson ladies" illuminates "the myth of the plantation system."

1293. Wibberley, Leonard. A Dawn in the Trees; Thomas Jefferson, the Years 1776-1789. New York: Farrar, Straus and Giroux, 1964. pp. 188.

Juvenile biography.

1294. Wibberley, Leonard. The Gales of Spring; Thomas Jefferson, the Years 1789-1801. New York: Farrar, Straus and Giroux, 1965. pp. 180.

Juvenile biography.

1295. Wibberley, Leonard. Man of Liberty; A Life of Thomas Jefferson. New York: Farrar, Straus and Giroux, 1968. pp. vii, 404.

Combines 4 separately printed books; good biography for younger readers.

1296. Wibberley, Leonard. Time of the Harvest; Thomas Jefferson, the Years

<u>1801-1826</u>. New York: Farrar, Straus and Giroux, 1966. pp. 170.

1297.   Wibberley, Leonard. <u>Young Man from the Piedmont; The Youth of</u>
        <u>Thomas Jefferson</u>. New York: Farrar, Straus and Giroux, 1963.
        pp. 184.

        Juvenile biography covering the years 1743-1776.

1298.   Wiggins, James Russell. <u>Jefferson Through the Fog</u>. Charlottesville:
        Thomas Jefferson Memorial Foundation, 1959. pp. 18.

        TJ and the issues of 1959, education, desegregation, science, etc.

1299.   Wilberger, Carolyn H. "A Tale of Four Travelers: American and
        Russian Views of Eighteenth-Century France." <u>Proceedings of the</u>
        <u>Pacific Northwest Conference on Foreign Languages</u>. 28(no. 2, 1977),
        39-42.

        Franklin, TJ, Fonvizin, and Karamzin; claims TJ "felt threatened by
        the sophistication of the French aristocracy."

1300.   Wilbur, Margaret Eyer. <u>Thomas Jefferson, Apostle of Liberty</u>. New
        York: Liveright, 1962. pp. 417.

        Popular biography with invented dialogue.

1301.   Wilkins, William. <u>Eulogium of Thomas Jefferson and John Adams,</u>
        <u>Pronounced at Pittsburgh, on the 24th August, 1826</u>. Pittsburgh:
        Johnston & Stockton, 1826. pp. 36.

        Also in <u>A Selection of Eulogies ...</u> . Hartford: D. F. Robinson, 1826.
        347-77.

1302.   Williams, Edwin. "Biographical Sketch" and "Administration of
        Jefferson" in <u>The Presidents of the United States, Their Memoirs and</u>
        <u>Administrations</u>. New York: E. Walker, 1849. 107-64.

        "... rather the policy of the politician than the policy of the states-
        man, the legislator, the lawgiver, or the patriot."

1303.   Williams, T. Harry. "On the Couch at Monticello." <u>Reviews in</u>
        <u>American History</u>. 2(1974), 523-29.

        Review essay prompted by Brodie's <u>Thomas Jefferson</u> argues that she
        has misused psychoanalytic and psychological techniques in inter-
        preting TJ's private life.

1304.   Wills, Garry. "Uncle Thomas's Cabin." <u>New York Review of Books</u>. 21
        (April 18, 1974), 26-28.

        Criticizes Fawn Brodie's inaccuracies.

1305.   Wilson, Rufus Rockwell. "The Jeffersonian Epoch" in Washington The
         Capital City and Its Part in the History of the Nation. Philadelphia:
         Lippincott, 1901. 1:67-96.

         Focus on life in Washington during TJ's presidency.

1306.   Wilson, Woodrow. "A Calendar of Great Americans." The Forum.
         16(1894), 715-27.

         Reprinted in Mere Literature. Boston, 1896. 196-99. "Jefferson was
         not a thorough American because of the strain of French philosophy
         that permeated and weakened all his thought."

1307.   Wilson, Woodrow. "Jefferson-Wilson, A Record and a Forecast.
         Extracts from 'A History of the American People' by Woodrow
         Wilson." North American Review. 197(1913), 289-94.

         The newly elected Democratic president on the first Democrat.

1308.   Wilson, Woodrow. "The Spirit of Jefferson." Princeton Alumni Weekly.
         6(1906), 551-54.

         "It is the spirit, not the tenets of the man, by which he rules us from
         his urn."

1309.   Wilstach, Paul M., ed. Correspondence of John Adams and Thomas
         Jefferson (1812...1826). Indianapolis: Bobbs-Merrill, 1925. pp. 197.

         Selected and abridged texts with editorial commentary.

1310.   Wilstach, Paul. "A Great Man's Gift to His Grandson." St. Nicholas.
         55(1928), 699-700.

         TJ willed Poplar Forest to Francis Eppes.

1311.   Wilstach, Paul. Jefferson and Monticello. New York: Doubleday, 1925.
         pp. xiii, 258.

         Biographical account of TJ's life at Monticello has interesting
         anecdotes. Comprehensive, although uncritical, social history of
         Monticello.

1312.   Wilstach, Paul. "Jefferson Out of Harness." American Mercury.
         4(1925), 63-68.

         TJ's sense of humor as revealed in his letters.

1313.   Wilstach, Paul. ed. "Reconciliation: Correspondence of John Adams
         and Thomas Jefferson." Atlantic Monthly. 138(1924), 811-19.

         Discussion of the correspondence from 1812 on, with extracts.

1314. Wilstach, Paul. "Thomas Jefferson" in Patriots Off Their Pedestals. Indianapolis: Bobbs-Merrill, 1927. 145-82.

Domestic, familiar TJ, told via anecdotes.

1315. Wilstach, Paul. "Thomas Jefferson's Secret Home." Country Life. 53(April 1928), 41-43.

On Poplar Forest.

1316. Windley, Lathan A. "Runaway Slave Advertisements of George Washington and Thomas Jefferson." Journal of Negro History. 63(1978), 373-74.

Prints an advertisement from the Virginia Gazette of Sept. 21, 1769, without any significant comment.

1317. Winstock, Melvin G. "Thomas Jefferson" in Making a Nation. Portland, Oregon: Making a Nation Co., 1923. 109-30.

1318. Winston, Alexander. "Mr. Jefferson in Paris." American Society Legion of Honor Magazine. 35(1964), 139-50.

Survey, nothing new.

1319. Wirt, F. A. "Thomas Jefferson Celebration." Agricultural Engineering. 25(1944), 192, 196.

Report on agriculturalists' pilgrimage to Monticello.

1320. Wirt, William. A Discourse on the Lives and Characters of Thomas Jefferson and John Adams, Who Both Died on the Fourth of July, 1826: Delivered at the Request of the Citizens of Washington, in the Hall of Representatives of the United States, on the Nineteenth of October, 1826. Washington: Gales & Seaton, 1826. pp. 69.

Often reprinted; includes a description of Monticello and its resident sage.

1321. Wise, Henry A. Seven Decades of the Union. The Humanities and Materialism, Illustrated by A Memoir of John Tyler, With Reminiscences of Some of His Great Cotemporaries. Philadelphia: Lippincott, 1871. 35-51.

Discusses TJ and events of his administration; claims one of his great contributions to science was bringing Ferdinand Hassler, the geodesist, to America.

1322. Wise, James Waterman. Thomas Jefferson Then and Now, 1743-1943— A National Symposium. New York: Bill of Rights Sesquicentennial

155

Committee, 1943. pp. 143.

54 prominent Americans contribute brief panegyrics.

1323.   Witt, Cornelis de. "Thomas Jefferson. Sa Vie et Sa Correspondance.
        I. La Revolution Americaine et la Revolution Francaise." Revue des
        Deux Mondes. ser. 2. 8(1857), 536-86.

        Discusses TJ's life through his mission to France and his arrival at the
        opinion that the decisions of one generation should not bind the next.

1324.   Witt, Cornelis de. "Thomas Jefferson. Sa Vie et Sa Correspondance.
        IV. Jefferson dans la Retraite." Revue des Deux Mondes. ser. 2.
        29(1860), 78-108.

        TJ's retirement of all his actions does him the most honor.

1325.   Wittke, Carl F. Jefferson Lives on. A Lecture Delivered at The Ohio
        State University, October 26, 1942. Columbus: Ohio State Univ.,
        (1942). pp. 22.

        Survey of TJ's character and achievements, calling on Americans "to
        expand his conception of individual rights."

1326.   Witty, Paul. "Thomas Jefferson" in A Free Nation; The Beginning of
        the United States. Columbus, Ohio: Highlights for Children, 1975.
        4-5.

*1327. Wold, Karl C. "Thomas Jefferson 1743-1826" in Mr. President, How Is
        Your Health? Saint Paul, Minn.: Bruce Publishing Co., 1948. 23-33.

1328.   Wolff, Philippe. "Jefferson on Provence and Languedoc." Proceedings
        of the Annual Meeting of the Western Society for French History.
        3(1975), 191-205.

        Examines TJ's letters written during his tour of southern France and
        compares him favorably as a traveller to Arthur Young.

1329.   Wolff, Philippe. "Le voyage de Thomas Jefferson en Provence et
        Languedoc en 1787." Annales Historiques de la Revolution Francaise.
        48(1976), 595-613.

        Similar to the previous item.

1330.   [Wood, Wallace]. "Jefferson, A.D. 1743-1826, American Statesman"
        in The Hundred Greatest Men. Portraits of the One Hundred
        Greatest Men of History. New York: Appleton, 1885. 438-40.

1331.   Woodbridge, Margaret. "Monticello." U.S. Tobacco Review. Winter
        1978. 4-8.

1332. Woodfin, Maude Hewlett. "Contemporary Opinion in Virginia of Thomas Jefferson" in Essays in Honor of William E. Dodd, ed. Avery Craven. Chicago: Univ. of Chicago Press, 1935. 30-85.

TJ rarely mingled in popular gatherings, but his reputation steadily increased in Virginia, with the exception of the setbacks caused by his governorship and the Mazzei letter. As he revealed himself as a republican reformer, he gained popular support but was also more sharply attacked by some members of his own class. He never attained the general respect tended to Washington.

1333. Woodward, Carl R. "Thomas Jefferson Survives." Agricultural History. 19(1945), 185.

Testimonial.

1334. Wootan, James B. Monticello, Its Sage, and His Home Town. Charlottesville: Monticello Hotel, 1927? pp. 14.

Jeffersonian folklore, preserved (or invented) by William Page, one of the first guides to Monticello after it opened to the public.

1335. "The World of Thomas Jefferson." Art and Man. 6(no. 3, 1976), 2-15.

Illustrated sketch of TJ as a man of the Enlightenment.

1336. Wranek, William. H. "Thomas Jefferson, Homebuilder." The Iron Worker. 15(Summer 1951), 1-9.

Sketch of the owner of Monticello.

1337. Wright, Chester. An Address, On the Death of the Venerable and Illustrious Adams and Jefferson, Ex-presidents of the United States, Delivered Before a Large Concourse of Citizens at Montpelier, Vermont, July 25, 1826. Montpelier: George W. Hill, 1826. pp. 19.

Stresses TJ's role as a defender of religious freedom and as a figure of national unity, as in "We are all Republicans, We are all Federalists."

1338. Young, Klyde and Lamar Middleton. "Thomas Jefferson" in Heirs Apparent: The Vice Presidents of the United States. New York: Prentice-Hall, 1948. 16-35.

Brief biographical sketch; suggests with little support that TJ intended to campaign for president as early as 1797.

III. POLITICAL STUDIES

III. POLITICAL STUDIES.

1339.   "Aaron Burr." United States Magazine and Democratic Review.
        1(1838), 221-49.

>   Review essay on Mathew L. Davis, Memoirs of Aaron Burr, focuses on
>   charges of treachery against TJ and rejects them.

1340.   Abernethy, Thomas Perkins. The Burr Conspiracy. New York: Oxford
        Univ. Press, 1954. pp. viii, 301.

>   Chapter XII, "Jefferson and Burr (183-98), describes TJ's uncertainty
>   about Burr's intentions and the quality of information he was
>   receiving; by the end of October 1806, he was ready to believe the
>   worst about Burr's activities in the West. Chapter XIV, "The Trial in
>   Richmond" (227-49), criticizes TJ for becoming a party to the
>   prosecution. Best book on this subject.

1341.   Adams, Henry. History of the United States of America During the
        First Administration of Thomas Jefferson. New York: Scribner's,
        1889. 2 vols. pp. 446; 456.

>   This, along with the two volumes appearing in 1890 on TJ's second
>   term, is a masterly account, one of the great works of American
>   historiography, but it must be read carefully because of Adams'
>   prejudices about TJ's character.

1342.   Adams, Henry. History of the United States of America During the
        Second Administration of Thomas Jefferson. New York: Scribner's,
        1890. 2 vols. pp. 471; 500.

1343.   Adams, James Truslow. "Jefferson and Hamilton To-Day: The
        Dichotomy in American Thought." Atlantic Monthly. 141(1928),
        443-50.

>   Both present day parties in somewhat different ways preach
>   Jefferson and practice Hamilton; if TJ was the more attractive man,
>   the past and the future still belong to Hamilton.

1344.   Adams, John Quincy. Correspondence Between John Quincy Adams,
        Esquire, President of the United States, and Several Citizens of
        Massachusetts Concerning the Charge of a Design to Dissolve the
        Union Alleged to Have Existed in That State. Boston: Daily
        Advertiser, 1829. pp. 80.

>   Controversy raised by the publication of TJ's letter of Dec. 25, 1825
>   to William Branch Giles, claiming J. Q. Adams had intimated
>   treasonous intentions on the part of the Massachusetts Federalists at
>   the time of the Embargo.

1345.   Adams, John Quincy. <u>Letter of the Hon. John Quincy Adams, in Reply to a Letter of the Hon. Alexander Smyth, to His Constituents.</u> Washington: Gales & Seaton, 1828. pp. 16.

Defends himself against charges of attempting to ridicule TJ and of voting against the Louisiana Purchase for reasons of faction; prints a letter from TJ to William Dunbar, dated July 17, 1803, showing similar constitutional scruples.

1346.   Adams, Mary P. "Jefferson's Military Policy with Special Reference to the Frontier, 1805-1809." Ph.D. dissertation. Univ. of Virginia, 1958. pp. 331.

Throughout his administration TJ "labored unceasingly to place the United States in an adequate state of military preparedness." After the Chesapeake affair of 1807 he made extensive preparations for war, trying to buy time with the Embargo, and he sent secret agents to Canada. DAI 19/06, p. 1350.

1347.   Adams, Mary P. "Jefferson's Reaction to the Treaty of San Ildefonso." <u>Journal of Southern History.</u> 21(1955), 173-88.

Contends the files of the War Department from April 1801 through mid 1803 "reveal a clear and positive Louisiana policy," including military preparations on the Mississippi, projection of the Lewis and Clark expedition, and Indian and land policy measures.

1348.   Adler, Bill, comp. <u>Washington: A Reader. The National Capitol as Seen Through the Eyes of: Thomas Jefferson, ...</u> New York: Meredith, 1967. 37-39.

Trivial collection of comments by assorted Washingtonians.

1349.   Agar, Herbert. "A Century of Progress" in <u>Land of the Free.</u> Boston: Houghton Mifflin, 1935. 29-85.

Breezy analysis of the failure to build a Jeffersonian, i.e. egalitarian, state upon a Hamiltonian system of finance.

1350.   Agar, Herbert. "John Adams and Jefferson" in <u>The People's Choice From Washington to Harding: A Study in Democracy.</u> Boston: Houghton Mifflin, 1933. 32-71.

Adams and TJ were part of the oligarchic class, "A little group of privileged and public-spirited men" which occupied the presidency during the first fifty years of the nation's existence. The election of 1800 was no revolution; "In fact, there was no important change."

1351.   Agar, Herbert. <u>Pursuit of Happiness: The Story of American Democracy.</u> Boston: Houghton Mifflin, 1938. pp. 387.

First 3 chapters (1-103) on TJ and his development of democratic principles and on the beginning of the Democratic party during his presidency.

1352. Alvord, Clarence Walworth. "Thomas Jefferson versus Alexander Hamilton." Landmark. 8(1926), 194-96.

Review essay on Bower's Jefferson and Hamilton.

1353. "Americana Page." Hobbies. 57(April 1952), 100.

Editorial praising TJ for removing "the fanatical nonsense from self-government.

1354. Ammon, Harry. "The Formation of the Republican Party in Virginia, 1789-1796." Journal of Southern History. 19(1953), 283-310.

Touches upon TJ's important but inconspicuous role in forming the Republican Party; claims Republicans attracted both anti-federalists and supporters of the Constitution.

1355. Ammon, Harry. "The Genet Mission and the Development of American Political Parties." Journal of American History. 52(1966), 725-41.

TJ at the time of the Genet affair was "far less deeply engaged than Hamilton in the direction of party policy. ...Madison, as in the previous years, was still the major figure in shaping party programs."

1356. Ammon, Harry. "James Monroe and the Election of 1808 in Virginia." WMQ. 3rd ser. 20(1963), 33-56.

Discusses cooling of relations between TJ and Monroe which led to the younger man's becoming the "Old Republican" presidential candidate.

1357. Anderson, Dice R. "Jefferson and the Virginia Constitution." AHR. 21(1915), 750-54.

TJ's 1776 draft of a constitution was "democratic and farseeing," probably too much so for the convention.

1358. Anderson, Frank Maloy. "Contemporary Opinion of the Kentucky and Virginia Resolutions." AHR. 5(1899-1900), 45-63, 225-52.

Examines responses to the Resolutions by state legislatures and in the press; responses were in terms of party division, and neither side perceived the constitutional implications. TJ and Madison are scarcely mentioned.

1359. Anderson, John R. "A Twentieth-Century Reflection of the American Enlightenment." Social Education. 29(1965), 159-63.

Inconclusive discussion of TJ and the school prayer issue.

1360.   Anderson, Philip J. "William Linn, 1752-1808: American Revolutionary and Anti-Jeffersonian." Journal of Presbyterian History. 55(1977), 381-94.

Portrait of a member of the black regiment, author of Serious Considerations on the Election of a President (1800).

1361.   Andrews, Robert Hardy. "How the CIA Was Born." Mankind. 5(no. 4, 1975), 14-15, 68.

Claims TJ sent John Ledyard off on the first peace-time intelligence gathering mission.

1362.   Andrews, Robert Hardy. "Mr. Jefferson's Two Declarations." Mankind. 5(June 1976), 51-53.

TJ's "first" Declaration attacked slavery before Congress dropped key phrases. Minor.

1363.   Andrews, Robert Hardy. "A President Is Not a King." Mankind. 4(February 1974), 8, 16-17, 66.

On the Burr trial and Marshall's subpoena of TJ; see reply and rejoinder in the June issue, pp. 8-9, 44-47.

1364.   Andrews, Stuart. "Thomas Jefferson and the French Revolution." History Today. 18(1968), 299-306.

Good account for a general audience, claims TJ's support of the Revolution through so many vicissitudes illustrates his faith in Enlightenment ideals and perhaps should encourage us to think more kindly of the Committee of Public Safety.

1365.   Angle, Paul M. "Jefferson Outlines a Better Democracy" in By These Words; Great Documents of American Liberty Selected and Placed in Their Contemporary Settings. New York: Rand McNally, 1954. 152-59.

Brief description of the first inaugural and the address.

1366.   Appleby, Joyce. "The Jefferson-Adams Rupture and the First French Translation of John Adams' Defence." AHR. 73(1967), 1084-91.

Excellent account of TJ's role in arranging, and failing to arrange, a French translation of Adams' Defence of the Constitutions, and of his initial enthusiasm and later criticism.

1367. Arieli, Yehoshua. "Free Society—The Formulation of the Jeffersonian Social Ideal" and "The Jeffersonian Ideal—Social and Political Democracy" in Individualism and Nationalism in American Ideology. Cambridge: Harvard Univ. Press, 1964. 123-80.

Contends TJ believed it was the function of the state to safeguard a social order that was inherently free and natural.

1368. "Arnold's Invasion, 1781. Jefferson's Official Conduct." WMQ. 2nd ser. 6(1920), 131-32.

Prints without comment affidavits by Daniel Hylton and James Currie testifying to TJ's diligence in safeguarding the military stores in Richmond.

1369. Aronson, Julian. "The Impulse of Equality in Jefferson's Virginia." Social Studies. 44(1953), 123-28.

Argues that TJ was supported by Virginia land owners in spite of and not because of his egalitarian ideas.

1370. Aronson, Sidney Herbert. "Status and Kinship in the Higher Civil Service: The Administrations of John Adams, Thomas Jefferson, and Andrew Jackson." Ph.D. dissertation. Columbia Univ., 1961. pp. 942.

TJ's higher appointive officials were somewhat more representative of American society than Adams's but less so than Jackson's. Examines social backgrounds of appointees in all 3 administrations. DAI 23/09, p. 3532.

1371. Aronson, Sidney H. Status and Kinship in the Higher Civil Service: Standards of Selection in the Administrations of John Adams, Thomas Jefferson, and Andrew Jackson. Cambridge: Harvard Univ. Press, 1964. pp. xiii, 274.

Version of the dissertation; analysis of the social origins of presidential appointees in three administrations, based on elaborate research into individuals and quantification of the results.

1372. Ashley, Maurice. "Thomas Jefferson" in Mr. President: An Introduction to American History. London: Jonathan Cape, 1948. 105-65.

TJ "did much to develop the presidential office into a major factor in American political affairs."

1373. Atkinson, George W. "Jefferson as a Tactician" in The Writings of Thomas Jefferson, ed. Lipscomb and Bergh. Washington: Thomas Jefferson Memorial Association, 1903. 6:i-xx.

Praises TJ's ability to move men.

1374.	Atwell, Priscilla Ann. "Freedom and Diversity: Continuity in the Political Tradition of Thomas Jefferson and John C. Calhoun." Ph.D. dissertation. Univ. of California, Los Angeles, 1967. pp. 332.

TJ and Calhoun had in common a "corporate conception of community and institutional approach to social problems; their efforts as statesmen to act for the good of the whole community; their attitude that party contests should be a contest of principle, not a struggle for power; and above all in the idea that political freedom in a republic characterized by diversity is conditional on specific circumstances and the habits, opinions, and prejudices of the citizens." DAI 28/11A, p. 4563.

1375.	Auguste, Yves. "Jefferson et Haiti." Revue d'Histoire Diplomatique. 86(1973), 333-48.

Traces the evolution of TJ's ideas about Haiti as he began to use it as a diplomatic playing card.

1376.	Bailey, Thomas A. "Federalism and the Birth of Parties" and "Jefferson and the Democratic-Republicans" in Democrats vs. Republicans: The Continuing Clash. New York: Meredith Press, 1968. 3-45.

Development of the Democratic Party portrayed as a result of conflict with the Federalists; argues for a "Janus-faced Jefferson."

1377.	Baldwin, Joseph G. Party Leaders: Sketches of Thomas Jefferson, Alex'r Hamilton, Andrew Jackson, Henry Clay, John Randolph of Roanoke. New York: Appleton, 1855. 17-134.

TJ contrasted with Hamilton: "He was more artificial as well as more original than Hamilton. ... a thorough-going party man ... the whole tone of his mind was partisan." Baldwin's hero is Clay.

1378.	Banning, Lance. The Jeffersonian Persuasion: Evolution of a Party Ideology. Ithaca: Cornell Univ. Press, 1978. pp. 307.

Focus on Jeffersonians rather than on TJ; contends that ideology of the Revolution shaped the thinking of the Republican party in the early national years.

1379.	Barrett, Jay A. "The Law of 1784; Jefferson's Draft" in Evolution of the Ordinance of 1787, With An Account of the Earlier Plans for the Government of the Northwest Territory. New York: Putnam's, 1891. 17-23.

Described TJ's 1784 committee report on a form of temporary government for the Northwest Territory.

1380. Barton, George. "When in the Course ..." Christian Science Monitor Magazine. July 1, 1936. 3, 14.

On the rough draft of the Declaration and TJ's authorship.

*1381. Bates, George Williams. The Establishment of American Independence as Related to the Louisiana Purchase, With a Review of the Historical Work of the National Society, Sons of the American Revolution. n.p., 1905? pp. 20.

1382. Bayard, James A. Remarks in the Senate of the United States, January 31, 1855, Vindicating the Late James A. Bayard, of Delaware, and Refuting the Groundless Charges contained in the "Anas" of Thomas Jefferson, Aspersing His Character. Washington: 1855. pp. 14.

Rpt. Wilmington, Del.: Thomas F. Bayard, 1907. pp. 38. In the Anas TJ claimed Bayard tried to bribe Samuel Smith to vote for Burr for president in 1800, or so Edward Livingston told him.

1383. Bayard, Richard H. Documents Relating to the Presidential Election in the Year 1801: Containing a Refutation of Two Passages in the Writings of Thomas Jefferson, Aspersing the Character of the Late James A. Bayard of Delaware. Philadelphia: Mifflin & Parry, 1831. pp. 14.

1384. Bean, W. G. "Anti-Jeffersonianism in the Ante-Bellum South." North Carolina Historical Review. 12(April 1935), 103-24.

Maps the Democratic Party's repudiation of the radical, democratic ideas of TJ, chiefly in terms of speeches in Congress. Sees slavery as the key issue.

1385. Beard, Charles A. Economic Origins of Jeffersonian Democracy. New York: Macmillan, 1915. pp. ix, 474.

A classic study. Final chapter focuses on "Jefferson's Economics and Politics" (415-67), and claims that TJ recognized the antagonism between capitalistic and agrarian interests and made the latter the peculiar concern of the Republican party. He claimed the Constitution as a Republican document, favored judicial control of legislation (until crossed by John Marshall), and came to espouse a wide suffrage free of property qualifications.

1386. Beard, Charles A. Jefferson, Corporations and the Constitution. Washington: National Home Library Foundation, 1936. pp. 93.

The Beard thesis popularized and applied to the development of corporations. TJ opposed to "monopolies," i.e. corporations, and thus he should not be co-opted by conservative politicians of 1936. TJ believed in strict construction, among other reasons, because of fears of the U. S. Bank's potential ability to drain the earnings of agriculture.

167

1387. Beard, Charles A. "Some Economic Origins of Jeffersonian Democracy." <u>AHR.</u> 19(1913), 282-98.

Members of Congress in 1790 voting on funding securities to assume state debts "represented the dominant interest of their respective constituencies rather than their personal interests" as TJ later charged in the Anas.

*1388. Beatty, James Paul. "Thomas Jefferson and Slavery." M.A. thesis. North Texas State Univ., 1973. pp. 141.

1389. Beckman, Gail M. "Three Penal Codes Compared." <u>American Journal of Legal History.</u> 10(1976), 148-73.

Compares TJ's code of 1776 for Virginia, Edward Livingston's for Louisiana, and David Dudley Field's for New York. Claims that TJ's was an expression of the Enlightenment and made way for penal code reforms in other states.

1390. Bell, Whitfield J., Jr. <u>The Declaration of Independence, Four 1776 Versions: Jefferson's Manuscript Copy, The First Official Printing by John Dunlap, The First Newspaper Printing, A Unique Printing on Parchment by John Dunlap.</u> Philadelphia: American Philosophical Society, 1976. pp. (24).

Historical introduction and notes.

1391. Bellamy, Francis. <u>Presidents of the United States in the Century, From Jefferson to Fillmore.</u> Philadelphia: Linscott, 1905. 17-108.

A volume in "The Nineteenth Century Series." Brief but perceptive account of TJ's administration tends to be critical of his inability to assess correctly practical problems of government.

1392. Belmont, Perry. <u>Survival of the Democratic Principle Including the Tariff Issue.</u> New York: Putnam's, 1926. pp. vi, 334.

Rambling, discursive account of the way in which TJ has been mis-read and underrated by subsequent political historians, often for partisan reasons, but also by thoughtlessly accepting the authority of Henry Adams.

1393. Bemis, Samuel Flagg. "Thomas Jefferson" in <u>The American Secretaries of State and Their Diplomacy.</u> New York: Knopf, 1927. 3-93.

TJ was the best man of his time to guide the diplomacy of his country, even though his handling of affairs was hampered by his rivalry with Hamilton and by Hamilton's actions.

1394. Berger, Raoul. "The President, Congress, and the Courts." Yale Law Review. 83(1974), 111-55.

Examines TJ's subpoena by Marshall in the Burr case and contends Marshall never recognized a principle of "executive privilege" exempting presidents from the force of law; goes on to examine the relevance of this for the Nixon-Watergate case. Shorter version published as "Jefferson v. Marshall in the Burr Case." American Bar Association Journal. 69(1974), 702-06.

1395. Berkhofer, Robert F., Jr. "Jefferson, the Ordinance of 1784, and the Origins of the American Territorial System." WMQ. 3rd ser. 29(1972), 231-62.

Argues that the Ordinance of 1784 is not so strictly in accord with TJ's views as has been previously assumed, nor is the Northwest Ordinance so divergent from his opinions on new territories or from the Ordinance of 1784 itself.

1396. Beveridge, Albert J. "Sources of the Declaration of Independence." PMHB. 50(1926), 289-315.

"All the ideas and much of the language" came from the Virginia Bill of Rights, but TJ gave final expression to "the general American thought and feeling."

1397. Bias, Randolph. "Jefferson and Hamilton." West Virginia Law Quarterly. 33(December 1926), 1-28.

Address to the State Bar Association; two giants.

1398. Binder, Frederick Melvin. "The Color Problem in Early National America as Viewed by John Adams, Jefferson and Jackson." Ph.D. dissertation. Columbia Univ., 1962. pp. 259.

TJ wished to lighten the burden of the negro slave and the Indian, but he was "governed by a desire to assure national unity ..." and he attempted to discourage the entry of slavery into national deliberation. DAI 24/05, p. 1987.

1399. Binder, Frederick M. The Color Problem in Early National America as Viewed by John Adams, Jefferson, and Jackson. The Hague: Mouton, 1968. pp. 177.

Slightly revised version of the 1962 dissertation.

1400. Blair, Albert L. "Was Jefferson a Democrat?" Arena. 21(1899), 633-45.

"He was far more the father of the second republican party than of the democracy.

169

*1401. Black, Chauncey F. A Contrast. Jefferson and Hamilton, Democracy and Federalism. 1800-1881. The Same Parties and the Same Principles. A Plain Question. Shall the People Rule or Shall They Be Ruled? York, Pa.: O. Stuck. (1880?). pp. 13.

1402. Black, Chauncey F. "1800-1900, Jefferson and Bryan." The Jeffersonian Democrat. 2(1899), 489-500.

"Where Jefferson stood then, William Jennings Bryan stands now." Draws parallels.

1403. Blanken, Maurice C. "Thomas Jefferson, Imperialist." Social Studies. 53(1962), 140-42.

TJ made possible the dream of manifest destiny; minor.

1404. Boardman, Fon W., Jr. America and the Virginia Dynasty, 1800-1825. New York: Henry Z. Walck, 1974. pp. 218.

Sketchy coverage of TJ as president, pp. 1-32.

1405. Bonger, Hendrik. Leraar der Mensenrechten: Thomas Jefferson. Arnhem: Van Loghum Slaterus, 1951. pp. 73.

On his work for civil rights with focus on years 1775-76.

1406. Boorstin, Daniel J. "The American Revolution: Revolution Without Dogma" in The Genius of American Politics. Chicago: Univ. of Chicago Press, 1953. 66-98.

Discusses the implications of the Declaration, arguing, "The awareness of the peculiarity of America had not yet by any means led Jefferson to a rash desire to remake all society and institutions."

1407. Borden, Morton. "A Neo-Federalist View of the Jeffersonians." Reviews in American History. 5(1977), 196-202.

Review essay taking to task Forrest McDonald's Presidency of Thomas Jefferson.

1408. Borden, Morton. "Thomas Jefferson" in America's Ten Greatest Presidents, ed. Borden. Chicago: Rand McNally, 1961. 57-80.

TJ's administration was "compounded of three ingredients—liberalism, nationalism, and a healthy dose of common sense." Emphasizes TJ's pragmatic approach, but on debatable strategies like the embargo simply weighs up the pros and cons.

1409. Bourgin, Frank P. and Charles E. Merriam. "Jefferson as a Planner of National Resources." Ethics. 53(1943), 284-92.

"Jefferson not only set forth the ends but also planned constructively the means of attaining liberty, equality, the pursuit of happiness, and the consent of the governed." He took at various times an interest in land planning, education, transportation, industrial enterprise, and planning for the general welfare.

1410. Bowers, Claude G. "Architect of the All-American System." VQR. 19(1943), 178-88.

TJ's Summary View justified the revolutionary movements of South America and led up to the Monroe Doctrine; discusses connections with South American revolutions.

1411. Bowers, Claude G. "Jefferson and Civil Liberties." Atlantic Monthly. 191(January 1953), 52-58.

Claims that the Kentucky and Virginia Resolutions and the election of TJ in 1800 forestalled "the most powerful attempt in our history to destroy the elemental freedoms."

1412. Bowers, Claude G. Jefferson and Hamilton; The Struggle for Democracy in America. Boston: Houghton Mifflin, 1925. pp. xvii, 531.

The first installment of this influential biography of TJ, this volume focuses on the years from 1789 to 1801 and on the political events and life of these years.

1413. Bowers, Claude G. "Jefferson and the Bill of Rights." Virginia Law Review. 41(1955), 709-29.

TJ's demand for a bill of rights was justified by the threats to civil liberty periodically generated by demagogues and sensationalists.

1414. Bowers, Claude G. Jefferson in Power; The Death Struggle of the Federalists. Boston: Houghton Mifflin, 1936. pp. xix, 538.

TJ's presidency which "marked the consolidation of the triumph of democracy."

1415. Bowers, Claude G. "Jefferson, Master Policitian." VQR. 2(1926), 321-33.

TJ was a master politican in the service of democracy because of his "soul." Impressionistic.

1416. Bowers, Claude G. Making Democracy a Reality, Jefferson, Jackson, and Polk. Memphis: Memphis State College Press, 1954. 1-39.

TJ chapter is a sentimental and imprecise paean to him as a defender of democratic freedom.

1417. Bowers, Claude G. "Thomas Jefferson and South America." Bulletin of the Pan American Union. 77(1943), 183-91.

Discusses TJ's South American connections: the Brazilian revolutionaries he met in Nimes, Francisco Miranda, etc., and his support of inter-American solidarity.

*1418. Bowers, Claude G. "Thomas Jefferson and the Courts." Proceedings of the North Carolina Bar Association. 29(1927), 26-45.

1419. Bowling, Kenneth R. "Dinner at Jefferson's: A Note on Jacob E. Cooke's 'The Compromise of 1790'." WMQ. 3rd ser. 28(1971), 629-48.

Rejects Cooke's argument (see below, #1501) that there was no real connection between the federal assumption of state debts and the decision to put the capital on the Potomac. Rejoinder by Cooke.

1420. Bowman, Albert H. "Jefferson, Hamilton, and American Foreign Policy." Political Science Quarterly. 71(1956), 18-41.

Argues that TJ and not Hamilton was the realist in foreign policy; TJ understood the national interest, but "Hamilton's foreign policy was based constantly upon what he wanted the United States to become, not upon what it was or was likely to be." The Nootka Sound crisis revealed the distance between their policies; the Jay Treaty "made war inevitable."

1421. Boyd, Julian P. "The Chasm That Separated Thomas Jefferson and John Marshall" in Essays on the American Constitution: A Commemorative Volume in Honor of Alpheus T. Mason, ed. Gottfried Dietze. Englewood Cliffs, N.J.: Prentice-Hall, 1964. 3-20.

Suggestive study of the "inexplorable protagonists of two opposed views of society." If neither was suited for the other's position, TJ ultimately is the more significant figure because of his relativism which enabled him to respect the role of an independent judiciary in spite of his temptations to curb it.

1422. Boyd, Julian P. The Declaration of Independence: The Evolution of the Text as Shown in Facsimiles of Various Drafts by Its Author, THOMAS JEFFERSON. Princeton: Princeton Univ. Press, 1945. pp. 46.

Analyzes facsimiles of all known drafts. Useful.

1423. Boyd, Julian P. "The Declaration of Independence—The Mystery of the Lost Original." PMHB. 100(1976), 438-67.

Conjectural account of the now missing draft of the Declaration as approved by Congress. The Historical Society of Pennsylvania has a

unique proof copy of the first half of the Declaration as printed by
John Dunlap.

1424.   Boyd, Julian P. "The Disputed Authorship of the Declaration on the
        Causes and Necessity of Taking up Arms, 1775." PMHB. 74(1950),
        51-73.

        The text finally adopted by Congress was the result of collaboration
        upon the part of TJ and John Dickinson, "however unwilling each was
        to accept the work of the other."

1425.   Boyd, Julian P. "Jefferson's Expression of the American Mind." VQR.
        50(1974), 538-62.

        Examines the conditions surrounding TJ's writing of A Summary View;
        discusses relationship of this to his Declaration of Rights for the
        Albemarle freeholders, and suggests the Survey may in its earliest
        form have been intended for delivery by Patrick Henry.

1426.   Boyd, Julian P. "New Light on Jefferson and His Great Task." New
        York Times Magazine. April 13, 1947. 17, 64-70.

        On the discovery of a mss. fragment of the Declaration, in TJ's hand.

1427.   Boyd, Julian P. "Two Diplomats Between Revolutions: John Jay and
        Thomas Jefferson." VMHB. 66(1958), 133-46.

        TJ's diplomatic skill played an important role in gaining an accept-
        able consular convention with France, despite Jay's opposition.

1428.   Bradford, Alden. History of the Federal Government for Fifty Years:
        From March 1789 to March 1839. Boston: Samuel G. Simpkins, 1840.
        119-68.

        A federalist view of TJ's presidency, charging that ultimately "his
        political opinions and conduct served to lessen, in some measure, the
        stability and permanency of the republic; by emboldening visionary
        and unprincipled men, many of whom were aliens, and who could
        vociferate most loudly for liberty, but had not a due respect for law
        or the Constitution."

1429.   Bradley, Jared W. "William C. C. Claiborne, the Old Southwest and the
        Development of American Indian Policy." Tennessee Historical
        Quarterly. 33(1974), 265-78.

        "... before Jefferson became President in 1801, the basic principles of
        his administration's Indian policy had been pre-determined for him by
        the 1796 Indian trade and intercourse act, and by Representative
        William C. C. Claiborne of Tennessee."

173

1430. Bradley, Jared W. "W.C.C. Claiborne and Spain: Foreign Affairs Under Jefferson and Madison." Louisiana History. 12(1971), 297-314; 13(1972), 5-28.

Claiborne's recommendations were far more bellicose than TJ's responses.

1431. Brant, Irving. "James Madison and His Time." AHR. 57(1952), 853-70.

Argues that Madison was not a mere satellite of TJ as suggested by Henry Adams and others; Madison in many cases led TJ in policy making, for example in pointing out to him the political implications of the French loss of Haiti, a base of support needed if the French were to retain Louisiana.

1432. Brant, Irving. "Two of a Size." Magazine of Albemarle County History. 16(1958), 5-17.

Good sketch of the Madison-TJ relationship, arguing for Madison as an independent thinker equal to TJ.

1433. Brent, Robert A. "The Triumph of Jacksonian Democracy in the United States." Southern Quarterly. 7(1968), 43-57.

American voters have accepted Jackson's version of democracy and rejected TJ's, partly because TJ preserves strong aristocratic tendencies.

1434. Brewer, Paul W. "Jefferson's Administration of Patronage: New York, 1801-1804." M.A. thesis. Univ. of Virginia, 1968. pp. 76.

There were only a small number of appointments made in New York, but they were moderately successful in the long run in helping to build a base for the Republican party.

1435. Briceland, Alan V. "The Philadelphia Aurora, The New England Illuminati, and the Election of 1800." PMHB. 100(1976), 3-36.

John C. Ogden wrote for Duane's Aurora a series of attacks upon New England Federalists, hurling the charges of illuminatism back upon them. Peripherally about TJ.

1436. Brisbane, Robert H., Jr. "Interposition: Theory and Practice." Phylon. 17(1956), 12-16.

TJ set forward the doctrine of interposition in its classic form in the Kentucky Resolutions.

1437. Bromfield, Louis. "Thomas Jefferson vs. Karl Marx" in A Few Brass Tacks. New York: Harper, 1946. 171-22.

174

Because of spoliation of the land and poor government planning TJ's dream of an independent citizenry is threatened by the specter of Marx's proletariat.

1438. Bronowski, Jacob and Bruce Mazlish. "Thomas Jefferson and the American Revolution" in The Western Intellectual Tradition from Leonardo to Hegel. New York: Harper, 1960. 373-91.

Sympathetic but only vaguely accurate sketch of TJ as a revolutionary politician.

1439. Broun, Heywood. "Shades of Thomas Jefferson." New Republic. 95(1938), 305.

It is less preposterous for Earl Browder and the Communist Party to claim TJ as comrade than it is for the extreme right to claim him as one of their own.

1440. Browder, Earl. "Jefferson and the People's Revolution" in The Heritage of Jefferson. New York: International Publishers, 1944. 30-39.

"Jefferson was no Communist, but the Communist Party can claim his as one of its principal precursors."

*1441. Brown, Edward A. "An Investigation of the Attitudes Expressed by Richmond's Press toward Thomas Jefferson in the Presidential Elections of 1800, 1804, and 1808." M.A. thesis. Univ. of Richmond, 1964.

1442. Brown, Everett Somerville. The Constitutional History of the Louisiana Purchase 1803-1812. Berkeley: Univ. of California Press, 1920. pp. xi, 248.

Detailed account of the constitutional issues raised by the Louisiana Purchase and the deliberations by TJ and Congress over them.

1443. Brown, Everett Somerville. "Intimate Sketches of Jefferson's Day." Michigan Alumnus Quarterly Review. 41(1935), 299-306.

Rpt. in The Territorial Delegate to Congress and Other Essays. Ann Arbor: G. Wahr, 1950. Anecdotes from William Plumer's diary, including dining at the White House with TJ.

1444. Brown, Everett S. "Jefferson's Manual of Parliamentary Practice." Michigan Alumnus Quarterly Review. 49(1943), 144-48.

Discusses TJ's preparation of his manual of parliamentary usage done for the U.S. Senate.

1445. Brown, Everett. S. "Jefferson's Plans for a Military Colony in Orleans Territory." MVHR. 8(1921), 373-76.

175

TJ proposed granting land in Orleans territory to recipients willing to perform military service if needed.

1446.   Brown, Robert E. and Katherine Brown. "The Revolution as a Social Movement" in Virginia 1705-1786: Democracy or Aristocracy? East Lansing: Michigan State Univ. Press, 1964. 284-306.

Argues that there was little if any internal revolution in Virginia and that TJ himself was not very radical; discusses legislative action on entail, primogeniture, franchise, education, and religion to show that only in the last two areas was TJ in advance of his peers.

1447.   Browne, Waldo R. "Backward Glance in History." Nation. 165(1947), 256-57.

TJ's resistance to the anti-French war hysteria of 1798 is worth thinking about for Americans in 1947.

1448.   Bruce, H. A. "Thomas Jefferson and the Louisiana Purchase." The Outlook. 88(1908), 433-46.

TJ was "the first of the long line of notable American expansionists."

1449.   Bruchey, Stuart. "Federal Government and Community Will" in The Roots of American Economic Growth, 1607-1861: An Essay in Social Causation. New York: Harper and Row, 1965. 113-22.

Examines the economic policies of TJ and Hamilton and minimizes their practical differences.

1450.   Bruckberger, R. L. Image of America. New York: Viking, 1959. 57-121.

Translation of La Republique Américaine. Paris: Gallimard, 1958. Discusses TJ's role in creating the American republic, comparing him to Saint-Just and seeing him as a revolutionary who recognized "the concrete dimension of time." Claims the Declaration is "totally devoid of ideological fanaticism, empty abstractions, all excess." Hamilton's economic system laid a solid foundation for national unity which TJ could not reject, yet his warnings about the Hamiltonian system remind us of the threat "a vast and complex machinery of industry" poses to individual liberty.

1451.   Buckley, Thomas E. Church and State in Revolutionary Virginia, 1776-1787. Charlottesville: Univ. Press of Virginia, 1977. pp. xiv, 217.

TJ discussed passim; covers the controversy over religion which culminated in 1786 with the passage of TJ's Bill for Establishing Religious Freedom.

176

1452. Bühler, Franz. Verwassungsrevision und Generationenproblem: Studie sur Verwassungsrevisionstheorie Thomas Jefferson. Arbeiten Aus dem Iuristischen Seminar der Universität Frieburg. Freiburg: Universitätsbuchhandlung, 1949. pp. xiii, 105.

Study of TJ's belief in the right of each generation to write its own laws.

1453. Burger, Warren E. "The Doctrine of Judicial Review: Mr. Marshall, Mr. Jefferson, and Mr. Marbury" in The Constitution and Chief Justice Marshall, William F. Swindler. New York: Dodd Mead, 1978. 383-94.

Explains Marbury vs. Madison and how it established the principle of judicial review.

*1454. Burke, Edmund J. Thomas Jefferson, Apostle of Freedom and Equality of Opportunity; the Solution of Our Economic and Social Ills. Cambridge, Mass.: Jefferson Club of Cambridge, 1934. pp. 14.

1455. Burns, James McGregor. "Jefferson and the Strategy of Parties" in The Deadlock of Democracy: Four-Party Politics in America. Englewood Cliffs, N.J.: Prentice-Hall, 1963. 24-46.

Argues that TJ was responsible for overturning the Madisonian model of the Constitution by leading the development of a strategy of majority rule through parties. An important statement.

1456. Burr, William Henry. "The Authorship of the Declaration of Independence" in Thomas Paine: Was He Junius? San Francisco: Freethought Publishing Co., 1890. 17-26.

Not only was Paine Junius, he also wrote the Declaration, or so it says here.

1457. Burr, William Henry. The Declaration of Independence A Masterpiece; But How It Got Mutilated (Washington? 1881?). pp. 11.

Argues for Tom Paine as the author of the Declaration.

1458. Busey, Samuel Clagett. "The Centennial of the First Inauguration of a President at the Permanent Seat of the Government." Records of the Columbia Historical Society. 5(1902), 96-111.

Description of TJ's first inauguration, arguing against the legend that he rode rather than walked to the ceremony.

1459. Butler, Nicholas Murray. "Spokesman of the Democratic Spirit: Thomas Jefferson" in Building the American Nation, An Essay in Reinterpretation. New York: Scribner's, 1923. 133-68.

177

Praises TJ for his principles and commitment to civil and political liberty, yet is deeply suspicious of those who supported him and whom he supported: "hack libellers, ... half-rebellious democratic societies made up chiefly of the mobs of the large cities, ... moonshiners of the mountains." Because of this and similar contradictions, "Perhaps no great writer on politics ... needs to have his sayings and acts analysed more carefully than does Jefferson."

1460. Butterfield, Lyman H. "Elder John Leland, Jeffersonian Itinerant." Proceedings of the American Antiquarian Society. 62(1952), 155-242.

Includes facsimile of "Ode to the Mammoth Cheese,..." Focus on Leland but discusses his support of TJ and relations with him.

1461. Butterfield, Lyman H. "Psychological Warfare in 1776: The Jefferson-Franklin Plan to Cause Hessian Desertions." Proceedings of the APS. 94(1950), 233-41.

The plan of preparing handbills encouraging Hessian officers and men to desert was not particularly successful because they did not reach the Germans in any quantity.

1462. Butts, R. Freeman. "The Struggle for Separation in Virginia" in The American Tradition in Religion and Education." Boston: Beacon, 1950. 45-67.

Presents TJ as thoroughgoing supporter of separation in church and state; nothing new.

1463. Cahn, Edmond. "Brief for the Supreme Court." New York Times Magazine. October 7, 1956. 9, 64-70.

Claims judicial review is not at odds with TJ's principles; see reply by Arthur Krock, October 28, 1956. p. 6.

1464. Cahn, Edmond. "The Doubter and the Bill of Rights." New York University Law Review. 33(1958), 903-16.

Contends against Henry Steele Commager that TJ believed in judicial as opposed to extra-judicial enforcement of the Bill of Rights.

1465. Cahn, Edmond. "The 'Establishment of Religion' Puzzle." New York University Law Review. 36(1961), 1274-97.

Explains Supreme Court inconsistency on church-state cases by contending the Justices have 2 different understandings of religion, a Jeffersonian-Enlightenment view and a Madisonian-dissenter view.

1466. Caldwell, Lynton K. The Administrative Theories of Hamilton and Jefferson: Their Contribution to Thought on Public Administration.

Chicago: Univ. of Chicago Press, 1944. pp. ix, 244.

TJ because of his overriding concern for individual liberty customarily thought of organization from the bottom up. He attempted to control the exercise of power in space by decentralization and to control it in time by regular rotation in office. "Hamilton is our great teacher of the organization and administration of public power; Jefferson, our chief expositor of its control."

1467. Caldwell, Lynton Keith. "Contributions to Thought on Public Administration: Hamilton and Jefferson." Ph.D. dissertation. Univ. of Chicago, 1943. pp. 466.

Published as item # 1466.

1468. Caplin, Mortimer. A Debt of Service. Charlottesville: Thomas Jefferson Memorial Foundation, 1975. pp. 14.

Founder's Day Address, Univ. of Virginia. Theme is TJ's remark in a letter to Edward Rutledge, "There is a debt of service due from every man to his country ..."

1469. Cappon, Lester J. "Men of Albemarle and the Louisiana Purchase." Magazine of Albemarle County History. 13(1953), 1-22.

Examines the parts played by TJ, Monroe, and Meriwether Lewis, all Albemarle men. Praises TJ's "forehanded ... timely" plans for exploration of the new territory.

1470. Cardwell, Guy A. "Jefferson Renounced: Natural Rights in the Old South." Yale Review. 58(1969), 388-407.

Argues that TJ's reputation in the South changed as Southerners were forced by abolitionism to reject natural law theory and its most famous advocate. Well researched but unannotated.

*1471. Carey, Paul Moseley. "Jefferson and Slavery." M.A. thesis. Univ. of Virginia, 1952. pp. iv, 132.

1472. Carlyle, Richard. The Earth Belongs to the Living. Los Angeles: Suttonhouse, Ltd., 1936. pp. 57.

A letter from the ghost of TJ with advice on the political and social issues of 1936. Author draws from TJ's writings to form a pastiche.

1473. Carneiro, David da Silva. "The Story of Jefferson and Maia." Brazil. 20(January 1946), 8ff.

TJ responded cautiously to Jose Joaquim de Maia's request for U.S. support of a Brazilian revolution for fear of antagonizing the Portuguese.

1474. Carr, James A. "John Adams and the Barbary Problem: The Myth and the Record." American Neptune. 26(1966), 231–57.

Contends the opinion that Adams wavered on action against the Barbary pirates and TJ took a firm hand is erroneous. Good account of controversies involving TJ and Adams on support and deployment of the Navy.

1475. Carter, Henry. "Why Not Jefferson?" Commonweal. 19(1934), 595–96.

The U.S. should return to TJ's policy of automatically recognizing whatever government comes to power in a foreign country, regardless of its security of tenure.

*1476. Case, Lyman W. "'A Hater of Shams' Discourses about the Declaration of Independence." Truth Seeker. 8(1881), 322–23.

1477. Cassell, Frank A. "General Samuel Smith and the Election of 1800." Maryland Historical Magazine. 63(1968), 341–59.

Smith was instrumental in breaking the electoral deadlock in February, 1801. "The evidence indicates Jefferson did not make a political bargain with (James A.) Bayard to secure his own election." Smith, however, seems to have suggested to Bayard that he was relaying Jefferson's assurances about Federalist office-holders.

1478. Catton, Bruce. "The Moment of Decision." American Heritage. 15(August 1964), 49–53.

5 presidential decisions; TJ's was to purchase Louisiana. Minor.

1479. Chambers, William Nisbet. Political Parties in a New Nation: The American Experience, 1776–1809. New York: Oxford Univ. Press, 1963. pp. 231.

TJ discussed throughout, particularly as president and party leader on pp. 170–90. TJ was able to consolidate the Republican's power in his first term, but infighting in his second term foreshadowed the difficulties his successors would meet.

1480. Channing, Edward. The Jeffersonian System, 1801-1811. New York: Harper, 1906. pp. xii, 299.

A history of TJ's administration strongly influenced by Henry Adams' history of the same period, but perhaps more federalist, more supercilious than Adams. Contends the War of 1812 discredited TJ's parsimonious defense spending, "philosophic" political weapons like the Embargo, and hostility to Britain.

1481. Channing, Edward. "Kentucky Resolutions of 1798." AHR. 20(1914), 333-36.

On the question of authorship; TJ the author and not John Breckinridge.

1482. Charles, Joseph. "Adams and Jefferson: The Origins of the American Party System." WMQ. 3rd. ser. 12(1955), 410-46.

"Jefferson did not create a party; a widespread popular movement recognized and claimed him as its leader."

1483. Charles, Joseph. "The Jay Treaty: The Origins of the American Party System." WMQ. 3rd ser. 12(1955), 581-630.

The Jay Treaty "altered party alignments and caused each group to close ranks."

1484. Charles, Joseph. The Origins of the American Party System: Three Essays. Williamsburg: Institute of Early American History and Culture, 1956. pp. vi, 147.

Essays originally appeared in WMQ, 12(1956), 217-67, and as in the two previous items (pp. 217-67 not relevant to TJ). Standard work.

1485. Charles, Joseph. "The Party Origins of Jeffersonian Democracy." Ph.D. dissertation. Harvard Univ., 1950. pp. 404.

Revised and published in part as The Origins of the American Party System (1956).

1486. Charlick, Carl. "Jefferson's NATO." Foreign Service Journal. 31(July 1954), 18-21, 58.

TJ attempted to organize European nations to engage with the U.S. in concerted action against the Barbary pirates.

1487. Chidsey, Donald Barr. Mr. Hamilton and Mr. Jefferson. Nashville: Thomas Nelson, 1975. pp. 207.

Popular, balanced account of the political struggles between the two men.

1488. Chuinard, E. G. "Thomas Jefferson and the Corps of Discovery: Creating the Lewis and Clark Expedition." American West. 12(November 1975), 4-13.

Points out six criticisms historians have directed towards TJ's role in the Lewis and Clark expedition, and concludes the only justifiable objection to his planning of the expedition concerns his failure to ensure that the Expedition journals were published immediately after the return.

1489. Clancy, Herbert J. The Democratic Party, Jefferson to Jackson. New York: Fordham Univ. Press, 1962. 3-97.

A somewhat superficial treatment of party organization and development.

*1490. Clark, J. Peyton. A View of the Services Rendered by Thomas Jefferson in the Cause of Civil Liberty; An Oration Delivered before the Jefferson Society of the University of Virginia .... Charlottesville: J. Alexander, 1850. pp. 20.

1491. Coe, Samuel Gwynn. The Mission of William Carmichael to Spain. Baltimore: Johns Hopkins Press, 1928. pp. vii, 116.

Carmichael was charge d'affaires in Spain while TJ was in Paris, and he continued there until 1794. Study based on correspondence between TJ and Carmichael but focus is on the latter.

1492. Cohn, David L. The Fabulous Democrats: A History of the Democratic Party in Text and Pictures. New York: Putnam's, 1956. pp. 192.

TJ discussed on pp. 9-27; popular.

1493. Cole, Charles C., Jr. "Brockden Brown and the Jefferson Administration." PMHB. 72(1948), 253-63.

Charles Brockden Brown, an admirer of TJ in the 1790's, became sharply critical of him and his administration, particularly in his pamphlet on the Embargo.

1494. Coles, Edward. History of the Ordinance of 1787. Philadelphia: Historical Society of Pennsylvania, 1856. pp. 33.

Argues that TJ's proposed plan of government for the Northwest Territory, made in 1784, was the model for the Ordinance of 1787. Coles was Monroe's private secretary and Governor of Illinois.

1495. Cometti, Elizabeth. "John Rutlege, Jr., Federalist." Journal of Southern History. 13(1947), 186-219.

Surveys Rutledge's career, concludes there is no evidence for his authorship of the Geffroy forgeries, but he may have been implicated in the publication of Callender's scurrilities.

1496. Commager, Henry Steele. Majority Rule and Minority Rights. New York: Oxford Univ. Press, 1943. pp. 92.

Contends that TJ because of his belief in man's right to govern himself opposed the principle of judicial review, but he also recognized the rights of minorities under "Nature's law" and judicial review is the only way to secure these.

1497. Conseil, L. P. "Essai sur les Memoires et la Correspondance de Jefferson, Consideres comme l'Expression la Plus Complete et la Plus Pure des Principes de l'Ecole Americaine" in Thomas Jefferson, Melanges Politiques et Philosophiques. Paris: Paulin, 1833. 1:1-126.

Argues that TJ as a model of republicanism applicable to French society; prefaces an abridged translation of T. J. Randolph's Memoirs, ... from the Papers of Thomas Jefferson.

1498. Conway, Moncure Daniel. "Randolph and Jefferson" in Omitted Chapters of History Disclosed in the Life and Papers of Edmund Randolph. New York: Putnam's, 1888. 187-210.

Discusses the relationship between Randolph, Washington's Attorney General, and TJ; finds that in 16 out of 19 "party divisions" in the Cabinet Randolph voted with TJ.

1499. Cook, Theodore Andrea. "The Original Intention of the 'Monroe Doctrine.' As Shown by the Correspondence of Monroe with Jefferson and Madison." Fortnightly Review. 70(1898), 357-68.

Claims that Monroe with the concurrence of TJ and Madison intended the Monroe Doctrine to set out a policy allying the U.S. and Britain as guarantors of South American independence against the Holy Alliance. "Into the Venezuelan question the Monroe Doctrine, as originally intended, never entered."

1500. Cooke, Jacob E. "The Collaboration of Tench Coxe and Thomas Jefferson. PMHB. 100(1976), 468-90.

Coxe, although a supporter of Hamilton's financial policies, was personally attracted to TJ and shared many of his ideas on commercial policy. He provided TJ with notes and data which were of material aid for the Report on Whale Fisheries and the Report on Commerce.

1501. Cooke, Jacob E. "The Compromise of 1790." WMQ. 3rd ser. 27(1970), 523–45.

Contends that the famous dinner table agreement among Hamilton, Madison, and TJ in June of 1790 had little real effect on the enactment of the compromise which provided for federal assumption of state debts and a national capital on the Potomac. However, see item # 1419.

1502. Cooke, John Esten. "The Virginia Declaration of Independence." Magazine of American History. 11(1884), 369–95.

Points out the similarity between TJ's Declaration and George Mason's Declaration of Rights.

1503. Cooke, William H. The Anniversary Address of the Jefferson Society of the University of Virginia, Delivered on the 13th of April, 1844. Charlottesville: James Alexander, 1844. pp. 20.

Notes the progress of liberty, praises TJ, and dreams of Western expansion and manifest destiny.

1504. Coon, Horace Campbell. "Intellectuals in the White House: Thomas Jefferson, Archetype of the Egghead in Politics" in Triumph of the Eggheads. New York: Random House, 1955. 24–46.

TJ demonstrated the usefulness of intelligence in democratic government, but "the intellectual leader in politics in those days was his own brains trust."

1505. Cooper, Joseph. "Jeffersonian Attitudes Toward Executive Leadership and Committee Development in the House of Representatives." Western Political Quarterly. 18(1965), 45–63.

TJ mentioned in passing as a typical "Jeffersonian"; describes the impact of Jeffersonian theory upon the House's assertion of independence from the Executive.

1506. Corbin, John. "From Jefferson to Wilson." North American Review. 210(1919), 172–85.

Claims that the "muddle-headed" president satirized by Washington Irving in The Knickerbocker History, who believed in hands-off government but tried forcibly to impose his intellectual fancies, is an earlier version of Wilson's espousal of the League of Nations.

184

1507. Corbin, John. "Toward the Revolution of 1800" and "Power Politics" in Two Frontiers of Freedom. New York: Scribner's, 1940. 193-220.

Claims that the contemporary crisis is reducible to the competing claims of liberty and social order under legal authority and the resolution lies in understanding the creation and development of the U.S. and a democratic republic. These chapters focus on the TJ-Hamilton rivalry, presenting TJ as a champion of liberty that undermines itself when taken to extremes.

1508. Corwin, Edward S. "Jefferson's War on the Judiciary" in John Marshall and the Constitution. New Haven: Yale Univ. Press, 1919. 53-85.

A volume in the popular Chronicles of America series.

1509. Cox, Isaac Joslin. "The American Intervention in West Florida." AHR. 17(1911), 290-311.

Peripherally about TJ. "Jefferson and his successors, largely influenced by his direct suggestion and advice," used every possible opportunity to gain the Floridas.

1510. Cox, Isaac Joslin. "The Pan-American Policy of Jefferson and Wilkinson." MVHR. 1(1914), 212-39.

TJ's desire to gain the Floridas influenced his whole attitude toward both Bonaparte and the Spanish colonies.

1511. Coyle, David Cushman. "Contemptible Egghead" in Ordeal of the Presidency. Washington: Public Affairs Press, 1960. 63-102.

Account of journalistic and literary attacks on TJ while in the White House. "He was the first of the Presidents to recover fully from the ordeal of the Presidency," since political calumny never touched his vanity as it had Adams, and, unlike Washington, he outlived his calumniators.

1512. Crabitès, Pierre. "President Roosevelt, Jefferson and the South." Catholic World. 146(1938), 405-11.

Contends that FDR in extending federal authority is following TJ's example and that the South from the beginning of the country has in fact favored such extension.

1513. Cragin, Aaron H. Jefferson against Douglas. Speech of Hon. A. H. Cragin, of New Hampshire, in the House of Representatives, August 4, 1856. Washington: Buell and Blanchard, 1856. pp. 14.

Another edition, Washington: n.p., 1856. pp. 28. Quotes TJ extensively on the evils of slavery in order to argue against its extension.

1514.   Crane, Fergus. "Thomas Jefferson and To-morrow." Eclectic Magazine. 148(1907), 485-91.

The new century requires new solutions for its problems, but the old principles of TJ are still the basis of a free society: states rights, separation of powers, honest men in office.

1515.   Crane, William. Anti-Slavery in Virginia: Extracts from Thomas Jefferson, Gen. Washington and others Relative to the "Blighting Curse of Slavery." Baltimore: J. F. Weishampel, 1865. pp. 23.

TJ quoted and cited as an anti-slavery advocate.

1516.   Craven, Avery. "Democratic Theory and Practice." VQR. 19(1943), 278-87.

The tendency to pay lip-service to TJ while practice has followed Hamilton is explained by "the fact that American democracy as it has evolved through the years is not the practice of theory but primarily of circumstances."

1517.   Croly, Herbert. "The Federalists and the Republicans" in The Promise of American Life. New York: Macmillan, 1909. 27-51.

TJ's "policy was at bottom the old fatal policy of drift ... Hamilton's ... one of energetic and intelligent assertion of the national good."

1518.   [Croly, Herbert]. "The Great Jefferson Joke." New Republic. 47(1926), 73-74.

The Democratic Party's "assiduous and indomitable attempts to revive Jeffersonian principles is the oldest and worst joke in American politics." FDR had recently appealed to the political thought of TJ as a standard for the Party.

1519.   Crosskey, William Winslow. Politics and the Constitution in the History of the United States. Chicago: Univ. of Chicago Press, 1953. 2 vols. pp. xi, 708; viii, 711-1410.

In order to explain how "our government became the queer, crippled thing which it is," contends that the original Constitution was subverted by "anti-federalist" Jeffersonians, who frustrated the establishment of a unitary system with a dominant central government by reinterpreting the Constitution according to their principles. Focus is on the early struggles in the Supreme Court, TJ. vs. Marshall, etc. and on the implications of the fourteenth amendment. Enormously documented, passionately argued legal history which will seem wrong-headed to many readers. Even so, throws light on TJ and his difficulties with the judiciary and with Marshall.

186

1520. Culberson, Charles A. "Jefferson and the Constitution" in The Writings
       of Thomas Jefferson, ed. Lipscomb and Bergh. Washington: Thomas
       Jefferson Memorial Association, 1903. 9:i-x.

       TJ as champion of states rights.

1521. Cullen, Joseph P. Declaration of Independence: The Keepsake Album of
       Its Creator. Gettysburg: Historical Times, 1969.

       Popular history of events leading up to the Declaration.

1522. Cunningham, Noble E., Jr. "The Jeffersonian Party to 1801: A Study of
       the Formation of a Party Organization." Ph.D. dissertation. Duke
       Univ., 1952. pp. 334.

       See the author's later The Jeffersonian Republicans.

1523. Cunningham, Noble E., Jr. The Jeffersonian Republicans: The Forma-
       tion of Party Organization, 1789-1801. Chapel Hill: Univ. of North
       Carolina Press, 1957. pp. x, 279.

       Focuses on the development of the Republican party on a broad front
       but also contains a good deal specifically on TJ's role. Rejects the
       idea of TJ as the organizing genius who singlehandedly brought it all
       together, although his political shrewdness made him an effective
       party leader after he returned to political life in 1796. The best book
       on this subject.

1524. Cunningham, Noble E., Jr. The Process of Government Under Jefferson.
       Princeton: Princeton Univ. Press, 1978. pp. xii, 357.

       TJ "brought to the presidency the most system in administration and
       the strongest leadership that the office had yet experienced," even
       though he left Federalist-designed structures essentially intact. He
       made the cabinet system work because of his talent for organization,
       his reliance on discussion and persuasion rather than authority, and his
       ability to preserve harmony among men of conflicting temperaments.
       He was also able to mobilize the power of his party, and he kept the
       government open to the people. A well-researched and significant
       book.

1525. Cunningham, Noble E., Jr. "Virginia Jeffersonians' Victory Celebrations
       in 1801." Virginia Cavalcade. 8(Summer 1958), 4-9.

1526. Current, Richard N. "That Other Declaration: May 20, 1775-May 20,
       1975." North Carolina Historical Review. 54(1977), 169-91.

       Detailed account of the scholarly and popular reputation of the
       Mecklenburg Declaration; TJ's rejection of it prompted anti-
       Jeffersonian reactions.

1527. Curtis, George M., III. "Thomas Jefferson" in The Virginia Law Reporters Before 1880. Charlottesville: Univ. Press of Virginia, 75-84.

Discussion on TJ's law career and of the Reports of 1769-72.

1528. Cutler, Lloyd N. "Thomas Jefferson, Won't You Please Come Home." Annals of the American Academy of Political and Social Science. 396(1971), 25-39.

Cites TJ's belief in generational revision of constitutions and calls for an "advisory urban constitutional convention" to address social injustices which are roots of crime.

1529. Dabney, Virginius. "Thomas Jefferson and John Marshall" in Virginia: The New Dominion. Garden City: Doubleday, 1971. 192-201.

Loosely organized sketch of TJ's antagonism to Marshall and Marshall's handling of the Burr trial.

1530. Dana, William F. "The Declaration of Independence." Harvard Law Review. 13(1900), 319-43.

Argues that since the Declaration by intention advanced accepted ideas, it is not an isolated document and must be interpreted in company with other state papers, e.g. the Virginia Bill of Rights, etc. Concludes the Declaration is a political, not a social, statement.

1531. Dane, Nathan. Appendix (9th Volume) to Dane's General Abridgment of American Law, etc. n.p., n.d. 5-16.

Bound with Dane's A General Abridgment and Digest of American Law, With Occasional Notes and Comments. vol. 9. Boston: Hilliard, Gray, Little, and Wilkins, 1829. The Appendix examines the relationship of state and federal governments in light of the debates on Foot's resolution in the U.S. Senate and the appearance of TJ's writings in the 1829 edition. Blames many of the loose constructions of the Constitution on TJ's writings since 1775 and criticizes his credulosity and jealousy concerning supposed monarchists and aristocrats.

1532. Daniel, John Warwick. "Jefferson" in Speeches and Orations. Compiled by His Son, Edward M. Daniel. Lynchburg, Va.: J. P. Bell Co., 1911. 637-48.

"...one distinction is Jefferson's, and Jefferson's alone—he founded a party, not for a day, but for all time."

1533. Daniel, John W. "Thomas Jefferson's Place in History" in Political History of the United States, by the Presidents; with Historical Reviews of Each Administration by ... Leading Statesmen of the Time. New York: Federal Book Concern, 1899. 78-84.

1534. Daniels, Josephus. "Jefferson's Contribution to a Free Press" in The Writings of Thomas Jefferson, ed. Lipscomb and Bergh. Washington: Thomas Jefferson Memorial Association, 1903. 18:i-xlviii.

A relatively early survey of TJ's activities in this field.

*1535. Daniels, Josephus. "Jefferson's Philosophy and the Present Crisis." Univ. of Virginia Alumni Bulletin. 3rd ser. 11(1918).

1536. Dargo, George. Jefferson's Louisiana: Politics and the Clash of Legal Traditions. Studies in Legal History. Cambridge: Harvard Univ. Press, 1975. pp. xii, 260.

Examines TJ's efforts to supplant civil law in Louisiana Territory with common law. Concentrates on controversy in Lower Louisiana (Orleans Territory).

1537. Dargo, George. "Legal Codification and the Politics of Territorial Government in Jefferson's Louisiana." Ph.D. dissertation. Columbia Univ., 1970. pp. 421.

TJ represented majority American opinion in thinking that the U.S. could incorporate Lower Louisiana only after its population and institutional foundations of its culture were thoroughly Americanized. The pivotal issue was the conflict between the Creoles' continental civil law and Anglo-American common law. DAI 33/07A, p. 3507. See previous item.

1538. Darling, Arthur Burr. "Jefferson's Policy: Peace and Expansion" and "Jefferson's Planning in America" in Our Rising Empire, 1763-1803. New Haven: Yale Univ. Press, 1940. 390-420, 456-84.

These chapters in a history of national expansion cover TJ's direction of diplomacy with France prior to actual negotiations for the Louisiana Purchase and the process itself of acquiring Louisiana. Suggestive.

1539. Daviess, Joseph H. "A View of the President's Conduct Concerning the Conspiracy of 1806." Quarterly Publications of the Historical and Philosophical Society of Ohio. 12(1917), 53-154.

A Kentucky Federalist's pamphlet on the Burr episode; brief notes by Isaac Joslin Cox and Helen Swineford.

1540. Davis, Curtis Carroll. "Mr Littlepage Briefs Mr. Jefferson on the European Situation: 1791." Northern Neck of Virginia Historical Magazine. 6(1956), 542-53.

Lewis Littlepage was an adviser to Stanislaus Augustus II of Poland and corresponded with TJ. His long letter of December 26, 1791, is a full report on European politics.

1541. Davis, David Brion. "Jefferson's Uncertain Commitment" in The Problem of Slavery in the Age of Revolution, 1770-1823. Ithaca: Cornell Univ. Press, 1975. 169-84.

Examines TJ's equivocal and indecisive position on slavery, pointing out that "when the chips were down" he was loyal to his class and society.

1542. Davis, David Brion. Was Thomas Jefferson the Authentic Enemy of Slavery? Oxford: Clarendon Press, 1970. pp. 29.

"...racism is not a sufficient explanation for the discrepancy between Jefferson's anti-slavery pronouncements and his long record of inaction. ... but rather ... his lifelong membership in a planter class whose wealth and power derived from the ownership of slaves."

1543. Davis, John W. "Thomas Jefferson, Attorney at Law." Proceedings of the Virginia State Bar Association. 38(1926), 361-77.

TJ's education and practice as a lawyer; rpt. in American Bar Association Journal. 13(February 1927), 63-68.

1544. Davis, Thomas J. A Sketch of the Life, Character, and Public Services of Thomas Jefferson, with Some Account of the Aid He Rendered in Establishing Our Independence and Government. Philadelphia: Claxton, Remsen, and Haffelfinger, 1876. pp. 179.

Despite the title, covers TJ only through the end of 1776; focuses on the writing of the Declaration and on TJ in the Continental Congress.

1545. Dawidoff, Robert. "The Fox in the Henhouse: Jefferson and Slavery." Reviews in American History. 6(1978), 503-11.

Review essay on John Chester Miller, The Wolf by the Ears, suggests that "Nature and Slavery were two great problems for Jefferson" in his use of 18th-century rationalist language.

1546. DeConde, Alexander. Entangling Alliance: Politics and Diplomacy Under George Washington. Durham: Duke Univ. Press, 1958. pp. xiv, 536.

Synthesizes diplomatic history and domestic political history of the period 1789-1797, considered in terms of the consequences and complications caused by the French alliance of 1778; TJ discussed passim.

1547. DeConde, Alexander. "Foreclosure of a Peacemaker's Career: A Criticism of Thomas Jefferson's Diplomatic Isolation." Huntington Library Quarterly. 15(1952), 297-304.

William Vans Murray criticizes TJ's closing of the legations at The Hague and Lisbon; DeConde portrays Murray as a conscientious diplomat, almost uniquely responsible for working out the Convention of 1800 with the French.

1548. DeConde, Alexander. This Affair of Louisiana. New York: Scribner's, 1976. pp. x, 325.

Argues that "an expansionist Anglo-American ethos, rooted in the colonial experience, ... continues into the first years of the new American nation and emerges during the Louisiana affair as a kind of pious imperialism." Focuses on the acquisition of Louisiana and discusses TJ throughout.

1549. DeConde, Alexander. "A Time for Candor and a Time for Tact." WMQ. 3rd ser. 17(1960), 341-45.

Account of TJ's difficulties with Gouverneur Morris as minister to France.

1550. DeConde, Alexander. "Washington's Farewell, the French Alliance, and the Election of 1796." MVHR. 43(1957), 641-58.

Pierre Auguste Adet, the Directory's minister to the United States, attempted to electioneer for TJ in 1796 in hopes of restoring the French alliance and overthrowing the Jay Treaty, but his efforts were counterproductive on the whole.

*1551. Deren, Štefica. "Nastanak I Razvoj Jeffersonovih Republikanaca." Politička Misao. 9(1972), 403-14.

Yugoslavia. Discusses TJ's role in the development of the Republican party.

1552. DeRosier, Arthur H., Jr. "Thomas Jefferson and the Removal of the Choctaw Indians." Southern Quarterly. 1(1962), 52-62.

Contends that TJ's policy of getting Indians off their land was practically successful in the short run but a moral failure which "will forever remain a blot" on his record.

1553. Dethlof, Henry C., ed. Thomas Jefferson and American Democracy. Lexington, Mass.: D. C. Heath, 1971. pp. xiv, 209.

A casebook in the "Problems in American Civilization" series.

*1554. Detweiler, Philip F. "The Declaration of Independence in Jefferson's Lifetime." Ph.D. dissertation. Tulane Univ., 1955. pp. 367.

1555. DeVoto, Bernard. "An Inference Regarding the Expedition of Lewis and Clark." Proceedings of the APS. 99(1955), 185-94.

Argues suggestively that TJ regarded the expedition, planned before the actual purchase, as a means to hasten the expansion of the U.S. to the Pacific.

1556. Dewey, Donald O. Marshall v. Jefferson: The Political Background of Marbury v. Madison. New York: Knopf, 1970. pp. ix, 195.

Competent introduction to the political and historical context of the Marbury case, which established the principle of judicial review. Discusses TJ's quarrels with Marshall and the consequences of the decision.

1557. Dixon, Lawrence W. "The Attitude of Thomas Jefferson Toward the Judiciary." Southwestern Social Science Quarterly. 28(1947), 13-19.

TJ disliked the judiciary's relative independence from the other branches and opposed the Supreme Court's custom of delivering a general opinion.

1558. Dodd, W. E. "Napoleon Breaks Thomas Jefferson." American Mercury. 5(1925), 303-13.

Napoleon's victory at Austerlitz made inevitable the Embargo, which destroyed TJ's popularity and political effectiveness.

1559. Dodd, William E. Statesmen of the Old South, or from Radicalism to Conservative Revolt. New York: Macmillan, 1911. 1-88.

TJ was from the time of his death until after the Civil War a forsaken prophet, except in so far as he was seen as the spokesman for states rights.

1560. Dodd, Willliam Edward. Thomas Jefferson's Ruckkehr zur Politik 1796. Leipzig: Grubel und Sommerlatte, 1899. pp. x, 88.

"Inaugural-Dissertation zur Bewerbung um die Doctorwurde bei der hohen philosophischen Facultat der Universitat." Covers TJ's political involvement in the early 1790's.

1561. Donovan, Frank. Mr. Jefferson's Declaration; The Story Behind the Declaration of Independence. New York: Dodd Mead, 1968. pp. 211.

Popular account of background, contents, and reception of the Declaration.

1562. Dornan, James E. "Thomas Jefferson and Foundations of American Foreign Policy." Occasional Review. 1(February 1974), 155-68.

Argues that TJ's peculiar fusion of idealistic morality and political realism in directing foreign policy laid the ground for subsequent difficulties.

192

1563. Dos Passos, John. The Men Who Made the Nation. New York: Double-day, 1957. pp. 469.

A novelist's history of the years from Yorktown until TJ's first term, played out in terms of the Hamilton-TJ rivalry, and closing with the Burr-Hamilton duel.

1564. Dos Passos, John. The Shackles of Power; Three Jeffersonian Decades. Garden City, N.Y.: Doubleday, 1966. pp. vi, 426.

Political and social history of the years 1800-1830 with TJ as a central figure.

1565. Douglass, Elisha P. "Thomas Jefferson and Revolutionary Democracy" in Rebels and Democrats; The Struggle for Equal Political Rights and Majority Rule During the American Revolution. Chapel Hill: Univ. of North Carolina Press, 1955. 287-316.

Claims that "When democracy is construed as political processes establishing political equality and majority rule, Jefferson cannot be considered a democrat to the same extent as the dissident groups in the Revolutionary era." Discusses TJ's draft of a constitution for Virginia and his reform bills during his governorship.

1566. Dowd, Morgan D. "Justice Joseph Story and the Politics of Appoint-ment." American Journal of Legal History. 9(1965), 265-85.

Analyzes TJ's role in the appointment of Story and reasons for his objections to him, including the fear that he would be on the Supreme Court if the batture case were appealed. Claims TJ had some in-fluence on Madison's appointments, but Madison was basically his own man. Well informed.

1567. Downes, Randolph Chandler. "Thomas Jefferson and the Removal of Governor St. Clair in 1802." Ohio Archaeological and Historical Pub-lications. 32(1927), 62-77.

Ohio Republicans acted to remove St. Clair as a response to the Territorial Legislature's Division Act of 1801.

1568. Drouin, Edmond G. "Madison and Jefferson on Clergy in the Legisla-ture." America. 138(1978), 58-59.

TJ changed his mind and was willing to admit clergymen to the legis-lature.

*1569. Dumbauld, Edward. "Introduction" to The Political Writings of Thomas Jefferson: Representative Selections. Indianapolis: Bobbs-Merrill, 1955. pp. xlii, 204.

1570. Dumbauld, Edward. "Jefferson and Local Government." The County Officer. 15(April 1950), 8-10, 28-29.

Contends that local government in which citizens most immediately participate is one of the basic features of Jeffersonian democracy.

1571. Dumbauld, Edward. "Thomas Jefferson and American Constitutional Law." Journal of Public Law. 2(1953), 370-89.

Surveys TJ's positions on constitutional law and the Constitution. Contends that he led the nation to view the Constitution as "an instrument of democracy."

1572. Dumbauld, Edward. Thomas Jefferson and the Law. Norman: Univ. of Oklahoma Press, 1978. pp. xv, 293.

The best book-length study of TJ's legal education, his achievements as a lawyer, his work as a lawmaker, and his stature as a legal scholar and commentator on the law.

1573. Dumbauld, Edward. "Thomas Jefferson and Pennsylvania Courts." Pennsylvania Bar Association Quarterly. 37(1966), 236-47.

Reviews TJ's career as lawyer; in 1816 Stephen Kingston asked his opinion on a case before the Pennsylvania courts, but TJ declined to become involved.

1574. Dunlap, John R. Jeffersonian Democracy, Which Means the Democracy of Thomas Jefferson, Andrew Jackson, and Abraham Lincoln. New York: The Jeffersonian Society, 1903. pp. 479.

Mostly concerned with attacking the "Rule of the Millionaires" by appealing to Jeffersonian principles; pp. 445-79 sketch TJ's accomplishments.

1575. Durrett, Reuben T. "The Resolutions of 1798 and 1799." The Southern Bivouac. 4(1886), 577-88, 658-64, 760-70.

Claims the Kentucky Resolutions were the foundation of the Republican organization against the Federalists and the "broad platform of the great Democratic party." Discusses authorship, by TJ then amended by John Breckinridge.

1576. Dwight, Theodore. History of the Hartford Convention: With A Review of the Policy of the United States Government, Which Led to the War of 1812. New York: N. & J. White, 1833. pp. 447.

First 100 pages attack TJ as secretary of state and as president; classic Federalist view.

*1577. E. The Declaration of Independence. Thomas Paine the Author. n. p., 1887? pp. 2.

1578. Eaton, Clement. "The Jeffersonian Tradition of Liberalism in
       America." South Atlantic Quarterly. 43(1944), 1-10.

       Much of TJ's doctrine is obsolete, but his liberalism—belief in equal-
       ity and democracy—is still relevant.

1579. Eckenrode, Hamilton J. "The Fall of Jefferson" in Revolution in
       Virginia. Boston: Houghton Mifflin, 1916. 195-231.

       Still useful account of TJ's governorship; claims TJ outlived this
       political disaster because at his return from France the "Zeitgeist"
       was ready for him.

1580. Edmunds, Sterling E. Thomas Jefferson: What His Pen Did and
       Attempted in Vain to Do, in the Formation of the Constitution.
       Chicago: Reprinted from The Public, 1909. pp. 16.

       TJ's mission in France prevented his securing a "more democratic
       document," and he was unable to deflect its interpretation by "an
       irremovable judiciary."

1581. Edwards, Everett E. "Thomas Jefferson and the Public Domain." Land
       Policy Review. 7(Summer 1944), 25-28.

       Praises TJ's work to provide democratic access to land.

1582. Egan, Clifford L. "United States, France, and West Florida, 1803-
       1807." Florida Historical Quarterly. 47(1969), 227-52.

       TJ's Florida policy failed because of his uncharacteristic rash actions
       and failure to listen to advice.

1583. Eggleston, George Cary. "Our Twenty-One Presidents. I. The First Ten
       —From Washington to Tyler." Magazine of American History.
       11(1884), 89-109.

       TJ on pp. 96-99; "His administration stamped the country with that
       republican character which it had never really possessed before."

1584. Elliott, Edward. "Thomas Jefferson: Growth Through Acquiescence" in
       Biographical Story of the Constitution: A Study of the American
       Union. New York: Putnam's, 1911. 77-100.

       Agrees with Hamilton's assessment that TJ's "temporizing" preserved
       Federalist systems even in the face of needed reforms of
       government. In fact, the Louisiana Purchase delivered an
       "irremediable hurt" to the doctrine of strict construction.

1585. Ellis, Richard E. The Jeffersonian Crisis: Courts and Politics in the
       Young Republic. New York: Oxford Univ. Press, 1971. pp. xii, 377.

       Argues that the Jeffersonian Republicans were not a monolithic party
       and that after the election of 1800 there was not simply one struggle
       over the federal judiciary system but various struggles on state

and national levels. Furthermore, the attack on the judiciary reflects the struggle between the radicals and moderates in TJ's own party, with the acquittal of Samuel Chase marking the turning point in favor of the moderates. An excellent work, but it has more to do with Jeffersonians than with TJ per se.

1586. Ellis, Richard E. "The Politial Economy of Thomas Jefferson" in Thomas Jefferson: The Man ... His World ... His Influence, ed. Lally Weymouth. New York: Putnam's, 1973. 81-95.

TJ's economic system "successfully forged a new political and economic synthesis from the old dichotomies of the Revolution," i.e. the dichotomy of the "agrarian minded" and the "commercial minded."

1587. Engelken, Ruth. "They Liked It, But..." Writers Digest. 55(July 1975), 9.

Even the Declaration underwent editorial revision, much to "Tom's" chagrin.

1588. Enloe, Cortez F. "The End of the Beginning: The Visionary Fox." Nutrition Today. 12(September/October 1977), 6-11, 31-40.

The Louisiana Purchase and national expansion as part of TJ's dreams for the American future.

1589. Evans, Emory G. "Indian Policy Under Thomas Jefferson." Essays in History. 1(1954), 18-37.

Although TJ wanted a benevolent policy toward the Indians, the whites' demands for land frustrated this. He mostly followed the policies set out under Washington and Adams, although the removal program was inaugurated under him.

1590. [Everett, Alexander Hill]. "Origin and Character of the Old Parties." North American Review. 39(1834), 206-68.

Review essay of Dwight's History of the Hartford Convention and Sullivan's Familiar Letters. Traces the Democratic party from the anti-federalists and characterizes the party under TJ as party of Liberty, the Federalists led by Hamilton as the party of Law. But since Britain is now on the side of Liberty, "The parties, into which our fathers were divided on the great argument of Liberty and Law, can therefore never be revived ... as it came up before, connected with the policy of Europe and the rival interests of France and England ... ." Still worth reading.

1591. Fahey, John H. The Principles of Thomas Jefferson and Their Application to Present Day Problems. New York: National Broadcasting Co., 1931. pp. 25.

An address on the anniversary of TJ's birth; TJ was an anti-monopolist and opposed the concentration of economic power.

1592. Farley, James A. Thomas Jefferson, Franklin Roosevelt, and the Federal Judiciary; Address ... Before the Alumni Association of Boston University Law School, April 22, 1937. Washington: Government Printing Office, 1937. pp. 8.

Also in Congressional Record of May 3, 1937. The New Deal version of TJ's opposition to courts.

1593. Fauntleroy, Cornelius H. "Thomas Jefferson and His Purchase of Louisiana." The Commonwealth Magazine (St. Louis). 2(March 1902), 5-14.

TJ's action was not the outcome of base commercialism nor of imperialism but of a sense of national self-preservation.

1594. Ferris, D. H. "Jefferson Made to Order." Georgia Review. 10(Summer 1956), 131-46.

The New Deal's "suggestion that Mr. Jefferson was a liberal is, of course, merely an absurd and very juvenile bit of apocrypha."

1595. Fish, Carl Russell. "Jefferson's Policy as to Public Office, 1801-1809" in The Civil Service and the Patronage. New York: Longmans Green, 1905. 29-51.

Claims TJ was so clever in satisfying his own followers and in not alienating the masses of the opposition that patronage ceased to be an issue by 1809.

1596. Fisher, Louis. "The Efficiency Side of Separated Powers." Journal of American Studies. 5(1971), 113-31.

Contends that TJ and other founding fathers advocated the principle of separation of powers not out of fear of executive power so much as out of a wish for greater administrative efficiency.

1597. Fitch, Robert E. "The American President as Philosopher-King." New Republic. 135(August 13, 1956), 11-13.

TJ's portrayal of George Washington suggests Eisenhower.

1598. Fitzpatrick, John C. "The Manuscript from Which Jefferson Wrote the Declaration of Independence." Daughters of the American Revolution Magazine. 55(1921), 363-67.

Rpt. in his The Spirit of the Revolution.... Boston: Houghton Mifflin, 1924. Describes a mss. in TJ's hand, endorsed "Constitution of Virginia first ideas of Th: J. communicated to a member of the Convention."

1599. [Flanders, Henry]. "A Glance at Two of Our Presidents." Lippincott's Magazine. 2(1868), 261-71.

Compares TJ and Adams as representative men of the American Revolution whose characters and careers bear closely on the origin of political parties in the U.S.

1600.   Fleming, Thomas J. "'A Scandalous, Malicious and Seditious Libel.'" American Heritage. 19(December 1967), 22-27, 100-06.

Jeffersonian prosecution of Harry Croswell for libel; he was editor of the Federalist journal, The Wasp, of Hudson, N.Y. and was defended in court by Hamilton.

1601.   Flood, Lawrence G. and Jean Grossholtz. "The Man on the Nickel: Does He Make Any Sense?" Mount Holyoke Alumnae Quarterly. 59(1975), 88-91.

Examines the contemporary relevance of TJ's political ideas. Many of them no longer apply and the only way to have equality as he wished is to contradict the principles of individualism and the right to acquire and own property. Attempts to be provocative, but not very thoughtful.

1602.   Flores, Dan L. "Rendezvous at Spanish Bluff: Jefferson's Red River Exploration." Red River Valley Historical Review. 4(Spring, 1979), 4-26.

Good account of plans to explore the Red River, particularly the freeman expedition of 1806; suggests that Spanish opposition here and the capture of Pike in 1807 put an end to TJ's exploration of the Louisiana Purchase.

*1603.   Floyd, Mildred D. "Thomas Jefferson and the Louisiana Purchase." M.A. thesis. Atlanta Univ., 1951.

1604.   Fohlen, Claude. "Jefferson et l'Achat de la Louisiane." Histoire. 5(1978), 75-77.

Review article on DeConde's This Affair of Louisiana.

1605.   Fohlen, Claude. "Jefferson et la France." Revue des Travaux de l'Academie des Sciences Morales et Politiques et Comptes Rendus de ses Seances. 129(1976), 553-67.

Discusses TJ's attitudes toward France; claims he was the only one of the founding fathers to remain a friend of France, largely because of his experiences while minister there.

1606.   Foley, William E. and Charles David Rice. "Visiting the President: An Exercise in Jeffersonian Indian Diplomacy." American West. 16(November/December 1979), 4-15, 56.

Account of visits by Indian delegates; argues that TJ's philanthropic attitudes toward the Indians were negated by the distance between white and Indian cultures. Illustrated by Saint-Memin portraits and with a note on him.

1607. Force, Gerald, comp. The Jefferson Drafts of the Declaration of Independence in Facsimile. Washington: Acropolis Books, 1963. pp. (12).

Facsimile of the rough draft and fragments, together with the Dunlap broadside; annotated, but not significant.

1608. Ford, Paul Leicester. "Jefferson's Drafts of the Kentucky Resolutions of 1798." The Nation. 62(1896), 156.

Compares what purports to be TJ's rough draft and the fair copy of the Resolutions.

1609. Ford, Worthington C. "The Federal Constitution in Virginia, 1787-1788." Proceedings of the Massachusetts Historical Society. 2nd Ser. 17(1902), 450-510.

Includes letters of Edward Carrington and others to TJ and Madison concerning ratification of the Constitution; no notes.

1610. Ford, Worthington C. "Jefferson and the Newspaper." Records of the Columbia Historical Society. 8(1905), 78-111.

Claims that TJ was weak in controversial writing and incompetent to reply to Hamilton's pseudonymous papers, so he encouraged Freneau, Duane, and Callender. Eventually he turned his back on the malignancy of the press which he had encouraged.

1611. Ford, Worthington C. "Jefferson's Constitution for Virginia." The Nation. 51(1890), 107-09.

Describes TJ's 1776 proposal.

1612. Ford, Worthington C. "Letters of James Cheatham, 1801-1807, Taken From the Jefferson Papers in the Library of Congress." Proceedings of the Massachusetts Historical Society. 3rd ser. 1(1907), 41-64.

Short introduction to letters from a Republican pamphleteer.

1613. Ford, Worthington C., ed. "Thomas Jefferson and James Thomson Callender." New England Historical and Genealogical Register. 50(1896), 321-33, 445-58; 51(1897), 19-25, 153-58, 323-28.

Brief introduction followed by correspondence relevant to the TJ-Callender relationship, including letters from Callender to TJ, letters to and from Madison, Monroe, and Abigail Adams. Rpt. Brooklyn Historical Printing Club, 1897. pp. 45.

1614. Forman, Sidney. "Thomas Jefferson on Universal Military Training." Military Affairs. 11(1947), 177-78.

Quotes TJ's letter to Monroe, June 18, 1813, on "the necessity of obliging every citizen to be a soldier." That and his comments on military training in the Rockfish Gap Report show that he would not be opposed to universal military training in spite of his opposition to European militarism.

1615. Foster, John W. "The Administration of Jefferson" in A Century of American Diplomacy, Being a Brief Review of the Foreign Relations of the United States. Boston: Houghton Mifflin, 1900. 185-232.

Gossipy acount of diplomatic affairs.

1616. Fouts, Levi N. "Jefferson the Inventor and His Relation to the Patent System." Journal of the Patent Office Society. 4(1922), 316-31.

Circumstantial account of TJ's establishment of the Patent Office.

1617. Franklin, John Hope. "The Dream Deferred" in Racial Equality in America. Chicago: Univ. of Chicago Press, 1976. 3-36.

Argues that TJ's racism and failure to act unequivocally in opposition to slavery demonstrate that "the ideology of the American Revolution was not really egalitarian."

1618. Franklin, Mitchell. "The Place of Thomas Jefferson in the Expulsion of Spanish Medieval Law from Louisiana." Tulane Law Review. 16(1942), 319-38.

Explains why TJ was ready to send troops to back up Gov. Claiborne's veto of the proposed legal system of 1806, supposedly because it claimed a "democratic" right to own slaves.

1619. Freund, Rudolph. "John Adams and Thomas Jefferson on the Nature of Land Holding in America." Land Economics. 24(1948), 107-19.

Claims Adams conceived of land tenure as basically personal in nature, depending on contracts between individual agents. TJ denied that the English King ever had a right to grant land in the colonies and held that Americans possessed their land in absolute domain like their Saxon forefathers.

1620. Fried, Albert, ed. The Jeffersonian and Hamiltonian Traditions in American Politics; A Documentary History. Garden City, N.Y.: Doubleday Anchor, 1968. pp. xii, 581.

Collection of documents illustrating the fortunes of the Jeffersonian politics of equality and human rights vs. property rights and limitless economic opportunity.

1621. Friedenwald, Herbert. "The Declaration of Independence." International Monthly. 4(1901), 102-21.

Analyzes text of the Declaration; suggests that TJ touches all the colonies in the course of the list of grievances, establishing a common interest in independence.

1622. Friedenwald, Herbert. The Declaration of Independence, An Interpretation and an Analysis. New York: Macmillan, 1904. pp. xii, 299.

Readable but dated account of the historical background of the Declaration, its composition and acceptance, its philosophical background (Lockean), and the nature of the grievances it claims.

1623. Fuller, Melville W. "Jefferson and Hamilton." Dial. 4(May 1883), 4-6.

Review essay on Morse's Jefferson and Lodge's Hamilton; TJ and Hamilton are types of the two great parties, one believing in strict, the other in free construction of the constitution. Faults Morse's bias.

1624. Gaines, William H., Jr. "A Son-in-Law in the House." Virginia Cavalcade. 16(Autumn 1966), 4-10.

On Thomas Mann Randolph's services in Congress in support of TJ's policies.

1625. Gaines, William H., Jr. "An Unpublished Thomas Jefferson Map, With a Petition for the Division of Fluvanna from Albemarle County, 1777." Papers of the Albemarle County Historical Society. 7(1946), 23-28.

TJ takes part in the creation of Fluvanna County.

1626. Galbreath, C. B. "Thomas Jefferson's Views on Slavery." Ohio Archaeological and Historical Publications. 34(1925), 184-202.

Argues that TJ opposed the extension of slavery and that there is no evidence for the claim that he favored Ohio's entry into the Union as a slave state.

1627. Garland, Hugh A. "Thomas Jefferson" in Life of John Randolph. New York: Appleton, 1850. 1:45-52.

TJ as a profound influence upon the young Randolph, but later replaced in his esteem by Edmund Burke. TJ also treated passim.

1628. Garraty, John A. "The Case of the Missing Commissions" in Quarrels That Have Shaped the Constitution. New York: Harper and Row, 1962. 1-14.

Explains how TJ's attempt to counter John Adams' midnight judges was met by John Marshall and the case of Marbury vs. Madison. Also published in essentially the same form in American Heritage. 14(June 1963), 6-9, 84-89.

1629. George, Henry. "Jefferson and the Land Question" in The Writings of Thomas Jefferson, ed. Lipscomb and Bergh. Washington: Thomas Jefferson Memorial Association, 1903. 16:i-xiv.

Claims TJ's political "axiom" has as a prerequisite a social or economic axiom, man's equal right to land.

1630.   Getchell, George H. "Thomas Jefferson" in Our Nation's Executives and Their Administrations. New York: Getchell and Fuller, 1885. 40-48.

Sketch.

1631.   [Giles, William Branch]. To the Public. (Richmond: T. W. White, 1828). pp. 17.

Letters and papers illuminating the contretemps between Giles and T. J. Randolph over the publication of TJ's letter to Giles dated December 25, 1825, in which it was purported TJ approved of John Adams' politics.

1632.   Gillet, Ransom H. Democracy in the United States. What It Has Done, What It Is Doing, and What It Will Do. New York: Appleton, 1868. 13-41.

A history of the Democratic Party; indicated pages cover election of 1800 through the Embargo, including a sketch of TJ's life and a section on his political principles.

1633.   Ginsberg, Robert, ed. A Casebook on the Declaration of Independence. New York: Thomas Y. Crowell, 1967. pp. 299.

A useful collection of pieces on the Declaration; includes the editor's own "The Declaration as Rhetoric," 219-44, an original essay which considers the Declaration in terms of audience, speaker, argument, style, etc.

1634.   Goetzmann, William H. "Clear-Eyed Men of Destiny" in When the Eagle Screamed: The Romantic Horizon in American Diplomacy, 1800-1860. New York: John Wiley, 1966. 1-20.

Deals with TJ and John Quincy Adams as the two men who laid "the foundations of American expansionism." Claims that news of Western explorations received in the 1780's and 1790's plus English expansionist activities enlarged TJ's views about Western expansion.

*1635.   Goldberg, Stephen H. "Thomas Jefferson and American Foreign Policy, 1783-1798: Prelude to Power." M.A. thesis. Queens College (CUNY), 1970.

1636.   Goldsmith, William M. The Growth of Presidential Power: A Documented History. The Formative Years. New York: Chelsea House, 1974. 346-81.

The chapters entitled "Presidential Leadership," "Jefferson's Early Initiative," "Thomas Jefferson and the Louisiana Purchase," and "Thomas Jefferson and the Embargo" cover, respectively, leadership of Congress, defense and the Barbary War, Constitutional issues raised by the Purchase, and the limits of presidential power.

1637. Gooch, Robert Kent. "Jeffersonianism and the Third Term Issue: A Retrospect." Southern Review. 6(1941), 735-49.

Those writers in 1940 quoting TJ on opposition to a presidential third term have little else in common with him.

1638. Gooch, Robert K. "Reconciling Jeffersonian Principles with the New Deal." Southwestern Social Science Quarterly. 16(June 1935), 1-13.

Thoughtful discussion, claiming TJ's democratic individualism can be preserved and strengthened by more emphasis on governmental authority; a New Deal defense.

*1639. Gordon, M. "Government/Happiness/Prosperity." Rights. 22(April 1976), 11.

1640. Gordy, J. P. "Thomas Jefferson" in Political History of the United States With Special Reference to the Growth of Political Parties. New York: Henry Holt, 1904. 1:132-58.

TJ treated as the "precise opposite" of Hamilton and the distance between the parties emphasized.

1641. Gordy, Wilbur Fisk. "Thomas Jefferson and the Louisiana Purchase" in American Leaders and Heroes. New York: Scribner's, 1901. 234-45.

1642. Granato, Leonard A. "Freneau, Jefferson, and Genet: Independent Journalism in the Partisan Press" in Newsletters to Newspapers: Eighteenth-Century Journalism, ed. Donovan H. Bond and W. Reynolds McLeod. Morgantown: West Virginia Univ. School of Journalism, 1977. 291-301.

Argues for Freneau's editorial independence on the National Gazette since he supported Genet after TJ realized the political danger of a pro-Genet stand.

1643. Granger, Moses M. Washington vs. Jefferson: The Case Tried by Battle in 1861-65. Boston: Houghton Mifflin, 1898. pp. 207.

Despite the title, little on TJ, who as author of the Kentucky Resolution "heresy" is made responsible for the Secession.

1644. Gray, Giles Wilkeson. "Thomas Jefferson's Interest in Parliamentary Practice." Speech Monographs. 27(1960), 315-22.

Discusses TJ's reading in and knowledge of parliamentary procedure before his assuming the presidency of the U.S. Senate in 1797, when he began to draw up his Manual of Parliamentary Practice, first published in 1801. He appealed to George Wythe for help and relied in the meantime on his commonplace pocketbook. Well-informed.

1645. Grayson, W. S. "The Legation of Thomas Jefferson.—Is the Declaration of Independence at War with the Institution of Domestic Slavery?" DeBow's Review. 31(1861), 136-47.

Doctrines of TJ and Christianity lead "by plain steps of logic, to agrarianism." All men were created equal, but since the creation, circumstances have changed and slavery is legitimate.

*1646. Green, Benjamin E. Opinions of John C. Calhoun and Thomas Jefferson on the Subject of Paper Currency. Philadelphia: Claxton, Remsen, and Haffelfinger, 1873. pp. 26.

1647. Green, Daniel. To Colonize Eden: Land and Jeffersonian Democracy. London: Gordon and Cremonesi, 1977. pp. 200.

Interesting attempt to use TJ's ideas about broad land ownership as a basic element of a democratic society to criticize present day British land policy. Sees TJ as the major influence on the Northwest Ordinance, by way of the Ordinance of 1784, and thus a definitive voice in shaping the economic and political structure of the new nation.

1648. Grigsby, Hugh Blair. The Virginia Convention of 1776. A Discourse Delivered before the Virginia Alpha of the Phi Beta Kappa Society, in the Chapel of William and Mary College in the City of Williamsburg, on the Afternoon of July 3, 1855. Richmond: J. W. Randolph, 1855. pp. 206.

Laudatory, apologetic sketch on pp. 168-87; also see pp. 20-33 on the Mecklenburg Declaration.

1649. Guinness, Ralph B. "The Purpose of the Lewis and Clark Expedition" MVHR. 20(1933), 90-100.

Contends that the expedition was not intended with an eye to eventual acquisition of further territory.

1650. H. B. D. "The Citizen Genet." Historical Magazine. 10(1866), 329-44.

Prints correspondence of TJ and Genet with extracts from newspapers of the period.

1651. Haines, Charles Grove. "The Views of Thomas Jefferson and of Leading Democrat-Republicans" in The American Doctrine of Judicial Supremacy. Second Edition Revised and Enlarged. Berkeley: Univ. of California Press, 1932. 241-53.

Discusses the antagonism of TJ and Marshall.

1652. Hall, Edward Hagaman. "Notes Concerning the Declaration of Independence, Including the Correction of Some Popular Errors." American Scenic and Historic Preservation Society, Annual Report. 18(1913), 467-83.

Distinguishes between the adoption on July 2 of Richard Henry Lee's resolution concerning independence and the later approval of TJ's Declaration.

1653. Halsey, J. J. "Nullification." The Dial. 8(1888), 245-47.

Review essay on Warfield's The Kentucky Resolution, taking issue with the contention that Breckinridge made radical changes to TJ's original proposal.

1654. Hamilton, J. G. deRoulhac. "The Pacifism of Thomas Jefferson." VQR. 31(1955), 607-20.

Argues that TJ was no pacifist in a post-1914 meaning of the term; although he would have preferred to avoid war, he supported it when it was inevitable.

1655. Hamilton, John Church. History of the Republic of the United States of America, as Traced in the Writings of Alexander Hamilton and of His Contemporaries. New York: D. Appleton, 1857-60. 7 vols.

When reprinted in 1879, more properly titled A Life of Alexander Hamilton; important statement of the Hamiltonian view of TJ.

1656. "Hamilton and Jefferson." Littell's Living Age. 81(1864), 613-16.

Review of Riethmuller's Alexander Hamilton and His Contemporaries presents TJ as the origin of slave-holding, secessionist, oligarchic principles and Hamilton as transmitter "to the thinkers of the North ... political sobriety, that sober respect for law, that preference for legal freedom to popular license, that belief in a true national life" which characterizes Lincoln.

*1657. Hanchette, William F., Jr. "Politics and the Judiciary Under Jefferson." M.A. thesis. Univ. of California, Berkeley, 1949.

1658. Hancock, James Denton. The Louisiana Purchase Treated in Its Relations to the Constitution of the United States and the Declaration of Independence. Address delivered ... before Sons of the American Revolution at Pittsburgh, Pa., February 22d, 1899. n.p., n.d.

TJ's reservations about the constitutionality of the Purchase indicate that settlement of the American West is no model to justify annexation of the Philippines.

1659. Hans, Nicholas. "Tsar Alexander I and Jefferson: Unpublished Correspondence." Slavonic and East European Review. 32(1954), 215-25.

Letters of 1802-07, both to and from Alexander and about Alexander from other correspondents; introduction and notes.

1660. Hanson, Galen. "Thomas Jefferson and Unity beyond Factions—Yet Unity with Vigorous Factions" in Candles in Conscience. Ventures in the Statecraft of Rigor and Restraint. Detroit: Harlo Press, 1965. 64-70.

Commonplace account of TJ on freedom of speech and opinion.

1661. Harrison, Lowell H. "John Breckinridge and the Acquisition of Louisiana." Louisiana Studies. 7(1968), 7-30.

Breckinridge worked closely with TJ on the Louisiana problem as he had earlier with the Kentucky Resolutions; focus on Breckinridge.

1662. Harrison, Lowell H. "John Breckinridge and the Jefferson Administration." Rocky Mountain Social Science Journal. 4(October 1967), 83-91.

Focus on Breckinridge and his importance for guiding legislation through Congress during TJ's presidency.

*1663. Hartman, Daniel W. "Thomas Jefferson's Theory of Ward Republics: Its Impact on the Practice of American Local Government." M.A. thesis. Mankato State Univ., 1971.

1664. Harvey, Alexander Miller. "Hamilton and Jefferson and the American Constitution." Collections of the Kansas State Historical Society. 17(1926-28), 744-87.

Argues that "these great antagonists really lived in harmony and labored to the same end, and that their battle of the century was a fixed fight."

1665. Harvey, Alexander M. Jefferson and the American Constitution. Topeka: Capper Printing Co., 1926. pp. 23.

TJ's great service was to drive the philosophy of the Declaration into the Constitution and to popularize it by demonstrating the possible strength of the government within its limitations.

1666. Harvey, Charles M. "Origins of the Democratic Party." The Chautauquan. 26(1898), 526-30.

The bank controversy of 1791 led to the establishment of the Republican party as TJ discovered serious differences with Hamilton. William McClay was not, as a descendant has claimed, the party's founder, but he may have been the "original Democrat."

1667. Harvey, Charles M. "Some Second Term Presidents." Atlantic Monthly. 92(1903), 736-42.

Second term presidents tend to make "a larger assertion of authority," e.g. TJ and the Embargo.

1668. Hatch, Louis Clinton. A History of the Vice-Presidency of the United States. Revised and edited by Earl L. Shoup. New York: American Historical Society, 1934. pp. viii, 437.

TJ set the example for the inauguration of subsequent vice-presidents. Discussion of the elections of 1796 and 1800 on pp. 120-33.

1669. Hawke, David. A Transaction of Freemen: The Birth and Course of The Declaration of Independence. New York: Scribner's, 1964. pp. 282.

An account of the Declaration focusing on TJ's role in conceiving and drafting it. Ably written popular history, contending that the Declaration revealed the appearance of a "solid ideological basis for unity" in the new country and has been a continuing force against the status quo and vested interests.

1670. Hayden, Ralston. "The Senate and the Treaties of Thomas Jefferson" in The Senate and Treaties, 1789-1817; The Development of the Treaty-making Functions of the United States During Their Formative Period. New York: Macmillan, 1920. 130-68.

Focuses on the role of the Senate in treaty-making and thus deals with the president as head of the executive branch and not with the Secretary of State; discusses the 1802 convention with Spain, the Louisiana Purchase Treaty, the King-Hawkesbury convention, and the 1805 treaty with Tripoli.

1671. Hays, Isaac Minis. "A Contribution to the Bibliography of the Declaration of Independence." Proceedings of the APS. 39(1900), 69-78.

Note on the first printed versions of the Declaration.

1672. Hays, Isaac Minis. "A Note on the History of the Jefferson Manuscript Draught of the Declaration of Independence in the Library of the American Philosophical Society." Proceedings of the APS. 37(1898), 88-107.

Useful note describing this and 5 other copies in TJ's hand; claims this mss. is a copy of the original rough draft made on or about June 27, 1776.

1673. Hazelton, John H. The Declaration of Independence: Its History. New York: Dodd Mead, 1906. pp. vii, 629.

A careful and intensive study of the Declaration and the circumstances of its creation; still useful.

1674. Hazelton, John H. "The Declaration of Independence." Case and Comment. 24(July 1917), 87-91.

Account of the negotiations in Congress.

1675. Hazen, Charles Downer. "Thomas Jefferson in France" in Contemporary Opinion of the French Revolution. Baltimore: Johns Hopkins Press, 1897. 1-53.

Focus is on TJ's official duties and on his consultations with the moderate revolutionaries; ends with his leaving at the outbreak of the revolution, unaware of how violent it will become.

1676. Heinlein, Jay C. "Albert Gallatin: A Pioneer in Public Administration." WMQ. 3rd ser. 7(1950), 64-94.

Includes observations on "how Gallatin's views [concerning public office] may have been shaped by the President, ... and the nature and effect of Gallatin's influence on Jefferson and administraiton policy."

1677. Hemphill, William Edwin. "'In a Constant Struggle.'" Virginia Cavalcade. 2(Spring 1953), 8-15.

How and why Virginians voted for TJ in 1800.

1678. Hemphill, W. Edwin. "The Jeffersonian Background of the Louisiana Purchase." MVHR. 22(1935), 177-90.

"... long before 1803 Thomas Jefferson was the primary statesman in the United States' struggle for unrestricted use of the greatest river system on the continent, and ... he followed for a number of years a systematic policy to attain this national good."

*1679. Hendrix, J. A. "Presidential Addresses to Congress: Woodrow Wilson and the Jeffersonian Tradition." Southern Speech Journal. 31(1966), 285-94.

1680. Henkels, Stan V. "Introduction" to The Confidential Letters From Thomas Jefferson to William Wirt. Being Reminiscences of Patrick Henry, Now, For the first time printed in full from the originals, In the collection belonging to John Gribbel of Philadelphia. Philadelphia: Privately printed, 1912. i-lv.

Discusses the correspondence, Patrick Henry; for the letters see PMHB. 34(1910), 358-418, but supposedly here they are "copied verbatim, et literatim, et punctuatim."

1681. Henrich, Joseph George. "Thomas Paine's Short Career as a Naval Architect, August-October 1807." American Neptune. 34(1974), 123-34.

On Paine's designs for gunboats; focus not on TJ but informative about his naval policy.

1682. Henrich, Joseph George. "The Triumph of Ideology: The Jeffersonians and the Navy, 1779-1807." Ph.D. disseration. Duke Univ., 1971. pp. vi, 420.

TJ was in 1800 sympathetic to anti-Navy ideology in his party, but not ready to give up his previous pro-Navy views. From 1801 to 1807 he generally supported the requests of the Navy for funds, despite Gallatin's urge to economize. There was no clear administrative naval policy, and only after the Chesapeake affair did the administration come up with a policy on the use of the new gunboats.

1683.   Herndon, G. Melvin. "Keeping an Eye on the British: William Tatham and the Chesapeake Affair." Virginia Cavalcade. 22(Summer 1972), 30-39.

Tatham sent TJ daily dispatches on the British fleet in July, 1806.

1684.   Hillard, George S. "Citizen Genet." Littell's Living Age. 72(1862), 729-40.

Discusses the Genet episode in light of correspondence published in Witt's Thomas Jefferson.

1685.   Hinsdale, Mary L. "Thomas Jefferson" in A History of the President's Cabinet. Ann Arbor: George Wahr, 1911. 39-47.

Superficial.

1686.   "An Historical Confrontation." Current. 131(July/August 1971), 6-7.

Reprints editorial from the Rutland Daily Herald, citing TJ on freedom of the press as relevant to the issue of the Pentagon Papers of 1971.

1687.   Hodgson, Joseph Jr. An Address Delivered Before the Jefferson Society of the University of Virginia, at Its Anniversary Celebration, Held in the Public Hall, April 13, 1857. Richmond: J. D. Hammersley, 1857. pp. 16.

Political progress and the error of secession; a pro-union appeal to the authority of TJ.

1688.   Hofstadter, Richard. The Idea of a Party System: The Rise of Legitimate Opposition in the United States, 1780-1840. Berkeley: Univ. of California Press, 1969. pp. xiii, 280.

First two chapters examine various conceptions of party; third and fourth chapters follow TJ and Madison from legitimate opposition to power. Suggests that among other reasons for TJ's preference for political moderation was his basically 18th-century notion of party. Suggestive.

1689.   Hofstadter, Richard. "Thomas Jefferson: The Aristocrat as Democrat" in The American Political Tradition and the Men Who Made It. New York: Knopf, 1948. 18-43.

Treats TJ as an agrarian, republican idealist who had to observe the "Federalization" of his own party, as by 1816 it took over "the whole complex of Federalist policies." TJ was sustained by his optimism despite this.

1690. Honeywell, Roy J. "President Jefferson and His Successors." AHR. 46 (1940), 64-75.

Examines TJ's correspondence with Madison in the latter's presidency and finds that although TJ gave advice in the interests of party unity, there is in fact little evidence for his dominating Madison as a "party oracle."

1691. Hooker, Richard J., ed. "John Marshall on the Judiciary, the Republicans, and Jefferson, March 4, 1801." AHR. 53(1948), 518-20.

Prints an accurate, annotated version of a Marshall letter written on the day of TJ's first inauguration.

1692. Horsman, Reginald. "The Ambivalence of Thomas Jefferson" in Expansion and American Indian Policy, 1783-1812. East Lansing: Michigan State Univ. Press, 1967. 104-14.

Contends that TJ was caught between a desire to civilize the Indians and a desire for their land. Competent, but see Sheehan, Seeds of Extinction, for a more recent statement.

1693. Horsman, Reginald. "American Indian Policy in the Old Northwest, 1783-1812." WMQ. 3rd ser. 18(1961), 35-53.

TJ "was able to combine an apparent genuine interest in the welfare of the Indian with a voracious appetite for Indian land."

1694. Hoskins, Janina W. "'A Lesson Which All Our Countrymen Should Study': Jefferson Views Poland." Quarterly Journal of the Library of Congress. 33(1976), 29-46.

Carefully describes TJ's knowledge of affairs in Poland; the lesson he recommends is to be aware of the suicidal results of dissension.

1695. Hoslett, Schuyler D. "Jefferson and England: The Embargo as a Measure of Coercion." Americana. 34(1940), 39-54.

The embargo had a measurable economic effect, but it was not continued for long enough to have a political effect.

1696. Hosmer, James K. The History of the Louisiana Purchase. New York: Appleton, 1902. pp. xiv, 230.

Popular history which gives ample space to TJ's role in the purchase and the subsequent debate over its constitutionality.

1697. Houghton, Walter R. "Thomas Jefferson's Administrations" in History of American Politics (Non-Partisan) Embracing a History of the Federal Government and of Political Parties in the Colonies and United States from 1607-1882. Indianapolis: F. T. Neeley, 1883. 159-72.

Republicanism becomes "responsible" once in power.

1698. Hughes, Thomas L. "Washington, Jefferson, and the Fault Lines of Foreign Policy." Vital Speeches. 45(August 1, 1979), 625-28.

1699. Huhner, Leon. "Jefferson's Contemplated Offer of the Post of Attorney General of the United States to Moses (?) Levy, of Philadelphia." American Jewish Historical Society Publications. 20(1911), 161-62.

In a letter to Gallatin, dated Sept. 1, 1804, he mentions the possibility of naming "Levy" as Attorney General; this was probably not Moses Levy nor his brother Sampson.

1700. Hunt, Gaillard. "Office Seeking During Jefferson's Administration." AHR. 3(1898), 270-91.

"The applications for office during Jefferson's administration prove beyond dispute that prevailing public sentiment on the subject of appointments and removals was in favor of their being made for political reasons. Jefferson recognized and followed this sentiment, and he achieved a popularity which increased instead of diminishing."

1701. Imaginary Conversation between President Jackson and the Ghost of Jefferson. Columbia, S.C.: Telescope Office, 1831. pp. 22.

A nullification fable.

1702. Infante, Luis C. "Tomás Jefferson y José Faustino Sanchez Carrión." IPNA (Organo del Instituto Cultural Peruano-Norteamericano). 30(1956), 41-45.

Argues that TJ and Sanchez Carrión, as men of the Enlightenment, show significant similarities which help explain the common historical process of the Americas.

1703. Irelan, John Robert. History of the Life, Administration, and Times of Thomas Jefferson, Third President of the United States. Chicago: Fairbanks and Palmer, 1886. pp. 541.

Concludes that TJ's most positive accomplishment as president was to leave the Federalist structures in place; accepts most of the old Federalist charges against TJ as truthful, or mostly so.

1704. Ireton, Robert E. "Jefferson and the Supreme Court." Boston University Law Review. 17(1937), 81-89.

Federalist view of the Chase impeachment effort and of Marbury vs. Madison.

1705. Jackman, S. W. "A Young Englishman Reports on the New Nation: Edward Thornton to James Bland Burges, 1791-1793." WMQ. 3rd ser. 18(1961), 85-121.

Prints letters of Thornton, secretary to the British Minister, which comment inter alia on TJ as Secretary of State.

1706. Jackson, Donald. "Jefferson, Meriwether Lewis, and the Reduction of the United States Army." Proceedings of the APS. 124(1980), 91-96.

Lewis advised TJ on which officers to retain and which to dismiss when the Army was reduced in size in 1801.

1707. Jahoda, Gloria. "John Beckley: Jefferson's Campaign Manager." Bulletin of the New York Public Library. 64(1960), 247-60.

Portrays Beckley as a committed party man who was an enthusiastic supporter of TJ, who in turn appointed him as the first Librarian of Congress in 1802.

1708. "Jefferson and Fox." United States Magazine and Democratic Review. 27(1850), 193-202.

Compares TJ and Charles James Fox as party leaders who "embodied in their principles and reflected in their measures, more fully and perfectly than any of their contemporaries, the progressive tendencies of their times."

1709. Jefferson Day Dinner, The Mayflower Hotel, City of Washington, April thirteenth 1945. Washington, 1945. unpag.

Democratic Party affair; one-page note on TJ.

1710. "Jefferson Letter on Third Term." Hobbies. 45(April 1940), 25.

Reports sale and quotes in part from an autograph letter of January 10, 1804, to the North Carolina Assembly in which he rejects the notion of a third term.

1711. "Jefferson Takes the Helm." The Month of Goodspeed's. 19(1948), 140-44.

Describes and gives a facsimile in part of a letter from TJ to Elbridge Gerry, March 29, 1801.

1712. "Jefferson to William Short on Mr. and Mrs. Merry, 1804." AHR. 33(1928), 832-35.

Prints with notes a letter of January 23, 1804, on the supposed affront offered to the British envoy and his wife at the White House.

1713. "Jefferson's Law Reports." Virginia Literary Museum. 1(1829), 129-33.

Notes that TJ's executor had recently published some reports from
the old General court, collected by or reported by TJ.

1714. Jenkinson, Isaac. Aaron Burr, His Personal and Political Relations with
Thomas Jefferson and Alexander Hamilton. Richmond, Ind.: M.
Cullaton & Co., 1902. pp. viii, 389.

An attempted vindication of Burr; development and expansion of the
author's 1898 paper.

1715. Jenkinson, Isaac. Jefferson and Burr: A Paper Read Before the
Thursday Club, Richmond, Indiana, February 8, 1898. Richmond, Ind.:
M. Cullaton & Co., 1898. pp. 55.

Argues that Burr was the victim, first of TJ's political intrigue to
keep him from a second term as vice-president, then again of TJ's
"vindictive persecution" in the matter of the treason trials.

1716. Jennings, Walter Wilson. The American Embargo, 1807-1809. Univ. of
Iowa Studies in the Social Sciences. Vol. 8. Iowa City: Univ. of Iowa
Press, 1921. pp. 242.

Detailed study of the effects of the Embargo and responses to it. It
"stimulated manufactures, injured agriculture, and prostrated commerce." TJ gave in reluctantly to opposition to the Embargo in order
to avert civil war.

1717. Johnson, Allen. Jefferson and His Colleagues: A Chronicle of the
Virginia Dynasty. New Haven: Yale Univ. Press, 1921. pp. ix, 343.

Volume in the Chronicles of America series; an account of the presidential administrations of Jefferson, Madison, and Monroe with
emphasis on the Louisiana Purchase, western expansion, spread of
democracy to the Spanish republics.

*1718. Johnson, Luciana. "Thomas Jefferson and the Beginning of the Republi-
can Party." M.A. thesis. Univ. of California at Riverside, 1956.

1719. Johnstone, Robert M., Jr. Jefferson and the Presidency: Leadership in
the Young Republic. Ithaca: Cornell Univ. Press, 1978. pp. 332.

Argues that TJ significantly developed techniques for presidential
leadership, particularly in finding extra-constitutional sources of
power. He used his immense prestige, patronage, the press, and the
social advantages of his office to capitalize upon his position as
leader of his party. "The effective use of this rudimentary machinery
of party as an instrument of presidential power was one of Jefferson's
most important contributions to the presidency." Excellent book.

1720. Johnstone, Robert Morton, Jr. "The Resources of Presidential Power:
The Jeffersonian Example." Ph.D. dissertation. Cornell Univ., 1972.
pp. 520.

Revised and published as Jefferson and the Presidency. DAI 33/12A, p. 6983.

*1721. Jones, Paul W. "Jefferson and the National Gazette." M.A. thesis. Bowling Green State Univ., 1961.

1722. Kaplan, Lawrence S. "The Consensus of 1789: Jefferson and Hamilton on American Foreign Policy." South Atlantic Quarterly. 71(1972), 91-105.

Contends that the differences between TJ and Hamilton have been exaggerated by historians, particularly those pertaining to the period 1789-91. The cabinet officers differed over means, not objectives.

1723. Kaplan, Lawrence S. Jefferson and France: An Essay on Politics and Political Ideas. New Haven: Yale Univ. Press, 1967. pp. ix, 175.

Good study of TJ's attachment to France, his friendships with French citizens, and his political dealings with that nation. Assesses the charge that TJ's Francophilia led him into the service of the French Revolution and Napoleon and concludes that his foreign policy was not determined by French influence but that he saw the necessity for a balance of power in Europe to safeguard American independence and believed the balance in his time was weighted in favor of the British.

1724. Kaplan, Lawrence S. "Jefferson's Foreign Policy and Napoleon's Ideologues." WMQ. 3rd ser. 19(1962), 344-59.

Claims TJ erred in his relations with the French Ideologues by "joining them in minimizing the evils of the Empire and in overestimating their influence in Napoleon's government."

1725. Kaplan, Lawrence. S. "Jefferson, the Napoleonic Wars, and the Balance of Power." WMQ. 3rd ser. 14(1957), 196-217.

Argues that TJ was most successful as a statesman when he showed an appreciation for the importance of a balance of power in Europe for America's fortunes, when he saw the need for freedom from foreign entanglement, and when he valued a cautious diplomacy in advancing westward expansion. His rationalizations of the Embargo and for involvement in the Napoleonic Wars departed from this policy.

1726. Kaplan, Lawrence S. "Thomas Jefferson: The Idealist as Realist" in Makers of American Diplomacy from Benjamin Franklin to Henry Kissinger, ed. Frank J. Merli and Theodore A. Wilson. New York: Scribner's, 1974. 53-79.

A continuous thread in TJ's public career was his belief in "British policy as part of a plot to subvert American liberties," and this belief played a part in his difficulties as Secretary of State when he had to deal with both Hamilton's Anglophilia and France's intransigent behavior.

1727. Kaplan, Lawrence S. "Toward Isolationism: The Jeffersonian Republicans and the Franco-American Alliance of 1778." Historical Reflections. 3(1976), 69-81.

Argues that despite TJ's affinity for French ideas and culture, the isolationist spirit of his first inaugural address is serious. The Franco-American alliance of 1778 was slow to mature.

1728. Kaplan, Sidney. "The 'Domestic Insurrections' of the Declaration of Independence." Journal of Negro History. 61(1976), 243-55.

Somewhat rambling discussion of the charge, "He has excited domestic insurrections among us...," as a phrase which recognizes the southerners' real fears of a slave rebellion as well as being a euphemistic recognition of the injustice of slavery.

1729. Katz, Stanley N. "Thomas Jefferson and the Right to Property in Revolutionary America." Journal of Law and Economics. 19(1976), 467-88.

Argues that "pure republican theory" triumphed for only a brief period in America when TJ's understanding of the relationship between property, virtue, and government was dominant.

1730. Keats, John. Eminent Domain: The Louisiana Purchase and the Making of America. New York: Charterhouse, 1973. pp. viii, 389.

Breezy, sweeping account of the Purchase, based on secondary sources, deals with TJ passim.

1731. Kean, Robert G. H. "Thomas Jefferson as a Legislator." Virginia Law Journal. 11(1887), 705-24.

TJ's career as a legislator was both effective and forward looking; rpt. separately, Lynchburg, 1887. pp. 20.

1732. Keller, Linda Quinne. "Jefferson's Western Diplomacy: The Lewis and Clark Expedition." M.A. thesis. Univ. of Virginia, 1971. pp. 64.

The expedition discussed in terms of diplomatic maneuvering intended to solidify U.S. claims to the West all the way to the mouth of the Columbia.

1733. Keller, William F. "Jefferson Refutes a Tory Argument." Americana Illustrated. 34(1940), 447-57.

Transcription of notes by TJ on early attempts to settle Virginia, particularly by Raleigh; links this to TJ's claim that Americans themselves financed American settlement.

1734. Kelley, Darwin. "Jefferson and the Separation of Powers in the States, 1776-1787." Indiana Magazine of History. 54(1958), 25-40.

In 1775 TJ approved Franklin's proposed Articles of Confederation which did not provide for separation of powers, but his experiences in Virginia, particularly as governor, led him to support the concept as a vital principle of government.

1735. Kennedy, William P. Matthew Lyon Cast the Deciding Vote Which Elected Thomas Jefferson President in 1801. 77th Congress, 2d. Session. House Document No. 825. Washington: Government Printing Office, 1942. pp. ii, 29.

Long-winded argument for Vermont's coming over to TJ on the 36th ballot before Maryland did.

1736. Kent, Frank R. "The Democratic Creed" in The Democratic Party, A History. New York: Century, 1928. 27-45.

Superficial account of TJ's election to and administration of the presidency.

1737. Kenyon, Cecilia M. "The Declaration of Independence" in Fundamental Testaments of the American Revolution. Washington: Library of Congress, 1973. 25-46.

Interprets the Declaration in terms of both the political revolution and the social revolution for which TJ continued to strive.

1738. Kerber, Linda K. Federalists in Dissent: Imagery and Ideology in Jeffersonian America. Ithaca: Cornell Univ. Press, 1970. pp. xii, 233.

Useful survey of the range and style of Federalist attacks on TJ.

1739. Ketcham, Ralph L. "Jefferson and Madison and the Doctrines of Interposition and Nullification: A Letter of John Quincy Adams." VMHB. 66(1958), 178-82.

Letter of October 10, 1836, to Edward Everett in which Adams sees TJ as the "father of South Carolina Nullification" but "Madison shrunk from his conclusions."

*1740. Kettell, Thomas Prentice. Constitutional Reform in a Series of Articles Contributed to the Democratic Review, upon Constitutional Guaranties in Political Government ... to Which Are Added Two Letters of the Hon. Michael Hoffman on a Re-organization of the Judiciary of the State of New York ... also, The Correspondence of Thomas Jefferson on Constitutional Reform. New York: Thomas P. Kettell, 1846. pp. 77.

1741. Kingdon, Frank. "Thomas Jefferson: Individual Liberty" in Architects of the Republic. New York: Alliance Publishing, 1947. 87-153.

Depicts TJ as "the man who established firmly in our democracy the principle of individual liberty."

1742. Kirkland, Frederic R. "Jefferson and Franklin." PMHB, 71(1947), 218-22.

Comments on an entry in the Anas concerning Washington's efforts to halt an attack on Franklin in Fenno's Gazette of the United States.

1743. Knode, Jay C. "Virtue and Talents." American Scholar. 12(1943), 490-502.

How the Jacksonian revolution has triumphed over TJ's political principles.

1744. Knudson, Jerry W. "The Case of Albert Gallatin and Jeffersonian Patronage." Western Pennsylvania Historical Magazine. 52(1969), 241-50.

Study of the federalist opposition in the press to TJ's appointment of Gallatin as his Secretary of the Treasury.

1745. Knudson, Jerry Wayne. "The Jefferson Years: Response by the Press, 1801-1809." Ph.D. dissertation. Univ. of Virginia, 1962. pp. 379.

Studies the reaction of four major Federalist and four Republican papers to seven major issues of TJ's presidency. TJ did not have the effective newspaper support later enjoyed by Jackson. His correspondence with William Duane suggests he cultivated the National Intelligencer as official reporter and the Aurora as "unofficial partisan scrapper." DAI 23/08, p. 2893.

1746. Knudson, Jerry W. "The Jeffersonian Assault on the Federalist Judiciary, 1802-1805: Political Forces and Press Reaction." American Journal of Legal History. 14(1970), 55-70.

Contemporary response to the attempt to impeach Samuel Chase.

1747. Knudson, Jerry W. "Political Journalism in the Age of Jefferson." Journalism History. 1(1974), 20-23.

Summary of Ph.D. dissertation; argues that political rhetoric of the attacks on TJ is not to be taken at face value.

1748. Knudson, Jerry W. "The Rage Around Tom Paine." New York Historical Society Quarterly. 53(1969), 34-63.

When Paine returned to America in 1802, the Federalist press seized the opportunity to smear both Paine and TJ. This was the first test for the effectiveness of TJ's newspaper support, failed by most papers except William Duane's Aurora.

1749. Koch, Adrienne. Adams and Jefferson: "Posterity Must Judge." Chicago: Rand McNally, 1963. pp. 60.

A casebook, leaving the answer up to the student.

1750.   Koch, Adrienne. Jefferson and Madison: The Great Collaboration. New
        York: Knopf, 1950. pp. xv, 294, xiv.

        Often suggestive study of the working relationship between TJ and
        Madison, arguing that Madison tempered TJ's opinions and led him to
        refine his positions in a number of important cases, most notably on
        the Constitution and the response to the Alien and Sedition Laws.
        Claims that TJ was ordinarily bolder and more imaginative in
        projecting hypotheses than Madison and that his thought was
        characteristically experimental and pragmatic, whereas Madison was
        more strictly logical.

1751.   Koch, Adrienne and Harry Ammon. "The Virginia and Kentucky Resolu-
        tions: An Episode in Jefferson's and Madison's Defense of Civil
        Liberties." WMQ. 3rd ser. 5(1948), 141-76.

        Concludes that Jefferson and Madison are "the only major authors of
        the Resolutions."

1752.   Koenig, Louis W. "'Consensus Politics,' 1800-1805." American
        Heritage. 18(February 1967), 4-7, 74-80.

        Discusses TJ's difficulties with John Randolph of Roanoke.

1753.   Kraus, Michael. "Jefferson Guides the Republic" in The United States
        to 1865. Ann Arbor: Univ. of Michigan Press, 1959. 297-326.

        Brief history of the TJ and Madison administrations; in TJ's terms he
        is portrayed as the author of all actions, but in Madison's the chief
        actors are variously "Congress," "the Americans," etc.

1754.   Kreisberg, Paul H. "Hamiltonian and Jeffersonian Ideals in the Admini-
        stration of the State." Journal of Social Studies. 6(Spring 1950),
        24-32.

        Derivative; calls TJ a "Rousseauist."

1755.   Krislov, Samuel. "Jefferson and Judicial Review: Refereeing Cahn,
        Commager, and Mendelson." Journal of Public Law. 9(1960), 374-81.

        Argues that TJ's position on judicial review was consistent. He ad-
        mitted the right of the judiciary to declare a law unconstitutional but
        held that judicial review did not necessarily imply judicial supremacy
        over the legislature.

1756.   Krock, Arthur. "Jefferson's Stepchildren." American Mercury.
        7(1926), 129-35.

        In 1926 "the Northern and Eastern Democracy happen to be the only
        Jeffersonian elements of the party," and this is accidental.

1757. Kuper, Theodore Fred. "Thomas Jefferson and Slavery." New York State Bar Journal. 42(1970), 125-32.

TJ's opposition to slavery; minor.

1758. Lacy, Alexander Bustard, Jr. "Jefferson and Congress: Congressional Method and Politics, 1801-1809." Ph.D. dissertation. Univ. of Virginia, 1964. pp. iii, 326.

By developing and using his role as party leader, TJ became an effective presidential leader. He effected little change in legal institutions, but he fostered "a pattern of political behavior which actually by-passed, and in effect made obsolete, certain aspects of the formal constitutional system." DAI 25/05, p. 3084.

1759. Langhorne, Elizabeth. "Edward Coles, Thomas Jefferson, and the Rights of Man." Virginia Cavalcade. 23(Summer 1973), 30-37.

Focus on Coles, TJ's private secretary who moved to Illinois in order to free his slaves after TJ declined to lead a campaign for emancipation.

1760. Larus, Joel. "Pell-Mell Along the Potomac." WMQ. 3rd ser. 17(1960), 349-57.

TJ and Anthony Merry, the British minister, clash over protocol as observed at a White House dinner.

1761. Latane, John Holladay. "Jefferson's Influence on American Foreign Policy." Univ. of Virginia Alumni Bulletin. 3rd ser. 17(1924), 245-69.

Discusses Woodrow Wilson's critical assessment of TJ and notes how similar the two presidents were. TJ would have hailed any system replacing physical coercion with moral force.

1762. Lemen, Joseph B. "The Jefferson-Lemen Anti-slavery Pact." Transactions of the Illinois State Historical Society for the Year 1908. Springfield: Illinois State Journal Co., 1909. 74-84.

Claims TJ sent James Lemen as a "confidential agent" into the Illinois section of the Northwest Territory to oppose slavery and later encouraged him to form a Baptist church with an anti-slavery platform. Evidence is extremely thin.

*1763. Lathrop, Mary F. "Jefferson's Contribution to the Law of the West" in Pennsylvania Bar Association. Report of the Thirty-third Annual Meeting. Philadelphia: Printed for the Association, 1927. 297-307.

1764. Leffmann, Henry. "The True Story of the Declaration of Independence." Philadelphia History. 2(1917), 21-35.

Background to TJ's writing of the Declaration; minor.

1765. Lerche, Charles O., Jr. "Jefferson and the Election of 1800: A Case Study in the Political Smear." WMQ. 3rd ser. 5(1948), 467-91.

Analyzes anti-Jefferson propaganda; the one achievement of the Federalist writers was to damage TJ's reputation "so badly that many of their charges linger today."

1766. Levy, Leonard W. "The Emergence of an American Libertarian Theory" in Legacy of Suppression: Freedom of Speech and Press in Early American History. Cambridge: Harvard Univ. Press, 1960. 249-312.

Gives TJ least possible amount of credit for evolving libertarian principles and most blame for contradictory practice during his administration.

1767. Levy, Leonard W. Jefferson & Civil Liberties, The Darker Side. Cambridge: Harvard Univ. Press, 1963. pp. xv, 225.

Argues that, although TJ was a libertarian who was an important worker for American civil liberties, he "never once risked career or reputation to champion free speech, fair trial, or any other libertarian value. On many occasions he was on the wrong side. On others he trimmed his sails and remained silent." Not all readers will agree with this book, but those wishing to deal with the subject must take account of it.

1768. Levy, Leonard. "Jefferson as a Civil Libertarian" in Thomas Jefferson: The Man ... His World ... His Influence, ed. Lally Weymouth. New York: Putnam's, 1973. 189-215.

The dark side of TJ's record. "A philosopher of freedom without a philosophy of freedom," he was poorly equipped to confront what he saw as challenges to freedom or to recognize how his own actions or those of his supporters threatened it.

*1769. Levy, Richard. "The First Inaugural Address of Thomas Jefferson: The Founding of the American Republic." M.A. thesis. Univ. of Chicago, 1966.

*1770. Lewis, Anthony Marc. "Jefferson and the American Union, 1769-1781." Ph.D. dissertation. Univ. of Michigan, 1946.

1771. Lewis, Anthony Marc. "Jefferson and Virginia's Pioneers, 1774-1781." MVHR. 34(1948), 551-88.

TJ was interested in encouraging settlers in Kentucky with cheap land, secure tenure, and military defense; he worked to control land speculators and as governor took an active interest in military affairs in the West.

1772. Lewis, Anthony M. "Jefferson's Summary View as a Chart of Political Union." WMQ. 3rd ser. 5(1948), 34-51.

Analysis of A Summary View shows that TJ "more clearly perhaps than did any of his contemporaries, ... forecast a desirable division of sovereign powers between the local and the imperial sphere." At the same time, it foretells "his constant support of an American confederacy."

1773. Libby, O. G. "Political Factions in Washington's Administrations." The Quarterly Journal. 3(July 1913), 293-318.

Contends that political factions in first four congresses did not reflect pre-constitutional divisions of federalists and anti-feds nor was there any real party organization, mostly because of the absence of talented party leaders. Hamilton "lacked ability to lead men," and TJ would find his key issues only during the Adams administration.

1774. Lichtenstein, Gaston. Thomas Jefferson as War Governor, Also Three Travel Articles and Some North Carolina History. Richmond, Va.: William Byrd Press, 1925. 9-42.

Quotes extensively from TJ's correspondence, but offers little critical or analytical comment and that diffuse and digressive.

1775. Lindsey, David. "George Canning and Jefferson's Embargo, 1807-1809." Tyler's Quarterly. 1(October 1952), 43-47.

On Canning, who felt U.S. supplies and markets were not essential to the success of England's war against France.

1776. Little, David. "Thomas Jefferson's Religious Views and Their Influence on the Supreme Court's Interpretation of the First Amendment." Catholic University Law Review. 26(1976), 57-72.

Contends that because religious beliefs "were finally irrelevant and unimportant to Jefferson ... he believed they should be set apart and fenced off from the world of action."

1777. Lokke, Carl Ludwig. "Jefferson and the Leclerc Expedition." AHR. 33(1928), 322-28.

TJ's support for French recovery of St. Domingo was exaggerated in Pichon's reports to Bonaparte.

1778. Long, Everett Lee. "Jefferson and Congress: A Study of the Jeffersonian Legislative System, 1801-1809." Ph.D. dissertation. Univ. of Missouri, 1966. pp. 494.

TJ as president took a pragmatic and moderate course in dealing with Congress in order to attract to the Republican party the broad center of political opinion and in order to respect the sensitivities of Congress members. Discusses executive initiative of legislation, use of floor leaders in Congress, the party caucus, and executive oversight of legislation. DAI 27/04A, p. 1017.

1779. Lorant, Stefan. "The Fourth Election—1800" and "The Fifth Election—1804" in The Presidency: A Pictorial History of the Presidential Elections from Washington to Truman. New York: Macmillan, 1951. 43-65.

Popular history with interesting illustrations.

1780. Lotts, Velma Capps. "Jefferson's Pre-Presidential Criticism of the Federal Judiciary." Marshall Review. 3(no. 3, 1940), 27-33.

Competent survey, but nothing new.

1781. Lovett, Robert Morss. "Thomas Jefferson and the Louisiana Purchase." New England Magazine. n.s. 1(1890), 569-77.

The Purchase as TJ's accomplishment.

1782. Luckwaldt, Friedrich. "Thomas Jefferson" in Meister der Politik. Eine Weltgeschichtliche Reihe von Bildnessen, hgb. Erich Marcks und Karl Alexander von Muller. Stuttgart: Deutsche Verlags-Anstalt, 1922. 2:275-324.

1783. Lydon, James G. "Thomas Jefferson and the Mathurins." Catholic Historical Review. 49(1963), 192-202.

TJ used members of the Mathurins, or Order of the Holy Trinity, to aid in redemption of American captives from the Barbary pirates in 1787-90.

1784. Lyman, Jane Louise. "Jefferson and Negro Slavery." Journal of Negro Education. 16(1947), 10-27.

Explains away TJ's views on race, presenting him as an opponent of slavery.

1785. Lynch, William O. "Jefferson the Liberal." Indiana Magazine of History. 40(1944), 41-47.

General sketch of TJ's political life.

1786. McBain, Howard Lee. "Jefferson and the New York Patronage" in DeWitt Clinton and the Origin of the Spoils System in New York. New York: Columbia Univ. Press, 1907. 139-58.

Argues that TJ tended to take the side of the Clintons rather than Burr in patronage decisions but denies that there was any collusion to separate Burr from the Republican party.

1787. McCaleb, Water Flavius. The Aaron Burr Conspiracy. A History Largely from Original and Hitherto Unused Sources. New York: Dodd Mead, 1903. pp. xviii, 309.

Contends that James Wilkinson accused Burr of treason to save his own skin and misled TJ. TJ interpreted criticism of his subsequent actions as partisan malice; he lost his temper and self-control, began to act obstinately and vindictively, and revealed his shortcomings. Rpt. in an expanded edition with introduction by Charles A. Beard, New York: Wilson-Erickson, 1936.

1788.   McCaleb, Walter F. "Early Pattern for Tyranny in the U.S." Texas Quarterly. 2(Winter 1959), 142-51.

Colorful, if somewhat careless, account of the Burr trial in which, the author contends, TJ set a pattern of tyranny for later generations.

1789.   McCaleb, Walter F. New Light on Aaron Burr. Austin: Texas Quarterly Studies, 1963. pp. xxi, 166.

See particularly in Chapter 9, "Jefferson's Conduct" (96-102), which charges "In relation to the Conspiracy, Thomas Jefferson occupies a meretricious position, unique, malevolent." Sees Burr as an innocent victim.

*1790.   McCarrell, David K. "The Formation of the Jeffersonian Party in Virginia." Ph.D. dissertation. Duke Univ., 1937.

1791.   McColley, Robert McNair. "Gentlemen and Slavery in Jefferson's Virginia." Ph.D. dissertation. Univ. of California, Berkeley, 1961.

Published in 1964 as Slavery and Jeffersonian Virginia.

1792.   McColley, Robert. Slavery and Jeffersonian Virginia. Urbana: Univ. of Illinois Press, 1964. pp. x, 227.

Covers approximately the years of 1776-1815; Virginia Jeffersonians developed "the model theory of American racism," and TJ was the model racist. But if TJ was well behind such public advocates of emancipation as John Jay, Anthony Benezet, and Robert Pleasants, he went as far as an elected representative of Virginia could go in attacking slavery.

1793.   McCormick, Robert R. An Address by Colonel Robert R. McCormick. Monticello, 1931. pp. (6).

Celebrates the Supreme Court decision of 1931, Near vs. State of Minnesota, as a confirmation of TJ's principles.

1794.   McCoy, Drew R. The Elusive Republic: Political Economy in Jeffersonian America. Chapel Hill: Univ. of North Carolina Press, 1980. pp. ix, 268.

On Jeffersonians rather than TJ, but he is frequently touched on, and this offers useful insights into his economic ideas and policies.

1795.   McDonald, Forrest. "A Mirror for Presidents." Commentary.
        62(December 1976), 34-41.

        Presidential experience of TJ described and offered as a model for
        Jimmy Carter in terms of a way to master both the ritualistic and
        executive functions of the presidency.

1796.   McDonald, Forrest. The Presidency of Thomas Jefferson. Lawrence:
        Univ. Press of Kansas, 1976. pp. xii, 201.

        Surveys TJ's eight years in the White House; traces influences of
        whig ideology, Bolingbroke, etc., but perhaps overstates the case.
        Argues that TJ made a serious mistake in insisting upon the elimina-
        tion of the public debt.

1797.   McGinnis, Charles A. "Thomas Jefferson and the Middle West." Negro
        History Bulletin. 5(no. 8, 1942), 173, 191.

        Credits TJ with keeping slavery out of the old Northwest.

*1798. McGrath, Paul Cox. "Secretary Jefferson and Revolutionary France,
        1790-1793." Ph.D. dissertation. Boston Univ., 1950.

1799.   McIlwaine, H. R., ed. Official Letters of the Governors of Virginia.
        II. Letters of Thomas Jefferson. Richmond: Virginia State Library,
        1928. pp. ix, 567.

        Prints letters of TJ and of those acting for him in his absence; brief
        notes.

1800.   MacKaye, Benton. "Genesis and Jefferson." Survey. 86(1950), 556-59.

        Claims TJ was a great "geotechnist," i.e. a sort of ecologist cum
        economist and regional planner.

1801.   McKee, George H. Th. Jefferson, Ami de la Revolution Francaise.
        Lorient: Imprimerie Al. Cathrine, 1928. pp. x, 325.

        Rpt. Paris: Nizet et Bastard, 1935. "Thèse pour le doctorat
        d'université preséntée à la Faculté des Lettres de Grenoble." Sees
        TJ too simply as friend of France; defines party orientation in the
        U.S. as democrates francophiles and federalistes anglophiles. Criti-
        cizes Genet more for his manners than for the substance of his
        actions.

1802.   McLaughlin, William G. "Thomas Jefferson and the Beginning of
        Cherokee Nationalism, 1806 to 1809." WMQ. 3rd ser. 32(1975),
        547-80.

        Argues that the rise of Cherokee nationalism was encouraged by the
        response to TJ's 1808 proposal to move the tribe to the West and to

his alternative offer of integration of Cherokees as fee simple farmer-citizens of the U.S. Focus on the Cherokees, not TJ.

1803. McLemore, R. A. "Jeffersonian Diplomacy in the Purchase of Louisiana, 1803." Louisiana Historical Quarterly. 18(1935), 246-53.

A letter from TJ to Robert Livingston, minister at Paris, shows his determination and skill in diplomatic moves to obtain Louisiana, despite Henry Adams' claims to the contrary.

1804. MacLeod, Julia H. "Jefferson and the Navy: A Defense." Huntington Library Quarterly. 8(1945), 153-84.

TJ understood the strategic use of naval power and was in some ways far in advance of his time; his support for the navy, however, was balanced by his concern to eliminate the national debt and by his recognition of the nation's financial inability to support a navy large enough to gain control of the seas from the much larger British fleet.

1805. Macmillan, Malcolm C. "Jeffersonian Democracy and the Origins of Sectionalism" in Writing Southern History: Essays in Historiography in Honor of Fletcher M. Green, ed. Arthur S. Link and Rembert W. Patrick. Baton Rouge: Louisiana State Univ. Press, 1965. 91-124.

In effect a bibliographical essay, useful for material written before 1964.

1806. MacNaul, Willard C. The Jefferson-Lemen Compact: The Relations of Thomas Jefferson and James Lemen in the Exclusion of Slavery from Illinois and the Northwest Territory, with Related Documents, 1781-1818. Chicago: Univ. of Chicago Press, 1915. pp. 59.

Details of the supposed agreement in which TJ encouraged Lemen to go to Illinois to work against the introduction of slavery. Reprints all the "evidence" which exists only in copies made by members of the Lemen family.

1807. Madison. James. Letters on the Constitutionality and Policy of Duties, for the Protection and Encouragement of Manufactures. Richmond: Thomas W. White, 1829. pp. 27, 4.

Prints extracts from TJ's letters in support of congressional power to set protective duties.

1808. Malone, Dumas and Garry Wills. "Executive Privilege: Jefferson & Burr & Nixon & Ehrlichman." New York Review of Books. 21(July 18, 1974), 36-40.

Malone replies to Wills' earlier review essay on the Burr trial (see below), and Wills rejoins at length.

225

1809.   Malone, Dumas. "Jefferson, Hamilton, and the Constitution" in Theory
        and Practice in American Politics, ed. William H. Nelson. Chicago:
        Univ. of Chicago Press, 1964. 13-23.

        TJ and Hamilton were important agents in the process of interpreting
        the Constitution, but constitutional interpretation cannot be divorced
        from historical circumstances. Discusses the bank question and the
        Alien and Sedition Laws.

1810.   Malone, Dumas. "Presidential Leadership and National Unity: The
        Jeffersonian Example." Journal of Southern History. 35(1969), 3-17.

        General survey of TJ's conduct of the presidency, contrasted with
        the situation and conduct of recent presidents.

1811.   Malone, Dumas. The Story of the Declaration of Independence.
        New York: Oxford Univ. Press, 1954. pp. 282.

        Background account of the drafting, lives of the signers; aimed at a
        general audience. Illustrated.

1812.   Malone, Dumas. "Thomas Jefferson as a Lawyer." Essential Books.
        1(December 1955), 5-8.

        Discusses the conditions of being a lawyer in Virginia circa 1770 and
        TJ's professional activities at that time.

1813.   Malone, Dumas. Thomas Jefferson as Political Leader. Berkeley: Univ.
        of California Press, 1963. pp. viii, 75.

        How TJ became a party leader, developed in biographical terms.

1814.   Mannix, Richard. "Gallatin, Jefferson, and the Embargo of 1808."
        Diplomatic History. 3(1979), 151-72.

        Contends that TJ was not concerned with the Embargo, did not see it
        as his measure, and was unaware of the details and requirements of
        its operation. Only Gallatin, somewhat reluctantly, made an effort
        to manage the Embargo.

1815.   Mansfield, Harvey C., Jr. "Thomas Jefferson" in American Political
        Thought, ed. Morton Frisch and Richard Stevens. New York:
        Scribner's, 1971. 23-50.

        Competent survey of TJ's political career, his ideas, and influence;
        balances idealism against partisanship.

1816.   Marchione, Margherita. Philip Mazzei: Jefferson's 'Zealous Whig.'
        New York: American Institute of Italian Studies, 1975. pp. x, 350.

Biographical chapter (15-34) focuses on Mazzei's American adventures, followed by facsimiles of correspondence and a translation of his Historical and Political Enquiries on the United States of North America.

1817. Marsh, Philip. "Jefferson and Freneau." American Scholar. 16(1947), 201-10.

Freneau, TJ, and the National Gazette.

1818. Marsh, Philip. "Jefferson and Journalism." Huntington Library Quarterly. 9(1946), 209-12.

TJ in the 1790's urged both Madison and Edmund Pendleton to write against Hamilton and the Federalists; apparently he solicited only these two to take up their pens.

1819. Marsh, Philip. "Jefferson's 'Conduct' of the National Gazette." Proceedings of the New Jersey Historical Society. 63(1945), 69-73.

Argues that TJ did not direct Freneau's paper.

1820. Marsh, Philip M., ed. Monroe's Defense of Jefferson and Freneau against Hamilton. Oxford, Ohio, 1948. pp. 56.

Reprints Hamilton's anonymous newspaper attacks on TJ and anonymous replies by Monroe, written in collaboration with Madison in 1792-93. Introduction and notes.

1821. Marsh, Philip. "Monroe's Draft of the Defense of Freneau." PMHB. 71(1947), 73-76.

Monroe defends TJ's appointment of Freneau as a translator.

1822. Marsh, Philip M. "Randolph and Hamilton: 'Aristides' Replies to 'An American,' 'Catullus,' and 'Scourge.'" PMHB. 72(1948), 247-52.

Edmund Randolph, "Aristides," replies to Hamilton, writing under three pseudonyms in attack upon TJ, but Randolph's middle of the road position ended up satisfying neither TJ nor Hamilton.

1823. Marshall, John. "John Marshall Renders His Opinion of Mr. Jefferson." Magazine of Albemarle County History. 30(1972), 15-18.

Letter of Marshall to Henry Lee, dated October 25, 1830, comments acerbly on the recent edition of TJ's writings and calls Lee's attention to the "peculiar asperity with which he speaks of your father." See item #689.

1824. Master, R. W. "Jefferson and the Constitution." World Review. 4(March 14, 1927), 87.

Outline for contestants in the National Oratorical Contest.

1825.   Mayer, Frederick. "The Historical Significance of the Struggle Between Hamilton and Jefferson." Social Studies. 40(1949), 165-67.

"Hamilton was the Hobbes of the United States. ... Jefferson was the first New Dealer." Superficial.

1826.   Mayes, R. B. "The Divine Legation of Thomas Jefferson.—Are All Men Created Free?—Are All Men Created White?" DeBow's Review. 30(1861), 521-32.

Taken literally, the Declaration contradicts the Bible, which suggests "man" as exlusively applicable to the white race.

1827.   Mead, Edwin D. "Washington, Jefferson, and Franklin on War." World Peace Foundation Pamphlet. 3(May 1913), 1-15.

TJ saw war as "The greatest of human evils."

*1828. Meisen, Adolph Frank. "Thomas Jefferson, War Governor of Virginia." Ph.D. dissertation. Univ. of North Carolina, 1943.

1829.   Mendelson, Wallace. "Cahn on Jefferson, Commager and Learned Hand." Texas Law Review. 37(1959), 721 ff.

Responds to 1958 article by Edmond Cahn by pointing out TJ changed his mind on judicial review after 1789.

1830.   Mendelson, Wallace and Samuel Krislov. "Jefferson on Judicial Review." Journal of Public Law. 10(1961), 113-24.

"A Reply to Professor Krislov" and "The Alleged Inconsistency: A Revised Version" debate Krislov's article in J. Pub. Law., 9(1960), on the consistency of TJ's views on judicial review.

1831.   [Mercer, Charles Fenton]. An Exposition of the Weakness and Inefficiency of the Government of the United States of North America. n.p.: Printed for the Author, 1845. pp. 380.

See especially the chapter on "Jeffersonian Policy" (234-58) for a detailed attack on TJ's political ideas and politics. "No matter what evil invades the land, what dreadful ruin breaks up our institutions, what disgrace attacks and leaves its foul spot on our character, all may be traced to the damnable policy of Thomas Jefferson and his party."

1832.   Merriam, Charles Edward. "The Jeffersonian Democracy" in A History of American Political Theories. New York: Macmillan, 1903. 143-75.

Argues that Jeffersonian theory was democratic although his practice was in many ways aristocratic; "its full realization was left for another time and another party."

1833. Merriam, J. M. "Jefferson's Use of the Executive Patronage." American Historical Association Papers. 2(1887), 47-52.

Abstract of a delivered paper contending that TJ made far more removals than commonly believed, and he increasingly emphasized political opposition as a cause for removal.

1834. Miller, John C. Crisis in Freedom: The Alien and Sedition Acts. Boston: Little Brown, 1951. pp. 253.

TJ touched on throughout; pp. 169-81 focus on his role and Madison's in drawing up the Kentucky and Virginia Resolutions, which offered the most forceful statement of the constitutional objections to the acts. Argues that their failure strengthened the Federalists' belief that public opinion was with them.

1835. Millspaugh, Arthur C. "The Jeffersonian Resolution" in Democracy, Efficiency, Stability: An Appraisal of American Government. Washington: Brookings Institution, 1942. 48-51.

Generalized assessment of TJ as a "strong" president.

1836. Minnegerode, Meade. Jefferson, Friend of France, 1793; The Career of Edmond Charles Genet, Minister Plenipotentiary from the French Republic to the United States, as Revealed by His Private Papers, 1763-1843. New York: Putnam's, 1928. pp. xiv, 447.

Focus on Genet; uncritically accepts Genet's charge that TJ betrayed him and presents a Hamiltonian view of TJ.

1837. Minnegerode, Meade. "The Mammoth of Democracy" in Presidential Years 1787-1860. New York: Putnam's, 1928. 77-121.

Popular social history focusing on the events leading up to TJ's election in 1800.

1838. Minor, Charles. Oration Delivered at the Request of the Jefferson Society of the University of Virginia, on the Anniversary of the Birth-Day of Thomas Jefferson, April 13, 1834, in the Episcopal Church, Charlottesville, Va. Charlottesville: Wm. Tompkins, 1834. pp. 14.

In praise of popular government, with a nod to TJ.

1839. Minor, Henry. "Democratic Dominance Under Jefferson" and "Democratic Government Fixed by Jefferson" in The Story of the Democratic Party. New York: Macmillan, 1928. 38-65.

TJ stopped the national government's tendency to assume power over the people, but he did not reject the idea of a powerful government ruled by the people.

1840.   Minor, Robert. "Titan of Freedom." New Masses. 47(April 13, 1943), 10-13.

TJ as a progressive, unfortunately dying before Marx discovered the truth about the forces of production; suggests that both TJ and Stalin understand constitutions as a technique of preventing political regress.

1841.   "Mr. Jefferson." Southern Literary Messenger. 7(1841), 287-88.

Claims TJ insisted upon "a uniformly strict construction of the Constitution."

1842.   Moley, Raymond. "The Wisdom of a Ghost." Newsweek. 12(November 21, 1938), 44.

TJ knew how to build a party, but the Democrats of 1938 fail to heed his example.

1843.   Moore, Justus E. The Warning of Thomas Jefferson; or a Brief Exposition of Dangers to Be Apprehended to Our Civil and Religious Liberties from Presbyterianism. Philadelphia: Wm. J. Cunningham, 1844. pp. 35.

Criticism of anti-Catholic rhetoric and riots.

1844.   Moore, R. Walton. "Farewell Address to Thomas Jefferson, President of the United States, and Resolution Relative Thereunto." WMQ. 2nd ser. 11(1931), 59-60.

Prints with notes address from Virginia General Assembly.

1845.   Morgan, Donald Grant. "The Origins of Supreme Court Dissent." WMQ. 3rd ser. 10(1953), 353-77.

Examines judicial career of Justice William Johnson, appointed to the Supreme Court in 1804, and his relationship with TJ.

1846.   Morgan, James Morris. "How President Jefferson Was Informed of Burr's Conspiracy." PMHB. 27(1903), 56-69.

TJ first heard of Burr's plans from Colonel John Morgan.

1847.   Morris, Roland S. "Jefferson as a Lawyer." Proceedings of the APS. 87(1943), 211-15.

Sketchy.

1848. Morse, Anson D. "The Significance of the Democratic Party in American Politics." International Monthly. 2(1900), 437-56.

TJ's policy prevented a revival of federalism, but it also federalized his own party. Suggests TJ "tried to make all classes democratic," but Jackson appealed to class interest.

1849. Moses, Ernest C. "The Signing of the Declaration, With Documental History. American Monthly Magazine. 23(1903), 107-10.

Questions TJ's reminiscences about signing the Declaration on the 4th.

1850. Mott, Frank L. Jefferson and the Press. Baton Rouge: Louisiana State Univ. Press, 1943. pp. 65.

TJ "adhered to the principle, but was deeply disappointed in the performance, of a free press."

1851. Mumper, James Arthur. "The Jefferson Image in the Federalist Mind, 1801-1809: Jefferson's Administration from the Federalist Point of View." Ph.D. dissertation. Univ. of Virginia, 1966. pp. 501.

The Federalists, even after Hamilton's eclipse, continued to attack TJ along the lines formed in May to October of 1792. The hard-core party line blinded them to the nature of the opposition and to the role of popular parties in a modern two-party system. DAI 27/10A, p. 3405.

1852. Munves, James. Thomas Jefferson and the Declaration of Independence. New York: Scribner's, 1978. pp. viii, 135.

An examination of the textual evolution of the Declaration, based on Becker and Boyd and aimed at a non-scholarly audience.

1853. Muresan, Camil. "Declaratia de Independenta a Statelor Unite ale America." Steaua. 27(no. 7, 1976), 18-19.

In Rumanian.

1854. National Association of Democratic Clubs. Thomas Jefferson. 1743-1897. One Hundred and Fifty-fourth Birthday Anniversary Celebration, Tuesday, April Thirteenth, 1897, ... Washington: N. T. Elliott, 1897. pp. 100.

Testimonials to TJ from Democratic political leaders; also words and music to William T. Whelan's "the Jeffersonian Banner."

1855. National Democratic Club. Banquet by the Democratic Club in Celebration of the 156th Birthday of Thomas Jefferson on Thursday, April 13th, 1899, at the Metropolitan Opera House. New York:

W. P. Mitchell & Son, 1899. pp. 80.

Tributes to TJ from leading Democrats.

1856.   Nevins, Allan. The American States During and After the Revolution, 1775-1789. New York: Macmillan, 1927. 324-33.

Discusses TJ's governorship of Virginia which exposed in him "certain real defects of capacity."

1857.   Nicolay, Helen. "Our Nation in the Building; The Romance of American Union." Century Magazine. 91(1914-15), 189-215, 456-65.

Popular treatment; these installments cover TJ's presidency.

1858.   Norcross, Jonathan. The History of Democracy Considered as a Party Name and as a Political Organization. New York: Published for the Author by G. P. Putnam's, 1883. 65-78.

Democrats are demagogues, dissolute and perpetually dissatisfied, but TJ was a Republican (GOP), "although he did many very naughty things that looked like Democratic deeds." Doubts that he wrote the "treasonable" Kentucky Resolutions.

1859.   Nunis, Doyce B., Jr. "Thomas Jefferson and the Rights of Man" in American Political Thought: Search for Nationhood. Menlo Park, Cal.: Addision-Wesley, 1975. 38-60.

Survey for undergraduates; emphasis on "Jefferson the doctrinaire."

1860.   Nussbaum, Frederick L. "American Tobacco and French Politics, 1783-1789." Political Science Quarterly. 40(1925), 497-516.

Examines TJ's efforts to end the control of the Farmers General over the American tobacco trade and to oppose the creation of monopolies such as that envisioned by Robert Morris.

1861.   O'Brien, Charles F. "The Religious Issue in the Presidential Campaign of 1800." Essex Institute Historical Collections. 107(1971), 82-93.

Survey of religious dimension of Federalist campaign against TJ.

1862.   "On the Question of Re-election." Current History. n.s. 7(September 1944), 178-80.

Prints selections from TJ's letters, with a comment that they are particularly appropriate at a time when for the first time an American president is seeking a fourth term.

1863.   The Ordinance of 1784 and Jefferson's Services for the Northwest Territory. Old South Leaflets, no. 127. Boston: Directors of the

Old South Work, 1902. pp. 24.

Prints TJ's report of 1784, supporting documents and letters, and commentary on his role in developing the Northwest Territory.

*1864. Osborn, Robert W. "Portrait of a Revolutionary: Thomas Jefferson and the Coming of the American Revolution." M.A. thesis. Fort Hays State College, 1969.

1865. "Our First Economy President, A Review of the First English Biography of Jefferson." World's Work. 51(1926), 666-67.

Praises Hirst's biography for its understanding of TJ's economic programs.

1866. Owsley, Frank Lawrence. "The Foundations of Democracy." Southern Review. 1(1936), 708-20.

Argues that through control of the courts the Hamiltonians have subverted TJ's vision of liberty, i.e. state rights, strict construction, and laissez faire; claims the Fourteenth Amendment is a plutocratic instrument.

1867. Padover, Saul K. "Jefferson's Prose Poem: The Declaration of Independence." American Mercury. 54(1942), 165-71.

Account of the composition of the Declaration.

1868. Padover, Saul K. "Thomas Jefferson and the Election of 1800." Lithopinion. 7(Fall 1972), 8-14.

Succinct account of conditions leading up to the election and the 36 ballots required to elect TJ.

1869. Page, Ralph W. "The British-American Adventures Toward Liberty." World's Work. 35(1917), 48-65.

TJ by purchasing Louisiana helped checkmate Napoleon, thus taking part in a long history of Anglo-American cooperation to preserve liberty. A novel view.

1870. Palmer, Robert R. "The Dubious Democrat: Thomas Jefferson in Bourbon France." Political Science Quarterly. 72(1957), 388-404.

Analyzes TJ's attitudes to the Revolution while in France; suggests he moved from tepid support in 1789 to become the leading American sympathizer in 1793 because of his fundamental belief in liberty and equality, his recognition of the possibility of attaining the ideals of the revolution, and his understanding of the real political issues involved.

1871. Pancake, John S. Thomas Jefferson & Alexander Hamilton. Woodbury,

N.Y.: Barron's Educational Series, 1974. pp. 521.

A "duo-biography" which focuses on the argument between TJ and Hamilton over the solution to the "federal problem," the correct balance between the demands of society and the rights of the individual.

1872. Park, Edwards. "Absolutely, Dr. Franklin?—Positively, Mr. Jefferson!" Smithsonian. 7(July 1976), 50-51.

"Two knowledgeable ghosts case modern America with incredulity and some feeling of regret."

1873. Patterson, Caleb Perry. Constitutional Principles of Thomas Jefferson. Austin: Univ. of Texas Press, 1953. pp. 211.

Contends TJ believed in "constitutional supremacy" in opposition to supremacy of the executive, legislative, or judiciary branches. This means opposition to centralization of power, strict construction, and the ultimate supremacy of the people over the Constitution, although TJ was no doctrinaire.

1874. Patterson, Caleb Perry. "Jefferson and Judicial Review." American Bar Association Journal. 30(1944), 431-51.

Competently examines TJ's changing opinions of judicial review in order to argue that he ultimately opposed making the Constitution "a blank paper by construction."

1875. Patterson, C. Perry. "Jefferson the Lawyer." Univ. of Pittsburgh Law Review. 11(1950), 369-96.

Extensive survey of TJ and major contemporaries leads to the conclusion that at the Virginia bar TJ and John Marshall are most similar in their contributions to the law; TJ's contribution is greater in private law, Marshall's in public.

1876. Patterson, Caleb Perry. "Thomas Jefferson and the Constitution." Minnesota Law Review. 29(March 1945), 265-79.

Survey of attitudes toward and opinions on the Constitution, arguing that he was "the most persistent advocate among the forefathers of the importance of a fundamental constitution," as well as being in favor of judicial review and of leaving power to amend in the hands of the people.

1877. Pattison, William D. Beginnings of the American Rectangular Land Survey System, 1784-1800. Dept. of Geography Research Paper No. 50. Chicago: Univ. of Chicago Press, 1957. pp. vii, 248.

TJ treated throughout in an interesting account of the surveying and establishing of boundaries in the Northwest Territory; see especially

"Jefferson's Plan for Western States" (15-36).

1878.   Patton, Jacob Harris. Political Parties in the United States, Their
        History and Influence. New York: New Amsterdam Book Co., 1896.
        pp. ix, 387.

        Extremely partisan account of parties in the U.S., repeating with un-
        diminished enthusiasm old Federalist charges against TJ; see
        pp. 9-52.

1879.   Pawelek, Dick. "Stormy Birth of U.S. Political Parties." Senior
        Scholastic. 112(November 1, 1979), 10-12.

        TJ provoked by Federalist excesses into forming a party.

1880.   Pease, Theodore Calvin. "The Days of Jeffersonian Simplicity" in
        The United States. New York: Harcourt Brace, 1927. 241-60.

        TJ's presidency treated with focus on TJ himself, principally in
        terms of his diplomatic successes and failures (the Embargo).

1881.   Pendleton, William C. "Organization of Virginia Government; Thomas
        Jefferson, Father of Virginia Government" and "Organization of
        Government under the Constitution; Political Battles Between
        Thomas Jefferson and Alexander Hamilton" in Political History of
        Appalachian Virginia 1776-1927. Dayton,Va.: Shenandoah Press,
        1927. 29-35, 45-97.

        Claims the people of Appalachian Virginia were "almost en masse"
        behind TJ in his fight for popular government, and "their devotion
        to human freedom helped to inspire his heart and nerve his mind for
        the mighty struggle." Doubtful.

1882.   Penman, John Simpson. The Irresistible Movement of Democracy.
        New York: Macmillan, 1923. 55-90.

        On "The Origin and Development of the Jeffersonian Democracy"
        and "The Political Revolution of 1800" with little sense of TJ's
        motives or why his democracy was supposedly irresistible.

1883.   Perry, Ralph Barton. "The Declaration of Independence" in Puritanism
        and Democracy. New York: Vanguard Press, 1944. 117-46.

        Discusses the historical and biographical context of the Declaration,
        arguing that it "contains the essential ideas of American democracy."
        The subsequent chapter (147-75) exposits the philosophical back-
        ground of the document, but doesn't link ideas to TJ.

1884.   Peterson, Merrill D. "Process and Personality in Jefferson's
        Administration." Reviews in American History. 7(1979), 189-98.

235

Review essay of Cunningham's Process of Government under Jefferson and Johnstone's Jefferson and the Presidency claims the most tantalizing issue raised here concerns the relationship between personal style and the process of government.

1885. Peterson, Merrill D. "Thomas Jefferson and American National Policy, 1783-1793." Charlottesville, 1964. pp. 30.

Mimeo typescript, "To be read at the Conference on Early American History, Williamsburg, Virginia, October 9, 1964." See the following item.

1886. Peterson, Merrill D. "Thomas Jefferson and Commercial Policy, 1783-1793." WMQ. 3rd ser. 22(1965), 584-610.

Argues that TJ's commercial policy as articulated in his Report on Commerce of 1793 "can only be appraised in the light of antecedent experience," and his ideal of free exchange and pacific intercourse among nations dominated his work and thought on national affairs from 1783-1793.

1887. Peterson, Norma Lois, ed. The Defence of Norfolk in 1807 as Told by William Tatham to Thomas Jefferson. Chesapeake, Va.: Norfolk County Historical Society of Chesapeake, 1970. pp. xiv, 118.

Tatham's letters to TJ from Norfolk subsequent to the Chesapeake-Leopard affair of June 22, 1807.

188. Phau, Donald. "The Treachery of Thomas Jefferson." The Campaigner. 13(March 1980), 4-32.

Contends TJ fought unceasingly to undermine the federal republic, but he could not destroy America's Platonic tradition, "being revived today in the 1980 presidential campaign of Lyndon H. LaRouche."

1889. Phayre, Ignatius [Fitzgerald, William George]. "The Apostle of Unrestraint" in Can America Last? A Survey of the Emigrant Empire from the Wilderness to World Power, Together with Its Claims to "Sovereignty" in the Western Hemisphere from Pole to Pole. London: J. Murray, 1933. 127-41.

TJ, "a muddled mischief-maker," is responsible for almost everything the author dislikes about the U.S.

1890. Phillips, James Duncan. "Jefferson's 'Wicked Tyrannical Embargo.'" New England Quarterly. 18(1945), 466-78.

Describes the effects of the Embargo on Salem, Mass. and gives a thorough going Federalist critique of TJ.

1891. Phillips, P. Lee. "The Jeffersonian States." Daughters of the American Revolution Magazine. 52(1918), 343-44.

Describes a map of the Northwest Territory in 1785 showing names of possible states as given by TJ.

1892. Pierce, D. T. "Thomas Jefferson on Cuba." Public Opinion. 24(1898), 454-55.

Suggests TJ was more interested in keeping European "despotisms" out of America than in annexing Cuba.

1893. Plaisted, Thais M. Thomas Jefferson Parliamentarian: With Annotated Citation Bibliography. Los Angeles: The Author, 1978. pp. 47.

Earlier edition in 1974, not seen. A note on sources for TJ's Manual of Parliamentary Practice and identification of the abbreviated citations.

1894. Pole, J. R. "Elective Despotism and Other Perils: Jefferson and Madison on the Shortcomings of the Constitution of 1776" in Political Representation in England and the Origins of the American Republic. London/New York: Macmillan/St. Martin's Press, 1966. 296-304.

Contends TJ's guiding principle was respect for will of the people, despite wavering in the direction of more orthodox Whig "persona and property" doctrine to which Madison was closer.

1895. Pole, J. R. "The Meanings of a Self-Evident Truth" in The Pursuit of Equality in American History. Berkeley: Univ. of California Press, 1978. 51-58.

Claims TJ's moral universalism as expressed in the phrase "all men are created equal" was "a vulnerable instrument of revolutionary policy;" being too easy to take literally, it was later turned against itself.

1896. Pole, J. R. "Personifications of the American Future: Hamilton and Jefferson" in Foundation of American Independence 1763-1815. Indianapolis: Bobbs-Merrill, 1972. 201-11.

Conventional sketch.

1897. Pollard, James E. "Thomas Jefferson" in The Presidents and the Press. New York: Macmillan, 1947. 52-95.

"Despite the buffeting he had suffered at the hands of the press, Jefferson carried to his grave his deep-rooted belief in the necessity for freedom of expression in a democracy."

1898. Poole, William Frederick. "Dr. Cutler and the Ordinance of 1787." North American Review. 122(1876), 235-39.

TJ not the author of the Ordinance of 1787, although in 1784 he did bring forward the anti-slavery provision in the act of 1784.

1899. Pound, Ezra. Jefferson And/or Mussolini: L'Idea Statale. Facism as I Have Seen It. London: Stanley Nott, 1935. pp. 128.

Also New York: Liveright, 1936. pp. xi, 128. An attempt to establish the fundamental likenesses of TJ and Mussolini; a bit of Poundian special pleading that has convinced no one. American edition contains an additional letter from Pound.

1900. Powell, Burt E. "Jefferson and the Consular Service." Political Science Quarterly. 21(1906), 626-38.

TJ more than any other was the creator and organizer of our consular system; he concluded the consular convention with France and as Secretary of State set up the consular service which was recognized by the act of 1792.

1901. Powers, Fred Perry. Jefferson and Jackson on Present Problems. New York: Present Problems Publ. Co., 1897. pp. 16.

On the "money problem," the tariff, and civil service.

1902. Prager, Frank D. "Trends and Developments in American Patent Law from Jefferson to Clifford." American Journal of Legal History. 6(1962), 45-62.

Pp. 45-48 give a succinct account of TJ's handling of the patent office.

1903. Price, John W. "Thomas Jefferson's Statute of Religious Freedom." Virginia State Bar Association Proceedings. 42 Annual Meeting. (1931), 245-57.

Focus is on historical background rather than on the Act or its passage per se.

1904. Price, William Jennings. "'The Characteristic Bent of a Lawyer' in Jefferson." Georgetown Law Journal. 16(1927), 41-54.

Discusses the Commonplace Book as evidence of TJ's assiduous study of law and looks at his diplomatic work as an application of it.

1905. Prince, Carl E. "The Passing of the Aristocrats: Jefferson's Removal of the Federalists, 1801-1805." Journal of American History. 57(1970), 563-75.

TJ's "patronage policy during his first term was decisive as it was thoroughly partisan."

1906. Proctor, L. B. "Jefferson and Chief Justice Marshall." Albany Law Journal. 44(1891), 342-43.

TJ's contempt of Marshall's opinions; claims that Marshall's associate justices usually agreed with him.

1907. Proctor, L. B. "Jefferson and Marshall. Historic Collision Between the Executive and the Judiciary." Albany Law Journal. 59(1899), 289-93.

Brief account of Marbury v. Madison and the Burr trial.

1908. Prufer, Julius F. "The Franchise in Virginia from Jefferson Through the Convention of 1829." WMQ. 2nd ser. 7(1927), 255-70; 8(1928), 17-32.

From 1769 on TJ was "progressively more democratic in his views."

1909. Pulley, Judith Ross. "Thomas Jefferson at the Court of Versailles: An American Philosophe and the Coming of the French Revolution." Ph.D. dissertation. Univ. of Virginia, 1966. pp. 340.

Although TJ's democratic principles made him sympathetic to the revolutionary movement, his reactions were more frequently governed by practical considerations pertaining to the welfare of the French people and the interests of the U.S. DAI 27/08A, p. 2485.

1910. Putnam, Samuel. "Jefferson and the Young Brazilians in France." Science and Society. 10(Spring 1946), 185-92.

Good account of TJ's influence on the Minas Gerais conspirators and of his meeting in Nimes with Jose Joaquim de Maia.

1911. Quarles, Benjamin. "Antebellum Free Blacks and the Spirit of '76." Journal of Negro History. 61(1976), 229-42.

Discusses criticism of the Declaration of Independence and by association of TJ made by black abolitionists.

1912. Quincy, Josiah Phillips. "The Louisiana Purchase, and the Appeal to Posterity." Proceedings of the Massachusetts Historical Society. 2nd ser. 18(1903), 48-59.

Defense of Josiah Quincy's objections to the Purchase; TJ established a dangerous precedent in being unfaithful to the Constitution, opening the way to imperialistic acquisitions and the extension of slavery. Also rpt. separately.

1913. The Race Problem. Jefferson's Prophecies. n.p., n.d. pp. 16.

Racist tract calling for repeal of the 14th and 15th amendments and appealing to the authority of TJ.

1914. Randall, J. G. "George Washington and 'Entangling Alliances.'"
       South Atlantic Quarterly. 30(1931), 221-29.

       The phrase is in fact TJ's and fits his conception of foreign policy,
       even though Washington gets credit.

1915. Randolph, Sarah N. "The Kentucky Resolutions in a New Light."
       Nation. 44(1887), 382-84.

       Role of TJ in promoting the Kentucky Resolutions by way of meet-
       ings with Wilson Cary Nicholas and the Breckinridges.

1916. Renault, Raoul. "Thomas Jefferson and the Loyal and Patriotic
       Society of Upper Canada." North American Notes and Queries.
       1(1901), 201-09, 233-44.

       After TJ lamented the burning of Washington, Rev. John Strachan
       of Upper Canada replied with an open letter of Canadian griev-
       ances; prints Strachan's letter.

1917. Republican Association. Celebration of Jefferson's Birthday in
       Washington. Wednesday, April 13, 1859. Washington: Buell &
       Blanchard, 1859. pp. 16.

       The young Republican Party (GOP) tries to capture TJ as one of its
       own; prints speeches by Francis P. Blair and Daniel R. Goodloe,
       emphasizing TJ's belief in the importance of gradual elimination
       of slavery.

1918. Rhinesmith, William Donald. "Joseph Dennie, Critic of Jeffersonian
       Democracy." Essays in History. 7(1962), 37-52.

       Focus on Dennie, High Federalist editor of The Port Folio,
       1801-1809.

1919. Rhodes, Irwin S. "What Really Happened to the Jefferson Subpoenas."
       American Bar Association Journal. 60(1974), 52-54.

       Contends TJ's "claim to an exclusive exercise of executive privi-
       lege ... was upheld by Chief Justice Marshall," and courts in the
       Watergate case seem to be denying Marshall's ruling. See, however,
       item #1394.

*1920. Rice, Philip A., II. "Thomas Jefferson and the Balance of Power
       Principle, 1783-1793." M.A. thesis. California State Univ.,
       Fullerton, 1969.

1921. Rich, Bennett Milton. "The Embargo Troubles" in The Presidents and
       Civil Disorder. Washington: The Brookings Institution, 1941. 31-37.

TJ's actions at times went beyond the letter of the law, but given the circumstances his response to resistance to the Embargo was creditable.

1922. Ridpath, John Clark. "Jeffersonian Democracy." The Jeffersonian Democrat. 2(1899), 438-44.

Campaign rhetoric.

1923. Riethmiller, Christopher James. "Thomas Jefferson" in Alexander Hamilton and His Contemporaries; or, The Rise of the American Constitution. London: Bell and Daldy, 1864. 269-302.

Noble, high-minded Hamilton opposed by TJ, the crafty, sans-culotte.

1924. Risjord, Norman K. "The Compromise of 1790: New Evidence on the Dinner Table Bargain." WMQ. 3rd ser. 33(1976), 309-14.

TJ's dinner invitation to Tench Coxe and James Madison, dated June 6, 1790, indicates negotiations over compromise concerning the assumption of state debts and location of the national capital were more complex than TJ later suggested in the Anas.

1925. Risjord, Norman K. "A New Meaning for Jefferson's Democracy." Reviews in American History. 1(1973), 88-95.

Review essay on Ellis, The Jeffersonian Crisis.

1926. Ritcheson, Charles R. "Collision with Secretary Jefferson" in Aftermath of Revolution: British Policy Toward the United States, 1783-1795. Dallas: Southern Methodist Univ. Press, 1969. 231-42.

Confrontation of TJ and George Hammond, British minister.

1927. Robertson, Walter S. "Report to the Founder on Foreign Affairs." U.S. Department of State Bulletin. 36(1957), 682-87.

Compares TJ's foreign policy with that of today.

1928. Robinson, Donald L. Slavery in the Structure of American Politics, 1765-1820. New York: Harcourt Brace Jovanovich, 1971. 81-97.

Characterizes TJ as the "only political leader of consequence in Revolutionary America who moved openly against Negro slavery," mostly on the basis of his rejected passage in the Declaration.

1929. Roche, George Charles, III. "The Real American Revolution." Freeman. 23(1973), 395-98.

241

The founders had two ideas: "the Tom Jefferson-limited government idea and the Adam Smith-free enterprise idea."

*1930. Rogers, Robert, Jr. "Thomas Jefferson's Leadership of the Republi-
        can Party, January, 1797 to June, 1798." M.A. thesis. Univ. of
        California, Berkeley, 1953.

1931.   Rooney, William E. "Thomas Jefferson and the New Orleans Marine
        Hospital." Journal of Southern History. 22(1956), 167-82.

        Describes first years of Marine Hospital Service in New Orleans;
        TJ's "efforts to provide medical care for seamen in an unhealthy
        port ... were typical of his humanitarianism."

1932.   Roosevelt, Franklin D. "We Seek Peace—Enduring Peace." Vital
        Speeches. 9(1945), 423-24.

        Speech FDR wrote the night before he died, to be delivered over
        radio on TJ's birthday.

1933.   Rose, U. M. "The Case Between Jefferson and Marshall." Colorado
        Bar Association Reports. 4(1902), 123-56.

        Surveys the whole TJ-Marshall relationship, sympathetically to
        each; claims TJ was in the wrong with Marshall, but a great man for
        all that.

1934.   Rosenberg, Arthur. "Robespierre and Jefferson" in Democracy and
        Socialism, A Contribution to the Political History of the Past 150
        Years. New York: Knopf, 1939. 10-21.

        Both Robespierre's and TJ's revolutions failed because of the
        "bourgeois-capitalistic spirit of the age" and because of the
        leaders' failure to understand "the actual social processes of their
        time."

1935.   Rostow, Eugene Victor. The Consent of the Governed.
        Charlottesville: Thomas Jefferson Memorial Foundation, 1968.
        pp. 27.

        TJ's case for revolution does not depend on his 18th-century natural
        law doctrine but on a more general theory about the nature of a free
        political community. Laws are tested by individuals, e.g. Thoreau,
        but when unable to persuade his fellow citizens of his rightness, a
        dissenter must follow the will of society. Vietnam War-era state-
        ment.

1936.   Roth, George L. "Verse Satire on 'Faction,' 1790-1815." WMQ.
        3rd ser. 17(1960), 473-85.

        Includes account of Federalist satire aimed at TJ by Thomas
        Fessenden and others.

1937.   Rowland, Kate Mason. "A Lost Paper of Thomas Jefferson." WMQ.
        1(1892), 34-45.

        Prints a draft of TJ's proposed constitution of 1776 for Virginia;
        this document does not, however, invalidate the role of George
        Mason.

1938.   Royster, Charles. "A Battle of Memoirs; Light-Horse Harry Lee and
        Thomas Jefferson." Virginia Cavalcade. 31(Autumn 1981), 112-27.

        Excerpted from the authors's Light-Horse Harry Lee, New York:
        Knopf, 1981. Covers conflicting memories of the British invasion
        of Virginia.

1939.   Rutland, Robert A. "The Jeffersonian Genesis" in The Democrats
        from Jefferson to Carter. Baton Rouge: Louisiana State Univ.
        Press, 1979. 1-28.

        Brief account of the building of the Democratic party during TJ's
        presidency.

1940.   Saint, Percy. "Thomas Jefferson and Government by Party."
        Louisiana Historical Quarterly. 8(1925), 41-51.

        TJ was unjust and unreasonable in disliking John Marshall and
        Patrick Henry, but he helped to establish "a government which
        requires organized self-restraint to perpetuate it," so we should
        ignore his rhapsodies and unrealities about liberty.

*1941.   Salstrom, P. "Individualism to Community Land." Green Revolution.
        32(February 1975), 1.

1942.   Sawvel, Franklin B. "Introduction" to The Complete Anas of Thomas
        Jefferson. New York: Round Table Press, 1902.

        Describes the background of the Anas, points out serious problems
        in editions relying on the H. A. Washington edition of 1854.

1943.   Scanlon, James E. "A Sudden Conceit: Jefferson and the Louisiana
        Government Bill of 1804." Louisiana History. 9(1968), 139-62.

        TJ composed the bill establishing a government for Louisiana, but
        John Breckinridge of Kentucky introduced it and the authorship was
        kept secret. Describes the debate on the bill.

1944.   Schachner, Nathan. "Jefferson: A Slippery Politician." American
        Mercury. 46(1939), 49-55.

        Politicians of every stripe quote him because "Jefferson was the
        most inconsistent of men."

1945. Schapsmeier, Edward L. and Frederick H. "The Hamilton-Jefferson Confrontation: Origins of the American Political System." Social Sciences. 46(1971), 139-47.

Argues that "A synthesis of ideas took place along with a readiness to compromise which gave birth to a nonideologically oriented political system."

1946. Schellenburg, T. R. "Jeffersonian Origins of the Monroe Doctrine." Hispanic American Historical Review. 14(1934), 1-31.

As early as August 1822 TJ began advocating an American system; influenced by the writings of the Abbe Pradt, he developed the idea in letters with the Abbe Correa and James Monroe. TJ "more than any other individual was responsible for the basic doctrine of Monroe's message of 1823."

1947. Scherr, Arthur. "The 'Republican Experiment' and the Election of 1796 in Virginia." West Virginia History. 37(1976), 89-108.

Members of each party in Virginia were aware of the importance of this election for the success of the democratic process; Virginians' pride in national history overcame sectional differ- when Adams won out over TJ.

1948. Schouler, James. "First Administration of Thomas Jefferson" and "Second Administration of Thomas Jefferson" in History of the United States of America, Under the Constitution. Vol. II. 1801-1817. New York: Dodd Mead, 1882. 1-204.

Balanced view of TJ and his administration; conceded the usual flaws, no "military instinct," dissimulation, etc., he is still a philosophic statesman who had some great successes as president and at least one failure (the Embargo). Suggests that had he made a tour of New England while president, much of the mutual distrust might have subsided.

1949. Schulte, Nordholt J. W. "De Onafhankelijkheidsverklaring: Droom of Richtsnoer." Kleio. 17(1976), 1071-84.

"The Declaration of Independence: Dream or Guidepost." Discusses Declaration and TJ's role, concluding that it remains a guide for most Americans.

1950. Schurman, Jacob G. "Jefferson and the Public Policies of Today." Univ. of Virginia Alumni Bulletin. 3rd ser. 4(1911), 219-36.

1951. Schwartz, Bernard. "Jefferson-Madision Correspondence" in The Great Rights of Mankind: A History of the American Bill of the American Bill of Rights. New York: Oxford Univ. Press, 1977. 115-18.

Inconclusive comments on the letters on proposed Bill of Rights.

1952. Scott, William B. In Pursuit of Happiness: American Conceptions of Property from the Seventeenth to the Twentieth Century. Bloomington: Indiana Univ. Press, 1977. pp. xi, 244.

TJ discussed passim, but not especially perceptively; conclusion is titled "The Lingering World of Thomas Jefferson."

1953. Scruggs, J. H., Jr. "Thomas Jefferson's Views of Democracy and the Negro." Alabama Historical Quarterly. 8(Spring 1946), 95-102.

Commenting, "Democracy is not a gift" but a "development of personality," quotes from Query XIV in Notes on the differences between black and white races.

1954. Sealove, Sandra. "The Founding Fathers as Seen by the Marques de Casa-Irujo." The Americas. 20(1963), 37-42.

Irujo became Spanish ambassador to the U.S. in 1796 and described TJ and others in letters now in the Archivo Historico Nacional, Madrid.

1955. Sears, Louis M. "British Industry and the Embargo." Quarterly Journal of Economics. 34(1919), 88-113.

Contends that the Embargo worked real hardships on British industry but that America lacked resolution to pursue the experiment.

1956. Sears, Louis Martin. "Jefferson and the Embargo." Ph.D. dissertation. Univ. of Chicago, 1922.

See next item.

1957. Sears, Louis M. Jefferson and the Embargo. Durham: Duke Univ. Press, 1927. pp. ix, 340.

"... in urging the embargo Jefferson was pursuing not a hasty opportunism, but rather the logic of his entire philosophy of life," i.e. his essentially pacific theories, and "the exigencies of the situation revealed Jefferson as an administrator of a high order."

1958. [Selden, Richard Ely]. Criticism on the Declaration of Independence as a Literary Document. By Mon Droit. New York: For Sale at the News Offices, 1846. pp. 44.

Charges that "its author had no distinct ideas on the subject he was writing about; or if he had, he possessed no faith in the truth of his assertions." Traces the effect of these "sophisms" on the South and on the "national genius."

245

1959. Semmes, Thomas, Jr. Oration, Delivered at the Request of the
        Jefferson Society of the University of Virginia, on the Anniversary
        of the Birth-Day of Thomas Jefferson, April 13, 1833, in the
        Episcopal Church, Charlottesville, Va. Charlottesville: Virginia
        Advocate Office, 1833. pp. 15.

        Sketches TJ's career, ends in an anti-"consolidation" states rights
        argument.

1960. Sensabaugh, George F. "Jefferson's Use of Milton in the Ecclesiasti-
        cal Controversies of 1776." American Literature. 26(1955), 552-59.

        TJ read Milton's Of Reformation in England and The Reason of
        Church Government Urged while drafting the "Resolutions for Dis-
        establishing the Church of England and for Repealing Laws Inter-
        fering with Freedom of Worship."

1961. Sestanovich, Stephen. "Thomas Jefferson, PAO." Foreign Service
        Journal. 43(July 1966), 23-25.

        Sketch on TJ as minister to France, emphasizing his work as the
        equivalent of a modern public affairs officer.

1962. Shackelford, George Green, ed. "Benedict Arnold in Richmond,
        January 1781: His Proposal Concerning Prize Goods." VMHB.
        60(1952), 591-99.

        Account of Arnold's raid and TJ's response.

1963. Shannon, Joseph B. A Revival of the Doctrines of Jefferson Necessary
        to Check the Rising Tides of Hamiltonian Privilege. Washington:
        Government Printing Office, 1932. pp. 24.

1964. Shannon, Joseph B. Thomas Jefferson, The Advocate of Truth, Freedom
        and Equality. Public Speeches of Joseph B. Shannon Touching upon
        Unfamiliar Phases of the Life and Teachings of The Great American
        Statesman. Kansas City, Mo.: Regular Democratic Club, 1930.
        pp. 32.

        TJ used to attack the "follies of the millionaires."

*1965. Sharswood, George. An Address Upon the Rights of the States,Deliver-
        ed Before the State Rights Association of Pennsylvania, and a Public
        Meeting of Citizens, on the 14th of April, 1834, at the Commission-
        er's Hall in the Northern Liberties of Philadelphia. Philadelphia:
        J. Harding, 1834. pp. 8.

1966. [Shaw, Albert]. "A Notable Anniversary." The American Monthly
        Review of Reviews. 27(1903), 515-20.

        Louisiana Purchase and TJ's part in it.

1967.   Shaw, Albert. "Political Parties in Perspective." Review of Reviews. 94(September 1936), 15-18.

Brief account of the rise of the party system behind TJ and Hamilton; criticizes Claude Bowers for partisanship.

1968.   Sheehan, Bernard W. Seeds of Extinction; Jeffersonian Philanthropy and the American Indian. Chapel Hill: Univ. of North Carolina Press, 1973. pp. xii, 301.

TJ wished to assimilate Indians into white society, but since he and those who shared his ideas tended to conceptualize the Indians abstractly, they failed to realize the profoundly destructive effects this would have for the Indians. Best book on TJ's Indian policy.

*1969   Shimakawa, Masashi. "Thomas Jefferson and the Indian Problem." Amerika Kenkyu/American Review. 12(1978), 214-15.

In Japanese; abstract in English.

1970.   Shiryaev, B. A. "Tomas Dzhefferson i Amerikanskaia Konstitutsiia." Vestnik Leningradskogo U.: Seriia Istorii Iazyka i Literatury. April 1977, 49-55.

TJ recognized some of the reasons for antidemocratic tendencies in the constitutional convention and, while seeing some good points in the Constitution, insisted on a Bill of Rights.

1971.   Shortridge, George D. "Mr. Jefferson—The Declaration of Independence and Freedom." DeBow's Review. 26(1859), 547-59.

"Mr. Jefferson's doctrine is the dream of an enthusiast or visionary," and does not justify abolition.

1972.   Showalter, William Joseph. "Jefferson as President." Virginia Journal of Education. 19(1926), 345-49.

Compares TJ to other presidents, particularly Wilson.

1973.   Shulim, Joseph I. "Thomas Jefferson Views Napoleon." VMHB. 60(1952), 288-304.

TJ's opinions of Napoleon varied with circumstances, but he ultimately saw him as "the author of more misery and suffering to the world than any being who has ever lived before him."

1974.   Shurr, Georgia Hooks. "Thomas Jefferson and the French Revolution." American Society Legion of Honor Magazine. 59(Winter 1979/80), 161-82.

Competent account from printed sources; claims the French Revolution was partly of TJ's making.

1975. Sigaud, Louis A. "The Tie That Severed." Tyler's Quarterly. 31(1949), 6-22.

Aaron Burr innocent of intriguing to become President in 1800, but TJ thought he did and this explains his "relentless animus" toward Burr.

1976. Sigaud, Louis A. "Tried and Not Found Wanting." Tyler's Quarterly. 31(1950), 225-52.

On TJ's "persecution" of Burr at his trial in 1807.

1977. Simpson, Joseph Bernard. Hamiltonism vs. Jeffersonism. A Refutation of the Popular Calumnies Against Alexander Hamilton. Chester, Ill.: Thomas J. Howarth & Co., 1904. pp. 64.

The usual Hamiltonian's case against TJ.

1978 Sisson, Daniel. The American Revolution of 1800. New York: Knopf, 1974. pp. xvii, 468.

Examination of the circumstances and significance of TJ's coming to power in 1800. Argues that he conceived a "strategy that will enable the people to negate the present or existing system. By a conversion of military to peaceful means, Jefferson produced a strategy and an organization whose means could be identified in spirit and principle with the purposes of the revolution. It enabled the people to identify with the emerging democratic sentiment that was a 'second city' within the body politic. ... the capacity of the Jeffersonians to combine a revolutionary ideology and a dynamic political organization culminated in the first modern theory of a politics of revolution." Suggestive study.

1979. Skeen, Carl. Jefferson and the West, 1798-1808. Columbus, Ohio: Anthony Wayne Parkway Board/Ohio State Museum, 1960. pp. 54.

Originally an M.A. thesis at Ohio State Univ.; discusses TJ's policies on Western expansion while president, with emphasis on the old Northwest. Concludes that "The West, in a sense, began with Jefferson."

1980. Skolnik, Richard, comp. 1803: Jefferson's Decision, The United States Purchases Louisiana. New York: Chelsea House, 1969. pp. xix, 194.

Collection of primary material for undergraduates; introduction and notes.

1981. Sloane, William M. "World Aspects of the Louisiana Purchase." AHR.

8(1904), 507-21.

TJ forced into the Purchase because of, among other reasons, a dangerous political situation at home with the West and South possibly ready to go over to the Federalists. Both the Federalists and the Republicans in the subsequent squabble over constitutionality tacitly abandoned the strict constructionist view of powers delegated to Congress.

1982. Small, Norman J. Some Presidential Interpretations of the Presidency. Johns Hopkins Univ. Studies in Historical and Political Science. Series 50, no. 2. Baltimore: Johns Hopkins Press, 1932. pp. 208.

Organized thematically; compares opinions of Washington, TJ, Lincoln, T. Roosevelt, and Wilson.

1983. Smelser, Marshall. "The Glorious Fourth—or, Glorious Second? or Eighth?" History Teacher. 3(February 1970), 25-30.

1984. Smith, Charles Emory. "The Louisiana Purchase" in The Writings of Thomas Jefferson, ed. Lipscomb and Bergh. Washington: Thomas Jefferson Memorial Association, 1903. 3:i-vii.

1985. Smith, Gaddis. "The U.S. vs. International Terrorists, A Chapter from Our Past." American Heritage. 28(August 1977), 37-43.

TJ's efforts to put down the Barbary pirates are not an adequate model for dealing with present-day terrorist highjackers.

1986. Smith, Glenn Curtis. "Notes on Thomas Jefferson's Summary View of the Rights of British Americans." VMHB. 59(1951), 494-98.

Uncritical description and brief account of the historical context.

1987. Smith, James Morton. Freedom's Fetters: The Alien and Sedition Laws and American Civil Liberties. Ithaca: Cornell Univ. Press, 1956. pp. xv, 464.

The definitive book on the subject, focusing particularly on the struggles in the press. TJ mentioned throughout, more as an object of political attention than as an active participant in this phase of the resistance to the Alien and Sedition Laws.

1988. Smith, James Morton. "The Grass Roots Origins of the Kentucky Resolutions." WMQ. 3rd ser. 27(1970), 221-245.

Argues for closer examination of events in Kentucky prior to the Resolutions as a balance to historians' concentration on TJ's involvement as theoretician and author.

1989. Smith, Robert Harold. "Albert Gallatin and American Fiscal Policy during Jefferson's First Administration." Ph.D. dissertation.

Syracuse Univ., 1954. pp. 276.

Discusses Gallatin's role in trying to achieve the three main financial goals of TJ's administration, prompt retirement of the federal debt, reduction of taxation, and economy in government. Although TJ and Madison had opposed the First Bank of the United States, under Gallatin's influence the Bank was strengthened and expanded. DAI 14/09, p. 1325.

1990. Smith, Sherwin D. "Forty-two Campaigns Ago." New York Times Magazine. October 25, 1964. 82-88.

On TJ, John Adams, and America's "first campaign" in 1796.

1991. Smith, William Raymond. "The Leader of the Consensus" in The Rhetoric of American Politics. Westport, Conn.: Greenwood Publishing, 1969. 125-42.

Rhetorical analysis of TJ's first inaugural speech.

1992. Soto Paz, Rafael. No es de Jefferson La Declaracion de Independencia. Havana: Editorial Lex, 1947. pp. 32.

Argues for Paine's authorship.

1993. Spencer, Donald S. "Appeals to the People: The Later Genet Affair." New York Historical Society Quarterly. 54(1970), 241-67.

TJ's role in the excitement about Genet's threat to appeal over Washington's head to the people. His letter demanding Genet's recall was in fact a demand for a reevaluation of French policy toward the United States and an attempt to protect American neutrality.

*1994. Spiker, Franklin A. "Thomas Jefferson as a Member of the Continental congress." M.A. thesis. Univ. of Virginia, 1934. pp. 93.

*1995. Spiro, Jeffery H. "Thomas Jefferson and the Origins of American Neutrality." M.A. thesis, 1975. Queens College (CUNY), 1975.

1996. Spivak, Burton. "Jefferson, England, and the Embargo: Trading Wealth and Republican Value in the Shaping of American Diplomacy, 1804-1809." Ph.D. Dissertation. Univ. of Virginia, 1975. pp. 539.

See the next item. DAI 35/08A, p. 5321.

1997. Spivak, Burton. Jefferson's English Crisis: Commerce, Embargo, and the Republican Revolution. Charlottesville: Univ. Press of Virginia, 1979. pp. xiii, 250.

Examines TJ's foreign policy toward England and his concern for the growth in the United States of English political forms, social ideas, and commercial development. Contends that "the commercial goals of Jefferson's English diplomacy encouraged the very kind of national economic development that he found so incompatible with his republican dreams."

1998.   "Sporadic Attacks on the Supreme Court." Congressional Digest. 16(March 1937), 70-73.

Covers TJ's attacks on the court and Marbury vs. Madison as a general background for FDR's difficulties with the court.

1999.   Sprague, Marshall. So Vast So Beautiful a Land: Louisiana and the Purchase. Boston: Little Brown, 1974. pp. xix, 396.

Discovery and eventual acquisition of the Louisiana Territory. A popular account which turns TJ into a Westerner of the spirit and imagination.

2000.   Sprague, Stuart Seely. "Jefferson, Kentucky and the Closing of the Port of New Orleans, 1802-1803." Kentucky Historical Society Register. 70(1972), 312-17.

"Rather than relaxing in 1802-1803, President Jefferson made strenuous efforts to keep Kentucky from exploding" into rash military action as a response to the French takeover of New Orleans.

2001.   Springer, William M. and George Willard. Counting the Electoral Votes. Proceedings and Debates of Congress Relating to Counting the Electoral Votes for President and Vice-President of the United States. Washington: Government Printing Office, 1877. 16-39.

44th Congress, 2nd Session. House of Representatives Misc. Doc. 13. Materials relating to counting the electoral votes in the elections of 1800 and 1804.

2002.   Stanwood, Edward. "Anticipation of the Monroe Doctrine." Proceedings of the Massachusetts Historical Society. 3rd ser. 1(1907), 39-41.

First enunciated in a letter from TJ to James Bowdoin, dated April 27, 1805.

2003.   Stanwood, Edward. "Jefferson and Burr" and "Jefferson Re-elected" in A History of Presidential Elections. Boston: J. R. Osgood, 1884. 30-50.

"This History ... professes to be little more than a record of the circumstances of such elections." A somewhat expanded account appears in his A History of the Presidency. Boston: Houghton Mifflin, 1898. 54-85.

2004. Steffen, Jerome O. <u>William Clark: Jeffersonian Man on the Frontier.</u> Norman: Univ. of Oklahoma Press, 1977. pp. xi, 196.

Biography of Clark, claiming to stress "his role in the implementation of Jeffersonian programs," treats TJ and Clark as two men of the Enlightenment.

2005. Steinberg, Alfred. "Thomas Jefferson: The Practical Idealist" in <u>The First Ten: The Founding Presidents and Their Administrations.</u> New York: Doubleday, 1967. 88-135.

TJ an idealist who was required by events to depart in practice from his philosophy. At the end of his second term the Embargo cost him his political control of Congress and led to his discouragement about his presidency.

2006. Stephens, Frank F. "Jefferson's Vision Realized in the Purchase of Louisiana." <u>Univ. of Missouri Bulletin.</u> 59(no. 29, 1958), unpag.

Six page sketch.

2007. Stevenson, Adlai E. "Jefferson and Our National Leadership." <u>VQR.</u> 36(1960), 337-49.

Discusses TJ as a model for American statesmen of the present day.

2008. Stewart, Donald Henderson. "Jeffersonian Journalism: Newspaper Propaganda and the Development of the Democratic-Republican Party, 1798-1801." Ph.D. dissertation. Columbia Univ., 1950. pp. 1223.

Extensive survey of the "Sarcasm, invective, logic, emotion, ridicule" employed by writers for the republican press. DAI 11/01, p. 164.

2009. Stuart, Reginald Charles. "Encounter with Mars: Thomas Jefferson's View of War." Ph.D. dissertation. Univ. of Florida, 1974. pp. 308.

See the next item; DAI 35/08A, p. 5323.

2010. Stuart, Reginald C. <u>The Half-Way Pacifist, Thomas Jefferson's View of War.</u> Toronto: Univ. of Toronto Press, 1978. pp. x, 93.

A suggestive monograph which argues that although TJ had a "defensive mentality," he "actively used violence either directly or indirectly in his policies against the Barbary pirates, Spain, England, and France to maintain his country's independence and security. ... He was more a pragmatist than a pacifist and continually weighed possibilities, risks and gains. ... If Jefferson seems a proto-Clausewitzian, it is because he emerged from the same age, with many of the same assumptions about the use of war, and he consistently operated on the basis of these assumptions while in and out of public office."

2011.   Stuart, Reginald C. "Thomas Jefferson and the Function of War: For
        Policy or Principle?" Canadian Journal of History. 11(1976),
        154-71.

        TJ saw war in political terms as "an instrument of last resort" with
        pragmatic limitations. He did not believe that "war was an aberra-
        tion, and he did not ignore the interest of the state in security."

2012.   Stuart, Reginald C. "Thomas Jefferson and the Origins of War." Peace
        and Change. 4(1977), 22-27.

        TJ became more pessimistic about the inevitability of war and came
        to feel that war stemmed from economic and political conditions but
        from human nature as well.

2013.   [Sullivan, William]. Familiar Letters on Public Characters, and
        Public Events, From the Peace of 1783, to the Peace of 1815.
        Boston: Russell, Odiorne, and Metcalf, 1834. pp. xi, 468.

        A diehard Federalist attacks TJ in detail; rpt. Boston, 1834;
        Philadelphia, 1847, as The Public Men of the Revolution.

2014.   [Sullivan, William]. Remarks on Article IX in the Eighty-fourth Number
        of the North American Review, entitled "Origin and Character of the
        Old Parties." Boston: Perkins, Marvin & Co., 1834. pp. 39.

        Federalist reply to Alexander Hill Everett's article, contending TJ
        was merely the "idol of a party." N.B. some libraries catalogue this
        under Everett.

2015.   Swindler, William F. "The Supreme Court and the President: United
        States v. Burr" in The Constitution and Chief Justice Marshall.
        New York: Dodd Mead, 1978. 34-46.

        Sketchy account of the Burr trial, e.g. does not discuss the subpoena
        issue, as the climax of TJ vs. Marshall; earlier chapter on Marbury vs.
        Madison also touches on TJ.

2016.   Taine, Hippolyte Adolphe. "Jefferson" in Nouveaux Essais de Critique
        et d'Histoire. Paris: Hachette, 1865. 171-87.

        Review essay on Witt's Thomas Jefferson, agrees with Witt that TJ
        was an ambivalent character, by turns "actif et impuissant," who was
        to a large degree responsible for the descent of the U.S. into "la
        démocratie brutale."

2017.   Tanner, Douglas W. "Thomas Jefferson, Impressment, and the Rejection
        of the Monroe-Pinckney Treaty." Essays in History. 13(1968), 7-26.

        TJ and Madison through the Monroe-Pinckney mission "made the issue
        of impressment a central one in Anglo-American relations ... (but)

In his excessive caution to avoid a decisive diplomatic confrontation, ... Jefferson lost the initiative on impressment."

2018. Taxay, Don. "Thomas Jefferson and the Founding of the Mint" in Studies on Money in Early America, ed. Eric P. Newman and Richard G. Doty. New York: American Numismatic Society, 1976. 209-16.

On TJ's work for a decimal coinage and for establishing the Mint.

2019. Tetley, Gerard. "Jefferson on the Verbosity of Statutes." Christian Science Monitor Magazine. April 3, 1948. 7.

TJ's letter of September, 1817 to Joseph C. Cabell is placed on the desks of modern Virginia legislators.

2020. Thomas, Charles Marion. American Neutrality in 1793; A Study in Cabinet Government. New York: Columbia Univ. Press, 1931. pp. 294.

A policy of American neutrality cannot be credited to TJ alone, but this study argues that his efforts were indispensable in laying down a policy so truly impartial as that of the U.S. in 1793.

2021. Thomas, Charles S. "Jefferson and Judiciary." Colorado Bar Association Report. 28(1925), 172-84.

Rpt. Constitutional Review. 10(April 1926), 67-76.

2022. "Thomas Jefferson." Niles Register. 38(1830), 344.

Prints a letter purportedly written from Monticello, May 25, 1823, praising Henry Clay and the American System. See note on p. 447 charging this to be a forgery.

2023. "Thomas Jefferson and the Constitution." Literary Digest. 88(March 20, 1926), 36.

TJ as upholder of the Constitution; an article designed for student orators.

2024. "Thomas Jefferson's Advice to the Cherokees." Journal of Cherokee Studies. 4(1979), 64-66.

Prints with note two speeches TJ made to Cherokee visitors, printed in the National Intelligencer in 1809. Urges acculturation and re-location.

2025. [Thompson, John R.]. "The Study of the Law. Ms. Letter of Th. Jefferson." Southern Literary Messenger. 14(1848), 187-90.

Prints the letter to Bernard Moore with introductory comments.

2026.   Thompson, Lewis O. "The Administration of Thomas Jefferson" in The
         Presidents and Their Administrations. A Handbook of Political
         Parties for Every Voter. Indianapolis: John W. Robinson, 1873.
         52-65.

2027.   Thompson, Walter. "Thomas Jefferson and Our Coinage." Numismatic
         Scrapbook. 25(1959), 3019-29.

         Prints TJ's 1784 report on establishing the Mint and explains why
         the Mint was placed under the State Dept.

2028.   Thornton, William M. "Who Bought Louisiana?" Univ. of Virginia
         Alumni Bulletin. 3rd ser. 6(1913), 390-412.

         On "the services of Thomas Jefferson in connection with the
         Louisiana Purchase." Separately printed, Washington: Government
         Printing Office, 1913. pp. 19. Address delivered at the Louisiana
         Purchase Exposition, April 30, 1913.

2029.   Tipple, John. A. Hamilton/Th. Jefferson: The New Order. Cleveland:
         Howard Allen, 1961. pp. 243.

         The old Hamilton-TJ story rehashed.

2030.   Tobin, Richard L. "Thomas Jefferson Buys Louisiana—On His Own" in
         Decisions of Destiny. Cleveland: World, 1961. 32-51.

         Popular history covering the diplomatic and constitutional issues
         involved in the Louisiana Purchase.

2031.   Trent, William P. "Thomas Jefferson" in Southern Statesmen of the
         Old Regime. New York: Crowell, 1897. 49-86.

         TJ's personality and character a mystery; claims TJ was a greater
         man than Hamilton, although the latter may have been a better exec-
         utive officer. TJ's flaw was suspicion; his were not "the direct,
         vigorous methods that have usually characterized Southern men," but
         he was "an eighteenth-century Matthew Arnold ... A Democracy of
         Sweetness and Light was what Jefferson wished to see established in
         this country."

2032.   Trescot, William Henry. The Diplomatic History of the Administrations
         of Washington and Adams, 1789-1801. Boston: Little Brown, 1857.
         pp. x, 283.

         The great achievement of diplomacy was to escape entanglement
         with Europe; pays attention to issues and events without looking
         at the nature of the participants in any detail.

2033.   Truman, Harry S. "A Year of Challenge: Liberalism or Conservatism."
         Vital Speeches. 14(1948), 290-94.

Speech at the Jefferson–Jackson Day Dinner, Washington, D.C., February 19, 1948; sees TJ as a "progressive liberal" whose party is still the party of progressive liberalism.

2034. Tucker, George. "Mr. Jefferson: His Interpretation of the Constitution." Southern Literary Messenger. 7(1841), 573-75.

Contends TJ was willing to give a liberal construction to the Constitution when it would "best promote the public good."

2035. Tugwell, Rexford G. "Thomas Jefferson" in How They Became President: Thirty-five Ways to the White House. New York: Simon & Schuster, 1964. 42-52.

Claims the election of 1800 shows on the Republican side a nearly perfect model of a campaign; it protected its presidential candidate, exposed only subordinates, and provoked the enemy to a self-defeating extremism.

2036. Turner, Frederick J. "The Origin of Genet's Projected Attack on Louisiana and the Floridas." AHR. 3(1898), 650-71.

TJ at first was sympathetic to Genet perhaps because he was not aware of "the ulterior designs of France to hold Louisiana and detach the West."

2037. Turner, Lynn W. "Thomas Jefferson Through the Eyes of a New Hampshire Politician." MVHR. 30(1943), 205-14.

Changing attitudes of Senator William Plumer toward TJ.

2038. Tyler, John. "Defence of Mr. Jefferson." WMQ. 1(1892), 106-7.

Reprints certificate of Tyler from the Richmond Enquirer of Sept. 10, 1805, defending TJ's conduct as governor.

2039. Tyler, Lyon G., ed. "Arnold's Invasion, 1781. Jefferson's Official Conduct." WMQ. 2nd ser. 6(1926), 131-32.

Prints without comment 2 affidavits justifying TJ's actions.

2040. Tyler, Lyon G., ed. "Election of Mr. Jefferson as Governor." WMQ. 15(1906), 161.

Reprints, without notes, from the Virginia Gazette announcement of TJ's election and his reply to the Assembly.

2041. [Tyler, Lyon G]. "Jefferson after Camden." Tyler's Quarterly. 7(1925), 81-86.

Documentation of TJ's effort to raise fresh troops after the battle of Camden, August 16, 1780.

2042. Tyler, Lyon G. "Jefferson as President." Tyler's Quarterly. 28(1946), 57-61.

2043. Tyler, Lyon G. "Jefferson's Second Term as President." Tyler's Quarterly. 28(1947), 133-38.

2044. Tyler, Lyon G. "Policies of Hamilton and Jefferson Concerning the Provisions of the Treaty of 1783." Tyler's Quarterly. 27(1945), 80-83.

Actually on TJ's dealings with John Hammond in 1791-92.

2045. [Tyler, Lyon G.]. "More Propaganda." Tyler's Quarterly. 3(1921), 149-54.

Protests the ignoring of TJ's role as author of the Declaration in a pamphlet issued by the American Luther League; another example of northern writers disregarding southerners' roles in American history.

2046. Tyler, Lyon G. "The Presidential Election of 1800." Tyler's Quarterly. 23(1946), 2-5.

2047. [Tyler, Lyon G.]. "The Virginia Dynasty." Tyler's Quarterly. 3(1921), 238-45.

Review of George Morgan's Life of James Monroe, argues that the political measures of TJ, Madison, and Monroe are the foundation of the present day Union and they have been misrepresented by northern writers.

2048. U.S. Congress. "Message from the President of the United States, Transmitting a letter from the King of France, communicated to the Senate." American State Papers. Foreign Relations. Washington: Gales and Seaton, 1832. 1:109.

Letter from the French Court, 11 September 1790, testifying to the esteem and approbation of TJ as minister.

2049. Van Der Linden, Frank. "The Presidential Election of 1800." American History Illustrated. 1(January 1967), 24-33.

Good popular history.

2050. Van der Weyde, William Manley. "Who Wrote the Declaration of Independence?" Americana. 6(January 1911), 8-15.

Rpt. separately; another claim for Thomas Paine as author.

2051. Van Loon, Hendrik Willem. "America: Jefferson and Hamilton Contribute Their Genius to a New Nation." Woman's Home Companion. 54(January 1927), 14-15, 106.

2052. Varg, Paul A. Foreign Policies of the Founding Fathers. Lansing: Michigan State Univ. Press, 1963. pp. xi, 316.

Covers the period from 1774 to 1812. TJ discussed passim, but particularly in the chapters entitled "Credit vs. Markets: The Origin of Party Conflict over Foreign Policy" and "Jefferson and Madison Formulate Foreign Policy." Sees foreign policy as shaped by party warfare and by the psychological forces vested in the symbols of an aristocratic Europe and a virtuous America.

2053. The Virginia and Kentucky Resolutions of 1798 and '99; With Jefferson's Original Draught Thereof. Also, Madison's Report, Calhoun's Address, Resolutions of the Several States in Relation to State Rights. With Other Documents in Support of the Jeffersonian Documents in Support of the Jeffersonian Doctrines of '98. Washington: Jonathan Elliott, 1832. pp. 82.

A Calhoun-Jefferson-States Rights package.

2054. Volz, Harry A. III. "The Opposition of Virginia Republicans to Jefferson's Embargo." Essays in History. 20(1976), 19-38.

The minority Republicans in Virginia who opposed the Embargo included men who had hoped TJ's election as president would lead to fundamental reforms and a dismantling of all Federalist programs.

2055. Vossler, Otto. Die Amerikanischen Revolutionsideale in ihren Verhaltnis zu den Europäischen; Untersucht an Thomas Jefferson. Munchen: R. Oldenbourg, 1929. pp. 197.

See R. R. Palmer, "A Neglected Work." WMQ. 3rd ser. 12(1955), 462-71, for an account of this. Also translated by Catherine Philippon and Bernard Wishy as Jefferson and the American Revolutionary Ideal. Washington: Univ. Press of America, 1980. pp. xxxvi, 235.

*2056. Waciuma, Wanjohi. Intervention in Spanish Floridas, 1801-1813: A Study in Jeffersonian Foreign Policy. Boston: Branden, 1976. pp. 371.

2057. Waite, Edward F. "Jefferson's 'Wall of Separation': What and Where?" Minnesota Law Review. 33(1949), 494-516.

Not on TJ but on subsequent judicial interpretations of the separation of church and state issue.

2058. Walker, Francis Amasa. "Jefferson's First Term" and "Jefferson's Second Term" in The Making of the Nation, 1783-1817. New York: Scribner's, 1895. 168-213.

Balanced and standard account of events.

2059. Wall, James M. "Consent of the Governed." Christian Century. 93(January 7, 1976), 3-4.

Editorial on TJ's basic principle of the necessary consent of the governed for a just government.

2060. Wallace, D. D. "Jefferson's Part in the Purchase of Louisiana." Sewanee Review. 19(1911), 328-38.

Argues that TJ did not seek the Louisiana acquisition but simply accepted it.

2061. Wallace, Henry A. Thomas Jefferson: Practical Idealist. Washington, 1935. pp. 21.

Addresses before the Jeffersonian Union, Atlanta, Georgia, April 13, 1935. pp. 21, printed here for release to the press. "Jeffersonian democracy must take on modern equipment ... if an agrarian liberalism is to achieve a balance between agriculture and industry, it must offer more than what has been called 'an amiable go-as-you-please individualism.'"

2062. Walsh, Richard, ed. "Letters of Morris and Brailsford to Thomas Jefferson." South Carolina Historical Magazine. 58(1957), 129-44.

Correspondence dealing with the exportation of rice to France; introduction and notes.

2063. Wandell, Samuel H. "Thomas Jefferson" in Aaron Burr in Literature; Books, Pamphlets, Periodicals, and Miscellany Relating to Aaron Burr and His Leading Political Contemporaries. Psyche Monographs: no. 6. London: Kegan Paul, 1936. 131-44.

Sketch and short bibliography.

2064. Warde, William F. "Jefferson, Lincoln and Dewey." International Socialist Review. 20(1959), 88-92.

Criticizes Dewey's liberal democracy, claiming TJ's and Lincoln's proclamation of the "right to revolution as the ultimate guarantee of all other democratic rights" brings them closer to Marxism than to "Deweyism."

2065. Warfield, Ethelbert D. "The Authorship of the Kentucky Resolutions of 1798." Magazine of Western History. 3(1886), 574-86.

John Breckinridge was the mover of the Resolutions, but their authorship is unclear.

2066. Warfield, Ethelbert Dudley. The Kentucky Resolutions of 1798, An Historical Study. New York: Putnam's, 1887. pp. ix, 203.

Background and authorship, effects of the Resolutions. TJ's draft supports a more radical states rights position than the toned down version of John Breckinridge, and Madison was more restrained yet.

2067. Warfield, Ethelbert D. "The New Light on the Kentucky Resolutions." Nation. 44(1887), 467-68.

Emphasizes the role of John Breckinridge.

2068. Warren, Charles. "How the President's Speech to Congress Was Instituted and Abandoned" in Odd Byways in American History. Cambridge: Harvard Univ. Press, 1942. 136-58.

TJ was the first president to send a written message to Congress instead of giving a speech; this was to end partisan friction over the custom.

2069. Warren, Charles. "Jefferson, the Essex Junto, and the Law Craft" in Jacobin and Junto, or Early American Politics as Viewed in the Diary of Dr. Nathaniel Ames, 1758-1822. Cambridge: Harvard Univ. Press, 1931. 146-82.

Fisher Ames' Republican brother reports on Federalist opposition to TJ.

2070. Warren, Charles. "Marshall, Jefferson, and the Judiciary" in The Supreme Court in United States History. Vol. I. 1789-1835. Boston: Little Brown, 1922. 169-230.

Focus on Marbury vs. Madison.

2071. Warren, Charles. The Trumpeters of the Constitution. Rochester: Univ. of Rochester, 1927. pp. 85.

TJ's services to American life and constitutional government discussed on pp. 44-52; generalities.

2072. Warren, Charles. "Why Jefferson Abandoned the Presidential Speech to Congress." Proceedings of the Massachusetts Historical Society. 57(1924), 123-72.

"The practice of making reply addresses had become an unmitigated nuisance, wasting the time of both branches of Congress in purely futile debate."

2073. Washburn, Charles G. "Who Was the Author of the Declaration of Independence?" Proceedings of the American Antiquarian Society. n.s. 38(1928), 51-62.

Examines pre-1776 declarations of rights and grievances, particularly the 1773 statement of Mendon, Mass., in order to suggest TJ was not the "author" of the Declaration so much as he was its draftsman. Poorly reasoned.

2074. "Washington, Jefferson and the Society of the Cincinnati." Researcher. 1(1927), 100-02.

Documents, without comment.

2075. Webster, Sidney. Two Treaties of Paris and the Supreme Court. New York: Harper, 1901. 1-27.

Discusses in the first chapter TJ's legal problems in annexing the Louisiana Territory to the U.S.

*2076. Weeder, Elinor Janet. "Wilson Cary Nicholas, Jefferson's Lieutenant." M.A. thesis. Univ. of Virginia, 1946. pp. iii, 144.

2077. Welling, James C. "The Mecklenburg Declaration of Independence." North American Review. 118(1874), 256-93.

Review essay of volumes arguing that TJ borrowed from the supposed Mecklenburg Declaration; finds the stories of the Mecklenburg Declaration belong "to the domain of fable."

2078. Welter, Rush. "The Adams-Jefferson Correspondence, 1812-1826." American Quarterly. 2(1950), 234-50.

Suggest that Adams tended to lead the correspondence in its rather fitful analysis of "the problem of man." He saw this problem under three heads: the nature of man, man's civil state, and the extent and uses of human learning.

2079. White, Andrew D. "Jefferson and Slavery." Atlantic Monthly. 9(1862), 29-40.

TJ continued to oppose slavery all his life, hoped younger men would take up the cause, and "in dealing with slavery was a real political seer and giver of oracles."

2080. White, Horace. "Jefferson-Lemen Compact." Nation. 101(1915), 144.

Argues for the existence of an agreement between TJ and James Lemen to work against introduction of slavery into the Northwest Territory.

2081.   White, Leonard D. The Jeffersonians: A Study in Administrative
         History, 1801-1829. New York: Macmillan, 1951. pp. xiv, 572.

         TJ in his First Inaugural typified the position of the "old
         Republicans," in his Second Inaugural he typified the position of the
         "new Republicans" who were dominant after 1815. Although not
         interested in the normal procedures of day to day administration, TJ
         was "as skillful as his Federalist predecessors in using administrative
         means for far-reaching political ends." His first term was marked by
         successful innovations in policy and administration, but his second
         ended in the disaster of the Embargo. TJ's "significance in American
         history flows much less from his contribution to the art of
         administration than from his convictions about democracy."

2082.   White, Leonard D. "Public Administration Under the Federalists" in
         The Gaspar G. Bacon Lectures on the Constitution of the United
         States, 1940-1950. Boston: Boston Univ. Press, 1953. 197-247.

         Examines the Hamilton-TJ feud on pp. 213-31 and concludes that
         Washington, TJ, and Hamilton "did not present a combination which
         long corresponded" to the requirements of effective administration.

2083.   Whitehill, Walter Muir, ed. Thomas Jefferson's Letter of 20 May 1826
         to James Heaton on the Abolition of Slavery. Washington:
         Dumbarton Oaks Garden Library, 1967. pp. 20.

         Intro. by the editor, facsimile, and note by Julian P. Boyd.

2084.   Wiggins, James R. "Jefferson and the Press" in Thomas Jefferson: The
         Man ... His World ... His Influence, ed. Lally Weymouth. New York:
         Putnam's, 1973. 141-57.

         Survey of TJ's attitudes toward and involvement with the press; he
         "believed in freedom of the press more unreservedly than any
         President of the United Sates before or since."

*2085.   Williams, Edna Glenn. "Thomas Jefferson, Slavery, and the Negro."
         M.A. thesis. Howard Univ., 1938.

2086.   Williams, John Sharp. Thomas Jefferson, His Permanent Influence on
         American Institutions. New York: Columbia Univ. Press, 1913.
         pp. ix, 330.

         Praise for TJ's influence as revolutionist, democratizer of state and
         federal institutions, diplomat, president, and for his encouragement
         of freedom of religion and of education.

2087.   Wills, Garry. "The Strange Case of Mr. Jefferson's Subpoena."
         New York Review of Books. 21(May 2, 1974), 15-19.

         Review essay of Malone's Jefferson the President: Second Term, focusing on the Burr trial and the subpoena of TJ. Worth attention, but see item #1806.

2088. Wills, Garry. "An Un-American Politician." New York Review of Books. 21(May 16, 1974), 9-12.

Continues review essay in previous item, discussing Malone's defense of TJ against the critique of Leonard Levy's Jefferson and Civil Liberties.

2089. Willson, Beckles. "Jefferson (1785-89)" in America's Ambassadors to France (1777-1927), A Narrative of Franco-American Diplomatic Relations. London: John Murray, 1928. 17-39.

Contends TJ failed to understand the situation in France because he did not recognize the lengths to which the revolution would go.

2090. Wilson, Clyde. "The Jeffersonian Conservative Tradition." Modern Age. 14(1969), 36-48.

Argues that modern conservatives must have a proper historic self-image that includes TJ as representative of republicanism, constitutionalism, and federalism (i.e. sharing of power among federated individual states).

2091. Wilson, Woodrow. "What Jefferson Would Do: Part of Address Delivered at Jefferson Day Banquet, Waldorf-Astoria Hotel, New York: April 13, 1912." Congressional Record, 62nd Congress, 2nd Session. 48:4747-48.

Rpt. in Wilson, College and State, Educational, Literary and Political Papers (1875-1913). New York: Harper, 1925. 2:424-29. TJ "would have acted upon the facts as they are" and called for tarrif and currency reforms.

2092. Witt, Cornelis de. Thomas Jefferson, Étude Historique sur la Démocratie Américaine. Paris: Didier et cie., 1862. pp. iv, 568.

Strongly critical of TJ; he put the American republic on its downward slide to mobbishness and rebellion. Translated by R. S. H. Church as Jefferson and the American Democracy: An Historical Study. London: Longman, 1862. pp. xxviii, 448. Originally published in part in four numbers of Revue des Deux Mondes.

2093. Witt, Cornelis de. "Thomas Jefferson. Sa Vie et Sa Correspondance. II. Formation et Triumphe du Parti Democratique aux États Unis." Revue des Deux Mondes. ser. 2. 15(1858), 332-72.

The struggles with Hamilton and the problems with foreign relations in the 1790's.

2094. Witt, Cornelis de. "Thomas Jefferson. Sa Vie et Sa Correspondance. III. Le Parti Democratique aux Affaires." Revue des Deux Mondes. ser. 2. 22(1859), 353-91.

Covers TJ's presidency, concluding that the executive power of the presidency has never recovered from his weakening of it and that the difficulties the country faces today are an almost inevitable consequence of his politics. Printed separately, Paris: J. Claye, 1859. pp. 39.

2095. Wood, John. The Suppressed History of the Administration of John Adams, (from 1797 to 1801), as Printed and Suppressed in 1802. By John Wood. ... Now Republished with Notes, and an Appendix, by John Henry Sherburne... . Philadelphia: Walker & Gillis, 1846. pp. 390.

A republican account of the period of the Alien and Sedition Laws, reprinted to connect the Federalists with the Whigs.

2096. Woodfin, Maude Howlett. "Ex-President Jefferson's Plans for Virginia." Social Science. 15(1940), 341-51.

TJ in retirement has many opinions but is reluctant to push any of them in public, except for the University.

2097. Woolery, William Kirk. The Relation of Thomas Jefferson to American Foreign Policy, 1783-1793. Johns Hopkins Univ. Studies in Historical and Political Science. Series 65, no. 2. Baltimore: Johns Hopkins Press, 1927. pp. viii, 128.

"As minister to France and as Secretary of State, (TJ) attacked every problem of American diplomacy, and the systems and principles he followed were, in practically every case, followed by the United States. It is the purpose of this study to investigate the chief problems and the reasoning Jefferson applied to them in the period 1783-1793." Originally a dissertation.

2098. Wright, Louis B. "The Founding Fathers and 'Splendid Isolation.'" Huntington Library Quarterly. 6(1942), 173-96.

Washington's and TJ's desire to keep out of European wars was prompted by realistic assessment of national strength and weakness, but "Jefferson's vision of collaboration between English-speaking peoples to maintain peace and justice in the Western Hemisphere" justifies eventual interventionism.

2099. Wyllie, John C., ed. "The Second Mrs. Wayland, An Unpublished Jefferson Opinion on a Case in Equity." American Journal of Legal History. 9(1965), 64-68.

Opinion dated August 16, 1782, on the estate of Adam Wayland.

2100. Wyman, William I. "Thomas Jefferson and the Patent System." Journal
       of the Patent Office Society. 1(September 1918), 5-8.

       Note on TJ's work as first patent commissioner and his changing atti-
       tude toward the value of the patent system.

2101. Young, Alfred. The Jeffersonian Republicans of New York: The
       Origins, 1763-1797. Chapel Hill: Univ. of North Carolina Press, 1967.
       pp. xv, 636.

       Only peripherally about TJ, but some information on his methods of
       encouraging party organization, e.g. pp. 194-201.

2102. Young, Andrew W. The American Statesman: A Political History,
       Exhibiting the Origin, Nature and Practical Operations of Constitu-
       tional Governments in the United States; The Rise and Progress of
       Parties; And the Views of Distinguished Statesmen Questions of
       Foreign and Domestic Policy. New York: J. C. Derby, 1855.
       95-156; 189-233.

       These pages deal with the formation of the Republican party and TJ's
       administration; avoids controversial issues and takes an objective
       point of view.

2103. Zaitseva, N. D. "Demokraticheskie Reformy Prezidenta T.
       Dzheffersona (1800-1804 GG)." Vestnik Leningradskogo U.: Seria
       Istorii, Iazyka i Literatury. April, 1978. 64-69.

       Argues that TJ's reforms during his first administration were deter-
       mined by the existing conditions of the development of capitalism
       and emerging bourgeois liberalism. TJ had not meant a radical
       break in the mode of life in the U.S. and favored capitalistic
       development.

*2104. Zipperer, Manfred. Thomas Jefferson's "Act for Establishing Religious
       Freedom in Virginia." vom 16 Januar 1786. Einverfassungsgeschicht-
       licher und rechtsvergleichender Beitrag zum Staatskirchenrecht.
       Erlangen, 1967. pp. xxi, 282.

2105. Zook, George F. "Proposals for a New Commercial Treaty Between
       France and the United States, 1778-1793." South Atlantic Quarterly.
       8(1909), 267-83.

       TJ as minister to France and as Secretary of State urged commercial
       reciprocity.

2106. Zvesper, John. "Thomas Jefferson" in Political Philosophy and Rheto-
       ric: A Study of the Origins of American Party Politics. Cambridge,
       England: Cambridge Univ. Press, 1977. 102-110.

       In the context of a discussion of the idealism of the Republican challenge to the Federalists, the author examines TJ's belief that a just politics must rest on the human moral sense and on moral virtue.

2107. Zyskind, Harold. "How to Read the Declaration of Independence" in Promoting Growth Toward Maturity in What Is Read, ed. William S. Gray. Supplementary Educational Monographs. Vol. 13, No. 74. Chicago: Univ. of Chicago Press, 1951. 7-12.

How to lead students to see the need for interpretation.

IV. PHILOSOPHICAL APPROACHES

AND

STUDIES IN THE HISTORY OF IDEAS

IV. PHILOSOPHICAL APPROACHES AND STUDIES IN THE HISTORY OF IDEAS.

2108.   Adair, Douglass. "Fame and the Founding Fathers" in Fame and the
        Founding Fathers, ed. Edmund P. Willis. Bethlehem, Pa., 1967.
        27-52.

        Rpt. in Fame and the Founding Fathers: Essays by Douglass Adair,
        ed. Trevor Colbourn. New York: Norton, 1974. 3-26. Argues that
        "love of fame" was a crucial motivating force for leaders of the
        Revolution and the early republic; examines attitudes of TJ and
        Hamilton in detail.

2109.   Adair, Douglass. "The Intellectual Origins of Jeffersonian Democracy:
        Republicanism, the Class Struggle, and the Virtuous Farmer." Ph.D.
        dissertation. Yale Univ., 1943. pp. ii, 310.

        Agrarian theory with which TJ and Madison have been closely iden-
        tified "was one of the most common political doctrines of the
        Enlightenment. It was also one of the most ancient theories in its
        origin." Traces this theory from Aristotle to TJ by way of Polybius,
        Plutarch, Roman authors, and Harrington and the English republicans.

        An important dissertation.

2110.   Adair, Douglass. "Rumbold's Dying Speech, 1685, and Jefferson's Last
        Words on Democracy." WMQ. 3rd ser. 9(1952), 521-31.

        Traces TJ's use of a trope used in his letter of June 24, 1826, to
        the mayor of Washington, D.C. to the scaffold speech of Col. Richard
        Rumbold a Whig martyr.

2111.   Adair, Douglass and T. V. Smith. Thomas Jefferson and the Declaration
        of Independence: A Radio Discussion .... Chicago: Univ. of Chicago
        Press, 1948. pp. 29.

        No. 537, July 4, 1948, in the Univ. of Chicago Round Table Series;
        discussion of TJ's political and ethical principles.

2112.   Adams, Dickinson Ward. "Jefferson's Politics of Morality: The Purpose
        and Meaning of His Extracts from the Evangelists, "The Philosophy of
        Jesus of Nazareth" and "The Life and Morals of Jesus of Nazareth."
        Ph.D. dissertation. Brown Univ., 1970. pp. 690.

        TJ's religious views before 1798 were those of a mild Deist, but after
        that he attempted to support the moral sense of a republican nation
        with the "pure doctrines" of Jesus. The concept of the moral sense is
        central to his thinking on religion, morality, and even politics. Con-
        tains a reconstruction of TJ's lost "Philosophy of Jesus" and a defini-
        tive text of "The Life and Morals." The second compilation, unlike
        the first, shows Jesus as something more than a mere man.
        DAI 36/06A, p. 3914.

2113. Adams, Hewitt D. "A Note on Jefferson's Knowledge of Economics." VMHB. 75(1967), 69-74.

List of books in TJ's library which were also cited in Smith's Wealth of Nations; TJ had 94 of the 149 authors cited.

2114. Adams, James Truslow, ed. Jeffersonian Principles: Extracts from the Writings of Thomas Jefferson. Boston: Little Brown, 1928. pp. xxii, 161.

Introduction argues for the centrality of TJ's belief in the ability of the common man, who would opt for limited government, no public debt, and the least restraint on individual freedom. Extracts from TJ deliver various opinions on political and ethical questions.

2115. Adams, John Quincy. "Thomas Jefferson." Old and New. 7(1873), 135-37.

Letter to the editor of the North American Review in 1830, taking exception to an article; despite his errors, "Mr. Jefferson had a mind. I did hope to see in the North American Review at least traces of a mind grappling with it."

2116. Adler, Cyrus. "Jefferson Bible." Cosmopolitan. 38(1905), 340-44.

A description of "The Life and Morals of Jesus of Nazareth" and how TJ put it together.

2117. Adler, Mortimer J. and William Gorman. The American Testament. New York: Praeger, 1975. pp. 160.

An "exegetical" reading of the Declaration of Independence, the Preamble to the Constitution, and the Gettysburg Address. Attempts to show the philosophical and historical background of the Declaration and what TJ "really meant." Minor.

2118. [American Unitarian Association]. What Kind of a Christian Was Thomas Jefferson? Boston: American Unitarian Association, 1947. pp. 17.

"Services of a commemoration at the Jefferson Memorial, Washington, D.C., on the 204th anniversary of Jefferson's birth, April 13, 1947, under the auspices of the American Unitarian Association, All Souls' Church (Unitarian) Washington D.C." Contains sermon by Frederick May Eliot on TJ's unitarianism.

2119. Anderson, Judith Lois. "Thomas Jefferson's Case for an Arcadian America." Ph.D. dissertation. Indiana Univ., 1970. pp. 251.

Drawing from the rhetorical sources of the classical period and the Enlightenment, TJ evolved "an eclectic ideal for the new nation" in which the principle of equality would not only regulate laws but would be present in the everyday lives of men. DAI 31/11A, p. 6194.

2120.   Angermann, Erich. "Ständische Rechtstraditionen in der American-ischen Unabhangigkeitserklärung." Historische Zeitschrift. 200(no. 1, 1965), 61-91.

"Traditions of the Rights of the Estates in the American Declaration of Independence." Compares the complaints against George III to similar complaints in the Dutch Declaration of 1581, the trial of Charles I in 1649, and the English Bill of Rights of 1689. Argues that each indicts monarchs for violating rights stemming not from natural law but from those belonging to feudal estates.

2121.   Backus, E. Burdette. Thomas Jefferson, Pioneer of Tomorrow's Reli-gion. Indianapolis: All Souls Unitarian Church, 1943. pp. 17.

"... we must have a religion which believes in men as Jefferson be-lieved in them."

2122.   Baker, Gordon E. "Thomas Jefferson on Academic Freedom." AAUP Bulletin. 39(1953), 377-87.

"His insistence on freedom of inquiry" is "equalled in eloquence by few;" yet at least once he "abandoned his high principles" by demand-ing that the University of Virginia's law professor be "uninfected with Federalist principles."

*2123.   Bar, Max. "Thomas Jefferson, eine Entwicklungsgeschichte seiner demokratischen Ideen." Ph.D. dissertation. University of Erlangen, 1951.

2124.   Barlieb, Calvin. "Thomas Jefferson's Conception of Democracy." School and Society. 59(1944), 241-43.

General sketch.

2125.   Barnes, Howard A. "The Idea That Caused a War: Horace Bushnell Versus Thomas Jefferson." The Journal of Church and State. 16(1974), 73-83.

Bushnell's organicism opposed TJ's individualism, and Bushnell be-lieved TJ had made the Civil War inevitable by substituting the social contract for the covenant.

2126.   Bauer, Gerald. "The Quest for Religious Freedom in Virginia." Historical Magazine of the Protestant Episcopal Church. 41(1972), 83-93.

Account of the passage of the Bill for Establishing Religious Freedom.

2127. Beach, Curtis. "The Freedom of Religion." New Outlook. 10(June 1957), 19-24.

Fanciful version of TJ's work for religious freedom, complete with imagined dialogue.

2128. Beard, Charles A. "Jefferson and the New Freedom." New Republic. 1(November 14, 1914), 18-19.

Argues that TJ's agrarianism is at the core of his political philosophy. If so, then in view of the triumph of capitalism and industrialism, what message has TJ for the Wilson Democrats who claim to derive their "New Freedom" from him?

2129. Beard, Charles A. "Thomas Jefferson: A Civilized Man." MVHR. 30(1943), 159-70.

"... republic--res publica--the public good, as incorporated in the idea of civilization, was for Mr. Jefferson a more fitting conception than democracy to be applied to American society..."

2130. Becker, Carl. The Declaration of Independence: A Study in the History of Political Ideas. New York: Harcourt Brace, 1922. pp. x, 286.

An important analysis of the premises underlaying the Declaration and its evolution from TJ's first draft. Considers also the literary qualities of the Declaration and its influence in the 18th century. A significant study which can be supplemented with but not replaced by Garry Wills' Inventing America. Rpt. with new introduction, New York: Knopf, 1942.

2131. Becker, Carl. "What Is Still Living in the Political Philosophy of Thomas Jefferson?" Proceedings of the APS. 87(1943), 201-10.

Also in AHR. 48(1943), 691-706. "In respect to fundamentals, Jefferson's political philosophy is still valid for us; in respect to what is more superficial—in respect to certain favorite institutional forms—it is outmoded." Latter particularly true in regard to "banks and speculation, cities and industrial communities," and TJ's laissez faire doctrines.

2132. Bell, Barry Ray. "The Ideology and Rhetoric of the American Revolution." Ph.D. dissertation. Univ. of Virginia, 1977. pp. 237.

TJ masked ideological differences among the Patriots by conflating the ideology of the Real Whigs with that of the Evangelicals. DAI 39/02A, p. 879.

2133. Belmont, Perry. "Jefferson" in Political Equality: Religious Toleration from Roger Williams to Jefferson. New York: Putnam's, 1927. 133-36.

Mostly quotations showing TJ was in favor of toleration.

2134. Bennett, H. Omer. "The Religion of Thomas Jefferson." Social Science. 5(1930), 460-65.

General survey.

2135. Benson, Carl W. Randolph. "Sociological Elements in Selected Writings and Works of Thomas Jefferson." Ph.D. dissertation. Louisiana State Univ., 1966. pp. 369.

TJ's thinking was based especially upon Locke's and Kames's theories on natural law and natural rights. He can be considered a proto-sociologist because of his insights into the elements of social control and socio-psychological determinants of human behavior. He was both a theorist and activist, a "practical idealist." DAI 27/08A, p. 2622.

2136. Benson, C. Randolph. Thomas Jefferson as Social Scientist. Rutherford, N.J.: Fairleigh Dickinson Univ. Press, 1971. pp. 333.

Revised version of dissertation noted above; as a man interested in finding a science of society, TJ was a precursor of modern social science.

2137. Bernstein, Samuel. "Jefferson on the French Revolution" in Essays in Political and Intellectual History. New York: Paine-Whitman Publishers, 1955. 57-76.

Surveys TJ's views of French society and character and gives a Marxist analysis of him as a thinker shocked by the "ugly manifestations" of capitalism in order to suggest that he had more in common with Robespierre and the Jacobins than with the Girondins. But since he derived most of his information from anti-Robespierrist sources, he leaned more toward the Girondins during their struggle with the Jacobins.

2138. Berryman, Charles. "Thomas Jefferson" in From Wilderness to Wasteland: The Trial of the Puritan God in the American Imagination. Port Washington, N.Y.: Kennikat, 1979. 98-103.

Jejune account of a deist TJ who waged rhetorical warfare on the Puritans.

2139. Blau, Joseph. "Enlightened Politics: Thomas Jefferson" in Men and Movements in American Philosophy. New York: Prentice-Hall, 1952. 46-55.

Sketch of TJ as philosopher; argues that he thinks of the moral sense in utilitarian terms and as answerable to reason and calculation. Therefore, it is not a conscience and its judgments are relative.

2140. Blinderman, Charles S. "Thomas Jefferson: Humanist." Humanist.
20(July/August 1960), 203-11.

Claims TJ can be a polemical weapon for the modern humanist in
"proselytizing of the masses."

2141. Boas, George. "La Philosophie dans la Vie de Jefferson." A.B.A. Bulletin de l'Association Belgo-Americaine. 6(October 1949), 4-7.

Discusses natural law doctrine and contends that TJ's use and understanding of this was dominated by a curious complex of traditions—
protestant, Aristotelian, Epicurean—which seemed axiomatic to him.
But he used his philosophy to regulate his life.

2142. Boller, Paul F., Jr. "Jefferson's Dreams of the Future." Southwestern
Review. 44(1959), 109-14.

TJ the Apostle of Democracy, etc.

2143. Bonn, Franklyn George, Jr. "The Idea of Political Party in the Thought
of Thomas Jefferson and James Madison." Ph.D. dissertation. Univ.
of Minnesota, 1964. pp. 305.

Both TJ and Madison disapproved of parties, but in "the face of an
opposition whose unity they exaggerated" they became increasingly
aware of the need for a cohesive and organized party. Yet, their
"suspicions of party activities in general ... account for a number of
their mistaken comments on the changed nature of American parties
as evident by the early 1800's." DAI 26/02, p. 1135.

2144. Boorstin, Daniel J. The Lost World of Thomas Jefferson. New York:
Holt, 1948. pp. xii, 306.

On the scientific ideas and work of a group of men associated for the
most part with the American Philosophical Society, called by
Boorstin "the Jeffersonian Circle" with TJ as the ordering center for
their discrete investigations. Valuable, informative study of
scientific ideas of the age, but generalizes too easily from one
particular figure to "Jeffersonian" in general. TJ treated passim.

2145. Bowers, Claude G. Civil and Religious Liberty, Jefferson: O'Connell:
Two Orations. Worcester, Mass.: Holy Cross College. 1930. pp. viii,
88.

TJ as an advocate of religious freedom, particularly as it has touched
Roman Catholics.

2146. Bowers, Claude G. "Jefferson and the Freedom of the Human Spirit."
Ethics. 53(1943), 237-45.

TJ fought for the freedom of speech, religious freedom, and academic freedom.

2147.	Boyd, Julian Parks. "A Perspective View from Monticello ... Phi Beta Kappa Address, Sweet Briar College, February 28, 1961." Bulletin of Sweet Briar College. 44(April 1961), 1-26?

Rpt. separately and thus seen. The importance of learning at a time of transition, illustrated with reference to TJ; peripheral.

2148.	Boyd, Julian P. "Subversive of What?" Atlantic Monthly. 132(August 1948), 19-23.

TJ's defense of freedom of speech and of opinion used as the basis for a tract for the times. Brief discussion of his defense of Nicholas Dufief, his Philadelphia provider of French books.

2149.	Boyd, Julian P. "Thomas Jefferson's 'Empire of Liberty.'" VQR. 24(1948), 538-54.

Argues that TJ's belief in reason and individual freedom was neither naive nor shallow and that "his understanding of the relation of a people to its land" was an important contribution to the bond of national union.

2150.	Boyd, Julian P. "Thomas Jefferson and the Police State." North Carolina Historical Review. 25(1948), 233-53.

Contends that TJ as political realist understood the need for, in Blackstone's words, "due regulation and domestic order," but he never swerved from opposition to any attempt to coerce opinion. "Dissent and the threat of revolution ... would serve as proof of our courage and strength." The Jeffersonian example particularly needs to be remembered today (1948).

2151.	Boykin, Edward. Thomas Jefferson and Religious Freedom. Washington: Thomas Jefferson Bicentennial Commission, 1942. pp. 15.

Illustrated pamphlet.

2152.	Brent, Robert A. "The Jeffersonian Outlook on Religion." Southern Quarterly. 5(1967), 417-32.

Contends TJ was "a deeply spiritual man," although his opposition to established churches and the doctrine of the Trinity antagonized various of his contemporaries. "In all things religious or political he was motivated by one consuming passion—that of the necessity of freedom for the human body, mind, and spirit."

2153.	Brent, Robert A. "Two Jeffersonian Myths Explored." American Studies in the Philippines. 1(December 1965), 47-61.

His belief in absolute equality, his being a thorough-going democrat are myths. Punctures straw men. Revised version published as

"Puncturing Some Jeffersonian Mythology." <u>Southern Quarterly</u>. 6(1968), 175-90.

2154. Brigham, Johnson. "Jefferson on Christianity and the Common Law. A Forgotten Chapter in the Life of Jefferson." <u>Green Bag</u>. 12(1900), 441-44.

Describes in some detail TJ's "Whether Christianity Is a Part of the Common Law" and his subsequent opinion on this.

2155. Brown, Barbara. "Jefferson Bible: Compilation of the Words of Jesus." <u>Mentor</u>. 17(July 1929), 57-59.

Account of <u>The Life and Morals of Jesus</u>.

2156. Brown, Esther Ernestine. <u>The French Revolution and the American Man of Letters</u>. University of Missouri Studies. Vol. 24, No. 1. Columbia: Curators of the Univ. of Missouri, 1951. pp. 171.

TJ discussed <u>passim</u>; argues that after his election to the presidency he was "able in his thinking to detach the principles of democracy from the French Revolution and attach them solely to America, where he believed they were assured by the Republican victory" of 1800.

2157. Brown, Stuart Gerry. <u>The First Republicans: Political Philosophy and Public Policy in the Party of Jefferson and Madison</u>. Syracuse: Syracuse University Press, 1954. pp. vii, 186.

Survey of the commonplaces of republican ideology.

2158. Brown, Stuart Gerry. "The Mind of Thomas Jefferson." <u>Ethics</u>. 73(1963), 79-99.

TJ's philosophical background, particularly Bacon, Locke, and Epicurus. This essay incorporated in the author's <u>Thomas Jefferson</u>.

2159. Brown, Stuart Gerry. <u>Thomas Jefferson</u>. New York: Washington Square Press, 1966. pp. viii, 247.

A volume in the Great American Thinkers series; competent introduction to TJ for non-specialists.

2160. Bryan, William Jennings. "Jeffersonian Principles." <u>North American Review</u>. 168(1899), 670-78.

TJ would not crucify mankind on a cross of gold, nor would he increase the permanent army, or attempt to make subjects of the Filipinos. "The Renaissance of Jeffersonian principles is at hand."

2161. Bryan, William Jennings. "The Statute for Establishing Religious Freedom" in <u>The Writings of Thomas Jefferson</u>, ed. Lipscomb and Bergh. Washington: Thomas Jefferson Memorial Association, 1903. 8:i-xi.

Meandering note on TJ's spiritual greatness in general.

2162.   Brydon, G. Maclaren. "Thomas Jefferson—The Churchman." Tyler's
        Quarterly. 25(1943), 73-75.

        Rejects the idea proposed in an earlier communication to this journal
        that TJ was an Episcopalian.

2163.   Cady, Edwin H. "Jefferson and the Democratic Aristoi" in The
        Gentleman in America; A Literary Study in American Culture.
        Syracuse: Syracuse Univ. Press, 1949. 85-102.

        Contends TJ's natural aristocracy of talent and virtue allowed the
        concept of the gentleman to become associated with that of democ-
        racy.

2164.   Caldwell, Lynton K. "The Jurisprudence of Thomas Jefferson."
        Indiana Law Journal. 18(1943), 193-213.

        Intelligent overview of TJ's conception of legal theory and his know-
        ledge of legal authorities.

2165.   Calisch, Edward N. "Jefferson's Religion" in The Writings of Thomas
        Jefferson, ed. Lipscomb and Bergh. Washington: Thomas Jefferson
        Memorial Association, 1903. 17:i-xi.

2166.   Campbell, Alexander. "Incidents on a Tour to the South. No. II."
        Millennial Harbinger. 3(February 1839), 54-60.

        The founder of the Disciples of Christ visits TJ's grave and describes
        the religious situation at the Univ. of Virginia—the University had
        come to be dominated by the major sects in the short time since TJ's
        death. Campbell admired TJ for his stand on religious freedom and
        individual rights.

2167.   Carter, Everett. "The Making of the Idea" in The American Idea: The
        Literary Response to American Optimism. Chapel Hill: Univ. of
        North Carolina Press, 1977. 30-36.

        TJ and Franklin gave "principal imaginative expression" to the idea
        of American progress in freedom; vaguely and generally developed
        statement.

2168.   Cawelti, John C. "Natural Aristocracy and the New Republic: The Idea
        of Mobility in the Thought of Franklin and Jefferson" in Apostles of
        the Self-Made Man. Chicago: Univ. of Chicago Press, 1965. 9-36.

        Argues that TJ favored an institutional framework to channel the
        mobility of his natural aristocracy, but that the anti-industrialism
        and suspicion of federal authority implicit in his thought obstructed
        the needed central planning, particularly by his political heirs.

2169. Chaudhuri, Joyotpaul. "Jefferson's Unheavenly City: A Bicentennial Look." American Journal of Economics and Sociology. 34(1975), 397-410.

Claims that TJ's notions of property, rights, and consent are more modern than Locke's and that his epistemological commitments are different. Revised version printed as "Jefferson's Unheavenly City: An Interpretation" in The Non-Lockean Roots of American Economic Thought, ed. Chaudhuri. Tucson: Univ. of Arizona Press, 1977. 17-29.

2170. Chaudhuri, Joyotpaul. "Possession, Ownership and Access: A Jeffersonian View of Property." Political Inquiry. 1(Fall 1973), 78-95.

Contends TJ conceives of property differently from Locke, and the "Jeffersonians' synthesis of rights and consent demonstrates the social basis of property without legitimizing the doctrines of laissez faire or social elitism."

2171. Cheetham, Henry H. Was Thomas Jefferson a Unitarian? Charlottesville: Thomas Jefferson Memorial Unitarian Church, 1956. pp. 12.

Yes, it says here.

2172. Chinard, Gilbert. "An American Philosopher in the World of Nations." VQR. 19(1943), 189-203.

"In his theories and his conduct can be distinguished a combination of international idealism, world-wide economic aspirations, and intense isolationism which cannot be reduced to a single formula."

2173. Chinard, Gilbert, ed. The Commonplace Book of Thomas Jefferson, A Repertory of His Ideas on Government, With an Introduction and Notes .... Baltimore: Johns Hopkins Press, 1926. pp. 403.

Useful introduction describes the mss. and comments in detail on TJ's entries.

2174. Chinard, Gilbert. "Introduction" in Pensées choisies de Montesquieu tirées du Commonplace Book de Thomas Jefferson. Paris: Societé de Edition "Les Belles Lettres," 1925. 7-29.

Charts TJ's changing responses from approval to reservation toward Montesquieu.

2175. Chinard, Gilbert. "Jefferson Among the Philosophers." Ethics. 53(1943), 255-68.

TJ was more influenced by readings in Bolingbroke, Cicero, and

Kames than by the philosophes he encountered after his trip to
France. He was reluctant to involve himself with the more abstract
speculations of the philosophers but took comfort in the doctrines of
Epicurus and Enfield's philosophical handbook. His concern to find a
practical rule of conduct and social morality made him an object of
admiration for later French thinkers such as Cabanis, Volney,
Thierry, and Comte.

2176. Chinard, Gilbert, ed. Jefferson et les Ideologues d'après sa correspon-
       dance inédite avec Destutt de Tracy, Cabanis, J.-B. Say, et Auguste
       Comte. Baltimore: Johns Hopkins Press/Paris: Les Presses
       Universitaires, 1925. pp. 295.

       TJ's correspondence reprinted, including letters to him, with ample
       commentary and explanation. Important on this topic.

2177. Chinard, Gilbert. "Jefferson and the Physiocrats." University of
       California Chronicle. 33(1931), 18-31.

       Contends the differences between TJ and the Physiocrats concerning
       economic ideas were greater than the similarities.

2178. Chinard, Gilbert. Volney et l'Amérique d'après des documents inédite
       et sa correspondance avec Jefferson. Baltimore: Johns Hopkins
       Press, 1923. pp. 296.

       Best account of the Volney-TJ relationship, although the focus is on
       Volney here.

2179. Christian, John T. "The Religion of Thomas Jefferson." Review and
       Expositor. 16(1919), 295-307.

       Rambling survey, concluding that if TJ were alive today, he would
       not be far removed from orthodox Christianity.

2180. Cohen, William. "Thomas Jefferson and the Problem of Slavery."
       Journal of American History. 56(1969), 503-26.

       Argues that "Jefferson's practical involvement with the system of
       black bondage indicates that, while his racist beliefs were generally
       congruent with his actions, his libertarian views about slavery tended
       to be mere abstractions. This is particularly true for the years after
       1785."

2181. Colbourn, Harold T. "The Saxon Heritage: Thomas Jefferson Looks at
       English History." Ph.D. dissertation. Johns Hopkins Univ., 1953.
       pp. 318.

       Author later publishes as H. Trevor Colbourn.

2182. Colbourn, H. Trevor. "Thomas Jefferson and the Rights of Expatriated Men" in The Lamp of History: Whig History and the Intellectual Origins of the American Revolution. Chapel Hill: Univ. of North Carolina Press, 1965. 158-84.

TJ's reading of whig history as background for his Summary View as well as for his whole career. This is the key to "his peculiar historical optimism, ... his staunch faith that the past could be successfully adapted to the future in America."

2183. Colbourn, H. Trevor. "Thomas Jefferson's Use of the Past." WMQ. 3rd ser. 15(1958), 56-70.

TJ developed a "persistent and enduring affection for whig history," including the myth of an Anglo-Saxon democracy which "he was optimistic enough to believe ... would be re-established on an enduring basis in America."

2184. Coleman, John. "The Concept of Equality as Held by Thomas Jefferson." University of Pittsburgh Bulletin. The Graduate School, Abstracts of Theses, Researches in Progress, and Bibliography of Publications. 10(1934), 3037.

Ph.D. dissertation abstract; claims TJ believed in equality of moral responsibility and moral action and in the equality of participants in the social contract but not in racial equality nor in equality of mind and character. Considers the implication of this for American institutions.

2185. Commager, Henry Steele. "The Americanization of History." Saturday Review. 52(November 1, 1969), 24-25, 54.

Popular condensation of item #2186.

2186. Commager, Henry Steele. "The Declaration of Independence" in Thomas Jefferson: The Man ... His World ... His Influence, ed. Lally Weymouth. New York: Putnam's, 1973. 179-87.

TJ considered as an Enlightenment man.

2187. Commager, Henry Steele. "Jefferson and the Enlightenment" in Thomas Jefferson: The Man ... His World ... His Influence, ed. Lally Weymouth. New York: Putnam's, 1973. 39-67.

Surveys TJ's connections with the Enlightenment; he alone "of the great galaxy of the philosophes embraced the whole of Enlightenment philosophy."

2188. Commager, Henry Steele. Jefferson, Nationalism, and the Enlightenment. New York: Braziller, 1975. pp. xx, 196.

Argues that the Old World imagined the Enlightenment, but the New World realized it in government based on faith in Nature and Reason.

2189. Commager, Henry Steele. "The Past as an Extension of the Present." Proceedings of the American Antiquarian Society. 79(1969), 17-27.

Claims that John Adams saw men as prisoners of the past, but TJ believed men could "triumph over history." The Jeffersonians Americanized the idea of progress.

2190. Cooke, J. W. "Jefferson on Liberty." Journal of the History of Ideas. 34(1973), 563-76.

Develops TJ's conception of freedom and observes no significant modification of his basic ideas in the fifty years of his life after 1776.

2191. Costanzo, Joseph F. "Thomas Jefferson, Religious Education and Public Law." Journal of Public Law. 8(1961), 81-108.

Claims TJ did not allow his own prejudices and animosities or his convictions on religious matters to affect his actions as a statesman and educator. TJ was impartial toward the exercise of religion, but he did not retreat into that "neutrality which is the benign disguise for wholly secular education."

2192. Cousins, Norman, ed. 'In God We Trust,' The Religious Beliefs and Ideas of the American Founding Fathers. New York: Harper, 1958. 114-294.

Selected comments of TJ on religion, with brief comments by the editor.

2193. Cragan, Thomas Mount. "Thomas Jefferson's Early Attitudes toward Manufacturing, Agriculture, and Commerce." Ph.D. dissertation. Univ. of Tennessee, 1965. pp. 331.

Focuses on attitudes before 1790; "There is considerable evidence that some of Jefferson's early views were not entirely inconsistent with the favorable attitudes toward manufacturing he later exhibited." DAI 26/04, p. 2158.

2194. Cramer, Frederick R. "Definitions of Freedom: Jefferson vs. Robespierre." Forum. 112(1949), 129-35.

Contrasts TJ and Robespierre as respectively the "ideological founding fathers of the liberal and totalitarian forms of popular government."

2195. Crawford, Nelson Antrim. "Thomas Jefferson and Religious Freedom." American Collector. 2(1926), 292-95.

Laudatory sketch on TJ as author of the Bill for Establishing Religious Freedom.

2196.   Craven, Avery O. "Thomas Jefferson and the Democratic Dogma" in Democracy in American Life, A Historical View. Chicago: Univ. of Chicago Press, 1941. 1-37.

Lecture on democracy for undergraduates; contends that TJ's theory of government rested on trust in the virtue of citizens, and if selfishness kept a good society from appearing, government would have to act as "widely as necessary," a la FDR.

2197.   Crothers, Samuel McChord. The Religion of Thomas Jefferson, Author of the Declaration of Independence. Boston: American Unitarian Association, 1926. pp. 15.

Rpt. as The Unitarianism of Thomas Jefferson. On TJ's rational religion.

2198.   "Cult of Jefferson." Commonweal. 37(1943), 604.

Editorial note. "What is basic in Jefferson's political philosophy, however, comes from Aristotle, Saint Thomas and John Locke."

2199.   Curti, Merle. "The American Enlightenment" in Human Nature in American Thought. Madison: Univ. of Wisconsin Press, 1980. 70-104.

Discusses TJ, pp. 80-88, stressing his thought on the role of environment in shaping men's thinking; mostly a generalizing sketch.

2200.   Dalton, David C. and Thomas C. Hunt. "Thomas Jefferson's Theories on Education as Revealed Through a Textual Reading of Several of His Letters." Journal of Thought. 14(1979), 263-71.

Authors discuss TJ's educational theories as consistent with his philosophy, public utterances, and public writings. Nothing new.

2201.   Davis, Charles Hall. "Jefferson's Thirteenth Amendment." Tyler's Quarterly. 26(1944), 248-70.

The 13th Amendment is "Jefferson's posthumous contribution to the cause of human freedom," as he expressed it in the Declaration of Independence. Neglects the complexities of TJ's attitude toward slavery.

2202.   Dawson, Joseph Martin. "Roger Williams and the Pattern of the American Republic." The Quarterly Review: A Survey of Southern Baptist Progress. 15(no. 2, 1955), 9-16.

Argues for a similarity of TJ's views to Williams' and for a Baptist influence on his ideas about religious liberty. Unconvincing. Similar material in the chapter of the same title in Dawson's <u>Baptists and the American Republic</u>. Nashville: Broadman Press, 1956. 15-45.

2203. DeFalco, Anthony A. "A Comparison of John Dewey's and Thomas Jefferson's Concept of Human Nature." Ed.D. dissertation. Rutgers Univ., 1976. pp. 100.

TJ's and Dewey's liberalism "is at least of the same 'family'; their view of human nature is not."

2204. D'Elia, Donald J. "Jefferson, Rush, and the Limits of Philosophical Friendship." <u>Proceedings of the APS</u>. 117(1973), 333-45.

Examines the correspondence and the friendship between Rush and TJ and contends that the differences between them were rooted in Rush's Christianity and TJ's deism. Discusses Rush's efforts to convert TJ and TJ's preference for Dugald Stewart and Tracy to the apologists Rush urged him to read.

2205. Densford, John P. "Educational Philosophy of Thomas Jefferson." <u>Peabody Journal of Education</u>. 38(March 1961), 265-75.

Abstract drawn from thesis; see following item.

2206. Densford, John Paul. "The Educational Philosophy of Thomas Jefferson." Ed.D. dissertation. Oklahoma State Univ., 1961. pp. 202.

The ends of education for TJ grew directly out of his theory of value; education was an instrument of society and was to be encouraged in order to realize individual and social possibilities of liberty and happiness. DAI 23/02, p. 551.

2207. Densford, John P. "Value Theory as Basic to a Philosophy of Education; with Special Reference to the Educational Theories of Thomas Jefferson and John Dewey." <u>History of Education Quarterly</u>. 3(1963), 102-06.

Contends TJ's educational philosophy rested on his epistomology, hence it is "an expression of his value theory."

2208. Dewey, John. "Thomas Jefferson and the Democratic Faith." <u>VQR</u>. 16(1940), 1-13.

"... The essentially moral nature of Jefferson's political philosophy is concealed from us at the present time because of the change that has taken place in the language in which moral ideas are expressed." Yet his position may well be the best one from which to defend democracy against contemporary critics.

2209.   Diamond, Martin. "The American Idea of Equality: The View from the
         Founding." Review of Politics. 38(1976), 313-31.

         Contends that the Declaration of Independence was not a democratic
         document, pledging the nation to a democratic form of government,
         but one that put the idea of equal liberty at the base of American
         political existence.

2210.   Diamond, Martin. "The Declaration and the Constitution: Liberty,
         Democracy, and the Fathers." Public Interest. 41(Fall 1975), 39-55.

         Attacks the interpretation of the Declaration as a democratic mani-
         festo and the Constitution as a reactionary check. Argues that the
         "social contract theory upon which the Declaration is based teaches
         not equality as such but equal political liberty."

2211.   Dickinson, John. "The Old Political Philosophy and the New." Proceed-
         ings of the APS. 87(1943), 246-62.

         TJ and statesmen of his time had an articulated philosophy of govern-
         ment, but present day politicians do not analyze their implicit politi-
         cal ideas. They must, however, if we are to preserve the free society
         envisioned by TJ.

2212.   Diggins, John P. "Slavery, Race, and Equality: Jefferson and the Pathos
         of the Enlightenment." American Quarterly. 28(1976), 206-28.

         Examines responses of historians from 1943-1975 to TJ's reasoning on
         racial equality. Argues that modern historians, like TJ, have been
         unable to resolve contradictory naturalistic and idealistic strains of
         Enlightenment thought.

2213.   Dorfman, Joseph. "The Economic Philosophy of Thomas Jefferson."
         Political Science Quarterly. 55(1940), 98-121.

         Claims TJ's underlying premise through all the shifts in his positions
         was a belief that "republican government would endure only as long
         as opportunities and resources for the acquisition of property were
         available to an ever increasing population."

2214.   Douglas, William O. "The Jefferson Philosophy" in Being an American.
         New York: John Day, 1948. 16-20.

         TJ spoke to the right of free choice and the right of dissent.

2215.   Draper, Theodore. "The Fantasy of Black Nationalism." Commentary.
         48(September 1969), 27-54.

         Finds the roots of the fantasy of "migrationism" in ideas like TJ's
         about colonization of free blacks; only a page on TJ.

2216. Dumbauld, Edward. The Declaration of Independence and What It Means Today. Norman: Univ. of Oklahoma Press, 1950. pp. xiii, 194.

Phrase by phrase examination of the Declaration which explores the intellectual and historical background of TJ's ideas and expressions. The second half of the title here is somewhat misleading.

2217. Dumbauld, Edward. "Independence Under International Law." American Journal of International Law. 70(1976), 425-31.

TJ on the theory of the law of nations.

2218. Dunning, William A. "An Historic Phrase." Annual Report of the American Historical Association for 1902. 1:82-85.

Traces the background of the phrase "are, and of right ought to be" from the Declaration of Independence to Swift's Drapier's Letters, the Bill of Rights of 1689, and Pope Boniface VIII.

2219. Dvoichenko-Markov, Eufrosina. "Jefferson and the Russian Decembrists." American Slavic and East European Review. 9(1950), 162-68.

Makes a tenuous argument for Jeffersonian influence on the Decembrists, mostly through Destutt de Tracy whom they read. Quotes no Russian who read TJ.

2220. Eidelberg, Paul. On the Silence of the Declaration of Independence. Amherst: Univ. of Massachusetts Press, 1976. pp. xv, 127.

Contends the underlying principle of the Declaration is aristocratic; interprets it as the product of the "statesmen of '76" rather than of TJ and as a rejection of "moral indifference or relativism" masquerading as egalitarianism.

2221. Eisinger, Chester E. "The Freehold Concept in Eighteenth-Century American Letters." WMQ. 3rd ser. 4(1947), 42-59.

Analyzes the "Jeffersonian myth" of the honest, republican farmer, the basis of which is freehold tenure of the land.

2222. Eliot, Frederick May. "What Kind of Christian Was Thomas Jefferson?" in Frederick May Eliot: An Anthology, ed. Alfred P. Stiernotte. Boston: Beacon Press, 1959. 33-40.

A christianity which could accept TJ would have to extend individual freedom of belief, be sympathetic to science, and drop its sectarian spirit.

2223.   Estee, Morris M. "Jeffersonian Principles; An Examination into Colonel
        Bryan's Statement of Them." Overland Monthly. n.s. 34(1899),
        50-52.

        "This is a commercial age and we are a commercial people," so TJ
        would not have flinched at the cry of imperialism. A reply to
        William Jennings Bryan's article in the North American Review,
        item 2178.

2224.   Fabian, Bernhard. "Jefferson's Notes on Virginia: The Genesis of Query
        xvii, The different religions received into that State?" WMQ. 3rd
        ser. 12(1955), 124-38.

        TJ's plea for religious liberty in this section embodies the substance
        of the argument of 1776 in support of his Resolutions for Disestab-
        lishing the Church of England and for Repealing Laws Interfering
        with Freedom of Worship.

2225.   Farnell, Robert Stewart. "Positive Valuations of Politics and Govern-
        ments in the Thought of the Five American Founding Fathers:
        Thomas Jefferson, John Adams, James Madison, Alexander Hamilton,
        and George Washington." Ph.D. dissertation. Cornell Univ., 1970.
        pp. 238.

        TJ valued politics and was eager to give American citizens the
        chance to participate in politics at various levels, but he was decid-
        edly "less enthusiastic in his valuation of government." DAI 31/09A,
        p. 4853.

2226.   Fesperman, Francis I. "Jefferson's Bible." Ohio Journal of Religious
        Studies. 4(October 1976), 78-88.

        Intelligent examination of TJ's beliefs, based upon a thoughtful dis-
        cussion of The Life and Morals of Jesus. Places TJ somewhere be-
        tween Priestley and Paine.

2227.   Fisher, George P. "Jefferson and the Social Compact Theory."
        American Historical Association Annual Report for 1893. 165-77.

        Contends that TJ enunciates Lockean social compact theory in the
        Declaration but offers a much more radical, "almost anarchical"
        version in his later statements about the earth belonging to the
        living.

2228.   Fisher, Sydney George. "The Twenty-eight Charges Against the King
        in the Declaration of Independence." PMHB. 31(1907), 257-303.

        Discusses the historical basis for the charges.

2229.   Foley, John P., ed. The Jeffersonian Cyclopedia: a comprehensive col-
        lection of the views of Thomas Jefferson classified and arranged in

alphabetical order under nine thousand titles relating to government, politics, law, education, political economy, finance, sciences, art, literature, religious freedom, morals, etc. New York: Funk and Wagnalls, 1900. pp. xxii, 1009.

TJ's statements on practically everything, referenced to the Washington edition of 1853-54 and the Ford edition of 1892-97. An after-dinner speaker's delight.

2230. Foote, Henry Wilder. "Introduction" to The Life and Morals of Jesus of Nazareth Extracted Textually from the Gospels of Matthew, Mark, Luke and John. By Thomas Jefferson. Boston: Beacon Press, 1951. 7-32.

Discusses Priestley's influence on TJ's views and the evolution of the Life and Morals out of the Syllabus of 1803. Useful.

2231. Foote, Henry Wilder. Thomas Jefferson: Champion of Religious Freedom Advocate of Christian Morals. Boston: Beacon Press, 1947. pp. ix, 70.

Surveys TJ's religious opinions and asserts he adopted Unitarian views late in life and would have joined a Unitarian church if Joseph Priestley had come to Charlottesville. Rpt. Boston: Beacon Press, 1960, under the title The Religion of Thomas Jefferson.

2232. Foote, Henry Wilder. Thomas Jefferson, Social Reformer. Boston: Beacon Press, 1947. pp. 15.

Survey points out the importance of an educated citizenry for TJ's trust in democratic reform.

2233. Ford, John Cuthbert. "The Natural Law and 'the Pursuit of Happiness.'" Notre Dame Lawyer. 26(1951), 429-61.

Examines the origins and implications of the phrase in the Declaration and compares it as a statement of natural law right to scholastic theory.

2234. Forrest, W. M. "Thomas Jefferson and Religious Freedom." Virginia Journal of Education. 19(1926), 355-57.

Argues that the greatest enemy to religious freedom has been the pulpit; TJ in his defense of religious freedom found his greatest opposition there.

2235. Foster, Franklin P. The World War, Jefferson and Democracy. Anderson, Ind.: The History Club, 1917. pp. 58.

World War I "reveals the march of Jefferson's ideals." Exposition of TJ's democracy for which the world is to be made safe.

2236. [Fowler, Samuel]. "The Political Opinions of Jefferson." North American Review. 101(1865), 313-35.

Review essay on Randall's biography. An Hegelian critique of TJ, claiming that for all of his great services and talents, his flaw was his commitment to individualism. Upon the "doctrine of state rights and local self-government ... will defend his reputation as statesman and philosopher." But "This is the day of great nations. ... We are at an immeasurable distance from the times when Jefferson could describe us as 'one nation towards others, separate governments among ourselves.'"

2237. Franklin, Francis. "The Democratic Philosophy of Thomas Jefferson" in The Heritage of Jefferson. New York: International Publishers, 1944. 40-48.

Contends Marxism is a perfected form of Jeffersonian democracy; "Lenin, in a more advanced age than that of Jefferson, voiced Jefferson's faith in democracy with his great slogan, 'Through democracy to socialism.'"

2238. Freehling, William W. "The Founding Fathers and Slavery." AHR. 77(1972), 81-93.

Emphasizes the positive side of TJ's position toward slavery in response to attacks on his failure to take a more aggressive position on abolition. Argues that TJ and his contemporaries set in motion the process leading toward abolition, even if in trying to have it both ways, TJ also gave informal sanction to the lower South's worst racial fears and helped to deepen those fears.

2239. Fritchman, Stephen Hole. "Thomas Jefferson" in Men of Liberty: Ten Unitarian Pioneers. Boston: Beacon Press, 1944. 83-102.

TJ's liberal religion.

2240. Fuller, Edmund and David E. Green. "Thomas Jefferson" in God in the White House: the Faiths of American Presidents. New York: Crown, 1968. 28-38.

Claims he is "among the most religious men to have been President, far more so than many who have been nominal members of churches."

2241. Funston, Janet and Richard. "Cesare Beccaria and the Founding Fathers." Italian American. 3(1976), 72-92.

Of all Americans, TJ was most influenced by Beccaria, particularly in the Declaration and the Virginia Bill for Proportioning Crimes and Punishments.

2242. Gabriel, Ralph H. "Thomas Jefferson and Twentieth-Century Rationalism." VQR. 26(1950), 321-35.

Explains the "paradox of the significance of Jefferson as a major folk hero in the middle of the twentieth century" by arguing that TJ's belief in universal moral values underlying society speaks to the crisis of the post-World War II age.

2243. Ganter, Herbert Lawrence. "Jefferson's 'Pursuit of Happiness' and Some Forgotten Men." WMQ. 2nd ser. 16(1936), 422-34; 558-85.

Explores the background of TJ's famous phrase; useful.

2244. Garrett, Leroy James. Alexander Campbell and Thomas Jefferson: A Comparative Study of Two Old Virginians. Dallas: Wilkinson Publishing Co., 1963. pp. 32.

Campbell, founder of the Disciples of Christ, admired TJ with reservations about his "infidelity," and made three visits to Monticello and TJ's grave. He frequently referred to TJ in his magazine The Millennial Harbinger. TJ would have approved of his anti-Calvinism.

2245. Garrision, Frank W. "Jefferson and the Physiocrats." Freeman. 8(1923), 180-82.

Contends TJ derived a number of political ideas, particularly those relating to limitation of power, from Dupont de Nemours and Turgot. A generally rejected view.

2246. Gillis, James M. "Flaw in Thomas Jefferson's Philosophy." Catholic World. 165(August 1947), 391-93.

TJ as skeptic contradicts the TJ who wrote "All men are endowed by their Creator ... ."

2247. Goebel, Julius. "Jus Connatum and the Declaration of the Rights of Man." J.E.G.P./Journal of English and Germanic Philology. 19(1920), 1-18.

Claims Christian Wolff influenced TJ's thinking about the law of nature as referred to in the Declaration. Originial version in German in Jahrbuch der deutschamerikanischen Gesellschaft von Illinois. 1918. 18-19, 80-83.

2248. Goodspeed, Edgar J. "Thomas Jefferson and the Bible." Harvard Theological Review. 40(1947), 71-76.

Identifies the editions of the Bible used by TJ for the Greek, Latin and French extracts in his Morals of Jesus.

2249. Gostkowski, Zygmunt. "T. Paine, T. Jefferson, R. W. Emerson, W. Whitman, Idealogia Wiary w Protego Człowieka." Przeglad Nauk Historycznychi i Spolecznych. 4(1954), 583-646.

Polish. "T. Paine, T. Jefferson, R. W. Emerson, W. Whitman, Ideology of Faith in the Common Man." Claims Whitman is of the four the real hero of American democracy since, unlike the others, he participated in the life of the masses.

*2250. Gould, William Drum. "The Religious Opinions of Thomas Jefferson." Ph.D. dissertation. Boston Univ., 1929.

2251. Gould, William D. "The Religious Opinions of Thomas Jefferson." MVHR. 20(1933), 191-208.

Argues that TJ was not a deist or atheist despite attacks on him; he believed in the "over ruling providence of God" and in religious freedom.

2252. Govan, Thomas P. "Jefferson and Hamilton: A Christian Evaluation." The Christian Scholar. 40(March 1957), 6-12.

TJ because of his optimistic view of man, was a heretic and idolater, a Gnostic, a Pelagian, and a Manichean, whose dislike of law let men unrestrained by tradition or law prey on their fellow citizens. Comments on this article by E. Harris Harbison, Leonard J. Trinterud, and Arthur M. Schlesinger, Jr. on pp. 13-20, rebuttal on pp. 126-27.

2253. Graebner, Norman A. "The Moral Foundations of American Constitutionalism" in Freedom in America: A 200-Year Perspective. University Park: Pennsylvania State Univ. Press, 1977. 77-88.

Focuses on TJ's belief in general moral instinct as basis for faith in men's ability to govern themselves.

2254. Grampp, William D. "Adam Smith and the American Revolutionists." History of Political Economy. 11(1979), 179-91.

Argues that utilitarianism is "the guide to Jefferson's ideas. He believed the purpose of government was to improve the character of the governed. ... (not) to maintain order so that there could be the widest possible expression of private interests."

2255. Grampp, William D. "A Re-examination of Jeffersonian Economics." Southern Economic Journal. 12(1946), 263-82.

Finds a threefold development in TJ's economic thought: a first period dominated by agrarianism, the second by a belief in laissez faire, and after 1805 he "proposed measures that were consistent with the objectives established by Hamilton, though his methods differed from those of Hamilton in revealing a greater concern with constitutional legitimacy."

2256. Grane, Sylvia E. "Thomas Jefferson, Philosophe des Lumieres." La Revue Liberale. 19(no. 3, 1957), 40-58.

TJ as an Elightenment thinker, humanist, revolutionary.

2257. Grimes, Alan P. "Conservative Revolution and Liberal Rhetoric: The Declaration of Independence." Journal of Politics. 38(August 1976), 1-19.

Argues that the self-evident truths of the Declaration supply an egalitarian ideology of political legitimacy which has had a continuing appeal because of the middle class orientation of the United States.

2258. Griswold, A. Whitney. "The Agrarian Democracy of Thomas Jefferson." American Political Science Review. 40(1946), 657-81.

TJ cannot be understood apart from the agrarian tradition which he, above all the other founding fathers, bequeathed the nation. His ideas come not from the physiocrats but from Locke's Second Treatise and from Adam Smith.

2259. Griswold, A. Whitney. Farming and Democracy. New York: Harcourt Brace, 1948. pp. ix, 227.

The first chapter, "The Jeffersonian Ideal," explores TJ's combination of agrarianism and democracy which forms the basis of American democratic society.

2260. Griswold, A. Whitney. "Jefferson's Republic: The Rediscovery of Democratic Philosophy." Fortune. 41(April 1950), 111-12, 126-42.

Presents TJ as a democratic thinker who speaks to the needs of the present—anti-totalitarian, egalitarian, moral, anti-centralist. See the editors' comments on p. 79, "Griswold's Jefferson," qualifying TJ for the Fortune reader.

2261. Grogan, Francis J. "The Traditional Background of the Declaration of Independence." Fordham University Dissertations Accepted for Higher Degrees. 17(part 2, 1950), 119-24.

Abstract of Ph.D. dissertation; contends the tradition of political liberty enshrined in the Declaration is objectively Catholic in origin and substance, although TJ and other founders were subjectively convinced they were enunciating Lockean, "protestant" principles.

2262. Gurley, James Lafayette. "Thomas Jefferson's Philosophy and Theology as Related to His Political Principles, Including Separation of Church and State." Ph.D. dissertation. Univ. of Michigan, 1975. pp. 253.

TJ's "uncritical eclecticism" combined elements of Stoicism, Epicureanism, Deism, and Unitarianism. DAI 36/03A, p. 1721.

2263.   Hall, J. Lesslie. "The Religious Opinions of Thomas Jefferson." Sewanee Review. 21(1913), 164-76.

Argues that TJ was not an atheist nor, as claimed by some, an Episcopalian nor a Unitarian in the mold of W. E. Channing, although he was an anti-Trinitarian. "He was a mere amateur, a mere dabbler in religion. ... why should young men be influenced by his crass views on religious subjects?"

*2264.   Hall, Richard. "Jefferson and the Physiocrats." M.A. thesis. Univ. of Virginia, 1950. pp. vii, 131.

2265.   Halliday, E. M. "Nature's God and the Founding Fathers." American Heritage. 14(October 1963), 4-7, 100-06.

TJ and Madison on the principles of freedom of religion.

2266.   Hamilton, J. G. deRoulhac. "Jefferson and Religion." Reviewer. 5(October 1925), 5-15.

Survey; argues attacks on TJ's religion were in fact attacks on his politics.

2267.   Hamowy, Ronald. "Jefferson and the Scottish Enlightenment: A Critique of Garry Wills's Inventing America: Jefferson's Declaration of Independence." WMQ. 3rd ser. 36(1979), 503-23.

Claims that "Despite Wills's conjectures ... the available data strongly suggest that it was Locke and not Hutcheson to whom Jefferson was indebted" when he drew up the Declaration. Charges that ultimately "Wills has invented a new Jefferson influenced by a Scottish moral philosophy which Wills has seriously misconstrued."

2268.   Hampton, Vernon B. "Jefferson Not a Church Member" in Religious Background of the White House. Boston: Christopher Publishing House, 1932. 374.

See also pp. 23-26; slight.

2269.   Hans, Nicholas. "Franklin, Jefferson, and the English Radicals at the End of the Eighteenth Century." Proceedings of the APS. 98(1954), 406-26.

Describes TJ's relations with religious and political reform societies in England, particularly the Deistic Society (Society of 13) and the Society of Constitutional Whigs.

2270. Hardon, John A. "The Jefferson Bible." American Ecclesiastical
       Review. 130(1954), 361-75.

       Detailed account of The Life and Morals of Jesus; claims TJ's idea of
       materialism has been frequently misunderstood.

2271. Harris, Herbert. "Jeffersonian Democracy." Current History.
       46(April 1937), 69-72.

       On TJ's political ideas; he was the "father of Populism," but he also
       "initiated the great American custom of driving the money changers
       out of the temple and inviting them home to lunch."

2272. Harrold, Frances Long. "Thomas Jefferson and the Commonwealth of
       Virginia: A Study in Constitutional Thought." Ph.D. dissertation.
       Bryn Mawr, 1960. pp. 368.

       Examines TJ's intellectual background and his life-long suspicion of
       unchecked power and authority. DAI 21/06, p. 1541.

2273. Harrold, Frances. "The Upper House in Jeffersonian Political Theory."
       VMHB. 78(1970), 281-94.

       TJ's opinions on the advantages of a bicameral legislature.

2274. Hellenbrand, Harold Leonard. "The Unfinished Revolution: Education
       and Community in the Thought of Thomas Jefferson." Ph.D. disserta-
       tion. Stanford Univ., 1980. pp. xi, 612.

       Examines the interplay between TJ's educational and political ideas;
       contends that in the early 1800's he was "cornered by his own philos-
       ophy and temperament into playing the political and pedagogical
       tyrant." DAI 41/08A, p. 3636.

2275. Henne, Anna Louise. "Die staatstheoretischen Anschauungen Thomas
       Jefferson's." Ph.D. dissertation. Univ. of Zurich, 1934. pp. 133.

2276. Herwald, Michelle. "Man from Monticello: Jefferson as an Enlightened
       Figure." Mount Holyoke Alumnae Quarterly. 59(1975), 82-84.

       Sketch.

2277. Heslep, Robert D. "Thomas Jefferson's Major Philosophical Principles."
       Educational Theory. 16(1966), 151-62.

       Argues that TJ's educational philosophy is controlled by a number of
       philosophically vague terms and hence his educational inquiries are
       not terribly helpful for solving present day problems. Challenging.

2278. Heslep, Robert D. "Thomas Jefferson's View of Equal Social Opportu-
       nity." Educational Theory. 13(1963), 142-48.

*2279. Heyer, William C. "Thomas Jefferson's Belief in Providence" in American Trust in Providence, An Outline of the Topic Along General Lines. Boston: R. G. Badger, 1925.

2280. Higgs, Robert J. "Versions of 'Natural Man' in Appalachia" in An Appalachian Symposium: Essays Written in Honor of Cratis D. Williams, ed. J. W. Williamson. Boone, N.C.: Appalachian State Univ. Press, 1977. 159-68.

Contends that Hobbes, Rousseau, and TJ offer three contradictory types of the natural man as found in the literature of Appalachia. Little of value on TJ.

2281. Hill, C. William. "Contrasting Themes in the Political Theories of Jefferson, Calhoun, and John Taylor of Caroline." Publius. 6(Summer 1976), 73-92.

Detailed examination of similarities and distinctions between the thought of Taylor and both TJ and Calhoun, contending the key is Taylor's "philosophic rationalism." Suggestive.

2282. Hodges, Wiley E. "Pro-governmentalism in Virginia, 1789-1836: A Pragmatic Liberal Pattern in the Political Heritage." Journal of Politics. 25(1963), 333-60.

Contends that many Virginians, TJ among them, "believed that government should regulate and promote the economic and other interests of individuals." Evidence for TJ's adherence to this view comes mostly from his action in support of public education.

2283. Hofstadter, Richard. "Parrington and the Jeffersonian Tradition." Journal of the History of Ideas. 2(1941), 391-400.

Criticizes Parrington for ascribing too much of TJ's agrarianism to the physiocrats.

2284. Holifield, E. Brooks. "Jefferson: Sensation" in The Gentlemen Theologians: American Theology in Southern Culture 1795-1860. Durham: Duke Univ. Press, 1978. 57-62.

Claims that religious reform for TJ entailed a progress "from sensation to a purified tradition and thence to a renewed moral sensibility." Discusses TJ's reading of Tracy, Cabanis, and Priestley; brief but intelligent.

2285. Holway, Hope. "Thomas Jefferson, The Radical Intellectual" in Radicals of Yesterday, Great American Tradition. Norman, Okla.: Cooperative Books, 1941. 11-23.

2286. Hook, Sidney. The Paradox of Freedom. Berkeley: Univ. of California Press, 1962. pp. ix, 152.

Claiming "The true Jeffersonian can recognize as supreme only that authority which Jefferson regarded as supreme in human affairs: the authority of human reason," tries to demonstrate how moral rights "develop out of the marriage of interests and intelligence."

2287. Horsley, Catherine Dunscombe. "Jefferson—The Churchman." Tyler's Quarterly. 25(1943), 1-3.

Claims TJ as an Episcopalian; see item #2162 for a refutation of this view.

2288. Horton, Andrew S. "Jefferson and Korais: The American Revolution and the Greek Constitution." Comparative Literature Studies. 13(1976), 323-29.

Argues for TJ's influence on Adamantios Korais and the Greek Constitution of 1827; a bit tenuous.

2289. Huntley, William B. "Jefferson's Public and Private Religion." South Atlantic Quarterly. 79(1980), 286-301.

Contends that TJ's religion had two foci, one expressed in public documents as a form of American civil religion, the other in private correspondence where he created a more tentative communal language of faith. Suggestive.

2290. Hunt, Gaillard. "The Virginia Declaration of Rights and Cardinal Bellarmine." Catholic Historical Review. 3(1917), 276-89.

Argues that TJ and George Mason derived the concept of the natural equality of man and the people's right of governing from Robert Bellarmine by way of Filmer's Patriarcha, Sidney, and Locke.

*2291. Hutchins, Robert Maynard. "Thomas Jefferson and the Intellectual Love of God" in No Friendly Voice. Chicago: Univ. of Chicago Press, 1936. 59-69.

2292. Jackson, Henry E., ed. The Thomas Jefferson Bible. New York: Boni and Liveright, 1923. pp. viii, 333.

Uses TJ's selections, but in the modern translation of the Bible by R. F. Weymouth. Long introduction by the editor, who describes himself as "President, College for Social Engineers, Washington, D.C." A curious, cranky performance.

2293. Jaffa, Harry V. "Agrarian Virtue and Republican Freedom: An Historical Perspective" in Goals and Values in Agricultural Policy, ed. I.S.U. Center for Agricultural and Economic Adjustment. Ames, Iowa: Iowa State Univ. Press, 1961. 45-62.

TJ's agrarian ideology strengthened the ante-bellum South's

"quasi-feudalism," but this could not prevail in a nation devoted to his proposition that all men are created equal. Rpt. in Jaffa's Equality and Liberty: Theory and Practice in American Politics. New York: Oxford Univ. Press, 1965. 42-66.

2294. Jaffa, Harry V. "Another Look at the Declaration." National Review. 32(July 11, 1980), 836-40.

On what TJ meant by man's equality; argues that it is a necessary basis for authority grounded on consent of the governed.

2295. Jaffa, Harry V. "On the Nature of Civil and Religious Liberty" in The Conservative Papers, intro. Melvin R. Laird. New York: Doubleday, 1964. 250-68.

"One cannot be equally tolerant then, and certainly Jefferson was not, of opinions destructive and of opinions not destructive of the regime of liberty itself." Rpt. in Equality and Liberty: Theory and Practice in American Politics. New York: Oxford Univ. Press, 1965. 168-89.

2296. "Jefferson and the Ketoctin Baptist Association." Bulletin of the Loudoun County Historical Society. 1(1958), 56-60.

The Ketoctin Baptists thanked TJ for the Statute for Religious Freedom.

2297. "Jefferson Edits the Bible." Time. 36(December 9, 1940), 70-71.

Brief comments on The Life and Morals of Jesus.

2298. "Jefferson on Religion." America. 69(1943), 126.

TJ not a "liberal" as many have claimed but "a devout member of the Episcopalian Church."

2299. Jefferson the Unitarian Speaks. Boston: American Unitarian Association, 1946. pp. 4.

2300. Johansen, Bruce Elliott. "Franklin, Jefferson and American Indians: A Study in the Cross-Cultural Communication of Ideas." Ph.D. dissertation. Univ. of Washington, 1979. pp. 254.

"An attempt to begin an examination of the means by which American Indian ideas figured into the formation of the emerging United States polity." DAI 40/12A, p. 6392.

*2301. Johnson, Peggy A. "'Diamonds in a Dunghill': The Gospel According to Thomas Jefferson." M.A. thesis. Univ. of California at Riverside, 1967.

2302. Johnson, U. Alexis. Thomas Jefferson and "The General Spread of the Light of Science." Charlottesville: Thomas Jefferson Memorial Foundation, 1969. pp. 16.

"We must continue to be willing to experiment" in social, political, and natural sciences.

2303. Jones, Edgar DeWitt. "Thomas Jefferson and Religion." Christian Century. 43(1926), 774-75.

Brief survey, praises TJ's planning for the interaction of separate secular and religious educational institutions at the Univ. of Virginia.

2304. Jones, Howard Mumford. "The Declaration of Independence: A Critique." Proceedings of the American Antiquarian Society. 83(1975), 55-72.

What TJ meant by the "common sense of the subject." "He wrote in general terms because he was making a general appeal to the enlightened minds of the Europe of his age," and these readers would have perceived the rhetorical nature of the accusations against George III. Also discusses the Declaration's place in American history.

2305. Jones, James F., Jr. "Montesquieu and Jefferson Revisited: Aspects of a Legacy." French Review. 51(1978), 577-85.

Restates accepted notion that TJ changed his opinion about Montesquieu for reasons both personal and political, but adds that in this change TJ "reflects a general movement of European critical opinion."

2306. Jordan, Winthrop D. White Over Black: American Attitudes Toward the Negro, 1550-1812. Chapel Hill: Univ. of North Carolina Press, 1968. 429-81.

Argues that TJ's "derogation of the Negro revealed the latent possibilities inherent in an accumulated popular tradition of Negro inferiority; it constituted, for all its qualifications, the most intense, extensive, and extreme formulation of anti-Negro 'thought' offered by any American in the thirty years after the Revolution. Yet Thomas Jefferson left to Americans something else which may in the long run have been of greater importance—his prejudice for freedom and his larger equalitarian faith." An important book.

2307. Kay, Miryam Neulander. "Separation of Church and State in Jeffersonian Virginia." Ph.D. dissertation. Univ. of Kentucky, 1967. pp. 407.

Focus on religious, denominational disputes as background to TJ's

297

Act for Establishing Religious Freedom. DAI 30/05, p. 1941.

2308. Kelly, Alfred H. "American Political Leadership: The Optimistic Ethical World View and the Jeffersonian Synthesis" in Leadership in the American Revolution. Washington: Library of Congress, 1974. 7-39.

Contends TJ resolved the contradictions among constitutionalism, the Enlightenment view of man, and political democracy, making possible the American myth which enjoined faith in constitutional democracy, progress, harmony of interest, and a special American destiny.

2309. Ketcham, Ralph. "The Puritan Ethic in the Revolutionary Era: Abigail Adams and Thomas Jefferson" in "Remember the Ladies," Perspectives on Women in American History, ed. Carol V. R. George. Syracuse: Syracuse Univ. Press, 1975. 49-65.

Explains how "they combined the same streams of thought, but in different measure."

2310. Kilgo, John Carlisle. "A Study of Thomas Jefferson's Religious Belief." Trinity Archive. 13(March 1900), 331-46.

Argues that TJ was a deist who derived most of his ideas in France; his deism has become the official dogme of the state college systems, from which "this nation will get the sources of its ruin."

2311. Kimball, Marie. "Jefferson's Four Freedoms." VQR. 19(1943), 204-21.

Claims TJ's early reading in political theory, especially Montesquieu, led to his lifelong advocacy of freedom of the land, of the body, of the mind, and of the soul. Thus, we should add abolition of slavery to the three accomplishments TJ wished noted on his grave marker.

2312. Kinsolving, Arthur B. "The Religious Opinions of Thomas Jefferson." Historical Magazine of the Protestant Episcopal Church. 20(1951), 325-27.

Note claiming that TJ's "horizontal mind" is secular and not religious, and he is not to be trusted on matters concerning religion.

2313. Klenner, Hermann. "Jefferson and Ho Chi Minh: Shingo Shibata's Conception of Human Rights." Social Praxis. 6(1979), 94-98.

Critique of Shibata's article of 1976 (item #2450) as an "unhistorical" attempt to "recharge socialistically Jefferson's bourgeois democratism." pp. 92-126 of this journal contain other responses to Shibata and Klenner; interesting for presentation of attitudes toward TJ of Marxist thinkers.

2314.   Kloman, William. "The Jefferson Theory of Revolution." Cybernetica.
        21(1978), 193-204.

        Compares TJ to Marx, claiming "Jefferson's man is the activist,
        ... the source of the revolution," whereas Marx sees men determined
        by historic process. TJ is concerned with "ultimate values and
        ideals" to be realized by the revolution.

2315.   Knoles, George Harmon. "The Religious Ideas of Thomas Jefferson."
        MVHR. 30(1943), 187-204.

        TJ hoped for a Christianity which had been cleansed of its priestly
        perversions in order to become a moral guide, but he believed that
        religion was a private matter.

2316.   Koch, Adrienne. The Philosophy of Thomas Jefferson. New York:
        Columbia Univ. Press, 1943. pp. xiv, 208.

        On TJ as philosophical thinker and on his philosophical background.
        Concentrates on his thought after 1785 and thus perhaps over-empha-
        sizes the importance of French influences by first encountering him
        during his stay in France. Still, a standard book; even if it can be
        supplemented with Colbourn's Lamp of Experience and Wills' Invent-
        ing America, they have not displaced it. Originally a Ph.D. disserta-
        tion at Columbia Univ. and published as such.

2317.   Koch, Adrienne. "Power and Morals and the Founding Fathers:
        Jefferson." Review of Politics. 15(1953), 470-90.

        "... the right to the pursuit of happiness consists of the right to
        pursuit, not of material advantages, but of the life of reason and the
        fulfillment of the human nature." This pursuit leads to the discovery
        and cultivation of moral virtue, the ultimate check on the abuse of
        power. Points to the use of the phrase by Locke. Rpt. as "Jefferson
        and the Pursuit of Happiness" in Power, Morals, and the Founding
        Fathers: Essays in the Interpretation of the American Enlightenment.
        Ithaca: Cornell Univ. Press, 1961. 23-49.

2318.   Koch, Adrienne. "Pragmatic Wisdom and the American Enlightenment."
        WMQ. 3rd ser. 18(1961), 313-29.

        TJ and Franklin are "touchstones for the character of the American
        Enlightenment" who typically synthesize theory and experience.

2319.   Koch, Adrienne. "Toward an American Philosophy." VQR. 29(1953),
        187-97.

        TJ and Madison are the richest resources for a reformulation of an
        American philosophic tradition because of the conjunction of power
        and liberty at the core of their political philosophy.

2320. Konvitz, Milton R. "Dewey's Revision of Jefferson" in John Dewey, Philosopher of Science and Freedom: A Symposium, ed. Sidney Hook. New York: Dial Press, 1950. 164-76.

Compares Dewey and TJ, claiming Dewey has reconciled TJ's ambiguous faith in human nature and fear of the transforming power of culture.

2321. Kuper, Theodore Fred. "Jefferson and the Freedom to Print." The Thistle. 13(September 1969), 85-91.

2322. Kuper, Theodore Fred. "Thomas Jefferson, Champion of Religious Freedom." The Courier. 2(February 1936), 9-10, 20.

TJ as a reproach to Hitler and the Nazis; urges Olympic athletes to turn their backs on the Swastika.

2323. Laing, Alexander. "Jefferson's Usufruct Principle." Nation. 223(July 3, 1976), 7-16.

Thoughtful, detailed examination of TJ's letter to Madison and the later responses to "The earth belongs in usufruct to the living."

2324. Landin, Harold William. "Thomas Jefferson and the French Revolution." Ph.D. dissertation. Cornell Univ., 1928. pp. 325, xxii.

Concerned with the development of TJ's political ideas; argues for the prime importance of political experience, particularly in struggles with the "aristocratic tidewater" early in his career. Locke only secondary in importance as an intellectual influence and the French Revolution not at all.

2325. Landy, A. "Marxism Is Democracy." New Masses. 47(April 13, 1943), 16-18.

TJ embodies the thought and experience which demonstrate the historic link between Marxism and democracy.

2326. Lane, Ann M. "The Classical Frontier: Republican Theory and the Jefferson-Cherokee Encounter." Ph.D. dissertation. Univ. of California, Santa Cruz, 1979. pp. 491.

DAI 40/12A, 6406.

2327. Lehmann, Karl. Thomas Jefferson American Humanist. New York: Macmillan, 1947. pp. xiv, 273.

TJ's humanism considered as a function of his response to the classical past. His ethics, aesthetics, ideas about education, sense of history, and political ideas were shaped by his reading of Latin and Greek authors and by knowledge of classical art. Still useful; rpt. Chicago: Univ. of Chicago Press, 1965.

2328. Lence, Ross Marlo. "The American Declaration of Independence: A Study of Its Polemical and Philosophical Antecedents." Ph.D. dissertation. Indiana Univ., 1973. pp. 278.

TJ along with Locke and certain eighteenth-century pamphleteers means by "the people" "nothing other than a majority of the whole community." Hence, "the Declaration's central concern is not the individual rights of man, but the rights of the political community." DAI 34/09A, p. 6071.

2329. Levin, David. "Cotton Mather's Declaration of Gentlemen and Thomas Jefferson's Declaration of Independence." New England Quarterly. 50(1977), 509-14.

Without claiming that TJ read Mather, asserts, "New England Puritanism gave to the American Revolution ... the concept, the language, and the historical example of a moderate revolution that would restore ancient liberties without turning loose an ungovernable mob."

2330. Levitsky, Ihor. "The Tolstoy Gospel in the Light of the Jefferson Bible." Canadian Slavonic Papers. 21(1979), 347-55.

Compares TJ's Life and Morals of Jesus with Tolstoy's My Confession and What I Believe. They share a belief in the necessity of discriminating between the teachings of Christ and the teachings of churches, but TJ, unlike Tolstoy, did not tamper with authorized text beyond selecting from it, and he eliminated the miraculous events which Tolstoy often retained.

2331. Lewis, Joseph. Jefferson the Freethinker. New York: Freethought Publishing Co., 1925. pp. (10).

TJ the materialist opposed by the forces of bigotry and superstition.

2332. Lichtenstein, Stanley. "Caricaturing the Fathers." Christian Century. 72(1955), 999.

Letter to the editor protesting the Indianapolis school system's presentation of TJ as favoring religious instruction in the university and tax support for the education of clergy.

*2333. Lindley, Thomas F., Jr. "The Philosophical Presuppositions of Thomas Jefferson's Social Theories." Ph.D. dissertation. Boston Univ., 1952.

2334. Lippmann, Walter. American Inquisitors: A Commentary on Dayton and Chicago. New York: Macmillan, 1928. pp. viii, 120.

TJ a character in a recurring "Dialogue on Olympus" as the author ponders the irony of the man who professes to be TJ's most loyal disciple acting as a prosecutor in the Scopes trial. Socrates, however, has the last word.

2335. Lipson, Leslie. "European Responses to the American Revolution." Annals of the American Academy of Political and Social Science. 428(November 1976), 22-32.

Europeans responded to the Declaration of Independence, the egalitarian claims it made, and the federalist structure of government. Jeffersonian and Hamiltonian versions of the Revolution each had their appeal. Competent overview.

2336. List, Frederick. Outlines of Political Economy, in a Series of Letters Addressed by Frederick List, esq. Late Professor of Political Economy at the University of Tubingen in Germany, to Charles J. Ingersoll, Esq., Vice-President of the Pennsylvania Society for the Promotion of Manufacturers and the Mechanic Arts. To Which is Added the Celebrated Letters of Mr. Jefferson to Benjamin Austin, and of Mr. Madison to the Editors of the Lynchburg Virginian. Philadelphia: Samuel Parker, 1827. pp. 40.

Attempt to enlist TJ posthumously as a partisan of the American System.

2337. Little, David. "The Origins of Perplexity: Civil Religion and Moral Belief in the Thought of Thomas Jefferson" in American Civil Religion, ed. Russell E. Richey and Donald G. Jones. New York: Harper and Row, 1974. 185-210.

Suggestive criticism of TJ's ethical position for obscuring disparities among religious belief, moral beliefs, and civic responsibility.

2338. Livermore, George. An Historical Research Respecting the Opinions of the Founders of the Republic on Negroes as Slaves, as Citizens, and and as Soldiers. Read Before the Massachusetts Historical Society, August 14, 1862. Boston: John Wilson, 1862, pp. 215.

Also in Proceedings of the Massachusetts Historical Society. 6(1863), 86-248. Touches on TJ and quotes from statements opposing slavery and from those describing the black race's supposed intellectual inferiority.

*2339. Luebke, Fred C. "The Development of Thomas Jefferson's Religious Opinions, 1743-1800." M.A. thesis. Claremont Graduate School, 1958.

2340. Luebke, Fred C. "The Origins of Thomas Jefferson's Anti-Clericalism." Church History. 32(1963), 344-56.

Argues that TJ's attitude toward the clergy had its origins in the slanderous attacks of Federalist ministers during the election of 1800.

2341. Luttrell, Clifton B. "Thomas Jefferson on Money and Banking: Disciple of David Hume and Forerunner of Some Modern Monetary Views." History of Political Economy. 7(1975), 156-73.

Contends that TJ's monetary views are consistent with those of David Hume and, allowing for the general substitution of demand deposits for bank notes, are similar to those of some leading economists today.

2342. Lynd, Staughton. "Beard, Jefferson and the Tree of Liberty." Mid-continent American Studies Journal. 9(Spring 1968), 8-22.

Claims TJ was most strongly influenced by the agrarian strain of Whiggism inherited from Bolingbroke rather than the artisan radicalism of Paine; in spite of many agreements, in the long run the two streams diverged. By the mid-19th century in Europe agrarianism was dead, but TJ's agrarianism lived on in an America of available unused land. Beard was a latter-day Jeffersonian who tried to impose the static dichotomy of agrarian whiggism on American history.

2343. Lynd, Staughton. "The Earth Belongs to the Living" in Intellectual Origins of American Radicalism. New York: Pantheon, 1968. 67-69.

Background to TJ's views on private property; contends TJ's theory was radical in principle but his practice was conservative.

2344. Lynn, Kenneth S. "Falsifying Jefferson." Commentary. 66(October 1978), 66-71.

Review essay criticizing Wills' Inventing America; "the tendentious report of a highly political writer whose unannounced but nevertheless obvious aim is to supply the history of the Republic with as pink a dawn as possible." Asserts TJ's position was essentially Lockean.

2345. Mabee, Charles. "Thomas Jefferson's Anti-Clerical Bible." Historical Magazine of the Protestant Episcopal Church. 48(1979), 473-81.

Suggests that TJ's scissors and paste method of compilation rather than just copying out desired sections is an attempt to preserve the authority of the Bible and also presents a "priestless Christianity." Thoughtful discussion.

2346. McAdoo, William Gibbs. State Rights and the Jeffersonian Idea. Address Delivered ... at the Convention of the Cooperative Club International, Des Moines, Iowa, May 25, 1926. Washington: Government Printing Office, 1926. pp. 14.

303

69th Congress, 1st Session. Senate Document No. 121. The essence of TJ's theory of government is for States to protect individual liberty and local concerns and the federal government to protect economic liberty.

*2347. McCarthy, Richard Joseph. "Some Philosophical Foundations of Thomas Jefferson's Foreign Policy." Ph.D. dissertation. St. John's University, 1958.

2348. McColley, Robert. "Slavery in Jefferson's Virginia." Journal of the Central Mississippi Valley American Studies Association. 1(Spring 1960), 23-31.

Contends TJ was one of the first to enunciate in a scientific manner the classic position of the Southern racist. More on slavery than on TJ.

2349. McCoy, Drew R. "Jefferson and Madison on Malthus: Population Growth in Jeffersonian Political Economy." VMHB. 88(1980), 259-76.

TJ praised Malthus's Essay on the Principle of Population because of its attack on the mercantile system and its restatement of pro-agrarian, laissez faire ideas, but he felt the population theory was not applicable to the U.S. and that Malthus had failed to consider emigration as a remedy.

2350. McCoy, Drew R. "The Republican Revolution: Political Economy in Jeffersonian America, 1776-1817." Ph.D. dissertation. Univ. of Virginia, 1976.

Discusses "ideological origins and influence of a Jeffersonian conception of republican political economy" and contends it "emphasized expansion across space—the American continent— as an alternative to development through time, with its attendant corruption and decay." DAI 37/09A, p. 6013.

2351. McWilliams, Wilson Carey. "The Jeffersonians" in The Idea of Fraternity in America. Berkeley: Univ. of California Press, 1973. 200-23.

Arguing that "Jefferson the moralist unites all Jeffersons," examines the moral and philosophical underpinning for TJ's attempt to unify Americans' loyalty to specific communities and local politics into a national union bound by fraternal affection. The danger in this was in making affection almost a self-sufficient good. Suggestive.

2352. Magnuson, Roger P. "Thomas Jefferson and the Separation of Church and State." Educational Forum. 27(1963), 417-21.

Argues that TJ never intended to build an impregnable wall between

304

church and state; his refusal to authorize a chair of divinity at the University is a rejection of sectarianism not of religion.

2353. Mallett, Marcus. "Foreword" to Jefferson on Plato. Charlottesville: Privately printed for John Wyllie, 1941. pp. (6).

TJ opinion of the virtue of the Univ. of Virginia lies "in its attempt to free the mind by eternal hostility to the tyranny of all imitations" whereas the Platonic view is to see education as learning to imitate the one good. Rpts. TJ on Plato from the letter to John Adams of July 5, 1814.

2354. Mangasarian, Mangasar Mugwiditch. The Religion of Washington, Jefferson and Franklin. A Lecture Delivered Before the Independent Religious Society, Orchestra Hall ... Chicago. (Chicago, 1907?) pp. 23.

Argues for the "brave and noble" unbelief in Christian religion of TJ et. al.

2355. Marshall, James F. "Stendhal and America." The French American Review. 2(1949), 240-67.

Circa 1817-1821 Stendhal saw himself as a "Jeffersonian democrat" and advised friends, "lisez Jefferson." However, he often used the name "Jefferson" to refer to Destutt de Tracy.

*2356. Martin, Edwin Thomas. "Thomas Jefferson and the Idea of Progress." Ph.D. dissertation. Univ. of Wisconsin, 1942.

See the author's later Thomas Jefferson, Scientist.

2357. May, Henry F. "The End of the Eighteenth Century" in The Enlightenment in America. New York: Oxford Univ. Press, 1976. 278-304.

Considers Adams and TJ as culminating figures of the American Enlightenment. Focuses on the "contradictions and complexities" of TJ.

2358. Mayer, Frederick. "Jefferson" in A History of American Thought, An Introduction. Dubuque: Wm. C. Brown, 1951. 105-19.

Simplistic sketch of TJ's ideas.

2359. Mayer, Frederick. "Jefferson and Freedom." Social Education. 18(March 1954), 107-09.

TJ's educational philosophy, pragmatic, skeptical, ethical, etc.

2360. Mead, Sidney E. "The 'Nation with the Soul of a Church.'" Church History. 36(1967), 262-83.

Wide-ranging essay, only touching on TJ but extremely suggestive
as to the nature of his "cosmopolitan, inclusive, universal theology."
An important statement.

2361. Mead, Sidney E. The Old Religion in the Brave New World: Reflections
on the Relation Between Christendom and the Republic. Berkeley:
Univ. of California Press, 1977. pp. xii, 189.

Jefferson Memorial Lectures for 1974. Only tangentially about TJ,
but suggestive about the contradictions between his enlightened,
civil religion and the evangelical orthodoxy of men like Timothy
Dwight and, later and less orthodox, Horace Bushnell.

2362. Mead, Sidney Earl. "Thomas Jefferson's 'Fair Experiment'—Religious
Freedom." Religion in Life. 23(1954), 566-79.

Thoughtful analysis of the religious consequences of TJ's rationalist
defense of religious liberty; explains "why it is that the religion of
many Americans is democracy."

2363. Mehta, M. J. "The Religion of Thomas Jefferson." Indo-Asian Culture.
16(1967), 96-103.

Standard summary of TJ's faith in religious freedom, but final paragraphs compare him to Raja Rammohan Roy (1774-1833), the "father
of modern Indian rationalism."

2364. Mellon, Matthew T. "Thomas Jefferson's Views on Negro Slavery" in
Early American Views on Negro Slavery. From the Letters and
Papers of the Founders of the Republic. Boston: Meador Publishing
Co., 1934. 89-122.

Rather one-sided view of TJ as an opponent of slavery.

2365. Merriam, C. E., Jr. "The Political Theory of Jefferson." Political
Science Quarterly. 17(1902), 24-45.

TJ not a great political theorist; he agreed on fundamental principles
with Locke but went beyond him in development of and deductions
from these principles. Source of his power was his genius as a party
leader, his gift for popular statement of popular ideas, and his con-
fidence in the people.

2366. Meyer, Donald H. "Thomas Jefferson and the Rhetoric of Republicanism" in The Democratic Enlightenment. New York: Putnam's, 1976.
109-28.

Competent survey for undergraduates of TJ's political and social
ideas.

306

2367. Miers, Earl Schenck. "Introduction" to The Declaration of Independence, as Written by Thomas Jefferson and Changed by the Congress Before Its Unanimous Adoption on July the Fourth 1776. Newark, Del: Printed for Friends of the Curtis Paper Co., 1955. pp. 22.

2368. Miller, John Chester. The Wolf By the Ears: Thomas Jefferson and Slavery. New York: Free Press, 1977. pp. xii, 319.

A wide-ranging, informative analysis of TJ's views on race and slavery and the actions to which they gave rise. Attentive to the ambivalences in TJ and aware of the ways in which his opinions were changed by changing historical circumstances, particularly by the events and conditions leading up to the Missouri Compromise. Argues that TJ began as a Virginian, became an American, ended as a Southern nationalist. Good discussion of the Callender scandals.

2369. Mirkin, Harris G. "Rebellion, Revolution, and the Constitution: Thomas Jefferson's Theory of Civil Disobedience." American Studies. 13(Fall 1972), 61-74.

Argues that TJ maintained in his thought a tension between the values of revolution and those of a preserved constitutional order. Rebellion or the threat of revolution held in check encroachment on the people's rights, yet a just revolutionary movement must convince the majority of its rightness or it is despotic.

2370. Montgomery, Henry C. "Epicurus at Monticello" in Classical Studies Presented to Ben Edwin Perry by His Students and Colleagues at the University of Illinois, 1924-1960. Illinois Studies in Language and Literature. No. 58. Urbana: Univ. of Illinois Press, 1969. 80-87.

Argues for an eclectic mixture of Stoicism and Epicureanism in TJ's philosophy.

2371. Moore, Leroy, Jr. "Religious Liberty, Roger Williams and the Revolutionary Era." Church History. 34(1965), 57-76.

No direct influence of Williams on TJ, but Williams ideas were passed through Locke, becoming anthropocentric in the process, and men like John Leland and Isaac Backus, religious heirs of Williams, admired and supported TJ's efforts for religious freedom.

2372. Morgan, Edmund S. "Challenge and Response: Reflections on the Bicentennial" in The Challenge of the American Revolution. New York: Norton, 1976. 196-218.

One challenge is TJ's egalitarianism, although with respect to slaves and women he "did not grasp the full implications of the creed he bequeathed to the nation."

2373.   Morgan, Edmund S. The Meaning of Independence, John Adams,
         George Washington, Thomas Jefferson. Charlottesville: Univ.
         Press of Virginia, 1976. 59-81.

         For TJ "it is difficult to discover personal qualities transformed by
         the Revolution into something larger." Independence meant for him
         primarily the independence of the individuals who made up the nation
         rather than the independence of the nation or the nation's govern-
         ment.

2374.   Morgan, Edmund S. "Slavery and Freedom: The American Paradox."
         Journal of American History. 59(1972), 5-29.

         Argues that the paradox of the coincidental rise of freedom and of
         slavery can be in part explained by the conception of freedom held
         by someone like TJ, "a freedom that sprang from the independence of
         the individual."

2375.   Morgan, H. Wayne. "The Founding Fathers and the Middle Ages."
         Mid-America. 42(1960), 30-43.

         TJ disliked the Middle Ages because he saw it as an era in which the
         arts and sciences were in eclipse. This attitude echoed that of his
         educated contemporaries and derived from the unfavorable treatment
         given by contemporary historians.

2376.   Morgan, Robert J. "'Time Hath Found Us': The Jeffersonian Revolu-
         tionary Vision." Journal of Politics. 38(August 1976), 20-36.

         Argues that TJ and the Jeffersonians saw the American Revolution
         as political rather than social, "liberation, not anomie."

2377.   Mott, Royden J. "Sources of Jefferson's Ecclesiastical Views." Church
         History. 3(1934), 267-84.

         TJ's legal and historical studies led him to the conclusion that the
         union of church and state was politically unsound.

2378.   Murdaugh, James Edmund Dandridge. "Political Thought in the Early
         American Essay." Ph.D. dissertation. Univ. of Virginia, 1925.
         pp. 221.

         Deals briefly with TJ's Summary View and Notes on the State of
         Virginia and with the press and pamphlet wars of the 1790's. Not
         unintelligent, but dated.

2379.   Nagley, Winfield E. Foundations of Thomas Jefferson's Philosophy.
         Honolulu: Univ. of Hawaii, 1976. pp. 35.

         Contends that "by joining actuality with philosophy in the threads
         of his many-faceted materialism, Jefferson united what Santayana

termed the two halves of the American mind, the hereditary and the practical." Relies on Koch and Stuart G. Brown, but suggestive.

*2380. Nagley, Winfield E. "The Materialism of Jefferson" in Two Centuries of Philosophy in America, ed. Peter Caws. Totowa, N.J.: Rowman & Littlefield, 1980. 52-60.

2381. Newton, Joseph Fort. "Thomas Jefferson and the Religion of American Life." Forum. 78(1927), 890-96.

TJ believed in salvation by education" and in religious democracy.

2382. Noonan, John T., Jr. "Virginia Liberators" in Persons and Masks of the Law: Cardozo, Holmes, Jefferson, and Wythe as Makers of the Masks. New York: Farrar, Straus and Giroux, 1976. 29-64.

On Wythe and TJ; contends their legal education, teaching them that decisions were to be made in terms of the abstract conditions of the law "without respect to persons," blinded them to the nature of slavery and of slaves as persons.

2383. Norlin, George. "Humanism in the Virginia Colony: Jefferson and the Declaration of Independence" in The Quest of American Life. Univ. of Colorado Studies. Series B. Studies in the Humanities. Vol. 2, No. 3. Boulder: Univ. of Colorado, 1945. 75-92.

Conventional generalities.

2384. Northrop, F. S. C. "The Declaration of Independence" in The Meeting of East and West. New York: Macmillan, 1946. 70-102.

Philosophical background, mostly Lockean, of the Declaration; better on Locke than on TJ.

2385. Northrop, F. S. C. "Jefferson's Conception of the Role of Science in World History." Cahiers d'Histoire Mondiale. 9(1966), 891-911.

Suggestive exploration of the connections and distinctions between the principles of mathematical physics and those of contractual law.

2386. Nye, Russel B. "Jeffersonian Democracy" in Main Problems in American History, ed. Howard H. Quint, Dean Albertson, and Milton Cantor. Homewood, Ill.: Dorsey Press, 1964. 126-35.

Sketches TJ's pragmatic evolution of a theory of government; revised edition, 1968.

2387. "On the Breeding of Kings." International Socialist Review. 17(1917), 597.

Letter from TJ, March 5, 1810, describing the degenerate state of

European royalty. No notes or comment.

2388. Ostrander, Gilman M. "Jefferson and Scottish Culture." Historical Reflections. 5(1978), 233-48.

Contrasts TJ's admiration for the thought of the Scottish Enlightenment to his vigorous disapproval of Scotch-Irish Presbyterianism in Virginia; he never thought of Scottish learning as distinctively Scottish.

2389. Ostrander, Gilman M. "Lord Kames and American Revolutionary Culture" in Essays in Honor of Russel B. Nye, ed. Joseph Waldmeir. East Lansing: Michigan State Univ. Press, 1978. 168-79.

Argues in rather general terms for the importance to TJ of Kames's Essays on Morality and Natural Religion.

2390. Ostrander, Gilman M. "New Lost Worlds of Thomas Jefferson." Reviews in American History. 7(1979), 183-88.

Review essay of books on TJ's philosophy; praises Garry Wills' emphasis on the importance of the Scottish Elightenment but points out this is hardly the new idea Wills thinks it is.

2391. Owsley, Frank L. "Two Agrarian Philosophers: Jefferson and DuPont de Nemours." Hound & Horn. 6(1932), 166-72.

Review essay emphasizes TJ as a southern thinker and contends his "whole national outlook changed after the Missouri controversy."

2392. Padover, Saul K. "Introduction" in Democracy By Thomas Jefferson. New York: Appleton-Century, 1939. 1-20.

TJ's thoughts on democracy are based on his belief in personal liberty.

2393. Padover, Saul K. Thomas Jefferson and the Foundations of American Freedom. Princeton: D. Van Nostrand, 1965. pp. 191.

Seventy page introduction to TJ's life and leading ideas about politics and society, followed by selected readings.

2394. Palmer, R. R. "A Neglected Work: Otto Vossler on Jefferson and the Revolutionary Era." WMQ. 3rd ser. 12(1955), 462-71.

Abstract of Vossler's Die Amerikanischen Revolutionsideale; see item #2055.

2395. Pancake, John S. Thomas Jefferson: Revolutionary Philosopher, A Selection of Writings. Woodbury, N.Y.: Barron's Educational Series, 1976. pp. 346.

Introductory biographical sketch and separate introductions to sections illustrating TJ's views on a wide variety of topics: economics, religion, education, diplomacy, slavery, Indians, etc.

2396. Parkes, Henry Bamford. "Jeffersonian Democracy." Symposium. 4(1933), 302-23.

Reconciles TJ's political theories with "communism" if not necessarily with Marxism.

2397. Parks, William. "The Influence of Scottish Sentimentalist Ethical Theory on Thomas Jefferson's Philosophy of Human Nature." Ph.D. dissertation. College of William and Mary, 1975. pp. 241.

TJ's faith in man's capability for self-government rested on his belief in the moral sense. DAI 36/03A, p. 1585.

2398. Parks, William. "Scottish Sentimentalist Ethics in Jefferson's America." Proceedings of the Conference on Scottish Studies. No. 1. Norfolk: Old Dominion Univ., 1973. 31-43.

Argues for the influence of the Scottish philosophers on TJ and his understanding of the moral sense theory.

2399. Parmelee, Mary Platt. "Jefferson and His Political Philosophy." Arena. 18(1897), 505-16.

"This continent has been supremely honored. ... If Jefferson's political philosophy was right, then we are right."

2400. Parrington, Vernon Louis. "Thomas Jefferson, Agrarian Democrat" in Main Currents in American Thought: The Colonial Mind, 1620-1800. New York: Harcourt, 1927. 342-56.

Claims TJ was strongly influenced by the Physiocrats and that he was centrally "concerned about responsive government—that it should faithfully serve the majority will."

2401. Paschall, G. Spurgeon. "Jefferson and the Baptists." The Quarterly Review: A Survey of Southern Baptist Progress. 15(No. 3, 1955), 54-56.

Suggests TJ attended meetings of the Buck Mountain Baptist Church near Monticello; not carefully researched.

2402. Pearson, Samuel C. "Nature's God: A Reassessment of the Religion of the Founding Fathers." Religion in Life. 46(1977), 152-65.

Surveys Franklin, Adams, and TJ, who was "unitarian, nationalistic, moralistic, anticlerical, and anticonfessional."

2403. Peebles, James Martin. Magic. One of a series of Lectures ... with an Addendum of Thomas Jefferson's Religious Convictions. San Francisco: Peebles Publishing House, 1895. pp. 16.

A lecturer on spiritualism praises TJ for freedom from sectarianism.

2404. Peterson, Merrill D. "The American Scholar: Emerson and Jefferson" in Thomas Jefferson and the World of Books. Washington: Library of Congress, 1977. 23-33.

Compares and contrasts the models of the American scholar offered by TJ, "the scholar as public man," and Emerson, an intellectual in "the modern sociological sense of self-conscious detachment and alienation from the surrounding society." Better on TJ than on Emerson.

2405. Peterson, Merrill D. Jefferson's 'Consent of the Governed': Convolutions of a Doctrine. An Address Delivered at Monticello on April 13, 1963. Charlottesville: Thomas Jefferson Memorial Foundation, 1963. pp. (17).

Development of the idea of the consent of the governed; using Lincoln's phrase, argues that government of the people came first, by the people in the mid-19th century, for the people in the 20th century.

2406. Peterson, Merrill D. "Mr. Jefferson's Sovereignty of the Living Generation." VQR. 52(1976), 437-47.

TJ's proposition that "the earth belongs in usufruct to the living" became after the French Revolution his rationale for sweeping social and political reform.

2407. Peterson, Merrill D. "Thomas Jefferson and the Enlightenment: Reflections on Literary Influence." Lex et Scientia. 11(1975), 89-127.

Taking on the question of what the Enlightenment means in America, suggestively examines TJ's reading of Bolingbroke, Montesquieu, and Beccaria, concluding that he resolved whig historicism and legalism into the rationalism and idealism of the Englightenment.

2408. Peterson, Merrill D. "Thomas Jefferson and the National Purpose." Proceedings of the APS. 105(1961), 517-20.

Contends that a renewed "National Purpose" cannot be founded on old doctrines and symbols of the native political tradition but that Jeffersonian symbol and value are still important in preserving institutions of freedom and self government and in insisting on the moral accountability of actions in the National Interest.

2409. Phelps, Wiliam Lyon. "As I Like It." Scribner's. 90(1931), 321-23.

Prints a letter of TJ's dated July 3, 1801, and uses it as text for a defense of freedom of speech and religious freedom.

2410. Plochl, Willibald M. "Thomas Jefferson, Author of The Statute of Virginia for Religious Freedom." The Jurist. 3(April 1943), 182-230.

Historical background and account of the passage of the Act for Establishing Religious Freedom. Argues for the basis of the law in a view of natural law as independent of human legislation. TJ believed that society must be based on true moral principles. Rpt. separately, Washington: Catholic Univ. of America, 1943. pp. 51.

2411. Pollin, Burton R. "Godwin's Letter to Ogilvie, Friend of Jefferson, and the Federalist Propaganda." Journal of the History of Ideas. 28(1967), 432-44.

Well-researched account of James Ogilvie, who was a correspondent of TJ's and a "conveyor of ideas" between TJ and William Godwin.

2412. Poole, William Frederick. Anti-Slavery Opinions Before the Year 1800, Read Before the Cincinnati Literary Club November 16, 1872 ... To Which is Appended a Fac Simile Rerint of Dr. George Buchanan's Oration on the Moral and Political Evil of Slavery. Cincinnati: Robert Clarke & Co., 1873. pp. 82, 20.

TJ's opinion of the evils of slavery quoted on pp. 25-41; Buchanan's oration was dedicated to TJ.

2413. The Pope and the Presbyterians. A Review of the Warnings of Jefferson Respecting the Dangers to Be Apprehended to Our Civil and Religious Liberties from Presbyterianism. Philadelphia: James M. Campbell, 1845. pp. 72.

Catholics, not Presbyterians, are the threat to religious freedom; anyway, TJ is no authority on the Presbyterians because he was an infidel. Answer to the pamphlet of Justus Moore; see item #1843.

2414. Powell, E. P. "Thomas Jefferson and Religion." The Open Court. 10(1896), 4943-45.

The election of 1800 was a victory for the separation of church and state, thanks to TJ's rational religion.

2415. Prescott, Frederick C. "Introduction" to Alexander Hamilton and Thomas Jefferson: Representative Selections, With Introduction Bibliography, and Notes. New York: American Book Co., 1934. xi-lxxii.

Traces two strains of thought in TJ, "one theoretical or philosophical, the other more strictly legal."

313

2416.   Prescott, F. C. "Jefferson and Bishop Burnet." American Literature.
        7(1935), 87.

        TJ's letter of June 24, 1826 to Roger C. Weightman draws upon
        Richard Rumbold's dying speech quoted in Burnet's History of His
        Own Times.

2417.   Quinn, Patrick F. "Agrarianism and the Jeffersonian Philosophy."
        Review of Politics. 2(1940), 87-104.

        The agrarian claim to a Jeffersonian tradition is valid, but it is not
        necessarily true that the American people is basically Jeffersonian as
        claimed.

2418.   Rager, John C. "Catholic Sources and the Declaration of
        Independence." Catholic Mind. 28(July 8, 1930), 253-68.

        Supports the Bellarmine/Declaration thesis, claiming the Declaration
        is an expression of both the American mind and "the Catholic mind,
        medieval and modern."

2419.   Reid, Bill G. "The Agrarian Tradition and Urban Problems." Midwest
        Quarterly. 6(1964), 75-86.

        TJ's agrarianism is still deeply rooted in American thinking.

2420.   Remsburg, John E. The Fathers of Our Republic: Paine, Jefferson,
        Washington, Franklin. A Lecture Delivered Before the Tenth Annual
        Congress of the American Secular Union, in Chickering Hall,
        New York, November 13, 1886. Boston: J. P. Mendum, 1887. pp. vi,
        45.

        TJ as freethinker, the enemy of priestcraft, on pp. 13-22.

2421.   Remsburg, John E. Jefferson an Unbeliever. Atchison, Kan.: Published
        by the Author, 1882. pp. 12.

        TJ as freethinker, anti-clerical and materialist.

2422.   Remsburg, John Eleazer. "Thomas Jefferson" in Six Historic Ameri-
        cans: Paine, Jefferson, Washington, Franklin, Lincoln, Grant, Fathers
        and Saviors of Our Republic, Freethinkers. New York: Truth Seeker
        Co., 1906. 65-96.

        Revised and expanded version of item #2420.

2423.   Renwick, John. "Marmontel on the Government of Virginia (1783)."
        Journal of American Studies. 1(1967), 181-89.

        Transcription of Marmontel's mss. "Observations d'un ami des
        Améreicains sur le Gouvernement de la Virginie." Notes Marmontel's

314

views follow TJ's closely but sees coincidence rather than influence.

2424. "Reviving a Controversy: To What Extent Bellarmine Influenced Jefferson." Extension. 37(January 1942), 20-21.

Inconclusive.

*2425. Riaume, Jean-Marc. "Thomas Jefferson et la frontiere." Seminaires 1979. (Talence: Centre de Recherches sur l'Amerique Anglophone, Univ. de Bordeaux III). 52-60.

2426. Richardson, William D. "The Possibility of Harmony Between the Races: An Inquiry into the Thought of Jefferson, Toqueville, Lincoln and Melville." Ph.D. dissertation. SUNY at Buffalo, 1979. pp. 286.

Uses Notes to examine TJ's attitudes to the possibility of racial harmony. DAI 39/12A, p. 1502.

2427. Riemers, Neal. "Revolutionary America: Jefferson's Empire of Liberty" in The Democratic Experiment: American Political Theory. Princeton: D. Van Nostrand, 1967. 1:91-121.

For undergraduates; on the concept of the continuing revolution and the continuing majority.

2428. Riley, I. Woodbridge. "Virginia and Jefferson" in American Philosophy: The Early Schools. New York: Dodd Mead, 1907. 266-95.

TJ "stood for liberty of thinking for its own sake." In his philosophy he was "more legal than logical," and was most influenced by Locke, Dugald Stewart, Cabanis, Destutt de Tracy. Emphasizes French influence.

2429. Robbins, Caroline. "The Pursuit of Happiness" in America's Continuing Revolution: An Act of Conservation, ed. Irving Kristol. Washington: American Enterprise Institute, 1975. 119-39.

On the 18th-century background of the phrase and what TJ meant by it, arguing that he intended public happiness, not individual, a "satisfaction of the aspirations of the majority."

2430. Robbins, Jan C. "Jefferson and the Press: The Resolution of an Antinomy." Journalism Quarterly. 48(1971), 421-30, 465.

Contends that TJ the libertarian defender of free speech and TJ the defender of prosecution of the press are profiles of the same man; both suppression and freedom arise from his belief that the ultimate law of men and nations is self-preservation.

2431. Rocker, Rudolf. "Thomas Jefferson" in Pioneers of American Freedom: Origin of Liberal and Radical Thought in America. ... Translated from the German by Arthur E. Briggs. Los Angeles: Rocker Publications Committee, 1949. 12-19.

Slight sketch of TJ as liberal thinker.

2432. Ross, Michael. "Homogeneity and Heterogeneity in Jefferson and Madison." International Review of History and Political Science. 13(November 1976), 47-50.

Note contrasting TJ's desire for a population uniform in occupation and political belief with Madison's belief that a great variety of interests will protect individuals from a tyrannical majority.

2433. Rothschild, Richard. Three Gods Give an Evening to Politics. New York: Random House, 1936. pp. viii, 216.

Jefferson, Lenin and Socrates in after dinner conversation.

2434. Ryavec, Ernest A. "Slovenians, Thomas Jefferson, and the Declaration of Independence." Officer Review. 16(November 1978), 12-14.

TJ could have learned of the Slovenian ritual for installing Dukes of Carinthia in Bodin's Republic.

2435. Sandler, S. Gerald. "Lockean Ideas in Thomas Jefferson's Bill for Establishing Religious Freedom." Journal of the History of Ideas. 21(1960), 110-16.

Claims to demonstrate the relation between TJ's reading notes on Locke, his Bill for Establishing Religious Freedom, and Locke's Letter Concerning Toleration.

2436. Sanford, Charles L. "The Art of Virtue: Franklin and Jefferson" in The Quest for Paradise: Europe and the American Moral Imagination. Urbana: Univ. of Illinois Press, 1961. 114-34.

TJ as a culture hero who virtually abandoned the Puritan view of unregenerate man and cleared the way for "the creation of an American Adam by romantic nationalism."

2437. Scaff, Lawrence A. "Citizenship in America: Theories of the Founding" in The Non-Lockean Roots of American Democratic Thought, ed. Joyotpaul Chaudhuri. Tucson: Univ. of Arizona Press, 1977. 44-73.

Argues that TJ "points us toward the prototypical American solution for democratic citizenship."

2438. Schaar, John H. "... And the Pursuit of Happiness." VQR. 46(1970), 1-26.

Discusses the changing notions of happiness in America, including

316

TJ's, which turns out to have ironic consequences.

2439.   Schaff, David S. "The Bellarmine-Jefferson Legend and the Declaration of Independence." Papers of the American Society of Church History. 2nd ser. 8(1928), 239-76.

Argues convincingly that the theory concerning Bellarmine's influence on TJ and George Mason is unsupported and there are essential differences between Bellarmine's theory of government and that behind the Declaration. Printed separately, New York: Putnam's, 1927. pp. 40.

2440.   Schlesinger, Arthur M. "The Lost Meaning of 'The Pursuit of Happiness'." WMQ. 3rd ser. 21(1964), 325-27.

"Pursuit" means practice of happiness.

2441.   Schneider, Herbert W. "The Enlightenment in Thomas Jefferson." Ethics. 53(1943), 246-54.

Argues that the enlightened quality of TJ's religion comes from "the merging of religious liberty and liberal religion." Temperamentally a stoic, he took an increasingly pessimistic view of history but maintained his faith in human nature.

2442.   Schulz, Constance B. "The Radical Religious Ideas of Thomas Jefferson and John Adams: A Comparison." Ph.D. dissertation. Univ. of Cincinnati, 1973. pp. 307.

TJ identified with the deists more readily than Adams did, in part because his opponents included conservative New England clergy and not, as in Adams' case, supporters of French radicalism. DAI 34/04A, p. 1839.

2443.   Sears, Louis Martin. "Democracy as Understood by Thomas Jefferson." Mid-America. n.s. 13(1942), 85-93.

TJ was a political democrat before he was a social democrat, but influenced by French thinkers and by native events like the Order of the Cincinnati, he hoped to transform society as well as the political order.

2444.   Sears, Louis M. "Jefferson and the Law of Nations." American Political Science Review. 13(1919), 379-99.

TJ was versed in the classic sources of international law, e.g. Grotius, Vattel, Puffendorf, but in face of the collapse of this "classical" school, he became a significant figure in the attempt to "reconstitute a new law of nations," even while appealing to the old authorities. The Embargo was a "grand experiment" whose failure was a "tragedy." Published in Spanish as "Jefferson y el derecho de las naciones." Inter-America. 4(1920), 181-93.

2445. Shalhope, Robert E. "Thomas Jefferson's Republicanism and Antebellum Southern Thought." Journal of Southern History. 42(1976), 529-56.

Examines TJ's thought in the last two decades of his life and claims his adherence to a pastoral republican ideology clarifies his paradoxical acceptance of slavery and commitment to a republican society. "To understand how Jefferson perceived antebellum American society is, perhaps, to recognize how an ever-increasing number of southerners came to view their circumstances."

2446. Shaw, Albert. Address at Meeting of the Phi Beta Kappa Society ... Held in Richmond, Virginia, April 13, 1904. n.p., n.d., pp. 27.

TJ "still entitled to be looked on as a prophet and guide" for society and government in a time of "undreamt of industrial combinations and prodigious aggregations of productive capital." Rpt. as "Jefferson's Doctrines Under New Tests" in The Outlook for the Average Man. New York: Macmillan, 1907; and in Representative Phi Beta Kappa Orations. Boston: Houghton Mifflin, 1915. 298-325.

2447. Sheehan, Bernard William. "Civilization and the American Indian in the Thought of the Jeffersonian Era." Ph.D. dissertation. Univ. of Virginia, 1965. pp. 395.

Argues that during the Jeffersonian period most informed opinion expected the Indians to be incorporated eventually into white civilization, but toward the end of the period a submerged doubt about the possibilities of such incorporation appeared and lent intellectual support to the removal program. Revised and published as item #1968. DAI 26/10, p. 6009.

2448. Sheehan, Bernard W. "Paradise and the Noble Savage in Jeffersonian Thought." WMQ. 3rd ser. 26(1969), 327-59.

Focus on "Jeffersonian generation" rather than on TJ; utopian belief in America as an untouched paradise "cast a progressivist spell over even the most mundane activities. ... Paradise was a mythic analogy for Western man's admitted desire to change himself and his surroundings." This program failed when the Indian was also conceived as a noble savage, for "noble savagism was (already) a simplistic statement of perfection."

2449. Sheldon, J. "Jefferson by the Light of 1863." Continental Monthly. 5(1864), 129-38.

"His works are an arsenal where these weapons of sedition are arranged ready for use."

2450. Shibata, Shingo. "Fundamental Human Rights and the Problem of Freedom: Marxism and the Contemporary Significance of the U.S. Declaration of Independence." Social Praxis. 3(1976), 157-86.

The Declaration "represents the essentials of modern democracy" but Marxism, which subsumes its most important features is "the most comprehensive theory of freedom."

2451. Simpson, Lewis P. "Literary Ecumenicalism of the American Enlightenment" in The Ibero-American Enlightenment, ed. A. Owen Aldridge. Urbana: Univ. of Illinois Press, 1971. 317-32.

Claims TJ's identification of the American landscape with Arcadia, as in Query xix of Notes, was instrumental in turning the Enlightenment ideal of a world of letters into a nationalistic, even parochial, ideal. Suggestive.

2452. Slicer, Thomas R. "Thomas Jefferson and the Influence of Democracy upon Religion" in Pioneers of Religious Liberty in America, Being the Great and Thursday Lectures Delivered in Boston in nineteen hundred and three. Boston: American Unitarian Association, 1903. 161-84.

TJ's democracy was "based in the essential dignity of human nature" and went hand in hand with a kind of religious liberty (later espoused by Channing) which saw as the only "great facts of religion" God and the soul.

2453. Smith, Dorothy Valentine. "Ideas and Ideals That Conceived the Declaration of Independence." Daughters of the American Revolution Magazine. 110(1976), 739-48.

Grudgingly admits TJ had a hand in it.

2454. Smith, T. V. "Thomas Jefferson and the Perfectibility of Mankind." Ethics. 53(1943), 293-310.

TJ's deepest credo was "It is not only permissible for liberal men to have diverse ends; it is inevitable and, indeed, desirable."

2455. Smithline, Arnold. "Thomas Jefferson" in Natural Religion in American Literature. New Haven: College and University Press, 1966. 56-64.

Brief and somewhat superficial discussion of TJ's deism and his concept of the moral sense.

*2456. Solomon, Charles. Karl Marx or Thomas Jefferson? A Debate on Individualism-Socialism Between Hon. Charles Solomon and Hon. George Gordon Battle. New York: Political Science Pocket Library, 1931. pp. 30.

2457. Somerville, John. "Contemporary Significance of the American Declaration of Independence." Philosophy and Phenomenological Research. 38(1978), 489-504.

Argues that the Declaration is even more important for us now because of TJ's recognition of the priority of civil rights and of the people's right of revolution.

2458. Spengler, Joseph J. "The Political Economy of Jefferson, Madison, and Adams" in American Studies in Honor of William Kenneth Boyd, ed. David K. Jackson. Durham: Duke Univ. Press, 1940. 3-59.

TJ's economic views owed little to the Physiocrats but much to Adam Smith, Hume, and Postlethwayte's dictionary.

2459. Sprague, Homer B. "The Mayflower Compact and the Jeffersonian Heresy." Our Day. 15(1895), 145-53.

The foundation of the Jeffersonian doctrine is distrust; its ruling sentiment antagonism; its inevitable tendency, disintegration." Links TJ to Hobbes; Mayflower Compact was written after the body politic existed.

2460. Stafford, John. "The Power of Sympathy." Midcontinent American Studies Journal. 9(Spring 1968), 52-57.

Survey of the importance of the concept of sympathy for TJ and contemporaries.

2461. Stead, John Prindle. "The Roots of Democracy in Thomas Jefferson and Mao-Tse-Tung." Ph.D. dissertation. Univ. of Southern California, 1976.

"A comparative analysis of the political thought of two great national leaders. ... both agree with ancient Chinese thought that participation and moral advancement are best guaranteed by a political system concerned with the people's relative material security." DAI 38/01A, p. 461.

2462. Steinfeld, Melvin. Our Racist Presidents From Washington to Nixon. San Ramon, Cal.: Consensus Publishers, 1972. 15-75.

Tendentious and uncritical sourcebook.

2463. Sternbach, Oscar. "The Pursuit of Happiness and the Epidemic of Depression." Psychoanalytic Review. 61(1974), 283-93.

Contends that the "authors of the Declaration of Independence ... resorted intuitively to conjuring up repressed childhood wishes" but focuses on supposed modern consequences.

2464.   Stewart, Randall. "A Doctrine of Man." Mississippi Quarterly.
        12(Winter 1959), 4-9.

        Looking at the "doctrine of man" in American literature, calls TJ
        "naive."

2465.   Stowe, Walter H. "The Religion of Thomas Jefferson." Historical
        Magazine of the Protestant Episcopal Church. 21(1952), 413-15.

        Minor note arguing that TJ was naive for believing Christian ethics
        could survive loss of belief in the divinity of Christ.

*2466. Stowe, William McF. "The Influence of Thomas Jefferson's Democratic
        Principles Upon Abraham Lincoln's Thinking on the Question of
        Slavery." Ph.D. dissertation. Boston Univ., 1938.

2467.   Sullivan, James. "The Antecedents of the Declaration of
        Independence." Annual Report of the American Historical
        Association for 1902. 1:66-81.

        Philosophical antecedents for the Declaration's ideas are in classic
        and medieval eras. The doctrines of the Declaration were originally
        advanced for purely partisan purposes and abandoned after the con-
        troversy; the same charge can be directed to the Declaration.

2468.   Swancara, Frank. Thomas Jefferson vs. Religious Oppression.
        New York: University Books, 1969. pp. 160.

        Poorly organized study of TJ's work for religious freedom, plus an
        overview of religious toleration and intolerance before his time.

2469.   Thomas, Elbert D. Thomas Jefferson, World Citizen. New York:
        Modern Age Books, 1942. pp. viii, 280.

        Discussion of the universal applicability of TJ's ideas.

2470.   Trainor, M. Rosaleen. "Thomas Jefferson on Freedom of Conscience."
        Ph.D. dissertation. St. John's Univ., 1966. pp. 201.

        Sees "two trends which defy synthesis in" TJ's thought on freedom
        of conscience: an empirical, modern trend which claims thought is
        the activity of a material organ and that man has an instinctive
        moral sense, and a classical trend which shows man governed by a
        natural law ordered by the Creator. Thus, TJ "did not discuss the
        difficulties of forming conscience, the possibilities of an erroneous
        conscience, or the problems of conflict between two persons differing
        conscientiously." DAI 28/09A, p. 3720.

2471.   Trivers, Howard. "Universalism in the Thought of the Founding
        Fathers." VQR. 52(1976), 448-62.

The founding fathers were men of the Enlightenment, characterized by its "universalism, the affirmation of universal principles in human affairs," and this has affected subsequent national behavior. TJ used as an example on pp. 452-56.

2472. Truman, Harry S. "World Unity; Requisites for Permanent Peace." Vital Speeches. 13(1947), 581-83.

Delivered at Monticello, July 4, 1947; world peace depends on recognizing what TJ knew: the necessity of providing in law for democratic freedoms, of respect for other's rights, of the free exchange of knowledge.

2473. Trumbull, Matthew Mark. Thomas Jefferson. The Father of American Democracy. His Political, Social, and Religious Philosophy. Chicago: George Schilling, 189?, pp. 20.

TJ's preference for a weak government led to anarchism, but an interfering government is the problem today. TJ thought Americans were mentally and morally qualified for self-government; maybe then, not now.

2474. [Tyler, Lyon Gardiner]. "Ideals of America." Tyler's Quarterly. 3(1921), 73-84.

The ideals of America today were established by Virginians, especially TJ, not in the New England colonies.

2475. [Tyler, Lyon Gardiner]. "What Jefferson Stood For." Tyler's Quarterly. 7(1926), 154-63.

2476. Ulich, Robert. "Thomas Jefferson" in History of Educational Thought. New York: American Book Co., 1950. 242-57.

Sketch of his ideas emphasizes educational theories.

2477. Underwood, Benjamin Franklin. Jefferson, The Free-Thinking Philosopher and Statesman; His Religious Views Presented from His Own Writings; His Views on Slavery, Religious Liberty and Other Subjects. Seymour, Ind.: Times Print, 188?. pp. 21.

Contends that TJ was a theist, but he rejected the ideas of the Bible as an inspired book or Christianity as a revealed religion. His views were the same as those of Paine, and they were far in advance of those of his age.

2478. Van Zandt, Roland. The Metaphysical Foundations of American History. The Hague: Mouton, 1959. pp. 269.

Argues on pp. 99-202 that TJ most clearly and fully enunciates the "closed system of ideas, ... a dialectic of opposed interests and

322

beliefs" through which American historians have come to understand their history.

*2479. Von Eckardt, Ursula M. "The Inalienable Right to the Pursuit of Happiness: The Meaning of the Concept Examined in the Declaration of Independence and in Related Texts." Ph.D. dissertation. New School for Social Research, 1953. pp. 336.

2480. Von Eckardt, Ursula M. The Pursuit of Happiness in the Democratic Creed: An Analysis of Political Ethics. New York: Praeger, 1959. pp. xvi, 414.

The right to the pursuit of happiness was not included in the Declaration "on the spur of the moment or as an after thought, but ... represents a central theme of Jefferson's complex political thought."

2481. Walton, Craig. "Hume and Jefferson on the Uses of History" in Philosophy and the Civilizing Arts: Essays Presented to Herbert W. Schneider, ed. Craig Walton and John P. Anton. Athens: Ohio Univ. Press, 1974. 103-25.

Contends that TJ because he wanted to use history ideologically rejected Hume less for his historical judgments than for his skepticism; suggestive. Slightly revised version of this in Hume: A Re-Evaluation, ed. Donald W. Livingstone and James T. King. New York: Fordham Univ. Press, 1976. 389-403.

2482. Waterman, Julian S. "Thomas Jefferson and Blackstone's Commentaries." Illinois Law Review. 27(1933), 629-59.

TJ opposed the Commentaries and the common law so interpreted because of Blackstone's Tory bias, his "Mansfieldism."

2483. Wayland, John Walter. The Political Opinions of Thomas Jefferson. New York: Neale, 1907. pp. 98.

A rather mechanical and simplistic analysis intended for "the busy, rushing people of to-day." Focus on practical organization and administration of government, not on political theory or intellectual background of TJ's opinions.

2484. Wettstein, A. Arnold. "Religionless Religion in the Letters and Papers from Monticello." Religion in Life. 45(1976), 152-60.

Thoughtful discussion of TJ's religion, claiming it is no vacuous deism but a notion of a religious a priori as foundational; compares him to Dietrich Bonhoeffer.

2485. Weyant, Robert V. "Helvetius and Jefferson: Studies of Human Nature and Government in the Eighteenth Century." Journal of the History of the Behavioral Sciences. 9(1973), 29-41.

Argues that Helvetius represents an egocentric view of man, descending from Locke, which holds that morality is the result of education, but that TJ's views are sociocentric in the tradition of Shaftesbury and the Scottish moralists and that he advocated a psychology of innate faculties.

2486. Whealon, John F. "American Liberalism: Its Meaning and Consistency." Mid-America. 39(1957), 73-84.

Contends that TJ can be seen as the norm for a genuine liberalism as opposed to the claims of conservatives for his patronage.

2487. Whealon, John F. "The Great 'Preamble': Did Bellarmine Influence Jefferson? A Look at the Record." Commonweal. 42(July 6, 1945), 284-85.

Finds no strong evidence for the influence of Robert Bellarmine on TJ.

2488. White, Lucia. "On a Passage by Hume Incorrectly Attributed to Jefferson." Journal of the History of Ideas. 37(1976), 133-35.

TJ's copy of Thomas Blackwell's An Enquiry into the Life and Writings of Homer contains on its fly leaf a quotation from Hume's "Of the Rise and Progress of the Arts and Sciences," also quoted by Hamilton in Federalist 85.

2489. White, Morton and Lucia. "The Irenic Age: Franklin, Crevecoeur, and Jefferson" in The Intellectual Versus the City, From Thomas Jefferson to Frank Lloyd Wright. Cambridge: Harvard Univ. Press, 1962. 6-20.

For TJ "the republic and the city joined hands only in a marriage of convenience."

2490. White, Morton. The Philosophy of the American Revolution. New York: Oxford Univ. Press, 1978. pp. xii, 299.

TJ discussed passim. Analyzes the philosophical backgrounds and positions of the founding fathers with particular attention to the issues of the self-evidence of truth, moral sense, natural law, and natural rights.

2491. Wicks, Elliott K. "Thomas Jefferson—A Religious Man with a Passion for Religious Freedom." Historical Magazine of the Protestant Episcopal Church. 36(1967), 271-83.

Intelligent survey, but nothing new.

324

2492. Williams, Kenneth Rayner. "The Ethics of Thomas Jefferson." Ph.D. dissertation. Boston Univ., 1962. pp. 247.

TJ believed that morality rested on the relation of man to man, but that religion was a private affair. The government had moral obligations to respect the natural rights of free men, although Indians and Negroes were barred from citizenship because of the supposed inferiority of their culture or race. DAI 23/05, p. 1744.

2493. Wills, Garry. Inventing America: Jefferson's Declaration of Independence. Garden City, N.Y.: Doubleday, 1978. pp. xxvi, 398.

Argues that the Declaration has been frequently misunderstood because of a failure to place its terms accurately in the context of eighteenth-century thought. An important book which reveals a great deal about TJ's attitudes toward science, ethics, slavery, etc. and illuminates his connections to Francis Hutcheson and the moral sense philosophers as well as to the Scottish common sense school; it is not so trail-breaking, however, as it pretends.

2494. Wills, Garry. "Prolegomena to a Reading of the Declaration" in Thomas Jefferson: The Man ... His World ... His Influence, ed. Lally Weymouth. New York: Putnam's, 1973. 69-79.

To understand the Declaration we must bring ourselves to understand the meaning TJ's words had for him, for example what he meant when he called himself a farmer.

2495. Wilson, Douglas. "The American Agricola: Jefferson's Agrarianism and the Classical Tradition." South Atlantic Quarterly. 80(1981), 339-54.

Excellent discussion of the classical foundations for TJ's agrarianism, particularly Virgil's Georgics.

2496. Wilson, Francis G. "On Jeffersonian Tradition." Review of Politics. 5(1943), 302-21.

Reviews TJ's positions and their continuity. If much of the intellectual tradition TJ admired has crumbled by our own time, his basic ideas are still valid; if we reject Destutt de Tracy, we hold on to the Declaration of Independence.

2497. Wiltse, Charles Maurice. "Jeffersonian Democracy; a Dual Tradition." American Political Science Review. 28(1934), 838-51.

Finds two streams of thought in TJ's political philosophy: a democratic emphasis on individualism and a socialist emphasis on the welfare of the whole. The democratic and socialist positions are closely linked; the first is a rejection of political absolutism, the second of economic absolutism.

2498. Wiltse, Charles Maurice. The Jeffersonian Tradition in American Democracy. Chapel Hill: Univ. of North Carolina Press, 1935. pp. xii, 273.

Thoughtfully examines how the "political liberalism of accumulated centuries passes through Jefferson into the Democratic tradition" by discussing his views on the state and on the law while emphasizing the flexibility and breadth of his ideas.

2499. Wiltse, Charles Maurice. "Thomas Jefferson: A Study of the Philosophy of the State." Ph.D. dissertation. Cornell Univ., 1932. pp. 264.

Thorough-going investigation of TJ's political ideas treated as a coherent system. Revised version published as item #2498.

2500. Wiltse, Charles M. "Thomas Jefferson on the Law of Nations." American Journal of International Law. 29(1935), 66-81.

TJ at times shows a tendency to move away from older natural law theory in favor of a sociological interpretation of international law. His theory of the social contract assumed the state of nature to be a state of peace, and he made this fundamental pacifism the goal of his dealings in international affairs.

2501. Wiltshire, Susan Lord. "Jefferson, Calhoun, and the Slavery Debate: The Classics and the Two Minds of the South." Southern Humanities Review. 11(Special Issue, 1977), 33-40.

Argues for two classical traditions in the South; one associated with the Enlightenment, looking to antiquity for models of freedom, the other looking for sanctions to maintain the status quo. TJ and Calhoun represent these.

2502. Wise, Jennings C. The Legacy of Jefferson: An Appeal to the Alumni of the University. n.p., n.d. pp. 15.

Claims TJ was an occult "mystic" of the cabbalistic, Masonic variety, e.g. the ten pavilions at the University symbolize "the ten Sephirothal emanations of the Great Wisdom." This lore needs to be taught in the law school in order to combat "the Browders and Tugwells" of the author's day.

2503. Wishy, Bernard. "John Locke and the Spirit of '76." Political Science Quarterly. 73(1958), 413-25.

Reviews the Lockean background of the Declaration and TJ's understanding of individual rights in view of Wilmoore Kendall's conservative interpretation of Locke; evidence does not support reading "radically individualistic political theory" into the Declaration.

2504. [Woodson, Carter G.]. "Thomas Jefferson's Thoughts on the Negro."
Journal of Negro History. 3(1918), 55-89.

Documents interspersed with comment, illustrating TJ's views on
blacks, slavery, and abolition.

2505. Wright, Esmond. "An Eighteenth-century Pragmatist; A Study of the
Sources of Jefferson's Political Ideas." M.A. thesis. Univ. of
Virginia, 1940. pp. 125.

His origins are English, not French, and his ideas were expressed in
terms of American situations.

2506. Wright, Esmond. "Thomas Jefferson and the Jeffersonian Idea" in
British Essays in American History, ed. H. C. Allen and C. P. Hill.
London: Edward Arnold, 1957. 61-82.

TJ as "rationalist, naturalist, and empiricist." If his ideas about the
function of government are outmoded, his values are of continuing
importance.

2507. Wright, Louis B. The Obligation of Intellectuals to Be Intelligent:
Some Commentary from Jefferson and Adams. Charlottesville:
Thomas Jefferson Memorial Foundation, 1974. pp. 15.

TJ as an intellectual was able to adapt his idealism "to the necessity of being practically intelligent." Both TJ and Adams disliked
foggy philosophers such as Plato or Rousseau; youthful academics of
today devoted to Marcuse or Marx should take notice. A veiled hit
at opponents of U.S. involvement in Viet Nam.

2508. [Wyllie, John Cook]. Jefferson's Prayer Book. Charlottesville:
Bibliographical Society of the Univ. of Virginia, 1952. pp. (20).

Facsimile of pages containing genealogical and other information
from the Book of Common Prayer belonging to Peter, then Thomas
Jefferson; commentary and bibliographical note.

2509. Yarbrough, Jean. "Republicanism Reconsidered: Some Thoughts on the
Foundation and Preservation of the American Republic." Review of
Politics. 41(1979), 61-95.

Examines the distinction made by Adams, Hamilton, Madison and TJ
between republicanism and liberal representative democracy. The
few pages on TJ emphasize his particular concern for the
preservation of the republic.

2510. Yellin, Jean Fagan. "Jefferson's Notes" in The Intricate Knot: Black
Figures in American Literature, 1776-1863. New York: New York
Univ. Press, 1972. 3-13.

TJ's <u>Notes on the State of Virginia</u> embody both "an assertion of human liberty, and a classic statement of ... racism," which he never rejected. A minor chapter in an otherwise good book.

*2511. Zakharova, M. N. "O genezise idei T. Dzheffersona." <u>Voprosy Istorii</u>. 1948. no. 3. 40-59.

U.S.S.R.

2512. Zwierlein, Frederick J. "Jefferson, Jesuits, and the Declaration." <u>America</u>. 49(1933), 321-23.

Rejects the Bellarmine influence on the Declaration theory because of TJ's prejudices against Jesuits.

*2513. Zwierlein, Frederick J. "Thomas Jefferson and Freedom of Religion." <u>American Ecclesiastical Review</u>. 109(1943), 39-58.

PRACTICAL AND FINE ARTS,

SCIENCE AND EDUCATION

V. PRACTICAL AND FINE ARTS, SCIENCE, EDUCATION.

2514. Abraham, Harold J. "The Chemical Library of Thomas Jefferson."
Journal of Chemical Education. 37(1960), 357-60.

Discusses TJ's interest in chemistry and gives an annotated list of
books on chemistry in his library. Useful on this.

2515. Abrahams, Harold J. "Thomas Jefferson's Library of Applied
Chemistry. Journal of the Elisha Mitchell Scientific Society.
77(1961), 267-74.

Surveys his chemical interests; documents books he owned relevant to
application of chemical knowledge, particularly to agriculture.

2516. Ackerman, James S. "Il Presidente Jefferson e il Palladianesimo
Americano." Bulletino del Centro Internazionali di Studi de
Architettura Andrea Palladio. 6(no. 2, 1964), 39-48.

Good survey of TJ's career as an architect, emphasizing his inspiration by Palladio; argues that TJ was attracted to his work because of
his intelligent evocation of Roman antiquity, the proportion and
reason of his architecture, and the naturalistic tendency of his
thinking.

2517. Adams, Herbert B. Thomas Jefferson and the University of Virginia.
Bureau of Education Circular of Information No. 1. Washington:
Government Printing Office, 1888. pp. 308.

Extensive but unfocused study of TJ and the University.

2518. Adams, Randolph G. Three Americanists: Henry Harrisse, Bibliographer; George Brinley, Book Collector; Thomas Jefferson,
Librarian. Philadelphia: Univ. of Pennsylvania Press, 1969. pp. 101.

TJ treated as the "Father of American Librarianship."

2519. Adams, William Howard, ed. The Eye of Thomas Jefferson.
Washington: National Gallery of Art, 1976. pp. xlii, 411.

Catalogue of a bicentennial exhibition; a veritable iconography of the
age with a text of some value.

2520. Adams, William Howard. "The Eye of Thomas Jefferson." The Lamp.
58(Spring 1976), 28-33.

Adapted from introduction to item #2519.

2521. Adams, William Howard, ed. Jefferson and the Arts: An Extended
View. Washington: National Gallery of Art, 1976. pp. 293.

An excellent collection of essays on TJ and the fine arts which are
described separately in these pages.

2522. Adams, William Howard. "Thomas Jefferson and the Art of the Garden." Apollo. 104(September 1976), 190-97.

Discusses the books and gardens that influenced TJ as a landscape architect.

2523. Adcock, Louis H. "Chemistry 200 Years Ago, Part I. Thomas Jefferson, Scientist." Chemistry. 48(September 1975), 14-15.

Sketch.

2524. Adler, Cyrus. "Jefferson as a Man of Science" in The Writings of Thomas Jefferson, ed. Lipscomb and Bergh. Washington: Thomas Jefferson Memorial Association, 1903. 19:iii-x.

2525. Aeppli, Felix. "Thomas Jefferson: The Urban Critic of the City." Ph.D. dissertation. Univ. of Zurich, 1975. pp. 139.

Surveys TJ's interests in city planning, his conception of the role of cities in the national economy, and the contradiction between his agrarianism and his view of history.

*2526. Akers, Barry H. "An Editor's Observation." Farmer. 69(no. 9, 1944), 8.

2527. Allan, Alfred K. "The Music Lover of Monticello." Music Journal. 13(September 1955), 39, 58.

Romanticized sketch of TJ's musical activities.

2528. Allen, E. A. "Thomas Jefferson and the Study of English." Academy. 4(1889), 1-10.

TJ as a pioneer in urging the study of language upon philological principles.

2529. Allen, John Logan. Passage Through the Garden: Lewis and Clark and the Image of the American Northwest. Urbana: Univ. of Illinois Press, 1975. pp. xxvi, 412.

TJ dealt with passim, but particularly see 59-72 for an account of TJ's interests in western exploration. A significant study of the Lewis and Clark expedition and the geographical ideas or "images" which supported it and resulted from it.

*2530. Allen, John Logan. "Thomas Jefferson and the Passage to India: A Pre-exploratory Image" in Pattern and Process: Research in Historical Geography, Ralph E. Ehrenberg. Washington: Howard Univ. Press, 1975. 103-13.

2531. Allen, Milford F. "Thomas Jefferson and the Louisiana-Arkansas Frontier." Arkansas Historical Quarterly. 20(1961), 39-64.

TJ's interest in gathering scientific information about the Louisiana Purchase lands led him to encourage the exploring expeditions of John Sibley, William Dunbar, and Thomas Freeman in the Red River and Ouachita River regions.

2532. Les Amis du Musée de Blérancourt. Jefferson. n.p., 1965. pp. 19.

Notes by various hands celebrating TJ upon the occasion of acquiring a bust of him by Houdon. In French.

2533. Andrews, Stuart. "Thomas Jefferson, American Encyclopaedist." History Today. 17(1967), 501-09.

Discusses TJ's interests in science, philosophy, and architecture in the context of Enlightenment ideals and of his experience and acquaintances in France.

2534. Anniversary Dinner at Monticello April 11, 1960 In Memory of Thomas Jefferson. Monticello: Thomas Jefferson Memorial Foundation, 1960. pp. (17).

Contains Julian P. Boyd's "Thomas Jefferson's Notes on Wines."

2535. Anniversary Dinner at Monticello April 13, 1962 In Memory of Thomas Jefferson. Monticello: Thomas Jefferson Memorial Foundation, 1962. pp. (12).

Note on "Thomas Jefferson, Gourmet" by Helen D. Bullock.

2536. Anniversary Dinner at Monticello April 9, 1963 In Memory of Thomas Jefferson. Monticello: Thomas Jefferson Memorial Foundation, 1963. pp. (16).

Contains note on TJ's love of music.

2537. Anniversary Dinner at Monticello April 13, 1967 In Memory of Thomas Jefferson. Monticello: Thomas Jefferson Memorial Foundation, 1967. pp. (12).

Note on "Jefferson's Marches" by James A. Bear, Jr.

2538. Anniversary Dinner at Monticello April 12, 1971 In Memory of Thomas Jefferson. Monticello: Thomas Jefferson Memorial Foundation, 1971. pp. (16).

Contains "Mr. Jefferson's Cook Books" by Susan Klaffky.

2539. Anniversary Dinner at Monticello April 12, 1972 In Memory of Thomas Jefferson. Monticello: Thomas Jefferson Memorial Foundation, 1972. pp. (12).

Has Helen L. Cripe's note, "Mr. Jefferson's Upright Piano," about TJ's misadventures with John Isaac Hawkins' patent piano.

2540. Anniversary Dinner at Monticello April 14, 1974 In Memory of Thomas Jefferson. Monticello: Thomas Jefferson Memorial Foundation, 1974. pp. (8).

Contains an account of James A. Bear, Jr. of TJ's model of the askos of Nimes.

2541. Anniversary Dinner at Monticello April 12, 1979 In Memory of Thomas Jefferson. Monticello: Thomas Jefferson Memorial Foundation, 1979. pp. 5, (2).

Includes recently discovered drawings by TJ for a town house and his notes on them.

2542. "Architectural Forum Master Detail Series: Historic American Buildings." Architectural Forum. 61(September 1934), 203-09.

Mistakenly calls TJ the architect of Liberty Hall in Frankfort, Kentucky, but the ascription rests only on family tradition. Illustrated.

2543. Arnold, Gustavus (pseud. Theodore G. Seemeyer?). "Farmington Country Club, Charlottesville, Virginia." Michigan Society of Architects Monthly Bulletin. 32(December 1958), 24-31.

Illustrated history of Farmington, for which TJ designed a wing.

2544. Arnold, Malcolm Heartwell. "Thomas Jefferson—American Pioneer in the Study of Old English." Ph.D. dissertation. Univ. of Virginia, 1915. pp. 242.

Rambling and poorly prepared; judges TJ by the standards of late 19th-century Teutonic philology.

2545. Arrowood, Charles Flinn, ed. Thomas Jefferson and Education in a Republic. New York: McGraw-Hill, 1930. pp. xii, 184.

TJ's contributions to the progress of education presented "in his own words so far as is practicable."

*2546. Ashley, Frederick W. "Two Pieces of Homespun. For the District of Columbia Library Association, December 5, 1934." D.C. Libraries. 6(January 1935), 27-31.

2547. Aymonin, Gérard G. "Thomas Jefferson et les naturalistes francais: un épisode des relations scientifiques franco-américaines." Annales de Bretagne. 84(1977), 303-06.

Discusses TJ's connections with Linnaean societies in America and France. 334

2548. Baeumer, Max L. "Simplicity and Grandeur: Winckelmann, French
       Classicism, and Jefferson." Studies in Eighteenth-Century Culture.
       7(1978), 63-78.

       Influence of Winckelmann and his definition of classical beauty as
       "noble simplicity and quiet grandeur" on TJ. He knew Winckelmann's
       Geschicte der Kunst das Althertums and also his friend Charles-Louis
       Clerisseau.

2549. Bailey, Liberty Hyde. "Monticello. The Country Seat of Thomas
       Jefferson. Present-Day Appearance of One of the Finest of the Es-
       tates of the Last Century." Country Life in America. 2(1902), 56-60.

       Sketch with interesting photographic illustrations.

2550. Bannon, Henry. "Thomas Jefferson, Naturalist." Forest and Stream.
       90(1920), 548-49.

       General note.

*2551. Barmore, Ida M. "Facts Worth Knowing About Thomas Jefferson."
       Popular Educator. 43(1926), 450-51.

2552. [Barnard, Henry?]. "Thomas Jefferson." American Journal of Educa-
       tion. 27(1877), 513-50.

       Memoir and survey of TJ's views on education and his work to further
       it.

2553. Barneaud, Charles. "Jefferson et l'éducation en Virginie." Revue
       International de l'Enseignement. 29(1895), 423-57.

       TJ's design for a university prompted reforms in established schools
       and became the model for the state land grant schools. The Univer-
       sity of Virginia has fallen on hard times, however, and does not fulfill
       its promise. Printed separately, Paris: Armand Colin, 1895. pp. 86.

2554. Barnwell, John. "Monticello: 1856." Journal of the Society of
       Architectural Historians. 34(1975), 280-85.

       Prints a mss. dated May 20, 1856, describing a visit to Monticello;
       visitors thought the sky room was a ball room.

2555. Baron, Sherry. "Thomas Jefferson: Scientist as Politician." Synthesis.
       3(Spring 1975), 6-21.

       Summarizes the dispute with Buffon and notices its political
       implications.

2556. Barr, Stringfellow. "'Jefferson's University'." Commonwealth, The
       Magazine of Virginia. 2(February 1935), 7-8.

       Sketch.   335

2557. Barrett, Clifton Waller. "The Struggle to Create a University." VQR. 49(1973), 494-506.

TJ's difficulties in bringing about the Univ. of Virginia; also printed separately, Charlottesville: Thomas Jefferson Memorial Foundation, 1973. pp. 18.

2558. Barth, Hans. Monticello Suite, Five Compositions For Piano. New York: J. Fischer, 1941.

No words.

2559. "Basin Battle." Time. 29(April 19, 1937), 33-36.

Full account of the dispute over the Jefferson Memorial.

2560. Bates, Kenneth. "The Eye of Thomas Jefferson." House and Garden. 148(July 1976), 32-33, 139.

Report on the National Gallery exhibit.

2561. Baugh, Albert C. "Thomas Jefferson, Linguistic Liberal" in Studies for William A. Read; A Miscellany Presented by Some of His Colleagues and Friends, eds. Nathaniel M. Caffee and Thomas A. Kirby. University, La.: Louisiana State University Press, 1940. 88-108.

Surveys TJ's interest in Old English and in the history of the language; contends his liberalism consisted of trust in usage rather than grammatic rules and a belief in the continuity of the development of English.

2562. Bean, William B. "Mr. Jefferson's Influence on American Medical Education: Some Notes on the Medical School of the University of Virginia." Virginia Medical Monthly. 87(1960), 669-80.

Rambling essay; TJ introduced or fostered among other innovations the first full time clinical teaching in America, conservatism in drugging and bloodletting, and the development of a medical school in a university setting. Considerable attention also to the contributions of Robley Dunglison.

2563. Bear, James A., Jr. "The Furniture and Furnishings of Monticello." Antiques. 102(July 1972), 112-23.

Good discussion of TJ's acquisition of furniture over the years. Illustrated.

2564. Bear, James A., Jr. Jefferson's Advice to His Children and Grand-children on Their Reading. Charlottesville: Univ. of Virginia, 1967. pp. 33.

While there is no list of TJ's recommendations for reading by the

336

very young, there are indications of books recommended to and read by his children and grandchildren prior to their 16th birthdays. Books are described and documented.

2565. Bear, James A., Jr. Old Pictures of Monticello. Charlottesville: Univ. Press of Virginia, 1957. pp. 31.

Includes some of TJ's drawings; shows the changing appearance.

2566. Bear, James A., Jr. "Thomas Jefferson, Manufacturer." The Iron Worker. 25(Autumn 1961), 1-11.

Account of TJ's nailery, joinery, and weaving shop operations at Monticello based on account books and archeological explorations.

2567. Bear, James A., Jr. "Thomas Jefferson's Art Collection." n.p., 1967. pp. 6.

Mimeographed sheets. Discusses the sale of part of TJ's collection in Boston in 1828-1833; lists 51 paintings with descriptions from TJ's 1809 catalogue.

2568. Bear, James A., Jr. Thomas Jefferson's Book-Marks. Charlottesville: Alderman Library of the Univ. of Virginia, 1958. pp. 10.

Issued to commemorate the visit of the Grolier Club to the University and to Monticello.

2569. Bear, James A., Jr. "Thomas Jefferson's Silver." Antiques. 74 (September 1958), 33-36.

Illustrated account of TJ's silver based on account books and letters, including an account of the basis for the widely reproduced "Jefferson cups."

2570. Beard, Eva. "Father of His Country's Housing." New York Times Magazine. April 14, 1946. 24.

Note on TJ as architect.

2571. Beard, Eva. "Thomas Jefferson, Statesman and Scientist." Nature Magazine. 51(April 1958), 202-04.

Survey of scientific interests, based on secondary sources.

2572. Bedini, Silvio A. "Godfather of American Invention" in The Smithsonian Book of Invention. New York: Smithsonian Exposition Books/W. W. Norton, 1978. 82-85.

TJ as tinkerer and first administrator of the patent office.

2573. Bedini, Silvio A. "Thomas Jefferson and His Watches." Hobbies.

61(February 1967), 38-39.

Brief, informative note.

2574. Bedini, Silvio A. Thomas Jefferson and Science. Exhibition
      Catalogue. Washington: National Museum of American History, 1981.
      pp. (16).

      Survey of TJ's scientific interests; abridged version in Colonial
      Homes. 7(November/December 1981), 80-83.

2575. Bedini, Silvio A. "Thomas Jefferson, Clock Designer." Proceedings of
      the APS. 108(1964), 163-80.

      Interesting and extensive description of TJ's interests in time pieces
      and time keeping as well as of his designs for various clocks,
      including the Great Clock at Monticello. Illustrated.

2576. Beiswanger, William L. "Thomas Jefferson's Designs for Garden
      Structures at Monticello." M.A. thesis. Univ. of Virginia, 1977.
      pp. 72.

2577. Beiswanger, William. "Jefferson's Designs for Garden Structures at
      Monticello." Journal of the Society of Architectural Historians.
      35(1976), 310-12.

      Describes plans and ideas from TJ's memorandum books and other
      sources; discusses the influence of Kames, Whately, and others. Only
      one garden structure is actually known to have been built.

2578. Benet, Stephen Vincent. "Thomas Jefferson 1743-1826" in A Book of
      Americans, Rosemary and Stephen Vincent Benet. New York: Farrar
      and Rinehart, 1933. 39-41.

      TJ's life in ballad form.

2579. Bennet, Hugh M. Thomas Jefferson Soil Conservationist. Washington:
      Department of Agriculture, 1944. pp. 16.

      Soil Conservation Service Misc. Pub. 548. TJ as pioneer soil conser-
      vationist who practiced crop rotation, deep plowing, and contour
      plowing. Discusses mid-20th-century condition of his land.

2580. Bennett, Richard. "A Confident Idealist." House and Garden. 83(May
      1943), 20-23.

      On the architecture and furnishings of Monticello.

2581. Berkeley, Francis L. "Farmer Thomas Jefferson." Wisdom. 1(March
      1956), 72-75.

338

Shortened version of an essay which originally appeared in Thomas Jefferson's Farm Book, ed. Betts.

2582. Berkeley, Francis L., Jr. "Mr. Jefferson's Rotunda: Myths and Realities." Univ. of Virginia Alumni News. 59(July/August 1972), 4-9.

Emphasizes TJ's innovative design for the Rotunda, pointing out it is no mere slavish copy of earlier buildings.

2583. Berman, Eleanor. Thomas Jefferson Among the Arts, An Essay in Early Aesthetics. New York: Philosophical Library, 1947. pp. xviii, 305.

Although TJ "had no philosophy of art, ... His esthetic ideas express ... a constellation of attitudes." TJ was "art as one of the first steps toward freedom." Claims a key to TJ's aesthetic principles is Hogarth's serpentine curve. A standard work, but a better is needed.

2584. Berman, Eleanor Davidson and E. C. McClintock, Jr. "Thomas Jefferson and Rhetoric." Quarterly Journal of Speech. 33(1947), 1-8.

Claims TJ's views on the art of rhetoric are valid and modern because he emphasized the social values of communication, the importance of accuracy, brevity and simplicity, and a balance between sound reasoning and effective presentation.

2585. Bestor, Arthur. "Thomas Jefferson and the Freedom of Books" in Three Presidents and Their Books. Urbana: Univ. of Illinois Press, 1955. 1-44.

Resolves TJ's defence of intellectual liberty and his seemingly contradictory attempts to combat erroneous positions he found in books like Montesquieu's Spirit, Hume's History, and Blackstone's Commentaries. Defends rationale of the Univ. of Virginia Board Visitor's resolution of March 4, 1825.

2586. Betts, Edwin. M. "The Correspondence Between Constantine Samuel Rafinesque and Thomas Jefferson." Proceedings of the APS. 87(1943), 368-80.

Correspondence reprinted with notes and commentary.

2587. Betts, Edwin M. "Groundplans and Prints of the University of Virginia, 1822-1826." Proceedings of the APS. 90(1946), 81-90.

Using TJ's letters and early views, discusses his interest in the early iconography of the University.

2588. Betts, Edwin M. "Jefferson's Gardens at Monticello." Agricultural History. 19(1945), 180-82.

Brief account of the Monticello gardens.

2589. Betts, Edwin Morris, ed. Thomas Jefferson's Farm Book, With Commentary and Relevant Extracts from Other Writings. Princeton: Princeton Univ. Press. for the American Philosophical Society, 1953. pp. xxii, 552.

Facsimile of the Farm Book with transcription, commentary, and supporting material arranged topically. Invaluable.

2590. Betts, Edwin M. and Hazlehurst B. Perkins. Thomas Jefferson's Flower Garden at Monticello. Richmond: Dietz Press, 1941. pp. 56.

Account of TJ's interest in gardening and the plans of his original gardens as now restored at Monticello. Rpt. Charlottesville: Univ. Press of Virginia, 1971. pp. ix, 60.

2591. Betts, Edwin Morris, ed. Thomas Jefferson's Garden Book, 1766-1824, With relevant extracts from his other writings. Philadelphia: American Philosophical Society, 1944. pp. xiv, 704.

TJ's record of his gardens, substantially augmented by relevant passages from his correspondence, and by significant annotations. A veritable botanical biography.

2592. Biancolli, Louis. "Thomas Jefferson, Fiddler." Life. 22(April 7, 1947), 13+.

TJ, his Amati "fiddle," and its supposed peregrinations after his death. Folklore, treated here with little skepticism.

2593. "Bicentennial Beat: Head and Heart." New Yorker. 52(June 21, 1976), 24-26.

Interview with W. Howard Adams on putting together the Eye of Thomas Jefferson exhibit.

2594. Binney, Marcus. "University of Virginia." Country Life. 163(January 12, 1978), 74-77; 163(January 19, 1978), 142-45.

Discussion of TJ's architectural designs, the possible influences on them—most interestingly by Charles Kelsall—and their realization.

2595. Bishop, William Warner. "Training in the Use of Books" in The Backs of Books and Other Essays on Librarianship. Baltimore: Williams and Wilkins, 1926. 99-124.

Discusses TJ's library and compares it to the size and complexity of modern libraries.

2596. Bitter, Karl. "Thomas Jefferson from the Statue." Century. 86(May 1913), 27.

Photograph of statue for the St. Louis Jefferson Memorial.

2597.   Blanck, Jacob. "News from the Rare Book Sellers." Publisher's Weekly. 143(1943), 1530-31.

Brief comments on TJ's library and its acquisition by the nation.

2598.   Blinderman, Abraham. "Thomas Jefferson, Administrator, Practitioner, and Patient." New York State Journal of Medicine. 70(March 1970), 690-96.

TJ's interest in science led him to pioneer in medical education.

2599.   Bloch, Harry. "Thomas Jefferson 1743 to 1826, Thoughts on Medicine, Child Care and Welfare." New York State Journal of Medicine. 72 (1972), 3030-32.

TJ's concern for children's diseases, mostly in his own family.

2600.   Bo, Jorgen and Borge Glahn. En Amerikansk Arkitekt. Kobenhavn: Schonbergske Forlag, 1953. pp. (28).

On TJ as architect, in Danish.

2601.   Boehm, Dwight and Edward Schwartz. "Jefferson and the Theory of Degeneracy." American Quarterly. 9(1957), 448-53.

TJ performed valuable service in refuting Buffon's theories which were used for political and propaganda purposes.

2602.   "Boston Museum Secures Houdon's Bust of Thomas Jefferson." Art News. 33(October 6, 1934), 11.

Marble bust acquired from the heirs of Destutt de Tracy; see also similar report in Art Digest. 9(November 1, 1934), 10.

2603.   Boutell, Lewis Henry. Thomas Jefferson, The Man of Letters. Chicago: Privately Printed, 1891. pp. 73.

Uncritical sketch of TJ's education, his interest in the classics, and early days at the Univ. of Virginia. Nothing of value on his literary art or practice.

2604.   Bowes, Mary M. "The Spirit of Jefferson: Wine Growing, The Adlum Letters" in Jefferson and Wine, ed. R. deTreville Lawrence, Sr. The Plains, Va.: Vinifera Wine Growers Association, 1976. 121-31.

Discusses TJ's difficulties in trying to grow vinifera grapes and his encouragement of efforts to use native grapes. Prints correspondence with John Adlum, who was growing vines on his estates in Maryland and Washington, D. C.

2605.   Bowman, Isaiah. "Jeffersonian 'Freedom of Speech' from the Standpoint of Science." Science. n.s. 82(1935), 529-32.

The Jeffersonian demand for freedom of speech is crucial for the protection and advancement of science, especially at a time when politicians are attempting to direct and dictate the course of science.

2606.   Boyd, Julian P. "Foreward" in Thomas Jefferson on Science and Freedom: The Letter to the Student William Greene Munford, June 18, 1799. With a Foreward by Julian P. Boyd. Worcester, Mass.: Achille J. St. Onge, 1964. pp. 60.

Discusses TJ as letter writer and identifies Munford; a miniature book.

2607.   Boyd, Julian P. "The Megalonyx, the Megatherium, and Thomas Jefferson's Lapse of Memory." Proceedings of the APS. 102(1958), 420-35.

Careful, extensive account of TJ's writing of his memoir on the megalonyx—how he initially was led to believe it was "of the lion kind," how he came to realize it was in fact related to the megatherium, a recently discovered fossil sloth. He might have avoided the initial error had he remembered the drawing of the megatherium by Juan Bautista Brú he had acquired in Paris.

2608.   Boyd, Julian P., Lyman H. Butterfield, and Walter M. Whitehill. Thomas Jefferson Among the Antiquities of Southern France in 1787. A Tribute to E. Harold Hugo. Princeton: Princeton Univ. Press, 1954. pp. (23).

Historical introduction to a letter dated March 20, 1787, from TJ to the Comtesse de Tessé on his travels in southern France and her reply.

2609.   Boyd, Julian P. "Thomas Jefferson and the Roman Askos of Nîmes." Antiques. 104(July 1973), 116-24.

Detailed, thorough account of TJ's wooden copy and subsequent model in silver of the askos belonging to Francois Séguier of Nîmes. Information also on TJ's visit to Nîmes and his relations with Charles Louis Clerisseau.

2610.   Brackenridge, Henry M. Speeches on the Jew Bill, in the House of Delegates of Maryland, by H. M. Brackenridge, Col. W. G. D. Worthington, and John S. Tyson, Esquire. Together with an Argument on the Chancery Powers, and An Eulogy of Thomas Jefferson and John Adams, etc by H. M. Brackenridge. Philadelphia: J. Dobson, 1829. pp. 276.

Reprints the Pensacola eulogy of August 1826, 157-82; includes also "Western Antiquities, Communicated in a Letter to Thomas
342

Jefferson," 192-205, arguing for Mexican influence on the mound-builders.

2611. Bradford, Gamaliel. "Thomas Jefferson" and "Ode to Thomas Jefferson" in The Enchanted Years, ed. John Calvin Metcalf and James Southall Wilson. New York: Harcourt Brace, 1921. 34-37.

Two poems.

2612. Bradford, M. E. "Faulkner and the Jefferson Dream: Nationalism in 'Two Soldiers' and 'Shall Not Perish.'" Mississippi Quarterly. 18(no. 2, 1965), 94-100.

Asserts that Faulkner's admiration for his farmers and hill folk is an allegiance to "the Jeffersonian ideal of 'independent' men.

2613. Brasch, Frederick E. "Thomas Jefferson, the Scientist." Science. n.s. 97(1943), 300-01.

Sketch.

2614. Bremo, Designed by Thomas Jefferson for General John Hartwell Cocke. n.p., 193? pp. 4.

Broadside accompanying a collection of postcards; it has been more recently decided that TJ did not have a hand in Bremo.

2615. Bridgman, Richard. "Jefferson's Farmer Before Jefferson." American Quarterly. 14(1962), 567-77.

Pre-revolutionary literature on farming was adapted for the most part from English sources and had little relevance for the American situation. Despite the idealizations of pastoral poetry, observers of actual American farmers often found them lazy and ignorant. "Jefferson's forceful idealism" claims the author, "rescued American pride."

2616. Brock, Macon A. "Roman Possesses Historical Clock." The Pendulum (Rome Georgia). 1(no. 1, 1929), 1.

TJ's descendant, H. P. Meikleham, owned a clock made in Paris for TJ by Paul Moinet; illustrated.

2617. Broglie, Axelle de. "Une Visite à Thomas Jefferson." Connaisance des Arts. No. 229(March 1971), 67-75.

TJ at Monticello was visited by Frenchmen like Chastellux, and his style of living showed the influence of his stay in France.

2618. Brooks, Joan Louise. "Jefferson and Bryant: The Embargoes." M.A. thesis. Univ. of Virginia, 1966. pp. 26.

343

Focus on Bryant and the composition of his anti-TJ satire.

2619. Brooks, Van Wyck. "Thomas Jefferson, Man of Letters." American Academy of Arts and Letters, Academy Papers. 2(1951), 174-82.

Character sketch, praising TJ as a prophetic idealist.

2620. Brown, Elizabeth Gaspar. "A Jeffersonian's Recommendations for a Lawyer's Education: 1802." American Journal of Legal History. 13(April 1969), 139-44.

Compares TJ's recommendations for aspiring lawyers with Augustus B. Woodward's memorandum of 1802.

2621. Brown, Glenn. "Letters from Thomas Jefferson and William Thornton, Architect, Relating to the University of Virginia." Journal of the American Institute of Architects. 1(January 1913), 21-27.

TJ asks Thornton for some sketches and gets a lengthy reply. Minimal supporting comment.

2622. Brown, J. Carter and Perry Wolff. On Thomas Jefferson. New York: Encyclopedia Americana/CBS News Audio Resource Library, 1971.

Cassette tape. "Vital History Cassettes, May 1976, no. 1." Brown and Wolff discuss TJ's aesthetic and political ideas.

2623. Brown, Ralph H. "Jefferson's Notes on Virginia." Geographical Review. 33(1943), 467-73.

Commentary on scientific aspects of Notes; claims the essay on climate in query vii may be the most influential section of the book.

2624. Brown, Roland W. "Jefferson's Contributions to Paleontology." Journal of the Washington Academy of Science. 33(1943), 257-59.

Recounts TJ's paper on the megalonyx.

2625. Brown, William Wells. Clotel; or The President's Daughter: A Narrative of Slave Life in the United States. London: Partridge and Oakey, 1853. pp. 253.

An antislavery novel, the first by an American black writer, it does not make a great deal of TJ's parentage of Clotel, but it does quote him on the evils of slavery and then accuse him of hypocrisy.

2626. Browne, Charles Albert. "Joseph Priestley and the American Fathers." American Scholar. 4(1935), 133-47.

Priestley found in TJ his most agreeable contact among the leaders of the American Revolution.

344

2627. Browne, C. A. "Thomas Jefferson and Agricultural Chemistry." Scientific Monthly. 60(1945), 55-62.

Well-informed paper puts TJ's chemical ideas in historical context.

2628. Browne, Charles A. "Thomas Jefferson and the Scientific Trends of His Time." Chronica Botanica. 8(1944), 363-423.

Wide-ranging but somewhat disjointed survey of TJ's scientific interests. Also bound separately.

2629. Browne, Charles Albert. "Thomas Jefferson's Relation to Chemistry." Journal of Chemical Education. 20(1943), 574.

Note on TJ's chemical interests; pp. 575-76 reprint his 1791 "Report on the Method for Obtaining Fresh Water from Salt," the first document of a chemical nature to be published by the U. S. government.

2630. Bruce, Philip Alexander. History of the University of Virginia, 1819-1919; The Lengthened Shadow of One Man. New York: Macmillan, 1920. 1: pp. xiv, 376.

The first volume in this five volume work covers TJ's involvement with the University as planner, architect, and rector. Best history of the University as a whole.

2631. Brunner, Karl. "Thomas Jefferson: An Essay on the Anglo-Saxon." Americana-Austriaca. Band I. Wien: Wilhelm Braumuller, 1966. 249-64.

In German. Examines TJ's interest in Old English against the background of a developing scholarship before and after his time.

2632. Bryan, Mina R. "Jefferson's Notes on Virginia in the Princeton Library." Princeton University Library Chronicle. 11(1950), 202-05.

Note on editions held.

2633. Bryan, Mina R. "Some General Observations of Jefferson Manuscripts." Autograph Collector's Journal. 4(no. 1, 1951), 12-16.

Offers information on his writing habits and his various systems for duplicating his letters, particularly the copying press and the polygraph. He began to use the press in 1785 and turned to the polygraph in 1804, after which copies are sometimes difficult to distinguish from originals.

2634. Buchman, Carl. "Jefferson and Liberty" in Seven Songs of the Early Republic, ed. Richard Franko Goldman, new settings by Carl Buchman. New York: Mercury Music Corp., 1942. 3.

2635. Bullock, Helen Duprey. "Mr. Jefferson—Musician." Etude. 61(October 1943), 633-34, 688.

Competent survey of TJ's musical interests.

2636. Bullock, Helen Duprey. Mr. Jefferson's Method of Preparing Glace from Petit's Recipe. Washington: The Author, 1963. Broadside.

2637. Burke, John G. and John C. Greene. The Science of Minerals in the Age of Jefferson. Transactions of the APS. 68(1978), pt. 4. pp. 113.

Focus on mineralogical activities of the APS, not much on TJ; he contributed specimens collected by Lewis and Clark and was aware of geologists' activities, but seems to have had little part in the Society's mineralogical enterprises.

2638. Burr, Horace. Thomas Jefferson, the Collector of Art. Charlottesville: Wayside Press, 1967. pp. (7).

Albemarle Art Association Pamphlets, No. 26. Describes TJ's collection at Monticello briefly, gives a "glossary" of ten paintings on the same subjects or by the same painters as listed in TJ's catalogues.

2639. Burrows, Edwin G. "Tom Writes a Declaration." New Masses. 47(April 13, 1943), 17.

Poem.

2640. Burruss, Julian A. "Jefferson and the Land-Grant College." Proceedings. Fifty-first Annual Convention. Association of Land Grant Colleges and Universities. Washington, D. C., November 14-17, 1937. 336-38.

TJ was not the father of the land-grant college, "but he was its prophet."

2641. Bush, Alfred L. The Life Portraits of Thomas Jefferson. Catalogue of an Exhibition at the University of Virginia Museum of Fine Arts, 12 through 26 April, 1962. Charlottesville: Thomas Jefferson Memorial Foundation, 1962. pp. 101.

Rpt. in Jefferson and the Arts: An Extended View, ed. William Howard Adams (item # 2521). Best catalogue on the life portraits; discusses their history, condition, iconographic importance, etc.

2642. Bush, Clive. "Origins of Natural History in America and First Syntheses" in The Dreams of Reason: American Consciousness and Cultural Achievements from Independence to the Civil War. London: Edward Arnold, 1977. 191-209.

Discusses Crevecoeur, William Bartram, and TJ's Notes; his "landscape of conflict" encouraged "pragmatic exploration."

346

2643. Butler, Jeanne F. "Competition 1792: Designing a Nation's Capitol." Capitol Studies. 4(no. 1, 1976), 11-96.

Illustrated account of the competition to design the U. S. Capitol; TJ treated passim and on 83-85.

2644. Butterfield, Lyman H. "An African Game Preserve: A Scholar's View of the Library of Congress." Library Journal. 90(1965), 5335-41.

Emphasizes TJ's collection as the Library's "true heart."

2645. Butterfield, Lyman H. "The Papers of Thomas Jefferson: Progress and Procedures in the Enterprise at Princeton." American Archivist. 12(1949), 131-45.

Describes the plans and editorial procedures of the edition of the Papers published by Princeton Univ. Press under the editorship of Julian P. Boyd.

*2646. Butterworth, Hezekiah. "The Death of Jefferson" in Songs of History. Boston: New England Publishing Co., 1887.

2647. Butterworth, Hezekiah. In the Days of Jefferson: or, The Six Golden Horseshoes, a Tale of Republican Simplicity. New York: Appleton, 1900. pp. 284.

Juvenile fiction.

2648. [Cabell, Nathaniel F.]. Early History of the University of Virginia, as Contained in the Letters of Thomas Jefferson and Joseph C. Cabell, Hitherto Unpublished. Richmond: J. W. Randolph, 1856. pp. xxxvi, 528.

Brief introduction, some annotation, but basic source material.

2649. Cahill, Helen S. "Thomas Jefferson Liked These." Woman's Home Companion. 69(April 1942), 88-89.

Recipes.

2650. Cairns, Dolores. "Country Squire from Virginia." Christian Science Monitor Magazine. April 9, 1949. 16.

Poem; rpt. NEA Journal. 42(1953), 248.

2651. Campbell, Orland and Courtney. The Lost Portraits of Thomas Jefferson. Painted by Gilbert Stuart. Recovered and Studied by Orland and Courtney Campbell. June 12-30, 1959, Mead Art Building, Amherst College. Amherst: Amherst College, 1959. pp. 31.

Authors claim to have discovered the lost original of Stuart's missing

347

first portrait of TJ. However, see article by David Meschutt, noted below.

2652. Campbell, Orland. The Lost Portraits of Thomas Jefferson Painted by Gilbert Stuart. Garden City: N.Y.: Adelphi Univ., Swirbul Library, 1965. pp. 27.

Slightly expanded version of the previous item; extensive scholarship but not necessarily the right conclusion.

2653. Cannon, Carl L. "Thomas Jefferson" in American Book Collectors and Collecting in Colonial Times to the Present. New York: H. W. Wilson, 1941. 38-49.

Overview of TJ as book collector.

*2654. Carey, Alma P. "Thomas Jefferson's Ideal University: Dream and Actuality." M.A. thesis. Univ. of Texas, 1937.

2655. Carey, John Peter. "Influences on Thomas Jefferson's Theory and Practice of Higher Education." Ph.D. dissertation. Univ. of Michigan, 1969. pp. 383.

TJ was most probably influenced by William Small and "the enlightened thinking of Scottish higher education" which he represented. Yet TJ's views on education were apparently formed early in his life, and it is difficult to conclude with certainty that he was definitely influenced by the ideas of other theorists. DAI 30/05A, p. 1835.

2656. Carlton, Jan. "Mr. Jefferson's Table." Commonwealth, The Magazine of Virginia. 47(1980), 49-52.

Cooking, includes recipes.

2657. Carrière, Joseph M. "The Manuscript of Jefferson's Unpublished Errata List for Abbé Morrelet's Translation of the Notes on Virginia." Papers of the Bibliographical Society of the University of Virginia. 1(1949), 3-24.

Explains why TJ was not fortunate in having Morellet as a translator.

2658. Carrière, J.-M. "Mr. Jefferson Sponsors a New French Method." French Review. 19(1946), 394-405.

TJ's correspondence with Nicholas Gouin Dufief, who published in 1804 Nature Displayed, proposing to teach French by having students memorize whole sentences at a time.

2659. Carter, James C. The University of Virginia: Jefferson Its Father and His Political Philosophy. Charlottesville: Univ. of Virginia, 1898. pp. 38.

348

An address calling for the continued teaching of the "fundamental political philosophy of Mr. Jefferson."

2660. Castiello, Kathleen Raben. "The Italian Sculptors of the United States Capitol: 1806-1834." Ph.D. dissertation. Univ. of Michigan, 1975. pp. 196.

Giuseppe Franzoni and Giovanni Andrei began the sculptural decoration of the Capitol building following a program set up by Latrobe and TJ. DAI 36/10A, p. 6346.

2661. Catalogue of an Exhibition of Thomas Jefferson Silver, University of Virginia Museum of Fine Arts, April 13 to June 15, 1958. Charlottesville: Univ. of Virginia, 1958. pp. 8.

Has a short note on TJ's plate and plated ware.

2662. Catalogue of a Private Library, Comprising a Rich Assortment of Rare Standard Works, Many in Fine Bindings, ... Also the Remaining Portion of the Library of the Late Thomas Jefferson ... the Whole to Be Sold by Auction at the Clinton Hall Sale Rooms. The Messers. Leavitt Auctioneers. n.p., 1873. pp. 44.

Pp. 36-41 describe items once belonging to TJ and now offered by his grandson Francis Eppes; also for sale are ten letters.

2663. Catalogue of President Jefferson's Library. A Catalogue of the extensive and valuable Library of the late President Jefferson (copied from the original MS., in his hand writing, as arranged by himself,) to be sold at auction, at the Long Room Pennyslvania Avenue, Washington City. By Nathaniel P. Poor, on the 27th February, 1829. Washington: Gales and Seaton, 1829. pp. 14.

The final library. Page 2 shows TJ's scheme of classification according to the faculties of the human mind.

2664. Catalogue of the Library of the University Arranged Alphabetically ... . Charlottesville: Gilmer, Davis and Co., 1828. pp. 114.

Facsimile edition, Charlottesville: Alderman Library, 1945. Catalogue of the original Univ. of Virginia library as shaped by TJ's recommendations.

*2665. Catalogue of Valuable Oil Paintings, Many of Them by the Old Masters, and All Choice Pictures, Being the Collection of the Late President Jefferson. To Be Sold at Auction on Friday, July 19th, at Mr. Harding's Gallery, School Street. (Boston, 1833). pp. 8.

2666. Cauthen, Irby, Jr. "'A complete and Generous Education': Milton and Jefferson." VQR. 55(1979), 222-33.

TJ's ideas of education echo Milton's, but there is no proof that he
read Milton's "Of Education."

2667.   "'Cellophane' at Monticello." DuPont Magazine. 28(October 1934),
        9-10.

        Note on TJ's inventions; cellophane (not invented by him!), used now
        to protect bedcovers.

2668.   Ceram, C. W. (Kurt W. Marek). "The President and the Mounds" in The
        First American: A Story of North American Archaeology. New York:
        Harcourt Brace, 1971. 3-10.

        Credits TJ with the invention of stratigraphy and describes his ex-
        cavation of the Indian mound; abridged version of this published as
        "Mr. Jefferson's 'Dig.'" American History Illustrated. 6(November
        1971), 38-41.

2669.   Chamberlain, Alexander F. "Thomas Jefferson's Ethnological Opinions
        and Activities." American Anthropologist. n.s. 9(1907), 499-509.

        Survey of TJ's archaeological interests, his interest in the race
        question and the origin of races, his method of approach to primitive
        peoples, and his interest in Indian languages.

2670.   Chandler, J. A. C. "Jefferson and the College of William and Mary."
        Virginia Journal of Education. 19(1926), 349-52.

        TJ's relationship with the college from student days to the time of
        the founding of the Univ. of Virginia.

2671.   "Charles and Ray Eames Take Center Stage in Los Angeles." Sunset.
        157(November 1976), 46-48.

        On the world of Franklin and Jefferson exhibit at the Los Angeles
        County Museum of Art.

2672.   "Charles Bellini, First Professor of Modern Languages in an American
        College." WMQ. 2nd ser. 5(1925), 1-29.

        Prints with some annotation letters of Bellini and TJ; Bellini came to
        Virginia in 1773 with Philip Mazzei and was appointed in 1779
        professor of modern languages at William and Mary.

2673.   Chase, Gilbert. "Thomas Jefferson y las Bellas Artes." Atlántico.
        3(1956), 5-20.

        TJ's artistic interests discussed; he is "un clasicista con tendencias
        románticas."

2674.   Chase-Riboud, Barbara. Sally Hemings: A Novel. New York: Viking,
        1979. pp. 348.

A controversial, prize-winning novel which assumes Sally Hemings was TJ's mistress and explores the situation primarily from her supposed point of view. A good novel, but suspect as history.

2675. Childs, Marquis W. "Mr. Pope's Memorial." Magazine of Art. 30(1937), 200-02.

Compares the grandiosity of the proposed Memorial to TJ's "almost Spartan simplicity;" explains how Pope got the commission.

2676. Chinard, Gilbert, ed. Houdon in America; A Collection of Documents in the Jefferson Papers in the Library of Congress. With an Intro- duction by Francis Henry Taylor. Baltimore: Johns Hopkins Press, 1930. pp. xxvi, 51.

TJ promotes Houdon. Taylor's introduction first appeared in The Pennsylvania Museum Bulletin. 24(1928).

2677. Chinard, Gilbert. "Introduction" to The Literary Bible of Thomas Jefferson: His Commonplace Book of Philosophers and Poets. Baltimore: Johns Hopkins Press, 1928. 1-37.

Analyzes the contents of a literary commonplace book and argues that it dates from an early period of TJ's life. Finds early evidence for an underlying stoic attitude, but also suggests several attitudes implied by some of the selections were merely of the moment.

2678. Chinard, Gilbert. "Jefferson and Ossian." Modern Language Notes. 38(1923), 201-05.

Prints TJ's letter to Charles Macpherson, asking him to obtain if possible a copy in Gaelic of the Ossian poems, plus MacPherson's reply and the letter of James MacPherson, the Ossian forger, to Charles. TJ's letter was heavily corrected during its composition, suggesting he was anxious to make a favorable impression.

2679. Chinard, Gilbert. "Jefferson and the American Philosophical Society." Proceedings of the APS. 87(1943), 263-76.

TJ's involvement with the Society surveyed.

2680. Chinard, Gilbert. "Les Michaux et leur Précurseurs" in Les Botanistes Francais en Amérique du Nord avant 1850. Paris: Centre National de la Recherche Scintifique, 1957. 280-83.

These pages are subheaded "Deux Grands Amateurs de Plantes: Chateaubriand et Thomas Jefferson." Brief.

2681. Chinard, Gilbert. "Thomas Jefferson as a Classical Scholar." Johns Hopkins Alumni Magazine. 18(1930), 291-303.

Rather slight discussion of TJ's interests; rpt. in American Scholar. 1(1932), 133-43.

2682. Choate, Florence and Elizabeth Curtis. The Five Gold Sovereigns, A Story of Thomas Jefferson's Time. New York: Frederick A. Stokes, 1943. pp. vii, 207.

Juvenile fiction, more fanciful than most of the stories featuring TJ.

2683. Christina, Sister M. "Thomas Jefferson, Architect." Catholic School Journal. 58(January 1958), 27-28.

Sketch.

2684. Churchill, Henry S. "The Jefferson Memorial." New Republic. 96(1938), 20.

Letter to the Editor protesting the proposed Jefferson Memorial design.

*2685. Ciolli, Antoinette. "Thomas Jefferson as a Man of Science." M.A. thesis. Brooklyn College, 1940.

2686. Claibourne, Craig. "Thomas Jefferson, An American in Paris with a Taste for French Food." Nutrition Today. 12(July/August 1977), 25-27.

2687. Clapp, Verner Warren. "Thomas Jefferson and His Libraries." Among Friends. 25(Winter 1961-62), 2-5.

Surveys TJ's librarianship and interest in books.

2688. Clark, Austin H. "Thomas Jefferson and Science." Journal of the Washington Academy of Science. 33(1943), 193-203.

Survey.

2689. Clark, Evert Mordecai. "An Unpublished Bit of Jeffersonian Verse." South Atlantic Quarterly. 26(1927), 76-82.

Explains the background of a brief bit of verse satirizing TJ as a tyrant written in 1808; unreliable in particulars.

2690. Clark, Kenneth. "Thomas Jefferson and the Italian Renaissance." VQR. 48(1972), 519-31.

TJ working in the spirit of Leon Battista Alberti who also influenced Palladio. Rpt. in Thomas Jefferson: The Man ... His World ... His Influence, ed. Lally Weymouth. New York: Putnam's, 1973. 97-105.

2691. Clark, William Bedford. "'Canaan's Grander Counterfeit': Jefferson and America in Brother to Dragons." Renascence. 30(1978), 171-78.

Examines R. P. Warren's use of TJ in his long narrative poem, where he is "less important as an individual reconstructed from the past than as a symbol embodying Warren's critique of America's history and his hopes for America's future."

2692.   Clemons, Harry, ed. "Some Jefferson Manuscript Memoranda of Colonial Virginia Records." VMHB. 65(1957), 154-68.

Prints with introduction and extensive annotation two fragmentary mss. in TJ's hand containing notes on the minutes of the Virginia Council and General Court of 1625 and 1626 and a memorandum based on the 1652 records of the House of Burgesses.

2693.   Clemons, Harry. The University of Virginia Library, 1825-1950: Story of a Jeffersonian Foundation. Charlottesville: Univ. of Virginia Library, 1954. pp. xix, 229.

History of the Univ. library told in terms of its Jeffersonian origins; early chapters describe TJ's plans, later ones describe a working out of those plans in the ensuing century and a quarter.

2694.   Coes, Frank L. "Jefferson Stamp." Hobbies. 48(April 1943), 78.

Postage stamps with TJ's portrait.

2695.   Cohen, I. Bernard. "Science and the Growth of the American Republic." Review of Politics. 38(1976), 359-98.

A wide-ranging article with a few incisive pages (366-69) on the influence of Newtonian science on TJ.

2696.   Cohen, I. Bernard, ed. Thomas Jefferson and The Sciences. New York: Arno Press, 1980. Separately paginated.

Volume in Three Centuries of Science in America Series reprints 29 articles or pamphlets, each noted separately here.

2697.   Cohen, Morris L. "Thomas Jefferson Recommends a Course of Law Study." Univ. of Pennsylvania Law Review. 119(1971), 823-44.

Prints facsimile and transcription of a letter dated August 30, 1814 to John Minor on a program of reading suitable for his son, who wished to become a lawyer. Lengthy introduction comments on the letter's background and the nature of its advice.

2698.   Colbourn, H. Trevor, ed. "The Reading of Joseph Carrington Cabell: 'A List of Books on Various Subjects Recommended to a Young Man ...'." Studies in Bibliography. 13(1960), 179-88.

Prints and comments on four reading lists given to Joseph C. Cabell, two of them from TJ.

2699. Collins, Peter. "Origins of Graph Paper as an Influence on Architectural Design." Journal of the Society of Architectural Historians. 21(1962), 159-62.

Meticulous account of TJ's early use of graph paper, but refrains from calling him the inventor of this method, although there is no evidence for anyone before him.

*2700. Coolidge, Harold T. "'Plan for a Botanick Garden...'." Bulletin of the Pacific Tropical Botanical Garden. 1(April 1971), 6-7.

2701. Cometti, Elizabeth, Ed. Jefferson's Ideas on a University Library. Charlottesville: Tracy W. McGregor Library, 1950. pp. 49.

Letters to Wm. Hilliard, Boston bookseller, pertinent to acquisitions for the new University. Interesting introduction by the editor.

2702. Cometti, Elizabeth. "Maria Cosway's Rediscovered Miniature of Jefferson." WMQ. 3rd ser. 9(1952), 152-55.

Miniature portrait by John Trumbull which TJ gave to Maria Cosway is rediscovered in Italy.

2703. Cometti, Elizabeth. "Mr. Jefferson Prepares an Itinerary." Journal of Southern History. 12(1946), 89-106.

Contends that TJ's travel notes prepared for John Rutledge, Jr. and Thomas Lee Shippen do not prove his philistinism as argued by Gilbert Chinard. Reprints the notes.

2704. Comstock, Helen. "Kosciuszko's Portrait of Thomas Jefferson." Connoisseur. 133(March 1954), 142-43.

Note on an aquatint portrait circa 1798 done by Kosciuszko.

2705. Comstock, Helen. "A Portrait of Jefferson in His Old Age." International Studio. 96(June, 1930), 17-18.

Reproduces and gives the history of the full-length portrait done by Thomas Sully in 1821.

2706. Conant, Howard S. "The Pursuit of Artistic Excellence." Intellect. 105(July 1976), 43-46.

Arts in America are not yet to the level TJ dreamed of.

2707. Conant, James. "Education for a Classless Society: The Jeffersonian Tradition." Atlantic Monthly. 165(1940), 593-602.

On the necessity of revitalizing the Jeffersonian tradition in education.

2708. Conant, James B. Thomas Jefferson and the Development of American Public Education. Berkeley: Univ. of California Press, 1962. pp. x, 164.

TJ was a genuine educational innovator who was concerned with education for everyone and at all levels; however, his notion of progressively selective education was not accepted, for "the doctrine of equality of status came in conflict with the notion of equality of opportunity." But the 1960's are different from previous times, and TJ's ideas are more relevant.

2709. Cooke, Giles B. and Clifton F. Schmidt, Jr. "Thomas Jefferson, Planter of Cork." The Crown (Crown Cork and Seal Co.). August 1943. 4 pp.

On TJ's efforts to introduce the cork oak in America, now being re-attempted during war time. Seen only as an offprint.

2710. [Cooke, John Esten]. The Youth of Jefferson or a Chronicle of College Scrapes at Williamsburg in Virginia, A.D. 1764. New York: Redfield, 1854. pp. 249.

Fiction.

2711. Coonen, Lester P. and Charlotte M. Porter. "Thomas Jefferson and American Biology." BioScience. 26(1976), 745-50.

Informed, thorough survey.

2712. Courain, Liz, et. al. The Rotunda at the University of Virginia. Charlottesville: Univ. of Virginia Alumni Fund, n.d. Broadside.

Informative accordion-fold broadside for visitors to the Rotunda.

2713. Cox, James M. "Jefferson's Autobiography: Recovering Literature's Lost Ground." Southern Review. 14(1978), 633-52.

Argues that TJ is a much more significant writer for American literature than Jonathan Edwards. His memoir (not referred to as an autobiography until the 20th century) shows how TJ's "life is, first of all, his writing." He suppresses his self "in order to make a life of representation and a representative life." He tends "toward seeing his life as a result of the history he has made by writing." Goes on to infer a "symbolic narrative" in the Autobiography, concerned with parricides and patrimonies.

2714. Cox, Nancy Lampton. Grandpappa Jefferson: Jefferson and His Grand-children at Monticello. New York: Vantage, 1973. pp. 48.

Juvenile fiction.

2715. Cox, R. Merritt. "Thomas Jefferson and Spanish: 'To Every Inhabitant, Who Means to Look Beyond the Limits of His Farm.'" Romance

Notes. 14(Autumn 1972), 116-21.

Note on TJ's interest in Spanish language and culture and his encouragement of others to study it.

2716.   Cox, Stephen D. "The Literary Aesthetic of Thomas Jefferson" in _Essays in Early Virginia Literature Honoring Richard Beale Davis_, ed. J. A. Leo Lemay. New York: Burt Franklin, 1977. 235-56.

Although TJ's critical statements on literary matters are scattered, he clearly valued emotive force in written expression, applying the term sublime rather generally to whatever he liked, but he did not divorce his sense of the sublime from the function of reason and the need for an ordered lucidity.

2717.   Cox, Warren. "The Mood of a Great Campus." _Architectural Forum._ 116(February 1962), 74-82.

TJ's architecture establishes his spirit at the Univ. of Virginia; mostly photographs. Rpt. _Univ. of Virginia Alumni News._ 48(March 1962), 4-12.

2718.   [Craig, Neville, B.?]. "Logan's Speech." _The Olden Time._ 2(1847), 49-67.

Full account of the controversy over Logan's speech; concludes that Logan gave a speech, but not that passing under his name, and TJ acted in good faith when writing the _Notes._

2719.   Crenshaw, Frank S. "Major Architectural Designs of Thomas Jefferson. The Executed and Non-executed Residential Designs and Executed Non-residential Designs." M.A. thesis. Univ. of Virginia, 1961. pp. 98.

Documents a variety of structures TJ had a hand in.

2720.   Cripe, Helen. "Music: Thomas Jefferson's Delightful Recreation." _Antiques._ 102(July 1972), 124-28.

Discusses instruments TJ bought or owned.

2721.   Cripe, Helen Louise Petts. "Thomas Jefferson and Music." Ph.D. dissertation. Univ. of Notre Dame, 1972. pp. 294.

Revised and published as the following item. DAI 33/04A, p. 1632.

2722.   Cripe, Helen. _Thomas Jefferson and Music._ Charlottesville: Univ. Press of Virginia, 1974. pp. xiv, 157.

A documented account of TJ's musical life, of the musical milieu in which he moved, the music he enjoyed, and the instruments he played. Reprints the 1783 catalogue of his music library and a catalogue of the Monticello music collection. Best book on this; authoritative.

2723. Culbreth, David M. R. The University of Virginia: Memories of Her Student-Life and Professors. New York: Neale, 1908. pp. 502.

Pp. 21-153 are on TJ as founder and planner.

2724. Cunningham, Noble E., Jr. The Image of Thomas Jefferson in the Public Eye: Portraits for the People, 1800-1809. Charlottesville: Univ. Press of Virginia, 1981. pp. xvii, 185.

Excellent illustrated study of contemporary portraits, engravings, medals, caricatures, etc.

2725. Cutright, Paul Russell. "Jefferson's Instructions to Lewis and Clark." Bulletin of the Missouri Historical Society. 22(1966), 302-20.

Discusses the rationale and motives behind TJ's instructions to Lewis and Clark, particularly in regard to the collection of scientific data.

2726. Cutright, Paul Russell. "Meriwether Lewis Prepares for a Trip West." Bulletin of the Missouri Historical Society. 23(1966), 3-20.

Lewis responds to TJ's instructions as he lays in supplies and equipment.

2727. Cutright, Paul Russell. "The Odyssey of the Magpie and Prairie Dog." Bulletin of the Missouri Historical Society. 23(1967), 215-28.

Account of the live specimens sent by Lewis and Clark in 1805.

2728. Dabney, Charles William. "Education and Democracy" in Universal Education in the South. Chapel Hill: Univ. of North Carolina Press, 1936. 1:3-21.

Covers TJ's plans for a Virginia school system; its weakness was its failure to provide for general supervision or leadership.

2729. Dabney, Charles W. Jefferson the Seer: An Address before the Conference for Education in the South in Session at the University of Virginia on April 25, 1903. n.p., n.d. pp. 15.

Praises TJ's educational ideals.

2730. Dabney, Virginius. "Today's University: Viewed in the Light of Its Founder's Dream." Virginia Journal of Education. 69(September 1966), 15-19.

2731. Daiker, Virginia. "The Capitol of Jefferson and Latrobe." Quarterly Journal of the Library of Congress. 32(1975), 25-32.

Discusses TJ's and Latrobe's correspondence on the design of the Capitol building.

2732. Daniel, Thomas Harrison. "Monticello." Watson's Jeffersonian Magazine. 1(1907), 575.

Poem.

2733. Darcy, Sam. The Second Revolution: The Ordeal and Dramatic Triumph of Thomas Jefferson. A Play in Three Acts. Chicago: Adams Press, 1977. pp. iv, 65.

Large cast, stilted dialogue, federalists as villains; focus on the election of 1800.

2734. Darling, J. S., ed. A Jefferson Music Book; Keyboard Pieces, Some with Violin Accompaniment. Williamsburg: Colonial Williamsburg Foundation, 1977. pp. x, 42.

Preface and notes, facsimiles of the music.

2735. Davenport, William L. "Collecting Jeffersoniana." Hobbies. 81(November 1976), 115-17.

Advice for those interested in collecting material relevant to TJ.

2736. Davis, Betty Elise. Young Tom Jefferson's Adventure Chest. New York: M. S. Mill, 1942. pp. 249.

Juvenile fiction.

2737. Davis, Richard Beale. The Abbé Corea in America, 1812-1820. The Contributions of the Diplomat and Natural Philosopher to the Foundations of Our National Life. Correspondence with Jefferson and Other Members of the American Philosophical Society and with Other Prominent Americans. Transactions of the APS. n. s. 45(part 2, 1955), 87-197.

The introduction focuses on Corea, but a sizeable portion of the well-annotated correspondence is to or from TJ.

2738. Davis, Richard Beale. A Colonial Southern Bookshelf; Reading in The Eighteenth Century. Athens: Univ. of Georgia Press, 1979. pp. x, 140.

Analyzes libraries and book holdings in the colonial South; TJ and his books discussed passim.

2739. Davis, Richard Beale. "Forgotten Scientists in Old Virginia." VMHB. 46(1938), 97-111.

TJ introduced Francis Walker Gilmer to the Abbé Corea and
encouraged interest in science in Virginia after 1800.

2740. Davis, Richard Beale. Intellectual Life in Jefferson's Virginia 1790-
1830. Chapel Hill: Univ. of North Carolina Press, 1964. pp. x, 507.

Examines a wide range of activity by a large number of characters,
but contains a great deal of information about TJ throughout. Very
useful for background.

2741. Davis, Richard Beale. "Jefferson as Collector of Virginiana." Studies
in Bibliography. 14(1961), 117-44.

Analyzes TJ's holdings; he "had posterity more in mind when he
acquired Virginiana than he did when gathering more general
materials." Rpt. with an added note in Literature and Society in
Early Virginia, 1608-1840. Baton Rouge: Louisiana State Univ. Press,
1973. 192-232.

2742. Davis, Richard Beale. "John Holt Rice vs. Thomas Jefferson on the
Great Deluge." VMHB. 74(1966), 108-09.

Rice made a marginal note in his copy of the Notes, arguing for
miraculous action in putting fossils on mountain tops.

2743. Davis, Richard Beale, ed. "A Postscript on Thomas Jefferson and His
University Professors." Journal of Southern History. 12(1946),
422-32.

Transcribes five letters to Francis Walker Gilmer about the search
for a faculty for the new university, with notes and commentary.
Letters not in Davis's Correspondence of TJ and Gilmer.

2744. Davis, Thurston N. and R. Freeman Butts. "Footnote on Church-State;
'Say Nothing of My Religion.'" School and Society. 81(1955), 180-87.

A debate over TJ's opinions on the proper relationship between
religious instruction and public education. Father Davis accuses
Butts of incorrectly turning TJ into an "ardent secularist"; Butts
points to TJ's insistence that schools of religion be independent of the
University of Virginia.

2745. "Death of Jefferson, July 4, 1826." Overland. n.s. 83(July 1925), 282.

Poem.

2746. DeTerra, Helmut, ed. "Alexander von Humboldt's Correspondence with
Jefferson, Madison and Gallatin." Proceedings of the APS.
103(1959), 783-806.

Humboldt in 1804 visited TJ, who was interested in his information on
Spanish America and in his scientific observation.

2747. DeTerra, Helmut. "Motives and Consequences of Alexander von Humboldt's Visit to the United States." Proceedings of the APS. 104(1960), 314-16.

Focus on Humboldt; TJ mentioned—meeting of the two in Washington was "the moral climax of Humboldt's American travels."

2748. De Vere, Maximilian Schele. "Mr. Jefferson's Pet." Harper's Magazine. 44(1872), 815-26.

On TJ and the founding of the University.

2749. Dickson, Harold E. "'Th.J.' Art Collector" in Jefferson and the Arts: An Extended View, ed. William Howard Adams. Washington: National Gallery of Art, 1976. 101-32.

Discusses aesthetic treatises which shaped TJ's taste, his acquisition and display of paintings and sculpture, and the eventual disposition of his collection. Claims that by 1790 TJ's collecting interests had moved from the "rather haphazard" to focus on representations of eminent men and things pertinent to American history.

2750. Dies, Edward Jerome. "Thomas Jefferson; Farmer of Monticello" in Titans of the Soil: Great Builders of Agriculture. Chapel Hill: Univ. of North Carolina Press, 1949. 21-29.

Sketch with emphasis on agricultural interests.

2751. Dillon, Richard. "Jefferson's Grand Design" in Meriwether Lewis, A Biography. New York: Coward-McCann, 1965. 1-5.

TJ's interests in the western territories and his visions of exploration presented as a key to Lewis's career.

2752. Dillon, Wilton S. Thomas Jefferson on Foreign Education. Phelps-Stokes Fund Occasional Papers No. 6. May, 1962. pp. 6.

TJ's advice for young Americans to be educated at home is similar to present day policies of countries such as Ghana. Reprints TJ's letter of October 15, 1785 to J. Bannister, Jr.

2753. Donnelly, Marian C. "Jefferson's Observatory Design." Journal of the Society of Architectural Historians. 36(1977), 33-35.

TJ's proposed observatory on Montalto next to Monticello was architecturally conservative, and the astronomical problems were not carefully considered as they were in the tower built by David Rittenhouse.

2754. Dorsey, John M., ed. The Jefferson-Dunglison Letters. Charlottesville: Univ. of Virginia Press, 1960. pp. 120.

360

Correspondence between TJ and Robley Dunglison, the physician he brought from London to be on the faculty of the University. Appendix discusses TJ's medical ideas.

2755. Dorough, C. Dwight. "Preach, My Dear Sir, a Crusade Against Ignorance." Phi Delta Kappan. 40(April 1959), 272-76.

TJ's work for education.

2756. Dos Passos, John. "Builders for a Golden Age." American Heritage. 10(August 1959), 65-77.

On TJ and architecture; misleadingly suggests he was inspired by Greek architecture. Adapted from the author's Prospects of a Golden Age. Englewood Cliffs, N.J.: Prentice-Hall, 1959.

*2757. Drake, G. W. J. "Jefferson and Vaccination." Virginia Medical Semi-Monthly. 4(1899), 5.

2758. Dresser, Louisa. "A Life Portrait of Thomas Jefferson." Worcester Art Museum News Bulletin. 17(no. 3, 1951), 9-10.

Note on the St. Memin drawing.

2759. Duboy, Philippe. "Thomas Jefferson, homme politique, et Charles-Louis Clérisseau, architect." Les Monuments Historiques de la France. 2(1976), 14-21.

"Jefferson illustre bien la 'conscience ambiguee' de l'intellectuel radical américain qui reconnaît certes les bases du système 'democratique' mais s'oppose à ses manifestations concrètes."

2760. Dumbauld, Edward. "Jefferson and Adams' English Garden Tour" in Jefferson and the Arts: An Extended View, ed. William Howard Adams. Washington: National Gallery of Art, 1976. 133-57.

Documents their visits to English estates: helpful.

2761. Dumbauld, Edward. "A Manuscript from Monticello: Jefferson's Library in Legal History." American Bar Association Journal. 38(1952), 389-92; 446-47.

TJ's library contained valuable legal mss. and a unique copy of the Virginia statutes from 1734 to 1772. The courts often treated his library as being in effect a depository of public records. Hening's Statutes at Large were in part a result of TJ's legal and historical scholarship.

2762. Dunbar, Gary S. "Thomas Jefferson, Geographer." Special Libraries Association. Geography and Map Division. Bulletin. No. 40(April 1960), 11-16.

TJ is best known to geographers for his studies in weather and climate, although a legitimate claim could be made for him as the Father of American Geography on the basis of the Notes.

2763.   D'Urso, Salvatore. "The Classical Liberalism of Robert M. Hutchins." Teachers College Record. 80(1978), 336-55.

Argues that much of Hutchin's philosophy derives from the classical liberalism of Locke and TJ.

2764.   Dwight, H. G. "Jeffersonian Simplicity." Harper's. 169(1934), 91-99.

TJ's success was an accident of history and luck; he is overrated as an architect and did not practice the simple life he is believed to have preached.

2765.   Eames, Charles and Ray. The World of Franklin and Jefferson. Washington: American Revolution Bicentennial Administration, 1976. pp. 77.

Handsomely illustrated catalogue of a bicentennial year museum exhibit covering TJ, his life and associates. Supporting text.

2766.   Echeverria, Durand. Mirage in the West: A History of the French Image of American Society to 1815. Princeton: Princeton Univ. Press, 1957. pp. xvii, 300.

TJ dealt with passim as a preeminent representer of American landscape, society and politics to a French audience.

2767.   Eddy, Helen L. "Thomas Jefferson's Land Practices." Land Policy Review. 7(Fall 1944), 22-25.

Brief survey.

2768.   Edward, Brother C. "Jefferson, Sullivan, and the Moose." American History Illustrated. 9(November 1974), 18-19.

Sketchy account of the moose hide and bones sent to Buffon.

2769.   Edwards, Everett E. Jefferson and Agriculture: A Sourcebook. Washington: U.S. Department of Agriculture, 1943. pp. iv, 93.

Rpts. papers by Henry A. Wallace and M. L. Wilson and collects statements by TJ on farming.

2770.   Edwards, Everett E. "The National Agricultural Jefferson Bicentenary Committee, Its Activities and Recommendations." Agricultural History. 19(1945), 167-78.

Farmers and historians pay tribute to TJ; notes activities of many agriculturally related groups.

2771. Edwards, Everett E. Washington, Jefferson, Lincoln and Agriculture. Washington: Bureau of Agricultural Economics, 1937. pp. 102.

Extracts from original material discussing farming.

2772. Egbert, Donald Drew. "A Bust of Washington Owned by Jefferson." Record of the Museum of Historic Art, Princeton University. 6(no. 1/2, 1947), 3-4.

Provenance of a bust by William Rush;; rpt. in Art Quarterly. 11(Autumn 1948), 376-78.

2773. Eidlitz, Robert James. "Medals Relating to Thomas Jefferson." Numismatist. 37(1924), 525-33.

Describes 48 medallic portraits; 10 illustrated.

2774. Ellsworth, Edward W. "Lincoln and the Education Convention: Education in Illinois—A Jeffersonian Heritage." Lincoln Herald. 80(no. 2, 1978), 69-78.

TJ's belief in education inspired Illinois residents from 1820-1855; Lincoln represented Sangamon County at the State General Education convention, showing a Jeffersonian faith in education for citizenship and a respect for the utilitarian needs of the frontier.

2775. Ernest, Joseph E. and H. Roy Merrens. "Praxis and Theory in the Writing of American Historical Geography." Journal of Historical Geography. 4(1978), 277-90.

Discusses Notes as an example of how subjective elements in an observer's personality affect the use of sources. Claims TJ had a vision of Virginia's future as the emporium of the West and this affected his discussion of "navigable waters."

*2776. Eubanks, Seaford W. "A Vocabulary Study of Thomas Jefferson's Notes on the State of Virginia." M.A. thesis. Univ. of Missouri, 1940.

2777. "Eulogies on Jefferson and Adams." American Quarterly Review. 1(1826), 54-77.

Reviews A Selection of Eulogies (1826); concentrates on the rhetorical performance of the speakers and has little to say about TJ and Adams.

2778. Ewan, Joseph. "How Many Botany Books Did Thomas Jefferson Own?" Missouri Botanical Garden Bulletin. 64(June 1976), unpag.

Informative but brief article on TJ's botanical knowledge and his botanical friends.

2779. Ewers, John C. "'Chiefs from the Missouri and Mississippi' and Peale's Silhouettes of 1806." Smithsonian Journal of History. 1(Spring 1966), 1-26.

Charles Willson Peale cut and sent to TJ silhouettes of members of the second delegation from tribes west of the Mississippi to visit Washington. Much information on the delegation's trip and reception.

2780. Fahy, Everett P., Jr. "The Sully Portrait of Jefferson." Univ. of Virginia Magazine. 124(February 1962), 22-24.

History of Sully's two portraits, the life study and the full length portrait.

2781. Fairley, Margaret Tynes. Mr. Jefferson and the Crocus. Charlottesville: The Author, 1952. pp. 12.

Contains four poems on TJ.

*2782. "Farmington." Historic Preservation. 10(no. 10, 1958), 22-23.

2783. Farrison, W. Edward. "Clotel, Thomas Jefferson, and Sally Hemings." College Language Association Journal. 17(1973) 147-74.

Good account of the development of the "Black Sal" legend and of the subsequent history of the Hemings family, but does not always treat sources critically.

2784. Farrison, William Edward. "Introduction" to Clotel; or The President's Daughter, William Wells Brown. New York: Citadel, 1969. 7-11.

Chronology of Clotel indicates TJ could not be father of Clotel or Althea.

2785. Farrison, W. Edward. "Origins of Brown's Clotel." Phylon. 15(1954), 347-54.

One source of William Wells Brown's novel was the Callender scandal about Sally Hemings.

2786. Faulkner, William Harrison. "The University of Virginia; Thomas Jefferson Architect." Indoors and Out. 3(December 1906), 103-13.

Illustrated account of TJ's plans.

2787. Faust, Joan Lee. "The Gardens at Monticello." Americana. 1(September 1973), 6-8.

Brief account of the flower gardens; illustrated.

2788. Ferguson, Eugene S. "Mr. Jefferson's Dry Docks." American Neptune. 11(1951), 108-14.

Details, both technical and political, on TJ's proposal to build a covered drydock at Washington large enough to hold 12 Constitution-class frigates.

2789. Ferguson, Henry N. "The Man Who Saved Monticello." American History Illustrated. 14(February 1980), 20-27.

On TJ, Monticello, and Uriah Phillips Levy's acquistion and renovation of it.

2790. Ferguson, Robert A. "'Mysterious Obligation': Jefferson's Notes on the State of Virginia." American Literature. 52(1980), 381-406.

Argues that TJ's Notes is an attempt to control the chaos he felt to be around him in the early 1780's, and to understand its coherent structure we must recognize the way in which it "turns upon English common law and the great, humanistic legal compendia of the Enlightenment." Suggestive.

2791. Fisher, Marvin. "An Answer to Jefferson on Manufactures." South Atlantic Quarterly. 61(1962), 345-53.

Argues that the best answer to TJ's Query xix in Notes is found in the reports of European travelers in America.

2792. Fitzhugh, Thomas, ed. Letters of Thomas Jefferson Concerning Philology and the Classics. Charlottesville: Univ. of Virginia, 1919. pp. 75.

About TJ's opinions on study of the classics and his educational plans for Virginia. "Reprinted from the Alumni Bulletin for April, 1918, October, 1918, and January and April, 1919."

2793. Flexner, James Thomas. "The Great Columbian Federal City." American Art Journal. 2(Spring 1970), 30-45.

The general assumption that the plan of Washington, D.C. results from the cooperation of TJ and L'Enfant is wrong; TJ looked on disapprovingly and was pleased when L'Enfant was discharged.

2794. Foley, Donald J. "Two Presidents Who Loved to Garden." Horticulture. 29(February 1951), 43.

Note on TJ and Washington as gardeners.

2795. Ford, Paul Leicester. "Jefferson's Notes on Virginia." Nation. 58(1894), 80-81, 98-99.

Discusses TJ's early revisions of the Notes.

2796. Ford, Susan. "Thomas Jefferson and John Adams on the Classics." Arion: A Journal of Humanities and the Classics. 6(Spring 1967), 116-32.

Editorial comment stringing together bits on the classics from their correspondence.

2797. Founder's Day Concert by the Glee Club Assisted by Members of the Concert Band in Honor of the Two Hundredth Anniversary of the Birth of Thomas Jefferson. Charlottesville: Univ. of Virginia, Division of Music, 1943. pp. ix.

Contains program notes by Helen Duprey Bullock and words for all songs, including texts for Randall Thompson's "Testament of Freedom" in its premiere performance.

2798. Fox, Mary Virginia. Treasure of the Revolution. New York: Abingdon, 1961. pp. 191.

Juvenile fiction; protagonists are fictional Randolph cousins of TJ during the British invasion of Virginia.

2799. Frary, Ihna Thayer. Thomas Jefferson, Architect and Builder. Richmond: Garrett and Massie, 1931. pp. xv, 139.

Discusses TJ's architecture with perhaps more enthusiasm than scholarship. Numerous illustrations. Rpt. 1939, 1950.

2800. Frary, Ihna T. "Virginia's Greatest Architect." Commonwealth, The Magazine of Virginia. 2(April 1935), 7-9.

Sketch.

2801. Fraser, Alexander David. "Thomas Jefferson, Field Archaeologist." Fine Arts, Dedicated to Artistic Virginia. 2(1935), 3-4, 15.

Account of TJ's excavation of an Indian mound.

2802. Friis, Herman R. "Alexander von Humboldt's Besuch in den Vereinigten Staaten von Amerika Vom 20. Mai bis zum 30. Juni 1804" in Alexander von Humboldt: Studien zu seiner unwersalen Geisteshaltung, ed. Joachim Schultze. Berlin: Walter de Gruyter & Co., 1959. 142-95.

Argues strongly that Humboldt did not visit TJ at Monticello.

366

2803. [Frye, Melinda Young]. Thomas Jefferson and Wine in Early America, Art and artifacts reflecting the cultural history of wine in the Colonies and the early Republic. San Francisco: The Wine Museum of San Francisco, 1976. pp. 24.

"Foreward" by Ernest G. Mittelberger; generalized comments on TJ and wine.

2804. Fuld Melvin. "Some Medals of Thomas Jefferson." Numismatist. 83(1970), 24.

2805. Fuller, Albert. "Thomas Jefferson and Music." High Fidelity and Musical America. 26(July 1976), 51.

Short generality.

2806. Fulling, Edward H. "Thomas Jefferson: His Interest in Plant Life as Revealed in His Writings." Bulletin of the Torrey Botanical Club. 71(1944), 563-98; 72(1945), 248-70.

Extensive survey of TJ's botanical interests and comments. Finds his botanical claim to fame rests not in adding to contemporary understanding of plants but in encouraging botanical activities on the Lewis and Clark expedition and at the Univ. of Virginia.

2807. "The Fur Cloak, A Reminiscence." The Token and Atlantic Souvenir. Boston: Gray and Bowen, 1833. 342-50.

Young woman wrapped by TJ in his fur cloak later hears how Kosciuszko was given the cloak by the Czar; fictional sketch.

2808. Gaines, William H. "Under a Jeffersonian Dome." Virginia Cavalcade. 5(Summer 1955), 20-25.

On the Rotunda.

2809. Gaither, Frances O. J. The Shadow of the Builder; The Centennial Pageant of the University of Virginia, As Presented on the Night June First, Nineteen Hundred Twenty-One. Charlottesville: Surber-Arundale, 1921. pp. 36.

Pageant in which TJ and the shade of Socrates rub elbows.

2810. Galtier, Gaston. La viticulture de l'Europe Occidentale à la veille de la Revolution francaise, d'après les notes de voyage de Thomas Jefferson. Montpellier: La journee vinicole, 1953. pp. 72.

Examines TJ's letters and notes of travel in France in 1787 and 1788 as essential documents for understanding the state of viticulture and the wine trade just prior to the Revolution. Claims TJ was interested in wine as a connoisseur, not with any eye toward establishing wineries in America.

2811. Garbett, Arthur S. "Thomas Jefferson's Life-Long Love of Music." Etude. 59(1941), 510, 568.

Chatty sketch.

2812. "Gardening President." House and Garden. 79(June 1941), 19.

2813. Garnett, W. E. "What Would Jefferson Say?" Virginia Journal of Education. 36(April 1943), 298-310.

He would want education for democracy and equality.

2814. Garrett, Wendell. "Mather Brown Portraits of Jefferson." Antiques. 106(1974), 82-83.

Note.

2815. Gassner, John. "Jefferson and Hamilton in Drama." Current History. n.s. 4(1943), 88-91.

Discusses Sidney Kingsley's The Patriots as drama and history; TJ may not be treated with absolute historical accuracy, but the play is still "another peak in the American theater."

2816. Gauss, Charles Edward. "Thomas Jefferson's Musical Interests." Etude. 51(1933), 367-68, 419.

Covers TJ's musicianship and interest in technological improvements, e.g. the metronome, Hopkinson's harpsichord improvements, etc.

2817. Geer, Henry Burns. "Thomas Jefferson on Pre-historic Americans." American Antiquarian and Oriental Journal. 24(1902), 224-28.

Reprints with minimal comment TJ's account of excavating an Indian mound.

2818. Gelder, Dorothy Beall. "The World of Music—For Thomas Jefferson and Other Presidents." Daughters of the American Revolution Magazine. 105(1971), 403-07, 475.

Focus on TJ; survey.

2819. Gerbi, Antonello. La Disputa del Nuovo Mondo: Storia di Una Polemica, 1750-1900. Milano: R. Ricciardi, 1955. pp. x, 783.

Revised and enlarged edition translated by Jeremy Moyle as The Dispute of the New World: The History of a Polemic, 1750-1900. Pittsburgh: Univ. of Pittsburgh Press, 1973. Discusses on pp.252-68 (1973) the role TJ and his Notes played in the response to Buffon's

368

theory concerning the inferiority of New World life forms. The best account of the whole controversy in its broadest outlines.

2820. Gibbs, James W. "Thomas Jefferson's 'Wonderful Clock'." Bulletin of the National Association of Watch and Clock Collectors. 16(December 1973), 56.

On the great clock at Monticello.

2821. Gillespie, A. H. "Thomas Jefferson's Monticello." American Landscape Architecture. 6(May 1932), 20-23.

Description.

2822. Gittleman, Edwin. "Jefferson's 'Slave Narrative': The Declaration of Independence as a Literary Text." Early American Literature. 8(1974), 239-56.

A close rhetorical analysis of the Declaration. Contends that it is unified by an underlying theme of slavery under tyranny, and that TJ's rejected slavery grievance was an essential element of the text's rhetorical progression and of its logic.

2823. Glass, Powell. "Jefferson and Plant Introduction." National Horticultural Magazine. 23(July 1944), 127-31.

Surveys TJ's interest in naturalizing plants such as upland rice, the olive, and the cork oak.

2824. Glassburn, Dorothy E. "Thomas Jefferson and the Thorne American Rooms." Carnegie Magazine. 16(November 1942), 180-82.

On a miniature of the Monticello dining and tea room by Mrs. James W. Thorne.

2825. Glenn, Frank. Quotation. Books from the Library of Thomas Jefferson. Kansas City, Mo., 1953. Broadside.

Offers for sale 6 volumes from TJ's library, including a copy of Volney's Ruins presented to Martha Jefferson Randolph by Nicholas Trist.

2826. Glenn, Garrard. "The University Created by Thomas Jefferson." Travel. 68(March 1937), 60-61.

Architectural and historical bits for potential tourists.

2827. Goff, Frederick R. "Freedom of Challenge (The 'Great' Library of Thomas Jefferson)" in Thomas Jefferson and the World of Books. Washington: Library of Congress, 1977. 9-17.

TJ's library as core and spiritual model of the Library of Congress.

2828. Goff, Frederick R. "Jefferson the Book Collector." Quarterly Journal of the Library of Congress. 29(1972), 32-47.

Principally describes the library sold to the nation in 1815; also comments on other L. C. acquisitions of books once in TJ's holdings.

2829. Goff, Frederick R. "T.I.: Mr. Jefferson's Books in Washington, D.C." in Records of the Columbia Historical Society of Washington, D.C. The Fiftieth Volume, ed. Francis Coleman Rosenberger. Washington: The Society, 1980. 81-94.

Describes TJ's activities as book collector; "T.I." refers to his well-known method of marking his books.

2830. Gold, Arthur and Robert Fizdale. "Bicentennial Dishes, Thomas Jefferson Style." Vogue. 166(July 1976), 137-38+.

Note on food, recipes.

2831. Granquist, Charles L. "Thomas Jefferson's 'Whirligig' Chairs." Antiques. 109(May 1976), 1056-60.

Informative account of TJ's two revolving chairs and related furniture.

2832. Greely, Arthur W. "Jefferson as a Geographer." National Geographic Magazine. 7(1896), 269-71.

General discussion of TJ's geographical interests.

2833. Greely, Arthur W. "Jefferson as a Geographer" in The Writings of Thomas Jefferson, ed. Lipscomb and Bergh. Washington: Thomas Jefferson Memorial Association, 1903. 13:i-vii.

Revision of previous item.

2834. Green, Kevin W. "Passive Cooling." Research & Design, The Quarterly of the AIA Research Corporation. 2(Fall 1979), 4-9.

Interesting account of the cooling strategies TJ used at Monticello: thick masonry walls, maximized ventilation, bringing shaded air into the house, etc.

2835. Green, Paul. The Common Glory. A Symphonic Drama of American History With Music, Commentary, English Folksong and Dance. Chapel Hill: Univ. of North Carolina Press, 1948. pp. ix, 273.

Pageant drama concerning the American Revolution in which TJ is a central character; the play closes with him on the bluffs of

Richmond, musing about the new nation. Bicentennial edition, revised and rewritten, published in New York: Samuel French, 1976.

2836.   Green, Paul. This Declaration: A Play in One Act. New York: Samuel French, 1954. pp. 20.

TJ and the committee to write the Declaration disagree over the importance of property.

2837.   Greene, John C. "Science and the Public in the Age of Jefferson." Isis. 49(1958), 13-25.

Background study, concluding that "scientists of Jefferson's day found their countrymen all too little interested in science" and they appealed to their patriotism, civic pride, utilitarian spirit, and to natural theology in order to cultivate an interest.

2838.   Greenlaw, Edwin. "Washington Irving's Comedy of Politics." Texas Review. 1(1916), 291-306.

Discusses Irving's satire of the Jeffersonians in the Knickerbocker History and identifies William the Testy as a "philosophic governor ... often suggestive of the Federalist opinion of Jefferson."

2839.   Gregory, Horace. "Our Writers and the Democratic Myth." Bookman. 75(1932), 377-82.

Contends H. L. Mencken, Vachel Lindsay, E. L. Masters, et. al. are passe because their version of the "heritage of the sage of Monticello" is "spiritually bankrupt."

2840.   [Griffin, Martin I. J., ed.]. "Thomas Jefferson Declares His Belief in the Good of Spiritual Paintings in Catholic Churches." American Catholic Historical Researches. 19(1902), 60.

Prints without comment an undated letter to Charles W. Peale.

2841.   Grigg, Milton L. "Restoration of Thomas Jefferson's Gardens at Monticello." Commonwealth, The Magazine of Virginia. 6(August 1939), 11-12.

TJ's ideas about gardens and attempts to realize them at Monticello.

2842.   Grigg, Milton L. "Thomas Jefferson and the Development of the National Capital." Records of the Columbian Historical Society. 53-56(1959), 81-100.

Surveys TJ's role in planning and design of Washington, D.C. in support of the contention that the form and architecture of the city today is his lengthened shadow.

2843. Griswold, A. Whitney. "Liberal Education and the Democratic Ideal" in Liberal Education and the Democratic Ideal. New Haven: Yale Univ. Press, 1959. 1-6.

Claims that TJ's scheme to rake the best geniuses from the soil is a democratic means of discovering and capitalizing for society the powers of worth and talent.

2844. "Guests and Gadgets." Christian Science Monitor Magazine. October 26, 1938. 15.

Monticello inventions.

2845. Guinness, Desmond and Julius Trousdale Sadler, Jr. Mr. Jefferson, Architect. New York: Viking, 1973. pp. 177.

A general survey, but generously illustrated.

2846. Guinness, Desmond and Julius Trousdale Sadler, Jr. "Thomas Jefferson: Architect." Albemarle Monthly. 2(June/July 1979), 19-29.

Emphasizes architecture at Univ. of Virginia.

2847. Guinness, Desmond. "Thomas Jefferson: Visionary Architect." Horizon. 22(April 1979), 50-55.

Comments on architecture for the University, with emphasis on the Rotunda.

2848. Gummere, Richard M. "Adams and Jefferson" in The American Colonial Mind and the Classical Tradition. Cambridge: Harvard Univ. Press, 1963. 191-97.

TJ's use of classical learning as evidenced in his correspondence with Adams.

2849. Guthrie, John D. "The Many-Sided Jefferson." Journal of Forestry. 42(April 1944), 237-42.

Sketch of TJ's scientific and technological interests.

2850. Hall, Courtney R. "Jefferson on the Medical Theory and Practice of His Day." Bulletin of the History of Medicine. 31(1957), 235-47.

Good account of Cabanis's influence on TJ, arguing that it was basic for his views of medicine.

2851. Halsey, Robert A. How the President Thomas Jefferson and Dr. Benjamin Waterhouse Established Vaccination as a Public Health Procedure. New York: New York Academy of Medicine, 1936. pp. 58.

Offers a nearly complete record of the correspondence on vaccination between TJ and Waterhouse, the first American physician to recognize the significance of Edward Jenner's discovery. In 1800 TJ successfully planted cowpox at Monticello and was distributing vaccination matter.

2852.   Hamlin, Talbot F. "A Previously Unpublished Perspective of the United States Capitol by B. H. Latrobe." Journal of the Society of Architectural Historians. 15(May 1956), 26-27.

A drawing Latrobe sent to TJ after a dispute about the design.

2853.   Hamlin, Talbot Faulkner. "Roman Influences in the South" in The American Spirit in Architecture. New Haven: Yale Univ. Press, 1926. 108-23.

TJ's enthusiasm for classic design deeply influenced the architecture of his region and that of the nation as a whole, particularly the official architecture.

2854.   Handler, Philip. "The University in a World in Transition." VQR. 46(1974), 177-97.

"How would the United States and its universities seem to Thomas Jefferson today?"

2855.   Hans, Nicholas. "The Project of Transferring the University of Geneval to America." History of Education Quarterly. 8(1968), 246-51.

Good account; deals with TJ's role in the negotiations.

2856.   Harbrecht, Rosemary. "Thomas Jefferson, Man of Culture." Social Studies. 41(1950), 258-60.

Sketch of TJ's interests in music, literature, and architecture.

2857.   Hart, Andrew De Jarnette, Jr. "Thomas Jefferson's Influence on the Foundation of Medical Instruction at the University of Virginia." Annals of Medical History. n.s. 10(1938), 47-60.

Discusses TJ's work for the University, particularly in terms of his search for a medical professor. He projected a broad training in fundamentals rather than in a narrowly practical course.

2858.   Hart, Charles Henry. "Life Portraits of Thomas Jefferson." McClure's Magazine. 11(1898), 47-55.

Reproduces seven portraits with commentary.

2859.   Haskell, Douglas. "Hamilton Captures Jefferson." Nation. 147(1938), 674.

"Lets not have an Andy Mellon memorial to the great Jefferson." Blames Mellon for picking John Russell Pope as architect of the Memorial.

2860. Haskins, Caryl P. "Mr. Jefferson's Sacred Gardens." VQR. 43(1967), 529-44.

TJ's interest in gardening and his correlative interest in natural history point to qualities that keep him relevant to later generations, his "wonder at the natural world" and his "dedication to vitality and innovation and growth and aspiration."

2861. Hastings, George E. "Notes on the Beginnings of Aeronautics in America." AHR. 25(1919), 68-72.

Describes the interest taken by TJ, Franklin, and Francis Hopkinson in hot air balloons.

2862. Hausmann, Ruth H. "Jefferson at Monticello." School Life. 18(January 1933), 90.

Poem.

2863. Hawke, David Freeman. Those Tremendous Mountains: The Story of the Lewis and Clark Expedition. New York: Norton, 1980. pp. xvi, 273.

Popular history; pp. 3-22 deal with TJ's initiation of and instructions to the expedition. Nothing new.

2864. Haworth, Paul Leland. "Thomas Jefferson—Poet." Bookman. 31(1910), 647-50.

Claims the poem "Lovely Peggy" in mss. at the Historical Society of Pennsylvania Library was in fact written by TJ and not merely copied. Highly dubious.

2865. Hazelton, Jean Hanvey. "Thomas Jefferson, Gourmet." American Heritage. 15(October 1964), 20-21, 102-05.

Discusses TJ's meals as prepared by his maître de hôtel, Etienne Lemaire, from 1806 to 1809; information gathered from Lemaire's Day Book.

2866. Healey, Robert Mathieu. "Jefferson on Religion in Public Education." Ph.D. dissertation. Yale Univ., 1959.

See following item.

2867. Healey, Robert M. Jefferson on Religion in Public Education. New Haven: Yale Univ. Press, 1962. pp. xi, 294.

Argues that TJ's belief in the principle of separation of church and
state and his belief in the importance of public education were not
mutually dependent but were "parallel developments rooted equally in
his total philosophy" and were both essential to democracy. Rpt.
Hamden, Conn.: Shoe String Press, 1970.

2868.   Heatwole, Cornelius J. "Thomas Jefferson and Education in Virginia."
        Virginia Journal of Education. 17(1924), 282-84.

        Historical sketch.

2869.   Heatwole, C. J. "Thomas Jefferson as an Architect." Virginia Journal
        of Education. 19(1926), 361-63.

        TJ's "influence on American architecture is evidenced everywhere in
        this country, particularly in the South."

2870.   Hellman, C. Doris. "Jefferson's Efforts towards the Decimilization of
        the United States Weights and Measures." Isis. 16(1931), 266-314.

        TJ in 1783 worked for the decimilization of coinage and later pro-
        posed similar rationalizations for all weights and measures. Although
        Congress took no action on this, he continued to promote the idea in
        his correspondence.

2871.   Hench, Atcheson L. "Jefferson and Ossian." Modern Language Notes.
        43(1928), 537.

        Points to Chastellux's account of TJ on Ossian; minor.

2872.   Henderson, Alfred. "Jefferson and the Submarine." Alumni Bulletin
        of the University of Virginia. 3rd ser. 11(1918), 82-85.

        Only a paragraph on TJ's correspondence with Fulton; rest is random
        jottings.

2873.   Henderson, John C. Thomas Jefferson's Views on Public Education.
        New York: Putnam's, 1890. pp. viii, 387.

        Discursive, unfocused.

2874.   Hendricks, Gordon. "A Wish to Please and a Willingness to Be Pleased."
        American Art Journal. 2(Spring 1970), 16-29.

        On Bass Otis and his portraits of TJ, Madison, and Monroe.

2875.   Henkels, Stan V. The Hampton L. Carson Collection of Engraved Por-
        traits of Jefferson, Franklin, and Lafayette. Catalogue 906, Part II.
        Compiled and Sale Conducted by Stan. V. Henkels. Philadelphia:
        Davis and Harvey, 1904. 1-20.

2876. Henline, Ruth. "A Study of Notes on the State of Virginia as an Evidence of Jefferson's Reaction against the Theories of the French Naturalists." VMHB. 55(1947), 233-46.

Contends the Notes are in part TJ's response to Buffon and his theory of the degeneration of species in the New World.

2877. Henneman, John B. "Two Pioneers in the Historical Study of English: Thomas Jefferson and Louis F. Klipstein." PMLA. 8(1893), xlii-xlix (Appendix).

The best early account of TJ's interest in Anglo-Saxon.

2878. "Herbert, Francis." "Ghosts on the Stage." The Talisman for 1830. New York: E. Bliss, 1829. 49-57.

Account of a visit to Monticello and a conversation with TJ demonstrating his love and knowledge of the classics and his opinions about presenting ghosts on stage in productions of plays like Hamlet, Macbeth, and some Greek tragedies. Interesting but perhaps fabulous.

2879. Herzberg, Max J. "Thomas Jefferson as a Man of Letters." South Atlantic Quarterly. 13(1914), 310-27.

TJ's writings on the whole are more interesting for historical value than for literary significance, except for the Declaration of Independence. All of his writings reveal the puzzling contradictions of his character.

2880. Heslep, Robert D. Thomas Jefferson and Education. New York: Random House, 1969. pp. 131.

Argues that TJ's view of education is important because it is grounded "on a fairly distinct philosophical basis" and can serve as a benchmark against which later programs' claims to be "democratic" can be exposed as lacking clarity and justification.

2881. Heslep, Robert Durham. "The Views of Jefferson and Dewey as Bases for Clarifying the Role of Education in an American Democratic State." Ph.D. dissertation. Univ. of Chicago, 1963.

See previous item.

2882. Hickey, Agnes McCarthy. "Monticello, The Home of Thomas Jefferson." Literary Digest. 101(April 13, 1929), 34.

A sonnet.

2883. Hicks, Clifford B. "Thomas Jefferson Lives Here." Popular Mechanics Magazine. 102(August 1954), 97-103, 212-16.

Illustrated article with emphasis on TJ's techniques of construction and on the restoration by the Memorial Foundation.

2884. Hillbruner, Anthony. "Word and Deed: Jefferson's Addresses to the Indians." Speech Monographs. 30(1963), 328-34.

"Simple logic and clear-cut structure were the major rhetorical features" of TJ's speeches to visiting Indians. Claims that after 1803 the tone of the addresses becomes paternal instead of fraternal, a response to changing historical and political pressures. Argues that TJ is a better speaker than he is given credit for, but that the evolving Indian policy revealed in the addresses shows him to be less of a democratic idealist than is sometimes thought.

2885. Hitchcock, Margaret R. "The Mastodon of Thomas Jefferson." Journal of the Washington Academy of Sciences. 21(1931), 80-86.

Describes the mastodon jawbones at the Univ. of Virginia which were given by TJ.

2886. Holmes, Lowell D. "Portrait in Science: Jefferson's Avocation." Natural History. 74(November 1965), 59-62.

Intelligent survey of TJ as an anthropologist, of his "visionary research methods and his role in promoting the collection and utilization of data."

2887. Honeywell, Roy J. The Educational Work of Thomas Jefferson. Cambridge: Harvard Univ. Press, 1931. pp. xvi, 295.

Argues that TJ was "among the foremost advocates of appropriate and progressive education for all, and of that cornerstone of democracy, the American public school." Still standard, but can be usefully supplemented. Rpt. in New York: Russell and Russell, 1964.

2888. Honeywell, Roy J. "A Note on the Educational Work of Thomas Jefferson." History of Education Quarterly. 9(1969), 64-72.

Surveys TJ's activities encouraging education.

2889. Hopkins, Frederick M. "Notes on Jefferson's Library." Publisher's Weekly. 139(1941), 1158-59, 1413.

Brief comment.

2890. Horn, Stanley F. "Thomas Jefferson on Lotteries and Education." Tennessee Historical Quarterly. 3(1944), 273-74.

Describes a letter of 1810 to the trustees in charge of a lottery for East Tennessee College; TJ disapproved of lotteries but gave advice on the ideal college.

2891.   Horn, William A. "The Jeffersonian Metrics." American Education.
         12(December 1976), inside cover.

         Note on TJ's proposed decimal measures.

2892.   Houlette, William D. "Books of the Virginia Dynasty." The Library
         Quarterly. 24(1954), 226-39.

         Discursive treatment of the reading and book-collecting habits of
         the first four presidents from Virginia; TJ discussed on pp. 229-35.

2893.   House, Ray. "Thomas Jefferson" in Some Souvenir Lines for the
         Bicentennial. Philadelplhia: Dorrance, 1975. 23-25.

         Poem.

2894.   "House." New Yorker. 34(June 14, 1958), 23-24.

         "Our man Stanley" reports on a visit to Monticello.

2895.   Howard, Seymour. "Thomas Jefferson's Art Gallery for Monticello."
         Art Bulletin. 59(1977), 583-600.

         On TJ's plans to acquire paintings and statues for Monticello. In the
         1770's and 1780's he most desired a copy of the Venus de Medicis, to
         which, reportedly, Martha Wayles Jefferson bore a striking resem-
         blance.

2896.   Howell, Wilbur Samuel. "The Declaration of Independence and
         Eighteenth-Century Logic." WMQ. 3rd ser. 18(1961), 463-84.

         Contends that "an unmistakable parallelism exists between the argu-
         mentative structure of the Declaration and the theory of argumenta-
         tive structure set forth in the most significant of the logics and
         rhetorics of Jefferson's time, particularly William Duncan's The
         Elements of Logick.

2897.   Howell, Wilbur Samuel. "The Declaration of Independence: Some
         Adventures with America's Political Masterpiece." Quarterly Journal
         of Speech. 62(1976), 221-33.

         Argues again for the rhetorical influence of William Duncan's
         Elements of Logick.

2898.   Howell, Wilbur Samuel. "Thomas Jefferson." Commentary.
         67(January 1979), 8-9.

         Summarizes two of his articles on rhetorical influences on the
         Declaration for the benefit of Garry Wills.

2899. Howland, William S. "The Oenologist of Monticello: Music, Art, Architecture, Poetry, Agriculture and Wine" in Jefferson and Wine, ed. R. deTreville Lawrence, Sr. The Plains, Va.: Vinifera Wine Grower's Association, 1976. 1-8.

Rambling survey of TJ's interest in wine and wine-making.

2900. Hubbard, William. "Looking at an Architecture of Convention" in Complicity and Conviction: Steps toward an Architecture of Convention. Cambridge: MIT Press, 1980. 159-201.

Interesting comparison of TJ's design for the Lawn at the Univ. of Virginia and the design for Kresge College at the Univ. of California at Santa Cruz. Claims the Lawn presents itself to us as a picture of what we could be.

2901. Hubbell, Jay Broadus. "Thomas Jefferson" in The South in American Literature. Durham: Duke Univ. Press, 1954. 122-34.

Surveys TJ's philosophy, discusses his literary interests, and comments on the literary quality of his writings. Notes of his style, "His comprehensive mind, like that ot Walt Whitman or Henry James, was too frequently unwilling to abandon qualifying phrases and clauses, even in the interest of the conciseness which he admired in Tacitus and Sallust."

2902. Hudnut, Joseph. "Classical Architecture Not Essential." Architectural Record. 82(August 1937), 54-55.

TJ himself was a progressive architect; on the Memorial design.

2903. Hudnut, Joseph. "Temple for Thomas Jefferson." New Republic. 98(1939), 190-91.

Criticizes the Jefferson Memorial for its pompously pretentious architecture.

2904. Hudnut, Joseph. "Twilight of the Gods." Magazine of Art. 30(1937), 480-84, 522-24.

Argues that the TJ Memorial has called into question the doctrinaire neo-classicism of Washington, D.C. Since TJ's own architecture was committed to his time, we should be committed to ours and consider the plan of Le Corbusier.

*2905. Huegli, Jon M. "Jeffersonian Rhetoric: Persistent Witness to Democratic Republicanism." M.A. thesis. Indiana Univ., 1967.

2906. Hughes, Robert. "Jefferson: Taste of the Founder." Time. 108(July 12, 1976), 51.

Report on the Eye of Thomas Jefferson exhibit.

2907. Humphrey, Henry B., Jr. "Homes of Our Presidents." Country Life. 50(May 1926), 37-39.

Derivative sketch.

2908. Hutcheson, John R. "A Tribute from the Land-Grant College Association." Agricultural History. 19(1945), 178.

TJ pioneered work carried on later by land-grant colleges.

2909. Huxtable, Ada Louise. "Jefferson's Virginia" in Kicked a Building Lately? New York: Quadrangle/New York Times Book Co., 1976. 198-202.

Discusses design for the Univ. of Virginia which "combines an intimate human scale with controlled, universal vistas." Originally in New York Times, March 9, 1975; rpt. as "Thomas Jefferson's Grand Paradox" in American Traditions: A House and Garden Guide. New York: House and Garden, 1976. 57.

2910. Huyck, Dorothy Boyle. "Thomas Jefferson's Greatest Service." The Iron Worker. 37(Summer 1973), 3-10.

TJ's service to agriculture, including the mouldboard of least resistance.

2911. Ide, John Jay. "A Discovery in Early American Portraiture: Portraits of John Jay and Thomas Jefferson by Caleb Boyle." Antiques. 25(1934), 99-100.

Identifies Boyle as painter of a portrait previously ascribed to Rembrandt Peale.

2912. "The Invisible Portrait." University: A Princeton Magazine. 6(Fall 1960), 32.

"Discovery" of the 1800 Rembrandt Peale portrait.

2913. Irland, Fred. "The Culture of Thomas Jefferson." Classical Weekly. 10(1917), 60-61.

Discusses in some detail the classical works in TJ's library sold to the nation.

2914. Isbell, Egbert R. "The Universities of Virginia and Michigania." Michigan History Magazine. 26(1942), 39-53.

Traces influence of TJ's educational ideas on Augustus B. Woodward and compares their university proposals.

2915. Isham, Norman Morrison. "Jefferson's Place in Our Architectural History." Journal of the American Institute of Architects. 2(1914), 230-35.

Criticizes Lambeth's book on TJ for exaggerating his accomplishments as an architect.

2916. Jackson, Donald. Thomas Jefferson & the Stony Mountains: Exploring the West from Monticello. Urbana: Univ. of Illinois Press, 1981. pp. xii, 339.

Informative account of TJ's interest in the trans-Mississippi West and its exploration. Although TJ "continually altered his policies to overtake reality," he held to three constant beliefs: the old confederacy east of the Mississippi should remain intact; the West should be developed by Americans, "forming whatever free and independent principalities they wished," and eventually the whole North and South American continents would be peopled by free and independent allies.

2917. Jackson, Sidney L. "The Encyclopédie Méthodique: A Jeffersonian Addendum." VMHB. 73(1965), 303-11.

TJ used and promoted Charles Joseph Panckoucke's Encyclopedie Methodique.

2918. Jacob, John J. Biographical Sketch of the Life of the Late Captain Michael Cresap. Cumberland, Md.: J. M. Buchanan, 1826. pp. 123.

Intended to refute TJ's accusation of Cresap as murderer of Logan's family.

2919. "Jefferson, First American Classicist, to Have Classic Memorial." Art Digest. 11(March 1, 1937), 9.

Mildly critical of the proposed design; illustrated.

2920. "Jefferson and His Indian Vocabulary." The Masterkey. 9(1935), 162-63.

Note on TJ's interest in Indian Languages and the loss of his vocabularies.

2921. "Jefferson and Music." Hobbies. 56(April 1951), 25.

Musical artifacts at Monticello.

2922. "Jefferson, Man of Science." Science. 97(April 9, 1943), 10.

Brief sketch.

2923. "Jefferson Memorial." New York Times Magazine. April 11, 1943. 8-9.

Handsome addition to the Washington scene.

2924. "Jefferson Memorial Raises Stormy Discussion." Architectural Record. 81(June 1937), 24-26.

Good account of the controversy over John Russell Pope's design for the Memorial; illustrated.

2925. "Jefferson Memorial Rises." New York Times Magazine. August 3, 1941. 16.

2926. "Jefferson on the Publication of State Papers." APS, Year Book, 1943. 75-76.

Prints TJ's letter to Ebenezer Hazard, dated April 30, 1775, and claims TJ and Hazard are the pioneers in the demand for the publication of official documents.

2927. "Jefferson Papers." Knickerbocker Magazine. 6(1835), 394-400, 537-40.

Portrays TJ's interest in "literature and the sciences" by reprinting with linking commentary selected letters, including an interesting letter debunking perpetual motion machines.

2928. "Jefferson, Pioneer American Collector." Hobbies. 48(April 1943), 6-7.

On his art and furniture purchases.

2929. "Jefferson Portrait Identified." Antiques. 76(1959), 250-51.

Contends a miniature by Paul Eugene duSimitiere is of TJ circa 1776.

2930. "Jefferson Portrait Returns to Monticello." Spinning Wheel. 15(June 1959), 30.

Trumbull miniature; suggests it was a gift to his wife Martha in 1788! Hardly.

2931. "Jefferson's Daughter." Tait's Edinburgh Magazine. 6(July 1839), 452.

Poem on "the daughter of Jefferson sold for a slave!" Rpt. The Liberator. May 26, 1848. 84.

2932. "Jefferson's Portable Writing Desk." Hobbies. 60(June 1955), 18.

Note on replicas of the desk often confused with the original.

2933. Jenkins, Starr. "American Statesmen as Men of Letters: Franklin, Adams, Jefferson, John Quincy Adams, Lincoln, Theodore Roosevelt and Wilson considered as Writers." Ph.D. dissertation. Univ. of New Mexico, 1972. pp. 293.

TJ in common with the rest of these figures was primarily a writer on politics and government, was centrally concerned with morality, was devoted to restraint of government, and saw America as "a new, special kind of nation." DAI 34/01A, p. 276.

2934. Jensen, Amy La Follette. "The Artful Gentry: Thomas Jefferson 1801-1809, James Madison 1809-1817" in The White House and Its Thirty-Two Families. New York: McGraw-Hill, 1958, 13-31.

Brief, illustrated account of life in the White House.

2935. Johnson, Louis. "Jefferson and Education." Vital Speeches. 16(1950), 418-20.

Education is essential for national defense; Founder's Day Address at the Univ. of Virginia, April 13, 1950.

2936. Johnson, William Dawson. History of the Library of Congress. Washington: Government Printing Office, 1904. 35-38, 65-104.

Describes TJ's role with particular attention to the process of acquisition of his library by the nation.

2937. Jones, Anna C. "Antlers for Jefferson." New England Quarterly. 12(1939), 333-48.

John Sullivan, governor of New Hampshire, gets a moose skin for TJ to present to Buffon in 1787; fullest article on this.

2938. Jones, Evan. "Down the Alimentary Canal with Thomas Jefferson." Saturday Review/World. 2(November 16, 1974), 44-46.

Cooking surveyed.

*2939. Jones, Howard, comp. Tah-jah-jute, or Logan, The Mingo Chief; With Material Pertaining to His "Speech" and the Times Taken from Thomas Jefferson's "Notes on Virginia," Printed in the Year 1800. Circleville, Ohio, 1937. pp. 47.

2940. Jones, Howard Mumford. "Jeffersonianism" in Jeffersonianism and the American Novel. New York: Teacher's College Press, 1966. 16-24.

Argues that TJ's faith in the moral sense, man's social duties, and the need for a responsible government are central to his philosophy, and American novelists have tended to surrender belief in all three.

2941. Jones, Robert W. "Thomas Jefferson and Pecan Breeding." 67th Annual Report of the Northern Nut Growers Association. 1976. 123-26.

Relies on Rodney H. True's 1916 article but speculates on the existence of pecan-hickory hybrids descended from TJ's pecan trees at Monticello.

2942. Judge, Joseph. "Mr. Jefferson's Monticello." National Geographic Magazine. 130(1966), 426-44.

Text describes how TJ lived at Monticello; numerous illustrations emphasize architecture and furnishings.

2943. Jullian, Philippe. "America Rediscovers Europe: Thomas Jefferson." Realites. 250(September 1971), 46-47.

TJ is responsible for Louis Seize style furnishings becoming the "official style of the United States almost to the present day."

2944. Kallen, Horace M. "The Arts and Thomas Jefferson." Ethics. 53(1943), 269-83.

Claims that TJ's aesthetic statements and preferences reflect his belief in the importance of function and of workmanship.

2945. Kallen, Horace M. "Jefferson's Garden Wall." American Bookman. 1(Winter 1944), 78-82.

Argues that TJ's serpentine wall at the Univ. of Virginia was inspired by Hogarth's serpentine line; quotes Gilbert Chinard, however, on the practical advantages of the design.

2946. Kellogg, Robert L. "Language and Culture in America." South Atlantic Bulletin. 41(January 1976), 3-8.

Associates TJ's linguistic interests with a cultural romanticism.

2947. Kennedy, John F. and Julian P. Boyd. "A White House Luncheon, June 17, 1963." New York History. 45(1964), 151-60.

Kennedy's remarks and Boyd's reply at a luncheon for sponsors and editors of projects under the aegis of the National Historical Publications Commission; JFK promises support for the Jefferson Papers and other editions; Boyd speaks on TJ's recognition of history as the basis for other knowledge.

*2948. Kenney, R. D. "Chief White Hair Medal with Portrait of President Jefferson, Dated 1801." American Numismatic Society Museum Notes. 5(1952), 191-92.

2949. Kent, Charles W. "Analogies Between Milton and Jefferson." Univ. of Virginia Alumni Bulletin. 3rd ser. 2(1909), 7-8.

Note draws analogies in matters of church, press, education, and
affairs of state.

2950. Kent, Charles W. "Jefferson's Quest of Knowledge" in The Writings of
Thomas Jefferson, ed. Lipscomb and Bergh. Washington: Thomas
Jefferson Memorial Association, 1903. 20:iii-xvi.

TJ was an educational innovator who aimed to develop an educational
system with a distinguished higher institution and a "compact completeness of the entire system from that high point down to the most
elementary school in the most remote precinct."

2951. Kent, Charles W. "Thomas Jefferson's University." Review of Reviews.
31(1905), 452-59.

Historical sketch of the University.

2952. Ketchum, Richard M. "The Case of the Missing Portrait." American
Heritage. 9(April 1958), 62-64, 85.

TJ's difficulties in getting delivery of his portrait from Gilbert
Stuart.

2953. Kibler, James Luther. "Ples for a Modern Edition of Jefferson's Notes
on Virginia." Tyler's Quarterly. 1(October 1952), 48-49.

2954. Kimball, Fiske. "The Beginnings of Landscape Architecture in
America." Landscape Architecture. 7(November 1917), 181-87.

The progress of knowledge of landscape gardening in the last third
of the eighteenth century is illustrated by TJ's growing sophistication.

2955. Kimball, Fiske. "A Church Designed by Jefferson." Architectural
Record. 53(1923), 184-86.

Note on a recently discovered photographic view of the Episcopal
church in Charlottesville, demolished in about 1895.

2956. Kimball, Fiske. "The Gardens and Plantations at Monticello."
Landscape Architecture. 17(April 1927), 173-80.

Discusses the variety of flowers and trees at Monticello.

2957. Kimball, Fiske. "Form and Function in the Architecture of Jefferson."
Magazine of Art. 40(1947), 150-53.

For TJ form did not follow function, "it was created in and with
function."

2958. Kimball, Fiske. "The Genesis of Jefferson's Plan for the University of Virginia." Architecture. 48(1923), 397-400.

Rejects the claim that TJ's design copied or depended upon Guennepin's Grands Prix of 1805.

2959. Kimball, Fiske. "The Grounds at Monticello in 1809." Landscape Architecture. 8(April 1918), 141-43.

Quotes Margaret Bayard Smith's description of landscaping as of summer, 1809.

2960. Kimball, Fiske. "Jefferson and the Arts." Proceedings of the APS. 87(1943), 238-45.

Surveys TJ's interests in painting, sculpture, gardening, music.

2961. Kimball, Fiske. "Jefferson and the Public Buildings of Virginia." Huntington Library Quarterly. 12(1949), 115-20; 303-10.

The first part describes TJ's architectural drawings, now in the Huntington, for buildings in Williamsburg circa 1770-1776. The second part covers drawings for buildings in Richmond; drawings for a proposed Capitol, done about 1780, show that he had arrived at the fundamental plan for the Capitol before he left America and before he met Clerisseau.

2962. Kimball, Sidney Fiske. "Jefferson as Architect." Nation. 98(1914), 33.

TJ, not Thornton, initiated the classic revival in the U.S. with his plans for the Capitol of Virginia.

2963. Kimball, Fiske. "Jefferson Memorial." Magazine of Art. 31(1938), 315-18.

On the controversy over the design.

2964. Kimball, Fiske and Marie. "Jefferson's Curtains at Monticello." Antiques. 52(1947), 266-68.

Illustrated; information from sketches by TJ.

2965. Kimball, Fiske. "Jefferson's Designs for Two Kentucky Houses." Journal of the Society of Architectural Historians. 9(October 1950), 14-16.

Discusses TJ's involvement in Liberty Hall in Frankfort and Farmington in Louisville; his suggestions arrived too late to be of any use for Liberty Hall.

2966.   Kimball, Fiske. Jefferson's Grounds and Gardens at Monticello.
        New York: Thomas Jefferson Memorial Foundation, 1927.

        Reprints articles from Landscape Architecture; items #2954, 2956,
        2959 above.

2967.   Kimball, Fiske. "Jefferson the Architect." Forum. 75(1926), 926-31.

        Account of TJ's "academical village;" if he had a prototype, it was
        probably Marly-le-Roi.

2968.   Kimball, Fiske. "The Life Portraits of Jefferson and Their Replicas."
        Proceedings of the APS. 88(1944), 497-534.

        Careful examination of the portraits of TJ, their circumstances and
        history; see item 2644.

2969.   Kimball, Fiske. "Monticello." Journal of the American Institute of
        Architects. 12(1924), 174-81.

        Slightly ecstatic note to accompany photographs.

2970.   Kimball, Fiske. "The Stuart Portraits of Jefferson." Gazette des
        Beaux-Artes. 6th ser. 23(1943), 329-44.

        Knowledgeable account of the portraits and copies of them made by
        Stuart, who took almost fifteen years from the sitting to deliver the
        second portrait of TJ.

*2971. Kimball, Fiske. "Thomas Jefferson and Civic Art" in City Planning at
        Yale: A Selection of Papers and Projects, ed. Christopher Tunnard
        and John N. Pearce. New Haven: Graduate Program in City Planning,
        Department of Architecture, Yale University, 1954. 25-32.

2972.   Kimball, Fiske. "Thomas Jefferson and the First Monument of the
        Classical Revival in America." Ph.D. dissertation. Univ. of
        Michigan, 1915.

        TJ and not Clerisseau was the real designer of the Virginia Capitol
        in Richmond; "Directly or indirectly, American classicism traces its
        ancestry to Jefferson's Capitol in Richmond." Rpt. Journal of the
        American Institute of Architects. 3(1915), 371-81; 421-33; 473-91.

2973.   Kimball, Fiske. "Thomas Jefferson and the Origins of the Classical
        Revival in America." Art and Archeology. 1(1915), 219-27.

        Particular attention to the Virginia and national Capitols; whereas
        Latrobe proposed Greek forms, TJ remained faithful to Roman
        models.

2974. Kimball, Fiske. Thomas Jefferson, Architect: Original Designs in the Collection of Thomas Jefferson Coolidge, Junior, with an Essay and Notes. Boston: Printed for Private Distribution at the Riverside Press, 1916. pp. vii, 205, xi.

Introduction deals with TJ's development as an architect, his architectural influence and his architectural library. Prints 233 drawings and related mss. A key book. Rpt. with a new introduction by Frederick Doveton Nichols, New York: Da Capo, 1968. Nichols' introduction is also useful for correcting some errors.

2975. Kimball, Fiske. "Thomas Jefferson as Architect: Monticello and Shadwell." Harvard University Architectural Quarterly. 2(June 1914), 89-137.

2976. Kimball, Fiske. "Thomas Jefferson's Windsor Chairs." Pennsylvania Museum Bulletin. 21(December 1925), 58-60.

Account of TJ's purchases at various times of Windsor chairs.

2977. Kimball, Fiske, ed. "Viewpoints: An Enthusiast on the Arts." Magazine of Art. 36(1943), 184.

Quotations from TJ; minimal comment.

2978. Kimball, Marie. "The Epicure of the White House." VQR. 9(1933), 71-81.

Account of TJ's interest in good cooking and good wines; one of the better efforts in this line.

2979. Kimball, Marie. "The Furnishing of Monticello." Antiques. 12(1927), 380-85; 482-86.

On TJ's furniture originally at Monticello and the process of bringing it back to the national shrine. Illustrated.

2980. Kimball, Marie. The Furnishing of Monticello. n.p., 1940. pp. 32.

Illustrated account of TJ's furniture then and now. Often reprinted; after 1946 in Charlottesville by the Thomas Jefferson Memorial Foundation.

2981. Kimball, Marie G. "Jefferson's Furniture Comes Home to Monticello." House Beautiful. 66(August 1929), 164-65, 186-90.

General description of restoration efforts.

2982. Kimball, Marie. "Jefferson's Works of Art at Monticello." Antiques. 59(1951), 297-99.

Describes the collection; Monticello as a building was "more sumptuous in its furnishings and adornments than any in the United States of its day."

2983. Kimball, Marie G. "More Jefferson Furniture Comes Home to Monticello." Antiques. 38(1940), 20-22.

Updates article in Antiques of 12(1927), item #2992 above.

2984. Kimball, Marie. "Notes on the Jefferson Sophocles." Princeton University Library Chronicle. 6(1945), 82-84.

Describes two volumes of Sophocles, owned and annotated by TJ.

2985. Kimball, Marie G. "The Original Furnishings of the White House." Antiques. 15(1929), 481-86.

Well-researched piece on TJ's furnishing of the White House, with his inventory of 1809. Although he admired French styles, he tended to patronize American craftsmen. Illustrated. Brief version of this rpt. in Antiques. 65(1952), 33-36.

2986. Kimball, Marie. "Thomas Jefferson, Patron of the Arts." Antiques. 43(1943), 164-67.

On TJ's acquisition of portrait paintings and busts.

2987. Kimball, Marie. Thomas Jefferson's Cook Book. Richmond: Garrett and Massie, 1938. pp. 111.

Introduction on TJ and cooking; recipes and notes from a mss. in the Massachusetts Historical Society as well as recipes from the book of Virginia Randolph Trist, TJ's granddaughter. Rpt. Charlottesville: Univ. Press of Virginia, 1976. pp. vii, 120.

2988. Kimball, Marie. "Thomas Jefferson's French Furniture." Antiques. 15(1929), 123-28.

Illustrated article on Furniture TJ acquired in France.

2989. Kimura, K. "Thomas Jefferson and Agriculture." Mita Gakkai Zasshi (Mita Journal of Economics). 42(July/August 1949), 45-59.

In Japanese.

2990. Kingsley, Sidney. The Patriots: A Play in a Prologue and Three Acts. New York: Random House, 1943. pp. 181.

Dramatization of the TJ-Hamilton conflict.

389

2991.   Kirby, Thomas Austin. "Jefferson's Letters to Pickering" in Philologia:
        The Malone Anniversary Studies, ed. Thomas A. Kirby and Henry
        Bosley Woolf. Baltimore: Johns Hopkins Press, 1949. 256-68.

        Prints with informative commentary TJ's letters to John Pickering of
        Salem and Boston, who shared TJ's interests in Indian languages and
        the proper pronunciation of classical Greek.

2992.   Kirtland, Jared Potter, ed. Song of Jefferson and Liberty. By Robert
        Treat Paine. Also Song of Moll Carey. By Theodore Dwight. History
        and Notes by Jared P. Kirtland. n.p., 1874. pp. 16.

        Gives words of both songs; Paine's song composed for the celebration
        at Wallingford, Conn. of TJ's first inaugural. Note describes the
        ceremony, claims the anniversary of the inauguration was celebrated
        in several towns in Connecticut for some years thereafter. Other
        song is anti-republican; Moll Carey was a notorious New York
        madam.

2993.   Kite, Elizabeth S., ed. L'Enfant and Washington, 1791-1792. Baltimore:
        Johns Hopkins Press, 1929. pp. xi, 182.

        Introduction by J. J. Jusserand, foreward by Charles Moore. Con-
        tains documents by L'Enfant, Washington, Jefferson, and others con-
        cerning L'Enfant's plan and the laying out of the city of Washington.
        Focus on L'Enfant, but sheds light on TJ's difficult relationship with
        him.

2994.   Kline, Alfred Allen. "The 'American' Stanzas in Shelley's Revolt of
        Islam: A Source." Modern Language Notes. 70(1955), 101-03.

        Finds parallels in ideas between stanzas of Shelley and TJ's first
        inaugural address, which supposedly the poet read in 1817 when he
        wrote the Revolt.

*2995. Klingensmith, Thelma H. "Thomas Jefferson's Contribution to Public
        Elementary Education." M.A. thesis. Univ. of North Dakota, 1962.
        pp. iii, 60.

2996.   Knight, Robert M. "Thomas Jefferson in Canto XXXI." Paideuma.
        5(1976), 79-93.

        Discusses Ezra Pound's extensive use in this canto of material from
        TJ's letters. Pound is more interested in the private than in the pub-
        lic TJ.

2997.   Knox, Fanona. "Jefferson's Choice." Library Journal. 77(1952),
        1574-76.

        On the collection in the Brush-Everard house in Williamsburg based
        on TJ's letter to Robert Skipwith.

2998. Kocher, Alfred Lawrence and Howard Dearstyne. "Discovery of Foundations for Jefferson's Addition to the Wren Building." Journal of the Society of Architectural Historians. 10(October 1951), 28-31.

The Revolutionary War put a stop to building operations. Good brief account of the proposed addition designed by TJ.

2999. Kreymborg, Alfred. "Ballad of the Common Man" in Ten American Ballads. New York: Dryden Press, 1942. unpag.

Poem for the Jefferson Memorial.

3000. Krnacik, John. "Thomas Jefferson's Interest in Italian Life, Language, and Art." Kentucky Foreign Language Quarterly. 13(1966), 130-37.

Survey.

3001. Kuper, Theodore Fred. "Thomas Jefferson, Lover of Music." Tempo. 1(January 1934), 18.

3002. Ladenson, Alex. "'I Cannot Live Without Books': Thomas Jefferson, Bibliophile." Wilson Library Bulletin. 52(1978), 624-31.

TJ's greatest contribution as a collector was his acquisition of material dealing with America.

3003. Lambeth, William Alexander and Henry Warren Manning. Thomas Jefferson as an Architect and Designer of Landscapes. Boston: Houghton Mifflin, 1913. pp. ix, 121.

Pioneering work on TJ as an architect; occasionally useful but needs to be used with more recent scholarship.

3004. Lammers, Claude C. "Jefferson's Aristocracy of Talent Proposal." Social Studies. 60(1969), 195-201.

On TJ's educational plans as a means for sifting out the best and brightest; condensed version published as "Jefferson and His Aristocracy of Talent Proposal." Education Digest. 35(January 1970), 45-47.

3005. LaMontagne, Leo E. "Jefferson as Classifier and "Jefferson and the Library of Congress" in American Library Classification, with Special Reference to the Library of Congress. Hamden, Conn.: Shoe String Press, 1961. 27-60.

On the historical background and subsequent development of TJ's system of library classification. Best work on this topic.

3006. Lancaster, Clay. "Jefferson's Architectural Indebtedness to Robert Morris." Journal of the Society of Architectural Historians.

10(March 1951), 3-10.

Morris, through his Rural Architecture (1755), influenced TJ for the first Monticello and to a lesser extent, the west pavilions at the University of Virginia.

3007. Lancaster, Dabney S. "The Influence of Thomas Jefferson on Higher Education." Virginia Journal of Education. 36(April 1943), 295-97, 309.

Conventional account of TJ as pioneer of quality education.

3008. Lancaster, Dabney S. "The Influence of Thomas Jefferson on Modern Education." Bulletin of Sweet Briar College. 21(May 1938), 11-20.

TJ advocated practical subjects, the elective system, use of original authors, and a broad system of public education.

3009. Lancaster, Dabney S. "Thomas Jefferson and Public Education." Virginia Journal of Education. 19(1926), 363-64.

Brief discussion of TJ's plan for public schools.

3010. Lane, Lawrence. "An Enlightened Controversy—Jefferson and Buffon." Enlightenment Essays. 3(Spring 1972), 37-40.

Minor sketch.

3011. Lange, Eugenie, ed. "Aus dem Briefwechsel Alexander von Humboldt (1769-1858) mit Thomas Jefferson (1743-1826)." Societe Suisse des Americanistes. Bulletin. 18(September 1959), 32-45.

Discusses the correspondence of TJ and Humboldt, but offers no new information.

3012. Langhorne, Elizabeth. "Black Music and Tales from Jefferson's Monticello." Folklore and Folklife in Virginia. 1(1979), 60-67.

Music and tales by blacks as remembered by Martha Jefferson Randolph; draws on work by Eugene Vail.

3013. Lawrence, R. deTreville, Sr., ed. Jefferson and Wine. The Plains, Va.: Vinifera Wine Grower's Association, 1976. pp. viii, 192.

Covers all aspects of the subject, TJ as wine appreciator, grower, etc., but often somewhat superficially. Individual essays are listed separately here under the contributors' names.

3014. League for Progress in Architecture. "The Jefferson Memorial." New Republic. 90(1937), 265.

Letter protesting the design.

3015.   Leavell, Byrd S. "Jeffersonian Ideals Endowed the University of
        Virginia." Virginia Medical Monthly. 104(1977), 91-96.

        Sketch of TJ's ideas on medicine, his promotion of vaccination, and
        the founding of the medical school. The usual.

3016.   Leavell, Byrd S. "Thomas Jefferson and Smallpox Vaccination."
        Transactions of the American Clinical and Climatological Associa-
        tion. 88(1976), 119-27.

        Finds TJ's accomplishments in this field impressive.

3017.   Le Coat, Gerard. "Thomas Jefferson et l'architecture metaphorique:
        le 'Village Academique' a l'Universite de Virginie." RACAR (Canadi-
        an Art Review). 3(no. 2, 1976), 8-34.

        Argues that in addition to its previously commented upon qualities of
        democratic pragmatism, the design for the University of Virginia
        "met en evidence une architecture-langage possedant une dimension
        metaphorique privilegiee." Suggestive analysis of the conception of
        the "Academical Village."

3018.   Lee, Gordon C., ed. Crusade Against Ignorance, Thomas Jefferson on
        Education. New York: Teachers College, Columbia Univ., 1961.
        pp. vi, 167.

        Largely an anthology of TJ's relevant writings but with an introduc-
        tion useful to students.

3019.   Lee, Lawrence. "Monticello" in Monticello and Other Poems.
        New York: Scribner's 1937. 3-9.

        A suite of six poems on TJ and Monticello.

3020.   Lee, Lawrence. "The Tomb of Thomas Jefferson." VQR. 16(1940),
        78-80.

        Poem; also in The Tomb of Thomas Jefferson. New York: Scribner's,
        1940. 43-45.

3021.   Lee, Lawrence. "The University of Virginia (I.M. Thomas Jefferson)."
        Scribner's. 85(1929), 300.

        A sonnet on TJ; revised version in The Tomb of Jefferson. New York:
        Scribner's, 1940. 17, as "... And Father of the University of
        Virginia ..."

3022.   Lehmann-Hartleben, Karl. "Thomas Jefferson, Archaeologist."
        American Journal of Archaeology. 47(1943), 161-63.

        TJ as a pioneer of modern archaeological technique.

3023. Leighton, Ann. "Thomas Jefferson as a Gardener." Country Life. 170(November 5, 1981), 1556-58.

Uses the Garden Book as the main source of information.

3024. Leikind, Morris C. "The Introduction of Vaccination into the United States." Ciba Symposia. 3(1942), 1114-24.

Surveys vaccination before 1820; touches on TJ's role.

3025. Lerch, Alice H. "Who Was the Printer of Jefferson's Notes?" in Bookmen's Holiday, Notes and Studies Written and Gathered in Tribute to Henry Miller Lydenberg. New York: New York Public Library, 1943. 44-56.

The first edition was printed by Philippe-Denis Pierres, who finished in May, 1785, although TJ went on reprinting revised versions of some leaves for another year and a half.

3026. Lerman, Louis. "Mr. Jefferson's Plow." New Masses. 47(April 13, 1943), 14-15.

Folksy monologue and ballad about TJ and the "plow" (figure of speech, not the mouldboard of least resistance) he invented to plant the Tree of Liberty.

*3027. Lerski, Hanna. "The British Antecedents of Thomas Jefferson's Architecture." Ph.D. dissertation. Johns Hopkins Univ., 1958.

3028. Lescaze, William. "America Is Outgrowing Imitation Greek Architecture." Magazine of Art. 30(1937), 366-69.

Criticizes classicism of the Jefferson Memorial and other official buildings.

3029. Lescure, Dolores. "Garden Week Visitors to See Homes Designed by Jefferson." Commonwealth, The Magazine of Virginia. 20(April 1953), 46.

3030. Levy, Uriah P. "Statue of Jefferson. Letters from Lieutenant Levy, of the United States Navy, Presenting to Congress a Statue of Thomas Jefferson." 23rd Congress, 1st Session. Ho. of Reps. Ex. doc. No. 240. Washington, 1834.

Presents a "colossal bronze statue" executed in Paris by "the celebrated David."

3031. Lewis, Clayton W. "Style in Jefferson's Notes on the State of Virginia." Southern Review. 14(1978), 668-76.

Claims that "In language, content, style, and organization, Notes

394

takes its form from reflexively related processes, and these in turn are reflexes of the activity and processes of nature itself." Content of Notes not so much the empirical State of Virginia as it is "the process of Jefferson's experience of the human and natural condition in Virginia." Suggestive.

3032. Lieuallen, Roy Elwayne. "The Jeffersonian and Jacksonian Conceptions in Higher Education." Ed.D. dissertation. Stanford Univ., 1955. pp. 355.

Concludes that "Since Jeffersonianism and Jacksonianism in education represent a single conception, that of equalitarianism, the terms are inappropriately used (by some twentieth-century educators) to designate contrasting conceptions." DAI 15/03, p. 355.

3033. A Life Portrait of Thomas Jefferson Drawn in 1804 by Févret de Saint-Mémin. Restruck From the Original Plate. Charlottesville: Univ. of Virginia, 1956. Broadside.

Folded broadside with notes on Saint-Mémin's physiognotrace portrait and a portrait laid in.

3034. Lincoln, A. "Jefferson and the West." Pacific Discovery. 17(no. 1, 1964), 24-29.

Sketch on sending out Lewis and Clark.

3035. Lincoln, A. "Jefferson the Scientist." Pacific Discovery. 17(July/August 1964), 10-15.

Sketch of TJ's natural history interests and the botanical specimens sent back by Lewis and Clark.

3036. Lindsay, Vachel. The Litany of Washington Street. New York: Macmillan, 1929. pp. xii, 121.

Basically a prose and verse celebration of Whitman as a Jeffersonian democrat. TJ treated passim; final chapter extolls his principles worked out in opposition to Hamilton. "... at the end of a thousand years, Jefferson's ideas will prevail."

*3037. Lindsay, Vachel. "Thomas Jefferson's One Thousand Years." World Review. 8(April 8, 1929), 129.

3038. Link, Patricia. "The Chien des Bergeres of Thomas Jefferson." Pure-Bred Dogs American Kennel Gazette. 93(August 1976), 25-28.

Discusses TJ's sheep dogs, which were probably Briards.

3039. Little, Ralph. "Portable Desks." Decorator. 6(no. 1, 1952), 6-7.

Describes TJ's desk and warns against accepting claims that the replicas made in 1876 are the original.

3040. "Living Faces." Saturday Evening Post. 211(April 15, 1939), 24.

On the J. H. I. Browere life mask.

*3041. Locigno, J. P. "Jefferson on Church and State in Education." Religious Education. 64(May 1969), 172-75.

*3042. Lokensgaard, Hjalmar O. "Aristocratic Elements in Jefferson's Educational Plans." M.A. thesis. Univ. of Iowa, 1932.

3043. Long, Edward John. "Living Links with Jefferson." American Forests. 60(November 1954), 20-23, 48-51.

On the grounds at Monticello, including seven trees of his planting.

3044. Long, O. W. Thomas Jefferson and George Ticknor: A Chapter in American Scholarship. Williamstown, Mass.: McClelland Press, 1933. pp. 39.

Ticknor visited TJ at Monticello, discussed books and education with him. "Through achievements at the University of Virginia, which was the idol of his old age, Jefferson inspired young Ticknor in his efforts for reforms at Harvard, especially in the direction of elective studies."

3045. Lucas, Frederic A. "Thomas Jefferson—Paleontologist." Natural History. 26(1926), 328-30.

Brief comments.

3046. Lucke, Jessie Ryon. "Some Correspondence with Thomas Jefferson Concerning the Public Printers." Papers of the Bibliographical Society of the University of Virginia. 1(1948), 25-37.

Letters to TJ from various printers, brief introduction.

3047. Luther, Frederick N. "Jefferson as a Naturalist." Magazine of American History. 13(1885), 379-90.

Survey of TJ's scientific interests.

3048. Mabbutt, Fred R. "The New Guardians: Education and Technology." Colorado Quarterly. 24(1975), 155-71.

TJ rightly understood the crucial importance of public education for the well-being of democracy, but at the present moment "communications technology" threatens to conflate politics and education, turning the latter into political propaganda; peripheral.

3049. Mabie, Hamilton W. "Some Famous Schools: The University of Virginia." The Outlook. 65(1900), 785-97.

Focus is on TJ's involvement with the University.

3050. McAdie, Alexander. "A Colonial Weather Service." Popular Science
       Monthly. 45(1894), 331-37.

       Discusses the weather observations of TJ and the Rev. James
       Madison; points out that July 4, 1776 was relatively cool, not
       sweltering as some authors claim.

3051. McClintock, Mike. "A Revolutionary Man with Contemporary Ideas."
       Popular Mechanics. 145(June 1976), 84-87, 158-59.

       Emphasis on TJ's gadgets.

3052. McCormick, Scott, Jr. "Thomas Jefferson's Ideas on Education." Davis
       and Elkins Historical Magazine. 5(1952), 8-14.

       Conventional survey.

3053. MacDonald, William. "Thomas Jefferson and the Tax on Knowledge."
       Nation. 64(1887), 298-99.

       TJ lobbied in 1821-24 for exemption from duties of all books and
       other articles generally used in acquiring information.

3054. McDowell, Frederick P. W. "Psychology and Theme in Brother to
       Dragons." PMLA. 70(1955), 565-86.

       Robert Penn Warren's TJ is unwilling to admit the complexity of
       moral and psychological values "because of his zeal to preserve the
       integrity of his vision."

*3055. McGirr, Newman F. "More Notes on the Thomas Jefferson Books in the
       Library of Congress." D.C. Libraries. 13(April 1942), 26-27.

*3056. McGirr, Newman F. "Notes on Thomas Jefferson and the National
       Library." D.C. Libraries. 9(January 1938), 27-28.

3057. McGoldrick, James H. "The Dream of Mr. Jefferson and Certain Other
       Men." The Clearing House. 38(1964), 552-55.

       Praises TJ's interest in public education; insignificant.

3058. McKie, D. "A Note on Priestley in America." Notes and Record of the
       Royal Society of London. 10(October 1952), 51-59.

       Prints a letter, dated March 21, 1801, from TJ to Priestley and
       Priestley's reply; gives historical background.

3059. McKim, Randolph. The Relations of the State to the University. An
       Address Delivered Before the Society of the Alumni of the University
       of Virginia, June 15, 1898. Charlottesville: Dominion Press, 1898.
       pp. 36.

       The Univ. is a monument to TJ's wisdom, particularly in preserving the distance between the church and the state in the direction of the Univ.

3060. MacLeish, Archibald. "Brave New World" in Act Five and Other Poems. New York: Random House, 1948. 61-63.

Poem.

3061. MacLeish, Archibald. The Great American Fourth of July Parade: A Verse Play for Radio. Pittsburgh: Univ. of Pittsburgh Press, 1975. pp. 51.

TJ, Adams, and assorted voices on the meaning of liberty.

3062. MacLeish, Archibald. "Our Lives, Our Fortunes, and Our Sacred Honor." Think. 27(July/August 1961), 2-23.

Short play on TJ and Adams.

3063. McMurran, Kristin. "New Black Novelist Explores Thomas Jefferson's Love Affair with a Beautiful Slave." People. 12(October 8, 1979), 97-98.

On Barbara Chase-Riboud's novel about Sally Hemings and TJ.

3064. McPeck, Eleanor M. "George Isham Parkyns: Artist and Landscape Architect, 1749-1820." Quarterly Journal of the Library of Congress. 30(1973), 171-82.

Discusses the influence on TJ of Parkyns, an English landscape architect who came to America.

3065. McReynolds, Allen. "George Caleb Bingham's Thomas Jefferson." Missouri Historical Review. 44(1949), 105-09.

Announces acquisition by Missouri Historical Society of a TJ portrait; Bingham copied Stuart's portrait.

3066. Maddox, William Arthur. The Free School Idea in Virginia Before the Civil War. New York: Teachers College, Columbia Univ., 1918. 12-89.

Discusses TJ's theories and work as part of the educational history of Virginia.

3067. Malone, Dumas, ed. The Jeffersonian Legacy. Boston: Beacon Press, 1954. pp. 165.

Dramatizations for radio performance by Morton Wishengrad, Milton Geiger, Joseph Mindel, and George Probst.

3068. Malone, Dumas. Thomas Jefferson and the Library of Congress. Washington: Library of Congress, 1977. pp. 31.

TJ's sale of his library to the nation and his inclusion of his catalogue which provided a system of classification.

3069. Malone, Dumas. "Thomas Jefferson, Educational Pioneer." Virginia Journal of Education. 19(1926), 352-54.

Discusses TJ's comprehensive system of education, especially the University.

*3070. The Mammoth Legend, as Related by Thomas Jefferson in His Notes on the State of Virginia, 1781, and Being One of the First Folk Tales or Legends of the Indians of the Ohio Valley Ever Recorded or Preserved in Printed Form, and an Account of the Shawnee Version of the Mammoth Legend as Related by N. Guilford, 1829. Chillicothe, Ohio: Ross County Historical Society, 1959.

3071. Mangeim, David Stephen. "Thomas Jefferson's 'Mouldboard of Least Resistance'." M.A. thesis. Wagner College, 1972. pp. 64.

Thorough study of TJ's plow, its acceptance and influence on subsequent designs. Most complete item on this topic.

3072. Martin, Henry Austin. "Jefferson as a Vaccinator." North Carolina Medical Journal. 7(January 1881), 1-34.

Pioneering article includes facsimiles of nine letters from TJ to Benjamin Waterhouse. TJ and Waterhouse were careful to propagate perfect vaccine, unlike some other early American vaccinators.

3073. Martin, Edwin T. Thomas Jefferson: Scientist. New York: Henry Schuman, 1952. pp. x, 289.

Best survey of this aspect of TJ's interests; portrays him as intelligent, enthusiastic amateur with a practical bent. Emphasizes TJ's efforts to answer Buffon's theory of American degeneration, and has a chapter on Federalist attacks on TJ for being a "philosophe." Covers the range of TJ's scientific interests.

3074. Martin, Edwin T. "Thomas Jefferson, A Scientist in the White House." Emory University Quarterly. 8(1952), 38-49.

Discusses TJ's pursuit of his scientific interests while president.

3075. Martin, Edwin T. "Thomas Jefferson's Interest in Science and the Useful Arts." Emory University Quarterly. 2(June 1946), 65-73.

See Martin's later book on the subject, item #3073 above.

399

3076. Martin, John S. "Rhetoric, Society and Literature in the Age of Jefferson." Midcontinent American Studies Journal. 9(Spring 1968), 77-90.

TJ's first inaugural address is a model of the new rhetoric of ideology, which offers a plan for action based on future possibilities, as opposed to the old rhetoric of typology, which appealed to the timeless authority of the past. Thus, in the Notes on the State of Virginia when the rhetorical moment of truth arrives, it is often couched in terms of the sublime.

3077. Marvel, Josiah P. and Henry S. Churchill. "The Jefferson Memorial." Nation. 144(1937), 448.

Letter protesting the proposed memorial in Washington: "it should be democratic architecture of today, not imperial pomp."

3078. Marx, Leo. "The Garden" in The Machine in the Garden; Technology and the Pastoral Idea in America. New York: Oxford Univ. Press, 1964. 73-144.

This chapter discusses in addition to Robert Beverley and Crevecoeur TJ's Notes as the most appealing, vivid, and thorough statement of the pastoral ideal in our literature. A suggestive and subtle analysis of style and intention, but the attempt to fit the book into a thematic category like pastoral may seem restricting.

3079. Massie, Susanne Williams. "Monticello" in Homes and Gardens in Old Virginia, ed. Massie and Frances Archer Christian. Richmond: Garrett and Massie, 1931. 301-05.

Rather superficial; revised ed. 1950.

3080. Mayer, Brantz. Tah-gah-jute; or, Logan and Captain Michael Cresap; A Discourse ... Before the Maryland Historical Society ... 9 May, 1851. Baltimore: John Murphy, 1851. pp. 86.

Little on TJ specifically; defends Cresap against the charge in Notes of murdering Logan's family and claims TJ seized upon the speech as an opportunity to refute Buffon.

3081. Mayo, Bernard. "Mr. Jefferson and the Way of Honor." The Jeffersonian (Univ. of Virginia). 1958-59. 40-48.

On the Jeffersonian basis of the Univ. of Virginia honor code.

3082. Mayor, A. Hyatt. "Jefferson's Enjoyment of the Arts." Metropolitan Museum of Arts Bulletin. 2(1943), 140-46.

Survey of TJ's art books, interest in architecture, collection of art.

3083. Mays, Jim. "Jefferson's Dream Comes True: A $5 Million Virginia Vineyard and Winery" in Jefferson and Wine, ed. R. deTreville Lawrence, Sr. The Plains, Va.: Vinifera Wine Growers Association, 1976. 176-79.

TJ's European root stocks were probably killed by phylloxera, but since the development of French hybrids resistant to the disease, a large vineyard is being developed on what was the plantation of his old friend and neighbor, James S. Barbour.

*3084. Mearns, David C. "The First White House Library." D.C. Libraries. 24(July 1953), 2-7.

3085. Mearns, David C. The Story Up to Now: The Library of Congress, 1800-1946. Washington: Library of Congress, 1947. 16-30.

Prints record of the vote in the House of Representatives on whether to acquire TJ's library.

*3086. Mearns, David C. "Virginia in the History of the Library of Congress, or, Mr. Jefferson's Other Seedlings." Virginia Library Bulletin. 16(1951), 1-4.

3087. Mehlinger, Howard D. "When I See Mr. Jefferson, I'm Going to Tell Him." Social Education. 42(1978), 54-60.

Telling TJ in heaven what is being done for "citizen education."

3088. Mellen, George Frederick. "Thomas Jefferson and Higher Education." New England Magazine. 26(1902), 607-16.

Laudatory survey of TJ's efforts to improve public knowledge.

3089. "Memorial Dispute." Literary Digest. 123(April 17, 1937), 6-7.

Brief account of the controversy over the Memorial design and the architect, John Russell Pope.

3090. Meschutt, David. "Gilbert Stuart's Portraits of Jefferson." American Art Journal. 13(Winter 1981), 2-16.

The best study of this disputed subject.

3091. Miller, Augustus C., Jr. "Jefferson as an Agriculturist." Agricultural History. 16(1942), 65-78.

Argues that if TJ eventually recognized the necessity of manufactures, he always believed agriculture to be the soundest of pursuits. Surveys his agricultural interests and practices.

3092. Miller, Helen Topping. Christmas at Monticello with Thomas Jefferson. New York: Longmans Green, 1959. pp. 61.

Juvenile fiction.

3093.   Miller, Sue Freeman. "The Grove at Monticello." Americana.
        8(July/August 1980), 46-51.

        On restoration of the grove to TJ's original intentions.

3094.   Miller, Sue Freeman. "Mr. Jefferson's Passion: His Grove at
        Monticello." Historic Preservation. 32(no. 2, 1980), 32-35.

        Illustrated account of the grove and its restoration.

3095.   Miller, Sue Freeman. "Whose Woods These Are." Albemarle Monthly
        Magazine. 1(August 1978), 42-43.

        TJ's plantings at Monticello.

3096.   "The Missing Minister." Time. 59(April 7, 1952), 74.

        Discovery of the Trumbull miniature given to Maria Cosway.

3097.   Mitchell, Henry. "Thomas Jefferson, The Young Gardener."
        Horticulture. n.s. 54(June 1976), 38-51.

        TJ's gardens told the world he was a romantic; illustrated.

3098.   Moe, Christian Hollis. "From History to Drama: A Study of the
        Influence of the Pageant, The Outdoor Epic Drama, and the Histori-
        cal Stage Play Upon the Dramatization of Three American Historical
        Figures." Ph.D. dissertation. Cornell Univ., 1958. pp. 386.

        Discusses dramatizations of TJ, Washington, and Lincoln.

*3099. Moffatt, Alexander D. "A Defense of the New World: Jefferson's Notes
        on Virginia and Some 18th-century Theories of American Degenera-
        cy." M.A. thesis. Southern Methodist Univ., 1966.

3100.   Moffatt, Charles H. "Jefferson's Sectional Motives in Founding the
        University of Virginia." West Virginia History. 12(1950), 61-69.

        Argues that TJ wanted the Univ. to be a stronghold against Federal-
        ism, and thus as much as Calhoun, Rhett, etc. he is responsible for
        Southern sectionalism.

3101.   Monjo, F. N. Grand Papa and Ellen Aroon; Being an Account of Some
        of the Happy Times Spent Together by Thomas Jefferson and His
        Favorite Granddaughter. New York: Holt, Rinehart, 1974. pp. 58.

        Juvenile fiction.

*3102. Montgomery, Henry C. "Thomas Jefferson and the Classical Tradition." Ph.D. dissertation. Univ. of Illinois, 1946.

3103. Montgomery, H. C. "Thomas Jefferson as a Philologist." American Journal of Philology. 65(1944), 367-71.

Discusses TJ's interest in Greek, Latin, American Indian languages. "By contemporary evaluation, ... it could hardly be said that he was a great classical scholar, or a philologist. But judged by the standards of his own time, he was, indeed, a philologist in the inclusive meaning of the term."

3104. Monticello Association. "Report of the Committee on Jefferson Furniture." Annual Report of the Monticello Association. 1926. 7-12.

Records furnishings once owned by TJ and now in the hands of descendants and others.

3105. "Monticello." Holiday. 3(April 1948), 48-49.

Illustrated spread.

3106. "Monticello, A Collector's Paradise." Hobbies. 48(April 1943), 7-9.

3107. "The Monticello Swag." House and Garden. 127(June 1965), 38-39.

Modern adaptations of TJ's curtains.

3108. Morison, Samuel Eliot. "Is 'Liberal Education' Democratic?: What Jefferson Advocated." Hispania. 27(February 1944), 78-79.

Short note contending that TJ's educational object was to create an intellectual aristocracy.

3109. Morris, Edwin Bateman. "Architectural Pilgrimage to Charlottesville." Architect. 13(January 1930), 385-89.

Chatty and trivial account of visit to Monticello to discover the Jeffersonian spirit.

3110. Morris, Mabel. "Jefferson and the Languages of the American Indians." Modern Language Quarterly. 6(1945), 31-34.

Briefly discusses TJ's interest in Indian language as shared by other members of the American Philosophical Society.

3111. Morrow, L. C. and J. M. Davis. "Thomas Jefferson's Philosophy of Education." Virginia Journal of Education. 15(1921), 141-42, 164-67.

Derivative sketch.

3112.　Mowbray, J. P. "That 'Affair' of Mrs. Atherton's." Critic. 40(1902), 501-05.

Protests that Gertrude Atherton's love for Alexander Hamilton has led her to misrepresent seriously the character of TJ in her novel The Conqueror.

3113.　Mugridge, D. H. "Thomas Jefferson and the Library of Congress." Wilson Library Bulletin. 18(1944), 608-11.

Comments briefly on TJ's role in reestablishing the Library's collection and more extensively on Jefferson scholarly projects underway with the library's help.

3114.　Mumford, Lewis. "The Universalism of Thomas Jefferson" in The South in Architecture; The Dancy Lectures, Alabama College 1941. New York: Harcourt Brace, 1941. 43-78.

Critical analysis of TJ as a renaissance man and his architecture which "struck a balance between ... the logic of building and the logic of life." A significant statement.

3115.　Murphy, Mabel Ansley. When Jefferson Was Young. Chicago: Whitman, 1942. pp. 262.

Juvenile fiction.

3116.　Murray, Elizabeth and Randolph Crawford. "Wild Flowers at Monticello." Virginia Wildlife. 38(March 1977), 32, 10.

Briefly discusses TJ's use of wild flowers in gardening.

3117.　"Museum Gets Jefferson's Music Books." Music Trade News. 9(August 1931), 18.

Gift to Monticello of some of TJ's music books owned by a great-great-granddaughter.

3118.　Myers, Mary C. "Ezekiel's Statue of Jefferson." University of Virginia Alumni Bulletin. 3rd ser. 3(August 1910), 361-78.

Account of ceremonies accepting the statue of TJ done by Sir Moses Ezekiel. Illustrated.

3119.　Nakosteen, Mehdi. "Thomas Jefferson" in The History and Philosophy of Education. New York: Ronald, 1965. 451-56.

Survey of TJ's reforming ideas on education.

3120.　Nason, Charles D. "Jefferson and Washington on National Education." Education. 19(1898), 157-67.

3121.   Needham, Charles Willis. "Jefferson as a Promoter of General Educa-
        tion" in The Writings of Thomas Jefferson, ed. Lipscomb and Bergh.
        Washington: Thomas Jefferson Memorial Association, 1903. 4:i-ix.

3122.   Newcomb, Rexford. "Thomas Jefferson, the Architect." Architect.
        9(1928), 429-32.

        Survey.

3123.   Nichols, Frederick D. "Belle Grove in the Developing Civilization of
        the Valley of Virginia." Historic Preservation. 20(no. 3/4, 1968),
        6-20.

        Ascribes Belle Grove's architecture to TJ on the basis of a recently
        discovered letter. Description.

*3124. Nichols, Frederick Doveton. Early Charlottesville Architecture; An
        Exhibition to Commemorate the Sesquicentennial Celebration by the
        Albemarle County Historical Society and the University of Virginia
        of the Signing of the Treaty for the Louisiana Purchase.
        Charlottesville: Charlottesville Public Library, 1953. pp. 8.

3125.   Nichols, Frederick D. "Jefferson: The Making of an Architect" in
        Jefferson and the Arts: An Extended View, ed. William Howard
        Adams. Washington: National Gallery of Art, 1976. 159-85.

        Informative discussion of the architecture TJ knew and admired in
        France and its influence on the buildings he designed.

3126.   Nichols, Frederick Doveton and James A. Bear, Jr. Monticello.
        Monticello: Thomas Jefferson Memorial Foundation, 1967. pp. 77.

        Guide book for sale at Monticello; a model of its kind.

3127.   Nichols, Frederick Doveton. "The Restoration of 'Academical Village'
        Gardens Completed." Univ. of Virginia Alumni News.
        53(March/April 1965), 2-7, 31-33.

        The East Lawn gardens at the University.

3128.   Nichols, Frederick Doveton. Thomas Jefferson's Architectural Draw-
        ings. A Massachusetts Historical Society Picture Book. Boston:
        Massachusetts Historical Society, 1960. pp. 10, (22).

        The foreword, "TJ's Architectural Development," contends the draw-
        ings show his growth as an artist; he became "the leading Romantic
        Classicist in America before Latrobe." See the revised editions of
        this listed as the next item.

3129.   Nichols, Frederick Doveton. Thomas Jefferson's Architectural Draw-
        ings Compiled and with Commentary and a Check List. Boston:
        Massachusetts Historical Society, 1961. pp. 46.

Adds a checklist of TJ's drawings to the foregoing; 3rd edition also published in 1961, adds Charlottesville: Thomas Jefferson Memorial Foundation and The University Press of Virginia as co-publishers, 48 pp. Useful research tool, especially these two editions.

3130. Nichols, Frederick Doveton and Ralph E. Griswold. Thomas Jefferson, Landscape Architect. Charlottesville: Univ. Press of Virginia, 1978. pp. xvii, 196.

Broad informative survey of TJ's interests in horticulture and land-scape architecture, influences on him, his plans for Monticello and the Univ. of Virginia, and his contributions to horticulture.

*3131. Nolan, Carolyn G. "Thomas Jefferson: Gentleman Musician." M.A. thesis. Univ. of Virginia, 1967. pp. 126, xiv.

3132. Noland, Nancy. "Jefferson and Palladio." Vassar Journal of Under-graduate Studies. 16(May 1943), 1-15.

Discriminating study of TJ's architecture, although it may over-emphasize the Palladian influence. Warns that TJ's work must be set apart from the styles that most closely surround it.

3133. Noll, Bink. "Air Tunnel, Monticello." Kenyon Review. 23(1961), 67.

Poem; the air tunnel is part of a waste removal system TJ devised.

3134. Norton, Paul F. "Jefferson's Plan for Mothballing the Frigates." U.S. Naval Institute Proceedings. 82(1956), 737-41.

TJ in 1802 proposed an enclosed dry dock to store unused frigates in time of peace. Benjamin Latrobe produced designs for this.

3135. Norton, Paul Foote. "Latrobe, Jefferson and the National Capitol." Ph.D. dissertation. Princeton Univ., 1952. pp. 442.

Follows "the exact contributions made by Jefferson's suggestions and by Latrobe's talent ... step by step through the years of Jefferson's presidency." DAI 15/04, p. 554. Printed, New York: Garland Pub-lishing, 1977, in series of "Outstanding Dissertations in the Fine Arts."

3136. Norton, Paul. "Latrobe's Ceiling for the Hall of Representatives." Journal of the Society of Architectural Historians. 10(May 1951), 5-10.

TJ and Latrobe differ over plans.

3137. Norton, Paul F. "Thomas Jefferson and the Planning of the National Capital" in Jefferson and the Arts: An Extended View, ed. William Howard Adams. Washington: National Gallery of Art, 1976. 187-232.

TJ's role in planning Washington, D.C., particularly in regard to his work with Benjamin Latrobe.

3138. Nunez, Bernard E. "Jefferson's Favorite Medicine, Wine" in Jefferson and Wine, ed. R. deTreville Lawrence, Sr. The Plains, Va.: Vinifera Wine Growers Association, 1976. 163-99.

TJ regarded a moderate amount of wine as a "necessity of life for me," and like many contemporaries believed in its medicinal efficacy.

3139. O'Callaghan, E. B. "Jefferson Notes of Virginia." Historical Magazine. 1(1857), 52.

Bibliographical note.

3140. O'Callaghan, E. B. "The Revised Proofs of Jefferson's Notes on Virginia." Historical Magazine. 13(1868), 96-98.

Bibliographic description.

3141. "Ode sur le Mort de Thomas Jefferson dediée à sa fille Madame Randolph." National Gazette. November 8, 1926.

Poem in French.

3142. O'Donnell, James H., III. "Logan's Oration: A Case Study in Ethnographic Authentication." Quarterly Journal of Speech. 65(1979), 150-56.

"Logan's Oration is a moving and legitimate expression of Native American oratory."

3143. Ogburn,Floyd, Jr. "Structure and Meaning in Thomas Jefferson's Notes on Virginia." Early American Literature. 15(1980), 141-50.

Using concepts of linguistic analysis such as foregrounding and collocation, attempts to get at the "deep structure" of TJ's "pastoral." But since these passages are supposedly the two sublime passages about the Potomac and the Natural Bridge, the conclusion that TJ understood nature as order and proportion seems incomplete.

3144. Oliver, John William. "Science and the 'Founding Fathers.'" Scientific Monthly. 48(1939), 256-60.

Discusses TJ and the patent office; he originally examined every patent application himself.

3145. Oliver, John W. "Thomas Jefferson—Scientist." Scientific Monthly. 56(1943), 460-67.

Examines TJ's scientific activities during five periods of his life.

3146.   O'Neal, Willaim Bainter and Frederick Doveton Nichols. "An Architectural History of the First University Pavilion." Magazine of
Albemarle County History. 15(1956), 36–43.

Account of the designing and construction of Pavilion VII under TJ's
direction.

3147.   O'Neal, William B. "Financing the Construction of the University of
Virginia: Notes and Documents." Magazine of Albemarle County
History. 23(1965), 5–34.

Difficulties of TJ and Joseph C. Cabell in obtaining funds to build
the University.

3148.   O'Neal, William B. Jefferson's Buildings at the University of Virginia:
The Rotunda. Charlottesville: Univ. of Virginia Press, 1960. pp. 62,
22 plates.

Introduction discusses design and building of the Rotunda; lists and
describes documents pertaining to construction; plates of influential
designs and TJ's drawings.

3149.   O'Neal, William Bainter. Jefferson's Fine Arts Library, His Selections
for the University of Virginia Together with His Own Architectural
Books. Charlottesville: Univ. Press of Virginia, 1976. pp. xviii, 409.

Full description and annotation of books in TJ's 1825 Catalogue of the
Library of the Univ. of Virginia, plus relevant items from John V.
Kean's 1825 Catalogue and the 1828 Catalogue, plus items from
Sowerby on the Monticello "great" library.

3150.   O'Neal, William B. Jefferson's Fine Arts Library for the University of
Virginia, With Additional Notes on Architectural Volumes Known to
Have Been Owned by Jefferson. Charlottesville: Univ. of Virginia
Press, 1956. pp. 53.

Includes a desiderata list for the Univ. of Virginia libraries, entries
having to do with fine arts from TJ's 1825 Catalogue of the Univ.
Library, and a list of books now in the Univ. library from TJ's own
libraries. Not the same as the previous item.

3151.   O'Neal, William B. "Michele and Giacomo Raggi at the University of
Virginia: With Notes and Documents." Magazine of Albemarle
County History. 18(1960), 5–31.

TJ's difficult dealings with Italian stonecutters hired to do the
Corinthian and Ionic capitols for the Pavilions and the Rotunda.

3152.   O'Neal, William B. "The Workmen at the University of Virginia, 1817–
1826, With Notes and Documents." Magazine of Albemarle County
History. 17(1959), 5–48.

Explores TJ's difficulties in obtaining competent workmen and the proposals he received from craftsmen.

3153. "On Time with Thomas Jefferson." Hobbies. 56(April 1951), 46.

Note on the great clock at Monticello.

3154. Oppenheimer, J. Robert. "Encouragement of Science." Science News Letter. 57(March 18, 1950), 170-72.

TJ's letter to William Green Munford is suffused with the idea of progress and with a recognition that science and political life are relevant to each other. Rpt. Science. 111(1950), 373-75.

3155. Ormsbee, Thomas Hamilton. "Thomas Jefferson's Own Oriental Lowestoft." American Collector. 14(January 1946), 5.

Illustrated note on TJ's Chinese-made Lowestoft punch bowl and pitcher.

3156. Osborn, Henry Fairfield. "Thomas Jefferson as a Paleontologist." Science, n.s. 82(1935), 533-38.

Sketch of TJ's interests in mammoths and the megalonyx.

3157. Osborn, Henry Fairfield. "Thomas Jefferson, The Pioneer in American Paleontology." Science. n.s. 69(1929), 410-13.

A speech recapitulating the history of American paleontology; only two paragraphs on TJ.

3158. Osgood, Ernest S. "A Prarie Dog for Mr. Jefferson." Montana: The Magazine of Western History. 19(April 1969), 54-56.

Account of a prarie dog sent to TJ by Lewis and Clark from Fort Madison.

3159. Osgood, John C. "How, Thomas Jefferson, Can We Provide Simultaneously for Excellence and Egalitarianism?" Mount Holyoke Alumni Quarterly. 59(1975), 85-88.

Remarks on TJ's ideas about education; title question not answered.

3160. "Our Architect President." Review of Reviews. 43(1911), 353-54.

"Architects generally do not appreciate the thoroughness of Jefferson's work."

3161. Owsley, Clifford. "Thomas Jefferson and His First Inaugural" in Inaugural. New York: Olympic Press, 1964. 126-41.

An eccentric rhetorical analysis of TJ's speech; finds it a "great speech" with a "Survival quotient" of 85 out of a possible 100 points.

3162. Padover, Saul K., ed. Thomas Jefferson and the National Capital. Preface by Harold L. Ickes. Washington: Government Printing Office, 1946. pp. xxxvi, 523.

Contains "notes and correspondence exchanged between Jefferson, Washington, L'Enfant, Ellicott, Hallett, Thornton, Latrobe, the commissioners, and others relating to the founding, surveying, planning, designing, constructing, and administering of the City of Washington, 1783-1818."

3163. Padover, Saul K. "Thomas Jefferson: Philosopher, Statesman—and Musician." Stereo Review. 21(November 1968), 82-86.

General survey of TJ's musical interests.

3164. Page, Thomas Nelson. "Jefferson and the University of Virginia" in Old Dominion. New York: Scribner's, 1908. 198-234.

TJ's university, the last product of his "comprehensive sweep of intellect," had an exemplary "spaciousness of design."

3165. Parks, Edd Winfield. "Jefferson as a Man of Letters." Georgia Review. 6(1952), 450-59.

Surveys TJ's literary tastes, interest in prosody, his literary style; characterizes him as a utilitarian with a broad definition of usefulness and as a classicist.

3166. Parks, Edd Winfield. "Jefferson's Attitude Toward History." Georgia Historical Quarterly. 36(1952), 336-41.

Conventional survey.

3167. "The Patriots, Sidney Kingsley's New Play, Brings Early American History to Broadway." Life. 4(March 8, 1943), 57-58.

Photographic illustrations of Kingsley's play about the conflict between TJ and Hamilton.

3168. Patton, John S. Jefferson, Cabell, and the University of Virginia. New York: Neale, 1906. pp. viii, 380.

TJ referred to throughout, but pp. 9-135 cover the years of his involvement with the University.

3169. Patton, John S. "Thomas Jefferson's Contributions to Natural History." Natural History. 19(1919), 405-10.

410

TJ's main contribution was sending out the Lewis and Clark expedition. Rpt. Univ. of Virginia Alumni Bulletin. 3rd ser. 12(1919), 409-15.

3170. Paullin, Charles O. "The Eugenic Views of Thomas Jefferson and John Adams." Journal of Heredity. 25(1934), 217-28.

Describes and quotes from letters by TJ and Adams commenting on a passage from Theognis of Megara on breeding.

3171. Peden, William. "Introduction" to Notes on the State of Virginia. Chapel Hill: Univ. of North Carolina Press, 1954. xi-xxv.

Good brief account of the circumstances of TJ's Notes, both of composition and publication.

3172. Peden, William. "Jefferson, Freneau, and the Poems of 1809." New Colophon. 1(1948), 394-400.

TJ had difficulties with Freneau's printer in regard to the size of his subscription.

3173. Peden, William H. Some Aspects of Jefferson Bibliography. Lexington, Va.: Journalism Laboratory Press, Washington and Lee University, 1941. pp. 22.

TJ's understanding and practice of bibliography; he was not a bibliographer in the modern sense. Also discusses research opportunities and the difficulties of making a Jefferson bibliography.

3174. Peden, William H. "Some Notes on Jefferson's Libraries." WMQ. 3rd ser. 1(1944), 265-72.

TJ's collecting interests in history, law, religion and science follow "the pattern of the average eighteenth-century Virginia gentleman of substance and position," but his wide range of interests and his collecting in the fields of Americana and philology show him to be "an innovator and a trailblazer."

3175. Peden, William Harwood. "Thomas Jefferson: Book Collector." Ph.D. dissertation. Univ. of Virginia, 1942. pp. 239.

An important study but superceded by Sowerby and other works more readily available.

3176. Peden, William H. "Thomas Jefferson and Charles Brockden Brown." Maryland Quarterly. 1(no. 2, 1944), 65-68.

Discusses Brown's letter of 25 December 1799, presenting a copy of, probably, Wieland, and TJ's reply of January 15, 1800. One of the few times TJ ever spoke kindly of novels.

3177. Peden, William. <u>Twilight at Monticello.</u> Boston: Houghton Mifflin, 1973. pp. xii, 241.

A thriller set at a meeting of Jefferson scholars at Monticello; much background given on TJ and various historians' interpretations of him.

3178. Peebles, John Kevan. "Thomas Jefferson, Architect." <u>Univ. of Virginia Alumni Bulletin.</u> 1(November 1894), 68-74.

Survey; rpt. <u>American Architect and Building News.</u> 47(January 19, 1895), 28-35.

3179. Penney, Annette C. "Cooking with Wines at the White House" in <u>Jefferson and Wine,</u> ed. R. deTreville Lawrence, Sr. The Plains, Va.: Vinifera Wine Growers Association, 1976. 56-57.

Brief discussion of TJ's stocking of the White House cellar and a recipe for "Mr. Jefferson's pannequaiques" (crepes) as prepared by his chef, Etienne Lemaire.

3180. Penney, Annette C. "Jefferson and South Carolina's Horticulture" in <u>Jefferson and Wine,</u> ed. R. deTreville Lawrence, Sr. The Plains, Va.: Vinifera Wine Growers Association, 1976. 86-90.

Comments on TJ's interest in encouraging viticulture in South Carolina; minor.

3181. Penney, Annette C. "North Carolina: Jefferson's 'Exquisite Wine'" in <u>Jefferson and Wine,</u> ed. R. deTreville Lawrence, Sr. The Plains, Va.: Vinifera Wine Growers Association, 1976. 81-85.

TJ said that scuppernong wine "would be distinguished on the best tables of Europe, for its fine aroma."

3182. Perkins, Mrs. C. D. "Jefferson's Monticello." <u>Bulletin of the Garden Club of America.</u> 48(March 1960), 30-32.

Note on restoration of the gardens.

3183. Perkins, Hazlehurst B. "Restoring the 'Monticello' Gardens." <u>Magazine of Albemarle County History.</u> 30(1972), 9-13.

Recounts experiences in reconstructing Monticello gardens by follow-ing plans and information in TJ's Garden Book.

3184. Pérouse de Montclos, J. M. "Jefferson and Architecture in the Second Half of the Eighteenth Century" in <u>The Eye of Thomas Jefferson,</u> ed. William Howard Adams. Washington: National Gallery of Art, 1976. 167-89.

On buildings and drawings TJ saw or could have seen in Paris.

412

3185. Perry, E. S. "Thomas Jefferson's Collection of Virginia Manuscripts" in "Time and the Land: The Work of American Historians During the Generation of the American Revolution." Ph.D. dissertation. Univ. of Cambridge, 1977. 373-423.

Gives a summary catalogue of all known Virginia mss. in TJ's collection; discusses provenance and documentary evidence.

3186. Peterson, Helen Stone. "Francis Gilmer's Mission." Virginia Cavalcade. 14(Autumn 1964), 5-11.

Sent by TJ to obtain professors for the University.

3187. Peterson, Martin Severin and Marvin Paul Grim. "The Farmer Who Founded Democracy; Thomas Jefferson Rotated Crops and Went Through Farm Depressions at Monticello." Wallace's Farmer. 54(July 26, 1929), 6, 17.

3188. Peterson, Merrill D. "Thomas Jefferson's Notes on the State of Virginia." Studies in Eighteenth-Century Culture. 7(1978), 49-62.

TJ articulated "a series of Enlightenment directives for the intelligence of the new American republic."

3189. Pevler, Herman H. Education: Jefferson and Today, An Address... . Roanoke, Va.: Old Dominion Chapter Public Relations Society of America, 1968. pp. 8.

TJ's real legacy is his conviction that old problems must be solved anew by each generation.

3190. Philbrick, Thomas. "Thomas Jefferson" in American Literature 1764-1789 The Revolutionary Years, ed. Everett Emerson. Madison: Univ. of Wisconsin Press, 1977. 145-69.

A sketch of TJ's activities during this period and brief rhetorical analysis of A Summary View, the Declaration, and Notes.

3191. Phipps, Frances. "Jefferson's Notes on Virginia" in Colonial Kitchens, Their Furnishings, and Their Gardens. New York: Hawthorn Books, 1972. 181-87.

Minor note on useful plants and gardening.

3192. Pickens, Buford. "Mr. Jefferson as Revolutionary Architect." Journal of the Society of Architectural Historians. 34(1975), 257-79.

Argues for TJ as an architectural innovator; "To be radically modern during these decades was not to invent but to transform," in part because of the limited options in technology. Important revaluation of TJ as architect.

3193.   Pierce, E. H. "Thomas Jefferson and His Violin." Etude. 47(1929),
        684-85.

        Sketch.

3194.   Pierson, William H. "American Neoclassicism, The Idealistic Phase:
        Thomas Jefferson" in American Buildings and Their Architects: The
        Colonial and Neoclassical Styles. Garden City, N.Y.: Doubleday,
        1970. 286-334.

        Suggestive study; focuses on Monticello and the University.

3195.   Pierson, William H., Jr. Thomas Jefferson, Educator and Architect.
        Williamstown, Mass.: Williams College, 1963. pp. 8.

        TJ's design for the Univ. of Virginia shows a "practical educator
        seeking to give order and cohesiveness."

3196.   Pi-Sunyer, Oriol. "Thomas Jefferson: Reluctant Manufacturer." Janus.
        51(1964), 226-34.

        Derivative discussion of TJ's nailery; argues that his apparent failure
        to manufacture nails on a commercial scale was a result of economic
        rather than technological factors.

3197.   Pleasants, Samuel A. "Thomas Jefferson—Educational Philosopher."
        Proceedings of the APS. 111(February 1967), 1-4.

        Surveys TJ's activities to encourage education.

3198.   Pope, Arthur Upham. "In Defense of the Jefferson Memorial."
        Magazine of Art. 30(1937), 362-65.

3199.   "Portrait Sculpture by Houdon." Boston Museum Bulletin. 32(1934),
        69-74.

        On the museum's 5 Houdons, including the recently acquired bust of
        TJ.

3200.   Powell, Edward Payson. "Jefferson and Hamilton in Education." New
        England Magazine. n.s. 14(1896), 699-706.

        TJ made the New England system of schools coherent; claims that
        "very soon these organized state systems will federalize at
        Washington in a great National University."

3201.   Pratt, Richard H. "Jefferson and His Fellow Architects." House and
        Garden. 52(July 1927), 74-75, 126, 148.

414

Contends TJ was the principal architect and stimulator of classicism in the young republic, a style revealing a kind of national self-consciousness.

3202. Presentation of the Restored East Lawn Gardens of the University of Virginia by the Garden Club of Virginia, May 4, 1965. Charlottesville, 1965. pp. (35).

Contains accounts of excavations and other research to determine original plans; also a short speech by Frederick D. Nichols, "Thomas Jefferson, Landscape Architect."

3203. Preston, Joseph Raine, ed. Correspondence between Thomas Jefferson and John Stuart." Journal of the Greenbrier Historical Society. 2(no. 5, 1973), 4-13.

Correspondence on matters paleontological; introduction and notes.

3204. Pritchett, Henry S. "Jefferson's Interest in Science." Univ. of Virginia Alumni Bulletin. 6(1899), 74.

Note; minor.

3205. A Profile of Thomas Jefferson from a Drawing by William Russell Birch. Charlottesville: Associates of the Univ. of Virginia Library, 1975. Broadside.

Facsimile and brief note.

3206. Purcell, Richard J. "Thomas Jefferson's Educational Views." Catholic Educational Review. 30(1932), 401-10.

Competent survey.

3207. Pyle, Mary Thurman. The Three Royal R's, Play in One Act. New York: Dramatists Play Service, 1941. pp. 25.

TJ as a student in a "field" school strikes a blow for public education.

3208. Radbill, Samuel X. "Dr. Robley Dunglison and Jefferson." Transactions and Studies of the College of Physicians of Philadelphia. 4th ser. 27(July 1959), 40-44.

Sketches TJ's relationship with Dunglison and the latter's career after 1826.

3209. Radbill, Samuel X. "Thomas Jefferson and the Doctors." Transactions and Studies of the College of Physicians of Philadelphia. 4th ser. 37(October 1969), 106-14.

Sketch of TJ's medical opinions and his doctor acquaintances, e.g. Waterhouse, Rush, Dunglison.

3210. Raffensperger, Edwin B. "Who Killed the Logan Family?" Potter's American Monthly. 11(1878), 187-93.

Claims Michael Cresap did not kill Logan's family and that Logan could not have made the speech ascribed to him in TJ's Notes.

3211. Raiden, Edward. Mr. Jefferson's Burr: A Play in Three Acts. Los Angeles: Thunder Publishing, 1960. pp. 140.

Shakespeare it's not.

3212. Ralston, Samuel Moffett. "The Thomas Jefferson Theory of Education" in Indiana University, 1820-1920; Centennial Memorial Volume. Bloomington: Indiana Univ., 1921. 179-91.

Survey.

3213. Randall, David. "'Dukedom Large Enough': III. Thomas Jefferson and the Declaration of Independence." Papers of the Bibliographic Society of America. 56(1962), 472-80.

Rare book dealer and librarian discusses collecting Jeffersoniana; rpt. in Dukedom Large Enough. New York: Random House, 1969. 273-80.

3214. Randolph, Frederick J. and Frederick L. Francis. "Thomas Jefferson as Meteorologist." Monthly Weather Review. 23(1895), 456-58.

Notes TJ's meteorological apparatus at Monticello, describes his record-keeping; TJ was the first American to describe the phenomenon of temperature inversion.

3215. Randolph, Jane Cary Harrison. Thomas Jefferson. Monticello Music, 1785. St. Louis: Cary N. Randolph, 1941. pp. 24.

Music and words for eight songs, no comment.

3216. Raphael, Henry. Thomas Jefferson, Astronomer. Leaflet No. 174. San Francisco: Astronomical Society of the Pacific, 1943. pp. 8.

Survey.

3217. Rauschenberg, Bradford L. "William John Coffee, Sculptor-Painter: His Southern Experience." Journal of Early Southern Decorative Arts. 4(November 1978), 26-48.

Includes discussion of the portrait busts done of TJ's family.

3218. Ravier, Xavier. "Thomas Jefferson et la Langue d'oc." Annales du Midi. 90(1978), 41-52.

Consideration of TJ's remarks on Provencal in his letter of March 29, 1787 to William Short as significant for "l'histoire de la langue occitane en particulier et l'histoire des idees linguistiques en general."

*3219. Reed, O. E. "Thomas Jefferson in Agriculture." Journal of Dairy Science. 27(1944), 613-66.

3220. Reps, John W. "Thomas Jefferson's Checkerboard Towns." Journal of the Society of Architectural Historians. 20(1961), 108-14.

TJ proposed an alternating open square plan for Jeffersonville, Ind. which was later tried in Jackson, Miss.; good account.

3221. Reston, James B. "New Washington Vista." New York Times Magazine. October 19, 1941. 23.

The Jefferson Memorial.

3222. Rice, Howard C., Jr. "A French Source of Jefferson's Plan for the Prison at Richmond." Journal of the Society of Architectural Historians. 12(December 1953), 28-30.

TJ had seen in France plans for a prison by Pierre-Gabriel Bugniet.

3223. Rice, Howard, C., Jr. "Jefferson's Gift of Fossils to the Museum of Natural History in Paris." Proceedings of the APS. 95(1951), 597-627.

Account of TJ's gift in 1808 of fossils from Big Bone Lick, Kentucky, to the National Institute of France; these gave Cuvier "essential evidence for his description and 'reconstruction' of two extinct species."

3224. Rice, Howard C., Jr. "A 'New' Likeness of Thomas Jefferson." WMQ. 3rd ser. 6(1949), 84-89.

Account of the portrait made by Edme Quenedey.

3225. Rice, Howard C., Jr. "Saint-Mémin's Portrait of Jefferson." Princeton University Library Chronicle. 20(1959), 182-92.

Account of Saint-Mémin's physiognotrace portrait of TJ and description of the two differing copperplate engravings he did from it.

3226. Richardson, E. P. "A Life Drawing of Jefferson by John Trumbull." American Art Journal. 7(November 1975), 4-9.

Reattribution of a pencil drawing from Latrobe to Trumbull; probably done in 1786 when Trumbull often saw TJ. Also printed in Maryland Historical Magazine. 70(1975), 363-71.

3227.   Rickey, Homer G. "Memorandum on the German Edition of Jefferson's Notes on Virginia." Charlottesville: Univ. of Virginia Library, 1952. pp. 4.

Mimeographed sheets; bibliographical note and translation of the introduction offered to the German edition (Leipzig, 1788-89), probably written by the publisher, Matthias Christian Sprengel.

3228.   Ridiman, Bob. "Scientist Thomas Jefferson." Humpty-Dumpty's Magazine for Little Children. 24(July 1976), 61-63.

3229.   Roberson, Samuel Arndt. "Thomas Jefferson and the Eighteenth-Century Landscape Garden Movement in England." Ph.D. dissertation. Yale Univ., 1974. pp. 163.

Discusses the influence of Thomas Whately's Observations on Modern Gardening (1770), and TJ's visits to many of the English gardens described there. His work at Monticello is an important forerunner of the American landscape movement of the nineteenth century. DAI 35/05A, p. 2684.

3230.   Roberts, John G. "An Exchange of Letters Between Jefferson and Quesnay de Beaurepaire." VMHB. 50(1942), 134-42.

TJ doubts the possibilities of success for Quesnay's French academy at Richmond.

*3231.   Roberts, Mary Fanton. "Brandon, With Its Memories of Perukes and Farthingales." Arts and Decoration. 43(January 1936), 6-9+.

3232.   Robinson, Geroid T. "Small Farms and Big Machines." Agricultural History. 27(April 1953), 69-71.

Compares TJ's agrarian ideas to those of the Russian Populists (Narodniks) and surmises that TJ would not have been hostile to cooperation among farmers, although he would certainly have opposed Soviet-style collectivization.

3233.   Robsjohn-Gibbings, T. H. "If Thomas Jefferson Visited Your Home." American Home. 32(July 1944), 26.

He would judge your furniture for its utility not for its antique charm.

3234.   Rocca, J. C. "Jefferson's Notes on Virginia and the Census of 1940." WMQ. 2nd ser. 23(1943), 153-59.

Compares TJ's comments on population and economic situation of
Virginia to data revealed in 1940 census. Not clear why.

3235. Rosen, George. "Political Order and Human Health in Jeffersonian
Thought." Bulletin of the History of Medicine. 26(1952), 32-44.

Argues that TJ and Benjamin Rush saw an analogy between the health
of the individual and the health of his society, and they viewed
(optimistically) the natural world in which man saw himself contained.

3236. Rosenbach, A. S. W. "The Libraries of the Presidents of the United
States." Proceedings of the American Antiquarian Society. 44(1934),
337-64.

TJ's library described, 346-51.

3237. Rosenberg, Pierre. "Salons: 1785, 1787, 1789" in The Eye of Thomas
Jefferson, ed. William Howard Adams. Washington: National Gallery
of Art, 1976. 152-66.

Account of the three salons TJ could have seen in Paris and some of
the paintings exhibited in them.

3238. Rosenberger, Francis Coleman. XII Poems. New York: Gotham Book
Mart, 1946. unpag.

Has four poems on TJ.

3239. Rossman, Wendell E. "Die Hoelzerne Saeulenarchitektur am Campus
von Jeffersons Universitaet von Virginia, Charlottesville, Va."
Phoenix, Ariz., 1965. pp. 164.

Detailed, illustrated study of the architectural facades of the
pavilions on the lawn at the University.

3240. Rothman, Irving N. "Structure and Theme in Samuel Ewing's Satire,
The 'American Miracle.'" American Literature. 40(1968), 294-308.

Ewing's poem is a "Federalist attack upon the Republicans and, particularly, Jefferson." Deals with the mammoth cheese and mammoth
bones.

3241. Ruck, William Sener. "Jefferson the Architect." VQR. 8(1932),
139-43.

Review essay of book by I. T. Frary criticizes the underemphasis on
TJ's European models.

3242. Ruskin, Mary. "Thomas Jefferson and Education." Social Studies.
41(1950), 349-50.

Conventional sketch.

3243. Rutledge, Anna Wells. "William John Coffee as a Portrait Sculptor." Gazette des Beaux Arts. ser. 6 28(November 1945), 297-312.

Coffee did terra cotta busts of TJ, Martha Jefferson Randolph, and four of her children. Account of his career with extensive quotations from correspondence with TJ.

3244. Sadler, Elizabeth Hatcher. The Bloom of Monticello. Richmond: Whittet and Shepperson, 1925. pp. 20.

TJ's life at Monticello with special attention to his plants and gardens; minor.

3245. Salamanca, Lucy. Fortress of Freedom; The Story of the Library of Congress. Philadelphia: Lippincott, 1942. pp. 445.

TJ's contributions discussed on pp. 93-116; the usual.

3246. Salmon, Myrene. "L'Enfant and the Planning of Washington, D.C." History Today. 26(1976), 699-706.

Describes L'Enfant's role in planning the city and his quarrels with the commissioners; TJ as Secretary of State was concerned about L'Enfant's progress.

3247. Sanchez, Ramon. "Jefferson, The Founder of the Ideology of Democratic Education." Journal of Education. 155(February 1973), 45-55.

Argues that to find a TJ who is the basis of a theory of democratic education we must turn to the author of the Declaration rather than the author of the Virginia proposals.

3248. Sand, Norbert. "Classics in Jefferson's Theory of Education." Classical Journal. 40(November 1944), 92-98.

TJ believed the classics were models of pure style and taste, their study was conducive to happiness and satisfaction, and they were "stores of real science." His sense of utility in educational matters was broad enough to provide a basic place for classics.

3249. Sandefur, Ray H. "Logan's Oration—How Authentic?" Quarterly Journal of Speech. 46(1960), 289-96.

Logan did indeed dictate the speech which "was probably as accurately reported as any speech given in similar circumstances could be." TJ's text probably came from the version published in New York in 1775.

3250. Sanders, Gold V. "Thomas Jefferson's Inventions." Popular Science.

148(January 1946), 104-13.

Monticello's gadgets.

3251. Sanford, Charles B. Thomas Jefferson and His Library. Hamden, Conn.: Archon, 1977. pp. 211.

Studies TJ's reading interests, book acquisition, and library organization and finds evidence for a deep interest in religion and Biblical scholarship as well as confirmation of wide reading in ethical literature. Best book on this subject.

3252. Sarton, May. "Monticello" in The Lion and the Rose. New York: Rinehart, 1948. 15.

Poem.

3253. Savin, Marion B. and Harold J. Abrahams. "The Botanical Library of Thomas Jefferson." Journal of the Elisha Mitchell Scientific Society. 74(1959), 44-52.

Discusses TJ's interest in botany; documents books on botany which he owned. Useful.

3254. Savin, Marion B. and Harold J. Abrahams. "The Zoological Library of Thomas Jefferson." Journal of the Elisha Mitchell Scientific Society. 74(1958), 98-109.

Comments on 43 books TJ owned on the subject.

3255. Schafer, Bruce H. "Thomas Jefferson: Architect and Statesman, 1743-1826." Telesis (The Architectural Student Journal). Spring 1976, 3-7.

Surveys architectural activities; insignificant.

3256. Scheick, William J. "Chaos and Imaginative Order in Thomas Jefferson's Notes on the State of Virginia" in Essays in Early Virginia Literature Honoring Richard Beale Davis, ed. J. A. Leo LeMay. New York: Burt Franklin, 1977. 221-34.

The ideal imaginative order of "a temperate liberty" is the underlying aesthetic vision of Notes, and TJ applies it variously to landscape, law, and the moral sense. Suggestive.

3257. Scheffel, Richard L. "Presidential Bird Watcher." Audubon Magazine. 63(May 1961), 138-39.

TJ could identify over 100 birds, knew Alexander Wilson's and Mark Catesby's work on ornithology.

*3258. Scheffel, Richard Leon. "Thomas Jefferson: Student of Natural

421

History, An Essay." M.S. thesis. Cornell Univ., 1960. pp. 61.

3259. Schick, Joseph S. "Poe and Jefferson." VMHB. 54(1946), 316-20.

Claims TJ could have met Poe and also influenced "the formulation of the principles of accuracy and brevity in the evolution of his literary technique."

3260. Schonberg, Harold C. "Jefferson and the Piano." The Piano Teacher. 4(July/August 1962), 11-12.

3261. "Scraps from a Note Book. The Capitol." Virginia Historical Register and Literary Advertiser. 1(October 1848), 169.

Short note on TJ's use of the Maison Carrée of Nimes as a model for the Richmond Capitol.

3262. Seeber, Edward D. "Critical Views on Logan's Speech." Journal of American Folklore. 60(1947), 130-46.

Discusses the varying reception of Logan's speech, including TJ's version of it, and examines the evidence for its authenticity and its provenance.

3263. Seeber, Edward D. "Diderot and Chief Logan's Speech." Modern Language Notes. 60(1945), 176-78.

Peripheral.

3264. A Selection of Original Plans and Drawings by Thomas Jefferson. San Marino, Cal.: Huntington Library, 1938. unpag.

An exhibit arranged for a visit of the Southern California chapter of the American Institute of Architects at the Huntington Library. Preface by William McCay; notes.

3265. Sellers, James Lee. "Thomas Jefferson's University." Prairie Schooner. 10(Summer 1936), 113-17.

Brief account of the creation of the Univ. of Virginia as a democratic institution.

3266. Senkevitch, Anatole. "The Competition for the President's House" in The Eye of Thomas Jefferson, ed. William Howard Adams. Washington: National Gallery of Art, 1976. 234-55.

TJ lost out to James Hoban; well-told version of the usual story.

*3267. Servies, James A. "Thomas Jefferson and His Bibliographic Classification." M.A. thesis. Univ. of Chicago, 1950. pp. iv, 119.

3268. Setzler, Edwin Boinest, Edwin Lake Setzler, and Hubert Holland Setzler. The Jefferson Anglo-Saxon Grammar and Reader. New York: Macmillan, 1938. pp. xiv, 198.

"The present text is an attempt—a belated attempt, it is true—to write the type of Anglo-Saxon grammar which Jefferson said should be prepared."

3269. Setzler, E. B. "Jefferson's Theory as to the Study of Anglo-Saxon: An Experiment conducted at the University of South Carolina." The Anglo-Saxon. Bulletin, Newberry College. 2(no. 3, 1930), 4-9.

Studying Anglo-Saxon in relation to its forms in modern English was a great success the author claims.

3270. Shackelford, George Green. "A Peep into Elysium" in Thomas Jefferson and the Arts: An Extended View, ed. William Howard Adams. Washington: National Gallery of Art, 1976. 233-69.

Discusses TJ's trip to Italy in 1787 and the architectural and artistic works he saw there.

3271. Shackelford, George Green. "Thomas Jefferson and the Fine Arts of Northern Italy: 'A Peep into Elysium,'" in America: The Middle Period. Essays in Honor of Bernard Mayo, ed. John D. Boles. Charlottesville: Univ. Press of Virginia, 1973. 14-35.

Similar to the previous item; contends TJ's interest in painting has been underestimated but is able to offer only speculations about much of what TJ saw and how it could have influenced him.

3272. Shapiro, Karl. "Jefferson" in V-Letter and Other Poems. New York: Reynal and Hitchcock, 1944. 19.

Poem.

3273. Shapley, Harlow. "Notes on Thomas Jefferson as a Natural Philosopher." Proceedings of the APS. 87(1943), 234-37.

"In general the natural philosophy of Jefferson was of the practical sort."

3274. Sharp, Wayne W. "La Revolutions de Thomas Jefferson." Comptes Rendus des Seances de L'Academie d'Agriculture de France. 62(1976), 1087-93.

Sketch emphasizing TJ's contributions to agriculture.

3275. Sheehan, Bernard W. "The Quest for Indian Origins in the Thought of the Jeffersonian Era." Midcontinent American Studies Journal. 9(Spring 1968), 34-51.

Discusses TJ's place among his contemporaries such as Benjamin Smith Barton and Peter S. Duponceau; they shared a belief in the utility of comparative linguistics and a desire to investigate without the encumbrance of an elaborate, or exotic, hypothesis.

3276. Shepherd, Henry E. "Thomas Jefferson as a Philologist." American Journal of Philology. 3(1882), 211-14.

TJ as friend to neology.

3277. Sherman, C. B. "Thomas Jefferson: Far-Sighted Farmer." Better Crops with Plant Food: The Pocket Book of Agriculture. 28(November 1944), 18-21, 44-45.

TJ as an innovative farmer in terms of stock, crops, and practices.

3278. Sherril, Sarah B. "The Eye of Thomas Jefferson." Antiques. 109(1976), 1104.

On the forthcoming exhibit.

3279. Shoemaker, Floyd C. "Remarks on Senator Allen McReynolds and the Bingham Portrait of Thomas Jefferson." Missouri Historical Review. 48(1953), 42-45.

On Bingham's 1857 copy of Stuart's portrait.

3280. Shonting, Donald Allen. "Romantic Aspects in the Works of Thomas Jefferson." Ph.D. dissertation. Ohio Univ., 1977. pp. 145.

TJ is a transitional figure between the neoclassic and the romantic. His emphasis on the essential worth of the individual, his appreciation of nature in all its variety, and his concern for freedom of expression are romantic elements. Although consciously neoclassic in his architecture, romantic elements mark his literary works and the development of his architecture. DAI 38/12A, p. 6998.

3281. Simms, L. Moody. "Thomas Jefferson and Architecture in the Early Republic." Illinois Quarterly. 33(December 1970), 6-15.

General discussion.

3282. Simpson, George Gaylord. "The Beginnings of Vertebrate Paleontology in North America." Proceedings of the APS. 86(1942), 130-88.

Discusses TJ's contributions to paleontology and argues that he was important as a publicist and encouraging force but that "he was not a vertebrate paleontologist in any reasonable sense."

3283. Simpson, Lewis P. "The Garden of the Covenant and the Garden of the Chattel" in The Dispossessed Garden, Pastoral and History in

Southern Literature. Athens: Univ. of Georgia Press, 1975. 1-33.

Argues that in Monticello and Notes TJ participated in the inherently alienating paradox of a pastoral ideal based on chattel slavery. This argument is recapitulated more briefly in "The Southern Literary Vocation" in Toward a New American Literary History: Essays in Honor of Arlin Turner, ed. Louis J. Budd, et. al. Durham: Duke Univ. Press, 1979. 25-28.

3284.   Simpson, Lewis P. "The Symbolism of Literary Alienation in the Revolutionary Age." Journal of Politics. 38(August 1976), 79-100.

Contends that TJ's "reversal of mind and society as paradigms for order" has resulted in a "radical displacement of the traditional community" and a "subjectification of American society."

3285.   Sinnott, John P. "Mr. Jefferson's Mothball Fleet." Navy Magazine. 13(April 1971), 22-26.

On TJ's proposed floating drydock.

3286.   "Sir Valentine." Literary Digest. 100(March 23, 1929), 29.

A poem purportedly by TJ, but in fact not.

3287.   Skallerup, Harry R. "'For His Excellency Thomas Jefferson, Esq.': The Tale of a Wandering Book." Quarterly Journal of the Library of Congress. 31(1974), 116-21.

How TJ's copy of Jose de Mendoza y Rios' A Complete Collection of Tables for Navigation and Nautical Astronomy ended up in the Naval Academy library instead of the Library of Congress.

3288.   Slonimsky, Nicolas. "Musical Miscellany." Etude. 68(February 1950), 4.

Short note on TJ's decision to buy a pianoforte instead of a clavichord.

3289.   Slosson, Edwin E. "Jefferson and State Education" in The American Spirit in Education; A Chronicle of Great Teachers. New Haven: Yale Univ. Press, 1921. 78-93.

Among TJ's innovations should be counted the elective system, vocational specialization, and the honor system. He also wanted to restrict drastically the university's control over students' personal lives and to do away with honorary degrees and titles.

3290.   Smith, B. M. "Loftiest Edifices Need the Deepest Foundations: Monticello." Hobbies. 56(April 1951), 58-60.

Describes design and furnishings of Monticello.

3291. Smith, C. Alphonso. "Thomas Jefferson" in Die Amerikanische
        Literatur. Bibliothek der amerikanischen Kulturgeschicte. hgb. von
        N. M. Butler und Wilhelm Paszkowski. Band II. Berlin: Weidmann,
        1912.

        Claims TJ influenced the course of American literature by the vigor
        of his style but more importantly by looking at every problem from
        the viewpoint of human freedom. "Jeffersonianism is today better
        exemplified in American literature than in American politics."
        Trans. by the author and rpt. in Southern Literary Studies; A
        Collection of Literary, Biographical, and Other Sketches. Chapel
        Hill: Univ. of North Carolina Press, 1927. 94-119.

3292. Smith, David Eugene. "Thomas Jefferson and Mathematics." Scripta
        Mathematica. 1(1932), 3-14.

        Describes TJ's interest in mathematics; he was more interested in
        application than in theory. Also printed separately and in Smith's The
        Poetry of Mathematics and Other Essays. New York: Scripta
        Mathematica, 1934. 49-70.

*3293. Smith, Doris N. "Thomas Jefferson's Proposals Concerning Public
        Education of an Educated Electorate." M.A. thesis. Bowling Green
        State Univ., 1962.

3294. Smith, Glenn C. "Thomas Jefferson Loved Flowers." Flower and
        Garden. 6(November 1962), 30-31.

3295. Smith, Gordon S. "Poplar Forest—Jefferson's Bedford Farm." Soil
        Conservation. 24(1959), 195-97.

        On conservation of farm lands at Poplar Forest; peripheral.

3296. Smith, Henry Nash. "A Highway to the Pacific: Thomas Jefferson and
        the Far West" in Virgin Land. Cambridge: Harvard Univ. Press, 1950.
        15-18.

        Brief chapter lauds TJ as "the intellectual father of the American
        advance to the Pacific."

*3297. Smith, Hugh P. "Some Limitations of the Educational Theory of
        Thomas Jefferson." Ph.D. dissertation. Univ. of North Carolina,
        1936.

3298. Smith, Russell. "Jefferson Program at Charlottesville." Musical
        America. 76(June 1956), 7.

        Report on a concert at Monticello of music from TJ's collection.

3299. "Some Favorite Recipes of Presidents Jefferson and Washington."
        Today's Living. 5(July 1974), 18-21, 50-52.

*3300. Southern Education Board. Thomas Jefferson on Public Education. Knoxville, Tenn., 1902. pp. 22.

3301. Sowerby, E. Millicent. Catalogue of the Library of Thomas Jefferson. 5 vols. Washington: Library of Congress, 1952-1959.

An essential piece of scholarship. Based on TJ's catalogue of the library he sold in 1815, this adds bibliographic description of the editions or probable editions he owned and annotates the entries, usually with comments from TJ's own writings. Volume 1 has a preface describing the compiler's method and covers entries on civil and natural history. Volume 2 covers moral philosophy, 3 includes politics, 4 concludes entries on philosophy with citations in mathematics, astronomy, and geography and begins the entries on the fine arts. 5 concludes the fine arts entries and adds a section on sources, etc. plus an index for the whole catalogue.

3302. Sowerby, E. Millicent. "Some Presentation Copies in the Library of Thomas Jefferson." Quarterly Journal of the Library of Congress. 8(November 1950), 78-87.

Jefferson's notation of author's names in some books is the only surviving record of their ownership.

3303. Sowerby, E. Millicent. "Thomas Jefferson and His Library." Papers of the Bibliographic Society of America. 50(1956), 213-28.

TJ was a bibliomaniac but not a bibliophile. Discusses the work involved in preparing the monumental Catalogue; anecdotal but suggestive. Translated into Spanish as "La Biblioteca de Thomas Jefferson." Revista Interamericana de Bibliografia. 8(no. 2, 1958), 115-24.

3304. Spencer, Thomas Eugene. "Education and American Liberalism: A comparison of the Views of Thomas Jefferson, Ralph Waldo Emerson, and John Dewey." Ph.D. dissertation. Univ. of Illinois, 1963. pp. 262.

"Despite obvious differences, Jefferson, Emerson, and Dewey had much in common." DAI 24/10, p. 4099.

3305. Spratt, John S. "Thomas Jefferson: The Scholarly Politician and His Influence on Medicine." Southern Medical Journal. 69(1976), 360-66.

Probably the best article on this subject; surveys previous scholarship, TJ's medical interests, and his influence real and potential on American medicine.

3306. Stafford, William. "New Letters from Thomas Jefferson." Esquire. 75(May 1971), 205.

Poem; rpt. in Someday, Maybe. New York: Harper and Row, 1973. 7-8.

3307. Stapley, Mildred. "Monticello and the Jeffersonian Style." Country Life. 20(October 1911), 43-46.

3308. Stapley, M. "Thomas Jefferson the Architect: A Tribute." Architectural Record. 29(1911), 177-85.

Describes Monticello, comments on other architectural projects. Argues that TJ is a significant architect who "grasped as a basic principle the value of sincerity between form and construction."

3309. Stiebing, William H., Jr. "Who First Excavated Stratigraphically?" Biblical Archaeology Review. 7(January/February 1981), 52-53.

TJ did; brief account.

3310. Stokes, Roy. "The Fourth." Library Journal. 88(1963), 2648.

TJ is "the symbol of all that librarianship stands for."

3311. Stolba, K. Marie. "Music in the Life of Thomas Jefferson." Daughters of the American Revolution Magazine. 108(1974), 196-202.

Sketch of TJ's interest in music, noting his correspondence on musical matters with Francis Hopkinson. Shorter version in American Music Teacher. 25(April 1976), 6-8.

3312. Stone, Peter and Sherman Edwards. 1776; A Musical Play. New York: Viking, 1970. pp. 174.

Book by Stone, music and lyrics by Edwards. The Declaration and its composition as musical comedy.

*3313. Storey, Helen Anderson. "Jefferson's Furniture at Monticello." Antiquarian. 15(July 1930), 38-40, 60-70.

3314. Surface, George Thomas. "Investigations into the Character of Jefferson as a Scientist." Journal of American History. 4(1910), 214-20.

TJ was "an observer in the field of geography before Morse had reached the age of ten years," and he was in the advance of any contemporary in the economic interpretation of geography.

3315. Surface, George Thomas. "Thomas Jefferson: A Pioneer Student of American Geography." Bulletin of the American Geographic Society. 41(1909), 743-50.

Discusses TJ's accomplishments as a geographer and contends for the innovative nature of his work.

3316. Suro, Dario. "Jefferson, The Architect." Américas. 25(November/ December 1973), 29-35.

TJ as Palladianist.

3317. Swift, David E. "Thomas Jefferson, John Holt Rice, and Education in Virginia, 1815-25." Journal of Presbyterian History. 49(1971), 32-58.

TJ and Rice had much in common, but Rice could not accept TJ's "deistic or Socinian" ideas about education. Informative about the struggles to establish the Univ. of Virginia and about Rice.

3318. Tate, Allen. "On the Father of Liberty." Sewanee Review. 38(1930), 20.

Poem.

3319. Taylor, Howard Singleton. "The Light of Jefferson." Watson's Jeffersonian Magazine. 1(1907), 564-65.

Poem.

3320. Taylor, Olivia A. "The Monticello Bust of Thomas Jefferson." Annual Report of the Monticello Association. 1956. 21-27.

Considers whether the "Monticello bust" is a copy of the lost Ceracchi, concludes it is probably a copy of the David d'Angers portrait commissioned by U. P. Levy.

3321. Thacker, William C. "The Structural Preservation of Monticello." n.p., 1955. pp. (11).

Report done for the Memorial Foundation, discusses work done in 1953 which included the removal of nearly 100 tons of the mud and brick nogging laid in between the floor joists.

3322. Thomas, James. "The Lost Ceracchi Bust of Thomas Jefferson." Antiques. 104(July 1973), 125-27.

The bust was destroyed in the Library of Congress fire of 1851, but daguerrotypes of it may have been made.

3323. Thomas Jefferson Memorial Foundation. Report of the Curator to the Board of Directors of the Thomas Jefferson Memorial Foundation. 1957— . Monticello: Thomas Jefferson Memorial Foundation, 1957— .

These reports, issued annually since 1957, are not listed separately here, but each one notes accessions at Monticello for the year as well as archaeological and structural repair activities.

3324. Thomas Jefferson Memorial Foundation. Thomas Jefferson, The Sage of Monticello And His Beloved Home. New York: Thomas Jefferson Memorial Foundation, 1926. pp. 45.

Issued as Monticello Papers Number Five. Includes essays by Fiske Kimball, "The Architecture of Monticello"; Mabel Mason Carlton, "The Life of Thomas Jefferson"; Henry Alan Johnston, "The Story of the Thomas Jefferson Memorial Foundation."

3325. Thomas Jefferson Memorial Foundation. Treasure from Monticello. The Charm and Beauty of Thomas Jefferson's Mansion Are Reproduced for the Modern Home. Harrisonburg, Va.: Harrisonburg Craftsmen, 1928? pp. 39.

Monticello furniture described and copies are for sale in the Monticello shop.

3326. "Thomas Jefferson." Science and Children. 13(January 1976), 38.

Inventions; juvenile.

3327. Thomas Jefferson and the College of William and Mary. Williamsburg: College of William and Mary, 1963. unpag.

Catalogue of "An Exhibit of Books, Manuscripts, and Artifacts Prepared in Observance of Charter Day, February Eighth, Nineteen Sixty-Three."

3328. "Thomas Jefferson and the Growth of American Technology." Intellect. 106(November 1977), 192.

Report on a Voice of America broadcast by Hugo A. Meier; insignificant.

3329. Thomas Jefferson and the World of Books. A symposium held at the Library of Congress September 21, 1976. Washington: Library of Congress, 1977. pp. 37.

Addresses by Frederick R. Goff and Merrill Peterson, noted separately here, and remarks by Daniel Boorstin and Dumas Malone.

3330. "Thomas Jefferson: Architect." American Society Legion of Honor Magazine. 11(1940), 187-89.

An appreciation of TJ's taste; superficial.

3331. The Thomas Jefferson Bicentennial Exhibition 1743-1943, April thirteenth to May fifteenth, 1943. Washington: National Gallery of Art, 1943.

Catalogue of fifty portraits of TJ and contemporaries; no illustrations or notes.

3332. "Thomas Jefferson Country Gentleman." Red Rose Farm Family Magazine. June/July 1962, Inside front cover-2, 15.

3333. "Thomas Jefferson, Farmer." Cooperative Farmer. 32(June/July 1976), 17, 34.

3334. Thomas Jefferson in High Street, Philadelphia One Hundred and Fifty Years Ago. Philadelphia: Strawbridge and Clothier, 1926. pp. 12.

Catalogue of furniture as supplied for the 'refurnishing' of the (supposed) house in which TJ wrote the Declaration. A dubious enterprise all around.

3335. The Thomas Jefferson Murals By Ezra Winter, N.A., in the Thomas Jefferson Room, Library of Congress. Washington: Government Printing Office, 1943? Folded broadside.

Black and white reproduction, plus description.

3336. "Thomas Jefferson—Paleontologist." Review of Reviews. 74(1926), 200.

Review of article by Frederick A. Lucas; minor.

3337. "Thomas Jefferson, Planter." Gourmet. 36(May 1976), 23, 56-62.

TJ as gastronome.

3338. "Thomas Jefferson Revealed as Art Collector." Art Digest. 10(May 15, 1936), 9.

On the rediscovery of Ribera's Penitent Magdalen which TJ purchased from the St. Severin collection in 1785.

3339. "Thomas Jefferson: The Sheepman." National Wool Grower. 66(April 1976), 10-11, 24-25.

Informative discussion of TJ's sheep raising and breeding, including his efforts to propagate Merino sheep.

3340. Thompson, Randall. The Testament of Freedom, A Setting of Four Passages from the Writings of Thomas Jefferson For Men's Voices with Piano or Orchestral Accompaniment. Boston: E. C. Schirmer, 1944. pp. 53.

Also published in E.C.S. miniature score series, pp. 95.

*3341. Thompson, Wilma. "Thomas Jefferson: Lifelong Musician." M. Mus. thesis. Southern Illinois Univ., 1973.

3342. Thomson, Robert Polk. "The Reform of the College of William and Mary, 1763-1780." Proceedings of the APS. 115(1971), 187-213.

Touches on TJ's role in the post-revolutionary reform of the College and concludes that its reorganization "was not simply a projection of Thomas Jefferson's ideas."

*3343. Thorpe, Russell W. "A Portrait of Thomas Jefferson, A Lost Picture Since 1897—Portrait by Robert Field (obit. 1819)." Antiquarian. 4(March 1925), 17-18.

3344. Thorup, Oscar A. "Jefferson's Admonition." Mayo Clinic Proceedings. 47(1972), 199-201.

TJ's caution against excessive physicking reminds of the danger of the "diseases of medical management."

3345. Thorup, Oscar A., Jr. "Thomas Jefferson and Academic Medicine." The Pharos of Alpha Omega Alpha. 40(April 1977), 16-22.

Sketch of TJ and the University of Virginia Medical School.

3346. "Thoughts on Visiting the Grave of Jefferson." Virginia Literary Magazine. 1(1829), 133.

Poem, signed "Zenobia."

3347. Tice, David A. "Jefferson's Country. American Forests. 83(May 1977), 24-27.

TJ and land management; general.

*3348. Tipton, Patricia Gray. "An Index to References to Music in Thomas Jefferson's Paris Letters." M.A. thesis. Memphis State Univ., 1972. pp. 79.

*3349. Todd, Terry E. "Thomas Jefferson and the Founding of the University of Virginia." M.A. thesis. University of California at Riverside, 1956.

3350. Towner, Lawrence W. "Introduction" in As Sweet as Madeira ... As Astringent as Bordeaux ... As Brisk as Champagne: Thomas Jefferson on Wines. Chicago: Privately Printed, 1965. unpag.

Facsimile of a mss. now in a private collection. A commentary on wines apparently sent by TJ in 1791-92 to Henry Sheaff, a

Philadelphia merchant. The wines TJ judged outstanding are still so, but the prices are long gone. Chateau d'Yquem in 1792 cost about the same as a pound of butter but in 1965 the price was at least 7 times that of butter.

3351. Trent, William P. English Culture in Virginia: A Study of the Gilmer Letters and an Account of the English Professors Obtained by Jefferson for the University of Virginia. Johns Hopkins University Studies in Historical and Political Science. 7th Ser. No. 5-6. Baltimore: Johns Hopkins Press, 1889. pp. 141.

The development of the University idea and Francis Walker Gilmer's role as TJ's friend and agent. Interesting but outdated.

3352. True, Rodney H. "Early Days of the Albemarle Agricultural Society." Annual Report of the American Historical Association ... 1918. 1:241-59.

Explains TJ's role in founding the Society.

3353. True, Rodney H. "A Sketch of the Life of John Bradbury, Including His Unpublished Correspondence with Thomas Jefferson." Proceedings of the APS. 68(1929), 133-50.

Touches on the relationship between TJ and Bradbury, an English botanist who traveled up the Missouri in 1809-11.

3354. True, Rodney H. "Some Neglected Botanical Results of the Lewis and Clark Expedition." Proceedings of the APS. 67(1928), 1-19.

Describes TJ's role in encouraging the cultivation of seeds brought home by Lewis and Clark. Samples were sent to Bernard McMahon, a Philadelphia gardener, and to William Hamilton; some were also planted at Monticello. TJ and McMahon held occasional correspondence about these.

3355. True, Rodney H. "Thomas Jefferson in Relation to Botany." Scientific Monthly. 3(1916), 344-60.

Details TJ's botanical activities; his cultivation of plants, his dissemination of seeds and specimens, his correspondence with other botanists. Still useful.

3356. True, Rodney H. "Thomas Jefferson's Garden Book." Proceedings of the APS. 76(1936), 939-45.

Descriptive account of the Garden Book.

3357. Trzeciakowski, Lech. "'The World of Jefferson and Franklin'— Exhibition at the National Museum in Warsaw." Polish Western Affairs. 16(no. 1, 1975), 98-99.

Review of the exhibit and its meaning for Poles.

3358. Tuttle, Kate A. "The Founding of the University of Virginia."
American Monthly Magazine. 22(1903), 108-13.

3359. Tutwiler, Henry. Address of H. Tutwiler, A.M., LL.D., of Alabama
Before the Alumni Society of the University of Virginia, Thursday,
June 29th, 1882. Charlottesville: Chronicle Book and Job Office,
1882. pp. 14.

An appeal not to change TJ's administrative structure of the Univ.
and an argument for its wisdom.

3360. Tyack, David. "Forming the National Character." Harvard Educational
Review. 36(1966), 29-41.

Reviews educational theories of TJ, Benjamin Rush, and Noah
Webster.

3361. [Tyler, Lyon G.]. "Ceracchi's Bust of Jefferson." Tyler's Quarterly
Historical and Genealogical Magazine. 8(1927), 243-46.

Prints the petition of "sundry citizens of the County of Albemarle"
who wished to keep the bust by Giuseppe Ceracchi within the state.
Long note on Ceracchi.

3362. Tyler, Lyon G. "Early Courses and Professors at William and Mary
College." WMQ. 14(1905), 71-83.

Touches upon TJ's relationship with William and Mary.

3363. Tyler, Lyon G., ed. "Two Unpublished Letters of Thomas Jefferson."
WMQ. 17(1908), 18-20.

Prints with notes letters, one dated Jan. 3, 1796, to Justin Pierre de
Rieux on farming and business matters.

3364. Tyler, Moses Coit. "Thomas Jefferson and the Great Declaration" in
The Literary History of the American Revolution, 1763-1783. New
York: Putnam's, 1897. 1:494-521.

Discusses the conditions of TJ's composition of the Declaration, the
response it evoked then and later, especially critical response, and its
literary quality. Finds the accusations of lack of originality and of
historical falsification beside the point and claims the document is
original because of TJ's own peculiar genius.

3365. Ultan, Roslye R. "A Comparative Study of the Educational Philosophies
of Thomas Jefferson and Benjamin Rush." unpub. typescript.
Dickinson College Library, 1958. pp. 35.

3366. U. S. Library of Congress. Catalogue of the Library of Thomas

Jefferson, 1815, A Prospectus. Washington: Government Printing
Office, 1943. pp. 17.

Prospectus for Sowerby's edition.

3367. Univ. of Chicago Libraries. "Jefferson Offers His Library."
Manuscripts. 15(1963), 3-7.

Prints letter, now at Chicago, of September 21, 1814, offering to sell
his library to the nation.

3368. Univ. of Virginia Development Fund. Thomas Jefferson's Other Spy-
glass. Charlottesville: Univ. of Virginia Development Fund, 1948.
pp. 16.

Fund raising brochure, dwelling on the TJ heritage and present need.

3369. The University of Virginia and Its Founder. Charlottesville: Univ. of
Virginia Alumni Fund, n.d. broadside.

Accordion-fold broadside for visitors on the history and architecture
of the University.

3370. Vail, Eugène A. "Littérature des Noirs ou Gens de Couleur." French
American Review. 1(1948), 135-42.

Translation of songs and tales collected by Martha Jefferson
Randolph from her father's slaves. First published in 1841.

*3371. Van Ward, Roland. "The Geological and Geographical Writings of
Thomas Jefferson." M.S. thesis. Univ. of Virginia, 1938. pp. 219.

*3372. Vaughan, G. B. "Thomas Jefferson, the Community College, and the
Pursuit of Education." Community College Frontiers. 8(Summer
1980), 4-10.

3373. Vaughan, Joseph Lee and Omer Allen Gianniny, Jr. Thomas Jefferson's
Rotunda Restored 1973-76. Charlottesville: Univ. Press of Virginia,
1981. pp. xxi, 170.

Introduction by Frederick Doveton Nichols; on TJ's original concept,
Stanford White's rebuilding, and the restoration. Generously illustrated.

3374. Verner, Coolie. "The Maps and Plates Appearing with the Several
Editions of Mr. Jefferson's 'Notes on the State of Virginia.'" VMHB.
59(1951), 21-33.

Careful bibliographical description.

3375. Verner, Coolie. "Mr. Jefferson Distributes His Notes, A Preliminary

Checklist of First Editions." Bulletin of the New York Public Library. 56(1952), 159-86.

How and to whom TJ sent copies of the 1st edition of Notes; varying states of the edition may suggest second thoughts on what TJ wished to include. Also printed separately, New York: New York Public Library, 1952. pp. 31.

3376. Verner, Coolie. "Mr. Jefferson Makes a Map." Imago Mundi. 14(1959), 96-108.

Scholarly account of how TJ made the 1786 map of Virginia intended to accompany the Abbe Morellet's translation of Notes. Claims that the map is the most detailed and accurate representation of Virginia in the last quarter of the 18th century.

3377. Verner, Coolie. "Mr. Jefferson's Crusade Against Ignorance." Journal of Education of the Faculty and College of Education of the University of British Columbia. 7(June 1962), 16-24.

Survey of TJ's work for public education; slight.

3378. Verner, Coolie and P. J. Conkwright. "The Printing of Jefferson's Notes, 1793-94." Studies in Bibliography. 5(1952), 201-03.

Mathew Carey engaged Parry Hall to print the second American edition of Notes.

3379. Verner, Coolie. "Some Observations on the Philadelphia 1794 Edition of Jefferson's Notes." Studies in Bibliography. 2(1949), 201-04.

Bibliographic description of two states of this edition.

3380. Via, Betty Davis. The Fourth of July Goose. n.p., 1958. Folding broadside.

Monticello juvenile fiction.

3381. A Virginia Gentleman's Library as Proposed by Thomas Jefferson to Robert Skipwith in 1771 and Now Assembled in the Brush-Everard House, Williamsburg, Virginia. Williamsburg: Colonial Williamsburg, 1952. pp. 15.

Introduction by Arthur Pierce Middleton.

3382. "The Virginia State Capitol." The Old Dominion. 5(August 15, 1871), 483-91.

Touches on TJ as architect.

3383. Wagoner, Jennings L. Thomas Jefferson and the Education of a New

<u>Nation</u>. Bloomington, Ind.: Phi Delta Kappa Educational Foundation, 1976. pp. 41.

Competent survey of TJ's educational interests, ideas, and accomplishments.

3384. Wall, Charles Coleman. "Students and Student Life at the University of Virginia, 1825 to 1861." Ph.D. dissertation. Univ. of Virginia, 1978. pp. 341.

Examines the distance between TJ's plans for the discipline of students and the disciplinary regime actually imposed after October, 1825. This led to serious student disorder until a reform in 1842 restored some of the positive elements of TJ's model. DAI 40/02A, p. 1035.

3385. Wallace, Henry A. "Thomas Jefferson: Farmer, Educator, and Democrat." <u>Proceedings of the Association of Land Grant Colleges and Universities</u>. 51(1937), 338-46.

Eulogistic portrait of TJ as archetypical progressive.

3386. Wallace, Henry A. "Thomas Jefferson's Farm Book." <u>Agricultural History</u>. 28(1954), 133-38.

Discusses TJ's interest in farming and the difficulties of experimental farming.

3387. Ward, James E. "Monticello: An Experimental Farm." <u>Agricultural History</u>. 19(1945), 183-85.

TJ experimented with crop rotation, farm machinery, deep plowing, horizontal plowing, new plants, and pest control.

3388. Ward, James E. "Thomas Jefferson's Contributions to American Agriculture." Ph.D. dissertation. Univ. of Virginia, 1935. pp. iii, 256.

3389. Ward, James E. "Thomas Jefferson's Contributions to Agriculture." <u>Congressional Record</u>. 78 Congress, 1 Session. 89 (Appendix): 1769-70.

Also in <u>Univ. of Virginia News Letter</u>. 19(April 15, 1943).

3390. Warren, Robert Penn. <u>Brother to Dragons: A Tale in Verse and Voices</u>. New York: Random House, 1953. pp. xii, 230.

A poem in dialogue dealing with events and characters involved in the Kentucky tragedy in which TJ's nephews butchered a slave. One of the speakers is TJ. A new version was published in New York: Random House, 1979. pp. xiv, 141. This version gives Meriwether

Lewis a more significant role, says Warren, and is the result of an extensive reworking of the text.

3391. Wasserman, Burton. "Exhibition in Sight." School Arts. 76(October 1976), 24-27.

On the Eye of Thomas Jefferson exhibit.

3392. Waterman, Thomas T. "Thomas Jefferson, His Early Works in Architecture." Gazette des Beaux Arts. ser. 6. 24(August 1943), 89-106.

On work before the Revolution and influences on it; identifies TJ's architectural mentor as Richard Taliaferro of Williamsburg. Attributes Brandon, Battersea, and the Randolph-Semple house in Williamsburg to him.

3393. Watlington, Pat. "The Building of 'Liberty Hall.'" Register of the Kentucky Historical Society. 69(1971), 313-18.

TJ sent a plan and suggestions for the house of John Brown in Frankfort.

3394. Watson, F. J. B. "American and French Eighteenth-Century Furniture in the Age of Jefferson" in Thomas Jefferson and the Arts: An Extended View, ed. William Howard Adams. Washington: National Gallery of Art, 1976. 271-93.

TJ bought more furniture than any of his contemporaries, and his interest in architecture and decoration plus his fascination with gadgetry and technique better enabled him to appreciate the qualities of Louis XVI furniture.

3395. Watson, Francis J. B. "America's First Universal Man Had a Very Acute Eye." Smithsonian. 7(June 1976), 88-95.

TJ's aesthetic preferences surveyed.

3396. Watson, Francis J. B. "The Eye of Thomas Jefferson." Antiques. 110(July 1976), 118-25.

Adapted from item #3394 above.

3397. Watson, Jane. "Jefferson Statue." Magazine of Art. 34(1941), 494-95.

Note on Rudulph Evan's statue for the Memorial.

3398. Watson, Lucille McWane. "Thomas Jefferson's Other Home." Antiques. 71(1957), 342-46.

On Poplar Forest; excellent description with illustrations. See also the amplifying note in Antiques, 72(1957), 154, on a visit by George Flower.

3399. Watts, George B. "Thomas Jefferson, the 'Encyclopédié' and the 'Encyclopédié méthodique.'" French Review. 38(1965), 318-25.

Informative note on TJ's interest in Diderot's Encyclopédié, Charles-Joseph Panckoucke's Encyclopédié méthodique, and Jean-Nicolas Demeunier's "dictionary," Économie Politique et diplomatique, to which he contributed.

3400. Wayland, John W. "Jefferson as a Scientist." Virginia Journal of Education. 19(1926), 358-59.

TJ was a scientist in both the broadest and the narrow senses of the term; more laudatory than informative.

3401. Wayland, John W. "The Poetical Tastes of Thomas Jefferson." Sewanee Review. 18(1911), 283-99.

Discusses a scrapbook of newspaper verse supposedly collected by TJ; highly unlikely.

3402. Weaver, Neal. "Thomas Jefferson: Statesman, Artist, Scientist, and One Man Horticultural Exchange." Garden Journal. 26(October 1976), 147-50.

Sketch emphasizing TJ's gardening and botanical interests.

3403. Webb, Gerald Fred. "Jeffersonian Agrarianism in Faulkner's Yoknapatawpha: The Evolution of a Social and Economic Standard." Ph.D. dissertation. Florida State Univ., 1972. pp. 157.

Focus on Faulkner; contends that the "fierce economic, political and moral independence seen in Faulkner's yeomen reflects an intellectual position substantially identical to that of Thomas Jefferson whose tenets Faulkner may simply have assimilated from his society." DAI 33/10A, p. 5754.

3404. Webster, Donald B., Jr. "The Day Jefferson Got Plastered." American Heritage. 14(June 1963), 24-27.

J. H. I. Browere makes a life-mask of TJ that almost proves to be his death-mask.

3405. Weil, Ann. My Dear Patsy, A Novel of Jefferson's Daughter. Indianapolis: Bobbs-Merrill, 1941. pp. 315.

Juvenile fiction; Martha, "Patsy," Jefferson falls in love with "Tom" Randolph.

3406. Weiss, Harry B. "Thomas Jefferson and Economic Entomology." Journal of Economic Entomology. 37(1944), 836-41.

Surveys TJ's references to insects; although he was not an entomologist, he was "the only president of the United States who thought seriously enough about insects to write about them in his letters and to stress the need for more specific study of them."

3407. Welsh, Frank. "The Art of Painted Graining." Historical Preservation. 29(no. 3, 1977), 32-37.

Discusses techniques of imitating wood grain with paint and describes its use at Monticello, where the author is paint and color conservator.

3408. Wharton, James. "Jefferson, Expert on Wines." The Commonwealth: The Magazine of Virginia. 26(June 1959), 4, 8, 65-66.

General account.

3409. "What Next, Mr. Jefferson?" Magazine of Art. 31(1938), 301.

On the Jefferson Memorial controversy.

3410. White, John W. "A Letter to Thomas Jefferson." New England Social Studies Bulletin. 14(1956), 5-13.

Informs TJ about what has happened to education since his death.

3411. Whitehill, Walter Muir. The Many Faces of Monticello. Charlottesville: Thomas Jefferson Memorial Foundation, 1965. pp. 14.

Architectural evolution of Monticello briefly considered.

3412. Whitehill, Walter Muir. "Thomas Jefferson, Architect" in Thomas Jefferson: The Man ... His World ... His Influence, ed. Lally Weymouth. New York: Putnam's 1973. 159-77.

Surveys TJ's architectural activities with a review of the most significant literature.

3413. Whiting, F. A., Jr. "Facts from the Fine Arts Commission; Further Light on the Jefferson Memorial Controversy." Magazine of Art. 31(1938), 348-49, 372-74.

Reviews the controversy.

3414. Whiting, Margaret A. "The Father of Gadgets." Stone and Webster Journal. 49(1932), 302-15.

TJ's inventions.

3415. Whitty, J. H. "Thomas Jefferson's Bull Moose." Nation. 95(1912), 211.

Notes TJ's gift to Buffon.

3416. Wickard, Claude R. "Thomas Jefferson—Founder of Modern American Agriculture." Agricultural History. 19(1945), 179-80.

TJ lauded as pioneer agricultural scientist.

3417. Wiley, Wayne Hamilton. "Academic Freedom at the University of Virginia: The First Hundred Years—From Jefferson through Alderman." Ph.D. dissertation. Univ. of Virginia, 1973. pp. 399.

TJ's radical measures to assure intellectual liberty at the University --faculty tenure, full powers of decision in the conduct of scholarly work, opportunity to assist in administering the affairs of the University (TJ provided not for a president but an annually rotating faculty chairmanship)—assured a tradition that held up well, with a few blemishes, for the first century. DAI 34/08A, p. 4817.

3418. Williams, Edward K. "Jefferson's Theories of Language." M.A. thesis. Univ. of Wyoming, 1948. pp. viii, 89.

3419. Williams, John Sharp. The University of Virginia and the Development of Thomas Jefferson's Educational Ideas: Speech ... delivered at the St. Louis Meeting of the Association of State Universities, June 28, 1904. Charlottesville? 1904. pp. 16.

Emphasizes the democratic features of the Univ. of Virginia as a consequence of TJ's ideas.

3420. Williams, Morley J. "The Gardens of Monticello." Landscape Architecture. 24(January 1934), 64-71.

Informative discussion of attempts to discover TJ's original gardens.

3421. Williams, Morley Jeffers. "A Site for a Memorial." Magazine of Art. 31(1938), 268-70.

Contends the logical site for the Memorial is across the Potomac.

3422. Wilson, James Southall. "Best Sellers in Jefferson's Day." VQR. 36(1960), 222-37.

Examines the day books of the Virginia Gazette in the 1750's and '60's; discusses, among others, TJ's purchases.

3423. Wilson, Judith. "Barbara Chase-Riboud: Sculpting Our History." Essence. 10(December 1979), 12-13.

Interview with the author of Sally Hemings.

3424. Wilson, M. L. "Agricultural Jefferson Recognized." Extension Service Review. 15(April 1944), 55.

"He truly had extension blood in his veins."

3425. Wilson, M. L. "Jefferson and His Moldboard Plow." Land. 3(1943), 59-64.

Detailed and informative account of the plow and TJ's farming practices.

3426. Wilson, Milburn L. "Jefferson, Father of Agricultural Science." Extension Service Review. 14(May 1943), 74.

Sketch.

3427. Wilson, M. L. "Jefferson's Interest in Farming and Scientific Agriculture." Virginia Polytechnic Institute Extension Division News. 25(July 1943), 12.

3428. Wilson, M. L. "Survey of Scientific Agriculture." Proceedings of the APS. 86(1942), 52-62.

Claims TJ's paper on the moldboard plow has the greatest historical significance among the agricultural publications included in the first six volumes of the APS Transactions.

3429. Wilson, M. L. "Thomas Jefferson and Agricultural Engineering." Agricultural Engineering. 24(1943), 299-303.

Full review of TJ's farming practices and farming technology.

3430. Wilson, M. L. "Thomas Jefferson-Farmer." Proceedings of the APS. 87(1943), 216-22.

Discursive survey of TJ's contributions to agricultural science and education.

3431. Wilson, M. L. "Why Agriculture Honors Jefferson." Congressional Record. 78 Congress, 1 Session. 89(Appendix), 4544-46.

3432. Wilstach, Paul M. "Jefferson's Little Mountain." National Geographic Magazine. 55(1929), 481-503.

Describes features of Monticello, its design and how TJ lived there. Illustrated.

3433. Wing, DeWitt C. "Thomas Jefferson: Pioneer in Genetic Science." Journal of Heredity. 35(June 1944), 173-74.

Note surveying TJ's interest in livestock breeding and scientific agriculture.

3434. Wolkowski, Leszek August. "Polish Commission for National Education,

1773-1794—Its Significance and Influence on Russian and American Education." Ph.D. dissertation. Loyola Univ. of Chicago, 1979. pp. 216.

Pierre Samuel DuPont de Nemours worked for the Polish Commission in 1774, drew upon his experience when he sent TJ his proposal for American Education in 1800. DAI 39/12A, pp. 7195-96.

3435. Woltz, Dawn Daniel. The Flowers Grown and Shown at Monticello. Charlottesville: Michie Company, 1977. pp. xv, 141.

Discusses present day plantings.

3436. Woodburn, Robert Orvis. "An Historical Investigation of the Opposition to Jefferson's Educational Proposals in the Commonwealth of Virginia." Ph.D. dissertation. American Univ., 1974. pp. 231.

Focuses particularly on response to TJ's "Bill for the More General Diffusion of Knowledge" (1779) and his "Bill for Establishing a System of Public Education" (1817). DAI 35/11A, p. 7096.

3437. Woodfin, Maude H. "Thomas Jefferson and William Byrd's Manuscript Histories of the Dividing Line." WMQ. 3rd ser. 1(1944), 363-73.

How TJ identified the author of the "History of the Dividing Line" and obtained the manuscript of the "Secret History" for the American Philosophical Society.

3438. Woodward, Charles L. "Do You Care Anything About This?" New York, 1895. Broadside.

Circular offering for sale copies of the separate printing of Ford's edition of TJ's Notes.

3439. Wranek, William H. "Charlottesville and the University: A Jeffersonian View." Magazine of Albemarle County History. 21(1963), 5-11.

TJ wished to appoint Thomas Cooper as professor of chemistry at the University; prints a recently discovered letter from him to Cooper, dated September 1, 1817.

3440. Wranek, William H. "Jefferson's Mountaintop Mansion." Commonwealth, The Magazine of Virginia. 19(April 1952), 33-35, 69.

Description.

3441. Wranek, William H. "Planned by Thomas Jefferson, The University of Virginia Continues to Progress Under Able Administration." The Iron Worker. 15(Autumn 1951), 1-15.

Sketch of TJ's University; peripheral.

443

3442. Wranek, William H. "The Renovation of Jefferson's House." Common-wealth, The Magazine of Virginia. 20(November 1953), 13-14, 39.

3443. Wright, John Kirtland. "Notes on Measuring and Counting in Early American Geography" and "Notes on Early American Geopiety" in Human Nature in Geography: Fourteen Papers, 1925-1965. Cambridge: Harvard Univ. Press, 1966. 204-93.

Two wide-ranging essays which touch at several points on TJ's accomplishments as a geographer in Notes. Suggestive and useful for background.

3444. Wright, Louis B. "Thomas Jefferson and the Classics." Proceedings of the APS. 87(1943), 223-33.

"Although Jefferson read widely and knew the French and English philosophers and historians of his own age, his thinking was chiefly influenced by the writers of antiquity."

3445. Wyllie, John Cook. "The Jefferson-Randolph Copies of An Anonymous Work Entered Three Ways by Sabin." VMHB. 56(1948), 80-83.

Describes presentation copies of John Francis Dumoulin's An Essay on Naturalization sent to TJ and prints Dumoulin's letters to him.

3446. Yancey, Sarah L., ed. Mr. Jefferson's Favorite Tunes. n.p., 1978. unpag.

Seventeen examples of TJ's music, with notes.

3447. Zurfluh, John, Sr. "Thomas Jefferson—Early American Stringed Instrument Enthusiast." American String Teacher. 26(Summer 1976), 4-5.

Sketch of TJ's interest in violins; derivative.

INDEX

SUBJECT INDEX

autographs, TJ's, 1036
Bacon, Edmund, 971, 1002
Bacon, Francis, 2158
Bailey, Lydia, 3172
balance of power, 1920
balloons, 360, 2861
Baltimore College, 968
Bank of the United States, 1386, 1809, 1989
Bankhead, Charles L., 1241
Banneker, Benjamin, 499
Baptists, 2202, 2296, 2371, 2401
Barbary Pirates, 1474, 1486, 1636, 1783, 1804, 1985, 2097
Barlow, Joel, 707
Barnwell, Dr. William, 1931
Barton, Benjamin Smith, 44, 2144, 2778, 3275
batture case, 1566
Bayard, James A., 1382, 1383, 1477
Beard, Charles A., 1354, 2342
Beccaria, Cesare, 1389, 2241, 2407
Beckley, John, 791, 794, 1707
Bellarmine, Robert, 2289, 2418, 2424, 2439, 2487, 2512
Belle Grove, 3123
Bellini, Charles, 673, 2672
Bentham, Jeremy, 244
Bible, 2112, 2116, 2248; see also Life and Morals of Jesus
bibliography, 3173
bicameralism, 2273
bicentennial of TJ's birth, 15, 44, 46, 149, 166, 297, 457, 549, 575, 595, 634, 1039, 1216, 1218, 1228, 1229, 2770, 2797
Bill for Establishing Religious Freedom, 520, 1451, 1903, 1960, 2104, 2126, 2161, 2296, 2307, 2410, 2435
Bill of Rights, 1413, 1464, 1465, 1951, 1970
Bingham, George Caleb, 3065, 3279
biology, 2711
Birch, William Russell, 3205
birch bark, 1157
Blackstone, William, 2482, 2585
Bodin, Jean, 2434
Bolingbroke, Lord, 2342, 2409
Bonaparte, Napoleon, 650, 1510, 1558, 1724, 1725, 1973
Bonhoeffer, Dietrich, 2484
book collecting, 2653, 2738, 2741, 2828, 2829, 3175, 3213, 3251

bookmarks, 2568
book trade, 2701, 2917, 3053, 3172, 3422
botany, 2680, 2700, 2739, 2778, 2806, 3035, 3253, 3353-55, 3402
Bowers, Claude G., 954, 1040
Boyle, Caleb, 2911
Bradbury, John, 3353
Brazil, 1473, 1910
Breckinridge, John, 533, 1481, 1575, 1653, 1661-62, 1915, 1943, 1988, 2065-67
breeding of livestock, 3433
Brehan, Madame, 265
Bremo, 2614
Brodie, Fawn, 325, 328, 352, 401, 627, 682, 826, 1304
brotherhood, 304
Browder, Earl, 1439
Browere, J. H. I., 3040, 3404
Brown, Charles Brockden, 1493, 3176
Brown, Mather, 2814
Brown, Samuel, 894
Brown, William Wells, 2784-85
Bru, Juan Bautista, 2607
Bryan, William Jennings, 1402, 2213, 2334
Bryant, William Cullen, 1123, 2618
Buffon, Comte de, 1278, 2601, 2768, 2817, 2876, 2937, 3073
Bugniet, Pierre-Gabriel, 3222
Burgesses, Virginia, 913
Burgandy, 748
Burk, John Daly, 395
Burke, Edmund, 309
Burnet, Gilbert, 2416
Burr, Aaron, 336, 592, 1339-40, 1539, 1714-15, 1767, 1786-87, 1789, 1846, 1868, 1975
—trial of, 1363, 1394, 1529, 1788, 1808, 1906-07, 1919, 1976, 2015, 2087
Burwell, Rebecca, 1030, 1106, 1147
Bushnell, Horace, 2125
business habits, 77, 1091
Byrd, William, 3437
Cabanis, Pierre J. B., 2176, 2284, 2850
Cabell, Joseph C., 2557, 2648, 2698, 3147, 3178
cabinet, presidential, 1498, 1524, 1685, 2020; see also secretary of state
Caesar, Julius, 493
Calhoun, John C., 1130, 1374, 1646, 2053,

Desert de Retz, 221
desk, TJ's portable, 67, 111, 198, 637, 1028, 1220, 1230, 2932, 3039
Dewey, John, 2064, 2203, 2320, 2881, 3304
Dickinson, John, 1424
diplomacy, 1393, 1475, 1486, 1491, 1546-48, 1615, 1675, 1678, 1726, 1904, 1961, 2032, 2086, 2097; see also foreign policy
diplomacy with England, 456, 1092, 1499, 1705, 1926, 1996-97, 2017, 2044
diplomacy with France, 1375, 1427, 1838, 1546, 1549, 1723, 1725, 1798, 1803, 1860, 2089, 2105; see also Louisiana Purchase
dissent, right of, 2214
diversity, 536, 553, 772, 1374, 2454
drama, interest in, 2878
dry dock, 2788, 3134, 3285
Duane, William, 1435, 1610, 1745, 1748, 1850
Dufief, Nicholas Gouin, 968, 2148, 2659
Dumoulin, John Francis, 3445
Dunbar, William, 2531
Duncan, William, 2896-97
Dunglison, Robley, 2562, 2598, 2754, 2857, 3015, 3208-09
Dunlap, John, 1423
Duponceau, Peter S., 3275
Dupont de Nemours, Pierre S., 49, 50, 260, 516, 752, 2245, 2391, 3434
Dwight, Theodore, 1033
economics, 1385, 1449, 1517, 1586, 1794, 1865, 1899, 2113, 2160, 2177, 2213, 2254-55, 2341, 2349-50, 2458
Edgehill, 813
education, encouragement of, 119, 426, 910, 2327, 2517, 2545, 2552-53, 2640, 2658, 2707-08, 2728-29, 2740, 2752, 2755, 2774, 2843, 2866-68, 2873, 2880-81, 2887-88, 2890, 2935, 2950, 2995, 3004, 3007-09, 3018, 2042, 3044, 3048, 3052, 3057, 3066, 3069, 3087-88, 3108, 3111, 3119-21, 3159, 3189, 3197, 3200, 3206, 3212, 3242, 3247-48, 3289, 3293, 3300, 3304, 3317, 3342, 3377, 3383, 3410, 3436
educational theory, 2200, 2205-07, 2274, 2277, 2359, 2476, 2654-66, 3032, 3297, 3360, 3365, 3434
Edwards, Bryan, 1542

egalitarianism, 1349, 1369, 1565, 1578, 1601, 1617, 1647, 1895, 2119, 2152, 2184, 2209-10, 2212, 2220, 2257, 2278, 2293-94, 2372, 3032
Eisenhower, Dwight D., 43, 1597
Election of 1796, 926, 1550, 1947, 1990
Election of 1800, 490, 928, 1244, 1268, 1350, 1382-83, 1411, 1435, 1441, 1472, 1525, 1677, 1715, 1735, 1765, 1779, 1837, 1861, 1868, 1975, 1978, 2001, 2008, 2035, 2046, 2049, 2733
Election of 1804, 1441, 1779, 2001
Election of 1808, 1356, 1441
Elk Hill, 1281
Embargo, 1344, 1558, 1636, 1667, 1695, 1716, 1720, 1725, 1775, 1814, 1890, 1921, 1955-57, 1995-97, 2009, 2054, 2444
Emerson, Ralph W., 2249, 2404, 3304
Encyclopedia, 2533, 3399
Encyclopedie Methodique, 2917, 3399
England, visit to, 1092, 1264, 1272, 2760, 3229
Enlightenment, 256, 1335, 2187, 2198, 2212, 2256, 2267, 2276, 2318, 2357, 2407, 2441, 2451, 2533
entail, 1446
entomology, 3406
environment, 2199
Epicurus, 2158, 2370
epistemology, 2169
Eppes, John Wayles, 323
Eppes, Francis, 323, 1310
Eppes, Maria Jefferson, 75, 519, 773, 950, 1203, 1240, 1275, 1292
Eppington, 1275
Essex County, Mass., 714
Essex Junto, 1344, 2069
ethics, 2492; see also moral virtue
ethnology, see anthropology
etiquette, 60
eugenics, 3170
eulogies of TJ, 94, 126, 175, 203, 228, 322, 341, 357, 379, 399, 411, 421, 437, 455, 481, 504, 530, 554, 569, 571, 585, 612, 615-16, 655, 657, 691, 704, 836, 977, 1011, 1045, 1072, 1074, 1086, 1116-18, 1124-25, 1127, 1129, 1133, 1189, 1194, 1210, 1213, 1227, 1301, 1320, 1337, 2610, 2777
Europe, TJ in, 52, 79, 383, 645, 1020,

1155, 1199
Ewing, Samuel, 3240
executive privilege, 1394, 1808, 1919
exhibits, museum and library, 46, 144, 149,
    394, 457, 1169, 1229, 2519, 2532, 2560,
    2574, 2593, 2661, 2671, 2765, 2906,
    3278, 3327, 3331, 3357, 3391
expansion, territorial, 209, 589, 1395, 1403,
    1503, 1538, 1548, 1555, 1634, 1692-93,
    1732, 1800, 1877, 1968, 1979, 2223,
    3296
exploration, western, 1602, 1634, 2529,
    2531, 2751, 2916
Ezekiel, Moses, 3118
fame, idea of, 2108
family, TJ's, 123, 172, 174, 307, 506, 804,
    844, 1079-80, 1153, 2564
Farm Book, 2589, 3386
Farmers General, 1860
farming, see agriculture
Farmington (Va.), 2543, 2782
Farmington (Louisville), 2965
fascism, 1899
fashion, 403
father figures, 130
Faulkner, William, 2612, 3403
Fauquier, Francis, 812, 1269
Federalist criticism of TJ, 241, 392, 825,
    949, 969, 974, 1360, 1511, 1738, 1744,
    1745, 1748, 1765, 1851, 1861, 1918,
    1936, 2013, 2618, 3073, 3240
Federalists, 1344, 1385, 1412, 1414, 1477,
    1495, 1576, 1834, 2069
Fessenden, Thomas Green, 1936
Few, Frances, 319
fiction, TJ in, 2625, 2674, 2710, 2783-85,
    2807, 3063, 3112, 3177, 3427; see also
    juvenile fiction
Field, David Dudley, 1389
Field, Robert, 3343
Firearms, 520-21
fireworks, 669
fiscal policy, 1989
Florida, 1430, 1509, 1582, 2056
Fluvanna County, Va., 1625
folk lore, 240, 1334, 3012, 3070, 3370
foreign policy, 1393, 1420, 1430, 1510,
    1538, 1562, 1582, 1635, 1963, 1722-26,
    1761, 1914, 1920, 1927, 1957, 1995,
    1997, 2010, 2020, 2052, 2056, 2097-98,
    2347

Foster, Sir Augustus John, 274, 1196
Fourth of July, 222, 266, 1267, 1287
Fox, Charles James, 1708
France, 89, 120, 163, 214, 258-60, 265
    510, 759, 776, 919, 1075, 1299, 1328
    29, 1605, 1675, 1723, 1727, 1909, 196]
    2048, 2089, 2394, 2608, 2766, 2988
    3125, 3223
franchise, 1908
francophilia, 629, 991, 1723, 2617
Franklin, Benjamin, 258, 272, 795, 146]
    1742, 1827, 1872, 2269, 2300, 2318
    2350, 2713
Franzoni, Giuseppe, 2660
fraternity, 2351
freedom of speech and opinion, 772, 168(
    2148, 2150, 2214, 2409, 2470, 2605
freedom of the press, 294, 967, 1534
    1686, 1766-67, 1793, 1850, 1897, 2084
    2321, 2430
Freeman, Thomas, 1602, 2531
freethinker, TJ as, 2331, 2420-22, 2477
French Academy (Richmond), 3230
French language, 2658
French Revolution, 137, 309, 449, 132?
    1364, 1675, 1801, 1909, 1974, 213?
    2156, 2324
Freneau, Philip, 789-90, 1610, 1642, 181?
    1819-21, 3172
friendship, 56
frontier, defense of, 1346
---idea of, 2425
Fuller, Margaret, 55
Fulton, Robert, 2872
furniture, 163, 2521, 2563, 2831, 294?
    2979-81, 2983, 2985, 2988, 3313, 332?
    3334, 3394
Gallatin, Albert, 1676, 1682, 1744, 181
    1989
garden book, 2591, 3356
garden structures, 2576-77
gardens and gardening, 221, 2521-2?
    2583, 2588, 2591, 2760, 2787, 279<
    2841, 2860, 2956, 2966, 3023, 309?
    3116, 3127, 3182, 3183, 3191, 320<
    3229, 3244, 3294, 3402, 3420, 3435
Garrett, Alexander, 234
Geffroy, Nicholas, 1495
genealogy, TJ's, 596, 841, 874, 946, 107?
    1126, 1153
Genet, Edmond Charles, 474, 925, 135<

1642, 1650, 1684, 1801, 1836, 1993, 2036, 2093
geography, 2529-30, 2762, 2775, 2832-33, 3314-15, 3371, 3443
geology, 2637, 3371
George III, 2120, 2228, 2304
geranium, 161
Germantown, Pa., 610, 973
Germany, 625, 649
Gerry, Elbridge, 1711
Gibbon, Edward, 324
Giles, William Branch, 1344, 1631
Gilmer, Francis W., 348, 2739, 2743, 3186, 3351
Girardin, Louis Hue, 968
Godwin, William, 2411
governor of Virginia, TJ as, 791, 917, 1368, 1565, 1579, 1771, 1774, 1799, 1828, 1856, 1938, 1962, 2038-41
Graff, J., 584
graph paper, 2699
grave, TJ's, 497, 593, 935, 945, 1219, 1256
graveyard, Monticello, 631-32, 1079
Greece, 2288
Gregg, Andrew, 984
Grigsby, Hugh Blair, 657, 1081, 1198
Griswold, Rufus W., 790
Grotjan, Thomas J., 393
grove at Monticello, 3093-95
Guennepin, 2758
gunboats, 1681-82
Hague, 649
Haiti, 1375, 1431, 1771
Hale, Salma, 517
Hall of Fame, 734
Hamilton Alexander, 124, 130, 291, 336, 420, 493, 558, 614, 660, 754, 793, 796, 836, 921, 924, 981, 1040, 1128, 1343, 1352, 1356, 1377, 1393, 1397, 1401, 1412, 1419-21, 1449-50, 1466-67, 1487, 1501, 1507, 1517, 1546, 1563, 1590, 1619, 1623, 1655-56, 1664, 1714, 1722, 1754, 1809, 1818, 1820, 1822, 1825, 1871, 1896, 1923, 1945, 1977, 2029, 2082, 2108, 2509, 3036, 3200
Hammond, George, 1926, 2044
harpsichord, 1092, 2816
Hartford Convention, 1576
Hassler, Ferdinand Rudolph 1321
Hawkins, John Isaac, 2539
health, TJ's, 221, 800, 1037, 1093, 1327, 2598

Heaton, James, 2083
Helvetius, Claude Adrien, 2485
Hemings, Madison, 770
Hemings, Sally, 41, 114, 117, 183-85, 328-29, 337-38, 401, 447, 495, 608, 661, 708, 742, 768, 830, 1303, 2368, 2674, 2785
Hemings family, 41, 100, 182, 186, 375, 540, 542, 682, 2783
Hening, W., 2761
Henrietta, ship, 163
Henry, Patrick, 398, 547-48, 936, 1278, 1425, 1680
Henry, Patrick (slave), 1197
heresy, 2752
Hessians, 641
Hilliard, Wm., 2701
historiography, 113, 158, 283, 546, 626, 629, 663, 829, 1015, 1033, 1046, 1087, 1303, 1392, 2212, 2267, 2283, 2394
history, TJ's knowledge of, 707, 1733, 2110, 2181-83, 2185, 2189, 2327, 2481, 2505, 3166
Hobbes, Thomas, 2459
Ho Chi Minh, 2313
Hogarth,William, 2583, 2945
homogeneity, political, 2432
honor code, academic, 3081
Hopkinson, Francis, 3311
horses, 448
hospitality, TJ's, 319, 433, 607, 642, 687, 805, 807, 1443
Hotel d'Langeac, 1019
Houdetot, Comtesse lalive d', 257
Houdon, Jean Antoine, 674, 2532, 2602, 2676, 3199
House of Representatives, U. S., 1505, 1624
Hudson, Christopher, 570, 638
human nature, 2199, 2203, 2280, 2320, 2397, 2464, 2485
humanism, 2140, 2327, 2383, 2690
humanitarian, TJ as, 871
Humboldt, Alexander von, 462, 1270, 2746-47, 2802, 3011
Hume, David, 2341, 2458, 2481, 2488, 2585
humor, TJ's, 1312
Huntington Library, 149
Hutcheson, Francis, 2267, 2493
Hutchins, Robert M., 2763
ice cream, 2634

453

ideologues, 752, 1723-24, 2175-76, 2766
ideology, 1378, 1796, 2132, 2257, 2445, 3076
Illinois, 1759, 1762, 1806, 2774
Illuminati, 1435
immigrants, 332
impressment, 2017
inaugural address, 1801, 1727, 1769, 1991, 3076, 3161
inaugurations, TJ's, 518, 1097, 1105, 1365, 1458
independence, idea of, 2373
Indian delegates, 1606, 2779, 2884
Indian languages, 2920, 2991, 3103, 3110, 3275
Indian mounds, 2610, 2668, 2801, 2817, 3022
Indian policy, 1347, 1429, 1552, 1589, 1692-93, 1802, 1968-69, 2004, 2447, 2884
Indians, culture of, 2300, 2447-48, 2610, 2669, 3142, 3275
influence, TJ's, 654, 684, 734, 892, 1131, 1343, 1516, 1619, 1743, 1761, 2086, 2436, 2763, 2772, 3291
influence abroad, 262, 820, 1059, 1497, 2219, 2288, 2335, 2355, 2994
Innes, Harry, 180
insurance, life, 674
intellectuals, 1504, 2404, 2507
interposition, doctrine of, 1436, 1739
inventions, 2572, 2844, 3051, 3250, 3328, 3414
Irving, Washington, 1506, 2838
isolationism, 1727, 2172
Italy, 673, 1155, 3000, 3270-71
Izard, Ralph, 578
Jackson, Andrew, 177, 393, 1130, 1370-71, 1398-99, 1433, 1743, 1848, 3032
Jay, John, 1427
Jay Treaty, 1420, 1483, 1550, 1560
Jefferson, Isaac, 101, 708
Jefferson, Jane Randolph, 422, 561, 1126
Jefferson, Martha Wayles, 519, 702, 731, 933, 1106, 1147, 1292, 2895
Jefferson, Peter, 286, 531, 946, 2508
Jefferson, Randolph, 810
"Jefferson and Liberty," 2992
Jefferson Club of St. Louis, 588
Jefferson Memorial, 429, 599, 635, 861, 862, 1039, 1060, 1174, 1229, 2559, 2675, 2684, 2859, 2902-04, 2919, 2923-25,

2963, 3014, 3028, 3077, 3089, 3198, 3397, 3409, 3413, 3421
Jefferson Memorial, St. Louis, 653, 862, 3221
Jefferson Monument Magazine, 605
Jefferson National Expansion Memorial Assoc., 589, 590, 1061, 1266
Jefferson Society (U. of Va.), 487, 886, 1055, 1490, 1503, 1687, 1838, 1959
"Jefferson's March," 2537
Jews, 664-65
Johnson, Samuel, 296
Johnson, William, 1845
joinery, TJ's, 2566
Jones, Joseph Seawell, 829
Jouett, Jack, 35, 71, 133, 277, 326-27, 404, 622, 638
judicial dissent, 1845
judicial review, 1453, 1463, 1464, 1496, 1556, 1651, 1755, 1829-30, 1874
judiciary, 1418, 1421, 1508, 1519, 1531, 1585, 1651, 1657, 1746, 1780, 1873, 1925, 2021
Jung, Carl, 87
juvenile fiction, TJ in, 2647, 2682, 2714, 2736, 2798, 3092, 3101, 3115, 3380, 3405
juvenile non-fiction, TJ in, 85, 92, 211, 231, 232, 236, 248-49, 271, 282, 287-88, 292, 311, 315-16, 343-45, 359, 374, 377, 402, 406-10, 416, 423, 438, 441, 475, 560, 572-73, 613, 618, 623, 666, 690, 746, 818, 827-28, 839, 843, 860, 867, 881, 887, 906, 948, 987, 1025, 1038, 1088, 1138, 1140-41, 1148, 1209, 1238, 1243, 1253-55, 1260, 1276, 1293-97, 1326, 3228, 3344
Kames, Lord, 2388-89, 2577, 2583
Kelsall, Charles, 2594
Kemp, John, 1156
Kentucky, 1771, 2000
Kentucky and Virginia Resolutions, 1358, 1411, 1436, 1481, 1575, 1608, 1643, 1653, 1739, 1750-51, 1834, 1858, 1915, 1988, 2053, 2065-67, 2449
King, William, 119
King-Hawkesbury Convention, 1670
Kingsley, Sidney, 2815, 3167
Korais, Adamantios, 2288
Kosciuszko, Thaddeus, 54, 505, 512, 891, 990, 1049, 2704, 2807

454

Lafayette, Marquis de, 255, 263, 273, 678, 679, 693, 807, 838, 1096, 1364
and grant colleges, 2640, 2908
and management, 3347
and ownership, 1581, 1622, 1629, 2221
and planning, 1409, 1647, 1800
landscape architecture, 2522, 2954, 2956, 2959, 2966, 3003, 3064, 3130, 3202, 3229
Langhorne forgery, 339, 486
Languedoc, 1328-29
Latin America, 816, 1410, 1417, 1499, 1702
Latrobe, Benjamin Henry, 2660, 2731, 2852, 2973, 3134-37
law, 1763, 1875, 2019, 2099, 2385, 2761, 2790
law, common, 1622, 2154, 2482
law, international, 2217, 2444, 2500
law practice, 356, 398, 543
law reports, 1527, 1572, 1713
law, study of, 911, 1572, 2025, 2620, 2697
law, theory of, 431, 1389, 1421, 1536-37, 1618, 2164, 2382
lawyer, TJ as, 361, 431, 676, 912, 1171, 1527, 1543, 1572-73, 1812, 1847, 1875, 1904
leadership, presidential, 1884, 2007
Leclerc, Charles V. E., 1777
Ledyeard, John, 1361
Lee, General Henry, 689, 1823, 1938
legal codification, 1536-37
Lego, 813, 1152
Leland, John, 199, 1005, 1460
Lemaire, Etienne, 2865, 3179
Lemen, James, 1762, 1806, 2080
L'Enfant, Pierre Charles, 2793, 2993, 3137, 3246
Lenin, V. I., 2237, 2433
letters, see correspondence
letters, facsimile, 350
letter-writer, TJ as, 2606
Levy, Jefferson M., 847, 1154
Levy, Moses, 1699
Levy, Uriah P., 997, 1233, 2789
Levy family, 227, 443, 465, 563, 1200
Lewis, Isham and Lilburne, 822, 3390
Lewis, Meriwether, 46, 81, 116, 583, 1469, 1706, 2726, 2751
Lewis and Clark Expedition, 81, 485, 836, 1347, 1488, 1555, 1649, 1732, 2529, 2726, 2751, 2863, 2916, 2034

—scientific aspects of, 2725, 2727, 2806, 2916, 2025, 3158, 3354
liberalism, 45, 2203, 2431, 2486, 3304
libertarian theory, 1766
liberty, 2190, 2210, 2286, 2319, 2374, 2450
Liberty Hall (Kentucky), 2542, 2965, 3393
librarianship, 2518, 2687, 2829, 3068, 3173, 3251
library, TJ's, 12, 498, 2113, 2514, 2515, 2595, 2597, 2662-63, 2687, 2738, 2741, 2825, 2828, 2889, 2892, 2983, 3002, 3055-56, 3149-50, 3174-75, 3236, 3251, 3253-54, 3287, 3301-03, 3366
library classification, 3005, 3068, 3251, 3267
Library of Congress, 290, 1101, 2518, 2644, 2829, 2913, 2936, 3005, 3056, 3068, 3085-86, 3113, 3245, 3329, 3335, 3366
library, sale of, 1083, 2683, 3367
"Life and Morals of Jesus of Nazareth," 2112, 2116, 2155, 2226, 2230-31, 2248, 2270, 2292, 2297, 2330, 2345
Lincoln, Abraham, 213, 320, 697, 756, 865, 994, 1139, 2064, 2426, 2466, 2774
Linn, William, 1360
Linnaean societies, 2547
literary style, 148, 756, 2130, 2716, 2822, 2901, 3031, 3076, 3078, 3143, 3165, 3190
literature, interest in, 2327, 2583, 2677, 2864, 2878, 2901, 3165, 3176, 3286, 3401
literature, national, 322
Little Sarah, ship, 925
Littlepage, Lewis, 1540
Littleton, Mrs. Martin W., 873, 1226, 1231
Livingston, Edward, 1389
Livingston, Robert R., 1803
local government, 1570, 1663
Locke, John, 1952, 2158, 2169-70, 2227, 2258, 2267, 2294, 2317, 2324, 2328, 2344, 2384, 2435, 2503
Logan, 270, 2718, 2918, 2939, 3080, 3142, 3210, 3249, 3262-63
Long, George, 732-33
lottery, 62, 561, 943, 986, 2890
Louisiana Government Bill, 1943
Louisiana Purchase, 81, 341, 522, 576, 588, 1345, 1347, 1381, 1431, 1442, 1448, 1469, 1478, 1538, 1548, 1555,

455

political hero, TJ as, 184, 435, 630, 1280
political practice, 1374, 1415
political principles, 451, 697, 1054, 1514, 1601, 1831, 2114, 2131, 2149, 2208, 2225, 2236, 2262, 2271, 2328, 2392–93, 2399, 2473, 2480, 2483, 2659
political theory, 558, 1374, 1569, 1729, 2106, 2123, 2139, 2143, 2157, 2173, 2194, 2211, 2274, 2281, 2311, 2319, 2325, 2346, 2365, 2378, 2433, 2461, 2478, 2497–99, 2505
political union, American, 1770, 1772, 2149
polygraph, 2633
Poplar Forest, 323, 396, 466, 480, 492, 851, 879–80, 1310, 1315, 3295, 3398
portraits of TJ, 76, 750, 2641, 2651–52, 2694, 2702, 2704–05, 2724, 2758, 2773, 2780, 2858, 2874–75, 2911–12, 2929–30, 2948, 2952, 2968, 2970, 3033, 3040, 3065, 3090, 3096, 3205, 3224–26, 3279, 3335, 3343, 3404; see also sculpture
positivism, 532
postage stamps, 43, 104, 370, 1265, 2694
Pound, Ezra, 2996
Pradt, Abbe de, 1946
prairie dog, 2727, 3158
prayer book, 2508
Presbyterianism, 1843, 2388, 2413
presidency, 73, 201, 285, 319, 343, 417, 511, 550, 699, 761–62, 814, 882, 929–30, 1120–21, 1302, 1341–42, 1350–51, 1372, 1391, 1404, 1407–08, 1414, 1428, 1466–67, 1478, 1480, 1504–06, 1511, 1524, 1583, 1636, 1667, 1690, 1697, 1703, 1717, 1719–20, 1736, 1745, 1753, 1758, 1795–96, 1810, 1835, 1857, 1880, 1948, 1972, 1982, 1989, 2003, 2005, 2026, 2042–43, 2058, 2094, 2102, 3074
presidential third term, 1637, 1710
press, 789–90, 796, 825, 1110, 1268, 1435, 1441, 1511, 1600, 1610, 1613, 1642, 1721, 1738, 1742, 1744–48, 1765, 1818, 1820, 1822, 1850, 2008
Priestley, Joseph, 2230, 2284, 2626, 3058
primogeniture, 1446
Princeton, N.J., 386
printers, 3025, 3046, 3778–79
prison, Richmond, 3222
private life of TJ, 185, 214, 380, 388, 708, 716, 727, 768, 970–71, 999, 1303, 1311
progress, idea of, 2167, 2189, 2356, 3154

prohibition, 740
propaganda, 1461
property, right to, 1729, 1952, 2169–70, 2258, 2343
protectionism, 1807, 2022
Provence, 1328–29, 3218
providence, 2279
psychological interpretations of TJ, 88, 531, 1150, 2463
public domain, 1581
public health, 3235
Puritans, 2138
pursuit of happiness, 439, 2233, 2243, 2317, 2429, 2438, 2440, 2463, 2479–80
Quenedy, Edme, 3224
Quesnay de Beaurepaire, Chevalier, 3230
Quincy, Josiah, 1912
race, 1784, 1953, 2085, 2212, 2306, 2368, 2426, 2504
racism, 1617, 1791–92, 1913, 2338, 2348, 2462, 2510
radical, TJ as, 568, 594, 1934, 2064, 2285
radio broadcasts on TJ, 239, 778, 2111, 3067
Rafinesque, Constantine S., 2586
Raggi, Michele and Giacomo, 3151
Raleigh, Sir Walter, 1733
Randall, Henry S., 388, 447, 592, 657, 724, 1015–16, 1081
Randolph, Edmund, 543, 1498, 1822
Randolph, John (loyalist), 738
Randolph, John, of Roanoke, 1624, 1627, 1752, 2054
Randolph, Martha Jefferson, 75, 192, 316, 519, 559, 601, 950, 1000, 1234, 1240, 1243, 1292, 3012, 3370
Randolph, Sarah Nicholas, 1198
Randolph, Thomas Jefferson, 61, 62, 447, 580, 1241–42, 1631
Randolph, Thomas Mann, 467, 1002, 1624
rationalism, 2242, 2286
reading for children, 2564
reading lists, 2697–98, 2997, 3381
Red River, 1602, 2531
reform, 1406, 1446, 1451, 1556, 2103, 2232, 2269
relevance of TJ, 165, 766, 775, 1143, 1298, 1447, 1472, 1514, 1591, 1601, 1950, 2091, 2469
religious affiliation, 2162, 2268, 2287
religious education, 2191, 2303, 2744

religious freedom, 288, 977, 1451, 1776, 2104, 2127, 2133, 2145, 2151, 2166, 2196, 2202, 2224, 2231, 2234, 2265, 2295, 2322, 2362-63, 2371, 2377, 2381, 2410, 2413, 2452, 2468, 2491, 2513, 2866-67
religious principles, 582, 624, 1651, 1776, 2112, 2118, 2121, 2134, 2151, 2165, 2171, 2179, 2192, 2197, 2204, 2222, 2226, 2230-31, 2239-40, 2244, 2246, 2250-51, 2263, 2266, 2268, 2284, 2290, 2301, 2303, 2310-11, 2315, 2337, 2339, 2354, 2363, 2402-03, 2414, 2442, 2465, 2470, 2484
reminiscences of TJ, 61, 68, 69, 121, 334, 587, 708, 971, 974, 992, 1002, 1112, 1184, 1187-88, 1193
renaissance, Italian, 2690
"Report on Commerce," 1500, 1885-86
"Report on ... Obtaining Fresh Water," 2629
"Report on Whale Fisheries," 1500
representation, political, 1894
republican party (Democratic), 1354, 1356, 1378, 1385, 1387, 1412, 1434, 1455, 1479, 1489, 1522-23, 1551, 1575, 1585, 1698-1700, 1718, 1719, 1778, 1930, 2008, 2094, 2157
Republican party (GOP), 1400, 1917
republicanism, 1497, 1729, 2109-10, 2129, 2206, 2326, 2366, 2445, 2509
reputation, TJ's, 42, 43, 45, 51, 55, 107, 113, 124, 159, 170, 184, 187, 209, 217, 227, 261, 293, 320, 353, 373, 457, 496, 513, 524, 539, 614, 630, 654, 657, 756, 764, 808, 954, 957-59, 1192, 1280, 1332, 1384, 1470, 1518, 1559, 1594, 1944, 2153, 2442, 2496
retirement, 525, 668, 763, 797, 804, 931, 1093, 1324, 2096
revolution, theory of, 2314, 2369, 2376, 2427, 2490
Revolution, American, 962, 1122, 1406, 1438, 1461, 1737, 1856, 1864, 1934, 2055, 2373, 2376, 2394
Revolutionary War in Virginia, 641, 688, 791, 1368, 1579, 1962, 2040-41
rhetoric, 1633, 1991, 2119, 2132, 2584, 2884, 2896-97, 2905, 3076, 3161
Rice, John Holt, 2742, 3317
Richmond, Va., 381, 1134, 1441, 1962

Riedesel, Baron von, 641, 1774
rights, civil, see civil liberty
rights of estates, 2120
Rives, William, 582
Robespierre, Maximilien, 1934, 2137, 2194
role models, 730
Roman Catholic Church, 1843, 2145, 2413
romanticism, 2946, 3097, 3280
Roosevelt, Franklin D., 429, 757, 769, 836, 954, 1512, 1592, 1637
Rotunda, 2582, 2712, 2808, 2847, 3148, 3373
Rousseau, Jean Jacques, 97, 2507
Roy, Raja Rammohan, 2263
Ruggieri, 669
Rumbold, Richard, 2110, 2416
Rush, Benjamin, 164, 219, 972, 2204, 3209, 3235, 3360, 3365
Rush, William, 2772
Russia, 1361, 1679, 2219, 3232
Rutledge, John, Jr., 1495, 2703
St. Clair, Arthur, 1567
Saint-Just, Louis Antoine, 1450
Saint-Memin, Fevret, 1606, 2758, 3033, 3225
Salem, Mass., 1890
salons, 3237
Sanchez Carrion, Jose Faustino, 1702
Saxe-Weimar-Eisenach, Bernhard Karl, Duke of, 122, 541
Say, J. B., 2176
scholar, role of, 2404, 3044
school prayer, 1359
school system, 2728, 2887, 2950, 3066
science, 126, 691, 837, 894, 1321, 2144, 2302, 2356, 2385, 2493, 2524, 2555, 2571, 2574, 2613, 2628, 2685, 2688, 2696, 2738, 2740, 2837, 2922, 2927, 3073-75, 3144-45, 3154, 3204, 3274, 3400
Scottish Enlightenment, 2267, 2388, 2390, 2397-98, 2493, 2655
sculpture, TJ in, 877, 1006, 1044, 1207, 1233, 1252, 2596, 2602, 3030, 3117, 3199, 3217, 3243, 3320, 3322, 3367, 3397
secession, 1687
secretary of state, TJ as, 351, 610, 790, 922-23, 973, 1393, 1412, 1420, 1497, 1500, 1546, 1722, 1726, 1798, 1832, 1885-86, 1900, 1926, 1993, 2020, 2035

2036, 2052, 2082, 2097, 2870
sectionalism, 1805, 2391, 3100
Senate, U.S., 1444, 1670
separation of church and state, 1359, 1446, 1451, 1462, 1465, 1568, 1776, 2057, 2191, 2307, 2332, 2352, 2361, 2377, 2866-67, 3041
separation of powers, 1596, 1734
serpentine wall, 2945
sexual attitudes, TJ's, 41, 1150, 2306
Shadwell, 639, 709, 813, 1007, 1029, 2975
Shecut, John, 2778
sheep, 3339
sheep dogs, 3038
Shelby, Isaac, 94
Shelley, Percy Bysshe, 2994
Shippen, Thomas Lee, 2703
shooting, 521
Short, William, 138, 1082, 1712
silver ware, 2569, 2661
Simitiere, Pierre Eugene du, 2929
skepticism, 188, 2246, 2481
Skinner, John S., 69
slavery, 41, 49, 77, 114, 182, 213, 375, 499, 526, 535, 909, 1139, 1145, 1316, 1362, 1384, 1388, 1398-99, 1470-71, 1513, 1515, 1541-42, 1545, 1617, 1626, 1645, 1728, 1757, 1759, 1762, 1784, 1791-92, 1797, 1826, 1898, 1911, 1917, 1928, 1958, 1971, 2079, 2083, 2085, 2180, 2201, 2212, 2238, 2293, 2306, 2338, 2348, 2364, 2368, 2374, 2382, 2412, 2445, 2466, 2493, 2501, 2504, 2510, 2625, 2822, 3283, 3370
Slovenians, 2434
Small, William, 468, 765, 812, 1269, 2655
Smith, Adam, 2113, 2254, 2258, 2458
Smith, Margaret Bayard, 161, 1244
Smith, Robert, 1781-82
Smith, Samuel Harrison, 1244, 1382-83, 1477
Smith, Thomas Jefferson, 817
snowstorm of 1772, 722
social contract, 2125, 2227, 2385, 2459
social ideas, 1367, 2136, 2168, 2333, 2443, 2940
Society of Constitutional Whigs, 2269
sociology, 2135-36, 2333
Socrates, 2433, 2809
soil conservation, 2579, 3295, 3430
songs about TJ, 78, 1854, 2537, 2634, 2797, 2992
Sophocles, 2983
Soviet view of TJ, 413
Spain, 1491, 1509-10, 1670, 1678
Spanish language, 2715
Sprengel, Matthias Christian, 3227
Stael, Madame de, 259, 317, 650
Stalin, Joseph, 1846
state colleges, 2310
state debts, assumption, 1387
state papers, 2926
states rights, 80, 1520, 1559, 1866, 1959, 1965, 2053, 2236, 2346
Stendhal, Henri Marie Beyle, 2355
Stevens, John, 1366
Stiles, Ezra, 1073
Story, Joseph, 1566
Strachan, John, 1916
strasbourg, 1021
stratigraphy, 2668, 3309
Stuart, Gilbert, 2651-52, 2952, 2970, 3090
Stuart, John, 3203
submarine, 2872
subpoena of TJ, 1363, 1394, 1808, 1919
Sullivan, John, 2768, 2937
Sully, Thomas, 2705, 2780
Summary View of the Rights of British America, 1150, 1410, 1425, 1792, 1986, 2182, 2378
Supreme Court, 1519, 1556-57, 1566, 1592, 1704, 1845, 1906, 2070
Suresnes, 1024
Swift, Jonathan, 2218
"Syllabus of the doctrines of Jesus," 1077, 2204
sympathy, 2460
Taliaferro, Richard, 3392
Tatham, William 1683, 1887
taxes, TJ's, 544
Taylor, John, of Caroline, 1367, 2281, 2445
Tesse, madame de, 265, 2608
Theognis of Megara, 3170
Thomas Jefferson Bicentennial Commission, 166, 173, 2150
Thomas Jefferson Centennial Commission, 1235-36
Thomas Jefferson Memorial Foundation, 51, 65, 237, 443, 555, 636, 671, 705, 939, 1161-62, 3323-25
Thomas Jefferson Society, 135, 1163
Thornton, Edward, 1705

Bates, Kenneth, 2560
Battle, George Gordon, 98, 2456
Bauer, Gerald, 2126
Baugh, Albert C., 2561
Bayard, James A., 1382
Bayard, Richard M., 1383
Beach, Curtis, 2127
Bean, W. G., 1384
Bean, William B., 2562
Bear, James A., Jr., 60–65, 67, 99–106, 123, 1091, 2540, 2563–69, 3126
Beard, Charles A., 107, 1385–87, 2128–29
Beard, Eva, 2570–71
Beard, Reed, 108
Beatty, James Paul, 1388
Beck, James M., 109–10
Becker, Carl, 2130
Beckman, Gail M., 1389
Bedini, Silvio, 111, 2572–75
Beiswanger, William L., 2576–77
Bell, Barry Ray, 2131
Bell, Landon C., 112
Bell, Whitfield J., Jr., 1390
Bellamy, Francis, 1391
Bellot, H. Hale, 113
Belmont, Perry, 1392, 2133
Beloff, Max, 114–15
Bemis, Samuel Flagg, 1393
Benet, Stephen Vincent, 2578
Benjamin, Mary, 116
Bennett, H. Omer, 2134
Bennett, Hugh M., 2579
Bennett, Lerone, 117
Bennett, Paul, 118
Bennett, Richard, 2580
Benson, Carl W. Randolph, 2135–36
Benson, Samuel P., 119
Benton, Tim, 428
Berenger, Henry, 120
Berger, Raoul, 1394
Berkeley, Francis L., Jr., 25, 26, 2581–82
Berkhofer, Robert F., Jr. 1395
Berman, Eleanor D., 2583–84
Bernard, John, 121
Bernhard, Karl, Duke of Saxe-Weimar, 122
Bernstein, Samuel, 2137
Berryman, Charles, 2138
Bestor, Arthur, 2585
Betts, Edwin Morris, 123, 2586–91
Beutin, Ludwig, 124
Bevan, Edith Rossiter, 125

Beveridge, Albert J., 1396
Biancolli, Louis, 2592
Bias, Randolph, 1397
Biddle, Nicholas, 126
Bierstadt, Edward Hale, 127
Bigelow, John, 128–29
Binder, Frederick Melvin, 1398–99
Binger, Carl, 130–31
Binney, Marcus, 2594
Birch, John J., 133
Birdwell, A. W., 134
Bishko, Jucretia R., 69
Bishop, Arthur, 2
Bishop, H. O., 136
Bishop, William Warner, 2595
Bitter, Karl, 2596
Bizardel, Yvon, 137–38
Black, Chauncey F., 1401–02
Blair, Albert L., 1400
Blanck, Jacob, 2597
Blanken, Maurice, 1403
Blau, Joseph, 2139
Blinderman, Abraham, 2598
Blinderman, Charles S., 2140
Bliven, Bruce, 139
Block, Harry, 2599
Bloss, George M. D., 140
Bo, Jorgen, 2600
Boardman, Fon W., Jr., 1404
Boas, George, 2141
Boehm, Dwight, 2601
Bogart, William H., 141
Bok-van Bork, Jacoba J., 142
Boller, Paul F., Jr., 2142
Bolton, Sarah Knowles, 143
Bonger, Hendrik, 1405
Bonn, George Franklyn, Jr., 2143
Bonnell, Ulane, 144
Boorstin, Daniel, 1406, 2144
Booth, Edward Townsend, 145
Borden, Morton, 1407–08
Borne, O. S., 146
Bottorf, William K., 147–48
Bourgin, Frank P., 1409
Boutell, Lewis Henry, 2603
Bowen, Dorothy, 149
Bowers, Claude G., 150–57, 1410–18, 2145–46
Bowes, Mary M., 2604
Bowling, Kenneth R., 1419
Bowman, Albert H., 1420

Ellett, Elizabeth F., 403
Elliott, Edward, 1584
Elliott, Mary Mallet, 404
Elliott, Milton J., 405
Ellis, Edward S., 406–10
Ellis, Richard E., 1585–86
Ellsworth, Edward W., 2774
Elson, Henry W., 948
Emmons, William, 411
Engelken, Ruth, 1587
Enloe, Cortez F., 1588
Erikson, Erik H., 414
Ernest, Joseph E., 2775
Eskew, Garnett L., 415
Espenshade, A. H., 416
Estee, Morris M., 2223
Eubanks, Seaford W., 2776
Evans, Charles H., 417
Evans, Emory G., 1589
Evans, Nancy, 418
Everett, Alexander H., 419–20, 1590
Everett, Edward, 421
Ewan, Joseph, 2778
Ewers, John C., 2779
Faber, Doris, 422
Fabian, Bernhard, 2224
Fahey, John H., 1591
Fahy, Everett P., Jr., 2780
Fairley, Margaret T., 2781
Faris, John T., 423
Farley, James A., 1592
Farnell, Robert Stewart, 2225
Farnum, George R., 424
Farrison, W. Edward, 2783–85
Faulkner, William Harrison, 2786
Fauntleroy, Cornelius H., 1593
Faust, Joan Lee, 2787
Feinstone, Sol, 633
Fenner, Mildred Sandison, 426–27
Ferguson, Eugene S., 2788
Ferguson, Henry N., 2789
Ferguson, John, 428
Ferguson, Robert, 2790
Ferris, D. H., 1594
Fesperman, Francis I., 2226
Fetter, Frank Whitson, 429
Fields, Joseph Edward, 430
Finkelnburg, Gustavus A., 431
Firestone, Linda, 436
Fish, Carl Russell, 1595
Fishburn, Eleanor C., 426–27
Fisher, George P., 2227

Fisher, Louis, 1596
Fisher, Marvin, 2791
Fisher, Sydney George, 2228
Fishwick, Marshall, 433–34
Fiske, John, 435
Fitch, Robert E., 1597
Fitzgerald, William G., 1889
Fitzhugh, Thomas, 2792
Fitzpatrick, F. B., 438
Fitzpatrick, John C., 1598
Fizdale, Robert, 2830
Flanders, Henry, 1599
Fleming, Anne Taylor, 439
Fleming, Thomas J., 440–45, 1600
Flexner, James T., 2793
Flood, Lawrence G., 1601
Flores, Dan L., 1602
Flower, B. O., 446
Flower, Milton E., 447
Floyd, Mildred D., 1603
Fohlen, Claude, 1604–05
Foley, D. J., 2794
Foley, John P., 448, 2229
Foley, William E., 1606
Foote, Henry Wilder, 2230–32
Force, Gerald, 1607
Ford, John Cuthbert, 2233
Ford, Paul Leicester, 449–51, 1608, 2795
Ford, Susan, 2796
Ford, Worthington C., 452–53, 1609–13
Forman, S. E., 454
Forman, Sidney, 1614
Forrest, W. M., 2234
Forsyth, John, 455
Foster, Sir Augustus John, 456
Foster, Franklin P., 2235
Foster, John W., 1615
Foster, W. E., 11
Fouts, Levi N., 1616
Fowler, Samuel, 2236
Fox, Mary Virginia, 2798
Francis, F. L., 3214
Frankfurter, Felix, 457
Franklin, Francis, 2237
Franklin, John Hope, 1617
Franklin, Mitchell, 1618
Frary, Ihna T., 2799, 2800
Fraser, Alexander David, 2801
Freehling, William W., 2238
Freidel, Frank, 458
Freudenberg, Anne, 26
Freund, Rudolph, 1622

Frey, Herman S., 459
Fried, Albert, 1619
Friedenwald, Herbert, 1620-21
Friederich, Werner P., 460
Friedman, Daniel, 461
Friis, Herman R., 462, 2802
Fritchman, Stephen Hole, 2239
Frost, John, 463
Frye, Melinda Young, 2803
Fuentes, German Alvarez, 464
Fuld, Melvin, 2804
Fuller, Albert, 2805
Fuller, Edmund, 2240
Fuller, Melville W., 1623
Fulling, Edmund H., 2806
Funston, Janet & Richard, 2241
Gabriel, Ralph H., 2242
Gaines, William H., Jr.,   465-67,   1624-25,
    2808
Gaither, Francis O., Jr., 2809
Galbreath, C. B., 1626
Galtier, Gaston, 2810
Ganter, Herbert L., 468, 2243
Garbett, Arthur S., 2811
Gardner, Joseph L., 469
Garland, Hugh A., 1627
Garnett, W. E., 470, 2813
Garraty, John A., 1628
Garrett, Leroy James, 2244
Garrett, Wendell D., 471-72, 2814
Garrison, Frank W., 2245
Garwood, Wilber St. John, 473
Gassner, John, 2815
Gauss, Charles E., 2816
Geer, Henry Burns, 2817
Gelder, Dorothy Beall, 2818
Genet, George Clinton, 474
George, Henry, 1629
Georgiady, Nicholas P., 475
Gerbi, Antonello, 2819
Getchell, George H., 1630
Gianniny, Omer Allen, Jr., 3373
Gibbs, James W., 2820
Giles, William Branch, 1631
Gillespie, A. H., 2821
Gillespie, David, 12
Gillett, Ransom H., 1632
Gillis, James M., 2246
Gilpin, Henry Dilwood, 476-78
Ginsberg, Robert A., 1633
Girouard, Mark, 479

Gittleman, Edwin, 2822
Glahn, Borge, 2600
Glass, Anna Cleghorne, 480
Glass, Powell, 2823
Glassburn, Doroth E., 2824
Gleason, Gene, 481
Glenn, Frank, 2825
Glenn, Garrard, 2826
Glenn, Thomas Allen, 482
Godwin, Mills E., 483
Godwin, Parke, 484
Goebel, Julius, 2247
Goetzmann, William, 485, 1634
Goff, Frederick R., 2827-29
Gold, Arthur, 2830
Goldberg, Stephen H., 1635
Goldsmith, William M., 1636
Golladay, V. Dennis, 486
Gooch, Richard Barnes, 487
Gooch, Robert Kent, 1637-38
Goodman, Nathan G., 488
Goodrich, Charles A., 489
Goodrich, Samuel Griswold, 490
Goodspeed, Edgar J., 2248
Goodwin, Lucia, 68
Goodwin, Katherine Calvert, 491
Gordon, M., 1639
Gordy, J. P., 1640
Gordy, Wilbur Fisk, 1641
Gorman, Ann C., 492
Gorman, William, 2117
Gostkowski, Zygmunt, 2249
Gould, William Drum, 2250-51
Govan, Thomas P., 493, 2252
Graebner, Norman A., 2253
Graff, Henry F., 494
Graham, Pearl M., 495
Grampp, William D., 496, 2254-55
Granato, Leonard A., 1642
Grane, Sylvia E., 2256
Granger, Moses M., 1643
Granquist, Charles L., 2831
Gray, Francis Calley, 498
Gray, Giles Wilkeson, 1644
Grayson, W. S., 1645
Greely, Arthur W., 2832-33
Green, Benjamin E., 1646
Green, Daniel, 1647
Green, David E., 2240
Green, Kevin W., 2834
Green, Paul, 2835-36

Greene, John C., 2637, 2837
Greenlaw, Edwin, 2838
Gregory, Dick, 499
Gregory, Horace, 2839
Gregory, Stephen S., 500
Gressman, Eugene, 501
Grosvenor, Charles Henry, 502
Grossholtz, Jean, 1601
Griffin, Martin I. J., 2840
Griggs, Edward Howard, 503
Griggs, Milton L., 2841-42
Grigsby, Hugh Blair, 1648
Grim, Marvin P., 3187
Grimes, Alan P., 2257
Griswold, A. Whitney, 2258-60, 2843
Griswold, Ralph E., 3130
Grogan, Francis J., 2261
Grundy, Felix, 504
Grzelonski, Bogdan, 505
Guernsey, A. H., 506
Guinness, Desmond, 2845-47
Guinness, Ralph B., 1649
Gummere, Richard M., 2848
Gunn, John W., 507
Gurley, James Lafayette, 2262
Gurney, Gene & Clara, 508
Guthrie, John D., 2849
Haber, Francis C., 510
Hadley, Arthur T., 511
Haiman, Miecislaus, 512
Haines, Charles Grove, 1651
Hale, Edward Everett, 513-15
Hale, Harrison, 516
Hale, Salma, 517
Hale, William Bayard, 518
Hall, Courtney R., 2850
Hall, Edward Hagaman, 1652
Hall, Gordon Langley, 519
Hall, J. Lesslie, 2263
Hall, Richard, 2264
Halliday, E. M., 2265
Halsey, Ashley, Jr., 520-21
Halsey, J. J., 1653
Halsey, Robert A., 2851
Halstead, Murat, 522
Hamilton, J. G. deRoulhac, 523-25, 1654, 2266
Hamilton, John Church, 1655
Hamlin, Talbot F., 2852-53
Hammond, Jabez D., 526
Hamowy, Ronald, 2267

Hampton, Vernon B., 2268
Hanchette, William F., Jr., 1657
Hancock, James Denton, 1658
Handler, Philip, 2854
Hannon, Stuart L., 527
Hans, Nicholas, 1659, 2269, 2855
Hanson, Galen, 1660
Haraszti, Zoltan, 528
Harbrecht, Rosemary, 2856
Hardon, John A., 2270
Harnit, Fanny, 529
Harper, Samuel H., 530
Harris, Herbert, 2271
Harris, Michael H., 12
Harris, Ramon I., 531
Harrison, Frederic, 532
Harrison, Lowell, 533, 1661-62
Harrison, Mary Louise, 534
Harrold, Frances Long, 2272-73
Hart, Andrew D., 2857
Hart, Charles H., 2858
Hartman, Daniel W., 1663
Harvey, Alexander M., 1664-65
Harvey, Charles M., 1666-67
Hash, Ronald J., 535
Haskell, Douglas, 2859
Haskins, Caryl P., 536, 2860
Hastings, George E., 2861
Hatch, Louis Clinton, 1668
Hausman, Ruth H., 2862
Hawgood, John A., 537
Hawke, David Freeman, 1669, 2863
Hawkes, Francis Lister, 538
Haworth, Paul Leland, 2864
Hay, Philip Courtland, 437
Hay, Robert P., 539
Hayden, Ralston, 1670
Hays, Isaac Minis, 1671-72
Hazelton, Jean Hanvey, 540, 2865
Hazelton, John H., 1673-74
Hazen, Charles Downer, 1675
Healey, Robert M., 2866-67
Heatwole, Cornelius J., 2868-69
Heinlein, Jay C., 1676
Hellanbrand, Harold Leonard, 2274
Heller, Francis H., 541
Hellman, C. Doris, 2870
Hemings, Madison, 542
Hemphill, John M., III., 543
Hemphill, William Edwin, 1677-78
Hench, Atcheson L., 2871
Henderson, Alfred, 2872

Henderson, John C., 2873
Henderson, Josie Duncan, 545
Hendricks, Gordon, 2874
Hendrickson, Walter B., 546
Hendrix, J. A., 1679
Henkels, Stan V., 547, 1680, 2875
Henline, Ruth, 2876
Henne, Anna Louise, 2275
Henneman, John B., 2877
Henrich, Joseph George, 1681-82
Herbert, Francis, 2878
Herndon, G. Melvin, 1683
Herwald, Michelle, 2276
Herzberg, Max J., 2879
Heslep, Robert D., 2277-78, 2880-81
Heyer, William C., 2279
Hickey, Agnes M., 2882
Hicks, Clifford B., 2883
Higginson, Thomas Wentworth, 550
Higgs, Robert J., 2280
Hill, C. William, 2281
Hillard, George S., 1684
Hillbruner, Anthony, 2884
Hinsdale, Mary L., 1685
Hirst, Francis W., 551
Hitchcock, Margaret R., 2885
Hoar, George Frisbie, 553
Hodges, Wiley E., 2282
Hodgson, Joseph, Jr., 1687
Hofstadter, Richard, 1688-89, 2283
Hoge, James, 554
Holifield, E. Brooks, 2284
Holland, Corabelle A., 555
Holliday, Carl, 556-57
Hollis, Christopher, 558
Holloway, Laura C., 559
Holmes, Lowell D., 2886
Holmes, Prescott, 560
Holmgren, Rod, 561
Holway, Hope, 2285
Holway, John, 562
Honeywell, Roy J., 1690, 2887-88
Hook, Sidney, 2286
Hooker, Richard J., 1691
Hopkins, Frederick M., 2889
Horn, Stanley F., 2890
Horn, William A., 2891
Horsley, Catharine D., 2287
Horton, Andrew S., 2288
Horsman, Reginald, 1692-93
Hoskins, Janina W., 1694

Hoslett, Schuyler D., 1695
Hosmer, Charles B., Jr., 563
Hosmer, James K., 1696
Houghton, W. M., 564
Houghton, Walter R., 1697
Houlette, William D., 2892
House, Ray, 2893
Howard, George Elliott, 565
Howard, Seymour, 2895
Howe, Henry, 566
Howell, Wilbur S., 2896-98
Howland, William S., 2899
Hubbard, Elbert, 567-68
Hubbard, Simeon, 569
Hubbard, William, 2900
Hubbell, Jay B., 2901
Huddleston, Eugene L., 13
Hudnut, Joseph, 2902-04
Hudson, Rector, 570
Huegli, Jon M., 2905
Hughes, Robert, 2906
Hughes, Thomas L., 1698
Huhner, Leon, 1699
Humphrey, Heman, 571
Humphrey, Henry B., 2907
Hunt, Gaillard, 1700
Hunt, Thomas C., 2200, 2289
Huntley, William B., 2290
Hutcheson, John K., 2908
Hutchins, Frank & Cortelle, 572
Hutchins, Robert Maynard, 2291
Huxtable, Ada Louise, 2909
Huyck, Dorothy, B., 2910
Ide, John J., 2911
Infante, Luis C., 1702
Ingersoll, Charles Jared, 576
Irelan, John Robert, 1703
Ireton, Robert E., 1704
Irland, Fred, 2913
Irwin, Frank, 577
Isbell, Egbert R., 2914
Isham, Norman M., 2915
Izard, Ralph, 578
Jackman, S. W., 1705
Jackson, Donald, 583, 1706, 2916
Jackson, Henry, E., 2292
Jackson, Joseph, 584
Jackson, Sidney L., 2917
Jacob, John J., 2918
Jaffa, Harry V., 2293-95
Jahoda, Gloria, 1707

James, John W., 585
James, Marquis, 586
Jefferson, Isaac, 587
Jeffries, Ona Griffin, 607
Jellison, Charles A., 608–09
Jenkins, Charles Francis, 610
Jenkins, Starr, 2933
Jenkinson, 1714–15
Jennings, Walter Wilson, 1716
Jensen, Amy L., 2934
Jobe, Brock W., 611
Johansen, Bruce E., 2300
Johnson,, Alfred, Jr., 612
Johnson, Allen, 1717
Johnson, Ann D., 613
Johnson, Gerald W., 614
Johnson, Louis, 2935
Johnson, Luciana, 1718
Johnson, Peggy A., 2301
Johnson, U. Alexis, 2302
Johnson, Walter Rogers, 615
Johnson, William, 616
Johnson, William D., 2936
Johnston, Johanna, 618
Johnston, John T. M., 617
Johnston, Richard Holland, 16
Johnstone, Robert M., Jr., 1719–20
Jones, Alfred H., 619
Jones, Anna C., 2937
Jones, Charles W., 620
Jones, Edgar Dewitt, 2303
Jones, Evan, 2938
Jones, Howard, 2939
Jones, Howard Mumford, 2304, 2940
Jones, James F., Jr., 2305
Jones, Joseph Seawell, 621
Jones, Paul W., 1721
Jones, Robert W., 2941
Jordan, Winthrop, 2306
Jouett, Edward S., 622
Judge, Joseph, 2942
Judson, Clara Ingram, 623
Judson, L. Carroll, 624
Jullian, Philippe, 2943
Kalkbrenner, Jurgen, 625
Kallen, Horace M., 2944–45
Kammen, Michael, 626–27
Kane, Joseph Nathan, 628
Kaplan, Lawrence S., 629, 1722–27
Kaplan, Sidney, 1728
Karsten, Peter, 630
Katz, Stanley N., 1729

Kay, Miryam Neulander, 2307
Kean, Jefferson Randolph, 631
Kean, Robert G. H., 1731
Kean, Robert H., 632
Keats, John, 1730
Keller, Linda Quinne, 1732
Keller, William F., 1733
Kelley, Darwin, 1734
Kelley, Joseph J., Jr., 633
Kellog, Charles E., 634
Kellogg, Robert L., 2946
Kelly, Alfred H., 2308
Kelly, Edward James, 635
Kemp, Verbon E., 636
Kennedy, John F., 2947
Kennedy, William P., 1735
Kenney, R. D., 2948
Kent, Charles W., 2949–51
Kent, Frank R., 1736
Kenyon, Cecilia M., 1737
Kerber, Linda K., 1738
Kerchendorfer, Paul R., 637
Ketcham, Ralph L., 1739, 2309
Ketchum, Richard M., 2952
Kettell, Thomas Prentice, 1740
Kibler, J. Luther, Jr., 638, 2953
Kilgo, John Carlisle, 2310
Kimball, Fiske, 639–40, 2954–77
Kimball, Marie G., 641–50, 2311, 2964, 2978–88
Kimura, K., 2989
Kingdon, Frank, 1741
Kingsley, Sidney, 2990
Kingsley, W. V., 652
Kinnaird, Anne, 653
Kinsolving, Arthur B., 2312
Kirby, Thomas A., 2991
Kirk, Russell, 654
Kirkland, Frederic R., 1742
Kirkland, John Thornton, 655
Kirtland, Jared P., 2992
Kite, Elizabeth S., 2993
Klaffky, Susan, 2538
Klare, Ralph E., 656
Kline, Alfred Allen, 2994
Klingberg, Frank J. & Frank W., 657
Klingensmith, Thelma H., 2995
Kloman, William, 2314
Knapp, Samuel L., 658
Knight, Robert M., 2996
Knode, Jay C., 1743

Mannix, Richard, 1814
Mansfield, Harvey C., Jr., 1815
Marchione, Margherita, 1816
Marienstras, Elise, 783
Marraro, Howard R., 784–88
Marsh, Philip M., 789–96, 1817–22
Marshall, James F., 2355
Martin, Asa E., 797
Martin, Henry A. 3072
Martin, Edwin T., 2356, 3073–75
Martin, H. Christopher, 798
Martin, John S., 3076
Martin, Pete, 799
Marvel, Josiah P., 3077
Marx, Leo, 3078
Marx, Rudolph, 800
Mason, F. Van Wyck, 801
Mason, J. E., 802
Massie, Susanne W., 3079
Masters, Edgar Lee, 803
Masters, R. W., 1824
May, Henry F., 2357
Mayer, Brantz, 3080
Mayer, Frederick, 1825, 2358–59
Mayes, R. B., 1826
Mayo, Barbara, 804
Mayo, Bernard, 805–10, 3081
Mayo, A. Hyatt, 3082
Mays, Jim, 3083
Mazlish, Bruce, 1438
Mazzei, Philip, 811
Meachan, William S., 812
Mead, Edward C., 813
Mead, Edwin Doak, 814–15, 1827
Mead, Robert G., Jr., 816
Mead, Sidney E., 2360–62
Mearns, David C., 817, 3084–86
Mehlinger, Howard D., 3087
Mehta, M. J., 2363
Meisen, Adolf Frank, 1828
Melbo, Irving R., 818
Mellen, George F., 3088
Mellon, Matthew T., 2364
Mendelson, Wallace, 1829–30
Menzies, Sir Robert, 820
Mercer, Charles Fenton, 1831
Merrens, H. Roy, 2775
Merriam, Charles E., 1409, 1832, 2365
Merriam, Harold G., 821
Merriam, J. M., 1833
Merrill, Boynton, Jr., 822

Merwin, Henry Childs, 823
Meschutt, David, 3090
Meyer, Donald H., 2366
Michael, William H., 824
Middlebrook, Samuel, 825
Middleton, Lamar, 1338
Midgeley, Louis, 826
Miers, Earl Schenck, 827–28, 2367
Miles, Edwin A., 829
Miller, Augustus C., 3091
Miller, Helen Topping, 3092
Miller, Hope Ridings, 830
Miller, John Chester, 1834, 2368
Miller, Joseph, 831
Miller, Sue Freeman, 832, 3093–95
Miller, Vincent, 833
Millspaugh, Arthur C., 1835
Milton, George F., 834
Minnegerode, Meade, 1836–37
Minor, Charles, 1838
Minor, Henry, 1839
Minor, Robert, 1840
Mintz, Max M., 835
Mirkin, Harris, G., 2369
Mitchell, Broadus, 836
Mitchell, Henry, 3097
Mitchell, Samuel Latham, 837
Moe, Christian Hollis, 3098
Moffatt, Alexander D., 3099
Moffatt, Charles H., 3100
Moffatt, L. G., 242
Moley, Raymond, 838, 1842
Monjo, F. N., 3101
Monsell, Helen Albee, 839
Montague, Andrew J., 840
Montgomery, Henry C., 2370, 3102–03
Moore, John Hammond, 849
Moore, Justus E., 1843
Moore, Leroy, Jr., 2371
Moore, R. Walton, 1844
Moreau, Henry, 850
Morgan, Donald Grant, 1845
Morgan, Edmund S., 2372–74
Morgan, Henry, 851
Morgan, H. Wayne, 2375
Morgan, James M., 852, 1846
Morgan, Robert J., 2376
Morison, Samuel Eliot, 853, 3108
Morrill, Justin S., 854
Morris, Charles, 855
Morris, Edwin B., 3109

Patterson, Augusta O., 937
Patterson, Caleb Perry, 1873-76
Pattison, William D., 1877
Patton, Jacob Harris, 1878
Patton, John S., 938-39, 3168-69
Paulding, C. G., 940
Paullin, Charles O., 3170
Pawelek, Dick, 1879
Pearson, Samuel C., 2402
Pease, Theodore C., 1880
Peattie, Donald Culross, 941
Peck, Mamie D., 942
Peden, William, 944-45, 3171-77
Peebles, James Martin, 2403
Peebles, John K., 3178
Pendleton, William C., 1881
Penman, John S., 1882
Penney, Annette C., 3179-81
Perkins, Mrs. C. D., 3182
Perkins, Hazlehurst B., 2590, 3183
Perry, Frances M., 948
Perkins, John L., 947
Perouse de Montclos, J. M., 3184
Perry, E. S., 3185
Perry, Ralph Barton, 1883
Peterson, Arnold, 949
Peterson, Helen Stone, 950, 3186
Peterson, Martin S., 3187
Peterson, Maud H., 951
Peterson, Merrill D., 952-65, 1884-86,
  2404-08, 3188
Peterson, Norma Louis, 1887
Pettengill, Samuel B., 966
Pevler, Herman H., 3189
Pew, Marlen, 967
Phau, Donald, 1888
Phelps, William Lyon, 2409
Philbrick, Thomas, 3190
Phillips, Edward H., 969
Phillips, James D., 1890
Phillips, P. Lee, 1891
Phipps, Edith, 968
Phipps, Frances, 3191
Pickens, Buford, 3192
Pierce, D. T., 1892
Pierce, E. H., 3193
Pierson, Hamilton W., 970-71
Pierson, William H., 3194-95
Pilling, Ron, 972
Pi-Sunyer, Oriol, 3196
Pitts, Carolyn, 973

Plaisted, Thais M., 1893
Pleasants, Samuel A., 3197
Plochl, Willibald A., 2410
Plume, William, 974
Pole, J. R., 1894-96
Pollard, James E., 1897
Pollin, Burton R., 2411
Pool, Gwinette, 975
Poole, William Frederick, 1898, 2412
Pope, Arthur Upham, 3198
Poppen, Richard S., 976
Porter, Charlotte M., 2711
Potter, Henry, 977
Pound, Ezra, 978, 1899
Powell, Burt E., 1900
Powell, Edward A., 979
Powell, Edward Payson, 980-81, 2414,
  3200
Powers, Fred Perry, 1901
Prager, Annabelle, 227
Prager, Frank D., 1902
Pratt, Richard, 982, 3201
Prescott, Frederick C., 2415-16
Preston, Joseph Raine, 3203
Price, John W., 1903
Price, William Jennings, 1904
Prince, Carl E., 1905
Pritchett, Henry S., 3204
Proctor, L. B., 1906-07
Prufer, Julius E., 1908
Pryor, John C., 989
Pula, James S., 990
Pulley, Judith Ross, 991-92, 1909
Purcell, Richard T., 3206
Putnam, Samuel, 1931
Pyle, Mary T., 3207
Quadros, Jose Antonio, 993
Quarles, Benjamin, 1911
Quimby, Laurie J., 994
Quincy, Josiah Phillips, 1912
Quinn, Patrick F., 2417
Radbill, Samuel X., 3208-09
Radcliff, Robert R., 995
Raffensperger, Edwin B., 3210
Rager, John C., 2418
Raiden, Edward, 3211
Ralston, S. M., 3212
Randall, David S., 3213
Randall, Henry S., 996
Randall, J. G., 997, 1914
Randall, Samuel Jackson, 998
Randolph, Frederick J., 3214

Sadler, Elizabeth, 3244
Sadler, Julius T., 2845–46
Saint, Percy, 1940
Sainte-Beuve, Charles A., 1058–59
Salamanca, Lucy, 3245
Salmon, Myrene, 3246
Salstrom, P., 1941
Sanchez, Ramon, 3247
Sand, Norbert, 3248
Sandburg, Carl, 1060
Sandefur, Ray H., 3249
Sanders, Gold V., 3250
Sandler, S. Gerald, 2435
Sanford, Charles B., 3251
Sanford, Charles L., 2436
Sarles, Frank B., 1061
Sarton, May, 3252
Savin, Marion B., 3253–54
Sawvel, Franklin P., 1942
Scaff, Lawrence A., 2437
Scanlon, James E., 1943
Schaar, John H., 2438
Schachner, Nathan, 1063–64, 1944
Schafer, Bruce H., 3255
Schaff, David S., 2439
Schamsmeier, Edward L. & Frederick H., 1945
Scheick, William J., 3256
Scheffel, Richard L., 3257–58
Schellenberg, T. R., 1946
Scherr, Arthur, 1947
Schick, Joseph S., 3259
Schlesinger, Arthur M., 2440
Schmidt, Clifton F., 2709
Schmidtchen, P. W., 1065
Schmucker, Samuel M., 1066
Schneider, Herbert W., 2441
Schonberg, Harold, 3260
Schouler, James, 1067, 1948
Schulte, Nordholt J. W., 1068, 1949
Schulz, Constance B., 2442
Schurman, Jacob C., 1950
Schwartz, Bernard, 1951
Schwartz, Edward, 2601
Scott, Clinton Lee, 1069
Scott, William B., 1952
Scribner, Robert Leslie, 1070
Scruggs, C. L., 1071
Scrugges, J. H., Jr., 1953
Sealove, Sandra, 1954
Sears, Louis M., 1955–57, 2443–44

Seeber, Edward D., 3262–63
Selden, Richard Ely, 1958
Selesky, Harold E., 1073
Sellers, James L., 3265
Semmes, Thomas, Jr., 1959
Semple, W. K., 847
Senkevitch, Anatole, 3266
Sensabaugh, George F., 1960
Sergeant, John, 1074
Serpell, Jean K., 1075
Servies, James A., 3267
Sestanovich, Stephen, 1961
Setzler, Edwin B., 3268–69
Severance, Frank H., 1077
Sevostianov, G. N., 1078
Shackelford, George G., 1079–82, 1962, 3270–71
Shaffer, Kenneth R., 1083
Shalhope, Robert E., 2445
Shannon, Joseph B., 1084, 1963–64
Shapiro, Karl, 3272
Shapley, Harlow, 3273
Sharp, Wayne W., 3274
Sharswood, George, 1965
Shaw, Albert, 1966–67, 2446
Shaw, C. P., 1085
Shaw, John Angier, 1086
Shaw, Peter, 1087
Sheean, Vincent, 1088
Sheehan, Bernard W., 1968, 2447–48, 3275
Sheldon, F., 1089
Sheldon, J., 2449
Shenker, Israel, 1090
Shenkir, William G., 1091
Shepherd, Henry E., 3276
Shepperson, Archibald B., 1092
Sherman, C. B., 3277
Sherman, E. David, 1093
Sherman, Stuart P., 1094–95
Sherrill, Sarah B., 3278
Shibata, Shingo, 2450
Shields, W. S., 1096
Shimakawa, Masashi, 1969
Shippen, Rebecca L., 1097
Shiryaev, B. A., 1970
Shoemaker, Floyd C., 3279
Shonting, Donald A., 3280
Shortridge, George D., 1971
Showalter, J. D., 1098
Showalter, William Joseph, 1972
Shulim, Joseph I., 1973

Shurr, Georgia H., 1974
Sidey, Hugh, 1099, 1100
Sifton, Paul G., 1101
Sigaud, Louis A., 1975–76
Simms, L. Moody, 3281
Simpson, George G., 3282
Simpson, Joseph B., 1977
Simpson, Lewis P., 2451, 3283–84
Simpson, Lloyd D., 1102
Simpson, Stephen, 1103–04
Sinnott, John P., 3285
Sisson, Daniel, 1978
Skallerup, Harry R., 3287
Skeen, Carl E., 1979
Skolnik, Richard, 1980
Slicer, Thomas R., 2452
Sloane, William M., 1981
Slonimsky, Nicholas, 3288
Slosson, Edwin E., 3289
Small, Norman J., 1982
Smelser, Marshall, 1105, 1983
Smith, B. M., 3290
Smith, Bessie W., 1106
Smith, C. Alphonso, 3291
Smith, Charles Card, 1107
Smith, Charles Emory, 1984
Smith, Datus C., Jr., 1108
Smith, David Eugene, 3292
Smith, Doris N., 3293
Smith, Dorothy Hunt, 1109
Smith, Dorothy Valentine, 2453
Smith, Gaddis, 1985
Smith, Glenn Curtis, 1110, 1986, 3294
Smith, Gordon S., 3295
Smith, Helen A., 1111
Smith, Henry Nash, 3296
Smith, Hugh P., 3297
Smith, James Morton, 1987–88
Smith, Margaret Bayard, 1112–13
Smith, Page, 1114
Smith, Paul H., 1115
Smith, Robert Harold, 1989
Smith, Russell, 3298
Smith, Samuel, 1116
Smith, Samuel Harrison, 1117
Smith, Sheldon, 1118
Smith, Sherwin D., 1990
Smith, T. V., 778, 2454
Smith, William Raymond, 1991
Smithline, Arnold, 2455
Smythe, Clifford, 1119

Sokolsky, Eric, 1120
Solomon, Charles, 2456
Somerville, John, 2457
Soto Paz, Rafael, 1992
Sowerby, E. Millicent, 3301–03
Sparks, Edwin E., 1121
Spencer, Donald S., 1993
Spencer, John Bassett, 1122
Spencer, Thomas E., 3304
Spengler, Jospeh J., 2458
Spiker, Franklin A., 1994
Spiro, Jeffery H., 1995
Spivey, Herman E., 1123
Sprague, Homer B., 2459
Sprague, Joseph E., 1124
Sprague, Marshall, 1999
Sprague, Peleg, 1125
Sprague, Stuart Seely, 2000
Spratt, John S., 3305
Springer, George M., 2001
Stafford, John, 2460
Stafford, William, 3306
Stanard, William G., 1126
Stanford, John, 1127
Stanley, Augustus O., 1128
Stanwood, Edward, 2002–03
Stapley, Mildred, 3307–08
Staughton, William, 1129
Stead, John P., 2461
Steffen, Jerome O., 2004
Steinberg, Alfred, 2005
Steinfeld, Melvin, 2462
Stenberg, Richard R., 1130
Stephens, Frank F., 2006
Stephenson, Nathaniel W., 1131
Sterling, Peter R., 1132
Sternbach, Oscar, 2463
Stevens, Charles, 1133
Stevenson, Adlai E., 2007
Stewart, Donald Henderson, 2008
Stewart, Randall, 2464
Stewart, Robert A., 1134
Stiebing, William H., Jr., 3309
Stockton, Frank R., 1135
Stoddard, William O., 1136
Stokes, Roy, 3310
Stokes, William E., Jr., 1137
Stolba, K. Marie, 3311
Stone, Gene, 1138
Stone, Peter, 3312
Storey, Helen A., 3313

van Loon, Hendrik W., 1245-46, 2051
van Pelt, Charles B., 1247
Van Vollenhoven, C., 1248
Van Ward, Roland, 3371
Van Wyck, P. V. R., 1249
Van Zandt, Roland, 2478
Varg, Paul A., 2052
Vaughan, G. B., 3372
Vaughan, Joseph L., 3373
Verner, Coolie, 32, 1250, 3374-79
Vest, George G., 1251-52
Via, Betty Elyse Davis, 343, 1253-55, 2736, 3380
Via, Vera V., 1256
Victor, O. J., 1257
Vogt, Per, 1258
Voorhees, Daniel W., 1259
Volz, Harry A., III, 2054
Von Eckardt, Ursula M., 2479-80
Vossler, Otto, 2055, 2394
Waciuma, Wanjohi, 2056
Wade, Mary H., 1260
Waite, Edward F., 2057
Wagner, Julia, 1261
Wagoner, Jennings L., 3383
Walker, Francis Amasa, 2058
Wall, Charles Coleman, 3384
Wall, James M., 2059
Wallace, D. D., 2060
Wallace, Henry A., 2061, 3385-86
Wallace, M. G., 1263
Walne, Peter, 1264
Walsh, Richard, 2062
Walter, L. Rohe, 1265
Walton, Craig, 2481
Wandell, Samuel H., 2063
Ward, James E., 3387-89
Ward, Paul W., 1266
Warde, William F., 2064
Warfield, Ethelbert, 2065-67
Warren, Charles, 1267-68, 2068-72
Warren, Robert Penn, 3390
Warner, Charles W. H., 1269
Washburn, Charles G., 2073
Wasserman, Burton, 3391
Wasserman, Felix M., 1270
Waterman, Julian S., 2482
Waterman, Thomas J., 3392
Watlington, Pat, 3393
Watson, F. J. B., 3394-96
Watson, Henry C., 1271

Watson, Jane, 3397
Watson, Lucille M., 3398
Watson, Ross, 1272
Watson, Thomas E., 1273-74
Watts, George B., 3399
Wayland, John W., 2483, 3400-01
Weaver, Bettie W., 1275
Weaver, George S., 1276
Weaver, Neal, 3402
Webb, Gerald Fred, 3403
Webster, Daniel, 1277-78
Webster, Donald B., Jr., 3404
Webster, Nathan B., 1279
Webster, Sidney, 2075
Wecter, Dixon, 1280
Weeder, Elinor J., 2076
Weeks, Elie, 1281
Weil, Ann, 3405
Weisman, Morris, 1282
Weiss, Harry B., 3406
Welling, James C., 2077
Welsch, Glenn A., 1091
Welsh, Frank, 3407
Welter, Rush, 2078
Wertenbaker, Thomas J., 1283
West, Murray, 1284
Wettstein, A. Arnold, 2484
Weyant, Robert V., 2485
Weymouth, Lally, 1285
Wharton, Anne H., 1286
Wharton, Isaac T., 1287
Wharton, James, 3408
Whealen, John J., 2486
Whealon, John F., 2487
White, Andrew D., 2079
White, Horace, 2080
White, John W., 3410
White, Leonard D., 2081-82
White, Lucia, 2488-89
White, Morton, 2489-90
Whitehill, Jane, 1289
Whitehill, Walter Muir, 66, 1290, 2083, 2608, 3411-12
Whiting, F. A., Jr., 3413
Whiting, Margaret, 3414
Whitney, David C., 1291
Whitton, Mary O., 1292
Whitty, J. H., 3415
Wibberley, Leonard, 1293-97
Wickard, Claude R., 3416
Wicks, Elliott K., 2491